Inside Earth

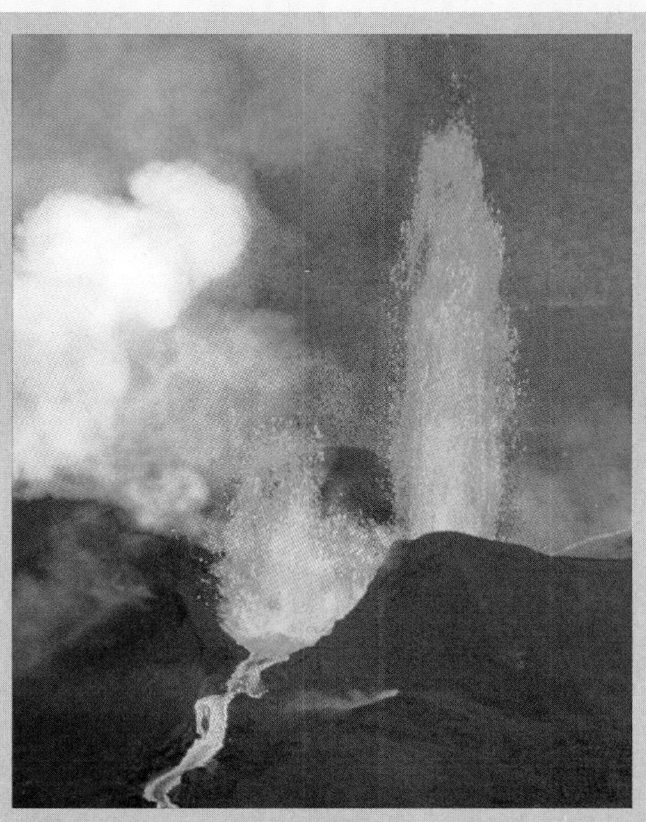

PRENTICE HALL
Needham, Massachusetts
Upper Saddle River, New Jersey

ISBN 0-13-434570-3
1 2 3 4 5 6 7 8 9 10 05 04 03 02 01 00 99 98

PRENTICE HALL

SCIENCE EXPLORER

GET READY FOR A CONTENT-RICH, HANDS-ON EXPLORATION!

15 Books In All

PRENTICE HALL SCIENCE EXPLORER Earth's Waters

PRENTICE HALL SCIENCE EXPLORER Motion, Forces and Energy

PRENTICE HALL SCIENCE EXPLORER Animals

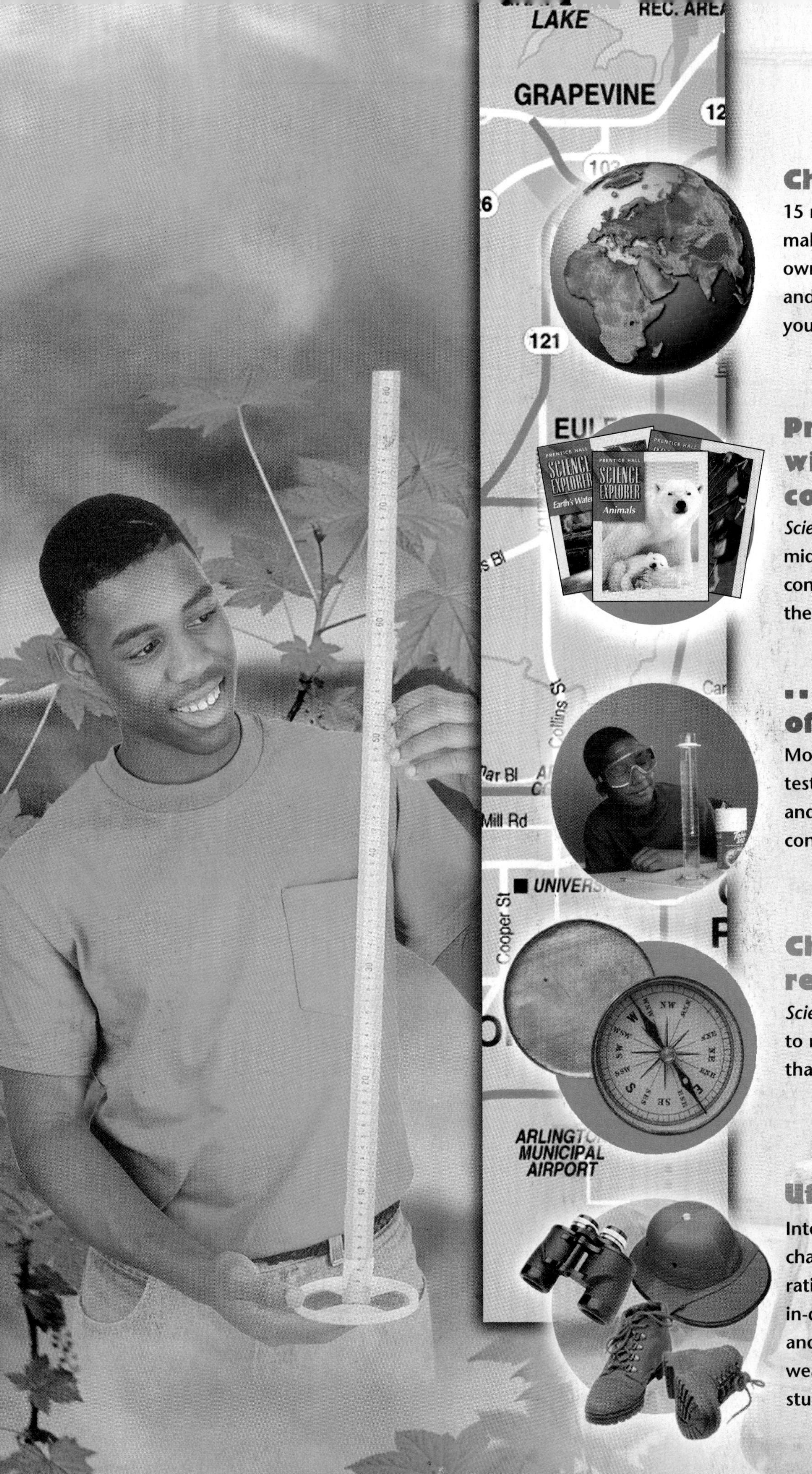

Chart your own course.

15 motivational hardcover books make it easy for you to create your own curriculum; meet local, state, and national guidelines; and teach your favorite topics in depth.

Prepare your students with rich, motivating content...

Science Explorer is crafted for today's middle grades student, with accessible content and in-depth coverage of all the important concepts.

...and a wide variety of inquiry activities.

Motivational student- and teacher-tested activities reinforce key concepts and allow students to explore science concepts for themselves.

Check your compass regularly.

Science Explorer gives you more ways to regularly check student performance than any other program available.

Utilize a variety of tools.

Integrated science sections in every chapter and Interdisciplinary Explorations in every book allow you to make in-depth connections to other sciences and disciplines. Plus, you will find a wealth of additional tools to set your students on a successful course.

Chart the course you want with 15 motivating books that easily match your curriculum.

Each book in the series contains:

- Complete and accessible coverage of core science topics
- Integrated Science sections in every chapter
- Interdisciplinary Explorations for team teaching at the end of each book
- Comprehensive skills practice and application—assuring that you meet the National Science Education Standards and your local and state standards

EXPLORATION TOOLS: BASIC PROCESS SKILLS

Observing
Measuring
Calculating
Classifying
Predicting
Inferring
Graphing
Creating data tables
Communicating

LIFE SCIENCE TITLES

From Bacteria to Plants
1 Living Things
2 Viruses and Bacteria
3 Protists and Fungi
4 Introduction to Plants
5 Seed Plants

Animals
1 Sponges, Cnidarians, and Worms
2 Mollusks, Arthropods, and Echinoderms
3 Fishes, Amphibians, and Reptiles
4 Birds and Mammals
5 Animal Behavior

Cells and Heredity
1 Cell Structure and Function
2 Cell Processes and Energy
3 Genetics: The Science of Heredity
4 Modern Genetics
5 Changes Over Time

Human Biology and Health
1 Healthy Body Systems
2 Bones, Muscles, and Skin
3 Food and Digestion
4 Circulation
5 Respiration and Excretion
6 Fighting Disease
7 The Nervous System
8 The Endocrine System and Reproduction

Environmental Science
1 Populations and Communities
2 Ecosystems and Biomes
3 Living Resources
4 Land and Soil Resources
5 Air and Water Resources
6 Energy Resources

 *Integrated Science sections in every chapter*

EXPLORATION TOOLS: ADVANCED PROCESS SKILLS

Posing questions

Forming operational definitions

Developing hypotheses

Controlling variables

Interpreting data

Interpreting graphs

Making models

Drawing conclusions

Designing experiments

EARTH SCIENCE TITLES

Inside Earth
1 Plate Tectonics
2 Earthquakes
3 Volcanoes
4 Minerals
5 Rocks

Earth's Changing Surface
1 Mapping Earth's Surface
2 Weathering and Soil Formation
3 Erosion and Deposition
4 A Trip Through Geologic Time

Earth's Waters
1 Earth: The Water Planet
2 Fresh Water
3 Freshwater Resources
4 Ocean Motions
5 Ocean Zones

Weather and Climate
1 The Atmosphere
2 Weather Factors
3 Weather Patterns
4 Climate and Climate Change

Astronomy
1 Earth, Moon, and Sun
2 The Solar System
3 Stars, Galaxies, and the Universe

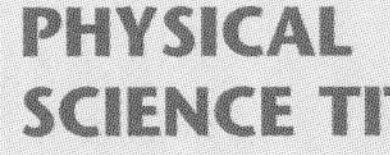

PHYSICAL SCIENCE TITLES

Chemical Building Blocks
1 An Introduction to Matter
2 Changes in Matter
3 Elements in the Periodic Table
4 Carbon Chemistry

Chemical Interactions
1 Chemical Reactions
2 Atoms and Bonding
3 Acids, Bases, and Solutions
4 Exploring Materials

Motion, Forces, and Energy
1 Motion
2 Forces
3 Forces in Fluids
4 Work and Machines
5 Energy and Power
6 Thermal Energy and Heat

Electricity and Magnetism
1 Magnetism and Electromagnetism
2 Electric Charges and Current
3 Electricity and Magnetism at Work
4 Electronics

Sound and Light
1 Characteristics of Waves
2 Sound
3 The Electromagnetic Spectrum
4 Light

 ***Integrated Science sections in every chapter***

Place your students in the role of science explorer through a variety of inquiry activities.

Motivational student- and teacher-tested activities reinforce key concepts and allow students to explore science concepts for themselves. More than 350 activities are provided for each book in the Student Edition, Teacher's Edition, Teaching Resources, Integrated Science Lab Manual, and Inquiry Skills Activity Book.

STUDENT EDITION ACTIVITIES

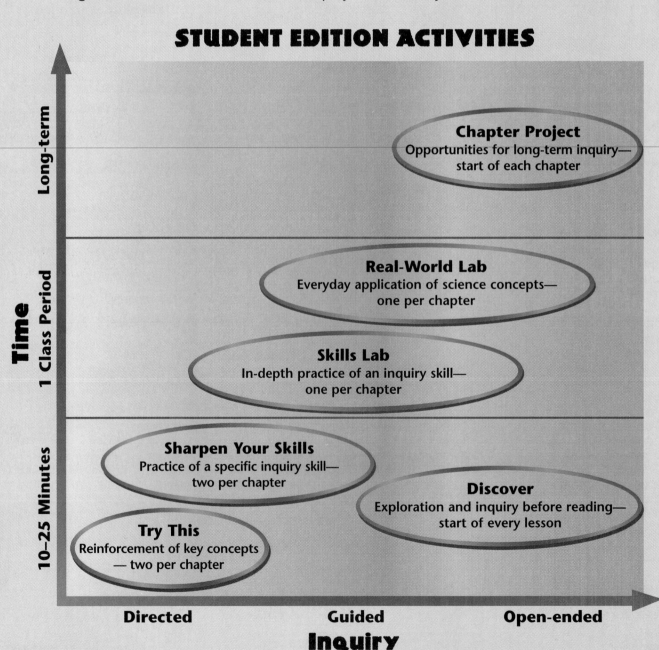

Time: Long-term / 1 Class Period / 10–25 Minutes
Inquiry: Directed / Guided / Open-ended

Chapter Project
Opportunities for long-term inquiry—start of each chapter

Real-World Lab
Everyday application of science concepts—one per chapter

Skills Lab
In-depth practice of an inquiry skill—one per chapter

Sharpen Your Skills
Practice of a specific inquiry skill—two per chapter

Discover
Exploration and inquiry before reading—start of every lesson

Try This
Reinforcement of key concepts — two per chapter

Check your compass regularly with integrated assessment tools.

Science Explorer gives you more ways to regularly assess student progress than any other program. A wide variety of assessment tools are built into every page of the Student Edition, and ongoing assessment options are woven throughout the Teacher's Edition and program resources. Now, you'll know exactly how your students are doing every step of the way.

Prepare for state and local exams with traditional and performance-based assessment.

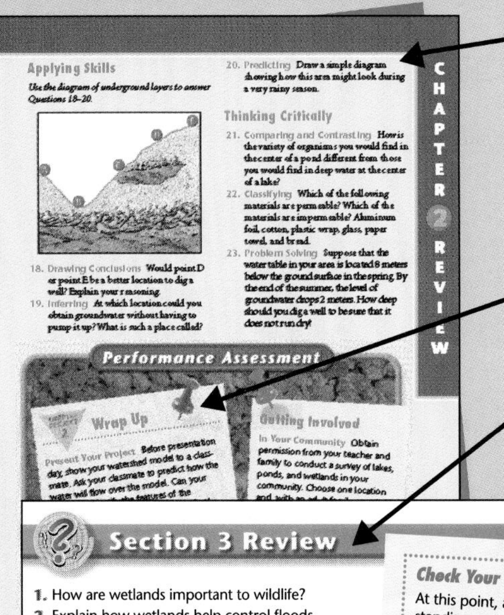

Applying Skills

Use the diagram of underground layers to answer Questions 18–20.

18. Drawing Conclusions Would point D or point E be a better location to dig a well? Explain your reasoning.
19. Inferring At which location could you obtain groundwater without having to pump it up? What is such a place called?
20. Predicting Draw a simple diagram showing how this area might look during a very rainy season.

Thinking Critically

21. Comparing and Contrasting How is the variety of organisms you would find in the center of a pond different from those you would find in deep water at the center of a lake?
22. Classifying Which of the following materials are permeable? Which of the materials are impermeable? Aluminum foil, cotton, plastic wrap, glass, paper towel, and bread.
23. Problem Solving Suppose that the water table in your area is located 8 meters below the ground surface in the spring. By the end of the summer, the level of groundwater drops 2 meters. How deep should you dig a well to be sure that it does not run dry?

CHAPTER 2 REVIEW

Performance Assessment

Wrap Up

Present Your Project Before presentation day, show your watershed model to a classmate. Ask your classmate to predict how the water will flow over the model. Can your ...

Getting Involved

In Your Community Obtain permission from your teacher and family to conduct a survey of lakes, ponds, and wetlands in your community. Choose one location ...

Section 3 Review

1. How are wetlands important to wildlife?
2. Explain how wetlands help control floods.
3. How are the Everglades unusual?
4. **Thinking Critically** Making Judgments Some of the plans to restore the Everglades will require millions of dollars and will negatively affect local farmers. What information would you want to have to help decide what plan of action to take to save the Everglades?

Check Your Progress — CHAPTER PROJECT 2

At this point, add the body of standing water to your watershed sketch. If your model will include any wetland areas, what materials will you use to model them? (*Hint:* Be sure to consider how water will enter and leave the body of water.)

- **Comprehensive Chapter Reviews** include a wide range of question types that students will encounter on standardized tests. Types include multiple choice, enhanced true/false, concept mastery, visual thinking, skill application, and critical thinking. Also includes Chapter Project "Wrap Up."
- **Chapter Projects** contain rubrics that allow you to easily assess student progress.
- **Section Reviews** provide "Check your Progress" opportunities for the Chapter Project, as well as review questions for the section.
- Additional *Science Explorer* assessment resources: **Assessment Resources with CD-ROM** and **Resource Pro® with Planning Express®.** See page 9 for complete product descriptions.

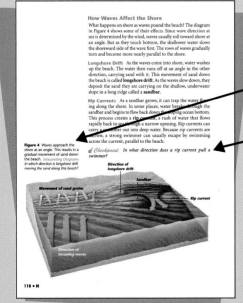

How Waves Affect the Shore

What happens on shore as waves pound the beach? The diagram in Figure 4 shows some of their effects. Since wave direction at sea is determined by the wind, waves usually roll toward shore at an angle. But as they touch bottom, the shallower water slows the shoreward side of the wave first. The rows of waves gradually turn and become more nearly parallel to the shore.

Longshore Drift As the waves come into shore, water washes up the beach. The water then runs off at an angle in the other direction, carrying sand with it. This movement of sand down the beach is called **longshore drift**. As the waves slow down, they deposit the sand they are carrying on the shallow, underwater slope in a long ridge called a **sandbar**.

Rip Currents As a sandbar grows, it can trap the water flowing along the shore. In some places, water breaks through the sandbar and begins to flow back down the sloping ocean bottom. This process creates a **rip current**, a rush of water that flows rapidly back to sea through a narrow opening. Rip currents can carry a swimmer out into deep water. Because rip currents are narrow, a strong swimmer can usually escape by swimming across the current, parallel to the beach.

Checkpoint In what direction does a rip current pull a swimmer?

Figure 4 Waves approach the shore at an angle. This results in a gradual movement of sand down the beach. *Interpreting Diagrams In which direction is longshore drift moving the sand along this beach?*

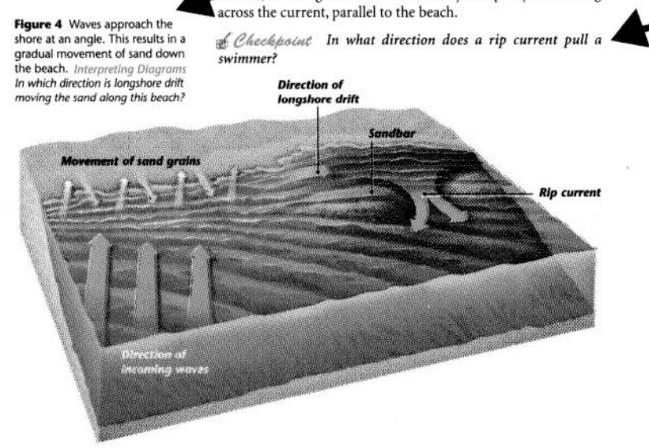

118 • H

Self-assessment opportunities help students keep themselves on course.

- **Caption Questions** throughout the text assess critical thinking skills.
- **Checkpoint Questions** give students an immediate content check as new concepts are presented.
- Plus, the **Interactive Student Tutorial CD-ROM** provides students with electronic self-tests, review activities, and Exploration activities.

Utilize a variety of tools.

Easy-to-manage, book-specific teaching resources

Teaching Resource Packages are available for each of the 15 titles. Packages contain a Teacher's Edition desk copy, Teaching Resources with Color Transparencies, Guided Reading Audiotapes, Materials Kit Order Form, and a Correlation to the National Science Education Standards.

Teacher's Edition three-step lesson plan—*Engage/Explore, Facilitate,* and *Assess*— is ideal for reaching all students. Chapter planning charts make it easy to find resources, as well as to plan for block scheduling and team teaching.

Teaching Resources with Color Transparencies are organized by chapter to make it easy for you to find what you need—when you need it.

- **Chapter Project Support**
- **Lesson Plans**
- **Section Summaries**
- **Review and Reinforcement**
- **Enrichment**
- **Skills Practice**
- **In-Text Lab Worksheets**
- **Interdisciplinary Explorations**
- **Performance Assessments with Rubrics**
- **Chapter Tests, Book Test**
- **Answer Key**
- **Color Transparencies (20 per book)**

Guided Reading Audiotapes provide section summaries for students who need additional guided reading support. Also available in Spanish.

Program-wide print and technology components to support the entire program

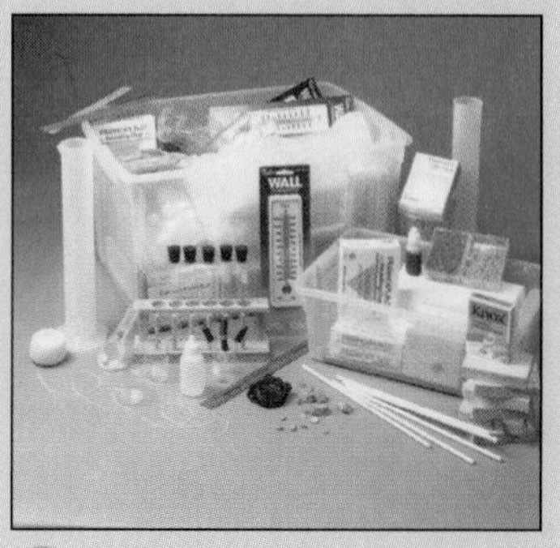

1

2 3

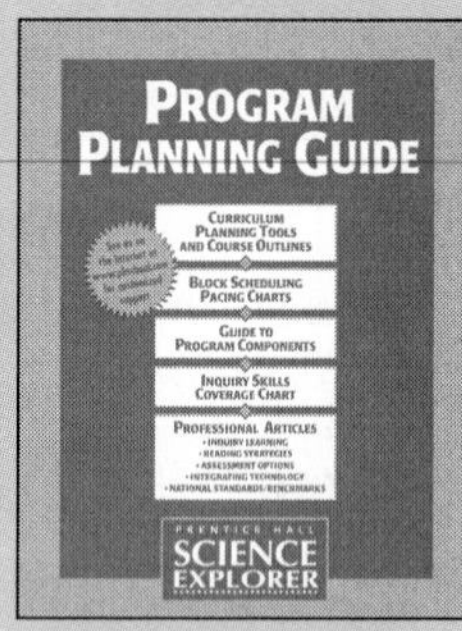

4 5 6

1. **Materials Kits**—Prentice Hall and Science Kit, Inc. have collaborated to develop a Consumable Kit and Nonconsumable Kit specific to each book. Electronic order forms make it easy for you to customize kits.

2. **Integrated Science Laboratory Manual**— 72 additional laboratory investigations, covering the entire *Science Explorer* curriculum.

3. **Integrated Science Laboratory Manual, Teacher's Edition**—information on safety, equipment, strategies, and answers to all questions in the student edition lab manual.

4. **Inquiry Skills Activity Book**—additional activities that introduce basic and advanced inquiry skills and reinforce skills on an as-needed basis.

7

8

9
10

11

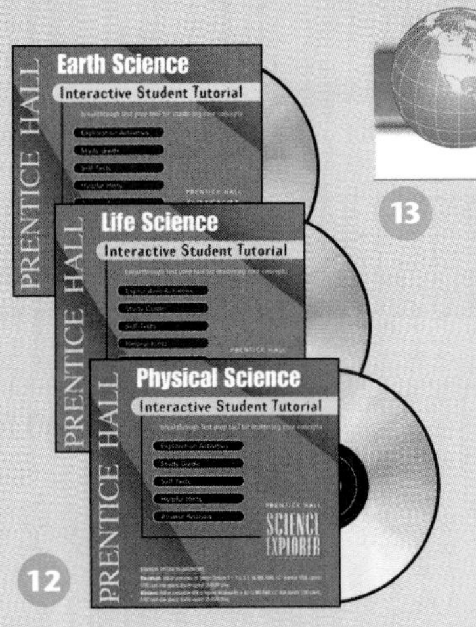

12

13
14

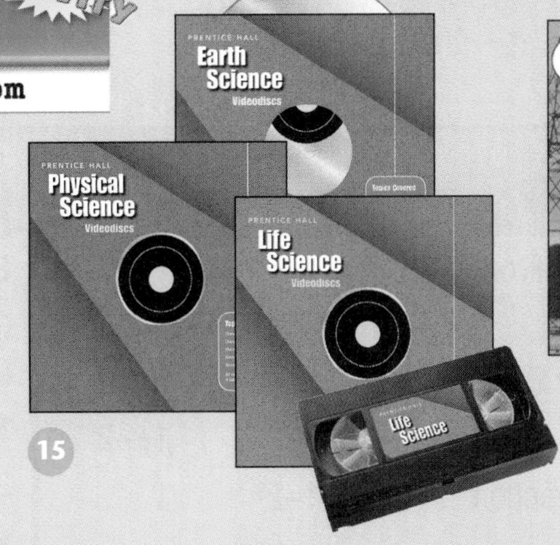

15

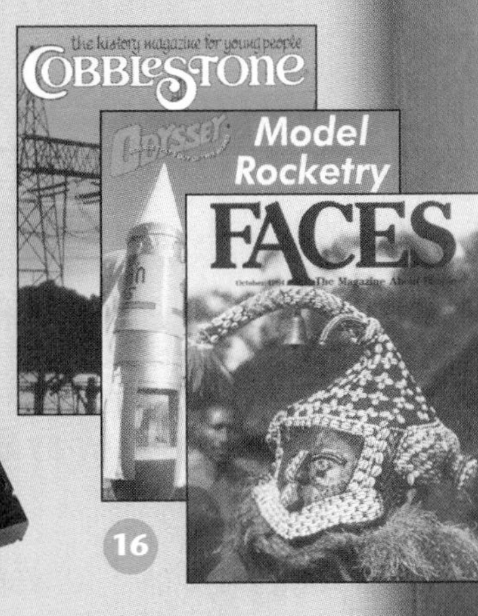

16

5. **Student-Centered Science Activities**—five regional activity books focused on the Northeast, Southeast, Midwest, Southwest, and West.

6. **Program Planning Guide**—course outlines, block scheduling pacing charts, correlations to the National Standards, and more.

7. **Product Testing Activities by *Consumer Reports***—19 student-oriented testing activities developed by Consumer Reports and Prentice Hall. Available in ten-packs for each activity and correlated to each book.

8. **Prentice Hall Interdisciplinary Explorations**—15 units designed to help you connect science topics to social studies, math, language arts—and students' daily lives.

9 & 10. **Professional Development Resources**—*How to Assess Student Work* and *How to Manage Instruction in the Block*

11. **Resource Pro® CD-ROM**—electronic versions of the Teaching Resources for all 15 books—ideal for creating integrated science lessons. Contains Planning Express® software and Computer Test Bank. Organized by chapter to save you time.

12. **Interactive Student Tutorial CD-ROMs**—provide students with self-tests, helpful hints, and Exploration activities. Tests are scored instantly and contain a detailed explanation of results.

13. ***Science Explorer* Internet Site**—additional activities and current data for every *Science Explorer* chapter. Check it out at www.science-explorer.phschool.com

14. **Assessment Resources with CD-ROM**—comprehensive collection of assessment resources containing **Computer Test Bank Software,** chapter and book tests, and performance assessments.

15. **Life, Earth, and Physical Science Videotapes and Videodiscs**—allow students to further explore and visualize concepts through spectacular short documentaries containing computer animations.

16. ***Cobblestone, Odyssey,* and *Faces* Magazines**—engaging magazines that support the Interdisciplinary Units and selected topics from each book.

Options for Pacing *Inside Earth*

The Pacing Chart below suggests one way to schedule your instructional time. The ***Science Explorer*** program offers many other aids to help you plan your instructional time, whether regular class periods or **block scheduling.** Refer to the Chapter Planning Guide before each chapter to view all program resources with suggested times for Student Edition activities.

Pacing Chart

	Days	Blocks
Nature of Science: Focus on Fronts	1	$\frac{1}{2}$
Chapter 1 Plate Tectonics		
Chapter 1 Project Cut-Away Earth	Ongoing	Ongoing
1 Earth's Interior	3–4	$1\frac{1}{2}$–2
2 Integrating Physics: Convection Currents and the Mantle	1–2	1
3 Drifting Continents	2–3	1–$1\frac{1}{2}$
4 Sea-Floor Spreading	4–5	2–$2\frac{1}{2}$
5 The Theory of Plate Tectonics	3–4	$1\frac{1}{2}$–2
Chapter 1 Review and Assessment	1	$\frac{1}{2}$
Chapter 2 Earthquakes		
Chapter 2 Project Shake, Rattle, and Roll	Ongoing	Ongoing
1 Earth's Crust in Motion	4–5	2–3
2 Measuring Earthquakes	3–4	2
3 Earthquake Hazards and Safety	2–3	1–2
4 Integrating Technology: Monitoring Faults	3–4	2
Chapter 2 Review and Assessment	1	$\frac{1}{2}$
Chapter 3 Volcanoes		
Chapter 3 Project Volcanoes and People	Ongoing	Ongoing
1 Volcanoes and Plate Tectonics	2–3	1–$1\frac{1}{2}$
2 Volcanic Activity	4–5	2–3
3 Volcanic Landforms	3–4	$1\frac{1}{2}$–2
4 Integrating Space Science: Volcanoes in the Solar System	1	$\frac{1}{2}$
Chapter 3 Review and Assessment	1	$\frac{1}{2}$

	Days	Blocks
Chapter 4 Minerals		
Chapter 4 Project Growing a Crystal Garden	Ongoing	Ongoing
1 Properties of Minerals	3–4	$1\frac{1}{2}$–2
2 How Minerals Form	2–3	1–$1\frac{1}{2}$
3 Integrating Technology: Mineral Resources	2–3	1–$1\frac{1}{2}$
Chapter 4 Review and Assessment	1	$\frac{1}{2}$
Chapter 5 Rocks		
Chapter 5 Project Collecting Rocks	Ongoing	Ongoing
1 Classifying Rocks	1–2	$\frac{1}{2}$–1
2 Igneous Rocks	2–3	1–$1\frac{1}{2}$
3 Sedimentary Rocks	2–3	1–$1\frac{1}{2}$
4 Integrating Life Science: Rocks From Reefs	1–2	$\frac{1}{2}$–1
5 Metamorphic Rocks	2–3	1–$1\frac{1}{2}$
6 The Rock Cycle	2–3	1–$1\frac{1}{2}$
Chapter 5 Review and Assessment	1	$\frac{1}{2}$
Interdisciplinary Exploration: Gold—The Noble Metal	2–3	1–$1\frac{1}{2}$

RESOURCE PRO®

The Resource Pro® CD-ROM is the ultimate scheduling and lesson planning tool. Resource Pro® allows you to preview all the resources in the *Science Explorer* program, organize your chosen materials, and print out any teaching resource. You can follow the suggested lessons or create your own, using resources from anywhere in the program.

Thematic Overview of *Inside Earth*

The chart below lists the major themes of ***Inside Earth***. For each theme, the chart supplies a big idea, or concept statement, describing how a particular theme is taught in a chapter.

	Chapter 1	Chapter 2	Chapter 3	Chapter 4	Chapter 5
Energy	Heat is transferred by radiation, conduction, and convection.	Stress is a force that acts on rocks. Seismic waves carry the energy of an earthquake away from the focus.	During a volcanic eruption, gases dissolved in magma rush out, carrying magma with them.	Magma heats water to a high temperature beneath Earth's surface. Smelting is necessary to remove the metal from an ore.	Forces inside Earth and at the surface produce a rock cycle that builds, destroys, and changes rocks in the crust.
Evolution	Plate tectonics explains how Earth's crust has changed over time.	Over time, fault movement can create mountains and valleys.	A volcano passes through three stages: active, dormant, and extinct.		The remains of living things may be preserved as fossils in sedimentary rock.
Patterns of Change	Temperature and pressure increase with depth inside Earth.	Stress causes rock to deform in various ways. Seismologists study seismic waves to locate an earthquake's epicenter.	Earthquake zones and volcanic belts are located along plate boundaries. The buildup of lava and magma creates landforms.		The processes of the rock cycle cause rocks to change continuously from one form to another.
Scale and Structure	Earth's interior is made up of crust, mantle, and core. The lithosphere is broken into a number of plates.	Earthquakes vary in intensity.	All volcanoes have a magma chamber, pipe, and vent.	The repeating pattern of a mineral's particles forms a solid called a crystal.	Rocks are made of minerals.
Systems and Interactions	No plate can move without affecting other plates.	An earthquake occurs when there is movement along a fault.	A volcano erupts when magma from the mantle breaks through the crust and lava flows over the surface.	Minerals form through crystallization of melted materials and through crystallization of materials dissolved in water.	Plate movements drive the rock cycle.
Unity and Diversity	Each layer of Earth's interior has its own conditions and materials.	Shearing, tension, and compression are different types of stress that produce different types of faults.	The silica content of magma helps determine whether a volcanic eruption is quiet or explosive. There are volcanoes on other planets and moons.	Minerals are identified by properties such as color, luster, hardness, density, streak, crystal shape, cleavage, and fracture.	Rocks are classified as igneous, sedimentary, or metamorphic. There are three types of coral reefs.
Stability	The formation of new crust at mid-ocean ridges is balanced by the destruction of old crust at deep-ocean trenches.			Each mineral has its own specific properties that can be used to identify it.	
Modeling	Students build a model and show sea-floor spreading and convection currents in Earth's mantle.	Students design a model of an earthquake-resistant structure.			

Inquiry Skills Chart

The Prentice Hall *Science Explorer* program provides comprehensive teaching, practice, and assessment of science skills, with an emphasis on the process skills necessary for inquiry. The chart lists the skills covered in the program and cites the page numbers where each skill is covered.

Basic Process SKILLS				
	Student Text: Projects and Labs	**Student Text: Activities**	**Student Text: Caption and Review Questions**	**Teacher's Edition: Extensions**
Observing	40–41, 48, 92, 108–109, 116–117, 140, 144–145, 165	27, 33, 64, 66, 118, 125, 146, 152, 154, 164, 180	17, 29, 89, 121, 143, 147, 156, 162, 173	21, 26, 32, 57, 59, 65, 122, 125, 131, 148, 180
Inferring	40–41, 48, 62–63, 92	16, 25, 150, 162, 180	30, 32, 51, 57, 76, 91, 97, 115, 129, 143, 160, 173	31, 57, 66, 94, 101, 106, 111, 129, 130 180
Predicting	52–53	43, 54, 72, 180	27, 39, 47, 51, 61, 85, 91, 115, 143, 161	76, 180
Classifying	62–63, 86–87, 144–145, 165	55, 121, 167, 181	51, 85, 115, 126, 143, 158, 173	67, 104, 119, 123, 125, 156, 181
Making Models	14–15, 40–41, 48, 52–53, 62–63, 108–109	30, 37, 77, 91, 94, 102, 103, 163, 175, 176, 181		18, 23, 35, 37, 43, 44, 45, 60, 61, 68, 73, 79, 105, 155, 160, 181
Communicating	14–15, 52–53, 86–87, 116–117, 144–145	32, 51, 85, 115, 138, 153, 173, 177, 179, 181	50, 84, 114, 142, 172	32, 34, 181
Measuring	116–117, 127, 140	59, 182–183	69	23, 122, 182–183
Calculating		74, 179, 183		183
Creating Data Tables	116–117, 165	21, 190		190
Graphing		190–192		190–192
Advanced Process SKILLS				
Posing Questions		28, 110, 134, 184–185	43, 73, 112	18, 184–185
Developing Hypotheses	108–109, 140	88, 93, 166, 184–185	104, 115	29, 184–185
Designing Experiments	170	185		19, 36, 96, 129, 185
Controlling Variables		185		185
Forming Operational Definitions	170	185	148	185

Advanced Process SKILLS *(continued)*				
	Student Text: Projects and Labs	**Student Text: Activities**	**Student Text: Caption and Review Questions**	**Teacher's Edition: Extensions**
Interpreting Data	14–15, 70–71, 92	185	124	185
Drawing Conclusions	70–71, 86–87, 127, 140, 144–145, 170	42, 78, 143, 156, 159, 185	38, 85, 102, 122, 143	31, 157, 185
Critical Thinking SKILLS				
Comparing and Contrasting	116–117	186	19, 20, 24, 51, 79, 85, 106, 112, 115, 119, 143, 149, 153, 158, 173	20, 21, 46, 58, 74, 96, 121, 135, 148, 151, 153, 186
Applying Concepts	14–15, 52–53	186	27, 35, 67, 85, 115, 125, 143, 169, 173	26, 56, 100, 186
Interpreting Diagrams, Graphs Photographs, and Maps		186	36, 43, 51, 65, 81, 85, 130, 132	186
Relating Cause and Effect	52–53	128, 187	24, 39, 51, 55, 69, 107, 132, 138, 143, 151, 155, 164, 173	37, 38, 187
Making Generalizations		187	51, 81, 115, 126	187
Making Judgments		187	169	187
Problem Solving		82, 133, 187	77	187
Information Organizing SKILLS				
Concept Maps		188	84, 114	132, 188
Compare/ Contrast Tables		188		24, 135, 158, 188
Venn Diagrams		189	142	189
Flowcharts		189		131, 139, 164, 189
Cycle Diagrams		189	50, 172	189

The *Science Explorer* program provides additional teaching, reinforcement, and assessment of skills in the Inquiry Skills Activities Book and the Integrated Science Laboratory Manual.

Throughout the *Science Explorer* program, every effort has been made to keep the materials and equipment *affordable, reusable,* and *easily accessible*.

The *Science Explorer* program offers an abundance of activity options so you can pick and choose those activities that suit your needs. To help you order supplies at the beginning of the year, the Master Materials List cross-references the materials by activity. If you prefer to create your list electronically,use the electronic order forms at:
www.science–explorer.phschool.com

There are two kits available for each book of the *Science Explorer* program, a Consumable Kit and a Nonconsumable Kit. These kits are produced by **Science Kit and Boreal Laboratories,** the leader in providing science kits to schools. Prentice Hall and Science Kit collaborated throughout the development of *Science Explorer* to ensure that the equipment and supplies in the kits precisely match the requirements of the program activities.

The kits provide an economical and convenient way to get all of the materials needed to teach each book. For each book, Science Kit also offers the opportunity to buy equipment and safety items individually. For a current listing of kit offerings or additional information about materials to accompany *Science Explorer*, please, contact Science Kit at:
1-800-828-7777
or at their Internet site at:
www.sciencekit.com

Master Materials List

Consumable Materials

*	Description	Quantity per class	Textbook Section(s)
C	Baking soda, 1 lb.	1	3-2 (TT)
C	Balloons, 9" round, pkg. of 16	1	3-3 (DIS)
SS	Bread, slice	10	5-3 (DIS)
SS	Butter, 1 stick	1	5-6 (Lab)
C	Candle, warming	5	4-2 (DIS)
C	Candle, white 10 cm × 1.75 cm	10	1-5 (Lab)
C	Cards, index, blank 3" × 5", pkg. of 100	1	5-6 (DIS)
C	Clay, modeling (cream), 1 lb.	3	1-5 (Lab) 5-5 (TT)
C	Clay, modeling (four colors), 1 lb.	2	2-1 (Lab)
SS	Crayons	5	5-6 (Lab)
C	Cup, plastic clear, 300 mL	5	1-2 (DIS) 3-3 (Lab)
C	Cupric sulfate, 100 g	1	4-3 (Lab)
C	Epsom salt, 500 g	1	4-1 (TT)
C	Food coloring, red, 30 mL	1	1-2 (DIS) 3-1 (TT) 3-3 (Lab)
C	Gelatin, box of 4 packets	2	3-3 (Lab)
C	Hydrochloric acid, 1M (1N), 50 mL	1	5-4 (DIS)
SS	Ice cube	5	4-2 (DIS)
SS	Ink, small bottle	5	5-6 (Lab)
C	Knife, plastic	5	2-1 (Lab) 3-3 (Lab)
C	Map, world, 10" × 15"	5	3-1 (Lab)
C	Marker, black, permanent	5	2-1 (Lab)
SS	Markers	10	1-4 (Lab)
C	Matches, wood safety, box of 30	5	4-2 (DIS)
C	Nails, 9 cm 16D, pkg. of 15	2	4-3 (Lab) 5-6 (Lab)
SS	Newspaper, sheet	30	1-3 (TT)
C	Paint, tempera, red, 8 oz.	1	5-6 (Lab)
C	Pan, aluminum foil, 13" × 10" × 2"	5	1-5 (Lab)
C	Pan, aluminum foil, 22.5 cm diameter	10	1-2 (DIS) 3-3 (DIS) 3-3 (Lab) 4-1 (TT) 5-3 (TT)
SS	Paper, construction, black, pkg. of 15	1	4-1 (TT)
SS	Paper, unlined, sheet	30	1-4 (Lab) 1-5 (DIS) 3-3 (Lab) 5-3 (DIS)
SS	Pen	5	2-2 (TT)
SS	Pencil	5	2-2 (TT) 4-3 (DIS)
SS	Pencils, colored, pkg. of 12	5	3-1 (Lab) 3-3 (Lab)
C	Phenyl salicylate (Salol), 100 g	1	4-2 (DIS)
SS	Raisins, box	1	3-2 (TT)
C	Salt, non-iodized, 737 g	1	4-1 (TT)
C	Sand, fine, 2.5 kg	1	3-3 (DIS)
SS	Sequins, pkg.	1	5-5 (TT)
C	Spoons, plastic, pkg. of 24	1	4-2 (DIS)
C	Sticks, craft, pkg. of 50	1	2-1 (DIS)
C	Straws, plastic (wrapped), pkg. of 50	1	2-3 (DIS) 3-3 (DIS)
C	String, cotton, 200 ft.	1	5-5 (TT)
C	Tape, adding machine roll, 2-1/4" × 100'	1	2-2 (TT)
C	Tape, cassette, blank	1	1-4 (TT)
SS	Tape, masking, 3/4" × 60 yd.	1	1-1 (DIS) 1-5 (DIS) 2-1 (SYS) 2-3 (DIS) 3-3 (DIS)
SS	Tape, transparent dispenser roll, 27 ft.	1	1-4 (TT)
SS	Tissues, facial, pkg. of 16	1	2-4 (DIS)
C	Tray, plastic foam, 8" × 10"	2	3-1 (TT)
C	Vinegar, 500 mL	1	3-2 (TT)

KEY: **DIS**: Discover; **SYS**: Sharpen Your Skills; **TT**: Try This; **Lab**: Lab
* Items designated **C** are in the Consumable Kit, **NC** are in the Nonconsumable Kit, and **SS** are School Supplied.

Master Materials List

Nonconsumable Materials

*	Description	Quantity per class	Textbook Section(s)
SS	Atlas	5	1-5 (DIS)
NC	Beaker, Pyrex, 400 mL	5	4-3 (Lab)
SS	Book	30	2-2 (TT) 3-3 (Lab) 5-3 (DIS)
SS	Bottle, 2-L plastic	5	3-2 (TT)
NC	Bottle, flint glass, narrow mouth with cap, 2 oz	5	3-1 (TT)
NC	Bowl, opaque, 2 L	5	3-3 (Lab)
SS	Box, plastic	5	3-1 (TT)
SS	Brick	30	1-5 (Lab)
NC	Brick veneer, 1/4" thick	1	5-5 (Lab)
SS	Brush, wire	5	5-6 (Lab)
SS	Can, aluminum	5	4-3 (DIS)
NC	Canister, film type with snap cap	15	1-1 (DIS)
SS	Compass with pencil	5	2-2 (Lab)
NC	Cylinder, graduated, polypropylene, 100 mL	5	3-2 (TT) 4-1 (Lab) 4-3 (Lab)
NC	Dropper, plastic	5	1-2 (DIS) 5-4 (DIS) 5-6 (Lab)
NC	Magnet, bar alnico, with marked poles, 3"	5	1-4 (TT)
NC	Magnifying glass, 3x and 6x	5	3-2 (DIS) 4-1 (TT) 4-2 (DIS) 5-1 (DIS) 5-2 (DIS) 5-3 (TT) 5-4 (DIS) 5-5 (DIS) 5-5 (Lab) 5-6 (Lab)
NC	Mineral, bauxite, tenpack	1	4-3 (DIS)
NC	Mineral, calcite, (5 pieces 2–3 cm, 20 chips)	1	4-1 (SYS)
NC	Mineral, galena, (5 pieces 2–3 cm, 20 chips)	1	4-1 (Lab)
NC	Mineral, graphite, (5 pieces 2–3 cm, 20 chips)	1	4-3 (DIS)
NC	Mineral, hematite, (5 pieces 2–3 cm, 20 chips)	1	4-1 (DIS)
NC	Mineral, magnetite, (5 pieces 2–3 cm, 20 chips)	1	4-1 (DIS)
NC	Mineral, pyrite, (5 pieces 2–3 cm, 20 chips)	1	4-1 (Lab)
NC	Mineral, quartz, (5 pieces 2–3 cm, 20 chips)	1	4-1 (SYS) 4-1 (Lab)
NC	Mineral, talc (5 pieces 2–3 cm, 20 chips)	1	4-1 (SYS)
SS	Pegboard	5	3-3 (Lab)
SS	Penny	5	4-1 (SYS) 5-1 (DIS)
NC	Pins, map, assorted colors, pkg. of 100	1	1-5 (Lab)
SS	Putty, plastic	5	2-1 (TT)
NC	Rock, conglomerate, (5 pieces 2–3 cm, 20 chips)	1	5-1 (DIS)
NC	Rock, gneiss, (5 pieces 2–3 cm, 20 chips)	1	5-5 (DIS) 5-5 (Lab) 5-6 (Lab)
NC	Rock, granite (pegmatite), (5 pieces 2–3 cm, 20 chips)	1	5-2 (DIS) 5-5 (DIS) 5-5 (Lab) 5-6 (Lab)
NC	Rock, limestone (coquina), (5 pieces 2–3 cm)	1	5-4 (DIS)

KEY: **DIS**: Discover; **SYS**: Sharpen Your Skills; **TT**: Try This; **Lab**: Lab
* Items designated **C** are in the Consumable Kit, **NC** are in the Nonconsumable Kit, and **SS** are School Supplied.

Nonconsumable Materials (cont.)

*	Description	Quantity per class	Textbook Section(s)
NC	Rock, limestone, (5 pieces 2–3 cm, 20 chips)	1	5-4 (DIS) 5-6 (Lab)
NC	Rock, marble, white, (5 pieces 2–3 cm, 20 chips)	1	5-1 (DIS) 5-6 (Lab)
NC	Rock, obsidian, (5 pieces 2–3 cm, 20 chips)	1	3-2 (DIS) 5-2 (DIS) 5-6 (Lab)
NC	Rock, pumice, (5 pieces 2–3 cm, 20 chips)	1	3-2 (DIS) 5-5 (Lab)
NC	Rock, sandstone, (5 pieces 2–3 cm, 20 chips)	1	5-3 (TT) 5-5 (Lab) 5-6 (Lab)
NC	Rock, shale, gray, (5 pieces 2–3 cm, 20 chips)	1	5-3 (TT) 5-5 (Lab) 5-6 (Lab)
NC	Rock, slate, (5 pieces 2–3 cm, 20 chips)	1	5-5 (Lab) 5-6 (Lab)
SS	Ruler, plastic, 12"/30 cm	5	1-4 (Lab) 2-4 (DIS)
NC	Sandpaper, medium, 9" × 11" sheet	5	2-1 (SYS)
SS	Scissors	5	1-4 (TT) 1-4 (Lab) 1-5 (DIS)
NC	Sinker, lead fishing, 4 oz.	5	2-1 (SYS)
NC	Slides, microscope, box of 72	1	4-2 (DIS)
NC	Slinky, plastic	5	2-2 (DIS)
NC	Sponge, 15 cm × 7.5 cm × 1.8 cm	10	1-5 (Lab)
NC	Spring scale, 500 g/5 N	5	2-1 (SYS)
NC	Streak plate, 50 mm × 50 mm × 3 mm	5	4-1 (DIS)
NC	Syringe, disposable, 10 cc	5	3-3 (Lab)
NC	Tongs, flask and test tube	5	4-2 (DIS)
SS	Washcloth	5	1-4 (DIS)
NC	Wood, block, 2" × 4" × 6"	10	5-5 (TT)

Equipment

*	Description	Quantity per class	Textbook Section(s)
SS	Apron, lab	30	3-2 (TT) 3-3 (Lab) 5-4 (DIS)
SS	Balance, triple beam	5	1-1 (DIS) 3-2 (TT) 4-1 (Lab) 4-3 (Lab) 5-3 (TT)
SS	Goggles, chemical splash, class set	1	2-1 (DIS) 3-2 (TT) 4-1 (TT) 4-1 (Lab) 4-2 (DIS) 4-3 (Lab) 5-4 (DIS) 5-6 (Lab)
SS	Gloves, medium, latex, box of 100	1	3-3 (Lab)
SS	Globe, physical features	5	1-3 (DIS)

KEY: **DIS**: Discover; **SYS**: Sharpen Your Skills; **TT**: Try This; **Lab**: Lab
* Items designated **C** are in the Consumable Kit, **NC** are in the Nonconsumable Kit, and **SS** are School Supplied.

Inside Earth

Program Resources

Student Edition
Annotated Teacher's Edition
Teaching Resources with Color Transparencies
Inside Earth Materials Kits

Program Components

Integrated Science Laboratory Manual
Integrated Science Laboratory Manual, Teacher's Edition
Inquiry Skills Activity Book
Student-Centered Science Activity Books
Program Planning Guide
Guided Reading English Audiotapes
Guided Reading Spanish Audiotapes and Summaries
Product Testing Activities by Consumer Reports™
Prentice Hall Interdisciplinary Explorations
Cobblestone, Odyssey, and *Faces* Magazines

Media/Technology

Science Explorer Interactive Student Tutorial CD-ROM
Resource Pro® (Teaching Resources on CD-ROM)
Assessment Resources CD-ROM with Dial-A-Test®
Internet site at www.science-explorer.phschool.com
Exploring Life, Earth, and Physical Science Videodiscs
Exploring Life, Earth, and Physical Science Videotapes

Science Explorer Student Editions

From Bacteria to Plants
Animals
Cells and Heredity
Human Biology and Health
Environmental Science
Inside Earth
Earth's Changing Surface
Earth's Waters
Weather and Climate
Astronomy
Chemical Building Blocks
Chemical Interactions
Motion, Forces, and Energy
Electricity and Magnetism
Sound and Light

Staff Credits

The members of the *Science Explorer* team—representing editorial, design, marketing, publishing processes, editorial services, production services, manufacturing, technology, electronic publishing, and advertising and promotion—and their managers are listed below. Bold type denotes core team members.

Joseph Berman, **Barbara A. Bertell,** Bruce Bond, Therese Bräuer, **Christopher R. Brown, Greg Cantone,** Arthur C. Germano, Christine A. Caputo, **Patrick Finbarr Connolly,** Edward de Leon, Robert G. Dunn, Loree Franz, **Paul J. Gagnon, Joel Gendler,** Elizabeth Good, David Graham, Maureen Grassi, Kerri Hoar, Jeffrey M. Ikler, Mimi Jigarjian, **Linda D. Johnson,** Russ Lappa, David Lippman, Eve Melnechuk, Thomas L. Messer, **Natania Mlawer,** Paul W. Murphy, **Cindy A. Noftle,** Beth A. Norman, Julia F. Osborne, Caroline M. Power, Edward A. Rock, Suzanne J. Schineller, **Susan W. Tafler,** Kira Thaler-Marbit, Robin L. Tiano, **Mark Tricca.**
We would like to thank National Science Consultants Terry Balko, Jeannie Dennard, Kathy French, and Brenda Underwood for their help in developing this program.

Activity on pages 108–109 is from *Exploring Planets in the Classroom,* ©Hawaii Space Grant Consortium. Used with permission.

ISBN 0-13-434570-3 Teacher's Edition

ISBN 0-13-434489-8 Student Edition

1 2 3 4 5 6 7 8 9 10 05 04 03 02 01 00 99 98

Cover: Lava flows down a mountainside on the Big Island of Hawaii.

Program Authors

Michael J. Padilla, Ph.D.
Professor
Department of Science Education
University of Georgia
Athens, Georgia

Michael Padilla is a leader in middle school science education. He has served as an editor and elected officer for the National Science Teachers Association. He has been principal investigator of several National Science Foundation and Eisenhower grants and served as a writer of the National Science Education Standards.

As lead author of *Science Explorer,* Mike has inspired the team in developing a program that meets the needs of middle grades students, promotes science inquiry, and is aligned with the National Science Education Standards.

Ioannis Miaoulis, Ph.D.
Dean of Engineering
College of Engineering
Tufts University
Medford, Massachusetts

Martha Cyr, Ph.D.
Director, Engineering
Educational Outreach
College of Engineering
Tufts University
Medford, Massachusetts

Science Explorer was created in collaboration with the College of Engineering at Tufts University. Tufts has an extensive engineering outreach program that uses engineering design and construction to excite and motivate students and teachers in science and technology education.

Faculty from Tufts University participated in the development of *Science Explorer* chapter projects, reviewed the student books for content accuracy, and helped coordinate field testing.

Book Authors

Carole Garbuny Vogel
Science Writer
Lexington, Massachusetts

Contributing Writers

Holly Estes
Science Instructor
Hale Middle School
Stow, Massachusetts

Greg Hutton
Science and Health
Curriculum Coordinator
School Board of
Sarasota County
Sarasota, Florida

Lauren Magruder
Science Instructor
St. Michael's Country
Day School
Newport, Rhode Island

Sharon M. Stroud
Science Instructor
Widefield High School
Colorado Springs
Colorado

Thomas R. Wellnitz
Science Instructor
The Paideia School
Atlanta, Georgia

Reading Consultant

Bonnie B. Armbruster, Ph.D.
Department of Curriculum
and Instruction
University of Illinois
Champaign, Illinois

Interdisciplinary Consultant

Heidi Hayes Jacobs, Ed.D.
Teacher's College
Columbia University
New York City, New York

Safety Consultants

W. H. Breazeale, Ph.D.
Department of Chemistry
College of Charleston
Charleston, South Carolina

Ruth Hathaway, Ph.D.
Hathaway Consulting
Cape Girardeau, Missouri

Tufts University Program Reviewers

Behrouz Abedian, Ph.D.
Department of Mechanical Engineering

Wayne Chudyk, Ph.D.
Department of Civil and Environmental Engineering

Eliana DeBernardez-Clark, Ph.D.
Department of Chemical Engineering

Anne Marie Desmarais, Ph.D.
Department of Civil and Environmental Engineering

David Kaplan, Ph.D.
Department of Chemical Engineering

Paul Kelley, Ph.D.
Department of Electro-Optics

George S. Mumford, Ph.D.
Professor of Astronomy, Emeritus

Jan A. Pechenik, Ph.D.
Department of Biology

Livia Racz, Ph.D.
Department of Mechanical Engineering

Robert Rifkin, M.D.
School of Medicine

Jack Ridge, Ph.D.
Department of Geology

Chris Swan, Ph.D.
Department of Civil and Environmental Engineering

Peter Y. Wong, Ph.D.
Department of Mechanical Engineering

Content Reviewers

Jack W. Beal, Ph.D.
Department of Physics
Fairfield University
Fairfield, Connecticut

W. Russell Blake, Ph.D.
Planetarium Director
Plymouth Community Intermediate School
Plymouth, Massachusetts

Howard E. Buhse, Jr., Ph.D.
Department of Biological Sciences
University of Illinois
Chicago, Illinois

Dawn Smith Burgess, Ph.D.
Department of Geophysics
Stanford University
Stanford, California

A. Malcolm Campbell, Ph.D.
Assistant Professor
Davidson College
Davidson, North Carolina

John M. Fowler, Ph.D.
Former Director of Special Projects
National Science Teacher's Association
Arlington, Virginia

Jonathan Gitlin, M.D.
School of Medicine
Washington University
St. Louis, Missouri

Dawn Graff-Haight, Ph.D.
Department of Health, Human Performance, and Athletics
Linfield College
McMinnville, Oregon

Deborah L. Gumucio, Ph.D.
Associate Professor
Department of Anatomy and Cell Biology
University of Michigan
Ann Arbor, Michigan

William S. Harwood, Ph.D.
Assistant Dean for Undergraduate Studies
University of Maryland
College Park, Maryland

Cyndy Henzel, Ph.D.
Department of Geography and Regional Development
University of Arizona
Tucson, Arizona

Greg Hutton
Science and Health Curriculum Coordinator
School Board of Sarasota County
Sarasota, Florida

Susan K. Jacobson, Ph.D.
Department of Wildlife Ecology and Conservation
University of Florida
Gainesville, Florida

Judy Jernstedt, Ph. D.
Department of Agronomy and Range Science
University of California, Davis
Davis, California

John L. Kermond, Ph.D.
Office of Global Programs
National Oceanographic and Atmospheric Administration
Silver Spring, Maryland

David E. LaHart, Ph.D.
Institute of Science and Public Affairs
Florida State University
Tallahassee, Florida

Joe Leverich, Ph. D.
Department of Biology
St. Louis University
St. Louis, Missouri

Dennis K. Lieu, Ph. D.
Department of Mechanical Engineering
University of California
Berkeley, California

Cynthia J. Moore, Ph.D.
Science Outreach Coordinator
Washington University
St. Louis, Missouri

Joseph M. Moran, Ph.D.
Department of Earth Science
University of Wisconsin–Green Bay
Green Bay, Wisconsin

Joseph Stukey, Ph.D.
Department of Biology
Hope College
Holland, Michigan

Seetha Subramananian, Ph.D.
Lexington Community College
University of Kentucky
Lexington, Kentucky

Carl L. Thurman, Ph.D.
Department of Biology
University of Northern Iowa
Cedar Falls, Iowa

Edward D. Walton, Ph.D.
Department of Chemistry
California State Polytechnic University
Pomona, California

Robert S. Young, Ph.D.
Department of Geosciences and Natural Resource Management
Western Carolina University
Cullowhee, North Carolina

Edward J. Zalisko, Ph.D.
Department of Biology
Blackburn College
Carlinville, Illinois

Teacher Reviewers

Stephanie Anderson
Sierra Vista Junior High School
Canyon County, California

John W. Anson
Mesa Intermediate School
Palmdale, California

Pamela Arline
Lake Taylor Middle School
Norfolk, Virginia

Lynn Beason
College Station Jr. High School
College Station, Texas

Richard Bothmer
Hollis School District
Hollis, New Hampshire

Jeffrey C. Callister
Newburgh Free Academy
Newburgh, New York

Judy D'Albert
Harvard Day School
Corona Del Mar, California

Betty Scott Dean
Guilford County Schools
McLeansville, North Carolina

Sarah C. Duff
Baltimore City Public Schools
Baltimore, Maryland

Melody Law Ewey
Holmes Junior High School
Davis, California

Sherri L. Fisher
Lake Zurich Middle School North
Lake Zurich, Illinois

Melissa Gibbons
Fort Worth ISD
Fort Worth, Texas

Debra J. Gooding
Kraemer Middle School
Placentia, California

Jack Grande
Weber Middle School
Port Washington, New York

Steve Hills
Riverside Middle School
Grand Rapids, Michigan

Carol Ann Lionello
Kraemer Middle School
Placentia, California

Patsy Partin
Cameron Middle School
Nashville, Tennessee

Bonnie Scott
Clack Middle School
Abilene, Texas

Charles M. Sears
Belzer Middle School
Indianapolis, Indiana

Barbara M. Strange
Ferndale Middle School
High Point, North Carolina

Jackie Louise Ulfig
Ford Middle School
Allen, Texas

Kathy Usina
Belzer Middle School
Indianapolis, Indiana

Heidi M. von Oetinger
L'Anse Creuse Public School
Harrison Township, Michigan

Pam Watson
Hill Country Middle School
Austin, Texas

Activity Field Testers

Nicki Bibbo
Russell Street School
Littleton, Massachusetts

Connie Boone
Fletcher Middle School
Jacksonville Beach, Florida

Rose-Marie Botting
Broward County School District
Fort Lauderdale, Florida

Colleen Campos
Laredo Middle School
Aurora, Colorado

Elizabeth Chait
W. L. Chenery School
Belmont, Massachusetts

Holly Estes
Hale Middle School
Stow, Massachusetts

Laura Hapgood
Plymouth Community
Intermediate School
Plymouth, Massachusetts

Sandra M. Harris
Winman Junior High School
Warwick, Rhode Island

Jason Ho
Walter Reed Middle School
Los Angeles, California

Joanne Jackson
Winman Junior High School
Warwick, Rhode Island

Mary F. Lavin
Plymouth Community
Intermediate School
Plymouth, Massachusetts

James MacNeil, Ph.D.
Concord Public Schools
Concord, Massachusetts

Lauren Magruder
St. Michael's Country Day School
Newport, Rhode Island

Jeanne Maurand
Glen Urquhart School
Beverly Farms, Massachusetts

Warren Phillips
Plymouth Community
Intermediate School
Plymouth, Massachusetts

Carol Pirtle
Hale Middle School
Stow, Massachusetts

Kathleen M. Poe
Kirby-Smith Middle School
Jacksonville, Florida

Cynthia Pope
Russner Middle School
Norfolk, Virginia

Anne Scammell
Geneva Middle School
Geneva, New York

Karen Riley Sievers
Callanan Middle School
Des Moines, Iowa

David M. Smith
Howard A. Eyer Middle School
Macungie, Pennsylvania

Sallie Teames
Rosemont Middle School
Fort Worth, Texas

Gene Vitale
Parkland Middle School
McHenry, Illinois

Zenovia Young
Meyer Levin Junior
High School (IS 285)
Brooklyn, New York

Contents

Inside Earth

Check your compass— regularly assess student progress.

Self-assessment tools are built right into the student text and **on-going assessment** is woven throughout the Teacher's Edition. You'll find a wealth of **assessment technology** in the Resource Pro®, Interactive Student Tutorial, and Assessment Resources CD-ROMs.

Prepare your students with rich, motivating content

Science Explorer is crafted for today's middle grades student, with accessible content and in-depth coverage. **Integrated Science Sections** support every chapter and the **Interdisciplinary Exploration** provides an engaging final unit.

Guide your students to become science explorers.

A wide range of student-tested activities, from guided to open-ended, with options for short- and long-term inquiry.

Activities

Inquiry Activities

CHAPTER PROJECT

Opportunities for long-term inquiry

DISCOVER

Exploration and inquiry before reading

Sharpen your Skills

Practice of specific science inquiry skills

TRY THIS

Reinforcement of key concepts

Draw upon the world around you.

Interdisciplinary Activities connect to every discipline and give science a **meaningful, real-world context.**

Skills Lab

In-depth practice of inquiry skills

Real-World Lab

Everyday application of science concepts

EXPLORING

Visual exploration of concepts

Interdisciplinary Activities

Science and History

Science and Society

Connection

Focus on Faults

Focus on Seismology

This four-page feature introduces the process of scientific inquiry by involving students in a high-interest, magazine-like account of an actual working scientist, geologist Carol Prentice. Using Dr. Prentice's investigation of ancient earthquakes and faults as an example, the article focuses on the dual skills of observing and making inferences as key elements of scientific inquiry.

Earthquakes and faulting are presented in Chapter 2 of this book. However, students need no previous knowledge of that chapter's content to understand and appreciate this feature.

Scientific Inquiry

- Before students read the feature, let them examine the pictures and read the captions on their own. Then ask: **What do the pictures on pages 11–13 focus on?** *(Cracks in Earth's surface)* **Why are cracks like these important?** *(They show where earthquakes occurred in the past.)*
- Ask: **How do you think geologists know what Earth looks like deep underground, as in the figure on page 13?** *(Based on the photograph on page 12, some students may think that geologists have dug trenches far below Earth's surface and have directly observed deep faults. Other students may suggest that geologists make "an educated guess" about what soil and rock look like deep underground. Accept all responses without comment at this time.)*

NATURE OF SCIENCE

FOCUS ON FAULTS

"When I was about fourteen, my family was living in Taiwan," Geologist Carol Prentice recalls. "One day I was playing pinball, and a little earthquake happened. It tilted my pinball machine."

Unlike most people experiencing their first quake, her reaction was not fright but fascination. "*What in the world is that?* I wondered. That was the first time I consciously remember thinking that earthquakes were something interesting." Later, she recalls, "When I was teaching earth science in high school, I realized that my favorite section to teach was on earthquakes and faults."

During an earthquake, forces from inside Earth fracture or break the surface of Earth, producing a powerful jolt called an earthquake. As Earth's crust moves and breaks, it forms cracks, or faults. Over the centuries, the faults may break again and again. Geologist Carol Prentice climbs into these faults to study the soil and rocks. She hunts for clues about the history of a fault and estimates the risk of a serious earthquake in the future.

Carol Prentice studied geology at Humboldt State University and the California Institute of Technology. She is currently a Research Geologist for the United States Geological Survey in Menlo Park, California.

10 ◆ F

Background

Geology is traditionally divided into two broad areas: physical geology and historical geology. Physical geology examines the materials that compose Earth and the processes that operate on and below its surface. Seismology, one of the many disciplines within physical geology, involves the study of the forces within Earth that create earthquakes and faults. Historical geology focuses on Earth's origins and the development of the planet through its 4.6-billion-year history. Paleoseismology, Dr. Prentice's specialty, combines these two broad areas.

Since the forces operating deep within Earth's crust cannot be observed directly, seismologists must rely on data gathered by seismographs and fault-monitoring devices. The seismologists then interpret the data to make inferences about Earth's interior.

Finding Clues to Ancient Earthquakes

Today, Dr. Prentice is an expert in the field of paleoseismology. *Paleo* means "ancient" and *seismology* is "the study of earthquakes." So it's the study of ancient earthquakes. "Paleoseismologists search for evidence of earthquakes that happened hundreds or thousands of years ago," explains Dr. Prentice.

There are written records about earthquakes that happened years ago. But the real story of a quake is written in the rocks and soil. Years after an earthquake, wind, rain, and flowing water can wear the fault lines away from Earth's surface. Then the evidence of the quake is buried under layers of sediment. But the fault is still there.

Choosing a Site

How do you pick a site to research? "First we study aerial photographs, geological maps, and satellite images of the fault line," Dr. Prentice explains. "We will have some sites in mind. Then, we go out and look at the sites and do some digging with a shovel to get samples."

"We look for places where sediments, such as sand and gravel, have been building up. If sediments have been depositing there for many thousands of years, you're likely to have a good record of prehistoric earthquakes at that site. When you dig, you're likely to see not only the most recent earthquake buried and preserved in the sediments, but also earlier earthquakes. That's a really good site." Once the site is established, the geological team begins digging a trench along the fault.

The cracks of recent earthquakes, such as the Gobi-Altay fault shown here, are sometimes visible for hundreds of kilometers. Because this quake happened in the Mongolian desert, it is especially easy to see.

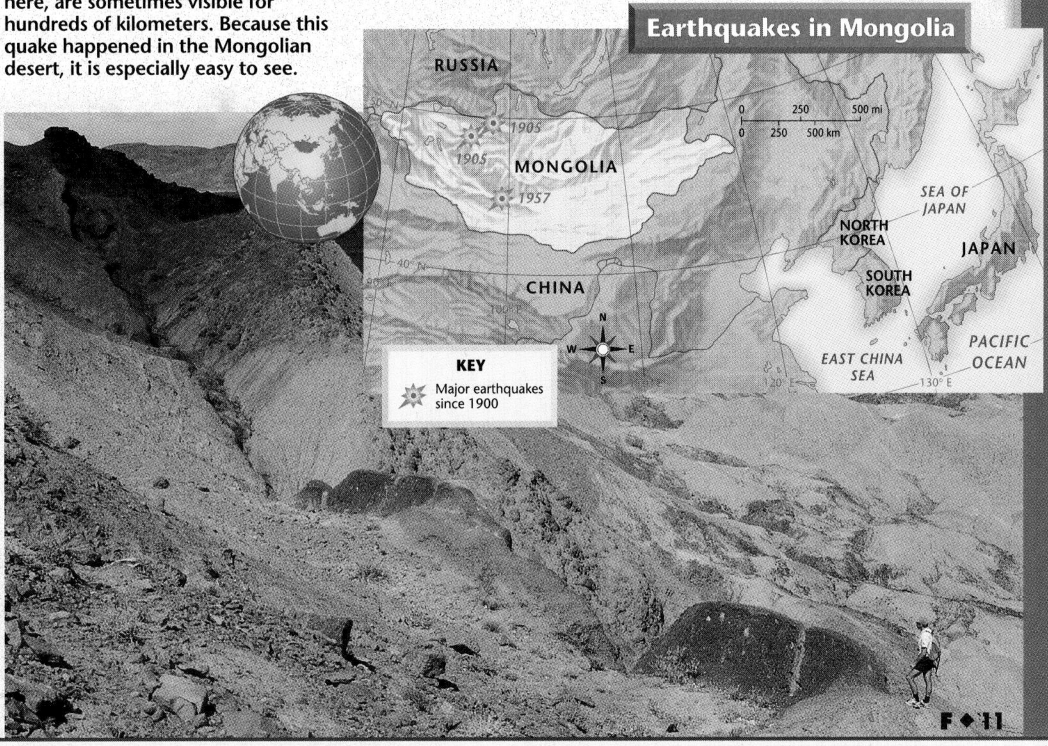

Earthquakes in Mongolia

- Encourage students to tell what they already know about earthquakes through their own direct experience or from news reports and documentary films. Particularly encourage them to describe cracks or deformations in the surface that they may have seen in person or in photographs.
- Help students with the pronunciation of *paleoseismology* (PAY lee oh size MOL uh jee) in the first paragraph on page 11.
- After students have read the text on these two pages, ask: **What evidence, or visible signs, of past earthquake activity does Dr. Prentice look for first when she's trying to find a site to study?** *(Cracks, or fault lines, on the surface)* **Why are they the first thing she looks for?** *(They're the easiest evidence to see.)* **What evidence does she look for next?** *(Sediments that have built up)* **Why does she look for sediments?** *(They show where prehistoric earthquakes occurred.)* **What do Dr. Prentice and her team do next?** *(They dig a deep trench along the fault.)*

- To give students an idea of how deep and narrow the trenches are, take them to a high wall inside the school building (such as in a gymnasium) or an outside wall of the building, and let each small group use a carpenter's metal tape measure to measure 4–5 meters ($13–16\frac{1}{2}$ feet) high on the wall. Encourage them to imagine themselves standing between two walls of that height and only about 1.25 meters apart (roughly the width of the trench shown in the photograph on this page). Emphasize that the trench walls are not stable, like the school's walls, but are made of gravel, sand, and other sediments packed tightly together. Ask: **How do you think you'd feel if you were working down in the trench? Why?** *(Let students share their thoughts about these dangerous working conditions.)*
- After students have read Looking at the Gobi-Altay Quake, have them turn back to the previous page and find the quake site on the map. Ask: **If the Gobi-Altay fault is in such a remote and unpopulated place, why are geologists so interested in it?** *(Its faults are similar to faults in other earthquake areas. By studying the Gobi-Altay earthquakes, geologists can learn about earthquakes that occur in heavily populated areas.)* Have students examine the map on page 58 showing the location of the San Andreas Fault and the photograph on page 56 showing an aerial view of the fault's surface.
- Before students read Interpreting the Data, ask: **What does *interpret* mean?** *(Translate, make sense of, figure out the meaning of)* After students have read the section, ask: **What specific kinds of data does Dr. Prentice collect?** *(Measurements that tell her when layers of rock and sediments formed and when they split and how fast the opposite sides of the fault are moving past each other)* **When she interprets the data, what does she find out?** *(Measurements about the formation and splitting of the layers tell her when and how frequently earthquakes occurred at that place in the past; measurements of the slip rate tell*

Working in the Trenches

What's it like to work in a spot where Earth's surface ruptured? Does Carol Prentice ever think that an earthquake might occur when she is digging in the fault? "It's always in the back of your mind when you are working in the trench," she admits.

But, she says, "The trenches are dangerous, not so much because there might be an earthquake while you are working there but because the trench can cave in. If a trench is 4 to 5 meters deep, or just over your head, it needs shores—braces and supports— or it might cave in. When sediments are soft, and the trench is deep, it's more likely to cave in. That could happen in a place like Mongolia."

Carol (in back) and another geologist in a deep trench.

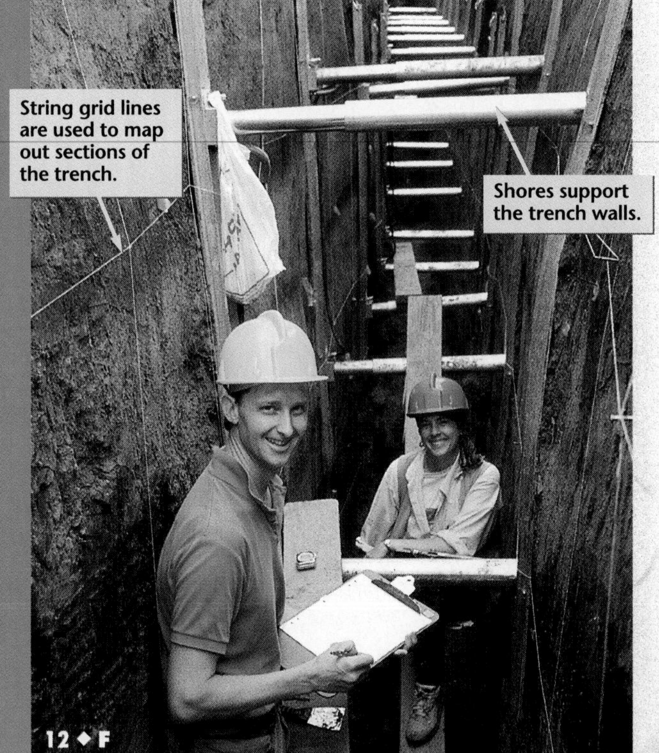
String grid lines are used to map out sections of the trench.
Shores support the trench walls.

In Mongolia, in northeast Asia, it's difficult for geologists to find the right materials to support a deep trench. It could cave in while someone is in it. "That would be very frightening," she says.

Looking at the Gobi-Altay Quake

Carol Prentice travels to earthquake sites around the world—Dominican Republic, Thailand, Mongolia—as well as to the San Andreas fault in California. One of Dr. Prentice's most recent research expeditions was to the site of the monster Gobi-Altay earthquake of 1957 in the Mongolian desert. In earthquakes like this one, the faults are easy to see. "We're taking a look at this Gobi Altay earthquake and seeing whether the next-to-last earthquake had the same pattern," Dr. Prentice says.

The faults of the Gobi-Altay earthquake are similar in some ways to the San Andreas fault and to the faults of other earthquakes in the United States. That's one of the reasons the Gobi-Altay is so interesting to geologists.

Interpreting the Data

When Dr. Prentice finds evidence of several earthquakes in one spot, she takes measurements that tell her when the layers of rocks, sand, and gravel formed and when they split. From that she knows when and how frequently earthquakes have occurred there.

She also determines how fast the opposite sides of the fault are slipping past each other. "Those two pieces of information— the dates of prehistoric earthquakes and the slip rate—are very, very important in trying to

Background

The vast Gobi Desert is one of the most sparsely populated areas on Earth. Despite its remote location, desolation, and fierce wind and sand storms, the Gobi is of intense interest to scientists. Artifacts of Bronze Age and earlier peoples have been found there, as well as fossilized dinosaur eggs from the Mesozoic Era 230-65 million years ago.

Paleontologists working in the Gobi in 1993 discovered the fossil of a 2.7-meter-long oviraptor (an ostrich-like dinosaur) squatting over an egg-filled nest—the strongest evidence to date that birds inherited brooding behavior from dinosaurs. In 1997 scientists reported finding bits of fur in 60-million-year-old fossilized dung deposits discovered in the Gobi—evidence that mammals developed hair millions of years earlier than scientists had thought.

Geologists look for sites where several earthquakes have occurred. Each earthquake moves and cracks Earth's surface to form a fault. Over the years, layers of sediment are deposited on top of the fault. Each new earthquake forms a new fault. The earlier faults are still there. You just cannot see them.

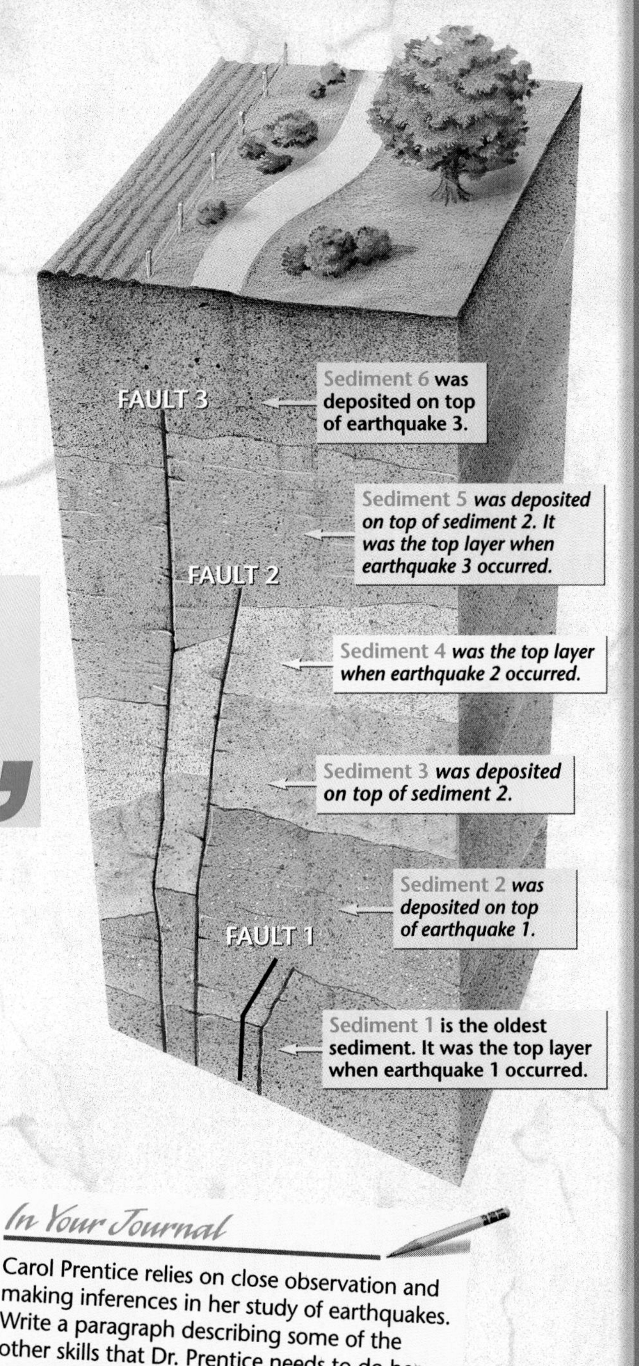
FAULT 3
Sediment 6 was deposited on top of earthquake 3.
Sediment 5 was deposited on top of sediment 2. It was the top layer when earthquake 3 occurred.
FAULT 2
Sediment 4 was the top layer when earthquake 2 occurred.
Sediment 3 was deposited on top of sediment 2.
Sediment 2 was deposited on top of earthquake 1.
FAULT 1
Sediment 1 is the oldest sediment. It was the top layer when earthquake 1 occurred.

figure out how dangerous a particular fault is," Dr. Prentice explains.

Since faults don't move every year, but over thousands of years, you can figure out the average slip per year and make some predictions. The faster the fault is moving, the greater the danger. "We can look at the landforms around a fault.

> **"... the real story of a quake is written in the rocks and soil."**

We can look at what our instruments record, and say: This is an active fault. Someday it might produce a big earthquake, but what we really want to know is when. Is that earthquake likely to happen in the next fifty years, in the next hundred years, or is it going to be a thousand years before the next big earthquake?"

In Your Journal

Carol Prentice relies on close observation and making inferences in her study of earthquakes. Write a paragraph describing some of the other skills that Dr. Prentice needs to do her work as a paleoseismologist.

her how active—and thus how dangerous—the fault is.) **How do geologists use this kind of information?** *(They try to predict future earthquakes along known faults.)*

- Direct students' attention to the diagram on this page, and ask: **How did geologists arrive at the idea behind this diagram?** *(Some things they observed when they examined trench walls or faults that have been exposed; other things they inferred from measurements and other data.)*

In Your Journal Students' paragraphs will vary. Most will probably describe the skills of measuring, recording data in an organized manner, calculating, and predicting. Students may also mention comparing and contrasting (of the slip rates along different faults, for example) and making inferences ("educated guesses") based on observable evidence.

Introducing Inside Earth

Encourage students to look through the book to find the parts that relate most closely to this feature. *(Chapter 2, Earthquakes, Section 1, Earth's Crust in Motion, particularly Kinds of Faults on pages 56–57, Friction Along Faults on page 58, and the lab activity Modeling Movement Along Faults on page 62)* Ask: **Besides faults, what other things about earthquakes will you be studying?** *(How they are measured and located, their hazards, safety precautions)* **What other topics in the book particularly interest you?** *(Accept all responses without comment.)*

Plate Tectonics

Sections	Time	Student Edition Activities	Other Activities
CHAPTER PROJECT 1 **Cut-Away Earth** p. 15	Ongoing (3 weeks)	Check Your Progress, p. 24 Check Your Progress, p. 39 Check Your Progress, p. 47 Wrap Up, p. 51	
1 Earth's Interior pp. 16–24 ◆ Describe what geologists do. ◆ List the characteristics of Earth's crust, mantle, and core.	3–4 periods/ $1\frac{1}{2}$–2 blocks	**Discover** How Do Scientists Determine What's Inside Earth?, p. 16 **Sharpen Your Skills** Creating Data Tables, p. 21	**TE** Inquiry Challenge, p. 18 **TE** Using the Visuals, p. 19 **TE** Building Inquiry Skills: Comparing and Contrasting, p. 20 **TE** Demonstration, p. 21 **TE** Demonstration, p. 22 **TE** Integrating Physics, p. 23
2 *Integrating Physics* **Convection Currents and the Mantle** pp. 25–27 ◆ Explain how heat is transferred. ◆ Identify what causes convection currents.	1–2 periods/ $\frac{1}{2}$–1 block	**Discover** How Can Heat Cause Motion in a Liquid?, p. 25 **Science at Home,** p. 27	**TE** Demonstration, p. 26 **TE** Building Inquiry Skills: Observing, p. 26
3 Drifting Continents pp. 28–32 ◆ Describe continental drift. ◆ Explain why Alfred Wegener's theory was rejected by most scientists of his day.	2–3 periods/ 1–$1\frac{1}{2}$ blocks	**Discover** How Are Earth's Continents Linked Together?, p. 28 **Try This** Reassembling the Pieces, p. 31 **Science at Home,** p. 32	**TE** Integrating Life Science, p. 31
4 Sea-Floor Spreading pp. 33–41 ◆ Describe the process of sea-floor spreading. ◆ Describe what happens to the ocean floor at deep-ocean trenches.	4–5 periods/ 2–$2\frac{1}{2}$ blocks	**Discover** What Is the Effect of a Change in Density?, p. 33 **Try This** Reversing Poles, p. 37 **Skills Lab: Making Models** Modeling Sea-Floor Spreading, pp. 40–41	**TE** Including All Students, p. 34 **TE** Including All Students, p. 35 **TE** Integrating Physics, p. 36 **TE** Including All Students, p. 37 **TE** Including All Students, p. 38
5 The Theory of Plate Tectonics pp. 42–48 ◆ Explain the theory of plate tectonics. ◆ Describe the three types of plate boundaries.	3–4 periods/ $1\frac{1}{2}$–2 blocks	**Discover** How Well Do the Continents Fit Together?, p. 42 **Sharpen Your Skills** Predicting, p. 43 **Skills Lab: Observing** Hot Plates, p. 48	**TE** Inquiry Challenge, p. 43 **TE** Demonstration, p. 44 **TE** Using the Visuals, p. 44 **TE** Inquiry Challenge, p. 45 **ISLM** F-1, "Mapping a Future World"
Study Guide/Chapter Review pp. 49–51	1 period/ $\frac{1}{2}$ block		**ISAB** Provides teaching and review of all inquiry skills

For Standard or Block Schedule The Resource Pro® CD-ROM gives you maximum flexibility for planning your instruction for any type of schedule. Resource Pro® contains Planning Express®, an advanced scheduling program, as well as the entire contents of the Teaching Resources and the Computer Test Bank.

CHAPTER PLANNING GUIDE

Program Resources	Assessment Strategies	Media and Technology
TR Chapter 1 Project Teacher Notes, pp. 8–9 **TR** Chapter 1 Project Student Materials, pp. 10–13 **TR** Chapter 1 Project Scoring Rubric, p. 14	**SE** Performance Assessment: Chapter 1 Project Wrap Up, p. 51 **TE** Check Your Progress, pp. 24, 39, 47 **TR** Chapter 1 Project Scoring Rubric, p. 14	
TR 1-1 Lesson Plan, p. 15 **TR** 1-1 Section Summary, p. 16 **TR** 1-1 Review and Reinforce, p. 17 **TR** 1-1 Enrich, p. 18 **SES** Book N, *Electricity and Magnetism,* Chapter 1	**SE** Section 1 Review, p. 24 **TE** Ongoing Assessment, pp. 17, 19, 21, 23 **TE** Performance Assessment, p. 24 **TR** 1-1 Review and Reinforce, p. 17	Exploring Earth Science Videodisc, Unit 2 Side 2, "A Trip Through the Earth" Audiotapes, English-Spanish Summary 1-1 Transparency 1, "Exploring Earth's Interior" Interactive Student Tutorial CD-ROM, F-1
TR 1-2 Lesson Plan, p. 19 **TR** 1-2 Section Summary, p. 20 **TR** 1-2 Review and Reinforce, p. 21 **TR** 1-2 Enrich, p. 22 **SES** Book M, *Motion, Forces, and Energy,* Chapter 6	**SE** Section 2 Review, p. 27 **TE** Performance Assessment, p. 27 **TR** 1-2 Review and Reinforce, p. 21	Exploring Physical Science Videodisc, Unit 4 Side 2, "Hot Is Hot, Cold Is Not" Audiotapes, English-Spanish Summary 1-2 Interactive Student Tutorial CD-ROM, F-1
TR 1-3 Lesson Plan, p. 23 **TR** 1-3 Section Summary, p. 24 **TR** 1-3 Review and Reinforce, p. 25 **TR** 1-3 Enrich, p. 26 **SES** Book G, *Earth's Changing Surface,* Chapter 4	**SE** Section 3 Review, p. 32 **TE** Ongoing Assessment, pp. 29, 31 **TE** Performance Assessment, p. 32 **TR** 1-3 Review and Reinforce, p. 25	Exploring Earth Science Videodisc, Unit 3 Side 1, "The Drifters" Audiotapes, English-Spanish Summary 1-3 Transparency 2, "Evidence for Continental Drift"
TR 1-4 Lesson Plan, p. 27 **TR** 1-4 Section Summary, p. 28 **TR** 1-4 Review and Reinforce, p. 29 **TR** 1-4 Enrich, p. 30 **TR** Skills Lab blackline masters, pp. 35–37	**SE** Section 4 Review, p. 39 **SE** Analyze and Conclude, p. 41 **TE** Ongoing Assessment, pp. 35, 37 **TE** Performance Assessment, p. 39 **TR** 1-4 Review and Reinforce, p. 29	Exploring Earth Science Videodisc, Unit 3 Side 1, "Journey to the Bottom of the Sea" Audiotapes, English-Spanish Summary 1-4 Transparencies 3, "Magnetic Stripes Along the Mid-Ocean Ridge"; 4, "Sea-floor Spreading and Subduction" Interactive Student Tutorial CD-ROM, F-1
TR 1-5 Lesson Plan, p. 31 **TR** 1-5 Section Summary, p. 32 **TR** 1-5 Review and Reinforce, p. 33 **TR** 1-5 Enrich, p. 34 **TR** Skills Lab blackline masters, pp. 38–39	**SE** Section 5 Review, p. 47 **SE** Analyze and Conclude, p. 48 **TE** Ongoing Assessment, pp. 43, 45 **TE** Performance Assessment, p. 47 **TR** 1-5 Review and Reinforce, p. 33	Exploring Earth Science Videodisc, Unit 3 Side 1, "Isto What?"; "Everything on Your Plate" Audiotapes, English-Spanish Summary 1-5 Transparencies 5, "Earth's Lithospheric Plates"; 6, "Exploring Plate Tectonics"; 7, "Continental Drift Since Pangaea"
TR Chapter 1 Performance Assessment, pp. 168–170 **TR** Chapter 1 Test, pp. 171–174	**SE** Chapter 1 Review, pp. 49–51 **TR** Chapter 1 Performance Assessment, pp. 168–170 **TR** Chapter 1 Test, pp. 171–174 **CTB** Chapter 1 Test	Interactive Student Tutorial CD-ROM, F-1 Computer Test Bank, Chapter 1 Test Science Explorer Internet Site

Key: **SE** Student Edition; **TE** Teacher's Edition; **TR** Teaching Resources; **CTB** Computer Test Bank; **SES** Science Explorer Series Text; **ISLM** Integrated Science Laboratory Manual; **ISAB** Inquiry Skills Activity Book; **PTA** Product Testing Activities by *Consumer Reports*; **IES** Interdisciplinary Explorations Series

Meeting the National Science Education Standards and AAAS Benchmarks

National Science Education Standards	Benchmarks for Science Literacy	Unifying Themes
Science As Inquiry (Content Standard A) ◆ **Develop descriptions, explanations, predictions, and models using evidence** Students build a model that shows Earth's surface and interior. Students model sea-floor spreading. *(Chapter Project; Skills Labs)* **Physical Science** (Content Standard B) ◆ **Transfer of energy** The three types of heat transfer are radiation, conduction, and convection. Students observe a model of convection currents in Earth's mantle. *(Section 2; Skills Lab)* **Earth and Space Science** (Content Standard D) ◆ **Structure of the Earth system** The crust, mantle, and core are the three main layers of Earth's interior. Molten material from the mantle rises at mid-ocean ridges and old crust sinks back into the mantle at deep-ocean trenches. Plate tectonics explains the formation, movement, and subduction of Earth's crust. *(Sections 1, 4, 5)* ◆ **Earth's History** Wegener used evidence from landforms, fossils, and climate to support his hypothesis of continental drift. About 260 million years ago the continents were joined together. *(Sections 3, 5)*	**1A The Scientific World View** Discovery of the mid-ocean ridge caused scientists to reconsider Wegener's hypothesis. *(Sections 4, 5)* **1B Scientific Inquiry** Wegener gathered evidence to support his hypothesis of continental drift. *(Section 3)* **1C The Scientific Enterprise** Geologists study the forces that make and shape Earth. *(Section 1)* **3A Technology and Science** Scientists used sonar, submersibles, and other technology to gather evidence to support sea-floor spreading. *(Section 4)* **4C Processes That Shape the Earth** Students build a model to show how Earth's interior affects its surface. The crust, mantle, and core are the three main layers of Earth. Heat inside Earth causes convection currents in the mantle. Molten material from the mantle rises at mid-ocean ridges and old crust sinks back into the mantle at deep-ocean trenches. Plate tectonics explains the formation, movement, and subduction of Earth's crust. Students investigate the movement of plates by convection currents. *(Chapter Project; Sections 1, 2, 4, 5; Skills Labs)* **4E Energy Transformation** Heat is transferred by radiation, conduction, and convection. Convection currents in the mantle cause movement of Earth's plates. *(Sections 2, 5; Skills Lab)*	◆ **Energy** Heat is transferred by radiation, conduction, and convection. The movement of Earth's plates is probably caused by convection currents in the mantle. *(Sections 2, 5; Skills Lab)* ◆ **Evolution** Plate tectonics explains how Earth's crust has changed. *(Section 5)* ◆ **Modeling** Students build a model of Earth and show sea-floor spreading and convection currents in Earth's mantle. *(Chapter Project; Skills Labs)* ◆ **Patterns of Change** Temperature and pressure increase as you approach Earth's center. Earth's magnetic poles reverse themselves about once every 600,000 years. *(Section 1)* ◆ **Scale and Structure** Earth's interior is made up of crust, mantle, and core. All the continents were once joined together in a single landmass. The lithosphere is broken into a number of plates. *(Sections 1, 3, 5)* ◆ **Stability** The formation of new crust at mid-ocean ridges is balanced by the destruction of old crust at deep-ocean trenches. *(Section 4; Skills Lab)* ◆ **Systems and Interactions** No plate can move without affecting other plates. Convection currents in the mantle probably cause the movement of Earth's plates. *(Section 5; Skills Lab)*

Media and Technology

Exploring Earth Science Videodiscs

◆ **Section 1** "A Trip Through the Earth" takes viewers from outer space to the center of Earth.

◆ **Section 3** "The Drifters" gives evidence supporting continental drift.

◆ **Section 4** "Journey to the Bottom of the Sea" provides evidence for sea-floor spreading.

◆ **Section 5** "Isto What?" explains the concept of isostasy. "Everything on Your Plate" illustrates activities at plate boundaries

Exploring Physical Science Videodiscs

◆ **Section 2** "Hot Is Hot, Cold Is Not" gives examples of radiation, conduction, and convection.

Interactive Student Tutorial CD-ROM

◆ **Chapter Review** Interactive questions help students to self-assess their mastery of key chapter concepts.

Student Edition Connection Strategies

◆ **Section 1** **Language Arts Connection**, p. 19; **Integrating Physics**, p. 24

◆ **Section 2** **Integrating Physics**, pp. 25–27

◆ **Section 3** **Integrating Life Science**, p. 31

◆ **Section 4** **Integrating Physics**, pp. 36–37

www.science-explorer.phschool.com

Visit the Science Explorer Internet site to find an up-to-date activity for Chapter 1 of *Inside Earth*.

ACTIVITY	Time (minutes)	Materials Quantities for one work group	Skills
Section 1			
Discover, p. 16	10	**Consumable** masking tape **Nonconsumable** 3 film canisters with tops, 3 different materials, permanent marker, scale	Inferring
Sharpen Your Skills, p. 21	15	No special materials are required.	Creating Data Tables
Section 2			
Discover, p. 25	10	**Consumable** hot water, cold water, food coloring **Nonconsumable** shallow pan, clear plastic cup, plastic dropper	Inferring
Science at Home, p. 27	home	No special materials are required.	Observing
Section 3			
Discover, p. 28	15	**Nonconsumable** globe that shows physical features	Posing Questions
Try This, p. 31	15	**Consumable** 1 sheet of newspaper	Making Models
Science at Home, p. 32	home	**Consumable** 1 piece of tracing paper **Nonconsumable** scissors	Communicating
Section 4			
Discover, p. 33	10	**Consumable** water **Nonconsumable** sink or large dishpan, washcloth	Observing
Try This, p. 37	15	**Consumable** audiotape, plastic tape **Nonconsumable** scissors, metric ruler, bar magnet	Making Models
Skills Lab, pp. 40–41	30	**Consumable** 2 sheets of unlined paper **Nonconsumable** blunt-tip scissors, metric ruler, 2 permanent markers of different colors and thicknesses	Making Models, Observing, Inferring
Section 5			
Discover, p. 42	20	**Consumable** tracing paper, sheet of paper, tape **Nonconsumable** world map in an atlas, scissors	Drawing Conclusions
Sharpen Your Skills, p. 43	10	No special materials are required.	Predicting
Skills Lab, p. 48	40	**Consumable** aluminum roasting pan, 2 10-cm-long candles, 2 L water **Nonconsumable** modeling clay, 6 bricks, 2 medium-sized kitchen sponges, 10 map pins	Observing, Making Models, Inferring

A list of all materials required for the Student Edition activities can be found on pages T14–T15. You can order Materials Kits by calling 1-800-828-7777 or by accessing the Science Explorer Internet site at **www.science-explorer.phschool.com.**

Cut-Away Earth

When most students think of what's under the surface of Earth, they generally think of a static ball of dirt and rock, unchanging through time. In this chapter, they will be introduced to the concepts of layers of Earth and plate tectonics. The Chapter 1 Project will reinforce their understanding of the relationship between Earth's interior and its surface features.

Purpose Students will make sketches of Earth's interior, plates, and plate boundaries. Then, within a group they will come to a final design for a model of Earth and build it to scale. In doing so, they will gain a better understanding of the structure of Earth.

Skills Focus After completing the Chapter 1 Project, students will be able to

- apply the concepts learned in the chapter to a model of Earth's interior;
- interpret data to make their model to scale;
- design and make a model of Earth's interior and features of the surface;
- communicate the features of their model in a presentation to the class.

Project Time Line The entire project will require about three weeks. Depending on how much class time students can spend working on the project each day, about two days may be required for each of the following phases.

- Make individual sketches of a possible three-dimensional model of Earth's interior.
- Take the sketches to a group meeting, in which all sketches can be considered in thinking about a final design.
- Discuss with the group possible materials in making the model.
- Experiment with possible materials and decide which might work best.
- Make individual sketches of how the model could incorporate the concept of sea-floor spreading.
- Take the second set of sketches to a group meeting, come to a consensus on a model design, and make the base of the model.

CHAPTER 1

Plate Tectonics

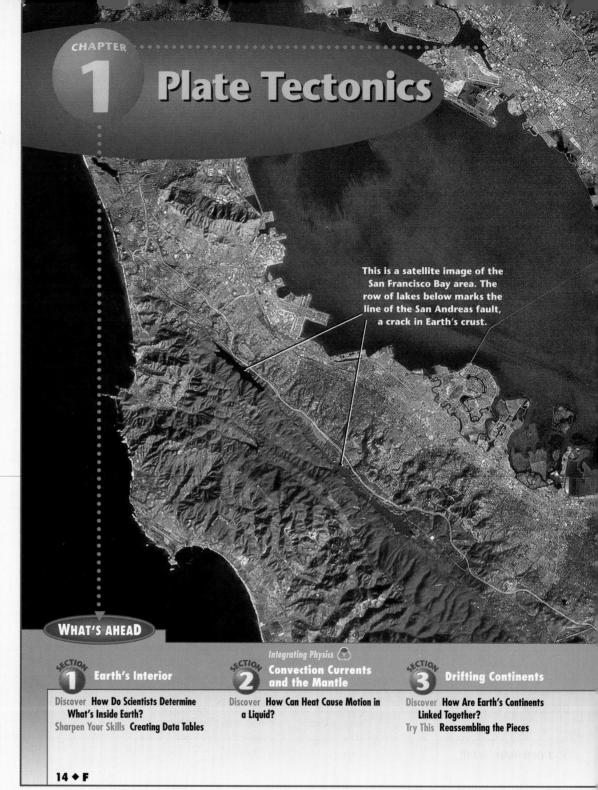

This is a satellite image of the San Francisco Bay area. The row of lakes below marks the line of the San Andreas fault, a crack in Earth's crust.

WHAT'S AHEAD

- Incorporate plate boundaries into the design and complete the construction of the model.
- Make a presentation to the class, explaining what the model shows about the structure of Earth.

For more detailed information on planning and supervising the chapter project, see Chapter 1 Project Teacher Notes, pages 8–9 in Teaching Resources.

Suggested Shortcuts You can make this project shorter and less involved in one of the following ways.

- Have students make their individual sketches and then design a model in their groups. Then invite the class as a whole to decide on a final design, incorporating the best aspects of all the groups' plans. Finally, have volunteers make the actual model in their free time.
- Have students individually complete the two worksheets. The final product would be a detailed sketch of Earth's interior by each student.

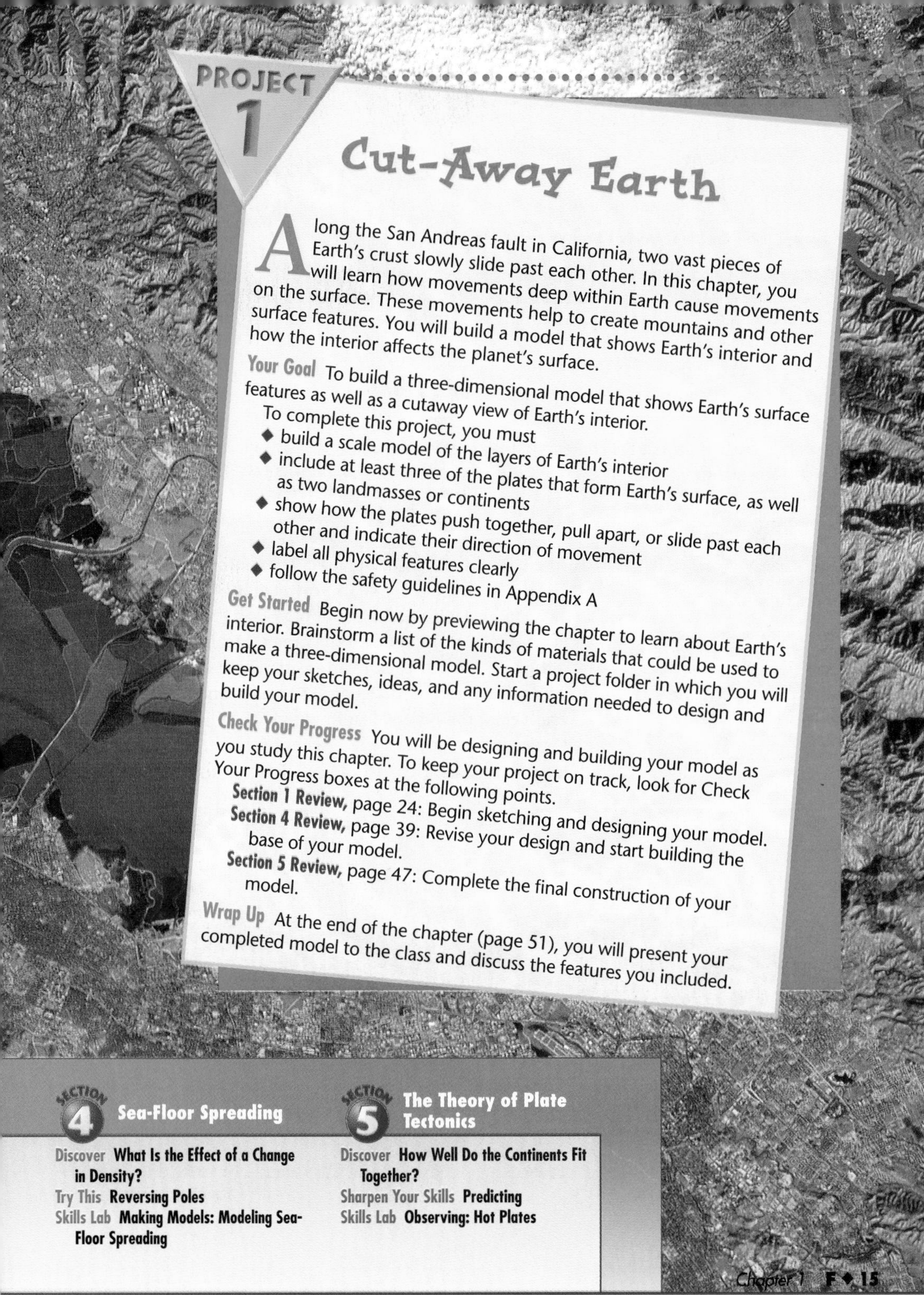

PROJECT 1

Cut-Away Earth

Along the San Andreas fault in California, two vast pieces of Earth's crust slowly slide past each other. In this chapter, you will learn how movements deep within Earth cause movements on the surface. These movements help to create mountains and other surface features. You will build a model that shows Earth's interior and how the interior affects the planet's surface.

Your Goal To build a three-dimensional model that shows Earth's surface features as well as a cutaway view of Earth's interior.

To complete this project, you must

- build a scale model of the layers of Earth's interior
- include at least three of the plates that form Earth's surface, as well as two landmasses or continents
- show how the plates push together, pull apart, or slide past each other and indicate their direction of movement
- label all physical features clearly
- follow the safety guidelines in Appendix A

Get Started Begin now by previewing the chapter to learn about Earth's interior. Brainstorm a list of the kinds of materials that could be used to make a three-dimensional model. Start a project folder in which you will keep your sketches, ideas, and any information needed to design and build your model.

Check Your Progress You will be designing and building your model as you study this chapter. To keep your project on track, look for Check Your Progress boxes at the following points.

Section 1 Review, page 24: Begin sketching and designing your model.
Section 4 Review, page 39: Revise your design and start building the base of your model.
Section 5 Review, page 47: Complete the final construction of your model.

Wrap Up At the end of the chapter (page 51), you will present your completed model to the class and discuss the features you included.

Section 4 Sea-Floor Spreading

Discover **What Is the Effect of a Change in Density?**
Try This **Reversing Poles**
Skills Lab **Making Models: Modeling Sea-Floor Spreading**

Section 5 The Theory of Plate Tectonics

Discover **How Well Do the Continents Fit Together?**
Sharpen Your Skills **Predicting**
Skills Lab **Observing: Hot Plates**

Launching the Project To introduce this project, show students a large world globe and ask: **If the inside of this globe reflected Earth's interior as well as it reflects Earth's surface, what would it show when cut in half?** *(Students might mention dirt, water, and rock.)* Tell them that in this chapter, they will learn that Earth's interior has several layers, each with different characteristics. Also point out that movements within the interior affect processes on the surface of the planet. Explain that in this project, they will work in groups to make a model of Earth's interior that shows a relationship between the surface and what's below. Then ask: **What kinds of materials are good for making three-dimensional models?** *(Students might mention a variety of materials, including clay and papier mâché.)* Then mention that they should be thinking of such materials in order to contribute to a group design for a model of Earth's interior. To help students get started, pass out Chapter 1 Project Student Materials, pages 10–13 in Teaching Resources. You may also wish to pass out the Chapter 1 Project Scoring Rubric, page 14, at this time.

- Challenge groups to make a detailed, color poster of Earth's interior instead of a three-dimensional model.

Possible Materials A variety of materials could be used for the base of the model. These include papier-mâché, modeling clay, chicken wire, cardboard, plywood, and wood blocks. Groups may also think of other materials to use. To bring the models to life, paints, paint brushes, and permanent markers will also be necessary.

Program Resources

- **Teaching Resources** Chapter 1 Project Teacher Notes, pp. 8–9; Chapter 1 Project Student Materials, pp. 10–13; Chapter 1 Project Scoring Rubric, p. 14

Performance Assessment

Use the Chapter 1 Project Scoring Rubric to assess students' work. Students will be assessed on

- how well they make their sketches and plan their models;
- how well they incorporate the required features and create an attractive model of Earth's interior.
- how effectively they present the model and explain its features to the class;
- how well they work in the group and how much they contribute to the group's effort.

SECTION 1

Earth's Interior

Objectives

After completing the lesson, students will be able to

- describe what geologists do;
- list the characteristics of Earth's crust, mantle, and core.

Key Terms geologist, rock, geology, constructive force, destructive force, continent, seismic wave, pressure, crust, basalt, granite, mantle, lithosphere, asthenosphere, outer core, inner core

1 Engage/Explore

Activating Prior Knowledge

Begin by having students recall times when they've dug a hole in the ground. Ask: **If you dig down far enough through the dirt, what does your shovel hit?** *(Most students will suggest that below the dirt is rock.)* **Other than rock, what else do you think is below the surface of Earth?** *(Students might mention oil and water.)* Remind them that Earth is large, and digging a hole or a well barely scratches the surface. Then challenge them to speculate about what Earth is like at its center.

DISCOVER

ACTIVITY

Skills Focus inferring
Materials *3 film canisters with tops, 3 different materials, masking tape, permanent marker, scale*
Time 10 minutes
Tips The different materials that could be used in the canisters include practically anything that will fit in the canisters. Try to include both liquids and solids and vary them in viscosity, density, size, and other physical characteristics.
Think It Over Answers will vary depending on the materials used. Some students may determine the contents of one or more canisters. Accept any reasonable explanation about how scientists gather evidence about Earth's interior.

SECTION 1

Earth's Interior

DISCOVER

How Do Scientists Determine What's Inside Earth?

1. Your teacher will provide you with three closed film canisters. Each canister contains a different material. Your goal is to determine what is inside each canister—even though you can't directly observe what it contains.
2. Stick a label made from a piece of tape on each canister.
3. To gather evidence about the contents of the canisters, you may tap, roll, shake, or weigh them. Record your observations.
4. What differences do you notice between the canisters? Apart from their appearance on the outside, are the canisters similar in any way? How did you obtain this evidence?

Think It Over

Inferring Based on your observations, what can you infer about the contents of the canisters? How do you think scientists gather evidence about Earth's interior?

GUIDE FOR READING

- **What does a geologist do?**
- **What are the characteristics of Earth's crust, mantle, and core?**

Reading Tip **Before you read, rewrite the headings in the section as what, how, or why questions. As you read, look for answers to these questions.**

In November 1963, the people of Iceland got to see how the world begins in fire. With no warning, the waters south of Iceland began to hiss and bubble. Soon there was a fiery volcanic eruption from beneath the ocean. Steam and ash belched into the sky. Molten rock from inside Earth spurted above the ocean's surface and hardened into a small island. Within the next several years, the new volcano added 2.5 square kilometers of new, raw land to Earth's surface. The Icelanders named the island "Surtsey." In Icelandic mythology, Surtsey is the god of fire.

The island of Surtsey

16 ◆ F

READING STRATEGIES

Reading Tip Students should rewrite the first heading of the section as the question, What is the science of geology? Encourage students to use this and subsequent questions as study aids by writing an answer to each question using information from the text. A typical answer to the first question might be: The science of geology is the study of planet Earth, including the forces that make and shape the planet.

Vocabulary Some students may have difficulty in both understanding and pronouncing the terms *lithosphere* and *asthenosphere.* Break the words apart and focus on the meaning and sound of *sphere,* an object in the shape of a ball. Both layers surround the rest of the planet. Thus the asthenosphere is a ball within the ball formed by the lithosphere.

The Science of Geology

Newspapers reported the story of Surtsey's fiery birth. But much of what is known about volcanoes like Surtsey comes from the work of geologists. **Geologists** are scientists who study the forces that make and shape planet Earth. Geologists study the chemical and physical characteristics of **rock,** the material that forms Earth's hard surface. They map where different types of rock are found on and beneath the surface. Geologists describe landforms, the features formed in rock and soil by water, wind, and waves. **Geologists study the processes that create Earth's features and search for clues about Earth's history.**

The modern science of **geology,** the study of planet Earth, began in the late 1700s. Geologists of that time studied the rocks on the surface. These geologists concluded that Earth's landforms are the work of natural forces that slowly build up and wear down the land.

Studying Surface Changes Forces beneath the surface are constantly changing Earth's appearance. Throughout our planet's long history, its surface has been lifted up, pushed down, bent, and broken. Thus Earth looks different today from the way it did millions of years ago.

Today, geologists divide the forces that change the surface into two groups: constructive forces and destructive forces. **Constructive forces** shape the surface by building up mountains and landmasses. **Destructive forces** are those that slowly wear away mountains and, eventually, every other feature on the surface. The formation of the island of Surtsey is an example of constructive forces at work. The ocean waves that wear away Surtsey's shoreline are an example of destructive forces.

Two hundred years ago, the science of geology was young. Then, geologists knew only a few facts about Earth's surface. They knew that Earth is a sphere with a radius at the equator of more than 6,000 kilometers. They knew that there are seven great landmasses, called **continents,** surrounded by oceans. They knew that the continents are made up of layers of rock.

Figure 2 The work of geologists often takes them outdoors—from mountainsides to caves beneath the surface. *Observing What are the geologists in each picture doing?*

2 Facilitate

The Science of Geology

Using the Visuals: Figure 1

Use the figure to reinforce the concept that the surface of Earth is constantly changing. Ask: **What are some other ways that Earth's surface is changed over time?** *(A typical answer might mention earthquakes, erosion, flooding, and glaciers.)* **Does the interior of Earth also change over time?** *(Accept any reasonable response.)* Explain that although this section is about the interior of the planet, students will learn that what occurs in the interior has a great effect on processes that shape the surface. **learning modality: visual**

Real-Life Learning

Invite a professional geologist to speak to the class about what a geologist does. This could be a teacher from a local university or a geologist from government or private industry. Mining and oil companies often hire geologists to help locate natural resources. Encourage students to make a list of questions to ask before the speaker comes to class. **learning modality: verbal**

Including All Students

To help students who have not mastered written English, have pairs of students of differing abilities work together to make a list of constructive forces and a list of destructive forces. Emphasize that their lists need not be confined to geologic forces. Then review the lists in a whole-class discussion. **cooperative learning**

Program Resources

- **Teaching Resources** 1-1 Lesson Plan, p. 15; 1-1 Section Summary, p. 16

Media and Technology

Audiotapes English-Spanish Summary 1-1

Answers to Self-Assessment

Caption Question

Figure 2 The geologists in the top picture are studying the characteristics of a cave. The geologist in the bottom picture is investigating rock layers.

Ongoing Assessment

Writing Have students write a short paragraph that explains in their own words what a geologist does.

Students can save their paragraphs in their portfolios.

The Science of Geology, continued

Building Inquiry Skills: Posing Questions

To start students thinking about the structure of Earth, have each student write down three questions that he or she would like answered about the structure and geologic forces of planet Earth. After giving them time to write their questions, have students share them in small groups. Then have each group read their questions. Discuss how students might find the answers. **learning modality: logical/ mathematical**

Using the Visuals: Figure 3

Ask students: **Who has ever visited a cave?** *(Some students may have visited local caverns or national parks with caves.)* Encourage students to relate their experiences to the class. Ask: **Why would a geologist study the interior of a cave?** *(To examine the materials below ground and try to determine the processes that formed the cave.)* Point out that even the deepest caves do not come close to reaching the center of Earth. **learning modality: logical/mathematical**

Inquiry Challenge

Materials *2-L bowl, small glass jar or bottle, pencil, water*
Time 15 minutes

To give students some idea of how geologists use seismic waves to investigate Earth's interior, have them investigate how an object in water changes the direction of waves. First, students might use the eraser end of a pencil to create waves in a bowl of water and observe how the waves move through the water. Then students could place a small jar or bottle in the middle of the bowl of water and predict how that jar or bottle will affect waves in the bowl. Students should sketch what they see happens to the waves produced and also write a description of how the changes in the waves show the location of the jar or bottle. **learning modality: kinesthetic**

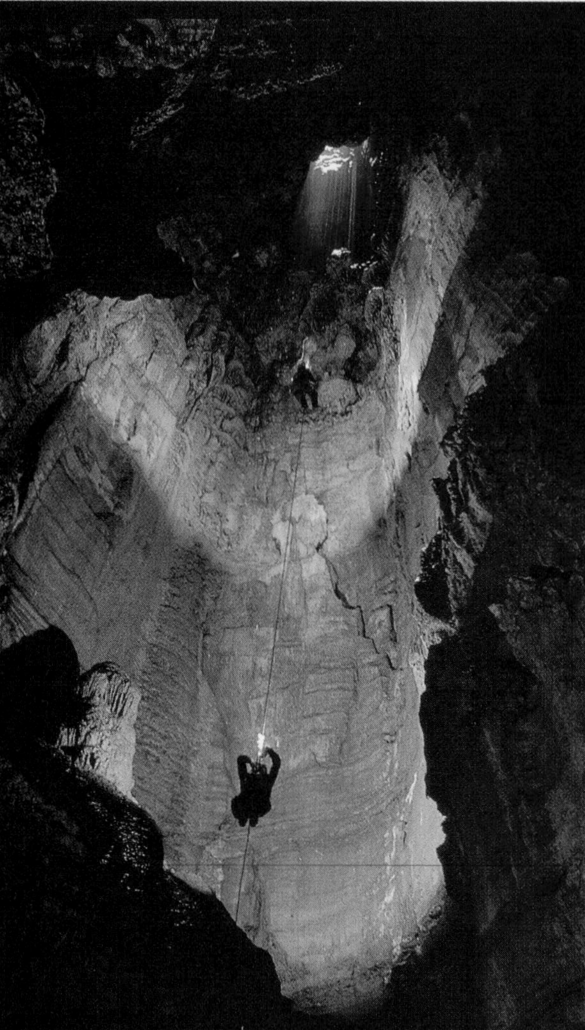

Figure 3 This cave in Georgia may seem deep. But even a deep cave is only a small nick in Earth's surface.

These layers can sometimes be seen on the walls of canyons and the sides of valleys. However, many riddles remained: How old is Earth? How has Earth's surface changed over time? Why are there oceans, and how did they form? For 200 years, geologists have tried to answer these and other questions about the planet.

Finding Indirect Evidence One of the most difficult questions that geologists have tried to answswer is, What's inside Earth? Much as geologists might like to, they cannot dig a hole to the center of Earth. The extreme conditions in Earth's interior prevent exploration far below the surface. The deepest mine in the world, a gold mine in South Africa, reaches a depth of 3.8 kilometers. But it only scratches the surface. You would have to travel more than 1,600 times that distance—over 6,000 kilometers—to reach Earth's center.

Geologists cannot observe Earth's interior directly. Instead, they must rely on indirect methods of observation. Have you ever hung a heavy picture on a wall? If you have, you know that you can knock on the wall to locate the wooden beam underneath the plaster that will support the picture. When you knock on the wall, you listen carefully for a change in the sound.

When geologists want to study Earth's interior, they also use an indirect method. But instead of listening for sounds, they use seismic waves. When earthquakes occur, they produce **seismic waves** (SYZ mik). Geologists record the seismic waves and study how they travel through Earth. The speed of these seismic waves and the paths they take reveal how the planet is put together. Using data from seismic waves, geologists have learned that Earth's interior is made up of several layers. Each layer surrounds the layers beneath it, much like the layers of an onion.

☑ *Checkpoint* ***What kind of indirect evidence do geologists use to study the structure of Earth?***

Background

Facts and Figures In studying Earth's interior, scientists use the principle that the speed and direction of a seismic wave depends on the material it travels through. For example, the crust and the mantle are composed of different materials. One type of seismic wave (P waves) travels through crust material at about 6 km/sec but travels through mantle material at 8 km/sec. As a result, a wave that travels through the mantle could reach a recording station faster than a wave that travels more directly through the crust. When moving from one type of material into another, seismic waves refract, or bend. Such changes of direction are evidence of different materials. One type of seismic wave (S waves) will not travel through a liquid. By studying those waves, scientists know that the outer core is liquid.

A Journey to the Center of the Earth

If you really could travel through these layers to the center of Earth, what would your trip be like? To begin, you will need a vehicle that can travel through solid rock. The vehicle will carry scientific instruments to record changes in temperature and pressure as you descend.

Temperature As you start to tunnel beneath the surface, you might expect the rock around you to be cool. At first, the surrounding rock is cool. Then at about 20 meters down your instruments report that the surrounding rock is getting warmer. For every 40 meters that you descend from that point, the temperature rises 1 Celsius degree. This rapid rise in temperature continues for several kilometers. After that, the temperature increases more slowly, but steadily.

Pressure During your journey to the center of Earth, your instruments also record an increase in pressure in the surrounding rock. The deeper you go, the greater the pressure. **Pressure** is the force pushing on a surface or area. Because of the weight of the rock above, pressure inside Earth increases as you go deeper.

As you go toward the center of Earth, you travel through several different layers. **Three main layers make up Earth's interior: the crust, the mantle, and the core. Each layer has its own conditions and materials.** You can see these layers in *Exploring Earth's Interior* on pages 22–23.

Language Arts CONNECTION

Imagine taking a trip to the center of Earth. That's what happens in a novel written by Jules Verne in 1864. At that time, scientists knew almost nothing about Earth's interior. Was it solid or hollow? Hot or cold? People speculated wildly. Verne's novel, called *Journey to the Center of the Earth*, describes the adventures of a scientific expedition to explore a hollow Earth. On the way, the explorers follow caves and tunnels down to a strange sea lit by a miniature sun.

In Your Journal

Write a paragraph that describes the most exciting part of your own imaginary journey to Earth's center.

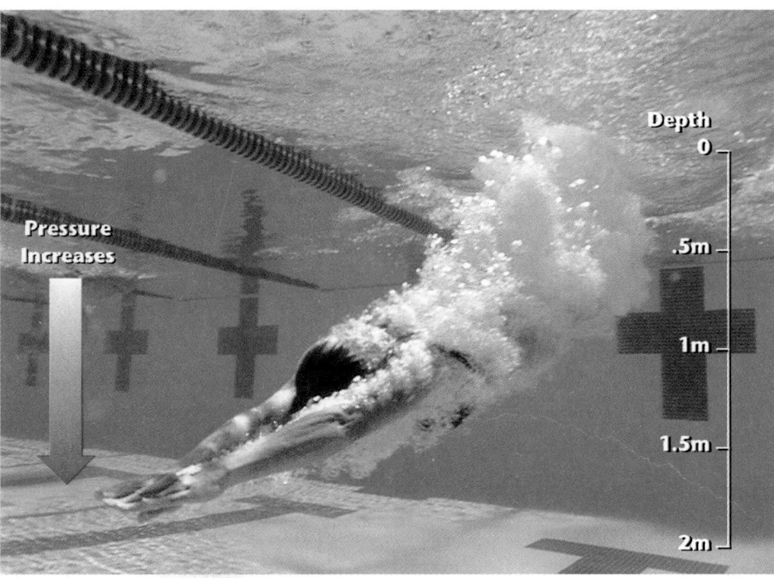

Figure 4 The deeper this swimmer goes, the greater the pressure from the surrounding water. **Comparing and Contrasting** *How is the water in the swimming pool similar to Earth's interior? How is it different?*

A Journey to the Center of the Earth

Using the Visuals: Figure 4

ACTIVITY

Materials *water, bucket, 2-L plastic soft-drink bottle, small plastic soft-drink bottle*
Time 15 minutes

Ask students: **How can you show that pressure increases with depth, as suggested in the figure?** *(Students may mention using gauges to measure pressure at various depths.)* Then divide the class into small groups and challenge them to devise an experiment that would demonstrate the concept. One way to show the concept is to immerse a small plastic soft-drink bottle with a cap on into a bucket filled with water. At the bottom of the bucket, the bottle will begin to collapse. **cooperative learning**

Language Arts CONNECTION

French writer Jules Verne (1828–1905) wrote tales of adventure that often remarkably anticipated the scientific inquiries of the twentieth century. Many libraries have the works in a form adapted especially for young people. Encourage students to read an adaptation of *Journey to the Center of the Earth* and make a report to the class.

In Your Journal Before students begin to write, have them study the *Exploring Earth's Interior* feature on pages 22–23. Then encourage them to use both that information and their imaginations to write a description of an exciting incident that might happen on a journey to the center of Earth. **learning modality: verbal**

Answers to Self-Assessment

Checkpoint

Geologists record seismic waves and study how they travel through Earth.

Caption Question

Figure 4 The deeper the water in the pool, the greater the pressure, just as pressure is greater the deeper you go beneath the surface of Earth. The water in the pool does not have layers, though.

Ongoing Assessment

Drawing Have students draw a diagram that shows a cross section of Earth with an indication of how pressure and temperature change with depth.

The Crust

Building Inquiry Skills: Comparing and Contrasting

Materials *small sample of basalt, small sample of granite, hand lens*
Time 10 minutes

Before students read the descriptions of basalt and granite, give them the opportunity to compare and contrast a small sample of each. Place the samples on a table at a central location. Students can then examine a sample of each and write a paragraph that compares and contrasts the two rocks in terms of color, weight, and texture. **learning modality: visual**

Addressing Naive Conceptions

Some students may misunderstand the idea that continental crust and oceanic crust consist mainly of granite and basalt, respectively. Display a piece of granite and ask: **Are all the rocks you see on land granite?** *(A typical answer might suggest that most do not look like granite.)* Explain that soil, water, and various other kinds of rocks cover much of the surface of the crust. Continental crust consists mainly, but not exclusively, of granite. **learning modality: verbal**

The Mantle

Including All Students

To help students who are having trouble understanding the boundaries between the various layers, draw three circles on the board to represent the crust, mantle, and core. Invite a volunteer to label Earth's three main layers. Call on another volunteer to use white chalk to shade the area that represents the lithosphere. *(The student should shade in the crust and the uppermost part of the mantle.)* Then invite another volunteer to use a different color of chalk to shade the area that represents the asthenosphere. *(The student should make a shaded circle just inside the lithosphere, wider than the lithosphere but still leaving most of the mantle unshaded.)* **learning modality: visual**

Figure 5 Two of the most common rocks in the crust are basalt and granite. **A.** The dark rock is basalt, which makes up much of the ocean floor. **B.** The light rock is granite, which makes up the core of the continents. *Comparing and Contrasting* *Which rock looks as if it's made up of one material? Of several materials?*

The Crust

Your journey to the center of Earth begins in the crust. The **crust** is a layer of rock that forms Earth's outer skin. On the crust you find rocks and mountains. But the crust also includes the soil and water that cover large parts of Earth's surface.

This outer rind of rock is much thinner than what lies beneath it. In fact, you can think of Earth's crust as being similar to the paper-thin skin of an onion. The crust includes both the dry land and the ocean floor. It is thinnest beneath the ocean and thickest under high mountains. The crust ranges from 5 to 40 kilometers thick.

The crust beneath the ocean is called oceanic crust. Oceanic crust consists mostly of the rock basalt. **Basalt** (buh SAWLT) is dark, dense rock with a fine texture. Continental crust, the crust that forms the continents, consists mainly of granite. **Granite** is a rock that has larger crystals than basalt and is not as dense. It usually is a light color.

The Mantle

Your journey downward continues. At a depth of between 5 and 40 kilometers beneath the surface, you cross a boundary. Above this boundary are the basalt and granite rocks of the crust. Below the boundary is the solid material of the **mantle,** a layer of hot rock.

The crust and the uppermost part of the mantle are very similar. The uppermost part of the mantle and the crust together form a rigid layer called the **lithosphere** (LITH uh sfeer). In Greek, *lithos* means "stone." The lithosphere averages about 100 kilometers thick.

Background

Facts and Figures One way scientists know about the composition of Earth's interior is by studying meteorites, the solid objects that fall through space and strike Earth. Astronomers theorize that meteorites formed when the solar system did. Therefore, meteorites are samples of the materials present when Earth formed, and Earth should generally have the same composition as all meteorites taken together. However, studies show that meteorites collectively have a much greater percentage of iron and nickel than does Earth's crust. Geologists think that during Earth's formation, when it was still molten, the more dense materials such as iron and nickel sank to the center. At the same time, less dense materials rose to the surface. According to this theory, Earth as a whole has the same percentages of iron and nickel as do meteorites.

Figure 6 At the surface, Earth's crust forms peaks like these in the Rocky Mountains of Colorado. Soil and plants cover much of the crust, which continues beneath to a depth of about 60 kilometers.

Next you travel farther into the mantle below the lithosphere. There your vehicle encounters material that is hotter and under increasing pressure. In general, temperature and pressure in the mantle increase with depth. The heat and pressure make the part of the mantle just beneath the lithosphere less rigid than the rock above. Like road tar softened by the heat of the sun, the material that forms this part of the mantle is somewhat soft—it can bend like plastic.

This soft layer is called the **asthenosphere** (as THEHN uh sfeer). In Greek, *asthenes* means "weak." Just because asthenes means weak, you can't assume this layer is actually weak. But the asthenosphere is soft. The material in this layer can flow slowly.

The lithosphere floats on top of the asthenosphere. Beneath the asthenosphere, solid mantle material extends all the way to Earth's core. The mantle is nearly 3,000 kilometers thick.

☑ *Checkpoint* ***How does the material of the asthenosphere differ from the material of the lithosphere?***

The Core

After traveling through the mantle, you reach the core. Earth's core consists of two parts—a liquid outer core and a solid inner core. Both parts of the core are made of the metals iron and nickel. The **outer core** is a layer of molten metal that surrounds the inner core. In spite of enormous pressure, the outer core behaves like a thick liquid. The **inner core** is a dense ball of solid metal. The great pressure at this depth squeezes the atoms of iron so tightly that they cannot spread out and become liquid.

The outer and inner cores make up about one third of Earth's mass, but only 15 percent of its volume. The inner and outer cores together are just slightly smaller than the moon.

Creating Data Tables ACTIVITY

Imagine that you have invented a super-strong vehicle that can resist extremely high pressure as it bores a tunnel deep into Earth's interior. You stop several times on your trip to collect data using devices located on your vehicle's outer hull. To see what conditions you would find at various depths on your journey, refer to *Exploring Earth's Interior* on pages 22–23. Copy the table and complete it.

Depth	Name of Layer	What Layer Is Made Of
20 km		
100 km		
2,000 km		
4,000 km		
6,000 km		

Demonstration

Materials *2 cans of window glazing, small pan, water, hot plate*
Time 10 minutes

Keep a can of window glazing—a puttylike material used to hold glass in place—in a refrigerator overnight. Invite students to touch the glazing to observe that it does not flow. Ask: **Is this substance a solid or a liquid?** *(Most students will say that it is a solid.)* Provide another can of glazing that you have heated beforehand in a pan of water on a hot plate. Invite students to observe how much more pliable the heated glazing is than the cold glazing. Ask: **How is the heated glazing like the material that makes up the mantle?** *(The heated glazing still has characteristics of a solid but can be shaped like plastic.)* **learning modality: kinesthetic**

The Core

Sharpen your Skills

Creating Data Tables

Time 15 minutes
Expected Outcome
A typical completed table may include the following information. At a depth of 20 km, the layer is the crust, which is made of solid rock, mostly granite and basalt. At 100 km, the layer is the mantle, which at this depth is solid rock. At 2,000 km, the layer is the mantle, which at this depth is may be either solid or molten material. At 4,000 km, the layer is the outer core, which is molten iron and nickel. At 6,000 km, the layer is the inner core, which is solid iron and nickel.
Extend Pairs of students could quiz each other using such depths as 5 km, 30 km, 1,000 km, and 5,000 km. **learning modality: logical/mathematical**

Media and Technology

Exploring Earth Science Videodisc
Unit 2, Side 2, "A Trip Through the Earth"

Chapter 1

Answers to Self-Assessment

Caption Question

Figure 5 The basalt looks like it's made of one material, while the granite looks like it's made of several materials.

The material of the asthenosphere is somewhat soft and can bend like plastic, while the material of the lithosphere is solid and rigid.

Ongoing Assessment

Oral Presentation Ask students to prepare a short oral presentation on the physical characteristics of the crust, mantle, inner core, and outer core. Then call on students at random to each give a description of one of the layers.

EXPLORING

Earth's Interior

Direct students' attention to the leftmost cutaway view of Earth's interior and invite volunteers to read the annotations about the three layers. Ask: **Does Earth's interior have three or four layers?** *(Three layers, with the core having two sublayers called the inner and outer core.)* **What characteristic causes geologists to consider the inner and outer cores as part of one layer instead of as two separate layers?** *(They both consist of the same materials, iron and nickel.)* Then turn students' attention to the cross-section from surface to center. Explain that scientists believe the elements separated during Earth's formation about 4.6 billion years ago. At that time, Earth was molten and the lightest elements rose to the top while the heaviest sunk to the center. Ask: **What general statement can you make about the change in temperature through Earth's interior?** *(Temperature increases as depth increases.)* **What about pressure?** *(Pressure also increases as depth increases.)* Finally, turn students' attention to what distinguishes the lithosphere from the asthenosphere. Make sure they understand that the lithosphere includes all of the crust and the topmost part of the mantle. **learning modality: visual**

Demonstration

Materials *apple, knife*
Time 5 minutes

Show students an apple and ask: **How is this apple like Earth?** *(They are both round.)* Then cut the apple in half and repeat the question. Students should be able to see the similarities. Both have layers, with a thin crust, a large middle layer, and a core. **learning modality: visual**

EXPLORING Earth's Interior

Earth's interior is divided into layers: the crust, mantle, outer core, and inner core. Although Earth's crust seems stable, the extreme heat of Earth's interior causes changes that slowly reshape the surface.

CRUST
The crust is Earth's solid and rocky outer layer, including both the land surface and the ocean floor. The crust averages 32 km thick. At the scale of this drawing, the crust is too thin to show up as more than a thin line.

Composition of crust:
oxygen, silicon, aluminum, calcium, iron, sodium, potassium, magnesium

MANTLE
A trip through Earth's mantle goes almost halfway to the center of Earth. The chemical composition of the mantle does not change much from one part of the mantle to another. However, physical conditions in the mantle change because pressure and temperature increase with depth.

Composition of mantle:
silicon, oxygen, iron, magnesium

CORE
Scientists estimate that temperatures within Earth's outer core and inner core, both made of iron and nickel, range from about 2,000°C to 5,000°C. If these estimates are correct, then Earth's center may be as hot as the sun's surface.

Composition of core:
iron, nickel

22 ◆ F

Background

Facts and Figures Have students consider these facts and figures about Earth's interior.

- Suppose you could drive a car at 100 km/hr (62 mi/hr) from Earth's surface to the center of the core. At that speed, the car would take about half an hour to drive through most continental crust, about another 29 hours to drive through the mantle, and about an additional 35 hours to drive to the center of the core.
- The mantle makes up about 80 percent of Earth's total volume.
- Pressure at the center of the inner core is 1 million times greater than air pressure at sea level.
- Crust material is 2.5–3.0 times denser than water; mantle material is 3.3–5.5 times denser than water; core material is 10–13 times denser than water.

◀ **CROSS-SECTION FROM SURFACE TO CENTER**
From Earth's surface to its center, the layers of Earth's interior differ in their composition, temperature, and pressure. Notice how temperature increases toward the inner core.

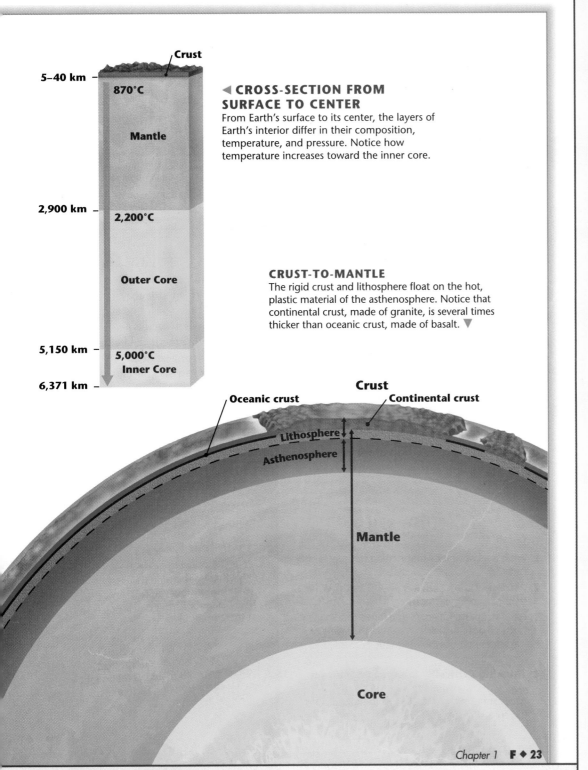

CRUST-TO-MANTLE
The rigid crust and lithosphere float on the hot, plastic material of the asthenosphere. Notice that continental crust, made of granite, is several times thicker than oceanic crust, made of basalt. ▼

Building Inquiry Skills: Measuring

Explain that the drawings of Earth's interior shown in *Exploring Earth's Interior* were done to scale, except for the thickness of the crust in the figures on page 23, which is slightly exaggerated. Ask: **Why should scientific illustrations be drawn to a scale?** *(Drawn to scale, the proportions between parts are accurate.)* Challenge students to determine what scale was used in preparing the cutaway view on the left and the cross-section view on the upper right. To determine the scale of a drawing, students must measure the distance from the outside boundary to the center, and then divide the distance in kilometers by that number. Students should find that the cutaway view uses a scale of about 1 cm = 1,000 km, and that the cross-section view uses a scale of about 1 cm = 600 km. **learning modality: logical/mathematical**

Earth's Magnetic Field

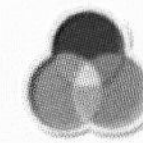

Integrating Physics

Materials *bar magnet, iron filings in a paper cup, sheet of paper*
Time 10 minutes

Ask students: **What is the shape of a bar magnet's magnetic field?** Then divide the class into pairs and give each pair the basic materials with which to investigate that question. The most common way to use these materials is to lay the bar magnet on a table, place the sheet of paper over it, and then sprinkle the iron filings over the sheet of paper. Make sure students do not place the iron filings directly on the magnet. Students should make a drawing of what they see. **learning modality: kinesthetic**

Media and Technology

Transparencies "Exploring Earth's Interior," Transparency 1

Program Resources

Science Explorer Series *Electricity and Magnetism*, Chapter 1, has more information on Earth as a magnet.

Ongoing Assessment

Drawing Have students make a diagram showing the layers of Earth, with brief descriptive phrases about each layer.

3 Assess

Section 1 Review Answers

1. Geologists study the processes that create Earth's features and search for clues about Earth's history.
2. Answers may vary. Students should write a sentence derived from the text about the crust, mantle, outer core, and inner core.
3. Currents in the liquid outer core force the solid inner core to spin at a different rate than the rest of the planet, causing the planet to act like a giant bar magnet. The outer core is a layer of molten material, while the inner core is a dense ball of solid metal.
4. Both the mantle and core are divided into two layers. The mantle has part of the rigid lithosphere and the soft asthenosphere; the core has the molten outer core and the solid inner core. The core is much hotter than the mantle, and pressure is much greater there. Both the mantle and core contain iron, but the mantle also contains silicon, oxygen, and magnesium and the core also contains nickel.

Check Your Progress

CHAPTER PROJECT 1

A review of the sketches in each student's folder will help you assess which students are having difficulty with the concepts involved, as well as give you an idea of what each student will contribute to the group's design. Then talk with each group during its initial meeting. Encourage students to brainstorm a list of possible materials for the model. Point out that the interior layers should be made to scale, while the surface features may be exaggerated for effect. Encourage groups to begin collecting materials and experimenting with a design.

Performance Assessment

Skills Check Have each student make a compare/contrast table that includes information about all the layers of Earth's interior.

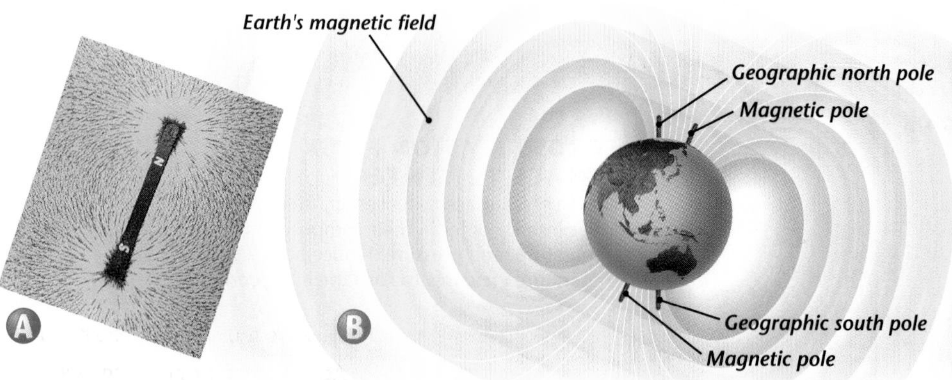

Figure 7 A. The pattern of iron filings was made by sprinkling them on paper placed over a bar magnet. B. Like a magnet, Earth's magnetic field has north and south poles. *Relating Cause and Effect If you shifted the magnet beneath the paper, what would happen to the iron filings?*

Earth's Magnetic Field

INTEGRATING PHYSICS Currents in the liquid outer core force the solid inner core to spin. Like a planet within a planet, the inner core spins inside Earth at a slightly faster rate than the rest of the planet. This movement creates Earth's magnetic field, which causes the planet to act like a giant bar magnet. As you can see in Figure 7, the magnetic field affects the whole Earth. However, the force is strongest at the magnetic poles. When you use a compass, the north-seeking end of the compass needle points to Earth's magnetic north pole.

Consider an ordinary bar magnet. If you place it beneath a piece of paper and sprinkle iron filings on the paper, the iron filings line up with the bar's magnetic field. If you could cover the entire planet with iron filings, they would form a similar pattern.

Section 1 Review

1. What are two things that geologists study about Earth?
2. What are the layers that make up Earth? Write a sentence about each one.
3. What happens in Earth's interior to produce Earth's magnetic field? Describe the layers of the interior where the magnetic field is produced.
4. **Thinking Critically Comparing and Contrasting** What are some of the differences and similarities between the mantle and the core? Explain.

Check Your Progress

CHAPTER PROJECT 1

Begin by drawing a sketch of your three-dimensional model. Think about how you will show the thicknesses of Earth's different layers at the correct scale. How can you show Earth's interior as well as its surface features? What materials can you use for building your model? Experiment with materials that might work well for showing Earth's layers.

Answers to Self-Assessment

Caption Question

Figure 7 The iron filings would move with the magnet, again forming the same pattern above the magnet's new position.

Program Resources

- **Teaching Resources** 1-1 Review and Reinforce, p. 17; 1-1 Enrich, p. 18

Media and Technology

Interactive Student Tutorial CD-ROM F-1

Section 2 Convection Currents and the Mantle

DISCOVER ACTIVITY

How Can Heat Cause Motion in a Liquid?

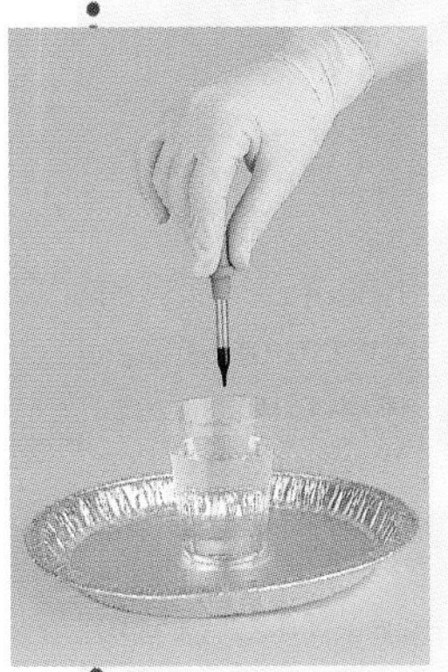

1. Carefully pour some hot water into a small, shallow pan. Fill a clear, plastic cup about half full with cold water. Place the cup in the pan.
2. Allow the water to stand for two minutes until all motion stops.
3. Fill a plastic dropper with some food coloring. Then, holding the dropper under the water surface and slightly away from the edge of the cup, gently squeeze a small droplet of the food coloring into the water.
4. Observe the water for one minute.
5. Add another droplet at the water surface in the middle of the cup and observe again.

Think It Over

Inferring How do you explain what happened to the droplets of food coloring? Why do you think the second droplet moved in a way that was different from the way the first droplet moved?

GUIDE FOR READING

- How is heat transferred?
- What causes convection currents?

Reading Tip As you read, draw a concept map of the three types of heat transfer. Include supporting ideas about convection.

Earth's molten outer core is nearly as hot as the surface of the sun. To explain how heat from the core affects the mantle, you need to know how heat is transferred in solids and liquids. If you have ever touched a hot pot accidentally, you have discovered for yourself (in a painful way) that heat moves. In this case, it moved from the hot pot to your hand. The movement of heat from a warmer object to a cooler object is called **heat transfer.**

Heat is always transferred from a warmer substance to a cooler substance. For example, holding an ice cube will make your hand begin to feel cold in a few seconds. But is the coldness in the ice cube moving to your hand? Since cold is the absence of heat, it's the heat in your hand that moves to the ice cube! **There are three types of heat transfer: radiation, conduction, and convection.**

Radiation

The transfer of heat through empty space is called **radiation.** Sunlight is radiation that warms Earth's surface. Heat transfer by radiation takes place with no direct contact between a heat source and an object. Radiation enables sunlight to warm Earth's surface. Other familiar forms of radiation include the heat you feel around a flame or open fire.

READING STRATEGIES

Vocabulary Call students' attention to the boldface terms *conduction* and *convection.* Students will notice that both terms begin with the prefix *con,* which means "together." Explain that one term is derived from a Latin word meaning "to lead together" *(conduction)* and the other term is derived from a Latin word meaning "to bring or carry together" *(convection).*

Program Resources

Science Explorer Series *Motion, Forces, and Energy,* Chapter 6, provides more information on heat transfer.

◆ **Teaching Resources** 1-2 Lesson Plan, p. 19; 1-2 Section Summary, p. 20

INTEGRATING PHYSICS

Section 2 Convection Currents and the Mantle

Objectives

After completing the lesson, students will be able to

- explain how heat is transferred;
- identify what causes convection currents.

Key Terms heat transfer, radiation, conduction, convection, density, convection current

1 Engage/Explore

Activating Prior Knowledge

Ask students: **In a room in a drafty house, why is it colder near the floor than near the ceiling?** *(Cold air sinks, while hot air rises.)* Students should understand that the air in such a room circulates as drafts of cold air move over the floor and warmer air rises. Point out that differences in temperature cause the circulation.

DISCOVER

Skills Focus inferring
Materials *shallow pan, clear plastic cup, hot water, cold water, plastic dropper, food coloring*
Time 10 minutes
Expected Outcome When students add the first droplet, food coloring should move toward the center, down to the bottom, and then upward along the edges of the cup toward the surface. When students add the second droplet, the coloring should move quickly to the bottom, spread out toward the edges of the cup, and then back upward.
Think It Over Heat is transferred from the hot water in the pan to the cold water in the cup. As the water in the bottom of the cup warms up, it becomes less dense and rises. The colder water at the top of the cup sinks, setting currents in the water in motion. The two droplets moved differently because they entered the currents at different places.

2 Facilitate

Radiation

Demonstration

Materials *heat lamp*
Time 5 minutes

Turn on a heat lamp and invite all students to walk within a meter of it. Ask: **How is the heat transferred from the lamp to your body?** *(The heat moves across the space by means of invisible rays.)* Challenge students to name other examples of heat transfer by radiation. *(Heat from the sun, a fire, and radiators)* **learning modality: kinesthetic**

Conduction

Real-Life Learning

Show students a meat thermometer and have a volunteer describe how and why it is used. Then ask: **How does this instrument measure the heat of a piece of meat?** *(The heat from the meat is transferred to the thermometer through direct contact, or conduction.)* Then challenge students to analyze whether a medical thermometer and a weather thermometer work in the same fashion. *(They all measure heat through conduction.)* **learning modality: logical/mathematical**

Convection

Building Inquiry Skills: Observing

Materials *beaker or clear glass saucepan, instant chicken soup mix, water, hot plate, oven mitt*
Time 10 minutes

Have small groups of students heat chicken soup in a beaker or saucepan on a hot plate. (**CAUTION:** *Students should wear goggles and aprons and handle hot materials very carefully.*) They should start with the soup cold, and use medium heat to prolong the process. *(Students should observe convection currents as the soup heats up.)* **learning modality: visual**

Figure 8 In conduction, the heated particles of a substance transfer heat to other particles through direct contact. That's how the spoon and the pot itself heat up.

Conduction

The direct transfer of heat in solid materials is called **conduction.** What happens as a spoon heats up in a pot of soup? Heat is transferred from the hot soup and the pot to the particles that make up the spoon. The particles near the bottom of the spoon vibrate faster as they are heated, so they bump into other particles and heat them, too. Gradually the entire spoon heats up. When your hand touches the spoon, conduction transfers heat from the spoon directly to your skin. Then you feel the heat. Look at Figure 8 to see how conduction takes place.

Convection

Conduction heats the spoon, but how does the soup inside the pot heat up? Heat transfer involving the movement of fluids—liquids and gases—is called convection. **Convection** is heat transfer by the movement of a heated fluid. During convection, heated particles of fluid begin to flow, transferring heat energy from one part of the fluid to another.

Heat transfer by convection is caused by differences of temperature and density within a fluid. **Density** is a measure of how much mass there is in a volume of a substance. For example, rock is more dense than water because a given volume of rock has more mass than the same volume of water.

When a liquid or gas is heated, the particles move faster. As the particles move faster, they spread apart. Because the particles of the heated fluid are farther apart, they occupy more space. The density decreases. But when a fluid cools, its particles move more slowly and settle together more closely. As it becomes cooler, the fluid's density increases.

If you look at Figure 9, you can see how convection occurs when you heat soup on a stove. As the soup at the bottom of the pot gets hot, it expands and therefore becomes less dense. The warm, less dense soup moves upward and floats over the cooler, denser soup. At the surface, the warm soup spreads out and cools, becoming denser. Then, gravity pulls this cooler, denser soup back down to the bottom of the pot, where it is heated again.

A constant flow begins as the cooler soup continually sinks to the bottom of the pot and the warmer soup rises. A **convection current** is the flow that transfers heat within a fluid.

Figure 9 In this pot, the soup close to the heat source is hotter and less dense than the soup near the surface. These differences in temperature and density cause convection currents.

Background

Integrating Science All the heat of Earth's interior was present at the planet's formation, and over time the total amount of heat has diminished as some heat is given off to space. Eventually, the core will be no hotter than the rest of the planet and will no longer produce convection in the mantle. Without convection in the mantle, movement of Earth's plates will come to a stop.

Media and Technology

Audiotapes English-Spanish Summary 1-2

Exploring Physical Science Videodisc Unit 4, Side 2, "Hot Is Hot, Cold Is Not"

Chapter 2

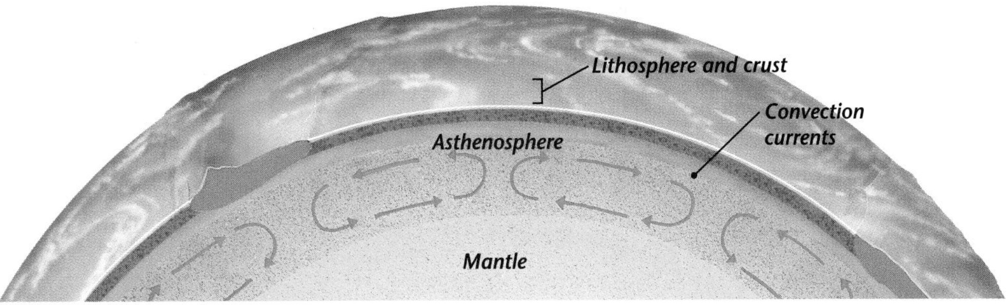

Figure 10 Heat from Earth's mantle and core causes convection currents to form in the asthenosphere. Some geologists think convection currents extend throughout the mantle. *Applying Concepts What part of Earth's interior is like the soup in the pot? What part is like the burner on the stove?*

The heating and cooling of the fluid, changes in the fluid's density, and the force of gravity combine to set convection currents in motion. Convection currents continue as long as heat is added. What happens after the heat source is removed? Without heat, the convection currents will eventually stop when all of the material has reached the same temperature.

Checkpoint What is convection?

Convection in Earth's Mantle

Like soup simmering in a pot, Earth's mantle responds to heat. Notice in Figure 10 how convection currents flow in the asthenosphere. The heat source for these currents is heat from Earth's core and from the mantle itself. Hot columns of mantle material rise slowly through the asthenosphere. At the top of the asthenosphere, the hot material spreads out and pushes the cooler material out of the way. This cooler material sinks back into the asthenosphere. Over and over, the cycle of rising and sinking takes place. Convection currents like these have been moving inside Earth for more than four billion years!

Section 2 Review

1. What are the three types of heat transfer?
2. Describe how convection currents form.
3. In general, what happens to the density of a fluid when it becomes hotter?
4. What happens to convection currents when a fluid reaches a constant temperature?
5. **Thinking Critically Predicting** What will happen to the flow of hot rock in Earth's mantle if the planet's core eventually cools down? Explain your answer.

Science at Home

Convection currents may keep the air inside your home at a comfortable temperature. Air is made up of gases, so it is a fluid. Regardless of the type of home heating system, heated air circulates through a room by convection. You may have tried to adjust the flow of air in a stuffy room by opening a window. When you did so, you were making use of convection currents. With an adult family member, study how your home is heated. Look for evidence of convection currents.

Convection in Earth's Mantle

Using the Visuals: Figure 10

Explain that each of the circular currents shown in the figure is called a convection cell. Ask: **Where in the convection cell is the densest material?** *(At the bottom, just as the material turns to move horizontally.)* **Where is the material the coolest?** *(At the top, where the cell turns downward.)* **learning modality: visual**

3 Assess

Section 2 Review Answers

1. Radiation, conduction, and convection
2. The heating and cooling of a fluid, changes in a fluid's density, and the force of gravity combine to set convection currents in motion.
3. In general, when heat energy increases, the density of a fluid decreases.
4. When a fluid reaches a constant temperature, the convection currents stop.
5. The flow of hot rock would slow and eventually stop because the heat from the core is what sets convection currents in the asthenosphere in motion.

Science at Home

ACTIVITY

Outcomes will vary depending on the type of heating system in a student's home. Students should be able to see that convection plays a part in all heating systems, though fans may also help circulate the air. They also may conclude that heating units or vents are best located near the floor, so that heat rises throughout the room.

Program Resources

- **Teaching Resources** 1-2 Review and Reinforce, p. 21; 1-2 Enrich, p. 22

Media and Technology

Interactive Student Tutorial CD-ROM F-1

Answers to Self-Assessment

Caption Question

Figure 10 The asthenosphere is like the soup in the pot. The core and mantle are like the burner on the stove.

Checkpoint

Convection is heat transfer by the movement of a heated fluid.

Performance Assessment

Drawing Have students draw labeled diagrams that show how heat is transferred by radiation, conduction, and convection.

Section 3 Drifting Continents

Objectives

After completing the lesson, students will be able to
- describe continental drift;
- explain why Alfred Wegener's theory was rejected by most scientists of his day.

Key Terms Pangaea, continental drift, fossil

1 Engage/Explore

Activating Prior Knowledge

Ask students: **What is a continent?** *(A continent is a one of Earth's seven large landmasses.)* **Can you name the continents?** *(Asia, Africa, North America, South America, Europe, Australia, Antarctica)* Then have students speculate about whether the continents have always had the same shape and been in the same place as they are today.

Discover

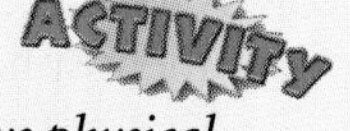

Skills Focus posing questions
Materials *globe that shows physical features*
Time 15 minutes
Tips Place several globes throughout the classroom where students can gather around them in small groups. Have students write the answers to the questions contained within the steps of the activity. *(Step 2: more than one third; Northern Hemisphere Step 3: at the North Pole; at the South Pole Step 4: through Europe and Asia)*
Think It Over Students' questions may vary. Accept any reasonable questions about the distribution of Earth's oceans, continents, and mountains.

Section 3 Drifting Continents

Discover Activity

How Are Earth's Continents Linked Together?

1. Find the oceans and the seven continents on a globe showing Earth's physical features.
2. How much of the globe is occupied by the Pacific Ocean? Does most of Earth's "dry" land lie in the Northern or Southern hemisphere?
3. Find the points or areas where most of the continents are connected. Find the points at which several of the continents almost touch, but are not connected.
4. Examine the globe more closely. Find the great belt of mountains running from north to south along the western side of North and South America. Can you find another great belt of mountains on the globe?

Think It Over
Posing Questions What questions can you pose about how oceans, continents, and mountains are distributed on Earth's surface?

Guide for Reading

- What is continental drift?
- Why was Alfred Wegener's theory rejected by most scientists of his day?

Reading Tip **As you read, look for evidence that supports the theory of continental drift.**

Five hundred years ago, the sea voyages of Columbus and other explorers changed the map of the world. The continents of Europe, Asia, and Africa were already known to mapmakers. Soon mapmakers were also showing the outlines of the continents of North and South America. Looking at these world maps, many people wondered why the coasts of several continents matched so neatly.

Look at the modern world map in Figure 11. Notice how the coasts of Africa and South America look as if they could fit together like jigsaw-puzzle pieces. Could the continents have once been a single landmass? In the 1700s, the first geologists thought that the continents had remained fixed in their positions throughout Earth's history. Early in the 1900s, however, one scientist began to think in a new way about this riddle of the continents. His theory changed the way people look at the map of the world.

World map drawn by Juan Vespucci in 1526. ▶

28 ◆ F

Reading Strategies

Reading Tip Encourage students to keep a list of supporting evidence that includes the type of evidence, the reason why it supports the theory, and the page of their text that the evidence is on. Tell students that the section headings should help them in this process. This list will eventually serve as a study guide to the chapter.

Vocabulary Call students' attention to the boldfaced term *Pangaea.* Have students look up the term *panacea* in a dictionary and compare the use of the prefix *pan.* Explain that *gaea* was an ancient Greek word for both "Earth" and the "goddess of the Earth," the personification of Earth.

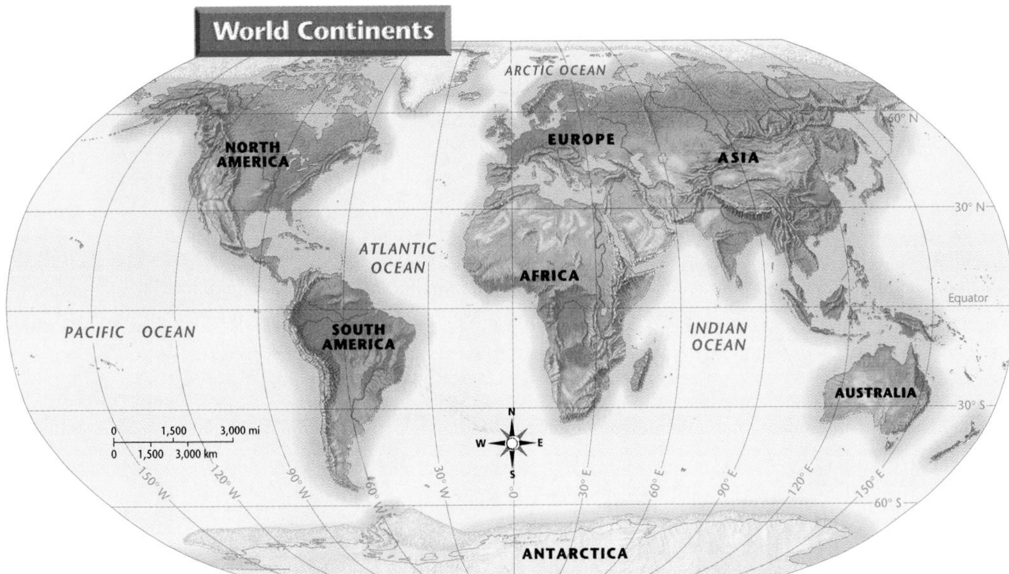

Figure 11 Today's continents provide clues about Earth's history. *Observing Which coastlines of continents seem to match up like jigsaw-puzzle pieces?*

The Theory of Continental Drift

In 1910, a young German scientist named Alfred Wegener (VAY guh nur) became curious about the relationship of the continents. He formed a hypothesis that Earth's continents had moved! **Continental drift is the hypothesis that all the continents had once been joined together in a single landmass.**

Wegener named this supercontinent **Pangaea** (pan JEE uh), meaning "all lands." According to Wegener, Pangaea existed about 300 million years ago. This was the time when reptiles and winged insects first appeared. Great tropical forests, which later formed coal deposits, covered large parts of Earth's surface.

Over tens of millions of years, Pangaea began to break apart. The pieces of Pangaea slowly moved toward their present-day locations, becoming the continents as they are today. Wegener's idea that the continents slowly moved over Earth's surface became known as **continental drift.**

Have you ever tried to persuade a friend to accept a new idea? Your friend's opinion probably won't change unless you provide some convincing evidence. Wegener gathered evidence from different scientific fields to support his ideas about continental drift. In particular, he studied landforms, fossils, and evidence that showed how Earth's climate had changed over many millions of years. Wegener published all his evidence for continental drift in a book called *The Origin of Continents and Oceans*, first published in 1915.

2 Facilitate

The Theory of Continental Drift

Using the Visuals: Figure 11

To understand the rest of this chapter, it is important for students to have a clear understanding of the distribution of land on Earth's surface. Have pairs of students quiz each other about the continents and the oceans that separate them. Identify students who have trouble with the basic geography of the world and give them a list of questions to answer by using a world map or globe. **learning modality: visual**

Including All Students

To help students place Wegener's theory in context, provide students with access to a geologic time scale, such as in *Earth's Changing Surface,* Chapter 4. All encyclopedias and most geology books also contain a detailed time scale of Earth's history. Then have students write a description of what Earth was like when Pangaea existed, using what they find on the time scale. **learning modality: verbal**

Students can keep their paragraphs in their portfolios.

Building Inquiry Skills: Developing Hypotheses

Ask students: **What force could have broken apart Pangaea and moved the continents into their present-day positions?** Challenge students in small groups to discuss this question and then develop a hypothesis that might answer it. Have each group read aloud its hypothesis to the class. Encourage questions and analysis of these hypotheses, though at this time do not make judgments about their validity. **cooperative learning**

Program Resources

◆ **Teaching Resources** 1-3 Lesson Plan, p. 23; 1-3 Section Summary, p. 24

Science Explorer Series *Earth's Changing Surface,* Chapter 4, includes a geologic time scale and provides more information on fossils.

Answers to Self-Assessment

Caption Question

Figure 11 The continents of Africa and South America best match up like jigsaw-puzzle pieces.

Media and Technology

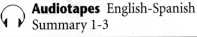

Audiotapes English-Spanish Summary 1-3

Ongoing Assessment

Writing Have each student write in his or her own words what Alfred Wegener's hypothesis was.

The Theory of Continental Drift, continued

Using the Visuals: Figure 12

Have students compare the coal beds indicated on the larger map with those indicated on the inset map. Ask: **What is different about these two maps?** *(The continents are pushed together in the inset map.)* **How does that make the location of coal beds important evidence?** *(The beds seem spread out at random in the map of present-day continents. When the continents are together, the coal beds create a pattern.)* Emphasize that this map shows three different types of evidence. Alone, each type may not prove the hypothesis. Taken together, though, they helped Wegener make a strong case. **learning modality: visual**

TRY THIS

Skills Focus making models
Materials *1 sheet of newspaper*
Time 15 minutes
Tips Provide pages of newspaper that are covered completely with lines of print, such as pages from a classified-ad section.
Expected Outcome When the lines of print line up correctly, the newspaper becomes readable and thus confirm that the pieces are reassembled correctly. The torn pieces of newspaper are like the continents that had drifted apart. Just as the print on the paper provides evidence that the paper was once one piece, the landforms on the continents provide evidence that the continents were once joined together.
Extend Students can make a bulletin board that explains Wegener's theory. For the continents, they can cut the shapes from one newspaper sheet. **learning modality: visual**

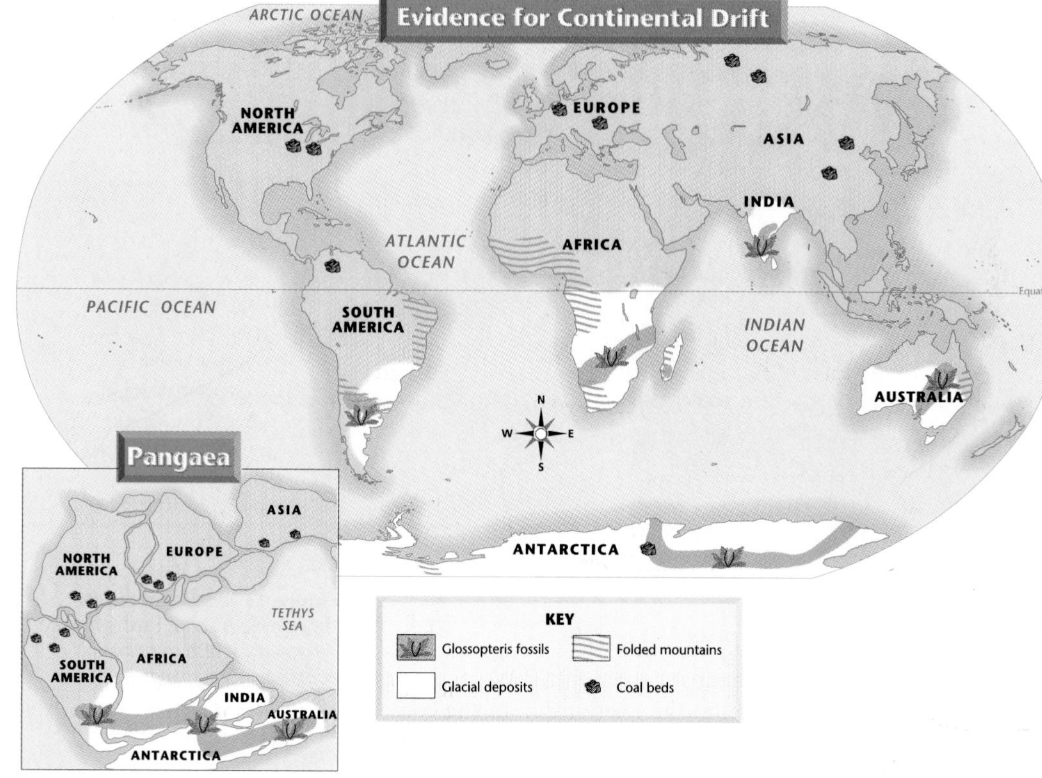

Figure 12 Wegener used several types of evidence to support his idea that the continents were once joined in a single landmass called Pangaea. *Inferring According to Wegener's theory, what does the presence of similar mountain ranges in Africa and South America indicate?*

Evidence from Landforms Mountain ranges and other features on the continents provided evidence for continental drift. For example, when Wegener pieced together maps of Africa and South America, he noticed some remarkable things. A mountain range running from east to west in South Africa lines up with a mountain range in Argentina. Brazilian coal fields match up with identical coal fields in South Africa. Wegener compared matching these features to reassembling a torn-up newspaper. If the pieces could be put back together, the "words" would match.

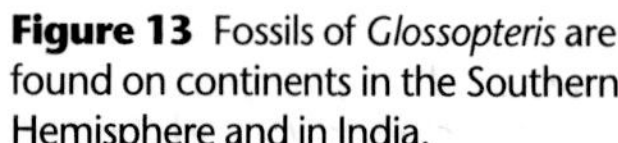

Figure 13 Fossils of *Glossopteris* are found on continents in the Southern Hemisphere and in India.

Evidence From Fossils Wegener also used fossils to support his argument for continental drift. A **fossil** is any trace of an ancient organism that has been preserved in rock. *Glossopteris* (glaw SAHP tuh ris) was a fernlike plant that flourished 250 million years ago. As shown in Figure 13, *Glossopteris* fossils have been found in rocks in Africa, South America, Australia, India, and Antarctica. The occurrence of *Glossopteris* on these widely separated landmasses convinced Wegener that the continents had once been united.

Background

History of Science Strong evidence for Wegener's theory is the geological similarities on both sides of the Atlantic, including how well mountain belts line up. "It is just as if we were to refit the torn pieces of a newspaper by matching their edges and then check whether the lines of print run smoothly across," Wegener wrote. "If they do, there is nothing left but to conclude that the pieces were in fact joined this way. If only one line was available for the test, we would still have found a high probability for the accuracy of fit, but if we have *n* lines, this probability is raised to the *n*th power." That is, the more evidence of a fit there can be found, the more the likelihood that the pieces were once joined together.

INTEGRATING LIFE SCIENCE The seedlike structures of *Glossopteris* could not have traveled the great distances that separate the continents today. The "seeds" were too large to have been carried by the wind and too fragile to have survived a trip by ocean waves. How did *Glossopteris* develop on such widely separated continents? Wegener inferred that the continents at that time were joined as the supercontinent Pangaea.

Evidence From Climate Wegener used evidence of climate change to support his theory—for example, from the island of Spitsbergen. Spitsbergen lies in the Arctic Ocean north of Norway. This island is ice-covered and has a harsh polar climate. But fossils of tropical plants are found on Spitsbergen. When these plants lived about 300 million years ago, the island must have had a warm and mild climate. According to Wegener, Spitsbergen must have been located closer to the equator.

Thousands of kilometers to the south, geologists found evidence that at the same time it was warm in Spitsbergen, the climate was much colder in South Africa. Deep scratches in rocks showed that continental glaciers once covered South Africa. Continental glaciers are thick layers of ice that cover hundreds of thousands of square kilometers. But the climate of South Africa is too mild today for continental glaciers to form. Wegener concluded that, when Pangaea existed, South Africa was much closer to the South Pole.

According to Wegener's theory, Earth's climate has not changed. Instead, the positions of the continents have changed. As a continent moves toward the equator, its climate becomes warmer. As a continent moves toward the poles, its climate becomes colder. But the continent carries with it the fossils and rocks that formed at its previous location. These clues provide evidence that continental drift really happened.

☑ *Checkpoint* ***What were the three types of evidence Wegener used to support his theory of continental drift?***

Figure 14 As evidence of continental drift, Wegener pointed to scratches on rocks made by glaciers. These scratches showed that places with mild climates today once had climates cold enough for glaciers to form.

TRY THIS

Reassembling the Pieces

ACTIVITY

Assembling a puzzle can reveal a hidden meaning.

1. Working with a partner, obtain one sheet of newspaper per person.
2. Tear your sheet of newspaper into six to eight large pieces. Trade your pieces with your partner.
3. Try to fit the pieces of newspaper together.

Making Models What evidence did you use to put the pieces together? How do your pieces of newspaper serve as a model of the theory of continental drift?

Integrating Life Science

Materials *variety of plant seeds*
Time 15 minutes

Bring a collection of seeds to class and allow students to examine them closely. Ask: **How are the different seeds moved from place to place?** Divide students in small groups and have them consider that question for each seed. Have each group make a list of the seeds and how they might be moved from one place to another. Groups should especially consider whether any seeds could have moved across an ocean. **learning modality: kinesthetic**

Using the Visuals: Figure 14

Ask students: **What are continental glaciers?** *(Some students may know that these are ice sheets that spread over a large area of land.)* Continental glaciers today cover Antarctica and Greenland. Ask: **What prevents a continental glacier from forming today over the United States?** *(The climate is too warm for glaciers to form.)* **What can you conclude about glacial scratches found in Vermont, Ohio, and other states?** *(The climate in these areas must have been much cooler at some time in the past.)* **learning modality: verbal**

Building Inquiry Skills: Drawing Conclusions

Divide students into small groups and invite each group to evaluate Wegener's evidence in terms of whether each piece is convincing and whether they add up to a proof of the hypothesis. Encourage each group to think of some aspect that would need to be proved before the hypothesis could be totally accepted as true. **learning modality: logical/mathematical**

Media and Technology

Transparencies "Evidence for Continental Drift," Transparency 2

Exploring Earth Science Videodisc
Unit 3, Side 1, "The Drifters"

Chapter 4

Answers to Self-Assessment

Caption Question

Figure 12 The presence of similar mountain ranges indicates that Africa and South America were once joined.

☑ *Checkpoint*

Evidence from landforms, evidence from fossils, and evidence from climate

Ongoing Assessment

Oral Presentation Call on students at random to explain the various kinds of evidence that Wegener put forward to support his hypothesis of continental drift.

Scientists Reject Wegener's Theory

Building Inquiry Skills: Observing

Several days before class, place an apple in a sunny place or over a heating duct, so that it dries quickly. Show students the apple. Ask: **Are the wrinkles on the apple's skin like the mountains on Earth? Would you expect that similar processes produced the wrinkles and mountains?** Students can discuss these questions in small groups. **learning modality: logical/mathematical**

3 Assess

Section 3 Review Answers

1. The continents had once been joined together in a single landmass.
2. Fossil leaves of *Glossopteris* are found in rocks in Africa, South America, Australia, India, and Antarctica. The "seeds" of that plant could not have been carried by wind or waves.
3. Wegener could not provide a satisfactory explanation for the force that pushes or pulls continents.
4. Coal is formed over time from plant material. Such plants could not have grown in the polar climate of present-day Antarctica. Either Earth's climate was much warmer or the continent was once closer to the equator.

Science at Home

Encourage students to do this activity at home. Then "debrief" them in a class discussion. Students can recount how receptive family members and others were to this idea and what any skeptics said in response.

Performance Assessment

Writing Challenge students to write a newspaper article reporting scientists' reactions to Wegener's theory.

Figure 15 Although scientists rejected his theory, Wegener continued to collect evidence on continental drift and to update his book. He died in 1930 on an expedition to explore Greenland's continental glacier.

Scientists Reject Wegener's Theory

Wegener did more than provide a theory to answer the riddle of continental drift. He attempted to explain how drift took place. He even offered a new explanation for how mountains form. Wegener thought that when drifting continents collide, their edges crumple and fold. The folding continents slowly push up huge chunks of rock to form great mountains.

Unfortunately, Wegener could not provide a satisfactory explanation for the force that pushes or pulls the continents. Because Wegener could not identify the cause of continental drift, most geologists rejected his idea. In addition, for geologists to accept Wegener's idea, they would need new explanations of what caused continents and mountains to form.

Many geologists in the early 1900s thought that Earth was slowly cooling and shrinking. According to this theory, mountains formed when the crust wrinkled like the skin of a dried-up apple. Wegener said that if the apple theory were correct, then mountains should be found all over Earth's surface. But mountains usually occur in narrow bands along the edges of continents. Wegener thought that his own theory better explained where mountains occur and how they form.

For nearly half a century, from the 1920s to the 1960s, most scientists paid little attention to the idea of continental drift. Then new evidence about Earth's structure led scientists to reconsider Wegener's bold theory.

Section 3 Review

1. What was Wegener's theory of continental drift?
2. How did Wegener use evidence based on fossils to support his theory that the continents had moved?
3. What was the main reason scientists rejected Wegener's theory of continental drift?
4. **Thinking Critically Inferring** Coal deposits have also been found beneath the ice of Antarctica. But coal only forms in warm swamps. Use Wegener's theory to explain how coal could be found so near the poles.

Science at Home

You can demonstrate Wegener's idea of continental drift. Use the map of the world in Figure 11. On a sheet of tracing paper, trace the outlines of the continents bordering the Atlantic Ocean. Label the continents. Then use scissors to carefully cut the map along the eastern edge of South America, North America, and Greenland. Next, cut along the western edge of Africa and Europe (including the British Isles). Throw away the Atlantic Ocean. Place the two cut-out pieces on a dark surface and ask family members to try to fit the two halves together. Explain to them about the supercontinent Pangaea and its history.

Program Resources

◆ **Teaching Resources** 1-3 Review and Reinforce, p. 25; 1-3 Enrich, p. 26

Media and Technology

Interactive Student Tutorial CD-ROM F-1

Sea-Floor Spreading

DISCOVER — ACTIVITY

What Is the Effect of a Change in Density?

1. Partially fill a sink or dishpan with water.
2. Open up a dry washcloth in your hand. Does the washcloth feel light or heavy?
3. Moisten one edge of the washcloth in the water. Then gently place the washcloth so that it floats on the water's surface. Observe the washcloth carefully (especially at its edges) as it starts to sink.
4. Remove the washcloth from the water and open it up in your hand. Is the mass of the washcloth the same as, less than, or greater than when it was dry?

Think It Over

Observing How did the washcloth's density change? What effect did this change in density have on the washcloth?

Deep in the ocean, the temperature is near freezing. There is no light, and living things are generally scarce. Yet some areas of the deep-ocean floor are teeming with life. One of these areas is the East Pacific Rise, a region of the Pacific Ocean floor off the coasts of Mexico and South America. Here, ocean water sinks through cracks, or vents, in the crust. The water is heated by contact with hot material from the mantle and then spurts back into the ocean.

Around these hot-water vents live some of the most bizarre creatures ever discovered. Giant, red-tipped tube worms sway in the water. Nearby sit giant clams nearly a meter across. Strange spiderlike crabs scuttle by. Surprisingly, the geological features of this strange environment provided scientists with some of the best evidence for Wegener's theory of continental drift.

GUIDE FOR READING

- **What is the process of sea-floor spreading?**
- **What happens to the ocean floor at deep ocean trenches?**

Reading Tip **Before you read, preview the art and captions looking for new terms. As you read, find the meanings of these terms.**

Figure 16 **Tube worms cluster near hot water vents in the ocean floor.**

READING STRATEGIES

Vocabulary Call students' attention to the boldface term *sonar* and explain that this is an acronym, or a word formed from the initial letters of the words of a compound term. This acronym is formed from the term *so*und *n*avigation *a*nd *r*anging. In this context, *ranging* means "determining distances."

Program Resources

- **Teaching Resources** 1-4 Lesson Plan, p. 27; 1-4 Section Summary, p. 28

Media and Technology

Audiotapes English-Spanish Summary 1-4

Sea-Floor Spreading

Objectives

After completing the lesson, students will be able to

- describe the process of sea-floor spreading;
- describe what happens to the ocean floor at deep-ocean trenches.

Key Terms mid-ocean ridge, sonar, sea-floor spreading, deep-ocean trench, subduction

1 Engage/Explore

Activating Prior Knowledge

Ask students: **At what places does material from Earth's interior flow out onto the surface?** *(At volcanoes)* Most students know that lava flows from a volcano and hardens to form a type of rock. Ask: **What causes the lava to harden?** *(It hardens as it cools.)* Have students speculate on whether there are any places where the opposite occurs, where material from the surface moves into Earth's interior and melts. Have students think about the consequences if there were no such areas.

DISCOVER

Skills Focus observing
Materials *sink or large dishpan, water, washcloth*
Time 10 minutes
Tips Review with students the difference between mass and density. The washcloth is about the same volume whether dry or wet, though it has more mass when wet. Therefore, the wet washcloth is denser than the dry washcloth.
Expected Outcome The washcloth should float for a short time on the water's surface. As it becomes soaked, the washcloth will gradually sink into the water. When removed from the water, the washcloth will be heavier than when dry.
Think It Over The washcloth's density increased as it became soaked with water. The increased density made the washcloth sink.

2 Facilitate

Mapping the Mid-Ocean Ridge

Using the Visuals: Figure 18

After students have studied the map, ask: **How is the mid-ocean ridge different under the Atlantic Ocean than it is under the Pacific Ocean?** *(It runs down the middle under the Atlantic, while it seems to outline the Pacific.)* Challenge students to think of any reason why this difference might be significant. *(Some students might infer that earthquakes and volcanoes are more common along the Pacific coasts than along the Atlantic coasts.)* **learning modality: visual**

Including All Students

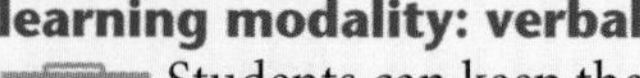

For students who have difficulty seeing, provide a relief map or globe that includes the ocean floor. Give them the opportunity to trace the path of the mid-ocean ridge around the world. Ask: **Does the mid-ocean ridge always go through the middle of oceans?** *(No, sometimes it is closer to land.)* **learning modality: kinesthetic**

Building Inquiry Skills: Communicating

Bring several baseballs to class and pass them out to students, allowing each to see and feel the seam that circles the ball. Then have each student write a short paragraph that explains why the mid-ocean ridge is like the seam on a baseball. *(Most students will realize that the seam is continuous on a baseball, as the ridge is practically continuous around Earth.)* **learning modality: verbal**

Students can keep their paragraphs in their portfolios.

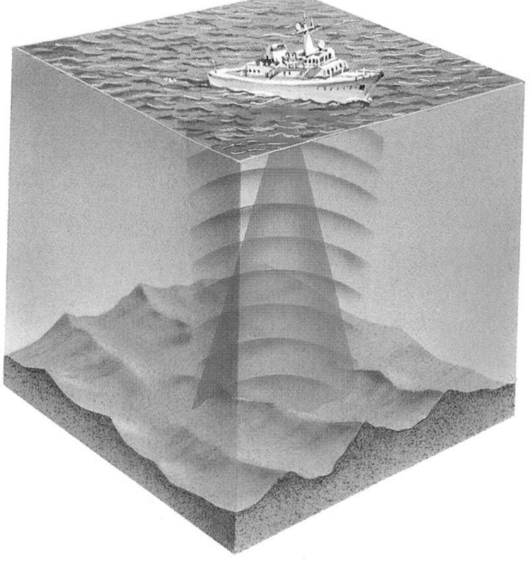

Figure 17 Scientists use sonar to map the ocean floor.

Mapping the Mid-Ocean Ridge

The East Pacific Rise is just one part of the **mid-ocean ridge,** the longest chain of mountains in the world. In the mid-1900s, scientists mapped the mid-ocean ridge using sonar. **Sonar** is a device that bounces sound waves off underwater objects and then records the echoes of these sound waves. The time it takes for the echo to arrive indicates the distance to the object.

The mid-ocean ridge curves like the seam of a baseball along the sea floor, extending into all of Earth's oceans. Most of the mountains in the mid-ocean ridge lie hidden under hundreds of meters of water. However, there are places where the ridge pokes above the surface. For example, the island of Iceland is a part of the mid-ocean ridge that rises above the surface in the North Atlantic Ocean. A steep-sided valley splits the top of the mid-ocean ridge for most of its length. The valley is almost twice as deep as the Grand Canyon. The mapping of the mid-ocean ridge made scientists curious to know what the ridge was and how it got there.

☑ *Checkpoint* *What device is used to map the ocean floor?*

Figure 18 The mid-ocean ridge is 75,000 kilometers long.

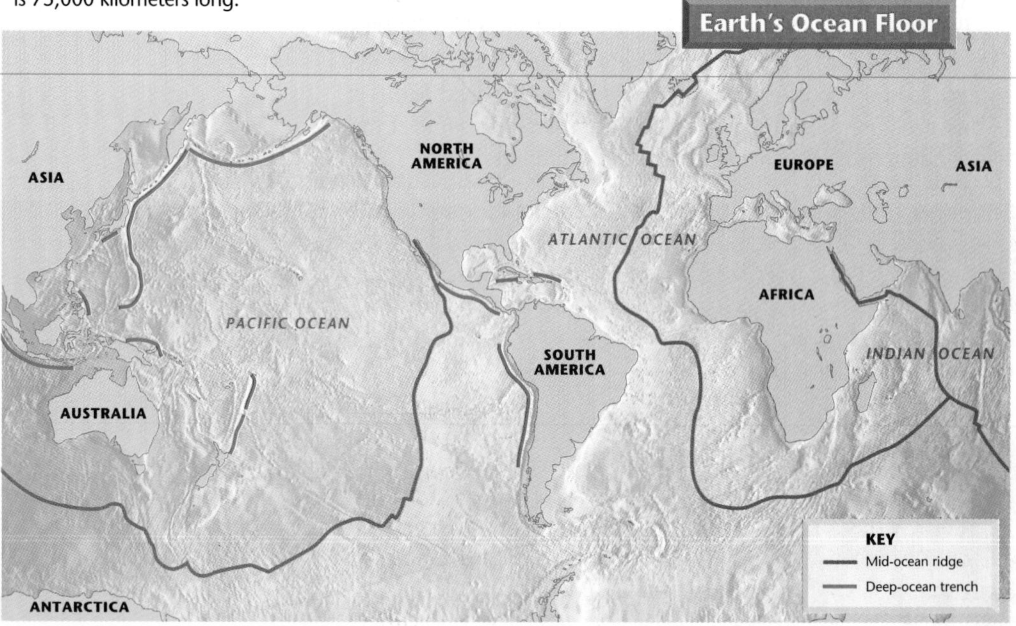

Background

Integrating Science The tube worms shown in Figure 16 are part of an extraordinary ecosystem that scientists have discovered around the hydrothermal vents of the mid-ocean ridge. Water at that depth normally has a temperature of about 2°C. The water from the vents is about 350°C. It doesn't boil because of the immense pressure at that depth. The warm water creates an environment with population densities that exceed those of warm coastal waters.

No sunlight penetrates to these depths, so no photosynthesis occurs. At the beginning of the food chain are bacteria that can generate energy from sulfur compounds in the water around the vents. The tube worms play a vital role in this process. The bacteria live inside the tube worms, which provide the bacteria with sulfides. The bacteria provide the tube worms with nutrients.

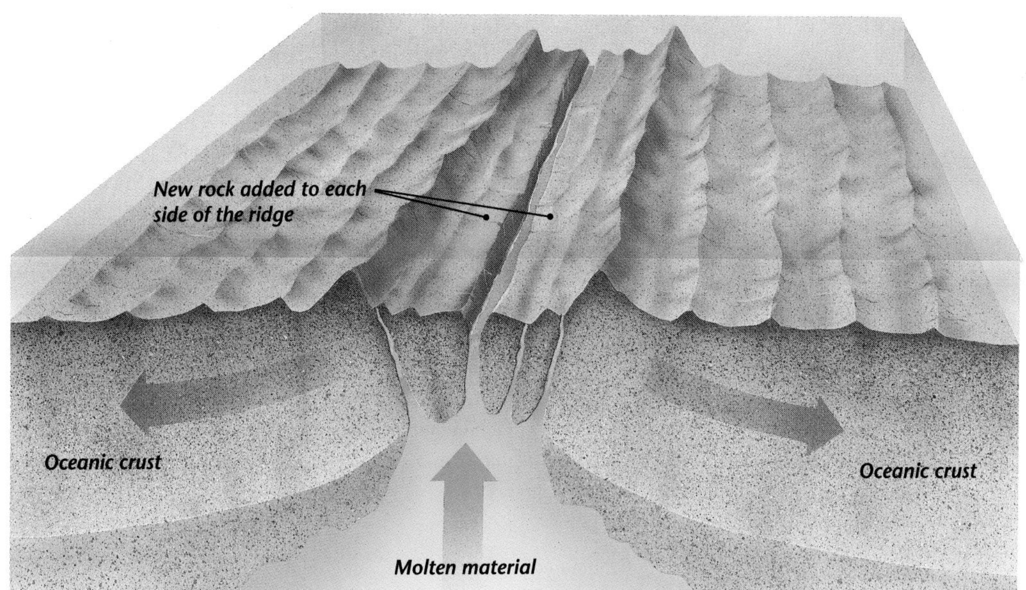

Figure 19 Molten material erupts though the valley that runs along the center of the mid-ocean ridge. This material hardens to form the rock of the ocean floor. *Applying Concepts What happens to the rock along the ridge when new molten material erupts?*

Evidence for Sea-Floor Spreading

Harry Hess, an American geologist, was one of the scientists who studied the mid-ocean ridge. Hess carefully examined maps of the mid-ocean ridge. Then he began to think about the ocean floor in relation to the problem of continental drift. Finally, he reconsidered an idea that he previously had thought impossible: Maybe Wegener was right! Perhaps the continents do move.

In 1960, Hess proposed a radical idea. He suggested that the ocean floors move like conveyor belts, carrying the continents along with them. This movement begins at the mid-ocean ridge. The mid-ocean ridge forms along a crack in the oceanic crust. **At the mid-ocean ridge, molten material rises from the mantle and erupts. The molten material then spreads out, pushing older rock to both sides of the ridge.** As the molten material cools, it forms a strip of solid rock in the center of the ridge. Then more molten material flows into the crack. This material splits apart the strip of solid rock that formed before, pushing it aside.

Hess called the process that continually adds new material to the ocean floor **sea-floor spreading.** He realized that the sea floor spreads apart along both sides of the mid-ocean ridge as new crust is added. Look at Figure 19 to see the process of sea-floor spreading.

Several types of evidence from the oceans supported Hess's theory of sea-floor spreading—evidence from molten material, magnetic stripes, and drilling samples. This evidence also led scientists to look again at Wegener's theory of continental drift.

Evidence for Sea-Floor Spreading

Using the Visuals: Figure 19

After students have studied the figure and read the caption, ask: **What part of the mantle contains molten material?** *(the asthenosphere)* **Therefore, the crack in the oceanic crust extends down through what layer?** *(the lithosphere)* **Through what other landforms on Earth does molten material rise to the surface?** *(volcanoes)* Point out that the mid-ocean ridge is like a huge string of volcanoes circling the planet. These volcanoes, though, don't generally erupt in the explosive way that people think of eruptions of volcanoes on land, and they are not cone-shaped like many volcanic mountains. **learning modality: visual**

Including All Students

ACTIVITY

To help students better understand the process of sea-floor spreading, place two chairs about a meter apart at the front of the room. Then have students form two lines to the back of the room. At your word, they should move in pairs through the opening and then turn away from each other, spreading out horizontally to the edges of the room. Ask: **What do the chairs represent?** *(the mid-ocean ridge)* **What does the space between the chairs represent?** *(the valley in the center of the ridge)* **What do you students represent?** *(First, the molten material from the mantle; then the spreading sea floor.)* **learning modality: kinesthetic**

Media and Technology

Exploring Earth Science Videodisc
Unit 3, Side 1, "Journey to the Bottom of the Sea"

Chapter 5

Answers to Self-Assessment

Checkpoint
Sonar is used to map the ocean floor.

Caption Question
Figure 19 The spreading molten material pushes the older rock to both sides of the ridge.

Ongoing Assessment

Drawing Pass out a sheet that contains the outlines of the world's continents and challenge students to draw the mid-ocean ridge on the map. Then have them check their drawings against the map in Figure 18 and make any corrections as necessary.

Evidence for Sea-Floor Spreading, continued

Building Inquiry Skills: Designing Experiments

Have students work in small groups to design an experiment that geologists could use to prove that rock "pillows" are an indication of molten material hardening underwater. *(A typical experiment might entail collecting rock from near a volcano, melting it in a furnace, and then allowing some to harden under water and some to harden out of water.)* Have groups compare and critique their experimental designs in a class discussion. **cooperative learning**

Using the Visuals: Figure 21

Show students a magnetic compass and have a volunteer explain how it's used. Then ask: **What does the indication "normal" refer to in Figure 21?** *(The magnetic field as it is today, in which a compass needle points to the magnetic North Pole.)* **Where would the compass needle point when Earth's magnetic field was reversed?** *(It would point to the magnetic South Pole.)* To illustrate this, flip the poles of a bar magnet held next to the compass, thereby causing the compass needle to reverse direction. Finally, ask a student to review for the class why Earth has a magnetic field, as explained in Section 1. **learning modality: verbal**

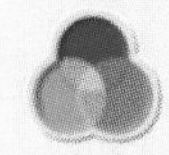

Integrating Physics

ACTIVITY

Have the class again act out the process of sea floor spreading, using two chairs a meter apart at the front of the room to represent the mid-ocean ridge. This time, though, announce every two or three pairs that Earth's magnetic field has reversed. At the announcement, the pair going through the "ridge" should turn to walk backwards. Each succeeding pair should also walk through backwards until you announce another reversal. **learning modality: kinesthetic**

Figure 20 The submersible *Alvin* photographed pillow lava along the mid-ocean ridge. These "pillows" form under water when cold ocean water causes a crust to form on erupting molten material. Each pillow expands until it bursts, allowing molten material to flow out and form the next pillow.

Evidence From Molten Material In the 1960s, scientists found evidence that new material is indeed erupting along the mid-ocean ridge. The scientists dived to the ocean floor in *Alvin,* a small submersible built to withstand the crushing pressures four kilometers down in the ocean. In the central valley of the mid-ocean ridge, *Alvin's* crew found strange rocks shaped like pillows or like toothpaste squeezed from a tube. Such rocks can form only when molten material hardens quickly after erupting under water. The presence of these rocks showed that molten material has erupted again and again from cracks along the central valley of the mid-ocean ridge.

Evidence From Magnetic Stripes When scientists studied patterns in the rocks of the ocean floor, they found more support for sea-floor spreading. *INTEGRATING PHYSICS* In Section 1 you read that Earth behaves like a giant magnet, with a north pole and a south pole. Earth's magnetic poles have reversed themselves about once every 600,000 years. If the magnetic poles suddenly reversed themselves today, you would find that your compass needle pointed south. Scientists discovered that the rock that makes up the ocean floor lies in a pattern of magnetized "stripes." These stripes hold a record of reversals in Earth's magnetic field.

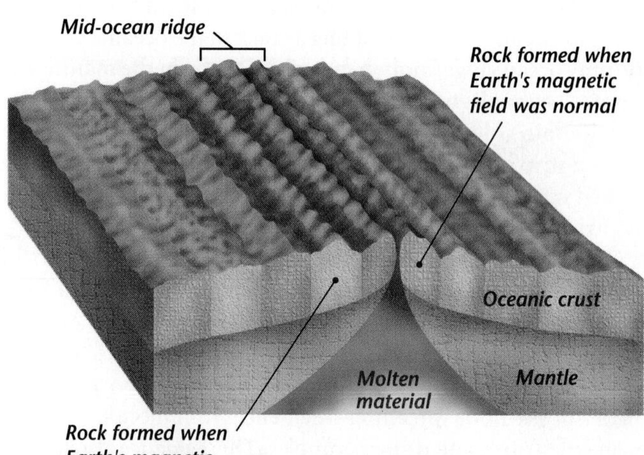

Figure 21 Magnetic stripes in the rock of the ocean floor show the direction of Earth's magnetic field at the time the rock hardened. *Interpreting Diagrams How are these matching stripes evidence of sea-floor spreading?*

Background

Facts and Figures Have students consider these facts and figures about the mid-ocean ridge.

- Its total length is more than 75,000 km. At places, it is more than 1500 km wide.
- Most of the ridge rises 2–3 km above the surrounding deep-ocean basins; the top of most of the ridge is about 2 km below the ocean's surface.
- The valley that splits most of the top of the ridge is 1–2 km deep and several kilometers wide.

The rock of the ocean floor, which contains iron, began as molten material. As the molten material cooled, the iron bits inside lined up in the direction of Earth's magnetic poles. When the rock hardened completely, it locked the iron bits in place, giving the rocks a permanent "magnetic memory." You can think of it as setting thousands of tiny compass needles in cement.

Using sensitive instruments, scientists recorded the magnetic memory of rocks on both sides of the mid-ocean ridge. They found that a stripe of rock that shows when Earth's magnetic field pointed north is followed by a parallel stripe of rock that shows when the magnetic field pointed south. As you can see in Figure 21, the pattern is the same on both sides of the ridge. Rock that hardens at the same time has the same magnetic memory.

Evidence From Drilling Samples The final proof of sea-floor spreading came from rock samples obtained by drilling into the ocean floor. The *Glomar Challenger*, a drilling ship built in 1968, gathered the samples. The *Glomar Challenger* sent drilling pipes through water six kilometers deep to drill holes in the ocean floor. This feat has been compared to using a sharp-ended wire to dig a hole into a sidewalk from the top of the Empire State Building.

Samples from the sea floor were brought up through the pipes. Then the scientists determined the age of the rocks in the samples. They found that the farther away from the ridge the samples were taken, the older the rocks were. The youngest rocks were always in the center of the ridges. This showed that sea-floor spreading really has taken place.

☑ *Checkpoint* ***What evidence did scientists find for sea-floor spreading?***

Figure 22 The *Glomar Challenger* was the first research ship designed to drill samples of rock from the deep-ocean floor.

Reversing Poles

1. Cut six short pieces, each about 2.5 cm long, from a length of audiotape.
2. Tape one end of each piece of audiotape to a flat surface. The pieces should be spaced 1 cm apart and line up lengthwise in a single line.
3. Touch a bar magnet's north pole to the first piece of audiotape. Then reverse the magnet and touch its south pole to the next piece.
4. Repeat Step 3 until you have applied the magnet to each piece of audiotape.
5. Sweep one end of the magnet about 1 cm above the line of audiotape pieces. Observe what happens.

Making Models What characteristic of the ocean floor did you observe as you swept the magnet along the line of audiotape pieces?

Skills Focus making models
Materials *audiotape, scissors, metric ruler, plastic tape, bar magnet*
Time 15 minutes
Tips Students can tape the pieces of audiotape to a desk or table. Advise them to tape only one end of each piece. Also, have them tape the pieces at least 1 cm apart so that the bar magnet will not accidentally magnetize an adjacent piece when magnetizing every other piece. Students should hold the magnet vertically in Step 5.
Expected Outcome Because every other piece of audiotape has been magnetized to an opposite pole than the one before, every piece will react differently than the pieces on either side. The pieces magnetized to the like pole will be attracted, while the pieces magnetized to the opposite pole will be repelled. The characteristic of the ocean floor modeled is its pattern of magnetic stripes.
Extend Have students write a paragraph that details the analogy suggested by this activity. **learning modality: kinesthetic**

Including All Students

Some students may have difficulty understanding the evidence from drilling samples. Have them draw a line down the middle of a piece of paper. The line represents the mid-ocean ridge, and the paper the ocean floor. Then have them mark three "drilling holes" at intervals away from each side of the line. Next, they should label the two "drilling holes" closest to the line as *1990*, the two middle ones *1980*, and the two outside ones *1970*. Explain that these dates are when the rock formed. Ask: **If you found these data in your research, what might you conclude about the process that created this ocean floor?** *(New floor periodically pushed the old floor aside on both sides of the ridge.)* **learning modality: visual**

Media and Technology

Transparencies "Magnetic Stripes Along the Mid-Ocean Ridge," Transparency 3

Answers to Self-Assessment

Caption Question

Figure 21 The pattern of stripes is the same on both sides of the ridge, indicating that the sea floor has spread from the mid-ocean ridge.

☑ *Checkpoint*

Evidence from molten material, evidence from magnetic stripes, and evidence from drilling samples

Ongoing Assessment

Skills Check Have students make a cause and effect chart to explain the processes that produced the three types of evidence discussed on these pages.

Subduction at Deep-Ocean Trenches

Using the Visuals: Figure 23

Ask students: **Where on this figure is the oceanic crust densest? Explain your reasoning.** *(It's densest near the trenches, because there it is as old as it can get, and oceanic crust becomes denser as it cools and ages.)* Then have students recall that continental crust and oceanic crust are composed of different materials. Ask: **Which is denser, continental crust or oceanic crust?** *(Oceanic crust is denser because it is composed mostly of basalt, while continental crust is composed of the less dense granite.)* Explain that these differences in density are important for them to remember when they read the next section. **learning modality: verbal**

Building Inquiry Skills: Relating Cause and Effect

Ask: **If the effect is the subduction of oceanic crust at a deep-ocean trench, what is the cause or causes?** Challenge each student to write a paragraph that answers this question. Explain that all the causes can be found in their text. *(Some students may correctly mention three causes: (1) a push from the rising molting material at the mid-ocean ridge, (2) a push from the convection currents underneath the lithosphere, and (3) a pull from gravity on the older, denser oceanic crust far away from the mid-ocean ridge.)* **learning modality: logical/mathematical**

Subduction and Earth's Oceans

Including All Students

Provide students with a relief map of the world that includes the ocean floor. Challenge them to find the locations of as many deep-ocean trenches as they can, keeping a record as they go. Seeing-impaired students can work with sighted students to find and record trenches. Ask: **Where do you find the most trenches? The least?** *(Most are in the Pacific basin; very few are in the Atlantic basin.)* **learning modality: kinesthetic**

ACTIVITY

Subduction at Deep-Ocean Trenches

How can the ocean floor keep getting wider and wider? The answer is that the ocean floor generally does not just keep spreading. Instead, the ocean floor plunges into deep underwater canyons called **deep-ocean trenches.** A deep-ocean trench forms where the oceanic crust bends downward.

Where there are deep-ocean trenches, subduction takes place. **Subduction** (sub DUK shun) is the process by which the ocean floor sinks through a deep-ocean trench and back into the mantle. Convection currents under the lithosphere push new crust that forms at the mid-ocean ridge away from the ridge and toward a deep-ocean trench.

New oceanic crust is hot. But as it moves away from the mid-ocean ridge, it cools and becomes more dense. Eventually, as shown in Figure 23, gravity pulls this older, denser oceanic crust down into the trench. The sinking crust is like the washcloth in the Discover activity at the beginning of this section. As the dry washcloth floating on the water gets wet, its density increases and it begins to sink.

At deep-ocean trenches, subduction allows part of the ocean floor to sink back into the mantle, over tens of millions of years. You can think of sea-floor spreading and subduction together as if the ocean floor were moving out from the mid-ocean ridge on a giant conveyor belt.

Figure 23 Oceanic crust created along the mid-ocean ridge is destroyed at a deep-ocean trench. In the process of subduction, oceanic crust sinks down through the trench into the mantle. *Drawing Conclusions Where is the oldest part of the ocean floor?*

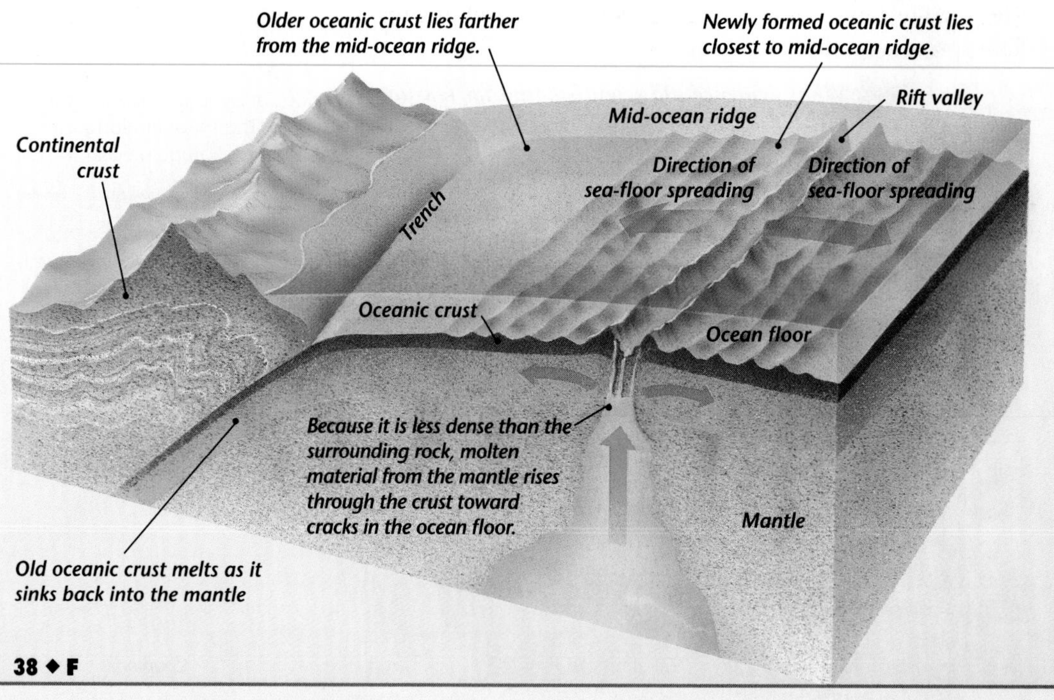

Older oceanic crust lies farther from the mid-ocean ridge.
Newly formed oceanic crust lies closest to mid-ocean ridge.
Rift valley
Mid-ocean ridge
Continental crust
Direction of sea-floor spreading
Direction of sea-floor spreading
Trench
Oceanic crust
Ocean floor
Because it is less dense than the surrounding rock, molten material from the mantle rises through the crust toward cracks in the ocean floor.
Mantle
Old oceanic crust melts as it sinks back into the mantle

Background

Facts and Figures Most deep-ocean trenches are found on the margins of the Pacific Ocean. Deep-ocean trenches are usually 8–10 km deep and thousands of kilometers long. The deepest known part of the ocean is Challenger Deep, which bottoms out at 10,915 m below sea level. This is in the Mariana Trench, under the Pacific Ocean north of the island of New Guinea. If Mt. Everest, the world's highest mountain, were placed inside Challenger Deep, its summit would still be more than 2,000 m under water.

Subduction and Earth's Oceans

The processes of subduction and sea-floor spreading can change the size and shape of the oceans. Because of these processes, the ocean floor is renewed about every 200 million years. That is the time it takes for new rock to form at the mid-ocean ridge, move across the ocean, and sink into a trench.

Subduction in the Pacific Ocean The vast Pacific Ocean covers almost one third of the planet. And yet it is shrinking. How could that be? Sometimes a deep ocean trench swallows more oceanic crust than the mid-ocean ridge can produce. Then, if the ridge does not add new crust fast enough, the width of the ocean will shrink. This is happening to the Pacific Ocean, which is ringed by many trenches.

Figure 24 It is cold and dark in the deep ocean trenches where subduction occurs. But even here, scientists have found living things, such as this angler fish.

Subduction in the Atlantic Ocean The Atlantic Ocean, on the other hand, is expanding. Unlike the Pacific Ocean, the Atlantic Ocean has only a few short trenches. As a result, the spreading ocean floor has virtually nowhere to go. In most places, the oceanic crust of the Atlantic Ocean floor is attached to the continental crust of the continents around the ocean. So as the Atlantic's ocean floor spreads, the continents along its edges also move. Over time, the whole ocean gets wider. The spreading floor of the North Atlantic Ocean and the continent of North America move together like two giant barges pushed by the same tugboat.

Section 4 Review

1. What is the role of the mid-ocean ridge in sea-floor spreading?
2. What is the evidence for sea-floor spreading?
3. Describe the process of subduction at a deep-ocean trench.
4. **Thinking Critically** **Relating Cause and Effect** Where would you expect to find the oldest rock on the ocean floor? Explain your answer.
5. **Thinking Critically** **Predicting** As you can see in Figure 18, the mid-ocean ridge extends into the Red Sea between Africa and Asia. What do you think will happen to the Red Sea in the future? Explain your answer.

Check Your Progress

CHAPTER PROJECT 1

Now that you have learned about sea-floor spreading, draw a revised sketch of your model. Include examples of sea-floor spreading and subduction on your sketch. Show the features that form as a result of these processes. How will you show what happens beneath the crust? Improve your original ideas and add new ideas. Revise your list of materials if necessary. Begin building your model.

3 Assess

Section 4 Review Answers

1. At the mid-ocean ridge, molten material rises from the mantle and erupts. The molten material then spreads out, pushing older rock to both sides of the ridge.
2. Evidence for sea-floor spreading includes evidence from molten material, evidence from magnetic stripes, and evidence from drilling samples.
3. In the process of subduction, oceanic crust sinks down through the trench into the mantle.
4. The oldest rock on the ocean floor would be found farthest away from the mid-ocean ridge, where new rock is formed.
5. The Red Sea will widen as the sea floor spreads out on both sides of the mid-ocean ridge there.

Check Your Progress

CHAPTER PROJECT 1

Check the folders of individual students to assess who is having trouble with the concepts involved in sea-floor spreading. Then meet with each group to discuss how they might modify their designs. Encourage groups to begin building the base of their models, using the materials that worked best in their experiments. Emphasize that they should change their designs to reflect new material they learned as well as to improve on the accuracy and attractiveness of the finished product.

Program Resources

◆ **Teaching Resources** 1-4 Review and Reinforce, p. 29; 1-4 Enrich, p. 30

Media and Technology

Transparencies "Sea-floor Spreading and Subduction," Transparency 4

Interactive Student Tutorial CD-ROM F-1

Answers to Self-Assessment

Caption Question

Figure 23 The oldest part of the ocean floor is farthest from the mid-ocean ridge.

Performance Assessment

Drawing Challenge students to make a detailed drawing of the process of sea-floor spreading, including subduction at a deep-ocean trench. Advise them to put as many labels as necessary on the drawing to explain the process.

Skills Lab

Making Models

Modeling Sea-Floor Spreading

Preparing for Inquiry

Key Concept Sea-floor spreading at the mid-ocean ridge continually adds new material to the ocean floor.

Skills Objectives Students will be able to:

- make a model of sea-floor spreading.
- observe how material rises through a center opening and sinks down through openings at the edges.
- infer how sea-floor spreading adds new crust and how that crust moves back down into the mantle.

Time 30 minutes

Advance Planning Gather all the materials at least one day prior to the activity. Prepare two sample sheets: a sheet with stripes predrawn, and a sheet folded and marked as in steps 3 and 4.

Alternative Materials Instead of small groups making several models, you could divide the class into larger groups and have each make a large model using butcher-block paper.

Guiding Inquiry

Invitation Help students focus on the key concept by asking: **What happens at the mid-ocean ridge?** *(Molten material rises from the mantle and erupts.)* **What forms when the molten material hardens?** *(New ocean floor)* **What happens as that new floor spreads out from the ridge?** *(It pushes older rock on both sides of the ridge.)* **How are magnetic stripes evidence of this process?** *(The magnetic stripes show that material has been pushed away from the ridge over time.)* **What happens at deep-ocean trenches?** *(Oceanic crust sinks back down into the mantle.)*

Introducing the Procedure

- Have students read through the entire activity. Then ask: **What is the purpose of this activity?** *(To make a model of sea-floor spreading)*

Skills Lab

Making Models

Modeling Sea-Floor Spreading

Along the entire length of Earth's mid-ocean ridge, the sea floor is spreading. Although this process takes place constantly, it is difficult to observe directly. You can build a model to help understand this process.

Problem

How does sea-floor spreading add material to the ocean floor?

Materials

scissors
metric ruler
2 sheets of unlined paper
2 markers of different colors and thicknesses

Procedure 

1. Draw stripes across one sheet of paper, parallel to the short sides of the paper. The stripes should vary in spacing and thickness.
2. Fold the paper in half lengthwise and write the word "Start" at the top of both halves of the paper. Using the scissors, carefully cut the paper in half along the fold line to form two strips.
3. Lightly fold the second sheet of paper into eighths. Then unfold it, leaving creases in the paper. Fold this sheet in half lengthwise.

4. Starting at the fold, draw lines 5.5 cm long on the middle crease and the two creases closest to the ends of the paper.

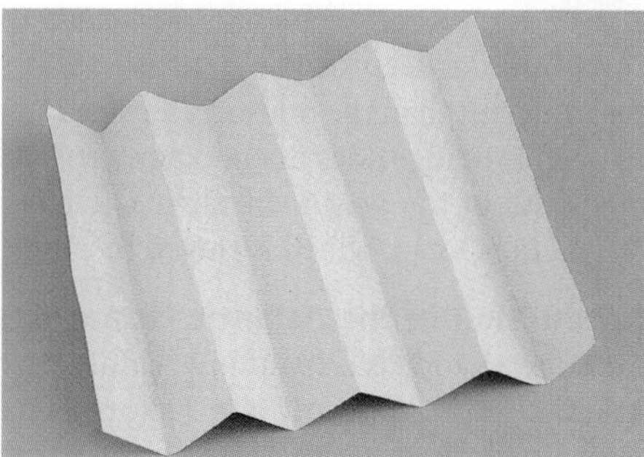

5. Now carefully cut along the lines you drew. Unfold the paper. There should be three slits in the center of the paper.

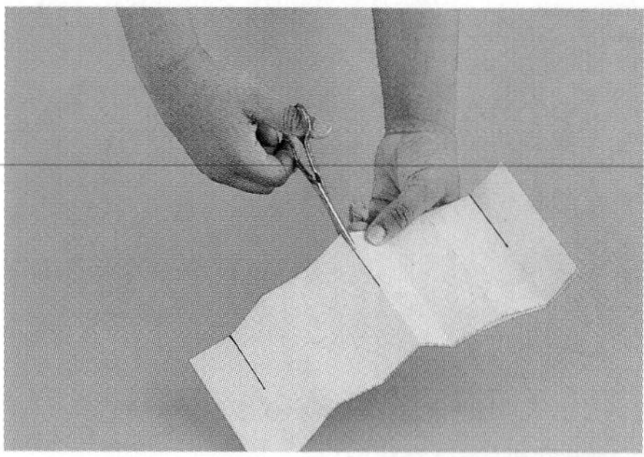

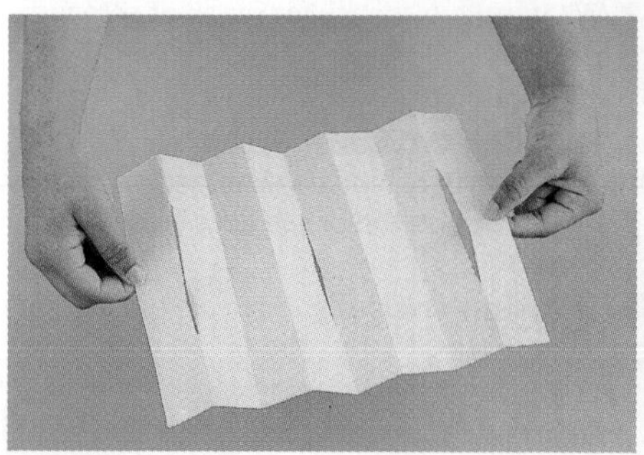

- **Why do you cut the first sheet in half?** *(The sea floor spreads out in both directions from the mid-ocean ridge. Cutting the sheet in half allows the model to represent movement on both sides of the ridge.)*
- **After you've cut the sheet in half, how does the pattern of stripes on one half sheet compare with the pattern on the other half?** *(The pattern is the same on each half.)*

Troubleshooting the Experiment

- Demonstrate how to begin to make each of the two sheets. Then show students your samples of the finished products. Allow them to refer to these sheets as they make their own.
- Check to see that students make the slits large enough to pull the paper through easily. They should cut a little more than halfway through the width of the sheet.

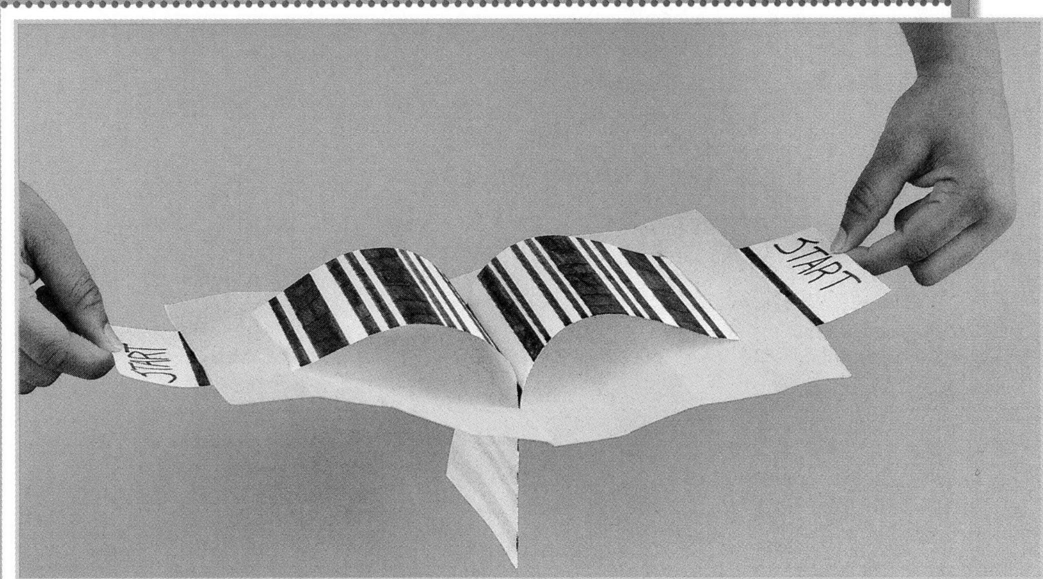

6. Put the two striped strips of paper together so their Start labels touch one another. Insert the Start ends of the strips up through the center slit and then pull them toward the side slits.
7. Insert the ends of the strips into the side slits. Pull the ends of the strips and watch what happens at the center slit.
8. Practice pulling the strips through the slits until you can make the two strips come up and go down at the same time.

Analyze and Conclude

1. What feature of the ocean floor does the center slit stand for? What prominent feature of the ocean floor is missing from the model at this point?
2. What do the side slits stand for? What does the space under the paper stand for?
3. How does the ocean floor as shown by the part of a strip close to the center slit differ from the ocean floor as shown by the part near a side slit? How does this difference affect the depth of the ocean?
4. What do the stripes on the strips stand for? Why is it important that your model have an identical pattern of stripes on both sides of the center slit?
5. Explain how differences in density and temperature provide some of the force needed to move the strips in your model.
6. **Think About It** Use your own words to describe the process of ocean-floor spreading. What parts of the process were not shown by your model?

More to Explore

Imagine that so much molten rock erupted from the mid-ocean ridge that an island formed there. How could you modify your model to show this island? How could you show what would happen to it over a long period of time?

Expected Outcome
Students will build a model that shows eruption of material through the mid-ocean ridge, the spreading of the sea floor on both sides of the ridge, and the subduction of the floor a deep-ocean trenches.

Analyze and Conclude
1. The center slit stands for the central valley of the mid-ocean ridge. The feature that is missing is the mountainous ridge.
2. The side slits stand for deep-ocean trenches. The space under the paper stands for the part of the mantle called the asthenosphere.
3. The ocean floor as shown by the strip near the center slit is younger, hotter, and less dense than ocean floor farther away. As the floor moves away from the ridge, it cools and becomes denser. The ocean floor as shown by the part near a side slit is older, cooler, and denser. The increased density causes the depth of the ocean to increase.
4. The stripes stand for the magnetic stripes in the rock of the ocean floor. The pattern of magnetic stripes is the same on both sides of the mid-ocean ridge.
5. Temperature differences in the mantle cause convection currents. These currents cause molten rock to erupt through the valley that runs along the center of the mid-ocean ridge. As more material erupts, the sea floor spreads, cools, and becomes denser. The denser material sinks back into the mantle when it reaches a trench.
6. Answers may vary. A typical answer should mention the eruption of molten material at the mid-ocean ridge, the spreading of the sea floor, and the subduction of oceanic crust at deep-ocean trenches. Parts of the process not shown by the model include changes in density and the melting of the crust as it sinks back into the mantle.

Extending the Inquiry

More to Explore Answers may vary. A typical answer might suggest drawing an island near the Start label on one of the strips. Then, through the movement of the strip through the model, the island's position would change, and it would eventually be subducted.

Program Resources

◆ **Teaching Resources** Skills Lab blackline masters, pp. 35–37

Safety

Caution students to use care when working with sharp instruments such as scissors. Review the safety guidelines in Appendix A.

Section 5 The Theory of Plate Tectonics

Objectives

After completing the lesson, students will be able to

- explain the theory of plate tectonics;
- describe the three types of plate boundaries.

Key Terms plate, scientific theory, plate tectonics, fault, transform boundary, divergent boundary, rift valley, convergent boundary

1 Engage/Explore

Activating Prior Knowledge

Ask students: **What is a plate?** *(A typical answer will describe a dinner plate.)* Challenge students to think of other contexts in which the word is used, such as metal plates that cover machinery, home plate in baseball, the plates or scales that cover a reptile, and the plates of photographs in a textbook. Help students form a general definition for *plate,* such as a broad, flat sheet of material.

Discover Activity

Skills Focus drawing conclusions
Materials *world map in an atlas, tracing paper, scissors, sheet of paper, tape*
Time 20 minutes
Tips To shorten the activity, provide students with a photocopy of the continent outlines.
Expected Outcome Students should be able to easily fit some of the continents together, such as South America and Africa. It may be more difficult to imagine how the other continents fit together. Accept all plausible configurations.
Think It Over Answers may vary. A typical answer might mention that some of the continents fit together quite well while others did not. The general fit between some continents suggests that the continents may once have been joined.

Section 5 The Theory of Plate Tectonics

Discover Activity

How Well Do the Continents Fit Together?

1. Using a world map in an atlas, trace the shape of each continent and Madagascar on a sheet of paper. Also trace the shape of India and the Arabian Peninsula.
2. Carefully cut apart the landmasses, leaving Asia and Europe as one piece. Separate India and the Arabian Peninsula from Asia.
3. Piece together the continents as they may have looked before the breakup of Pangaea. Then attach your reconstruction of Pangaea to a sheet of paper.

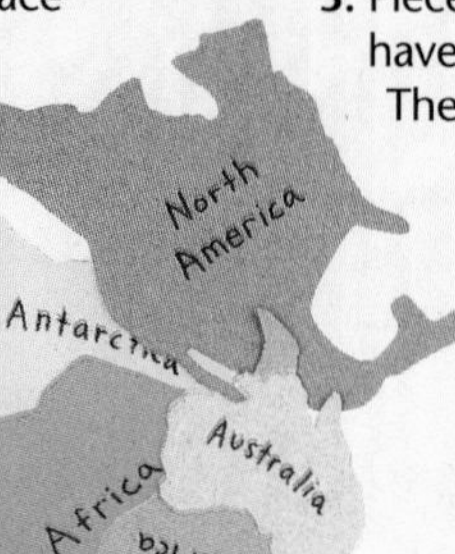

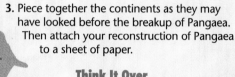

Think It Over
Drawing Conclusions How well did the pieces of your continents fit together? Do your observations support the idea that today's landmasses were once joined together? Explain.

Guide for Reading

- What is the theory of plate tectonics?
- What are the three types of plate boundaries?

Reading Tip Before you read, preview *Exploring Plate Tectonics* on pages 46–47. Write a list of any questions you have about plate tectonics. Look for answers as you read.

Have you ever dropped a hard-boiled egg? If so, you may have noticed that the eggshell cracked in an irregular pattern of broken pieces. Earth's crust, its solid outer shell, is not one unbroken layer. The crust is more like that cracked eggshell. It's broken into pieces separated by jagged cracks.

A Canadian scientist, J. Tuzo Wilson, observed that there are cracks in the continental crust similar to those on the ocean floor. In 1965, Wilson proposed a new way of looking at these cracks. According to Wilson, the lithosphere is broken into separate sections called **plates.** The plates fit closely together along cracks in the crust. As shown in Figure 26, the plates carry the continents or parts of the ocean floor, or both.

Figure 25 The Great Rift Valley in east Africa is a crack in Earth's crust where two pieces of crust are pulling apart.

Reading Strategies

Reading Tip Typical questions students might write include, What are plates? What are convergent and divergent boundaries? What is a rift valley? Advise students to leave enough space between each question to write the answers when they find them in the text.

Program Resources

- **Integrated Science Laboratory Manual** F-1, "Mapping a Future World"

A Theory of Plate Motion

Wilson combined what geologists knew about sea-floor spreading, Earth's plates, and continental drift into a single theory—the theory of plate tectonics (tek TAHN iks). A **scientific theory** is a well-tested concept that explains a wide range of observations. **Plate tectonics** is the geological theory that states that pieces of Earth's crust are in constant, slow motion, driven by convection currents in the mantle. **The theory of plate tectonics explains the formation, movement, and subduction of Earth's crust.**

How can Earth's plates move? The plates of the lithosphere float on top of the asthenosphere. Convection currents rise in the asthenosphere and spread out beneath the lithosphere. Most geologists think that the flow of these currents causes the movement of Earth's plates.

No plate can budge without affecting the other plates surrounding it. As the plates move, they collide, pull apart, or grind past each other, producing spectacular changes in Earth's surface. These changes include volcanoes, mountain ranges, and deep-sea trenches.

Predicting

ACTIVITY

Study the map of Earth's plates in Figure 26. Notice the arrows that show the direction of plate movement. Now find the Nazca plate on the map. Which direction is it moving? Find the South American plate and describe its movement. What do you think will happen as these plates continue to move?

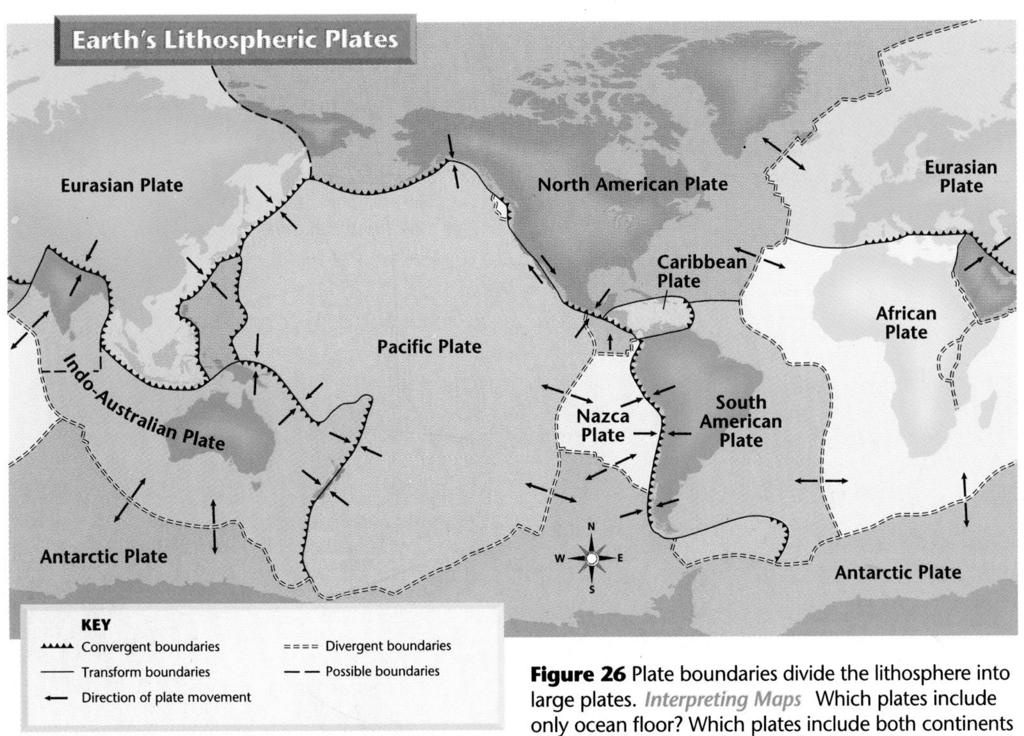

Figure 26 Plate boundaries divide the lithosphere into large plates. *Interpreting Maps* Which plates include only ocean floor? Which plates include both continents and ocean floor?

Media and Technology

Audiotapes English-Spanish Summary 1-5

Transparencies "Earth's Lithospheric Plates," Transparency 5

Program Resources

◆ **Teaching Resources** 1-5 Lesson Plan, p. 31; 1-5 Section Summary, p. 32

Answers to Self-Assessment

Caption Question

Figure 26 Plates that include only ocean floor are the Pacific Plate and the Nazca Plate. All the other labeled plates in the figure include both continents and ocean floor.

2 Facilitate

A Theory of Plate Motion

Inquiry Challenge

ACTIVITY

Materials *large clear bowl, water, block of rigid plastic foam slightly smaller than diameter of bowl, sand or gravel, metric ruler*
Time 15 minutes
Ask students: **Do you think plates with high mountains float higher or lower on the asthenosphere than those without mountains?** Then encourage students to investigate this question by using the plastic foam block to represent a plate, water to represent mantle material, and sand or gravel to create "mountains." *(Students should find that an area of a plate with mountains floats lower.)* **learning modality: kinesthetic**

Sharpen your Skills

Predicting

ACTIVITY

Time 10 minutes
Challenge students to make their prediction after they have learned about all three types of boundaries. The Nazca plate is moving east, while the South American plate is moving west. Thus, this is a convergent plate boundary. Because the Nazca plate carries dense oceanic crust and the South American plate carries less dense continental crust, the Nazca plate plunges beneath the South American plate.
Extend Challenge students to describe each of the boundaries associated with the North American plate and predict what will happen at each. **learning modality: logical/mathematical**

Ongoing Assessment

Writing Have each student write a paragraph explaining in his or her own words the theory of plate tectonics.

Plate Boundaries

Demonstration

Materials *2 large wooden blocks*
Time 10 minutes

Introduce the three types of plate boundaries by demonstrating each type using wooden blocks. For a transform boundary, slide one block past the other. For a divergent boundary, pull two blocks away from each other. For a convergent boundary, push two blocks together. For each type, encourage students to make a drawing with labels and arrows showing the direction of each block's movement. **learning modality: visual**

Using the Visuals: Figure 27

Materials *large, flat rock*
Time 10 minutes

Before class, break a large, flat rock into two pieces. Invite students to examine the boundary between the two pieces and then model two plates slipping past each other. Students will observe that the process is far from smooth, as the two pieces grind against one another. Emphasize that this likely would be a jerky process, in which the boundary would catch for a moment and then let go. Ask: **Why do you think earthquakes occur frequently at transform boundaries?** *(The plates cannot move smoothly past one another because of the irregular nature of faults.)* **learning modality: kinesthetic**

Addressing Naive Conceptions

Many students may be misled into thinking that geologists can observe movements at plate boundaries, just as a person might observe other forces of nature, such as hurricanes and volcanoes. Ask: **How fast do you think Earth's plates are moving?** *(Only a few centimeters per year)* Emphasize that the movements involved in plate tectonics occur over millions of years. Geologists infer what processes are occurring by studying evidence of the past. **learning modality: verbal**

Plate Boundaries

The edges of different pieces of the crust—Earth's rigid shell—meet at lines called plate boundaries. Plate boundaries extend deep into the lithosphere. **Faults**—breaks in Earth's crust where rocks have slipped past each other—form along these boundaries. There are three kinds of plate boundaries: transform boundaries, divergent boundaries, and convergent boundaries. For each type of plate boundary, there is a different type of plate movement.

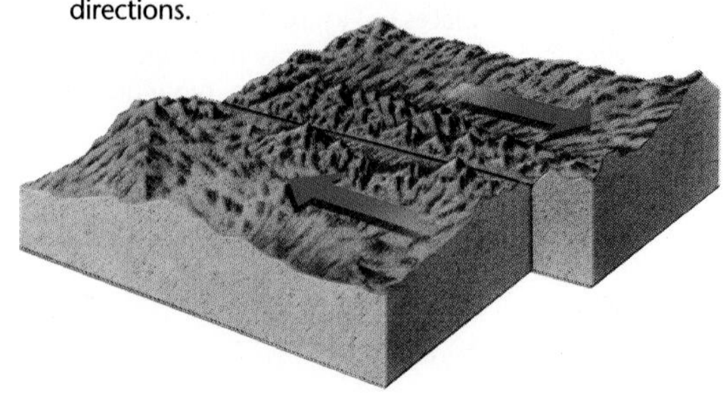

Figure 27 At a transform boundary, two plates move along the boundary in opposite directions.

Transform Boundaries Along transform boundaries, crust is neither created nor destroyed. A **transform boundary** is a place where two plates slip past each other, moving in opposite directions. Earthquakes occur frequently along these boundaries. Look at Figure 27 to see the type of plate movement that occurs along a transform boundary.

EXPLORING *Plate Tectonics*

Plate movements have built many of the features of Earth's land surfaces and ocean floors.

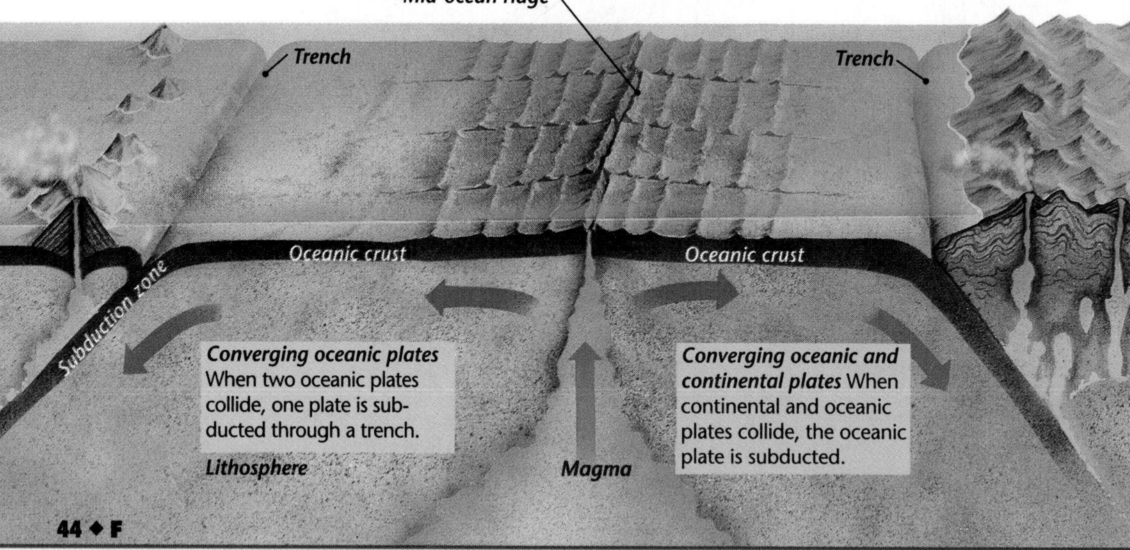

Diverging oceanic plates The mid-ocean ridge marks a divergent boundary where plates move apart.

Converging oceanic plates When two oceanic plates collide, one plate is subducted through a trench.

Converging oceanic and continental plates When continental and oceanic plates collide, the oceanic plate is subducted.

44 ◆ F

Background

Facts and Figures

- The San Andreas Fault is an example of a transform boundary. The Pacific plate is sliding past the North American plate.
- The Rio Grande rift is a divergent boundary on land that extends from southern Colorado to El Paso, Texas.
- The Appalachian Mountains formed as a result of a convergent boundary in which two plates of continental crust collided.

Media and Technology

Exploring Earth Science Videodisc
Unit 3, Side 1, "Isto What?"

Chapter 1

Divergent Boundaries The place where two plates move apart, or diverge, is called a **divergent boundary** (dy VUR junt). Most divergent boundaries occur at the mid-ocean ridge. In Section 4, you learned how oceanic crust forms along the mid-ocean ridge as sea-floor spreading occurs.

Divergent boundaries also occur on land. When a divergent boundary develops on land, two slabs of Earth's crust slide apart. A deep valley called a **rift valley** forms along the divergent boundary. For example, the Great Rift Valley in east Africa marks a deep crack in the African continent that runs for about 3,000 kilometers. Along this crack, a divergent plate boundary is slowly spreading apart. The rift may someday split the eastern part of Africa away from the rest of the continent. As a rift valley widens, its floor drops. Eventually, the floor may drop enough for the sea to fill the widening gap.

☑ *Checkpoint* *What is a rift valley? How are rift valleys formed?*

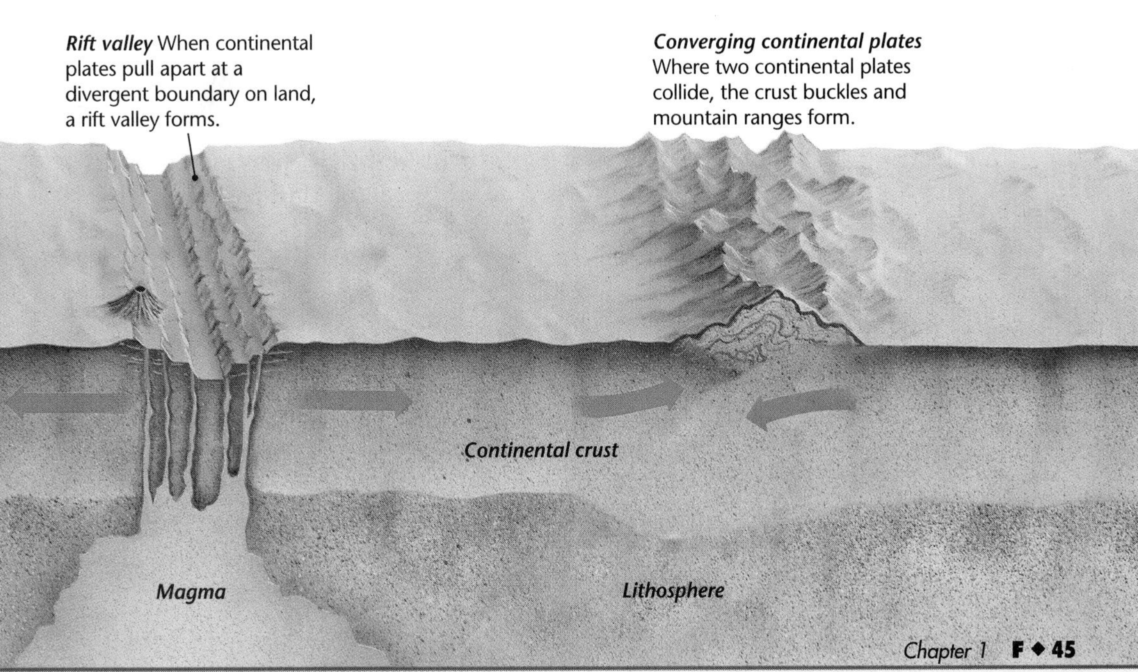
Rift valley When continental plates pull apart at a divergent boundary on land, a rift valley forms.
Converging continental plates Where two continental plates collide, the crust buckles and mountain ranges form.
Continental crust
Magma
Lithosphere

Media and Technology

Transparencies "Exploring Plate Tectonics," Transparency 6

Exploring Earth Science Videodisc Unit 3, Side 1, "Everything on Your Plate"

Chapter 6

Answers to Self-Assessment

☑ *Checkpoint*

A rift valley is a deep valley that forms along a divergent boundary on land. Rift valleys form as two slabs of Earth's crust slide apart.

EXPLORING

Plate Tectonics

Give students a chance to study the visual essay and then call on students to read the annotations. Ask: **What is magma?** *(Some students will know that magma is hot, molten material from beneath Earth's surface.)* **Where is the magma coming from that is shown erupting through the mid-ocean ridge and the rift valley?** *(The magma comes from the asthenosphere, the part of the mantle that can flow.)* Point out that most of what is shown they already know from learning about sea-floor spreading. Ask: **What new processes are shown?** *(Movements on land, including divergent boundaries on land and converging continental plates.)* **learning modality: visual**

Inquiry Challenge

Materials *candy bar, paper towel*
Time 10 minutes

Have all students wash their hands. Then give pairs of students a candy bar with a thick chocolate top and caramel and nougat layers below. As a model, the chocolate represents the crust, the caramel represents the mantle part of the lithosphere, and the nougat represents the asthenosphere. Ask: **How can you use this candy bar to model what happens at divergent and convergent boundaries?** Students will find that when pulled apart, a valley will form between the break in the chocolate top. When pushed together, the chocolate top will buckle and form a ridge. Have students make sketches of what they see. (**CAUTION:** *Check for allergies to chocolate if you allow students to eat the candy bars.*) **learning modality: kinesthetic**

Ongoing Assessment

Oral Presentation Call on students at random to explain what occurs at each of the different types of plate boundaries.

Plate Boundaries, continued

Including All Students

Ask students: **When two continental plates collide, why isn't one subducted beneath the other?** *(Both are approximately the same density and also less dense than the mantle, so neither one sinks beneath the other.)* Point out that not all mountains form this way, but many do. The Appalachian Mountains in the United States are another example of what results when continental plates collide. Ask: **When these plates collide, can local people hear a crash?** *(Of course not, since this collision occurs over millions of years.)* **learning modality: verbal**

Building Inquiry Skills: Comparing and Contrasting

Have students make a table that compares and contrasts the three types of plate boundaries. Their tables should include all the possibilities of what could happen at each kind of boundary, including two possibilities at divergent boundaries and three possibilities at convergent boundaries. **learning modality: verbal**

The Continents' Slow Dance

Using the Visuals: Figure 29

Call on students at random to read the annotations for each map in the sequence. Then ask: **What evidence of sea-floor spreading can you see on these maps occurring from 135 million years ago to today?** *(The Atlantic Ocean formed during that period as the sea floor spread at the mid-ocean ridge.)* **From what has occurred in the past, what do you predict will happen to the Atlantic and Pacific oceans in the future?** *(The Atlantic Ocean will expand, and the Pacific Ocean will shrink.)* **learning modality: visual**

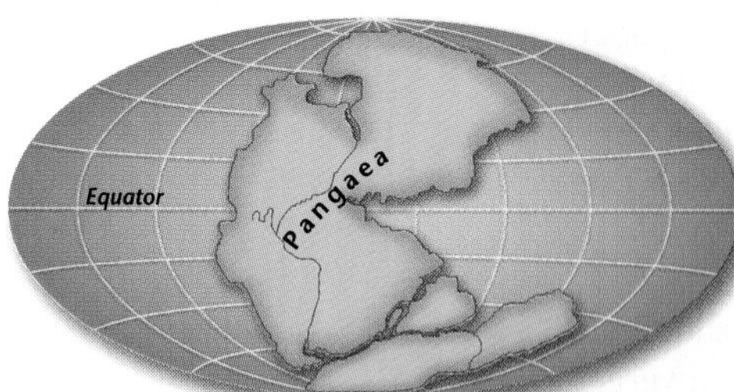

225 million years ago
All Earth's major landmasses were joined in the supercontinent Pangaea before plate movements began to split it apart.

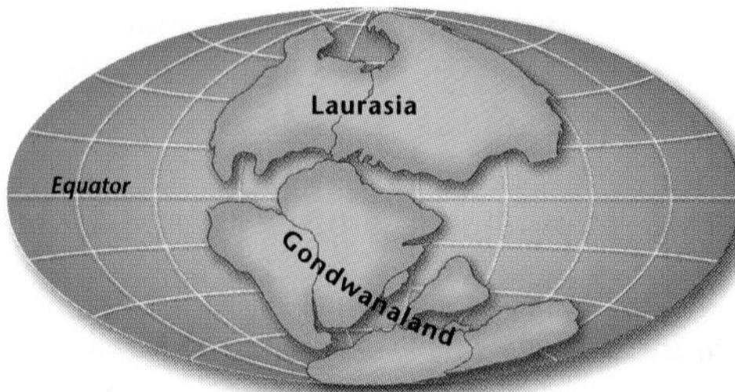

180–200 million years ago
Pangaea split apart, opening narrow seas that later became oceans.

Figure 29 It has taken more than 200 million years for the continents to move to their present locations. *Posing Questions* What questions would you need to answer in order to predict where the continents will be in 50 million years?

Figure 28 A collision between two continental plates produced the majestic Himalayas. The collision began 50 million years ago, when the plate that carries India slammed into Asia.

Convergent Boundaries The place where two plates come together, or converge, is called a **convergent boundary** (kun VUR junt). When two plates converge, the result is called a collision. Collisions may bring together oceanic crust and oceanic crust, oceanic crust and continental crust, or continental crust and continental crust.

When two plates collide, the density of the plates determines which one comes out on top. Oceanic crust, which is made mostly of basalt, is more dense than continental crust, which is made mostly of granite. And oceanic crust becomes cooler and denser as it spreads away from the mid-ocean ridge.

Where two plates carrying oceanic crust meet at a trench, the plate that is less dense dives under the other plate and returns to the mantle. This is the process of subduction that you learned about in Section 4.

Sometimes a plate of oceanic crust collides with a plate made of continental crust. The less dense continental crust can't sink under the more dense oceanic crust. Instead, the oceanic plate begins to sink and plunges beneath the continental plate.

When two plates made of continental crust collide, subduction does not take place. Both continental plates are mostly low-density granite rock. Therefore, neither plate is dense enough to sink into the mantle. Instead, the plates crash head-on. The collision squeezes the crust into mighty mountain ranges.

☑ *Checkpoint* ***What types of plate movement occur at plate boundaries?***

Background

Integrating Science Scientists measure the movement of plates using two technologies. In Satellite Laser Ranging, scientists bounce laser pulses off satellites orbiting Earth. By timing how long the laser pulse takes to reach the satellite and return to a station on Earth, scientists can calculate any movement of that station over time. In Very Long Baseline Interferometry, scientists use radio telescopes to record signals from quasars billions of light-years away at two stations on Earth. Over time, any change in the difference of when the same signal arrives at the two stations indicates that the stations are moving in relation to each other. Using these methods, scientists have determined, for example, that the state of Maryland is moving away from England at a rate of 1.7 cm/yr. And Hawaii is moving toward Japan at a rate of 8.3 cm/yr.

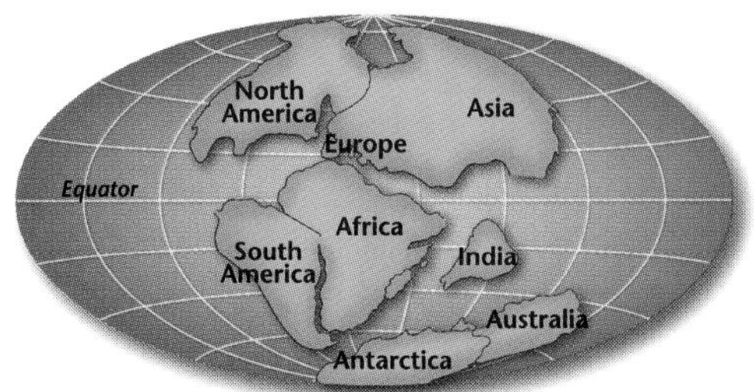

135 million years ago Gradually, the landmasses that became today's continents began to drift apart.

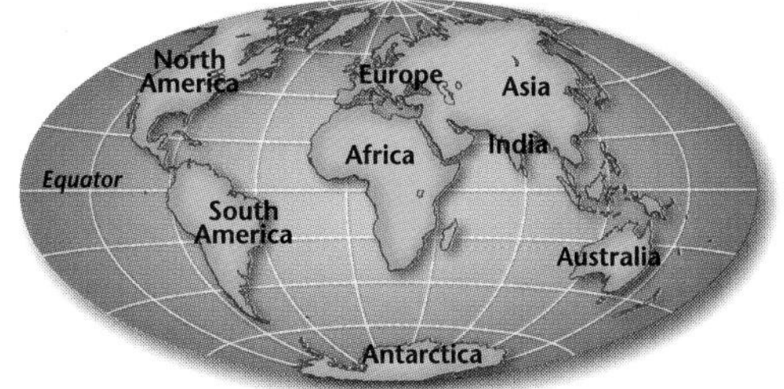

Earth today
Note how far to the north India has drifted—farther than any other major landmass.

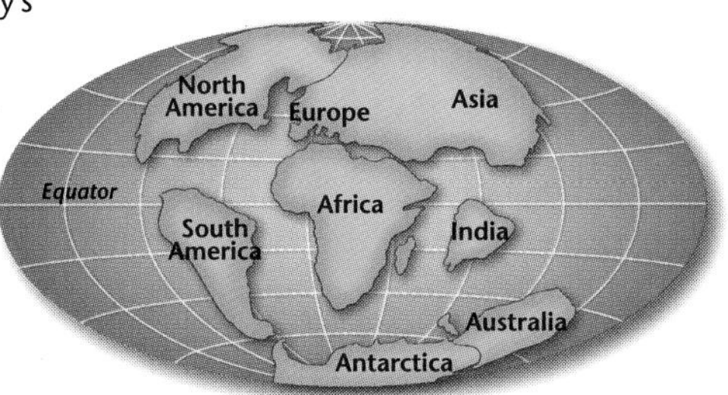

65 million years ago
India was still a separate continent, charging toward Asia, while Australia remained attached to Antarctica.

The Continents' Slow Dance

The plates move at amazingly slow rates: from about one to ten centimeters per year. The North American and Eurasian plates are floating apart at a rate of 2.5 centimeters per year—that's about as fast as your fingernails grow. This may not seem like much, but these plates have been moving for tens of millions of years.

About 260 million years ago, the continents were joined together in the supercontinent that Wegener called Pangaea. Then, about 200 million years ago, Pangaea began to break apart. Figure 29 shows how Earth's continents and other landmasses have moved since the break-up of Pangaea.

Section 5 Review

1. What is the theory of plate tectonics?
2. What are the different types of boundaries found along the edges of Earth's plates?
3. What major event in Earth's history began about 200 million years ago? Explain.
4. **Thinking Critically Predicting** Look at Figure 26 on page 43 and find the divergent boundary that runs through the African plate. Predict what could eventually happen along this boundary.

Check Your Progress

CHAPTER PROJECT 1

Now that you have learned about plate tectonics, add examples of plate boundaries to your model. If possible, include a transform boundary, a convergent boundary, and a divergent boundary. Complete the construction of your model by adding all the required surface features. Be sure to label the features on your model. Include arrows that indicate the direction of plate movement.

3 Assess

Section 5 Review Answers

1. The theory of plate tectonics explains the formation, movement, and subduction of Earth's crust.
2. Transform boundaries, divergent boundaries, and convergent boundaries
3. The supercontinent Pangaea began to break apart.
4. If the rift valley continues to grow, it could someday split the eastern part of Africa away from the rest of the continent.

Check Your Progress

CHAPTER PROJECT 1

Discuss with each group how they can incorporate plate boundaries and the movement of plates in their model. Review their designs and give them feedback about the materials they might use. Then encourage them to make any changes necessary and construct the model of a cut-away Earth. Also, give them some guidelines of how they could best make their presentation to the class.

Program Resources

◆ **Teaching Resources** 1-5 Review and Reinforce, p. 33; 1-5 Enrich, p. 34

Media and Technology

 **Transparencies** "Continental Drift Since Pangaea," Transparency 7

 **Interactive Student Tutorial CD-ROM** F-1

Answers to Self-Assessment

Caption Question

Figure 29 You would need answers to how fast and in what direction each plate is moving.

Checkpoint

Plates slip past each other at transform boundaries, move apart at divergent boundaries, and come together at convergent boundaries.

Performance Assessment

Drawing Divide students into small groups and give each group a piece of posterboard. Encourage each group to make a poster that includes all the information they've learned about sea-floor spreading and plate tectonics. They could use colored pencils, chalk, or water paints to make their posters.

Skills Lab

Observing

Hot Plates

Preparing for Inquiry

Key Concept Convection currents in the mantle cause the movement of Earth's plates.

Skills Objectives Students will be able to:

- make a model of two layers of Earth's interior.
- observe how convection currents can move objects on the surface of a liquid.
- infer how similar convection currents in the mantle move Earth's plates.

Time 40 minutes

Advance Planning Gather the materials at least a day in advance. Buy disposable roasting pans at a grocery store. Then try out the activity. Pay close attention to how best to position the sponges together in the pan so that this can be demonstrated to students. Also, time how long it takes the sponges to reach the pan's edges with your setup.

Alternative Materials Books can be used instead of bricks. The length of the candles is dependent on the height of the pan; shorter candles should be used if the pan is raised less than three bricks high. The tip of the candle flame should be 2–3 cm below the bottom of the pan. To nudge the sponges together in Step 5, a pencil or ruler is helpful, because it disturbs the water less than hands do.

Guiding Inquiry

Invitation Help students think of prior experiences with convection currents by asking: **What happens to noodles and other solids in soup as the water heats up?** *(The solids begin to move around.)* **What causes this movement?** *(The solids move with the movement of water in convection currents, which are created by the heat of a stove's burner.)*

Introducing the Procedure

- Have students read through the entire activity. Then ask: **What is the purpose of the map pins?** *(They prevent the sponges from sticking together.)*

Skills Lab

Observing

HOT PLATES

In this lab, you will observe a model of convection currents in Earth's mantle.

Problem

How do convection currents affect Earth's plates?

Materials

1 aluminum roasting pan
2 candles, about 10 cm long
clay to hold the candles up
6 bricks
2 medium-sized kitchen sponges
10 map pins
2 L water

Procedure

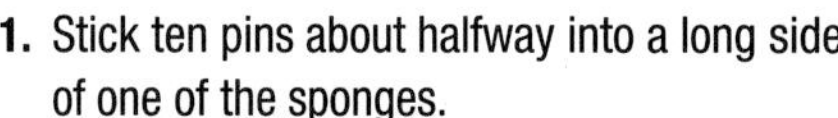

1. Stick ten pins about halfway into a long side of one of the sponges.
2. Place an aluminum pan on top of two stacks of bricks. **CAUTION:** *Position the bricks so that they fully support both ends of the pan.*
3. Fill the pan with water to a depth of 4 cm.
4. Moisten both sponges with water and float them in the pan.
5. Slowy nudge the two sponges together with the row of map pins between them. (The pins will keep the sponges from sticking together.)
6. Carefully let go of the sponges. If they drift apart, gently move them back together again.
7. Once the sponges stay close together, place the candles under opposite ends of the pan. Use clay to hold up the candles.
8. Draw a diagram of the pan, showing the starting position of the sponges.
9. Carefully light the candles. Observe the two sponges as the water heats up.
10. Draw diagrams showing the position of the sponges 1 minute and 2 minutes after placing the candles under the pan.

Analyze and Conclude

1. What happens to the sponges as the water heats up?
2. What can you infer is causing the changes you observed?
3. What material represents the mantle in this activity? What represents Earth's plates?
4. What would be the effect of adding several more candles under the pan?
5. **Think About It** How well did this activity model the movement of Earth's plates? What type of plate movement did you observe in the pan? How could you modify the activity to model plate movement more closely?

More to Explore

You can observe directly the movement of the water in the pan. To do this, squeeze a single drop of food coloring into the pan. After the drop of coloring has sunk to the bottom, place a lit candle under the pan near the colored water. How does the food coloring move in the water? How does this movement compare with convection currents in the mantle?

- Ask: **After you light the candles, where will the water in the pan be hottest and coolest?** *(The water will be hottest at the bottom of the pan and coolest at the surface.)*

Troubleshooting the Experiment

- Demonstrate how to place the pins in the sponges. Only about 0.5 cm of each pin should stick out of the sponge.
- Check that students have the pan at the right height, with the bricks positioned at the edges and the candles just inside the bricks.

Safety

Caution students to be careful when placing the map pins into the sponges and to be very careful with the open flame of the candles. Review the safety guidelines in Appendix A.

STUDY GUIDE

CHAPTER 1 REVIEW

Section 1 Earth's Interior

Key Ideas

- A geologist studies the materials that make up the Earth and the processes that shape its surface and interior.
- Earth's interior is divided into the crust, the mantle, the outer core, and the inner core.
- The lithosphere includes the crust and the rigid upper layer of the mantle; beneath the lithosphere lies the soft layer of the mantle called the asthenosphere.

Key Terms

geologist	crust
rock	basalt
geology	granite
constructive force	mantle
destructive force	lithosphere
continent	asthenosphere
seismic wave	outer core
pressure	inner core

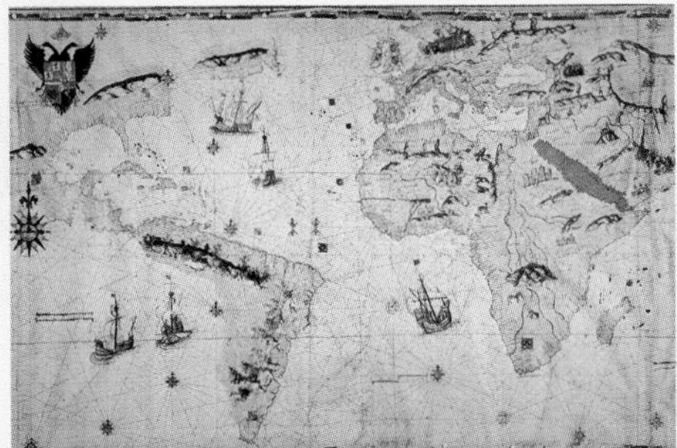

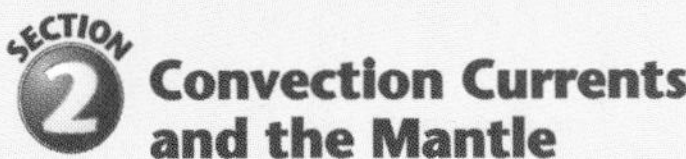

Section 2 Convection Currents and the Mantle

Integrating Physics

Key Ideas

- Heat can be transferred in three ways: radiation, conduction, and convection.
- Differences of temperature and density within a fluid cause convection currents.

Key Terms

heat transfer	convection
radiation	density
conduction	convection current

Section 3 Drifting Continents

Key Ideas

- Alfred Wegener developed the idea that the continents were once joined and have since drifted apart.
- Most scientists rejected Wegener's theory because he could not identify a force that could move the continents.

Key Terms

Pangaea continental drift fossil

Section 4 Sea-Floor Spreading

Key Ideas

- In sea-floor spreading, molten material erupts along the mid-ocean ridge and hardens to form rock.
- In subduction, the ocean floor sinks back to the mantle through deep ocean trenches.

Key Terms

mid-ocean ridge	deep-ocean trench
sonar	subduction
sea-floor spreading	

Section 5 The Theory of Plate Tectonics

Key Ideas

- The theory of plate tectonics explains plate movements and how they cause continental drift and sea-floor spreading.
- Plates slip past each other at transform boundaries, move apart at divergent boundaries, and come together at convergent boundaries.

Key Terms

plate	transform boundary
scientific theory	divergent boundary
plate tectonics	rift valley
fault	convergent boundary

ACTIVITY
USING THE INTERNET
www.science-explorer.phschool.com

Program Resources

- **Teaching Resources** Skills Lab blackline masters, pp. 38–39
- **Teaching Resources** Chapter 1 Project Scoring Rubric, p. 14; Chapter 1 Performance Assessment, pp. 168–170; Chapter 1 Test, pp. 171–174

Media and Technology

Interactive Student Tutorial CD-ROM F-1

Computer Test Bank Chapter 1 Test

- Remind students not to move the pans once they have been filled, since any movement will likely cause a collapse.
- Demonstrate how to nudge the sponges together. Encourage students to do this as delicately as possible—the less movement the better.
- Before students light the candles, close all windows and doors to cut down on drafts.

Expected Outcome

As the candles heat the water on the bottom of the pan, convection currents will form throughout the pan. The currents will carry the sponges from the center to the edges of the pan.

Analyze and Conclude

1. The sponges begin to move apart to the edges of the pan.
2. The heat from the candles has heated the water, creating convection currents. The convection currents carry the sponges to the edges of the pan.
3. The water represents the mantle; the sponges represent Earth's plates.
4. Answers may vary. A typical answer may suggest that adding candles near to the original candles would heat the water faster and thus create faster currents. The result would be that the sponges would move apart faster.
5. Answers may vary. A typical answer may suggest that the activity models the movement of Earth's plates well. The movement in the pan models divergent plate movement. Some ways to modify the experiment would be to use a thicker liquid than water in which to create convection currents, reposition the candles to get the plates to converge, and have several irregularly shaped sponge "continents."

Extending the Inquiry

More to Explore Encourage students to repeat the activity after a class discussion that explores the techniques of groups that had the most success. Then give each group access to a drop of food coloring so that they can observe the convection currents that move the sponges. The food coloring should move up to the top and then out to the sides, finally sinking back down at the edges of the pan. The basic movement is quite similar to the currents in the mantle.

CHAPTER 1 REVIEW

Reviewing Content

Multiple Choice

1. a **2.** d **3.** d **4.** b **5.** b

True or False

6. crust **7.** inner core **8.** true **9.** deep-ocean trenches **10.** diverge

Checking Concepts

11. The inner core is a dense ball of solid iron and nickel that spins. The outer core, by contrast, is a layer of molten iron and nickel that behaves like a thick liquid.
12. Heat from Earth's core and the mantle itself create convection currents in the asthenosphere. Hot columns of soft mantle material rise slowly. At the top of the asthenosphere, the material spreads out and pushes cooler material out of the way. This cooler material then sinks.
13. Evidence includes fossils of tropical plants found in polar regions and scratches made by continental glaciers found in places with mild climates.
14. The importance of that discovery is that it supported the theory of sea-floor spreading. It also led scientists to look again at Wegener's theory of continental drift.
15. Iron bits inside molten material lock in place as rock hardens, showing the direction of the magnetic field at that time. Rock magnetized in one direction forms along the mid-ocean ridge until Earth's magnetic poles reverse themselves. This happens about once every 600,000 years. Then rock magnetized in the opposite direction forms a new stripe of rock along each side of the mid-ocean ridge.
16. Oceanic crust is more dense than continental crust. As a result, when a plate carrying oceanic crust collides at a convergent boundary with a plate carrying continental crust, the oceanic plate begins to sink and plunges beneath the continental plate.
17. Answers may vary. A typical interview should include mention of a variety of evidence that supports Wegener's theory, including evidence from landforms, fossils, and climate. Students should also mention evidence for the more modern theories of sea-floor spreading and plate tectonics.

CHAPTER 1 REVIEW

Reviewing Content

For more review of key concepts, see the Interactive Student Tutorial CD-ROM.

Multiple Choice

Choose the letter of the answer that best completes each statement.

1. The layer of the upper mantle that can flow is the
   a. asthenosphere.
   b. lithosphere.
   c. inner core.
   d. continental crust.
2. Most scientists rejected Wegener's theory of continental drift because the theory failed to explain
   a. coal deposits in Antarctica.
   b. formation of mountains.
   c. climate changes.
   d. how the continents move.
3. Subduction of the ocean floor takes place at
   a. the lower mantle.
   b. mid-ocean ridges.
   c. rift valleys.
   d. trenches.
4. The process that powers plate tectonics is
   a. radiation. b. convection.
   c. conduction. d. subduction
5. Two plates collide with each other at
   a. a divergent boundary
   b. a convergent boundary
   c. the boundary between the mantle and the crust.
   d. a transform boundary.

True or False

If the statement is true, write true. If it is false, change the underlined word or words to make the statement true.

6. The Earth's <u>outer core</u> is made of basalt and granite.
7. The spinning of the <u>asthenosphere</u>, made of iron and nickel, explains why Earth has a magnetic field.
8. <u>Convection currents</u> form because of differences of temperature and density in a fluid.
9. <u>Magnetic stripes</u> on the ocean floor are places where oceanic crust sinks back to the mantle.
10. When two continental plates <u>converge</u>, a rift valley forms.

Checking Concepts

11. How is the inner core different from the outer core?
12. Why are there convection currents in the mantle? Explain.
13. What evidence of Earth's climate in the past supports the theory of continental drift?
14. What was the importance of the discovery that molten rock was coming out of cracks along the mid-ocean ridge?
15. How do magnetic stripes form on the ocean floor? Why are these stripes significant?
16. What happens when a plate of oceanic crust collides with a plate of continental crust? Why?
17. **Writing to Learn** Imagine that Alfred Wegener is alive today to defend his theory of continental drift. Write a short interview that Wegener might have on a daytime talk show. You may use humor.

Thinking Visually

18. To show the processes that link a trench and the mid-ocean ridge, copy the cycle diagram into your notebook and fill in the blanks. (For more on cycle diagrams, see the *Skills Handbook.*)

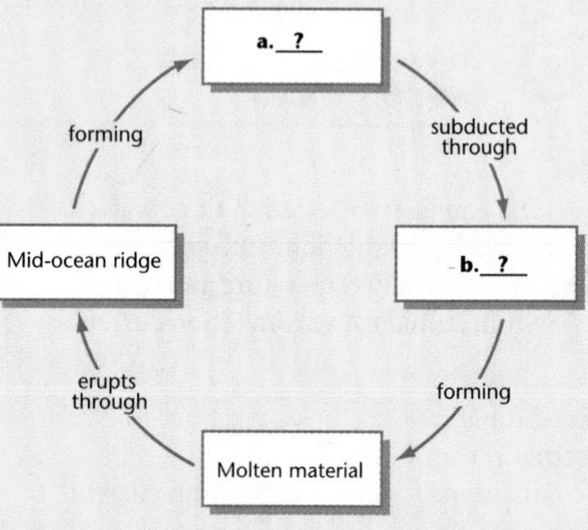

Thinking Visually

18. a. oceanic crust **b.** deep-ocean trenches

Applying Skills

19. The part carrying Australia is moving to the northeast; the part carrying India is moving to the north.
20. Because the parts are moving in different directions, a divergent plate boundary will form between them.
21. Students should infer that this is a convergent plate boundary where two plates made of continental crust are colliding. When the plates converge, the collision squeezes the crust into mountain ranges.

Thinking Critically

22. Crust, lithosphere, inner core—solid; asthenosphere—solid but able to flow slowly; outer core—liquid
23. Both continental crust and oceanic crust are part of the solid outer layer of rock that forms Earth's outer skin. Continental crust consists mainly of granite, while oceanic crust

Applying Skills

Geologists think that a new plate boundary is forming in the Indian Ocean. The plate carrying Australia is twisting away from the plate carrying India.

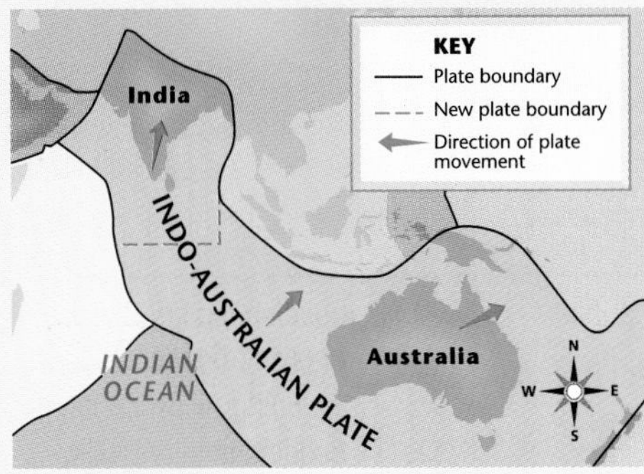

19. **Interpreting Maps** Look at the arrows showing the direction of plate motion. In what direction is the part of the plate carrying Australia moving? In what direction is the part carrying India moving?

20. **Predicting** As India and Australia move in different directions, what type of plate boundary will form between them?

21. **Inferring** On the map you can see that the northern part of the Indo-Australian plate is moving north and colliding with the Eurasian plate. What features would occur where these plates meet? Explain.

Thinking Critically

22. **Classifying** Classify these layers of Earth's crust as liquid, solid, or solid but able to flow slowly: crust, lithosphere, asthenosphere, outer core, inner core.

23. **Comparing and Contrasting** How are oceanic and continental crust alike? How do they differ?

24. **Relating Cause and Effect** What do many geologists think is the driving force of plate tectonics? Explain.

25. **Making Generalizations** State in one sentence the most significant discovery that geologists established through their study of plate tectonics.

CHAPTER 1 REVIEW

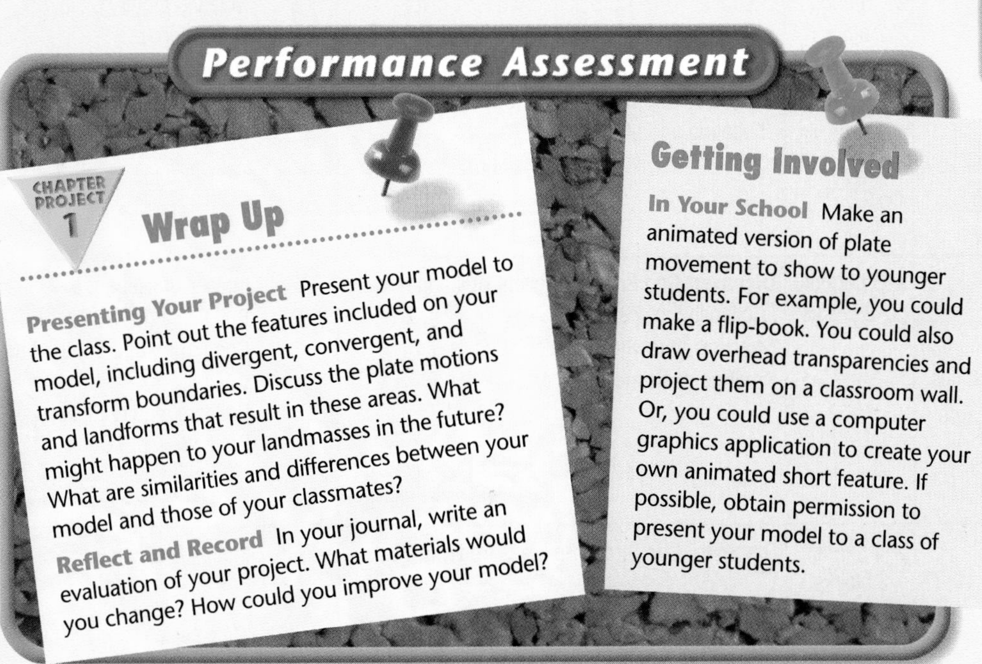

Performance Assessment

CHAPTER PROJECT 1

Wrap Up

Presenting Your Project Present your model to the class. Point out the features included on your model, including divergent, convergent, and transform boundaries. Discuss the plate motions and landforms that result in these areas. What might happen to your landmasses in the future? What are similarities and differences between your model and those of your classmates?

Reflect and Record In your journal, write an evaluation of your project. What materials would you change? How could you improve your model?

Getting Involved

In Your School Make an animated version of plate movement to show to younger students. For example, you could make a flip-book. You could also draw overhead transparencies and project them on a classroom wall. Or, you could use a computer graphics application to create your own animated short feature. If possible, obtain permission to present your model to a class of younger students.

consists mainly of basalt. As a result, oceanic crust is denser than continental crust.

24. Heat from Earth's core is the driving force of plate tectonics. The plates float on top of the partially molten asthenosphere. The heat of Earth's core cause convection currents in the asthenosphere. The flow of those currents causes the movement of the plates.

25. Answers may vary. A typical answer: Pieces of Earth's lithosphere are in constant, slow motion, driven by convection currents in the mantle.

Program Resources

- **Inquiry Skills Activity Book** Provides teaching and review of all inquiry skills

Performance Assessment

CHAPTER PROJECT 1

Wrap Up

Presenting Your Project

As each group presents its model of a cut-away Earth, assess how well the model reflects the concepts of Earth's layers, sea-floor spreading, and plate tectonics. Also assess how attractive and well-constructed the model is. Students should explain what their model shows and how Earth's interior relates to the surface.

Reflect and Record In assessing the accuracy and attractiveness of the group's model, students should compare it with other groups' models. If the materials and designs differ, they should consider how those differences might have affected the final product. They should include in their reflections which concepts were difficult to show in the model, what materials worked best, what design elements had to be revised in the process of making the model, and what improvements could be made to make a better model. Have students write their reflections in their journals.

Getting Involved

In Your School Divide students into groups and allow each group to plan the form the animation will take. After groups have had time to discuss the possibilities, advise each about the direction they should take. Make sure all groups aren't making a flip-book or a series of transparencies. At least one group should use computer graphics. Challenge each group to send representatives to classes of younger students to set up a presentation. Have groups report back to the class about how well their presentations taught the material to the younger students.

Earthquakes

Sections	Time	Student Edition Activities	Other Activities
CHAPTER PROJECT 2 **Shake, Rattle, and Roll** p. 53	Ongoing (2–3 weeks)	Check Your Progress, p. 61 Check Your Progress, p. 69 Check Your Progress, p. 81 Wrap Up, p. 85	
1 Earth's Crust in Motion pp. 54–63 ◆ Describe how stress forces affect rock. ◆ Explain why faults form and where they occur. ◆ Describe how movement along faults changes Earth's surface.	4–5 periods/ 2–3 blocks	**Discover** How Does Stress Affect Earth's Crust?, p. 54 **Try This** It's a Stretch, p. 55 **Sharpen Your Skills** Measuring, p. 59 **Skills Lab: Making Models** Modeling Movement Along Faults, pp. 62–63	**TE** Building Inquiry Skills: Applying Concepts, p. 56 **TE** Including All Students, p. 57 **TE** Building Inquiry Skills: Comparing and Contrasting, p. 58 **TE** Real-Life Learning, p. 59 **TE** Inquiry Challenge, p. 60
2 Measuring Earthquakes pp. 64–71 ◆ Describe how the energy of an earthquake travels through Earth. ◆ Identify the different kinds of seismic waves. ◆ Name the scales used to measure the strength of an earthquake.	3–4 periods/ 2 blocks	**Discover** How Do Seismic Waves Travel Through Earth? p. 64 **Try This** Recording Seismic Waves, p. 66 **Real-World Lab: Careers in Science** Locating an Epicenter, pp. 70–71	**TE** Building Inquiry Skills: Observing, p. 65 **TE** Demonstration, p. 68 **ISLM** F-2, "Investigating the Speed of Earthquake Waves"
3 Earthquake Hazards and Safety pp. 72–77 ◆ Describe the kinds of damage that an earthquake causes. ◆ Explain what can be done to reduce earthquake hazards.	2–3 periods/ 1–2 blocks	**Discover** Can Bracing Prevent Building Collapse?, p. 72 **Sharpen Your Skills** Calculating, p. 74 **Science at Home,** p. 77	**TE** Inquiry Challenge, p. 73 **TE** Building Inquiry Skills: Comparing and Contrasting, p. 74 **TE** Building Inquiry Skills: Predicting, p. 76
4 *Integrating Technology* **Monitoring Faults** pp. 78–82 ◆ Describe how geologists monitor faults. ◆ Explain how geologists determine earthquake risk.	3–4 periods/ 2 blocks	**Discover** Can Stress Be Measured?, p. 78	**TE** Inquiry Challenge, p. 79
Study Guide/Chapter Review pp. 83–85	1 period/ $\frac{1}{2}$ block		**ISAB** Provides teaching and review of all inquiry skills

For Standard or Block Schedule The Resource Pro® CD-ROM gives you maximum flexibility for planning your instruction for any type of schedule. Resource Pro® contains Planning Express®, an advanced scheduling program, as well as the entire contents of the Teaching Resources and the Computer Test Bank.

CHAPTER PLANNING GUIDE

Program Resources	Assessment Strategies	Media and Technology
TR Chapter 2 Project Teacher Notes, pp. 40–41 **TR** Chapter 2 Project Student Materials, pp. 42–45 **TR** Chapter 2 Project Scoring Rubric, p. 46	**SE** Performance Assessment: Chapter 2 Project Wrap Up, p. 85 **TE** Check Your Progress, pp. 61, 69, 81 **TR** Chapter 2 Project Scoring Rubric, p. 46	
TR 2-1 Lesson Plan, p. 47 **TR** 2-1 Section Summary, p. 48 **TR** 2-1 Review and Reinforce, p. 49 **TR** 2-1 Enrich, p. 50 **TR** Skills Lab blackline masters, pp. 63–64 **SES** Book M, *Motion, Forces, and Energy,* Chapter 2	**SE** Section 1 Review, p. 61 **SE** Analyze and Conclude, p. 63 **TE** Ongoing Assessment, pp. 55, 57, 59 **TE** Performance Assessment, p. 61 **TR** 2-1 Review and Reinforce, p. 49	Exploring Earth Science Videodisc, Unit 3 Side 1, "Why Worry" Audiotapes, English-Spanish Summary 2-1 Transparency 8, "Shearing, Tension, and Compression" Transparency 9, "Strike-Slip, Normal, and Reverse Faults" Interactive Student Tutorial CD-ROM, F-2
TR 2-2 Lesson Plan, p. 51 **TR** 2-2 Section Summary, p. 52 **TR** 2-2 Review and Reinforce, p. 53 **TR** 2-2 Enrich, p. 54 **TR** Real-World Lab blackline masters, pp. 65–67	**SE** Section 2 Review, p. 69 **SE** Analyze and Conclude, p. 71 **TE** Ongoing Assessment, pp. 65, 67 **TE** Performance Assessment, p. 69 **TR** 2-2 Review and Reinforce, p. 53	Exploring Earth Science Videodisc, Unit 2 Side 2, "Waves in the Earth" Audiotapes, English-Spanish Summary 2-2 Transparency 10, "Earthquake Focus and Epicenter and P Waves and S Waves" Interactive Student Tutorial CD-ROM, F-2
TR 2-3 Lesson Plan, p. 55 **TR** 2-3 Section Summary, p. 56 **TR** 2-3 Review and Reinforce, p. 57 **TR** 2-3 Enrich, p. 58	**SE** Section 3 Review, p. 77 **TE** Ongoing Assessment, pp. 73, 75 **TE** Performance Assessment, p. 77 **TR** 2-3 Review and Reinforce, p. 57	Exploring Earth Science Videodisc, Unit 3 Side 1, "Rock and Roll" Audiotapes, English-Spanish Summary 2-3 Transparency 11, "Exploring an Earthquake-Safe House" Interactive Student Tutorial CD-ROM, F-2
TR 2-4 Lesson Plan, p. 59 **TR** 2-4 Section Summary, p. 60 **TR** 2-4 Review and Reinforce, p. 61 **TR** 2-4 Enrich, p. 62 **SES** Book H, *Earth's Water,* Chapter 5	**SE** Section 4 Review, p. 81 **TE** Ongoing Assessment, pp. 79 **TE** Performance Assessment, p. 81 **TR** 2-4 Review and Reinforce, p. 61	Audiotapes, English-Spanish Summary 2-4 Interactive Student Tutorial CD-ROM, F-2
	SE Chapter 2 Review, pp. 83–85 **TR** Chapter 2 Performance Assessment, pp. 175–177 **TR** Chapter 2 Test, pp. 178–181 **CTB** Chapter 2 Test	Interactive Student Tutorial CD-ROM, F-2 Computer Test Bank, Chapter 2 Test Science Explorer Internet Site

Key: **SE** Student Edition
CTB Computer Test Bank
ISAB Inquiry Skills Activity Book
TE Teacher's Edition
SES Science Explorer Series Text
PTA Product Testing Activities by *Consumer Reports*
TR Teaching Resources
ISLM Integrated Science Laboratory Manual
IES Interdisciplinary Explorations Series

Meeting the National Science Education Standards and AAAS Benchmarks

National Science Education Standards	Benchmarks for Science Literacy	Unifying Themes
Science As Inquiry (Content Standard A) ◆ **Use appropriate tools and techniques to gather, analyze, and interpret data** Students locate an epicenter. *(Real-World Lab)* **Physical Science** (Content Standard B) ◆ **Transfer of energy** Stress is a force that acts on rock. Seismic waves carry energy from an earthquake through Earth. *(Sections 1, 2)* **Earth and Space Science** (Content Standard D) ◆ **Structure of the Earth system** Earthquakes result from the movement of rock beneath Earth's surface. Movement of rock along a fault causes changes in the land surface. *(Section 1; Skills Lab)* **Science and Technology** (Content Standard E) ◆ **Design a solution or product** Students design a model earthquake-resistant structure. *(Chapter Project)* **Science in Personal and Social Perspectives** (Content Standard F) ◆ **Natural hazards** Earthquakes can cause great damage. *(Section 3; Science and Society)* ◆ **Science and technology in society** Structures can be designed to reduce earthquake damage. Geologists have invented instruments to monitor faults. Students analyze the risk of an earthquake. *(Chapter Project; Sections 3, 4; Science and Society)*	**3A Technology and Science** A seismograph records ground movements. Structures can be designed to reduce earthquake damage. Geologists have invented instruments to monitor faults. *(Sections 2, 3, 4)* **3B Design and Systems** Students design a model earthquake-resistant structure. *(Chapter Project)* **4C Processes That Shape the Earth** Earthquakes result from movement of rock beneath Earth's surface. Movement of rock along a fault causes changes in the land surface. *(Sections 1, 3; Skills Lab)* **4E Energy Transformation** Stress is a force that acts on rock. Earthquakes create vibrations called seismic waves. *(Sections 1, 2)* **4F Motion** Seismic waves carry the energy of an earthquake away from the focus. Seismologists use seismic waves to locate an epicenter. *(Section 2; Real-World Lab)* **7D Social Trade-Offs** Students analyze the risk of an earthquake. *(Science and Society)* **11B Models** Students make a model of an earthquake-resistant structure. Students model movements along faults. *(Chapter Project; Skills Lab)* **11C Constancy and Change** Stress builds up along a fault until an earthquake releases it. *(Section 1)* **12B Computation and Estimation** Students locate an epicenter. *(Real-World Lab)*	◆ **Energy** Stress is a force that acts on rocks. Seismic waves carry the energy of an earthquake away from the focus. Earthquakes can cause great damage. *(Sections 1, 2, 3)* ◆ **Evolution** Over time, fault movement can create mountains and valleys. *(Section 1)* ◆ **Modeling** Students design a model of an earthquake-resistant structure. Students model movement along faults. *(Chapter Project; Skills Lab)* ◆ **Patterns of Change** Stress causes rock to deform in various ways. A seismograph records ground movements. Seismologists use seismic waves to locate an epicenter. Geologists use various instruments to monitor ground movements. *(Sections 1, 2, 4; Skills Lab; Real-World Lab)* ◆ **Scale and Structure** Earthquakes vary in intensity. Structures can be made earthquake-resistant. *(Sections 2, 3; Chapter Project)* ◆ **Stability** An area can appear stable, but still have the risk of an earthquake. *(Science and Society)* ◆ **Systems and Interactions** An earthquake occurs when there is movement along a fault. The energy of an earthquake produces seismic waves. Earthquakes can cause great damage. *(Sections 1, 2, 3)* ◆ **Unity and Diversity** Shearing, tension, and compression are different types of stress that produce different types of faults. P waves, S waves, and surface waves are the three types of seismic waves. *(Sections 1, 2; Skills Lab; Real-World Lab)*

Media and Technology

Exploring Earth Science Videodiscs

◆ **Section 1** "Why Worry" defines and describes the three major earthquake zones on Earth.

◆ **Section 2** "Waves in the Earth" features Earth's interior and discusses Earth's layers and the nature of seismic waves.

◆ **Section 3** "Rock and Roll" shows the 1989 San Francisco Bay earthquake and explains the cause of quakes.

Interactive Student Tutorial CD-ROM

◆ **Chapter Review** Interactive questions help students self-assess their mastery of key chapter concepts.

Student Edition Connection Strategies

◆ **Section 1** **Integrating Physics**, p. 58 

◆ **Section 2** **Integrating Mathematics**, p. 69 

◆ **Section 3** **Integrating Technology**, p. 76
Integrating Health, p. 77 

◆ **Section 4** **Integrating Technology**, pp. 78–81 
Integrating Space Science, p. 80
Language Arts Connection, p. 80
Science and Society, p. 82

www.science-explorer.phschool.com

Visit the Science Explorer internet site to find an up-to-date activity for Chapter 2 of *Inside Earth*.

ACTIVITY	Time (minutes)	Materials Quantities for one work group	Skills
Section 1			
Discover, p. 54	5	**Consumable** popsicle stick	Predicting
Try This, p. 55	10	**Nonconsumable** plastic putty	Classifying
Sharpen Your Skills, p. 59	10	**Consumable** masking tape **Nonconsumable** small weight, spring scale, sandpaper	Measuring
Skills Lab, pp. 62–63	40	**Consumable** modeling compound in two or more colors **Nonconsumable** marking pen, plastic butter knife	Making Models, Inferring, Classifying
Section 2			
Discover, p. 64	10	**Nonconsumable** spring toy	Observing
Try This, p. 66	10	**Consumable** paper strip 1 m long **Nonconsumable** large book, pencil, pen	Observing
Real-World Lab, pp. 70–71	35–40	**Consumable** outline map of the United States **Nonconsumable** drawing compass with pencil	Interpreting Data, Drawing Conclusions
Section 3			
Discover, p. 72	10	**Consumable** 5 straws, tape	Predicting
Sharpen Your Skills, p. 74	10	**Consumable** paper **Nonconsumable** pencil (calculator optional)	Calculating
Science at Home, p. 77	home	**Nonconsumable** two small towels, various-sized books	Making Models
Section 4			
Discover, p. 78	5	**Consumable** facial tissue **Nonconsumable** ruler	Drawing Conclusions

A list of all materials required for the Student Edition activities can be found on pages T14–T15. You can order Materials Kits by calling 1-800-828-7777 or by accessing the Science Explorer internet site at **http://www.science-explorer.phschool.com.**

Shake, Rattle, and Roll

Students may not realize that the design of a building or other structure and the materials of which it is made affect the amount of damage it sustains in an earthquake. This project will give students an opportunity to model and test ways to reduce structural damage during a quake.

Purpose This project is designed to enhance students' knowledge of design features and materials that make structures more earthquake-resistant. Students will research how earthquakes cause damage to structures and will learn how actual structures are designed and built to reduce damage. They will build model structures, test them in simulated earthquakes, improve the structures to make them stronger, and retest them. Finally, students will demonstrate their models in a class presentation and communicate what they have learned about building design.

Skills Focus After completing the Chapter 2 Project, students will be able to

- make a model structure that incorporates construction methods and materials used to reduce damage to actual structures during an earthquake;
- relate cause and effect to evaluate "earthquake" damage to their model;
- apply concepts from the text to improve their model;
- communicate how the design and materials of their model help to make it earthquake-resistant;
- predict how well an actual structure built on the model's design would survive an earthquake.

Project Time Line The project requires two to three weeks to complete. Each student should first sketch a preliminary design for his or her model structure, choose materials for making the model, and discuss his or her design with classmates. Students should complete the first design based on what they have learned, discuss possible improvements with classmates, build the model, and test it in a simulated earthquake, making note of any design flaws. Students should use what they have learned to improve their models, then retest them and make any final changes. Each student should then prepare a class presentation of the model. See Chapter 2 Project Teacher Notes on pages 40–41 in Teaching Resources for more detailed instructions.

CHAPTER 2 Earthquakes

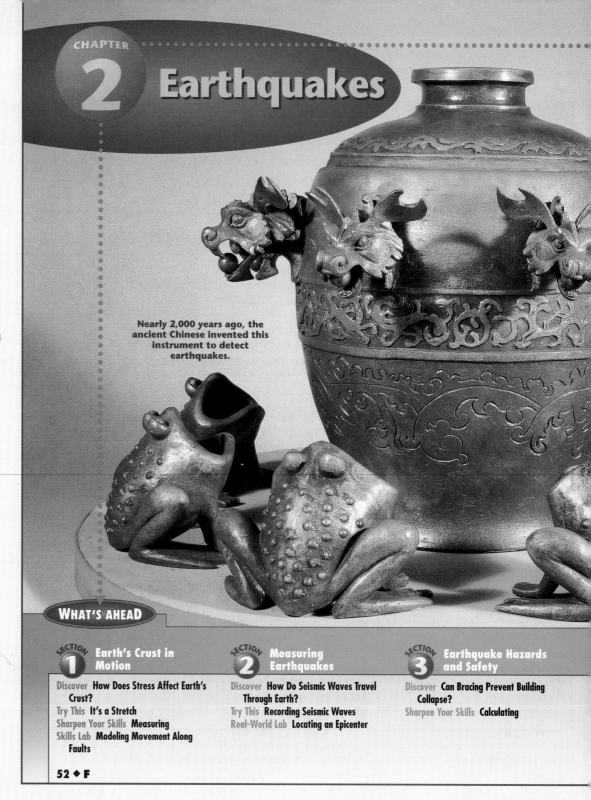

Nearly 2,000 years ago, the ancient Chinese invented this instrument to detect earthquakes.

WHAT'S AHEAD

Possible Materials

- Provide a wide variety of materials for making the model structures, including popsicle sticks, pretzels, toothpicks, straws, wooden dowels, very thin crackers (such as crispbread), wooden dowels, uncooked pasta, bread sticks, tissue paper, pieces cut from plastic bottles, foam-plastic, aluminum foil, tape, glue, rubber cement, gumdrops, small marshmallows, clay, staples, paper clips, foam rubber, rubber washers, cotton batting, pieces of carpet padding, and small springs. Discourage students from using materials that would not behave realistically in a simulated earthquake—for example, modeling walls with index cards that would

PROJECT 2

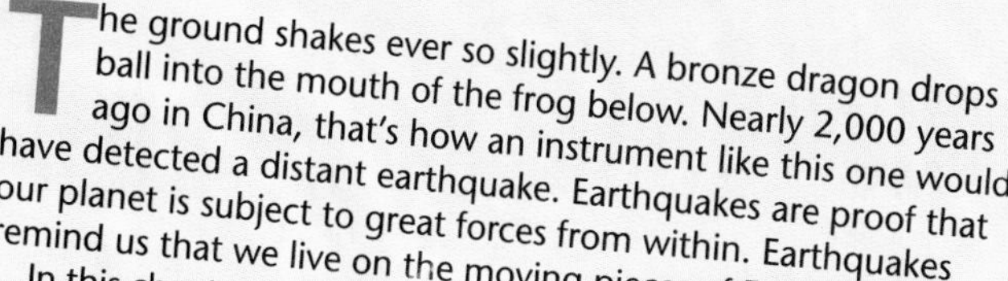

Shake, Rattle, and Roll

The ground shakes ever so slightly. A bronze dragon drops a ball into the mouth of the frog below. Nearly 2,000 years ago in China, that's how an instrument like this one would have detected a distant earthquake. Earthquakes are proof that our planet is subject to great forces from within. Earthquakes remind us that we live on the moving pieces of Earth's crust.

In this chapter, you will design a structure that will withstand earthquakes.

Your Goal To design, build, and test a model structure that is earthquake resistant.

Your model should

- be made of materials that are approved by your teacher
- be built to specifications agreed on by your class
- be able to withstand several simulated earthquakes of increasing intensity
- be built following the safety guidelines in Appendix A

Get Started Before you design your model, find out how earthquakes cause damage to structures such as homes, office buildings, and highway overpasses. Preview the chapter to find out how engineers design structures to withstand earthquakes.

Check Your Progress You will be working on this project as you study this chapter. To keep your project on track, look for Check Your Progress boxes at the following points.

Section 1 Review, page 61: Design your model.
Section 2 Review, page 69: Construct, improve, and test your model.
Section 4 Review, page 81: Test your model again, and then repair and improve it.

Wrap Up At the end of the chapter (page 85), you will demonstrate how well your model can withstand the effects of a simulated earthquake and predict whether a building that followed your design could withstand a real earthquake.

Integrating Technology 

Section 4 **Monitoring Faults**

Discover **Can Stress Be Measured?**

not tear when the structure is shaken. Also students should not use construction toys such as Legos™ and Tinker Toys™, as these would make the structures too solid.

- To simulate earthquakes, students could place their model structures on a cafeteria tray, piece of plywood, small table, or other base, hold the base at opposite ends, and shake it back and forth.

Launching the Project To introduce the project, let each student build a very simple structure using toothpicks and tape, subject it to a simulated earthquake, and observe what happens to it. Ask: **How could you improve your structure so it would be stronger in an earthquake?** *(Accept all responses at this time, and encourage creative thinking.)*

Allow time for students to read the project description on page 53. At this time, you might hand out Chapter 2 Project Overview on pages 42–43 in Teaching Resources. Encourage discussion of the different kinds of structures they could model and the materials they could use. Also discuss and agree on a list of specifications for the models.

Program Resources

- **Teaching Resources** Chapter 2 Project Teacher Notes, pp. 40–41; Chapter 2 Project Student Materials, pp. 42–45; Chapter 2 Project Scoring Rubric, p. 46

Performance Assessment

The Chapter 2 Project Scoring Rubric on page 46 in Teaching Resources will help you evaluate how well students complete the Chapter 2 Project. You may want to share the scoring rubric with your students so they are clear about what will be expected of them. Students will be assessed on

- designing their models, including the selection of appropriate building materials and effective construction methods;
- their creativity and neatness in building the models;
- how well they work with others in testing the models and devising improvements;
- how well they present their models to the class.

SECTION 1 Earth's Crust in Motion

Objectives

After completing the lesson, students will be able to
- ◆ describe how stress forces affect rock;
- ◆ explain why faults form and where they occur;
- ◆ describe how movement along faults changes Earth's surface.

Key Terms earthquake, stress, shearing, tension, compression, deformation, fault, strike-slip fault, normal fault, hanging wall, footwall, reverse fault, fault-block mountain, folds, anticline, syncline, plateau

1 Engage/Explore

Activating Prior Knowledge

Encourage any students who have experienced an earthquake to describe the event—where they were at the time, how they first became aware that an earthquake was occurring, what happened to buildings and objects around them, how they felt during and after the quake, and so on. If students have not experienced an earthquake, let them relate what they have learned from television reports, movies, newspaper and magazine articles, and other sources.

DISCOVER

Skills Focus predicting
Materials *popsicle stick*
Time 5 minutes
Tips In Step 2, advise students to increase the pressure on the stick slowly and gradually. In Step 3, caution students to maintain a firm grip on one end of the popsicle stick as they release the pressure so the stick does not fly off into the air and cause injury.
Expected Outcome When students release the pressure in Step 3, the stick will spring back to straighten. As they continue bending in Step 4, the stick will break.
Think It Over The crust will break.

SECTION 1 Earth's Crust in Motion

DISCOVER — ACTIVITY

How Does Stress Affect Earth's Crust?

1. Put on your goggles.
2. Holding a popsicle stick at both ends, slowly bend it into an arch.
3. Release the pressure on the popsicle stick and observe what happens.
4. Repeat Steps 1 and 2. This time, however, keep bending the ends of the popsicle stick toward each other. What happens to the wood?

Think It Over
Predicting Think of the popsicle stick as a model for part of Earth's crust. What do you think might eventually happen as the forces of plate movement bend the crust?

GUIDE FOR READING
- ◆ How do stress forces affect rock?
- ◆ Why do faults form and where do they occur?
- ◆ How does movement along faults change Earth's surface?

Reading Tip **Before you read, use the headings to make an outline about stress in the crust, faults, and mountain building.**

You are sitting at the kitchen table eating breakfast. Suddenly you notice a slight vibration, as if a heavy truck were rumbling by. At the same time, your glass of orange juice jiggles. Dishes rattle in the cupboards. After a few seconds, the rattling stops. Later, when you listen to the news on the radio, you learn that your region experienced a small earthquake. Earthquakes are a reminder that Earth's crust can move.

Stress in the Crust

An **earthquake** is the shaking and trembling that results from the movement of rock beneath Earth's surface. The movement of Earth's plates creates powerful forces that squeeze or pull the rock in the crust. These forces are examples of **stress,** a force that acts on rock to change its shape or volume. (Volume is the amount of space an object takes up.) Because stress is a force, it adds energy to the rock. The energy is stored in the rock until the rock either breaks or changes shape.

Figure 1 Stress in the crust folded this rock like a sheet of ribbon candy.

READING STRATEGIES

Vocabulary Use the following procedure to develop understanding of the term *deformation.* Write the word on the board and circle the root *form.* Ask: **What does the verb "to form" mean?** *(To shape something)* Underline the suffix *-ation* and ask: **What does this suffix do to the verb?** *(Makes it a noun)* **What does** ***formation*** **mean?** *(The process or act of shaping something)* Underline *de-* and ask: **What does this prefix mean?** *("the opposite of")* **So what does** ***deformation*** **mean?** *(The process or act of changing something's normal shape)*

Use a similar procedure to develop understanding of the terms *anticline* and *syncline.* (Root *cline* meaning "slope," from the Greek *klinein,* "to lean"; prefix *anti-,* meaning "opposite to" from the Greek *anti,* "opposite, against"; prefix *syn-,* meaning "with," from the Greek *sun-,* "together, with")

Types of Stress

Three different kinds of stress occur in the crust—shearing, tension, and compression. **Shearing, tension, and compression work over millions of years to change the shape and volume of rock.** These forces cause some rocks to become brittle and snap. Other rocks tend to bend slowly like road tar softened by the heat of the sun.

Stress that pushes a mass of rock in two opposite, horizontal directions is called **shearing.** Shearing can cause rock to break and slip apart.

The stress force called **tension** pulls on the crust, stretching rock so that it becomes thinner in the middle. The effect of tension on rock is somewhat like pulling apart a piece of warm bubble gum. Tension occurs where two plates are moving apart.

The stress force called **compression** squeezes rock until it folds or breaks. One plate pushing against another can compress rock like a giant trash compactor.

Any change in the volume or shape of Earth's crust is called **deformation.** Most changes in the crust occur so slowly that they cannot be observed directly. But if you could speed up time so a billion years passed by in minutes, you could see the deformation of the crust. The crust would bend, stretch, break, tilt, fold, and slide. The slow shift of Earth's plates causes this deformation.

☑ *Checkpoint* ***How does deformation change Earth's surface?***

TRY THIS

It's a Stretch

You can model the stresses that create faults. ACTIVITY

1. Knead a piece of plastic putty until it is soft.
2. Push the ends of the putty toward the middle.
3. Pull the ends apart.
4. Push half of the putty one way and the other half in the opposite direction.

Classifying Which types of stress do Steps 2, 3, and 4 represent?

Figure 2 Deformation pushes, pulls, or twists the rocks in Earth's crust. *Relating Cause and Effect If shearing continues to tug at the slab of rock in **B**, what will happen to the rock?*

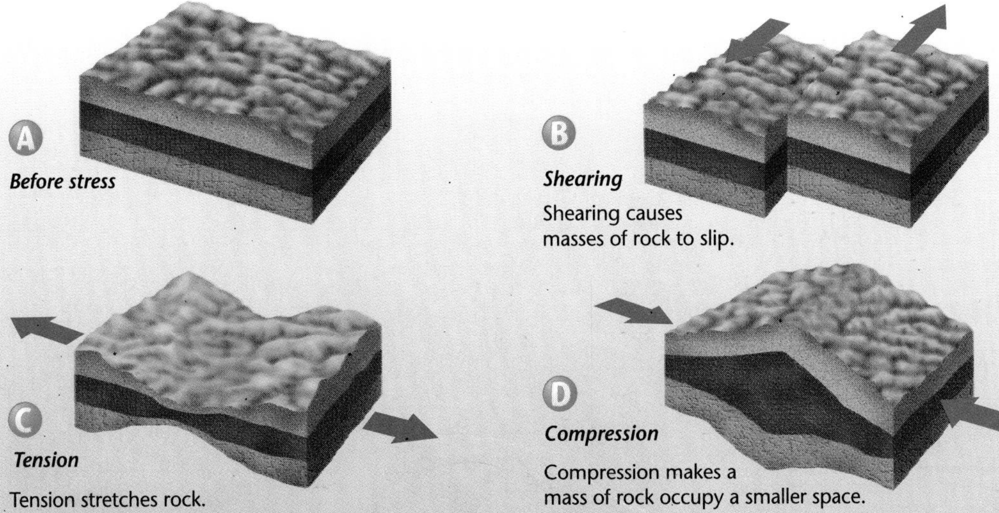

A
Before stress
B
Shearing
Shearing causes masses of rock to slip.
C
Tension
Tension stretches rock.
D
Compression
Compression makes a mass of rock occupy a smaller space.

2 Facilitate

Stress in the Crust

Including All Students

If students did the Discover activity, ask: **When you bent the popsicle stick the first time and held it in an arch shape, what was happening?** *(Energy—the "push" applied by the hands—was being transferred to the stick and stored in it.)* **What would have happened if you had suddenly let go of one end of the bent stick, and why?** *(The stick would have sprung back to its original shape because the stored energy was quickly released.)* **Where did this stored energy go?** *(It was transferred to the surrounding air.)* **learning modality: logical/mathematical**

Types of Stress

TRY THIS

Skills Focus classifying
Materials *plastic putty*
Time 10 minutes
Tips After students soften the putty in Step 1, tell them to form it into a tube shape before they do each subsequent step.
Expected Outcome Step 2 represents compression, Step 3 represents tension, and Step 4 represents shearing.
Extend Let students repeat the activity with a stiffer material, such as modeling clay, and compare the results.
learning modality: kinesthetic

Program Resources

◆ Teaching Resources 2-1 Lesson Plan, p. 47; 2-1 Section Summary, p. 48

Media and Technology

Audiotapes English-Spanish Summary 2-1

Transparencies "Shearing, Tension, and Compression," Transparency 8

Answers to Self-Assessment

☑ *Checkpoint*

It causes it to bend, stretch, break, tilt, fold, and slide.

Caption Question

Figure 2 The rock will break; the two parts will move in opposite directions.

Ongoing Assessment

Oral Presentation Ask each student to explain with the aid of a diagram how the directions of force differ in compression, tension, and shearing.

Kinds of Faults

Using the Visuals: Figure 3

Make sure students understand that the fault is the irregular, shadowed line running up the middle of the photograph. Point out the road running left-to-right at the bottom of the photograph and ask: **If a strong earthquake occurred, what do you think would happen to the road where it crosses the fault? Why?** *(The road would be bent out of alignment or broken because the two slabs of crust on opposite sides of the fault are moving in different directions.)* **What other things might be deformed or broken at a fault?** *(Fences, rivers and streams, bridges, driveways, straight rows of trees or crops, and the like)* **learning modality: logical/mathematical**

Building Inquiry Skills: Applying Concepts

ACTIVITY

As students read the description of each type of fault and examine its accompanying diagram, ask: **How could you use your hands to show a strike-slip fault?** *(Hold the edges of the open hands against each other with the palms down, the fingers pointing away from the body, and the thumbs tucked below, then slide one hand away from the body and the other hand toward the body.)* **A normal fault?** *(Hold the open hands with the fingers pointing toward each other, lay the fingers of one hand over the fingers of the other hand, then move the hands away from each other.)* **A reverse fault?** *(Hold the hands as described for a normal fault, but move them toward each other.)* **learning modality: kinesthetic**

Figure 3 A strike-slip fault that is clearly visible at the surface is the San Andreas Fault in California.

Kinds of Faults

If you try to break a caramel candy bar in two, it may only bend and stretch at first. Like a candy bar, many types of rock can bend or fold. But beyond a certain limit, even these rocks will break. And it takes less stress to snap a brittle rock than it does to snap one that can bend.

When enough stress builds up in rock, the rock breaks, creating a fault. A **fault** is a break in Earth's crust where slabs of crust slip past each other. The rocks on both sides of a fault can move up or down or sideways. **Faults usually occur along plate boundaries, where the forces of plate motion compress, pull, or shear the crust so much that the crust breaks.** There are three main types of faults: strike-slip faults, normal faults, and reverse faults.

Strike-Slip Faults Shearing creates strike-slip faults. In a **strike-slip fault,** the rocks on either side of the fault slip past each other sideways with little up-or-down motion. Figure 3 shows the type of movement that occurs along a strike-slip fault. A strike-slip fault that forms the boundary between two plates is called a transform boundary. The San Andreas fault in California is an example of a strike-slip fault that is a transform boundary.

Normal Faults Tension forces in Earth's crust cause normal faults. In a **normal fault,** the fault is at an angle, so one block of rock lies above the fault while the other block lies below the fault. The half of the fault that lies above is called the **hanging wall.** The half of the fault that lies below is called the **footwall.** Look at Figure 4 to see how the hanging wall lies above the

Figure 4 A normal fault created the Sandia Mountains in New Mexico.

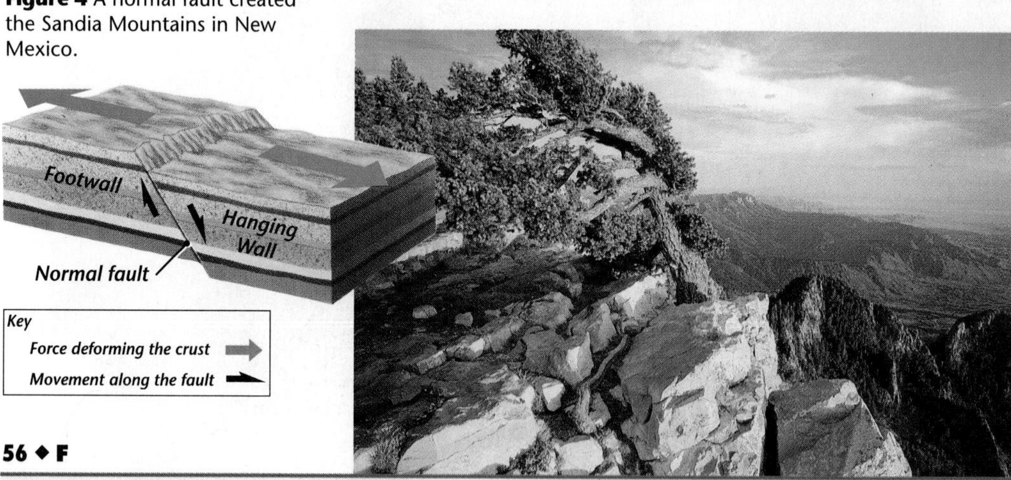

Background

Facts and Figures The terms *hanging wall* and *footwall* are believed to have originated with miners who excavated shafts to reach ore deposits in fault zones. As they worked, the miners walked on the rocks below the fault (the footwall) and hung their lanterns on the rocks above the fault (the hanging wall).

Normal and reverse faults are types of *dip-slip faults.* The movement in dip-slip faults is largely vertical, with the displacement (the "slip") occurring along the tilt (the "dip") of the fault plane.

A fourth type of fault, not named in the student text, is the *thrust fault.* A thrust fault is similar to a reverse fault in that the hanging wall moves upward. However, the tilt of the fault plane is not as steep as in a dip-slip fault.

footwall. When movement occurs along a normal fault, the hanging wall slips downward. Tension forces create normal faults where plates diverge, or pull apart. For example, normal faults occur along the Rio Grande rift valley in New Mexico, where two pieces of Earth's crust are diverging.

Reverse Faults Compression forces produce reverse faults. A **reverse fault** has the same structure as a normal fault, but the blocks move in the opposite direction. Look at Figure 5 to see how the rocks along a reverse fault move. As in a normal fault, one side of a reverse fault lies at an angle above the other side. The rock forming the hanging wall of a reverse fault slides up and over the footwall. Reverse faults produced the Appalachian Mountains in the eastern United States.

A type of reverse fault formed the majestic peaks in Glacier National Park in Montana shown in Figure 5. Over millions of years, a huge block of rock slid along the fault, moving up and over the surface rock. Parts of the overlying block then wore away, leaving the mountain peaks.

☑ *Checkpoint* *What are the three types of fault? What force of deformation produces each?*

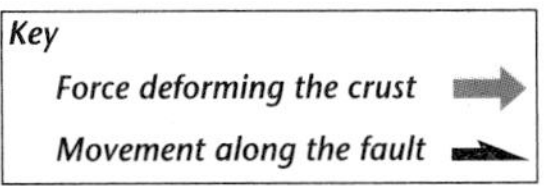

Figure 5 A reverse fault formed Mt. Gould in Glacier National Park, beginning 60 million years ago.
Inferring Which half of the reverse fault slid up and across to form this mountain, the hanging wall or the footwall? Explain.

Including All Students

The San Andreas fault is particularly interesting because the deformations it produces in surface features are so clearly visible. Encourage students who need additional challenges to look through books and magazines to find photographs of such deformations and make multiple photocopies for the class to examine. Using evidence in the photographs, students could locate and mark the fault line in each photograph and draw arrows to indicate the directions in which the two opposing rock slabs moved. **learning modality: visual**

Building Inquiry Skills: Inferring

Instruct students to look back at Figure 26 in Chapter 1 on page 43. Ask: **What are some places on or near land where plates are converging—moving toward each other?** *(At the boundaries between the Eurasian and Indo-Australian plates, the Eurasian and Pacific plates, the Indo-Australian and Pacific plates, the Nazca and South American plates, and the Pacific and North American plates)* **What do you think happens to Earth's crust in those places as the plates move toward each other?** *(Students should be able to reason that over long periods of time, the crust compresses, forming mountains and other landforms.)* **What do you think happens to the solid rock?** *(It breaks to form faults.)* **What type of stress force is occurring along those boundaries between plates?** *(compression)* **What type of fault would you expect to find there?** *(reverse faults)* Point out that there are other faults in those areas besides the major fault along the plate boundary. **learning modality: logical/mathematical**

Media and Technology

Transparencies "Strike-Slip, Normal, and Reverse Faults," Transparency 9

Answers to Self-Assessment

The three types of faults are strike-slip faults, produced by shearing; normal faults by tension; and reverse faults by compression.

Caption Question

Figure 5 The hanging wall slipped up and across. If the footwall had moved up, the fault would be called a normal fault.

Ongoing Assessment

Drawing Have each student make a simple sketch of each type of fault without referring to the diagrams on these pages, add arrows to show the block movements, and label each sketch with the name of the type of fault it shows.

Students can save their labeled drawings in their portfolios.

Friction Along Faults

Integrating Physics

Before students read about friction, invite them to define the term in their own words. *(Students' definitions will vary but should include the idea of resistance as one surface rubs against another.)* Ask: **What are some examples of low friction that you've experienced?** *(Students may mention slipping on ice or a polished floor.)* **What are some examples of high friction?** *(Sliding a heavy box across a concrete floor is one example.)* **What are some examples of times when people use high friction to their advantage?** *(Students may mention using sandpaper to smooth rough wood, wearing rubber-soled sneakers on a slippery gym floor, and filing fingernails.)* **learning modality: logical/mathematical**

Building Inquiry Skills: Comparing and Contrasting

ACTIVITY

Materials *two ceramic tiles, each with one side glazed and the other side unglazed*
Time 5 minutes

Use the following activity to help students understand how the amount of friction affects movement along a fault. Let each student rub two ceramic tiles together in different combinations—the two glazed surfaces against each other, the glazed surface of one tile against the unglazed surface of the other tile, and the two unglazed surfaces against each other—and compare how the tiles move each time. Ask: **When did the tiles move most easily?** *(When the two smooth sides were rubbed against each other)* **When were they hardest to move?** *(When the two rough sides were rubbed together)* **What do you think would happen if the unglazed sides were so rough that they caught on each other when you tried to slide them?** *(At first the tiles would not move, but with more pressure they would jerk free and slide abruptly.)* **How do these tiles show what happens along a fault?** *(The rougher the rock faces along the fault, the more difficult it is for the blocks to slip and slide past each other. A strong earthquake occurs when the blocks suddenly break free from each other and move abruptly.)* **learning modality: kinesthetic**

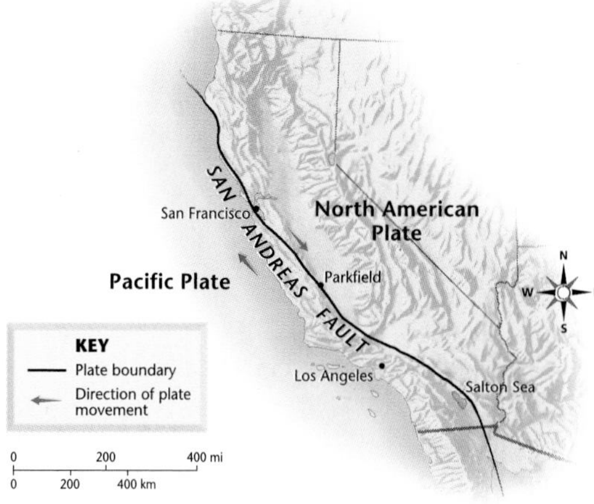

Figure 6 The San Andreas fault extends from the Salton Sea in southern California to the point in northern California where the plate boundary continues into the Pacific Ocean.

Friction Along Faults

INTEGRATING PHYSICS How rocks move along a fault depends on how much friction there is between the opposite sides of the fault. Friction is the force that opposes the motion of one surface as it moves across another surface. Friction exists because surfaces are not perfectly smooth.

Where friction along a fault is low, the rocks on both sides of the fault slide by each other without much sticking. Where friction is moderate, the sides of the fault jam together. Then from time to time they jerk free, producing small earthquakes. Where friction is high, the rocks lock together and do not move. In this case, stress increases until it is strong enough to overcome the friction force.

The San Andreas fault forms a transform boundary between the Pacific plate and the North American plate. In most places along the San Andreas fault, friction is high and the plates lock. Stress builds up until an earthquake releases the stress and the plates slide past each other.

Mountain Building

The forces of plate movement can build up Earth's surface. **Over millions of years, fault movement can change a flat plain into a towering mountain range.**

Mountains Formed by Faulting When normal faults uplift a block of rock, a **fault-block mountain** forms. You can see a diagram of this process in Figure 7. How does this process begin?

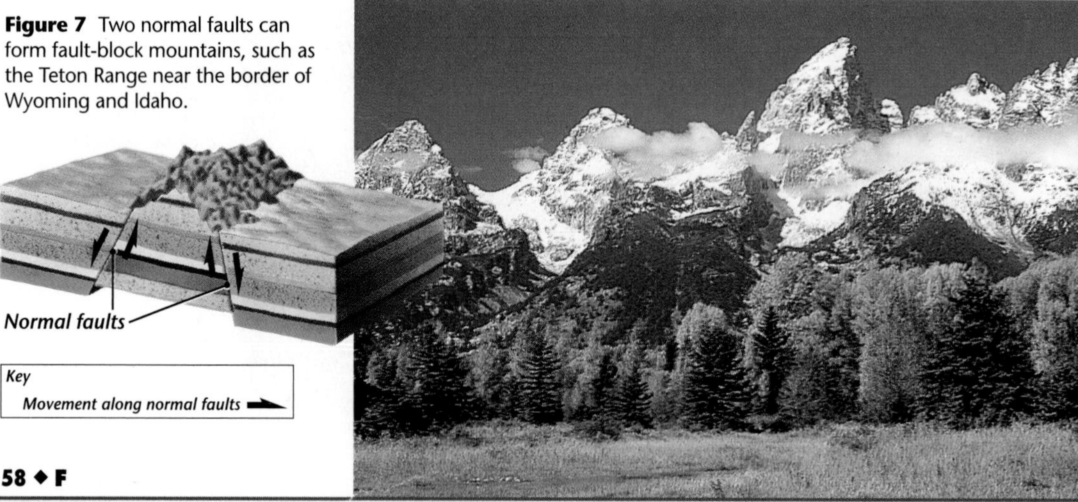

Figure 7 Two normal faults can form fault-block mountains, such as the Teton Range near the border of Wyoming and Idaho.

Background

History of Science The San Andreas fault played a major role in the formulation of a hypothesis to explain how earthquakes are generated. Following the 1906 San Francisco earthquake, geologist H.F. Reid of Johns Hopkins University conducted a study of the San Andreas fault. Reid discovered that during the 50 years prior to the 1906 quake, the land at distant points on both sides of the fault showed a relative displacement of slightly more than 3 m. From this information, Reid deduced the earthquake-generation mechanism in which rocks store energy as they are deformed until eventually, when frictional resistance is overcome, they abruptly slip, releasing the stored energy in the form of seismic waves. Because this slippage allows the deformed rock to spring back to its original shape, Reid termed the process *elastic rebound.*

Where two plates move away from each other, tension forces create many normal faults. When two of these normal faults form parallel to each other, a block of rock is left lying between them. As the hanging wall of each normal fault slips downward, the block in between moves upward. When a block of rock lying between two normal faults slides downward, a valley forms.

If you traveled by car from Salt Lake City to Los Angeles you would cross the Great Basin, a region with many ranges of fault-block mountains separated by broad valleys, or basins. This "basin and range" region covers much of Nevada and western Utah.

Mountains Formed by Folding Under certain conditions, plate movement causes the crust to fold. Have you ever skidded on a rug that wrinkled up as your feet pushed it across the floor? Much as the rug wrinkles, rock stressed by compression may bend slowly without breaking. **Folds** are bends in rock that form when compression shortens and thickens part of Earth's crust.

The collisions of two plates can cause compression and folding of the crust. Some of the world's largest mountain ranges, including the Himalayas in Asia and the Alps in Europe, formed when pieces of the crust folded during the collision of two plates. Such plate collisions also lead to earthquakes, because folding rock can fracture and produce faults.

Individual folds can be only a few centimeters across or hundreds of kilometers wide. You can often see small folds in the rock exposed where a highway has been cut through a hillside.

Measuring

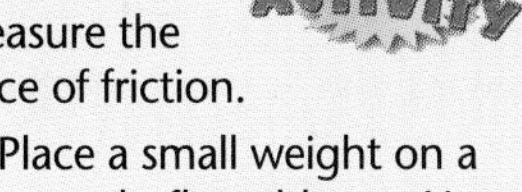

You can measure the force of friction.

1. Place a small weight on a smooth, flat tabletop. Use a spring scale to pull the weight across the surface. How much force is shown on the spring scale? (*Hint*: The unit of force is newtons.)
2. Tape a piece of sandpaper to the tabletop. Repeat Step 1, pulling the weight across the sandpaper.

Is the force of friction greater for a smooth surface or for a rough surface?

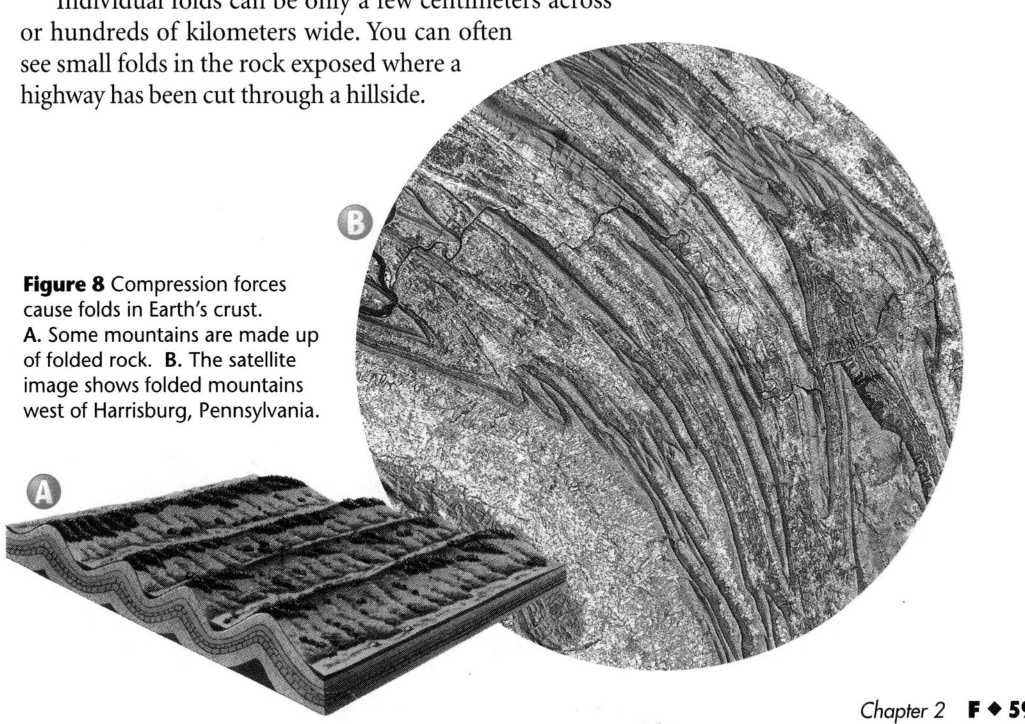

Figure 8 Compression forces cause folds in Earth's crust. **A.** Some mountains are made up of folded rock. **B.** The satellite image shows folded mountains west of Harrisburg, Pennsylvania.

Program Resources

Science Explorer Series *Motion, Forces, and Energy,* Chapter 2, provides additional information about the force of friction.

Media and Technology

Exploring Earth Science Videodisc
Unit 3, Side 1, "Why Worry"

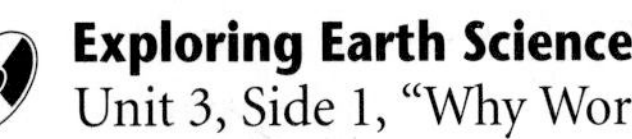

Chapter 3

Sharpen your Skills

Measuring

Materials *small weight, spring scale, sandpaper, masking tape*
Time 10 minutes
Tips If necessary, let students first practice using the spring scale by weighing several small objects and reading the measurements on the scale. Remind them to calibrate the scale to zero when no weight is added. Point out that when they do the activity, they must read the measurement while they are pulling the weight across the surface.
Expected Outcome The force of friction (the scale reading) is greater for a rough surface.
Extend Students could repeat the activity with other materials taped to the surface, such as waxed paper, aluminum foil, and a terrycloth towel. **learning modality: logical/mathematical**

Mountain Building

Real-Life Learning

ACTIVITY

Encourage students to look for actual examples of rock folds. (Draw students' attention to Figure 9 on the next page.) Roadways cut through rocky hillsides often have exposed folds. Tell students to note the locations of the folds they find and to sketch the fold patterns they see. In a follow-up class session, let students share their observations and drawings. **learning modality: visual**

Ongoing Assessment

Writing Have students write a brief explanation, in their own words, of why earthquakes are so common—and so often violent—along the San Andreas fault.

Mountain Building, continued

Inquiry Challenge

Challenge students to use any simple materials available in the classroom to model the folding process that produces anticlines and synclines. *(Students can use any material that buckles and folds when compressed, such as a stack of several sheets of construction paper of different colors to represent different rock layers. To model an anticline, lay the stack on a desktop and push the two short ends toward each other; the stack will bend upward in the middle. To model a syncline, lay the stack across a space between two desks and push the ends; the stack will bend downward in the middle.)* **learning modality: kinesthetic**

ACTIVITY

Cultural Diversity

Display a detailed regional map that includes South Dakota and also shows the locations of Indian reservations in the Black Hills area. (Map 4, "The North Central States," in The National Geographic Society's *Close-Up: U.S.A.* map set is an excellent choice.) Let students first locate the Black Hills along the boundary between South Dakota and Wyoming. Explain that since ancient times, Native Americans living in that region have regarded the Black Hills as a sacred place. However, the Black Hills were taken from the native peoples when valuable minerals, including gold, were discovered there. Invite students to locate and name the present-day Indian reservations in the area and find out the name of the Native American tribe living there. *(The Pine Ridge and Rosebud reservations are home to the Oglala Sioux.)* Encourage interested students to find out more about the history of this area and how the type of geology there made it easy for people to find gold and other minerals. Students could also find pictures and descriptions of famous tourist attractions in the Black Hills, including the Mount Rushmore National Memorial and the Crazy Horse Memorial being carved on Thunderhead Mountain. **learning modality: visual**

Anticlines and Synclines Geologists use the terms anticline and syncline to describe upward and downward folds in rock. You can compare anticlines and synclines in the diagram in Figure 9. A fold in rock that bends upward into an arch is an **anticline.** A fold in rock that bends downward in the middle to form a bowl is a **syncline**. Anticlines and synclines are found on many parts of Earth's surface where compression forces have folded the crust.

One example of an anticline is the Black Hills of South Dakota. The Black Hills began to form about 65 million years ago. At that time, forces in Earth's crust produced a large dome-shaped anticline. Over millions of years, a variety of processes wore down and shaped the rock of this anticline into the Black Hills.

You may see a syncline where a valley dips between two parallel ranges of hills. But a syncline may also be a very large feature, as large as the state of Illinois. The Illinois Basin is a syncline that stretches from the western side of Indiana about 250 kilometers across the state of Illinois. The basin is filled with soil and rock that have accumulated over millions of years.

Figure 9 **A.** Over millions of years, compression and folding of the crust produce anticlines, which arch upward, and synclines, which dip downward. **B.** The folded rock layers of an anticline can be seen on this cliff on the coast of England.

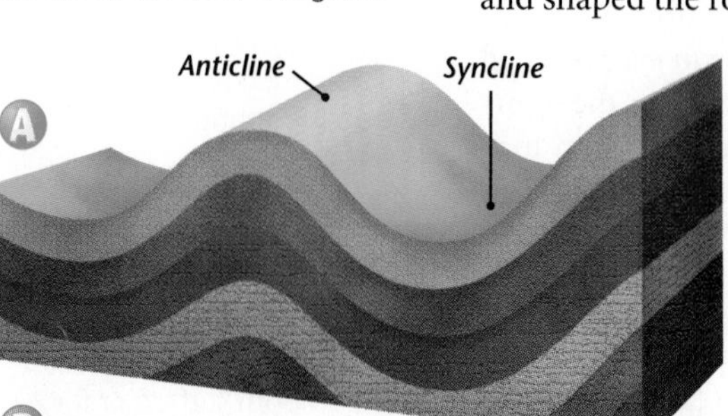

B

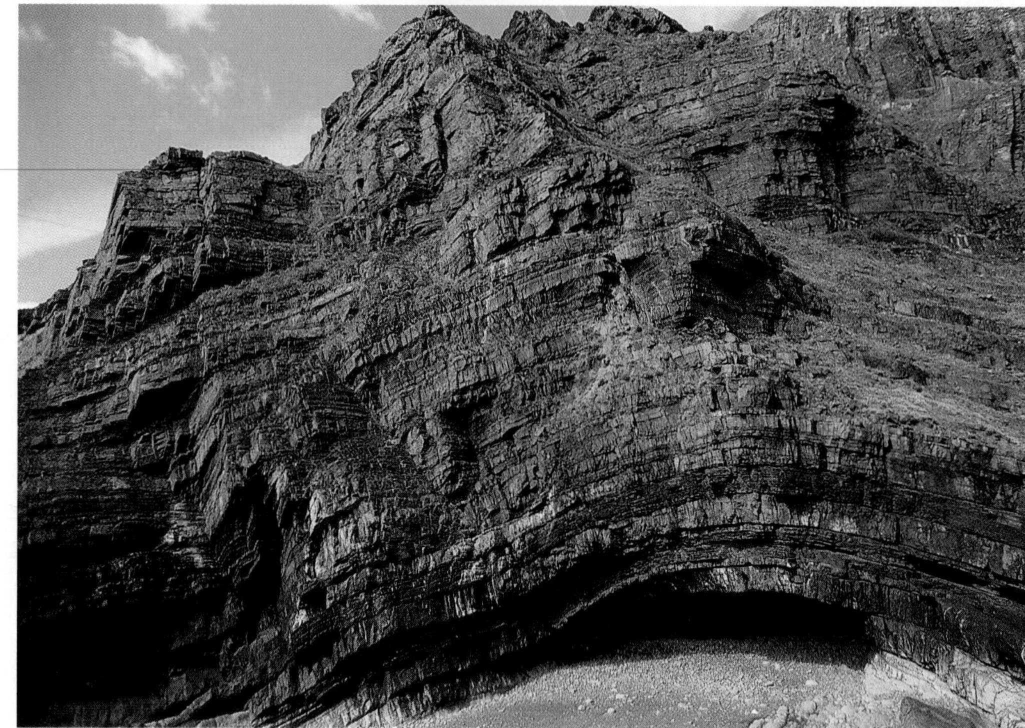

Background

Facts and Figures Anticlines and synclines are usually not found in isolation. Rather, they occur one after another in a series. Folds often occur in three dimensions, forming a basin or a dome.

Anticlines and synclines are classified based on their orientation. If each flank of the fold dips at the same angle, the fold is called *symmetrical.* If one flank is steeper than the other, the fold is called *asymmetrical.* In extreme forms of folding, the rock layers may turn back and collapse on one another, like a flattened letter S. Such a fold is described as *recumbent.* Recumbent folds are known as *nappes,* from the French word for "tablecloth." An *isoclinal* fold is so compressed that the rock layers are parallel to one another.

Figure 10 The flat land on the horizon is the Kaibab Plateau, which forms the North Rim of the Grand Canyon in Arizona. The many layers of rock that make up the plateau are visible in the canyon walls.

Plateaus The forces that raise mountains can also raise plateaus. A **plateau** is a large area of flat land elevated high above sea level. Some plateaus form when vertical faults push up a large, flat block of rock. Like a fancy sandwich, a plateau consists of many different flat layers, and is wider than it is tall.

Forces deforming the crust uplifted the Colorado Plateau in the "Four Corners" region of Arizona, Utah, Colorado, and New Mexico. The Colorado Plateau is a roughly circular area of uplifted rock more than 500 kilometers across. This vast slab of rock once formed part of a sea floor. Today, much of the plateau lies more than 1,500 meters above sea level.

Section 1 Review

1. What are the three main types of stress in rock?
2. Describe the movements that occur along each of the three types of faults.
3. How does Earth's surface change as a result of movement along faults?
4. **Thinking Critically Predicting** If plate motion compresses part of the crust, what landforms will form there in millions of years? Explain.

Check Your Progress

CHAPTER PROJECT 2

Discuss with your classmates the model you plan to build. What materials could you choose for your earthquake-resistant structure? Sketch your design. Does your design meet the guidelines provided by your teacher? How will you use your materials to build your model? (*Hint*: Draw the sketch of your model to scale).

Program Resources

◆ **Teaching Resources** 2-1 Review and Reinforce, p. 49; 2-1 Enrich, p. 50

Media and Technology

Interactive Student Tutorial CD-ROM F-2

3 Assess

Section 1 Review Answers

1. Shearing, tension, and compression
2. *Strike-slip fault:* The rocks on either side of the fault slip sideways past each other with little up-or-down motion. *Normal fault:* The hanging wall slips downward past the footwall. *Reverse fault:* The hanging wall slides up and over the footwall.
3. Movement along faults can create mountains and valleys.
4. Compression produces reverse faults, upward folds called anticlines, and downward folds called synclines. Over time, faulting and folding create mountains, plateaus, and valleys.

Check Your Progress

CHAPTER PROJECT 2

Provide graph paper so students can draw their models to scale. Suggest that they list the materials they plan to use and attach the list to the scale drawing. Allow time for students to show their drawings to classmates and explain how they plan to build the models. Encourage the other students to comment on the plans, ask questions, and offer suggestions. If any students are having difficulty devising a plan, meet with those students individually to offer guidance. Also encourage them to talk with classmates to get ideas.

Performance Assessment

Skills Check To evaluate students' understanding of different types of faults and their ability to represent those concepts in a model, have each student use two dry kitchen sponges to show the movements involved in strike-slip, normal, and reverse faulting and explain the processes as they demonstrate them.

Skills Lab

Making Models

Modeling Movement Along Faults

Preparing for Inquiry

Key Concept The directions of stress forces are different for strike-slip, normal, and reverse faults.

Skills Objectives Students will be able to

- make a simple model to show block movements in a strike-slip fault, a normal fault, and a reverse fault;
- infer how faulting can change the land surface;
- classify deformations in surface features caused by different types of faults.

Time 40 minutes

Guiding Inquiry

Invitation Remind students of the three fault models they made with their hands in Building Inquiry Skills, page 56. Ask: **What was different about the directions of movement in the three types of faults?** *(In the strike-slip fault, movement was sideways and in opposite directions; in the normal fault, the hanging wall moved down; in the reverse fault, the hanging wall moved up.)*

Introducing the Procedure

Tell students that in this activity, they will be using blocks of clay to represent blocks of Earth's crust. Ask: **How will blocks of clay more closely resemble real blocks of rock than your hands did?** *(They can show several layers of rock and the actual shape of the hanging wall and footwall.)*

Troubleshooting the Experiment

Have students first cover the desktop with a sheet of waxed paper or plastic to protect it.

- In Step 2, make sure students cut the squares in half from one side to the opposite side, not from corner to corner.
- In Step 4, if any students cut the block straight down instead of at an angle, have them press the two pieces firmly back together and recut the block.
- In Step 6, the hanging wall is the block with the larger surface area on top and the footwall is the lower block. The fault is the cut between the two blocks.
- In Step 7, the land surface is the top surface of the two blocks. Make sure students draw the arrows to show the river flowing *toward* the fault on the surface of the footwall and *away from* the fault on the surface of the hanging wall.
- In Step 9, the blocks should be moved sideways, with no up or down movement. In Step 10, the upper block should be moved down. In Step 11, the upper block should be moved up.

Skills Lab

Making Models

MODELING MOVEMENT ALONG FAULTS

Faults are cracks in Earth's crust where masses of rock move over, under, or past each other. In this lab, you will make a model of the movements along faults.

Problem

How does the movement of rock along the sides of a fault compare for different types of faults?

Materials

Modeling compound in two or more colors
Marking pen
Plastic butter knife

Procedure 

1. Roll some modeling compound into a sheet about 0.5 centimeter thick and about 6 centimeters square. Then make another sheet of the same size and thickness, using a different color.
2. Cut each square in half and stack the sheets on top of each other, alternating colors. **CAUTION:** *To avoid breaking the plastic knife, do not press too hard as you cut.* The sheets of modeling compound stand for different layers of rock. The different colors will help you see where similar layers of rock end up after movement occurs along the model fault.
3. Press the layers of modeling compound together to form a rectangular block that fits in the palm of your hand.
4. Use the butter knife to slice carefully through the block at an angle, as shown in the photograph.
5. Place the two blocks formed by the slice together, but don't let them stick together.
6. Review the descriptions and diagrams of faults in Section 1. Decide which piece of your block is the hanging wall and which is the footwall. Using the marking pen, label the side of each block. What part of your model stands for the fault itself?
7. What part of the model stands for the land surface? Along the top surface of the two blocks, draw a river flowing across the fault. Also draw an arrow on each block to show the direction of the river's flow. The arrow should point from the footwall toward the hanging wall.
8. Make a table that includes the headings Type of Fault, How the Sides of the Fault Move, and Changes in the Land Surface.

Type of Fault	How the Sides of the Fault Move	Changes in the Land Surface

9. Using your blocks, model the movement along a strike-slip fault. Record your motion and the results on the data table.
10. Repeat Step 9 for a normal fault.
11. Repeat Step 9 for a reverse fault.

Analyze and Conclude

Refer to your data table to draw a chart that will help you answer questions 1 through 4.

1. On your chart, show the direction in which the sides of the fault move for each type of fault.
2. On your chart, show how movement along a strike-slip fault is different from movement along the other two types of fault.
3. Add to your chart a column that shows how the river on the surface might change for each type of fault.
4. Assuming that the river is flowing from the footwall toward the hanging wall, which type of fault could produce small waterfalls in the surface river? (*Hint:* Recall how you tell which block is the hanging wall and which block is the footwall).
5. If you could observe only the land surface around a fault, how could you tell if the fault is a strike-slip fault? A normal fault?
6. If you slide the hanging wall of your fault model upward in relation to the footwall, what type of fault forms? If this movement continues, where will the slab of rock with the hanging wall end up?
7. From an airplane, you see a chain of several long, narrow lakes along a fault. What type of fault would cause these lakes to form?
8. **Think About It** In what ways does the model help you picture what is happening along a fault? In what ways does the model not accurately reflect what happens along a fault? How is the model still useful in spite of its inaccuracies?

More to Explore

On Earth's surface, individual faults do not exist all by themselves. With one or more of your classmates, combine your models to show how a fault-block mountain range or a rift valley could form. (*Hint:* Both involve normal faults.) How could you combine your models to show how reverse faults produce a mountain range?

Sample Data Table

Type of Fault	How Hanging Wall Moves	Changes in the Land Surface
Strike-slip fault	sideways	Riverbed is broken and moved sideways.
Normal Fault	down	Downstream part of river drops below upstream part.
Reverse fault	up	Downstream part of river may form a lake where it meets hanging wall.

Safety

Students should handle the knife carefully during this activity. Review the safety guidelines in Appendix A.

Program Resources

◆ **Teaching Resources** Skills Lab blackline masters, pp. 63–64

Expected Outcome

In Step 9, the riverbed will be displaced horizontally in a zig-zag shape. In Step 10, the downstream part of the river on the surface of the upper block will be displaced downward so it is lower than the upstream part. In Step 11, the downstream part will be displaced upward so it is higher than the upstream part.

Analyze and Conclude

1. *Strike-slip fault:* The hanging wall moves sideways. *Normal fault:* The hanging wall moves downward. *Reverse fault:* The hanging wall moves upward.
2. Students' charts should indicate that there is no upward or downward movement along a strike-slip fault.
3. *Strike-slip fault:* The continuous line of the riverbed would be broken and displaced horizontally. *Normal fault:* The downstream part of the river would drop below the upstream part, creating a waterfall at the fault. *Reverse fault:* The downstream part of the river would be thrust above the upstream part; water would collect at the fault to form a lake.
4. A normal fault
5. A strike-slip fault would be indicated by sideways displacement of a feature where it crossed the fault. A normal fault would be indicated by a break in the feature where the two blocks moved away from each other at the fault; the part of the feature on the surface of the hanging wall would be lower than the part on the surface of the footwall.
6. A reverse fault; above the footwall
7. A reverse fault
8. The model demonstrates actual rock movements. The model's fault is much more regular and smooth than real faults between rock surfaces, so the model's movements involve far less friction and are less abrupt and "jerky." The model enables you to see block movements that are hidden underground in real faulting.

Extending the Inquiry

More to Explore Encourage students to model fault-block mountains and rift valleys. They can refer to Figure 7, Page 58, for fault-block mountains and *Exploring Plate Tectonics,* pages 44–45, for a rift valley.

Measuring Earthquakes

Objectives

After completing the lesson, students will be able to
- describe how the energy of an earthquake travels through Earth;
- identify the different kinds of seismic waves;
- name the scales used to measure the strength of an earthquake.

Key Terms focus, epicenter, seismic waves, P waves, S waves, surface waves, seismograph, magnitude, Mercalli scale, Richter scale, moment magnitude scale

1 Engage/Explore

Activating Prior Knowledge

Ask: **What kinds of waves have you observed?** *(Students will probably mention ocean waves and waves in a lake, pond, swimming pool, or even a bathtub.)* **How do waves move in water?** *(They will probably say that the waves move outward from a "push" on the water.)*

DISCOVER

Skills Focus observing
Materials *spring toy*
Time 10 minutes
Tips Advise students to hold both ends of the spring securely as they make the waves. If they have difficulty observing differences in the two wave types, let them repeat each step several times.
Expected Outcome In Step 2, the coils will move forward and backward along the spring in a straight line. In Step 3, the coils will move sideways.
Think It Over In Step 2, the coils move forward and back as a wave moves from the compressed end of the spring to the other end in a straight line. In Step 3, the coils move from side to side as a wave moves in a bulge from the jerked end of the spring to the other end.

Section 2 Measuring Earthquakes

DISCOVER — ACTIVITY

How Do Seismic Waves Travel Through Earth?

1. Stretch a spring toy across the floor while a classmate holds the other end. Do not overstretch the toy.
2. Gather together about 4 coils of the spring toy and release them. In what direction do the coils move?
3. Once the spring toy has stopped moving, jerk one end of the toy from side to side once. In what direction do the coils move? Be certain your classmate has a secure grip on the other end.

Think It Over
Observing Describe the two types of wave motion that you observed in the spring toy.

GUIDE FOR READING

- How does the energy of an earthquake travel through Earth?
- What are the different kinds of seismic waves?
- What are the scales used to measure the strength of an earthquake?

Reading Tip Before you read, preview the illustrations and captions. Predict how energy from earthquakes travels through the crust.

Earth is never still. Every day, worldwide, there are about 8,000 earthquakes. Most of them are too small to notice. But when an earthquake is strong enough to rattle dishes in kitchen cabinets, people sit up and take notice. "How big was the quake?" and "Where was it centered?" are two questions just about everyone asks after an earthquake.

To know where an earthquake was centered, you need to know where it began. Earthquakes always begin in rock below the surface. Most earthquakes begin in the lithosphere within 100 kilometers of Earth's surface. An earthquake starts at one particular point. The **focus** (FOH kus) is the point beneath Earth's surface where rock that is under stress breaks, triggering an earthquake. The point on the surface directly above the focus is called the **epicenter** (EHP uh sen tur).

Seismic Waves

If you have ever played a drum, you know that the sound it makes depends on how hard you strike it. Like a drumbeat, an earthquake produces vibrations called waves. These waves carry energy as they travel outward through solid material. During an earthquake, seismic waves race out from the focus in all directions. The seismic waves move like ripples in a pond. **Seismic waves** are vibrations that travel through Earth carrying the energy released during an earthquake. An earthquake's seismic waves first reach Earth's surface at the epicenter. Look at Figure 11 to see how seismic waves travel outward from the focus.

READING STRATEGIES

Reading Tip To predict how energy reaches the surface, students must understand that earthquake waves move outward from the focus in all directions. Direct students' attention to the focus and the concentric rings of seismic waves shown in Figure 11 and ask: **What do these waves remind you of?** *(The ripples that spread outward on the surface of a pond when something is dropped into the water)*

Vocabulary Students may wonder where the terms *seismic, seismograph, seismologist,* and *seismology* came from. Encourage students to look up the origin of the root word *seism. (From* seismos, *the Greek word for earthquake, derived from* seiein, *meaning "to shake")* Also discuss the meanings of the suffixes -graph *("a device that writes or records")*, -ology *("the study of" something)*, and -ologist *("a person who studies" something)*.

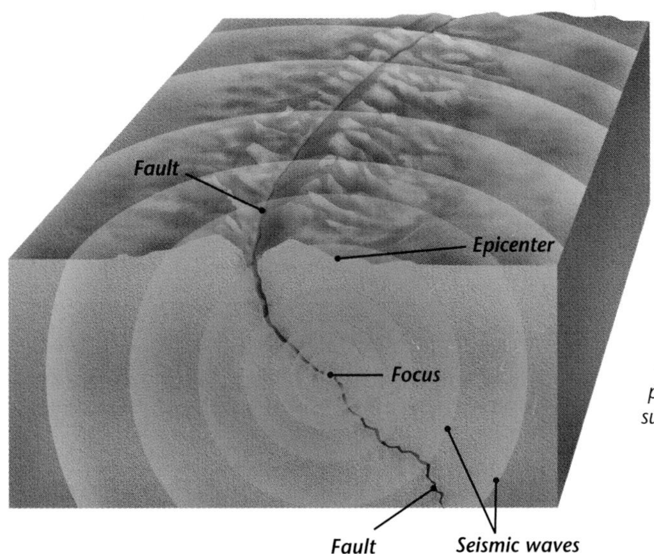

Figure 11 An earthquake occurs when rocks fracture at the focus, deep in Earth's crust. *Interpreting Diagrams* *At what point do seismic waves first reach the surface?*

Seismic waves carry the energy of an earthquake away from the focus, through Earth's interior, and across the surface. The energy of the seismic waves that reach the surface is greatest at the epicenter. The most violent shaking during an earthquake, however, may occur kilometers away from the epicenter. The types of rock and soil around the epicenter determine where and how much the ground shakes. You will learn more about the effects of seismic waves in Section 3.

There are three types of seismic waves: P waves, S waves, and surface waves. An earthquake sends out two types of waves from its focus: P waves and S waves. When these waves reach Earth's surface at the epicenter, surface waves develop.

Primary Waves The first waves to arrive are primary waves, or P waves. **P waves** are earthquake waves that compress and expand the ground like an accordion. P waves cause buildings to contract and expand. Look at Figure 12 to compare P waves and S waves.

Secondary Waves After P waves come secondary waves, or S waves. **S waves** are earthquake waves that vibrate from side to side and thrust the ground up and down, or back and forth. When S waves reach the surface, they shake structures violently. Unlike P waves, which travel through both solids and liquids, S waves cannot move through liquids.

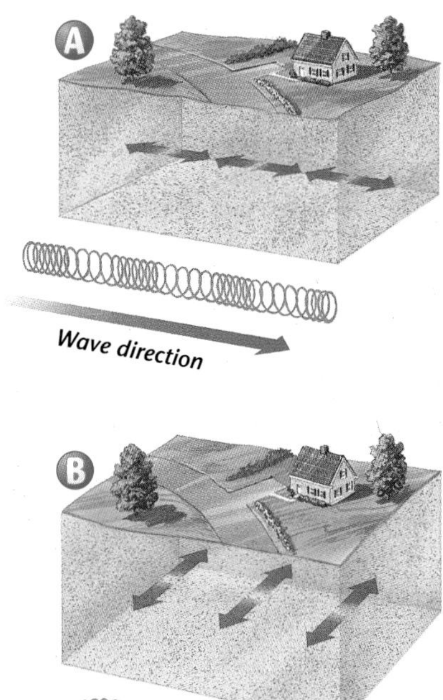

Figure 12 A. In P waves, the particles of the crust vibrate forward and back along the path of the wave. B. In S waves, the particles of the crust vibrate from side to side.

2 Facilitate

Seismic Waves

Building Inquiry Skills: Observing

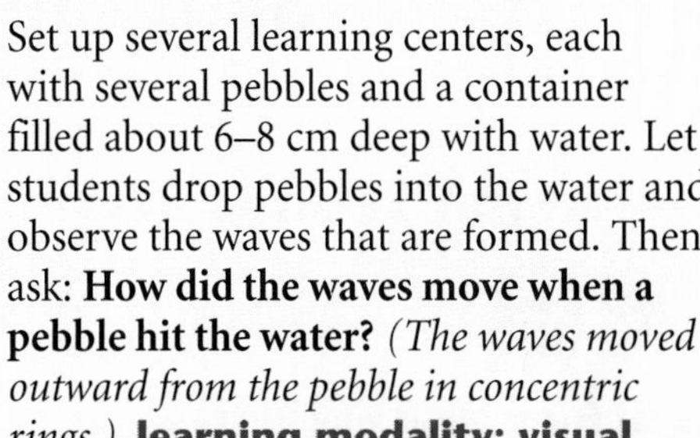

Materials *dishpans or other wide, shallow containers; water; pebbles*
Time 10 minutes

Set up several learning centers, each with several pebbles and a container filled about 6–8 cm deep with water. Let students drop pebbles into the water and observe the waves that are formed. Then ask: **How did the waves move when a pebble hit the water?** *(The waves moved outward from the pebble in concentric rings.)* **learning modality: visual**

Using the Visuals: Figure 11

Draw students' attention to the pattern of seismic waves shown in the diagram and ask: **How are seismic waves like the waves you made when you dropped pebbles into water?** *(Seismic waves also move outward in concentric rings.)* **How are they different?** *(Seismic waves move outward three-dimensionally in all directions, whereas the water waves moved only on the surface. Seismic waves move through solid materials.)* **learning modality: visual**

Including All Students

Remind students of their experience creating waves with the spring toy in the Discover activity. Ask: **When the wave moved straight ahead along the spring, which type of earthquake wave did it model?** *(a P wave)* **When the spring moved from side to side, which type of wave did it model?** *(an S wave)* **When you used the spring, where was the focus of the model earthquake?** *(At the end that was compressed and jerked)* **learning modality: logical/mathematical**

Media and Technology

Audiotapes English-Spanish Summary 2-2

Transparencies "Earthquake Focus and Epicenter and P Waves and S Waves," Transparency 10

Answers to Self-Assessment

Caption Question
Figure 11 the epicenter

Program Resources

- **Teaching Resources** 2-2 Lesson Plan, p. 51; 2-2 Section Summary, p. 52

Ongoing Assessment

Writing Have each student describe the major difference between P waves and S waves.

Seismic Waves, continued

Building Inquiry Skills: Inferring

After students read about surface waves, ask: **Why do you think surface waves produce more severe ground movements than P waves and S waves do?** *(Students should infer that because the surface consists of loose soil, sand, gravel, mud, small rocks, and the like rather then solid rock, it is susceptible to greater movement as the particles shift and slide.)* **learning modality: logical/ mathematical**

Detecting Seismic Waves

TRY THIS ACTIVITY

Skills Focus observing
Materials *large book, pencil, paper strip 1 m long, pen*
Time 10 minutes
Tips Make sure students hold the pencil and rolled strip *parallel* to the book and tabletop.
Expected Outcome The pen will first draw a straight line, then a jagged back-and-forth line as the book is jiggled. The line's spikes will be larger with stronger jiggling.
Extend Encourage students to try different types of "earthquakes"—long, slow movements; strong, abrupt movements; a strong quake followed by calm and then a smaller quake (an aftershock); and so forth. **learning modality: kinesthetic**

Using the Visuals: Figure 13

After students have studied the figure and read the caption, ask: **Which type of seismograph did you model in Try This?** *(A mechanical seismograph)* **What similarities do you see between the real seismograph record and the marks you made on the paper strip?** *(Students should mention the back-and-forth jiggles in the line and the different sizes of the spikes caused by different strengths of the movements.)* **learning modality: visual**

Recording Seismic Waves

ACTIVITY

You and two classmates can simulate a seismograph.

1. Place a big book on a table.
2. With one hand, hold a pencil with a strip of paper about one meter long wound around it.
3. In your other hand, hold a pen against the paper.
4. As you hold the pen steady, have one student slowly pull on the paper so it slides across the book.
5. After a few seconds, have the other student jiggle the book for 10 seconds—first gently, then strongly.

Observing How did the line on the paper change when the earthquake began? When it grew stronger?

Surface Waves When P waves and S waves reach the surface, some of them are transformed into surface waves. **Surface waves** move more slowly than P waves and S waves, but they produce the most severe ground movements. Some surface waves make the ground roll like ocean waves. Other surface waves shake buildings from side to side.

✓ *Checkpoint* *What are the three types of seismic waves?*

Detecting Seismic Waves

To record and measure the vibrations of seismic waves, geologists use instruments called seismographs. A **seismograph** (SYZ muh graf) records the ground movements caused by seismic waves as they move through the Earth.

Until recently, scientists used mechanical seismographs. As shown in Figure 13, a mechanical seismograph consists of a heavy weight attached to a frame by a spring or wire. A pen connected to the weight rests its point on a rotating drum. When the drum is still, the pen draws a straight line on paper wrapped around the drum. During an earthquake, seismic waves cause the drum to vibrate. Meanwhile, the pen stays in place and records the drum's vibrations. The height of the jagged lines drawn on the seismograph's drum is greater for a more severe earthquake.

Today, scientists use electronic seismographs that work according to the same principle as the mechanical seismograph. The electronic seismograph converts ground movements into a signal that can be recorded and printed.

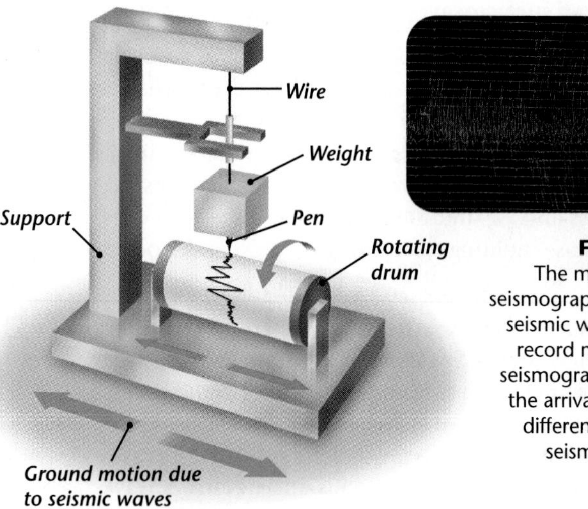

Figure 13 The mechanical seismograph records seismic waves. The record made by a seismograph shows the arrival times of different types of seismic waves.

Background

History of Science Early seismic instruments, known as seismoscopes, detected the occurrence of an earthquake but created no written record of the event. The first seismoscope—the bronze dragon-and-frog device pictured on pages 52–53—was invented by Chinese astronomer and geographer Chang Heng in A.D. 132. In 1795, Italian naturalist and clockmaker Ascanio Filomarino invented a seismoscope in which the shaking of the ground made bells ring and a clock tick.

The first seismograph was invented by Italian scientist Luigi Palmieri in 1856. This instrument has two parts. One, containing tubes of mercury, detects earthquakes, and the other prints a record. Using this device, Palmieri found that small foreshocks may precede large quakes and that tremors accompany volcanic eruptions.

The Mercalli Scale	
Earthquake Intensity	**Earthquake Effects**
I–II	Almost unnoticeable
III–IV	People notice vibrations like those from a passing truck. Unstable objects disturbed.
V–VI	Dishes and windows rattle. Books knocked off shelves. Slight damage.
VII–VIII	People run outdoors. Moderate to heavy damage.
IX–X	Buildings jolted off foundations or destroyed. Cracks appear in ground and landslides occur.
XI–XII	Severe damage. Wide cracks appear in ground. Waves seen on ground surface.

Figure 14 An earthquake in 1997 damaged the tower of this city hall in Foligno, Italy (left). The Mercalli scale (right) uses Roman numerals to rank earthquakes by how much damage they cause.
Applying Concepts How would you rate the damage to the Foligno city hall on the Mercalli scale?

Measuring Earthquakes

When geologists want to know the size of an earthquake, they must consider many factors. As a result, there are at least 20 different measures for rating earthquakes, each with its strengths and shortcomings. Three ways of measuring earthquakes, the Mercalli scale, the Richter scale, and the moment magnitude scale, are described here. **Magnitude** is a measurement of earthquake strength based on seismic waves and movement along faults.

The Mercalli Scale Early in the twentieth century, the **Mercalli scale** was developed to rate earthquakes according to their intensity. An earthquake's intensity is the strength of ground motion in a given place. The Mercalli scale is not a precise measurement. But the 12 steps of the Mercalli scale describe how earthquakes affect people, buildings, and the land surface. The scale tells roughly how much damage may be caused by earthquakes of different strengths. Figure 14 summarizes the Mercalli scale.

The Richter Scale The **Richter scale** is a rating of the size of seismic waves as measured by a particular type of mechanical seismograph. The Richter scale was developed in the 1930s. Geologists all over the world used this scale for about 50 years. Eventually, electronic seismographs replaced the mechanical seismographs used for the Richter scale. The Richter scale provides accurate measurements for small, nearby earthquakes. But the scale does not work well for large or distant earthquakes.

Measuring Earthquakes

Including All Students

Students may wonder how the Mercalli and Richter scales got their names. Explain that the scales were named after the men who developed them—Italian volcanologist Giuseppe Mercalli and American seismologist Charles Richter. Then ask: **How are the Mercalli scale and the Richter scale similar?** *(Both describe the "strength" of an earthquake.)* **How are they different?** *(The Mercalli scale describes an earthquake's strength in terms of its effects—to what extent people notice it and the amount of damage it causes. The Richter scale describes an earthquake's strength in terms of the size of its seismic waves; it is a precise measurement.)* **On which scale would an earthquake's strength vary from one place to another, and why?** *(The Mercalli scale; the amount of shaking that people would feel and the damage to objects would be greater in a place closer to the quake's epicenter and less in a place farther away, so the intensity ratings in the two places would be different.)* **learning modality: verbal**

Building Inquiry Skills: Classifying

Direct students to examine the photograph of the 1906 San Francisco earthquake in Figure 16 on the next page. Ask: **Where do you think this earthquake rated on the Mercalli scale?** *(Probably IX or X)* Ask volunteers to find photographs of other areas damaged by earthquakes, including moderate quakes as well as severe ones, and make photocopies of the pictures for the class to examine. Let students try to estimate each quake's Mercalli rating based on evidence they see in the photograph. *(Students may have some difficulty differentiating between categories VII–VIII and IX–X and between categories IX–X and X–XII. Accept all reasonable responses.)* **learning modality: visual**

Media and Technology

Exploring Earth Science Videodisc
Unit 2 Side 2, "Waves in the Earth"

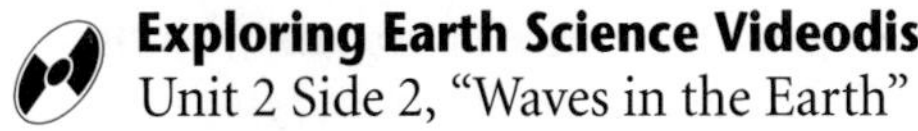

Chapter 9

Answers to Self-Assessment

Checkpoint

The three types of seismic waves are P waves, S waves, and surface waves.

Caption Question

Figure 14 The damage would probably rate VII–VIII.

Ongoing Assessment

Drawing Have each student draw and label a simple diagram explaining how a mechanical seismograph works.

Locating the Epicenter

Demonstration

Time 10–15 minutes

ACTIVITY

Do the following activity in a roomy area such as a gym. Choose two students to roleplay a P wave and an S wave. Position both students at a starting point, and position a third student some distance away to represent a seismograph. When you say "Earthquake!" the two students should start walking toward the third student, with the "P wave" student taking long forward strides and the "S wave" student taking shorter steps in a waddling gait to represent the side-to-side vibration of S waves. After a few seconds, say "Stop" and ask: **Which wave is closer to the seismograph?** *(The P wave)* Repeat the activity with six students roleplaying three pairs of P and S waves. Assign a number to each pair, and have all three pairs start walking at your signal. Say "One, stop," "Two, stop," and "Three, stop" at intervals. Have the students who are observing compare the distances between the P-wave and S-wave students in the three pairs. Ask: **Are all three distances the same?** *(No)* **How do they vary?** *(The P and S students who were walking for the shortest time are the closest together, while the P and S students who were walking for the longest time are the farthest apart.)* **How would this difference help a geologist tell how far away an earthquake's epicenter is?** *(If the S waves arrive at a seismograph a very short time after the P waves, the epicenter is close to the seismograph; the longer the interval between the arrival times of the P and S waves, the farther away the epicenter is.)* **learning modality: kinesthetic**

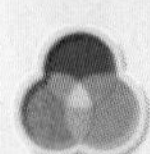

Integrating Mathematics

Ask: **Why would drawing only two circles not be enough to locate the earthquake's epicenter?** *(Two circles would intersect at two points, not one, and identify two possible epicenters. If students have difficulty visualizing this, let them lay a sheet of tracing paper over the map in Figure 17, trace each circle in a different color, and mark the two points where each pair of circles intersect.)* **learning modality: logical/mathematical**

Earthquake Magnitudes

Earthquake	Moment Magnitude
San Francisco, California, 1906	7.7
Southern Chile, 1960	9.5
Anchorage, Alaska, 1964	9.2
Loma Prieta, California, 1989	7.0
Northridge/ Los Angeles, California, 1994	6.7

Figure 15 The table lists the moment magnitudes for some of the twentieth century's biggest earthquakes.

The Moment Magnitude Scale Today, geologists use the **moment magnitude scale,** a rating system that estimates the total energy released by an earthquake. **The moment magnitude scale can be used to rate earthquakes of all sizes, near or far.** You may hear news reports that mention the Richter scale. But the magnitude number they quote is almost always the moment magnitude for that earthquake.

To rate an earthquake on the moment magnitude scale, geologists first study data from modern electronic seismographs. The data show what kinds of seismic waves the earthquake produced and how strong they were. The data also help geologists infer how much movement occurred along the fault and the strength of the rocks that broke when the fault slipped. Geologists combine all this information to rate the earthquake on the moment magnitude scale.

Earthquakes with a magnitude below 5.0 on the moment magnitude scale are small and cause little damage. Those with a magnitude above 5.0 can produce great destruction. A magnitude 6.0 quake releases 32 times as much energy as a magnitude 5.0 quake, and nearly 1,000 times as much as a magnitude 4.0 quake.

☑ *Checkpoint* ***What are three scales for measuring earthquakes?***

Locating the Epicenter

Geologists use seismic waves to locate an earthquake's epicenter. Seismic waves travel at different speeds. P waves arrive first at a seismograph, with S waves following close behind. To tell how far the epicenter is from the seismograph, scientists measure the difference between the arrival times of the P waves and S waves.

Figure 16 In terms of magnitude, the 1906 San Francisco earthquake was not the strongest of the century. But it toppled buildings and caused fires that devastated the city.

Background

Facts and Figures Students might be interested to learn that American astronauts left seismographs on the moon to record moonquakes. Many such quakes are caused by meteorites hitting the moon's surface. Other moonquakes seem to occur most often when the moon is closest to Earth.

Program Resources

- **Integrated Science Laboratory Manual** F-2, "Investigating the Speed of Earthquake Waves"

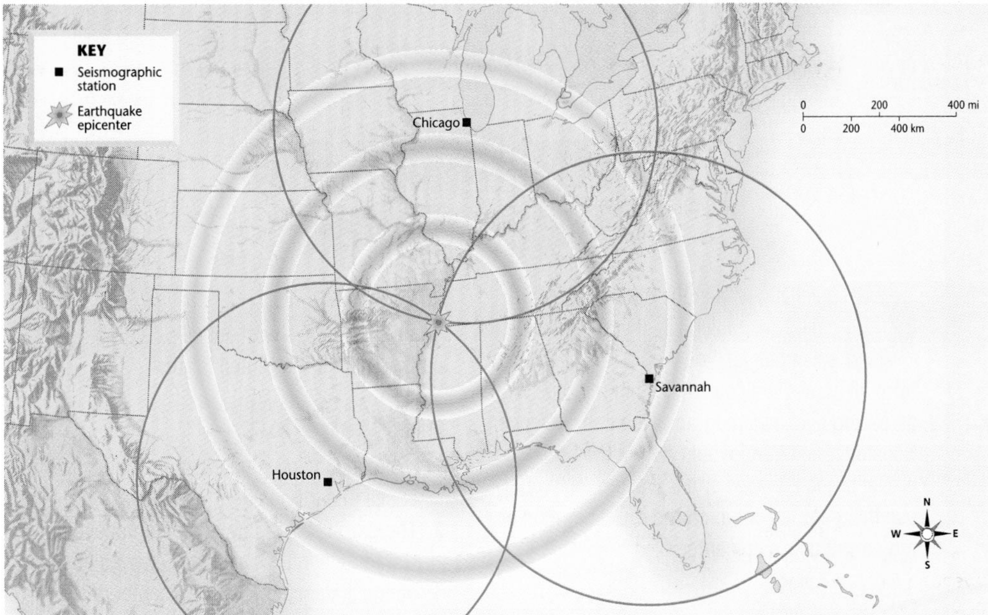

Figure 17 The map shows how to find the epicenter of an earthquake using data from three seismographic stations. *Measuring Use the map scale to determine the distances from Savannah and Houston to the epicenter. Which is closer?*

The farther away an earthquake is, the greater the time between the arrival of the P waves and the S waves.

INTEGRATING MATHEMATICS Geologists then draw at least three circles using data from different seismographs set up at stations all over the world. The center of each circle is a particular seismograph's location. The radius of each circle is the distance from the seismograph to the epicenter. The point where the circles intersect is the location of the epicenter. If you look at Figure 17, you can see why two circles would not give enough information to pinpoint the epicenter.

Section 2 Review

1. How does the energy from an earthquake reach Earth's surface?
2. Describe the three types of seismic waves.
3. What method do geologists use today for measuring the strength of an earthquake?
4. **Thinking Critically Relating Cause and Effect** Describe how energy released at an earthquake's focus, deep inside Earth, can cause damage on the surface many kilometers from the epicenter.

Check Your Progress

CHAPTER PROJECT 2

Now it is time to complete your design and construct your model. From what you have learned about earthquakes, what changes will you make in your design? Have a classmate review your model and make suggestions for improvements. When you have made the changes, test your model's ability to withstand an earthquake. Take notes on how well it withstands the quake.

3 Assess

Section 2 Review Answers

1. Seismic waves carry the energy of an earthquake away from the focus. Some of those waves reach the surface and become surface waves.
2. *P waves:* Travel straight outward from the focus; compress and expand the ground; move through solids and liquids; are the fastest-moving seismic waves. *S waves:* Vibrate from side to side as they travel outward from the focus; move only through solids. *Surface waves:* Move along the surface; move more slowly than P and S waves; produce the most violent ground movements.
3. Data from electronic seismographs, which convert ground movements into signals that can be recorded and printed, are used to rate the strength of earthquakes on the moment magnitude scale.
4. Some of an earthquake's P and S waves travel to the surface, where they are transformed into surface waves that spread out horizontally from the epicenter and reach distant surface areas.

Check Your Progress

CHAPTER PROJECT 2

Encourage volunteers to describe any changes they made in their initial design based on what they learned from the text and from other students. Have the class review their agreed-upon criteria for simulating earthquakes so all models are subjected to the same degree of shaking. Emphasize that they should take notes about any damage their models sustain and any weaknesses that are revealed.

Program Resources

◆ **Teaching Resources** 2-2 Review and Reinforce, p. 53; 2-2 Enrich, p. 54

Media and Technology

Interactive Student Tutorial CD-ROM F-2

Answers to Self-Assessment

☑ Checkpoint

Three scales for measuring earthquakes are the Mercalli scale, the Richter scale, and the moment magnitude scale.

Caption Question

Figure 17 Houston (about 800 km compared with about 900 km for Savannah)

Performance Assessment

Drawing Have each student draw and label a sketch, without referring to figures 11 or 12, showing an earthquake's focus underground, its epicenter on the surface, the different motions of P waves and S waves moving outward from the focus, and surface waves moving outward from the epicenter.

Real-World Lab

Careers in Science

Locating an Epicenter

Preparing for Inquiry

Key Concept Data from seismographs in three different locations can be used to identify an earthquake's epicenter.

Skills Objectives Students will be able to
- ◆ interpret data to determine the distances of three seismographs from an earthquake's epicenter;
- ◆ draw a conclusion about the location of the earthquake's epicenter.

Time 35–40 minutes

Advance Planning Make a photocopy of the map for each student.

Guiding Inquiry

Invitation Ask: **Why is it important for scientists to know where an earthquake's epicenter is located?** *(Accept all reasonable responses, such as the usefulness of this information in predicting future earthquakes.)* Then have students look back at Figure 17 on the previous page. Explain that they will use the same technique in this activity to find an earthquake's epicenter.

Introducing the Procedure

Before students begin, review the use of a drawing compass and a map scale. Ask: **What do the numbers on the compass represent?** *(The distance in centimeters between the compass's metal point and pencil point.)* **If you set the compass at 7 and drew a circle, what would the circle's diameter be?** *(14 cm)* **What would its radius be?** *(7 cm)*

Next, ask: **What does a map scale show?** *(The distance on the map that represents a certain number of kilometers or miles on the real land surface)* **What is this map's scale?** *(Each centimeter on the map represents 300 km on land. If students cannot answer your question, have them lay a metric ruler along the scale line to see how many kilometers are represented by each centimeter.)* **Suppose you wanted to show a distance of 1800 km from Denver on this map. How would you figure out the length of that map measurement in centimeters?** *(Divide the distance you want to show by the number of kilometers represented by 1 cm on the map: 1800 km ÷ 300 km = 6 cm on the map.)* Then ask: **How would you use the compass to measure that distance?** *(Set the compass arm at 6 cm, hold the metal point on the dot for Denver, and draw a circle. To determine the compass setting, students also could hold the metal point on the 0 end of the scale line and adjust the compass arm so the pencil point is at 1800 km on the line.)* **What does the circle show?** *(All the points 1800 km from Denver)* If students need more practice, give them additional examples, not including the distances they will use in the activity.

Troubleshooting the Experiment

- ◆ In Step 2, point out that the arrival-time differences listed in the table include seconds as well as minutes, whereas the labels on the *y*-axis give only whole minutes. Thus, students will need to use the

---

Real-World Lab

Careers in Science

Geologists who study earthquakes are called seismologists. If you were a seismologist, you would receive data from all across the country. Within minutes after an earthquake, seismographs located in Denver, Houston, and Miami would record the times of arrival of the P waves and S waves. You would use this data to zero in on the exact location of the earthquake's epicenter.

Problem

How can you locate an earthquake's epicenter?

Skills Focus

interpreting data, drawing conclusions

Materials

drawing compass with pencil
outline map of the United States

Procedure

1. Make a copy of the data table showing differences in earthquake arrival times.
2. The graph shows how the difference in arrival time between P waves and S waves depends on the distance from the epicenter of the earthquake. Find the difference in arrival time for Denver on the *y*-axis of the graph. Follow this line across to the point at which it crosses the curve. To find the distance to the epicenter, read down from this point to the *x*-axis of the graph. Enter this distance in the data table.

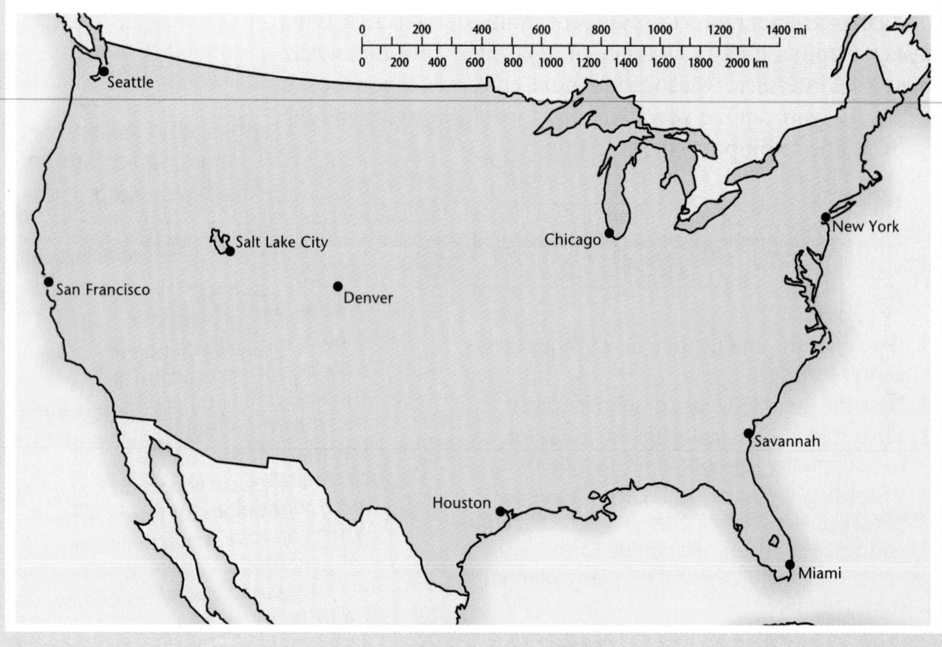

Data Table

City	Difference in P and S Wave Arrival Times	Distance to Epicenter
Denver, Colorado	2 min 10 s	
Houston, Texas	3 min 55 s	
Miami, Florida	5 min 40 s	

3. Repeat Step 2 for Houston and Miami.
4. Set your compass at a radius equal to the distance from Denver to the earthquake epicenter that you recorded in your data table.
5. Draw a circle with the radius determined in Step 4, using Denver as the center. Draw the circle on your copy of the map. (*Hint:* Draw your circles carefully. You may need to draw some parts of the circles off the map.)
6. Repeat Steps 4 and 5 for Houston and Miami.

Analyze and Conclude

1. Observe the three circles you have drawn to locate the earthquake's epicenter.
2. Which city on the map is closest to the earthquake epicenter? How far, in kilometers, is this city from the epicenter?
3. In which of the three cities listed in the data table would seismographs detect the earthquake first? Last?
4. When you are trying to locate an epicenter, why is it necessary to know the distance from the epicenter for at least three recording stations?
5. About how far is the epicenter that you found from San Francisco? What would the difference in arrival times of the P waves and S waves be for a recording station in San Francisco?
6. What happens to the difference in arrival times between P waves and S waves as the distance from the earthquake increases?
7. **Apply** Working as a seismologist, you find the epicenters of many earthquakes in a region. What features of Earth's crust would you expect to find in this region?

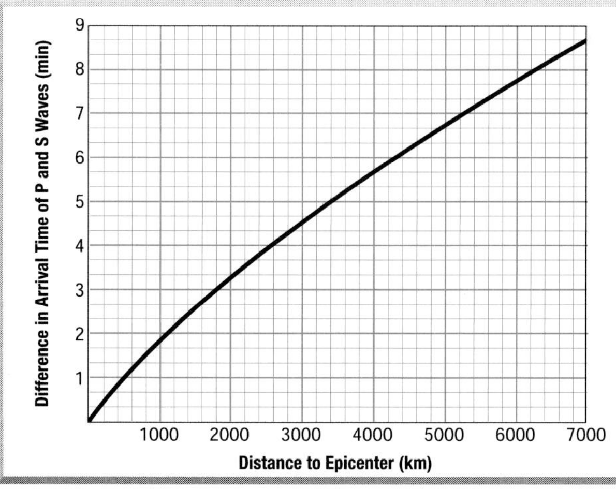

More to Explore

You have just located an earthquake's epicenter. Find this earthquake's location on the earthquake risk map on page 81. Judging from the map, was this earthquake a freak event? What is the risk of earthquakes in the area of this quake? Now look at the map of Earth's plates on page 43. What conclusions can you draw from this map about the cause of earthquakes in this area?

lighter lines on the graph to estimate the partial-minute differences as closely as they can. (Since there are three lighter lines dividing each whole-minute interval, each lighter line represents 20 seconds.)

◆ Remind students that they must use the map scale to determine where to set the compass arm for each distance in steps 4 and 6.

Expected Outcome
The correct compass settings are 4 cm for Denver, 8.4 cm for Houston, and 13.3 cm for Miami. The point on the map at which all three circles intersect will be about 600 km south southeast of Seattle.

Analyze and Conclude
1. The epicenter is located about 600 km south southeast of Seattle.
2. Seattle; 600 km
3. *First:* Denver; *Last:* Miami
4. Using three recording stations enables you to identify one epicenter location, whereas using only two stations identifies two possible epicenter locations
5. 650 km from San Francisco; 1 min 20 s
6. The difference in arrival times also increases.
7. You would expect to find faults in Earth's crust in the region.

Extending the Inquiry

More to Explore This earthquake was not a freak event, as it occurred in an area of moderate risk. Earthquakes in this area are caused by movement along the boundary between the Pacific and North American plates.

Sample Data Table

City	Difference in P and S Wave Arrival Times	Distance to Epicenter
Denver, Colorado	2 min 10 s	1,200 km
Houston, Texas	3 min 55 s	2,600 km
Miami, Florida	5 min 40 s	4,000 km

Program Resources

◆ **Teaching Resources** Real-World Lab blackline masters, pp. 65–67

Safety

Students should take care with the compass point in this activity. Review the safety guidelines in Appendix A.

Earthquake Hazards and Safety

Objectives

After completing the lesson, students will be able to
- ◆ describe the kinds of damage that an earthquake causes;
- ◆ explain what can be done to reduce earthquake hazards.

Key Terms liquefaction, aftershock, tsunamis, base-isolated building

1 Engage/Explore

Activating Prior Knowledge

Ask: **What kinds of structures have you seen used to make buildings, bridges, and highway overpasses stronger?** *(Students may mention heavy wooden or steel beams, supporting buttresses, diagonal beams, and the like.)* **Do you think these structures would help protect against damage in an earthquake? Why, or why not?** *(Accept all reasonable answers. Encourage students to rely on their own direct observations or on what they have seen in news reports and documentary films.)*

DISCOVER

Skills Focus predicting
Materials *5 straws, tape*
Time 10 minutes
Tips In Step 3, make sure students tape the fifth straw roughly halfway up the square.
Expected Outcome In Step 2, the frame will collapse sideways. In Step 3, it will remain standing for a time but will fall over if more pressure is exerted.
Think It Over The fifth straw provided additional support to the frame. Cardboard would provide even stronger support. Without additional supporting structures, a house's frame would probably collapse in an earthquake.

Section 3 Earthquake Hazards and Safety

DISCOVER ACTIVITY

Can Bracing Prevent Building Collapse?

1. Tape four straws together to make a square frame. Hold the frame upright on a flat surface in front of you.
2. Hold the bottom straw down with one hand while you push the top straw to the left with the other. Push it as far as it will go without breaking the frame.
3. Tape a fifth straw horizontally across the middle of the frame. Repeat Step 2.

Think It Over

Predicting What effect did the fifth straw have? What effect would a piece of cardboard taped to the frame have? Based on your observations, how would an earthquake affect the frame of a house?

GUIDE FOR READING

- ◆ **What kinds of damage does an earthquake cause?**
- ◆ **What can be done to reduce earthquake hazards?**

Reading Tip **Before you read preview the headings of the section. Then predict some of the ways that people can reduce earthquake hazards.**

On a cold, bleak morning in January 1995, a powerful earthquake awoke the 1.5 million residents of Kobe, Japan. In 20 terrifying seconds, the earthquake collapsed thousands of buildings, crumpled freeways, and sparked about 130 fires. More than 5,000 people perished.

Most of the buildings that toppled were more than 20 years old. Many were two-story, wood-frame houses with heavy tile roofs. These top-heavy houses were about as stable in an earthquake as a heavy book supported by a framework of pencils. In contrast, many of the more modern buildings remained standing. The newer buildings had been designed to withstand intense shaking.

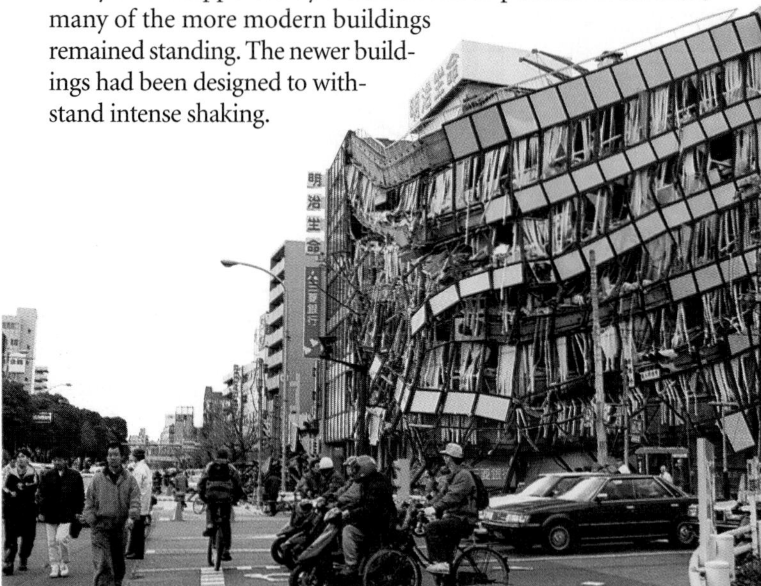

Figure 18 Many buildings in Kobe, Japan, could not withstand the magnitude 6.8 earthquake that struck in 1995.

READING STRATEGIES

Asking Questions Draw a two-column table on the board, with the first column labeled *Location Conditions* and the second column labeled *Construction Methods.* Let students quickly skim through the section and suggest questions about the text and illustrations that occur to them. List each question in the appropriate column. For example, under *Location Conditions,* students' questions might include, "Why do soil conditions affect the amount of damage an earthquake causes?" "What type of land is safest to build on in an earthquake zone?" and "What is a tsunami, and where do tsunamis occur?" For *Construction Methods,* questions might include, "What kinds of building materials are most earthquake-resistant?" "How can support be added to existing buildings?" and "What is a base-isolated building?" Encourage students to note answers to these questions as they read.

Figure 19 An earthquake caused the soil beneath this house to liquefy. Liquefaction caused by seismic waves can change solid soil to liquid mud within seconds. *Posing Questions What are some questions people might ask before building a house in an area that is at risk for earthquakes?*

How Earthquakes Cause Damage

When a major earthquake strikes, it can cause great damage. **The severe shaking produced by seismic waves can damage or destroy buildings and bridges, topple utility poles, and fracture gas and water mains.** S waves, with their side-to-side movement, cause the most damage. As the twisting forces of S waves sweep through the ground, the S waves put enough stress on buildings to tear them apart. Earthquakes can also trigger landslides or avalanches. In coastal regions, giant waves pushed up by earthquakes can cause more damage.

Local Soil Conditions When seismic waves move from hard, dense rock to loosely packed soil, they transmit their energy to the soil. The loose soil shakes more violently than the surrounding rock. The thicker the layer of soil, the more violent the shaking will be. This means a house built on solid rock will shake less than a house built on sandy soil.

Liquefaction In 1964, when a powerful earthquake roared through Anchorage, Alaska, cracks opened in the ground. Some of the cracks were 9 meters wide. The cracks were created by liquefaction. **Liquefaction** (lik wih FAK shun) occurs when an earthquake's violent shaking suddenly turns loose, soft soil into liquid mud. Liquefaction is likely where the soil is full of moisture. As the ground gives way, buildings sink and pull apart.

Liquefaction can also trigger landslides. During the 1964 Anchorage earthquake, liquefaction caused a landslide that swept an entire housing development down a cliff and into the sea. Figure 19 shows the damage liquefaction can cause.

Aftershocks Sometimes, buildings weakened by an earthquake collapse during an aftershock. An **aftershock** is an earthquake that occurs after a larger earthquake in the same area. Aftershocks may strike hours, days, or even months later.

2 Facilitate

How Earthquakes Cause Damage

Cultural Diversity

After students have read the section opening, point out that in addition to being top-heavy with tile roofs, traditional Japanese homes are built of wood with paper walls. Ask: **How do you think this kind of construction would stand up to an earthquake?** *(Lightweight wood and paper would be more easily damaged than stronger building materials.)* **learning modality: logical/mathematical**

Inquiry Challenge

Materials *small containers such as storage boxes, shoe boxes, and baking pans; sandy soil; building materials such as index cards, popsicle sticks, straws, cardboard, paper clips, and tape*
Time 20 minutes

Challenge small groups of students to devise a model showing that structures built on loose soil shake more violently in an earthquake than structures built on solid rock. *(To model an earthquake's effects on a structure built on loose soil, students can make a small model building, put it on top of soil in a container, then shake the container. To model the effects on a structure built on solid rock, students can tape the model building directly to a desktop, then shake the desk with the same intensity.)* In a follow-up class discussion, let students describe their models and the effects they observed. **cooperative learning**

Program Resources

◆ **Teaching Resources** 2-3 Lesson Plan, p. 55; 2-3 Section Summary, p. 56

Media and Technology

Audiotapes English-Spanish Summary 2-3

Answers to Self-Assessment

Caption Question

Figure 19 Students might suggest the following questions: Will the house be built on dense rock or loose soil? What is the slope of the land? Have other houses in the area been damaged by earthquakes? What building techniques helped protect the houses that were not damaged?

Ongoing Assessment

Writing Have each student describe, in his or her own words, the different ways in which earthquakes cause damage. *(Students should describe how shaking caused by seismic waves, local soil conditions, liquefaction, aftershocks, and tsunamis contribute to earthquake damage.)*

How Earthquakes Cause Damage, continued

Using the Visuals: Figure 20

To help students understand why tsunami waves are so high when they strike a coast, ask: **What do you see happening to the *length* of the waves as they move through shallow water?** *(The length decreases.)* **What do you see happening to the wave *height* as the length decreases?** *(The height increases.)* **learning modality: visual**

Building Inquiry Skills: Comparing and Contrasting

Materials *long, narrow, clear-plastic box; clay; water; ruler or other flat object*
Time 5 minutes

ACTIVITY

Set up the following learning station so students can observe how wave height increases as wavelength decreases. Place the box on a flat surface. Use clay to create a sloping "beach" at one end of the box. Fill the "ocean" end of the box about one-third full of water. Let pairs of students take turns making waves in the "ocean" by repeatedly pushing a ruler or other flat object toward the "beach." As one partner makes the waves, the other should watch the waves from the side. **learning modality: kinesthetic**

Sharpen your Skills

Calculating

Materials *pencil and paper (calculator optional)*
Time 10 minutes

ACTIVITY

Tips If students are uncertain about what math operations to use, lead them through the steps. *To calculate time for seismic waves to reach Hawaii:* 3600 km ÷ 560 km/min = 6.429 (6.5) min. *To calculate time for tsunami to reach Hawaii:* 3600 km ÷ 640 km/hr = 5.625 hrs (5 hrs, 37.5 min)
Expected Outcome Hawaii will have about $5\frac{1}{2}$ hrs advance warning (5 hrs, 37.5 min − 6.5 min).
Extend Ask: **What should people in Hawaii do during that time to prepare for the tsunami? learning modality: logical/mathematical**

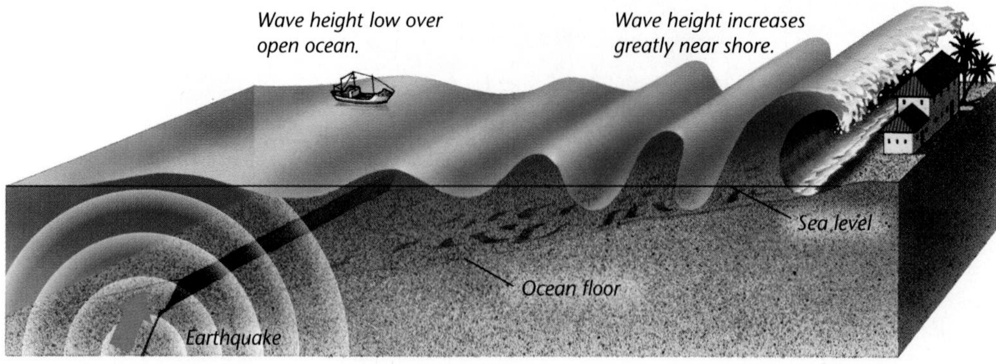

Figure 20 A tsunami begins as a low wave, but turns into a huge wave as it nears the shore.

Tsunamis When an earthquake jolts the ocean floor, plate movement causes the ocean floor to rise slightly and push water out of its way. If the earthquake is strong enough, the water displaced by the quake forms large waves, called **tsunamis** (tsoo NAH meez). Figure 20 follows a tsunami from where it begins on the ocean floor.

A tsunami spreads out from an earthquake's epicenter and speeds across the ocean. In the open ocean, the distance between the waves of a tsunami is a very long—between 100 and 200 kilometers. But the height of the wave is low. Tsunamis rise only half a meter or so above the other waves. However, as they approach shallow water near a coastline, the waves become closer together. The tsunami grows into a mountain of water. Some are the height of a six-story building.

Calculating

ACTIVITY

The Tsunami Warning System alerts people who live near the Pacific Ocean. When geologists detect an earthquake on the ocean floor, they notify coastal areas.

An earthquake in the Gulf of Alaska occurs 3,600 kilometers from Hawaii. The quake's seismic waves travel about 560 kilometers per *minute*. The quake triggers a tsunami that travels at 640 kilometers per *hour*. The seismic waves arrive in Hawaii within minutes and are recorded on seismographs. The seismic waves' arrival warns of the dangerous tsunami that may follow. About how much advance warning will Hawaii have that a tsunami is on the way?

☑ *Checkpoint* ***What are the major causes of earthquake damage?***

Making Buildings Safer

Most earthquake-related deaths and injuries result from damage to buildings or other structures. **To reduce earthquake damage, new buildings must be made stronger and more flexible. Older buildings must be modified to withstand stronger quakes.** A structure must be strong in order to resist violent shaking in a quake. It must also be flexible so it can twist and bend without breaking. *Exploring an Earthquake-Safe House* shows how a house can be made safer in an earthquake.

Choice of Location The location of a building affects the type of damage it may suffer during an earthquake. Steep slopes pose the danger of landslides. Filled land can shake violently. Therefore, people should avoid building on such sites. People should also avoid building structures near earthquake faults. As seismic waves pass through the earth, their strength decreases. So the farther a structure is from a fault, the less strong the shaking will be.

Background

Facts and Figures Although tsunamis are commonly called "tidal waves," their cause has nothing to do with tidal action. For this reason, scientists prefer the Japanese word *tsunami*, meaning "harbor wave."

Tsunamis can cause horrendous damage. For example, after the cataclysmic volcanic eruption on the island of Krakatoa, Indonesia, in 1883, walls of water up to 30 m high crashed into the surrounding islands, flattening many villages and killing 36,000 people.

Although we tend to think of tsunamis as Pacific Ocean phenomena, they are known to occur elsewhere as well. In 1755, for example, a major earthquake destroyed much of the city of Lisbon on Portugal's Atlantic coast. Tsunamis produced by the quake destroyed Lisbon's harbor and killed more than 10,000 people.

EXPLORING an Earthquake-Safe House

People can take a variety of steps to make their homes safer in an earthquake. Some steps strengthen the house itself. Others may help to keep objects from tipping or falling.

B. Secure brick chimneys with light, metal brackets.
C. In the attic, nail plywood to the ceiling joists around the chimney for protection against falling bricks.
D. Remove heavy items from the walls above beds. Locate beds away from plate-glass windows.
A. To prevent bookshelves, cabinets, and tall dressers from toppling, fasten them to wall studs with L-shaped brackets.
E. Use plywood panels to strengthen the walls that surround the crawl space beneath a house.
H. Bolt the house to its concrete foundation to prevent it from slipping off.
F. To help the house withstand shaking, use metal connectors to strengthen joints in the house's frame.
G. To reduce the risk of fire, strap the water heater to the wall to prevent it from toppling over and breaking a gas line. Learn how to shut off the gas, water, and electricity.

Making Buildings Safer

EXPLORING
An Earthquake-Safe House

Review each step with the class and encourage students to infer the reasoning for each precautionary measure. Then ask: **Which of these steps could be done after the house is built?** *(All but steps F and H)* If students live in an area that is at risk for earthquakes, encourage them to review these precautions with their families, make a safety survey of their homes, and implement as many steps as they can. **learning modality: logical/mathematical**

Including All Students

Have students look back at the map of the San Andreas fault in Figure 6 on page 58 and compare that map with a political map of California. Ask: **You've just read that people should avoid building near earthquake faults. Have the people in California followed that safety guideline?** *(No; many cities, towns, bridges, highways, and smaller roads are close to the fault.)* **Have any of these structures ever been damaged in an earthquake?** *(Students saw a photograph of the effects of the 1906 San Francisco quake on page 68 and may have seen pictures of the damage caused by the quakes that struck San Francisco in 1989 and Northridge in 1994.)* **Now that people have already built structures near the San Andreas fault, what could be done to protect those structures in an earthquake?** *(Accept all reasonable responses, such as adding support beams to buildings and rebuilding destroyed highway overpasses so they are more earthquake-resistant.)* **learning modality: visual**

Media and Technology

Transparencies "Exploring an Earthquake-Safe House," Transparency 11

Exploring Earth Science Videodisc Unit 3, Side 1, "Rock and Roll"

Chapter 2

Answers to Self-Assessment

☑ Checkpoint

The major causes of earthquake damage are the shaking caused by seismic waves as well as local soil conditions (loose soil underlying buildings), liquefaction, aftershocks, and tsunamis.

Ongoing Assessment

Writing or Drawing Have each student list or draw a simple sketch to show three ways in which his or her own home could be made safer in the event of an earthquake.

Making Buildings Safer, continued

Building Inquiry Skills: Predicting

Materials *5 straws, scissors, tape*
Time 10 minutes

Instruct students to repeat Step 3 of the Discover activity at the beginning of this section, this time placing the fifth straw diagonally across the square from corner to corner. Before students test the reinforced frame, ask: **How do you think this support will affect the frame's strength?** *(The diagonal support will greatly increase the frame's resistance to a lateral force.)* Encourage students to make use of this observation as they build their model structures for the chapter project. **learning modality: kinesthetic**

Integrating Technology

After students have read about base-isolated buildings and have examined Figure 22, ask: **If you were going to build a base-isolated building for the chapter project, what kind of material could you use for the shock-absorbers?** *(Students might suggest small springs, pieces of foam rubber or spongy plastic, silicone putty, and the like.)* **learning modality: logical/mathematical**

Protecting Yourself During an Earthquake

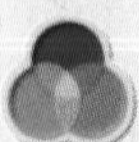

Integrating Health

Ask: **Where would you store emergency supplies so they'd be easy to reach but also protected from being buried by debris or ruined in a quake?** *(Students may suggest storing them inside a metal box or in a basement.)* **What other supplies would you add to the kit?** *(Accept all reasonable suggestions, such as candles and matches, flashlights and batteries, and blankets.)* **Besides earthquakes, for what other natural disasters would an emergency kit be useful?** *(Tornadoes, hurricanes, blizzards, floods)* **learning modality: logical/mathematical**

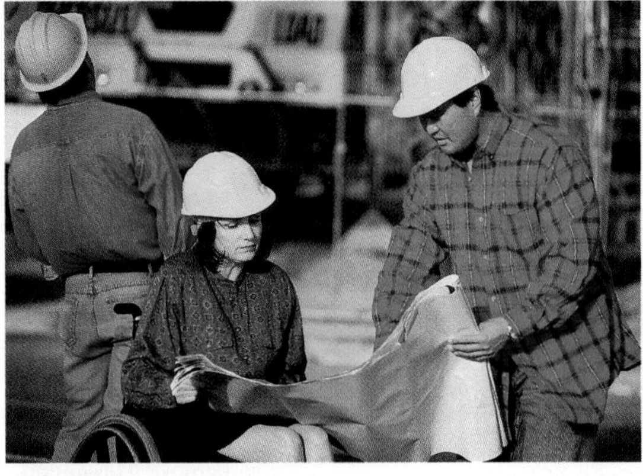

Figure 21 Architects and engineers work to design buildings that will be able to withstand earthquakes.

through the earth, their strength decreases. So the farther a structure is from a fault, the less strong the shaking will be.

Construction Methods The way in which a building is constructed determines whether it can withstand an earthquake. During an earthquake, brick buildings as well as some wood-frame buildings may collapse if their walls have not been reinforced, or strengthened. Sometimes plywood sheets are used to strengthen the frames of wooden buildings.

To combat damage caused by liquefaction, new homes built on soft ground should be anchored to solid rock below the soil. Bridges and highway overpasses can be built on supports that go down through soft soil to firmer ground.

INTEGRATING TECHNOLOGY A building designed to reduce the amount of energy that reaches the building during an earthquake is called a **base-isolated building.** As you can see in Figure 22, a base-isolated building rests on shock-absorbing

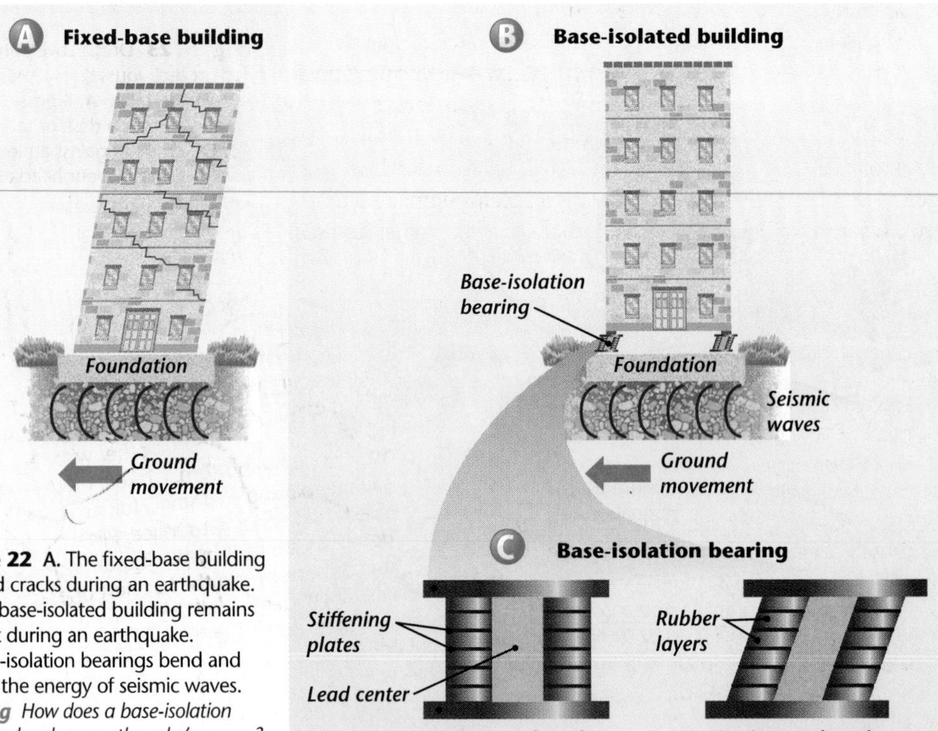

Figure 22 A. The fixed-base building tilts and cracks during an earthquake. B. The base-isolated building remains upright during an earthquake. C. Base-isolation bearings bend and absorb the energy of seismic waves. *Inferring How does a base-isolation bearing absorb an earthquake's energy?*

Background

Integrating Science Architect Frank Lloyd Wright was a pioneer in designing earthquake-resistant buildings. Wright's Imperial Hotel in Tokyo survived the city's 1923 earthquake—with a magnitude of 8.3 on the Richter scale—with only minor damage.

Many modern cities located in earthquake-prone areas have enacted building codes designed to reduce damage to structures and resulting injury or death. Architects often go beyond these codes to further insure public safety. For example, the Transamerica Pyramid in San Francisco was designed to be twice as strong as required by the Bay Area's building codes. Structures at the base of the building are expected to reduce its sway by a third during a major quake.

rubber pads or springs. Like the suspension of a car, the pads and springs smooth out a bumpy ride. During a quake, a base-isolated building moves gently back and forth without any violent shaking.

Much earthquake damage is not the direct result of shaking. Earthquakes indirectly cause fire and flooding when gas pipes and water mains break. Not much can be done to prevent pipes and mains from breaking. But automatic shut-off valves can be installed on these lines to cut off gas and water flow.

Protecting Yourself During an Earthquake

What should you do if an earthquake strikes? The main danger is from falling objects and flying glass. **The best way to protect yourself is to drop, cover, and hold.** This means you should crouch beneath a sturdy table or desk and hold on to it so it doesn't jiggle away during the shaking. The desk or table will provide a barrier against falling objects. If no desk or table is available, crouch against an inner wall, away from the outside of a building, and cover your head and neck with your arms. You can also brace yourself in a door frame. Avoid windows, mirrors, wall hangings, and furniture that might topple.

If you are outdoors, move to an open area such as a playground. Avoid vehicles, power lines, trees, and buildings, especially ones with brick walls or chimneys. Sit down to avoid being thrown down.

INTEGRATING HEALTH After a major earthquake, water and power supplies may fail, food stores may be closed, and travel may be difficult. People may have to wait several days for these services to be restored. To prepare for such an emergency, families living in a region at high risk for damaging quakes may want to put together an earthquake kit. The kit should con-

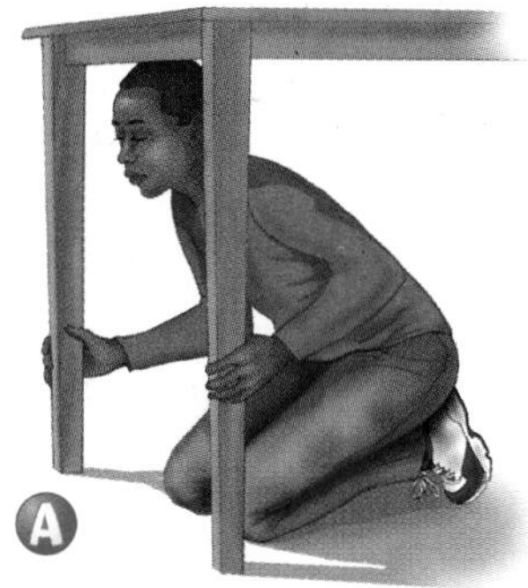

Figure 23 Drop, cover, and hold to protect yourself indoors during an earthquake. **A.** If possible, crouch under a desk or table. **B.** Or, crouch against an interior wall and cover your head and neck with your hands.

Section 3 Review

1. Explain how liquefaction occurs and how it causes damage during an earthquake.
2. What can residents do to reduce the risk of earthquake damage to their homes?
3. Describe safety measures you can take to protect yourself during an earthquake.
4. **Thinking Critically Problem Solving** You are a builder planning a housing development where earthquakes are likely. What types of land would you avoid for your development? Where would it be safe to build?

Science at Home

Show your family how an earthquake can affect two different structures—one with more weight on top, the other with more weight on the bottom. Make a model of a fault by placing two small, folded towels side by side on a flat surface. Pile a stack of books on the fault by placing the light books on the bottom and the heaviest ones on top. Then, gently pull the towels in opposite directions until the pile topples. Repeat the process, but this time with the heavier books on the bottom. Discuss with your family which makes a more stable structure.

3 Assess

Section 3 Review Answers

1. An earthquake's shaking turns loose, soft, moist soil into liquid mud that gives way, causing buildings to sink and tear apart. Liquefaction can also trigger a landslide.
2. Students may mention any of the steps presented in the visual essay on page 75.
3. Drop, cover, and hold; students may also cite other precautions described on this page.
4. Avoid building on loose, sandy soil and on hillsides. Construct buildings on solid rock in flat areas. In coastal areas, buildings should be located away from places that might be exposed to tsunamis.

Science at Home

Tips Tell students to make a tall stack of about 10 books—first with several light books such as paperbacks on the bottom, several medium-size books next, and several large, heavy books (such as dictionaries, one-volume encyclopedias, and cookbooks) on top, then reversing the order. Demonstrate the procedure in class so students understand what to do when they try the activity at home. With the heavier books on top, the stack will topple when the towels are pulled in opposite directions. With the heavier books at the bottom, the stack will wobble a bit but remain intact.

Program Resources

◆ **Teaching Resources** 2-3 Review and Reinforce, p. 57; 2-3 Enrich, p. 58

Media and Technology

Interactive Student Tutorial CD-ROM F-2

Answers to Self-Assessment

Caption Question

Figure 22 The bearing acts as a shock-absorber that smooths out vibrations.

Performance Assessment

Drawing Have each student draw and label a sketch showing three ways to make the model building for the chapter project more earthquake-resistant.

Students can save their drawings in their portfolios.

SECTION 4 Monitoring Faults

Objectives

After completing the lesson, students will be able to
- ◆ describe how geologists monitor faults;
- ◆ explain how geologists determine earthquake risk.

1 Engage/Explore

Activating Prior Knowledge

Ask: **Why is it important for scientists to develop ways to predict earthquakes?** *(A warning would allow people who live in the area to protect themselves by reinforcing buildings and other structures, preparing emergency supplies, and the like.)* **Do you think earthquake predictions will ever be very accurate? Why, or why not?** *(Accept divergent responses so long as students support their views with well-reasoned explanations.)*

DISCOVER ACTIVITY

Skills Focus drawing conclusions
Materials *facial tissue, ruler*
Time 5 minutes
Tips To make the measuring process easier, have students lay the ruler along the tissue's lower edge and grasp the tissue just above its two lower corners.
Expected Outcome Depending on the flexibility of the tissue used, it may lengthen by 1.5–2 cm when it is stretched. The tissue will suddenly tear when tugged.
Think It Over The tissue is like the ground along a fault in that both absorb some degree of tension force without breaking but snap suddenly when an abrupt, strong force is applied. The more stress that builds up in the ground, the greater the likelihood of a sudden earthquake.

SECTION 4 Monitoring Faults

DISCOVER ACTIVITY

Can Stress Be Measured?

1. Unfold a facial tissue and lay it flat on your desk.
2. Measure the length of the tissue with a ruler.
3. Grasping the ends of the tissue with both hands, gently pull it. As you are stretching it, hold the tissue against the ruler and measure its length again.
4. Stretch the tissue once more, but this time give it a hard tug.

Think It Over
Drawing Conclusions How is the tissue like the ground along a fault? How might measuring stress in the ground help in predicting an earthquake?

GUIDE FOR READING
- ◆ **How do geologists monitor faults?**
- ◆ **How do geologists determine earthquake risk?**

Reading Tip **As you read, make a list of devices for monitoring earthquakes. Write a sentence about each.**

The small town of Parkfield, California, lies on the San Andreas fault about halfway between Los Angeles and San Francisco. Geologists are fascinated by Parkfield because the town had a strong earthquake about every 22 years between 1857 and 1966. Scientists have not found any other place on Earth where the time from one earthquake to the next has been so regular.

In the early 1980s, geologists predicted that a strong earthquake was going to occur in Parkfield between 1985 and 1993. The geologists eagerly set up their instruments—and waited. They waited year after year for the predicted earthquake. But it didn't happen. Finally, several medium-sized earthquakes rumbled along the San Andreas fault near Parkfield in 1993–1994.

Did these quakes take the place of the larger earthquake that geologists had expected? Or had the San Andreas fault itself changed, breaking the pattern of 22 years between quakes? Geologists still don't know the answers to these questions. Nonetheless, geologists continue to monitor the San Andreas fault. Someday, they may find a way to predict when and where an earthquake will occur.

Figure 24 This laser beam detects movement along the San Andreas Fault in Parkfield, California.

READING STRATEGIES

Reading Tip Encourage students to describe each monitoring device in their own words rather than copy the text information. Let students share their sentences in a follow-up class discussion. Guide students to agree on one "best sentence" for each device that incorporates the most important points mentioned in students' sentences.

Caption Writing Ask each student to write a new caption for Figure 24 that briefly describes how a laser-ranging device works and explains why detecting movement along a fault may help geologists predict future earthquakes in that area.

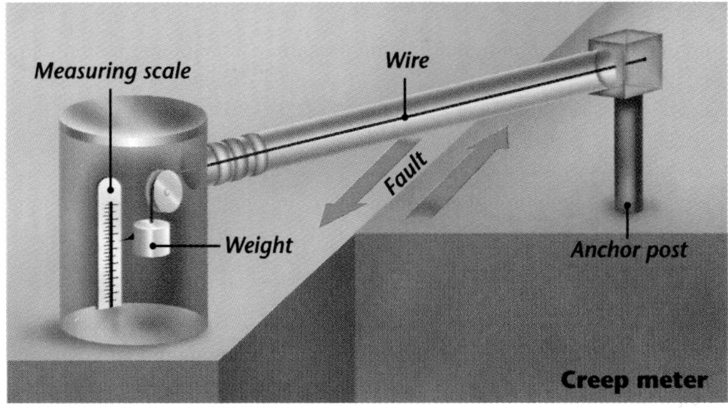

Figure 25 A creep meter can be used to measure movement along a strike-slip fault.

Devices that Monitor Faults

In trying to predict earthquakes, geologists have invented instruments to record the ground movements that occur along faults. **To observe these changes, geologists put in place instruments that measure stress and deformation in the crust.** Geologists hypothesize that such changes signal an approaching earthquake.

Unfortunately, earthquakes almost always strike without warning. The only clue may be a slight rise or fall in the elevation and tilt of the land. Instruments that geologists use to monitor these movements include creep meters, laser-ranging devices, tiltmeters, and satellites.

Creep Meters A creep meter uses a wire stretched across a fault to measure horizontal movement of the ground. On one side of the fault, the wire is anchored to a post. On the other side, the wire is attached to a weight that can slide if the fault moves. Geologists can measure the amount that the fault has moved by measuring how much the weight has moved against a measuring scale.

Laser-Ranging Devices A laser-ranging device uses a laser beam to detect even tiny fault movements. The device calculates any change in the time needed for the laser beam to travel to a reflector and bounce back. Thus, the device can detect any change in distance to the reflector.

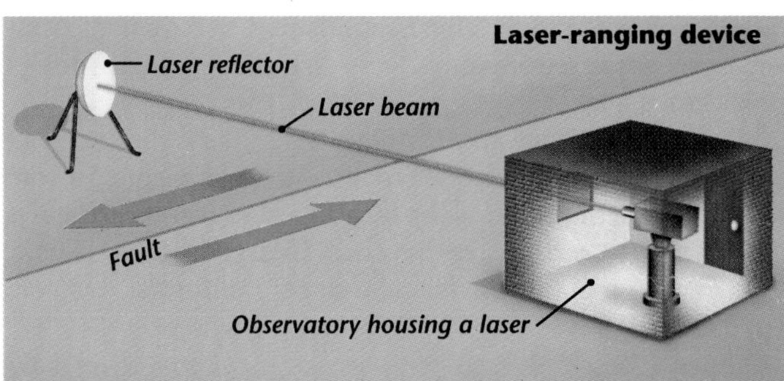

Figure 26 A laser-ranging device monitors fault movement by bouncing a laser beam off a reflector on the other side of the fault. *Comparing and Contrasting How are a laser-ranging device and a creep meter (shown above) similar? How are they different?*

2 Facilitate

Devices that Monitor Faults

Including All Students

After students read about monitoring faults, ask: **What might be happening deep under the ground to cause small changes in the elevation or tilt of the land surface before an earthquake?** *(The blocks of rock might be moving just slightly along a normal or reverse fault. In a normal fault, the hanging wall's surface would fall. In a reverse fault, its surface would rise.)* **What types of changes might indicate movement along a strike-slip fault?** *(Sideways distortions in objects that cross the fault, such as roads, fences, and so forth)* **learning modality: logical/mathematical**

Inquiry Challenge

ACTIVITY

Materials *clay or other material to represent fault blocks; popsicle sticks, wooden matchsticks, or paper clips for posts; metal washer or other small weight; string or wire; mirror; penlight*
Time *20 minutes*

Challenge students to devise a simple model of a creep meter or a laser-ranging device based on a description and diagram on this page. Let students use the model to demonstrate how the device indicates land movements along a strike-slip fault, a normal fault, and a reverse fault. **learning modality: logical/mathematical**

Program Resources

◆ **Teaching Resources** 2-4 Lesson Plan, p. 59; 2-4 Section Summary, p. 60

Media and Technology

Audiotapes English-Spanish Summary 2-4

Answers to Self-Assessment

Caption Question

Figure 26 *Similarity:* Both measure movement along a fault. *Differences:* A creep meter measures horizontal movement only; a laser-ranging device measures any change in distance from the reflector. A creep meter provides gross measurements; a laser-ranging device provides precise measurements.

Ongoing Assessment

Oral Presentation Have students explain how measuring changes in the land along a fault might help scientists predict earthquakes.

Devices that Monitor Faults, continued

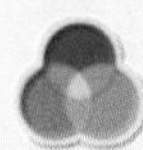

Integrating Space Science

Ask: **Which of the other three kinds of fault-monitoring devices is a satellite monitor like, and why?** *(A laser-ranging device; both involve bouncing a signal off something.)* **What other kinds of measurements are made by bouncing a signal off something?** *(Students may be familiar with sonar and radar used to measure the depths and contours of the ocean floor.)* **learning modality: logical/mathematical**

Language Arts CONNECTION

Provide newspaper articles about one or more major earthquakes, and have students circle the words or phrases that identify Who, What, Where, When, and Why.

In Your Journal Let students share their bulletins by role-playing newscasters and reading them aloud.

Monitoring Risk in the United States

Including All Students

Encourage interested students to research the locations and dates (and magnitudes, if known) of notable earthquakes that have occurred in the continental United States, Alaska, and Hawaii during the past 200 years. Suggest that they compile the data chronologically in a class master chart. Let students label a large U.S. map with tags identifying the earthquake locations, dates, and magnitudes. Students could also compare the locations of the earthquakes that occurred in the continental U.S. with the risk areas shown in Figure 28. **cooperative learning**

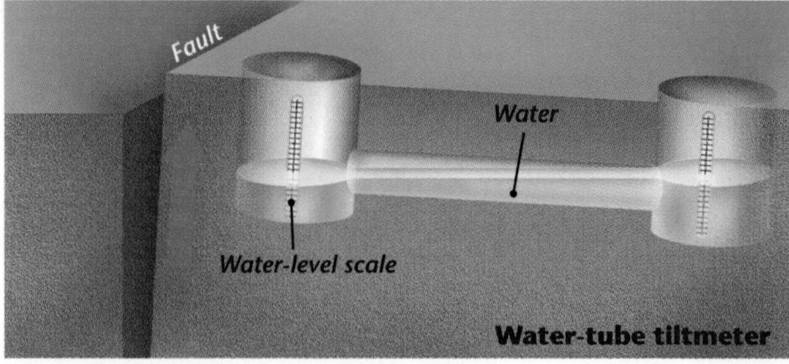

Figure 27 A tiltmeter monitors vertical movement along a fault.

Tiltmeters A tiltmeter measures tilting of the ground. If you have ever used a carpenter's level, you have used a type of tiltmeter. The tiltmeters used by seismologists consist of two bulbs that are filled with a liquid and connected by a hollow stem. Look at the drawing of a tiltmeter in Figure 27. Notice that if the land rises or falls even slightly, the liquid will flow from one bulb to the other. Each bulb contains a measuring scale to measure the depth of the liquid in that bulb. Geologists read the scales to measure the amount of tilt occurring along the fault.

INTEGRATING SPACE SCIENCE **Satellite Monitors** Besides ground-based instruments, geologists use satellites equipped with radar to make images of faults. The satellite bounces radio waves off the ground. As the waves echo back into space, the satellite records them. The time it takes for the radio waves to make their round trip provides precise measurements of the distance to the ground. The distance from the ground to the satellite changes with every change in the ground surface. By comparing different images of the same area taken at different times, geologists detect small changes in elevation. These changes in elevation result when stress deforms the ground along a fault.

☑ *Checkpoint* *What do fault-monitoring instruments measure?*

Language Arts CONNECTION

In an emergency broadcast, the television newscaster must not only provide information on the disaster, but also grab the viewer's attention. To state the facts as briefly as possible, journalists use the 5 W's: Who, What, Where, When, and Why.

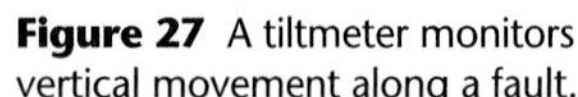

In Your Journal

You are a local newscaster presenting the news. During your broadcast, you receive information that a major earthquake has struck a city in another part of the country. You must interrupt the regular news to present an emergency news bulletin. Write that bulletin, following the 5 W's.

Monitoring Risk in the United States

Even with data from many sources, geologists can't predict when and where a quake will strike. Usually, stress along a fault increases until an earthquake occurs. Yet sometimes stress builds up along a fault, but an earthquake fails to occur. Or, one or more earthquakes may relieve stress along another part of the fault. Exactly what will happen remains uncertain—that's why geologists cannot predict earthquakes.

Geologists do know that earthquakes are likely wherever plate movement stores energy in the rock along faults. **Geologists can determine earthquake risk by locating where faults are active and where past earthquakes have occurred.** In the United States, the risk is highest in the states of California, Oregon,

Background

Facts and Figures The first and only successful short-range earthquake prediction occurred in 1975, when Chinese seismologists forecast a large earthquake that was about to hit Liaoning Province. About 3 million residents were evacuated from a major city, sparing thousands of lives.

In the 1980s, the U.S. Geological Survey conducted a survey that predicted the long-range probability of earthquakes along the San Andreas fault during the 30-year period from 1988 to 2018. The Parkfield section of the fault was given the highest probability, 90 percent. Then in 1994, a 6.7 magnitude quake struck the Los Angeles community of Northridge, some 50 km from the San Andreas fault. This quake caused seismologists to recognize the hazard of blind thrust faults, which are associated with the main fault but are unknown until they break.

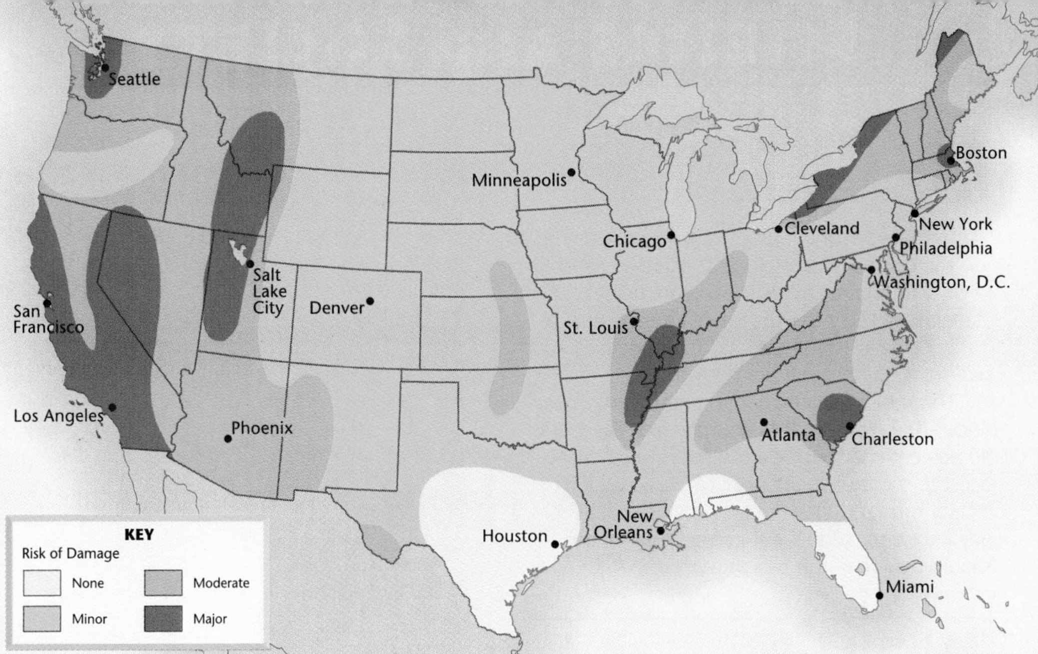

Figure 28 The map shows areas of the United States, excluding Alaska and Hawaii, where earthquakes are likely to occur and the relative damage they are likely to cause. *Interpreting Maps Where are damaging earthquakes least likely to occur? Most likely to occur?*

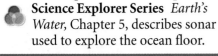

Washington, and Alaska. The risk of quakes is high because that's where the Pacific and North American plates meet.

Other regions of the United States also have some risk of earthquakes. Serious earthquakes are rare east of the Rockies. Nonetheless, the region has experienced some of the most powerful quakes in the nation's history. Scientists hypothesize that the continental plate forming most of North America is under stress. This stress could disturb faults that formed millions of years ago. Today, these faults lie hidden beneath thick layers of soil and rock. Find your state in Figure 28 to determine your area's risk of a damaging quake.

Section 4 Review

1. What equipment do geologists use to monitor the movement of faults?
2. What two factors do geologists consider when determining earthquake risk for a region?
3. Explain how satellites can be used to collect data on earthquake faults.
4. **Thinking Critically Making Generalizations** Why can't scientists predict the exact time and place an earthquake is going to occur?

Check Your Progress

CHAPTER PROJECT 2

Use what you have learned about making buildings earthquake resistant to repair and improve your structure. Test your model again. Are your changes successful in preventing damage? Make additional repairs and improvements to your structure.

3 Assess

Section 4 Review Answers

1. Creep meters, laser-ranging devices, tiltmeters, satellites
2. The locations of active faults and the locations of past earthquakes
3. The satellite bounces radio waves off the ground and measures the time required for a round trip. If the ground elevation changes, the time for the bounce-back will change. By comparing bounce-back times, scientists can detect small changes in elevation.
4. Fault-block movements occur deep under ground, and instruments monitor only surface movements. Scientists do not fully understand the relationship between slight deformations in the land surface and the likelihood of an earthquake. Not every area throughout the world is monitored with instruments. (Accept other reasonable explanations.)

Check Your Progress

CHAPTER PROJECT 2

Encourage students to make use of the information in Section 3 as they consider improvements to their models—particularly ways to convert them to base-isolated structures. Remind students to test their improvements and, if necessary, make repairs and further changes before they settle on a final design for the class presentation.

Program Resources

- **Teaching Resources** 2-4 Review and Reinforce, p. 61; 2-4 Enrich, p. 62
- **Science Explorer Series** *Earth's Water,* Chapter 5, describes sonar used to explore the ocean floor.

Media and Technology

Interactive Student Tutorial CD-ROM F-2

Answers to Self-Assessment

Checkpoint

The movement of the ground along a fault—horizontal movement, tilting, and changes in elevation

Caption Question

Figure 28 *Least likely:* areas on the map with no shading; *Most likely:* areas on the map with the darkest shading.

Performance Assessment

Oral Presentation Have students name the four types of fault-monitoring devices described in this section and describe how they work.

Science and Society

What's the Risk of an Earthquake?

Purpose

To challenge students to identify the drawbacks and benefits of modifying structures located in areas where there is some possibility of serious earthquake damage, even though major earthquakes are infrequent, and develop an earthquake-preparedness plan for critical structures.

Panel Discussion

Time 80–90 minutes

After students have read the introductory text and the three paragraphs under The Issues, ask: **If you owned a house in the New Madrid fault area, would you want to renovate your house to protect it against possible earthquake damage? Why, or why not?** Let students discuss this issue freely until opposing viewpoints are clear. Then ask: **What if you were a contractor who was building a new housing development? Would you make the houses more earthquake-proof?** After students discuss this question, list *home-owners* and *building contractors* on the board, and ask: **What other groups of people would be interested in earthquake preparedness?** *(Students may mention community officials, safety associations such as the Red Cross, directors of utility companies, hospital directors, highway engineers, and the like. Add these groups to the list as students identify them.)* Divide the class into as many groups as are listed on the board. Provide time for each group to meet and discuss the pros and cons of spending funds on earthquake preparedness from that group's viewpoint. Ask each group to select one representative to serve on an "Earthquake-Preparedness Committee" to discuss and decide on how to spend the funds that the community has received.

What's the Risk of an Earthquake?

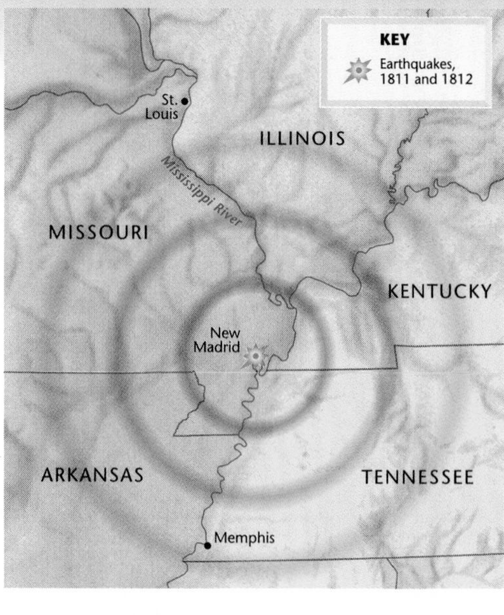

The New Madrid fault system stretches beneath the central Mississippi River Valley. East of the Rocky Mountains, this is the region of the United States most likely to experience an earthquake. But because the faults are hidden under soil and sediment, the hazards are not obvious.

This region has not had a serious earthquake since 1812. Yet scientists estimate that there is a 90 percent chance that a moderate earthquake will occur in this area in the next 50 years. Which locations might be at risk for heavy damage? No one knows for sure. What preparations, if any, should people of this region make?

The Issues

How Much Money Should People Spend? In areas where earthquakes are rare, such as the New Madrid fault region, communities face hard choices. Should they spend money for earthquake preparation now in order to cut costs later? Or should they save the money and risk the consequences?

Which Buildings Should Be Modified? It's clear that the best way to save lives is to make buildings that can withstand severe shaking. Since damaged or collapsing buildings cause most injuries and deaths during earthquakes, modifying existing buildings could save lives. Unfortunately building renovations are costly.

Most new houses can withstand moderate earthquakes. But many older houses—especially brick or masonry houses—are not safe. Unfortunately, few homeowners can afford the cost of making their houses safer. They might need financial aid or a tax break to help them make these changes.

What Other Structures Need Improvement? Imagine what would happen if your community were without utility stations and lines for electricity, gas, and water, or without bridges, schools, and hospitals. Engineers who understand earthquake hazards have worked out design standards to reduce damage to these structures. Today, many cities follow these standards in their building codes. But not all structures can be made earthquake-safe. Furthermore, some structures are more crucial for public health and safety than others.

You Decide

1. Identify the Problem
Summarize the dilemma that communities face in regard to earthquake preparations. Which structures in a community are most important to make earthquake-resistant?

2. Analyze the Options
Consider what would happen if communities spent more money, less money, or nothing on earthquake preparations. In each case, who would benefit? Who might be harmed?

3. Find a Solution
Your community near the New Madrid fault system has received a large sum of money to spend on earthquake preparedness. Develop a plan for building and modifying structures. Explain and defend your use of funds.

Background

Facts and Figures Although the central Mississippi River valley is considered to be at lower earthquake risk than other areas of the United States, it was along the New Madrid fault that the most severe earthquakes in U.S. history occurred—a series of quakes that started in December 1811 and continued until March 1812.

The New Madrid earthquakes shook more than two thirds of the United States and were even felt in Canada. The quakes changed the level of the land by as much as 6 m, altered the course of the Mississippi River, and created new lakes, including Reelfoot Lake in Tennessee and Lake St. Francis west of the Mississippi. Because the area was sparsely populated at the time, the quakes caused no known deaths.

STUDY GUIDE

Section 1 Earth's Crust in Motion

Key Ideas

- Stresses on Earth's crust produce compression, tension, and shearing in rock.
- Faults are cracks in Earth's crust that result from stress.
- Faulting and folding of the crust cause mountains and other features to form on the surface.

Key Terms

earthquake
stress
deformation
shearing
tension
compression
fault
strike-slip fault
normal fault
hanging wall
footwall
reverse fault
fault-block mountain
folds
anticline
syncline
plateau

Section 2 Measuring Earthquakes

Key Ideas

- As seismic waves travel through Earth, they carry the energy of an earthquake from the focus to the surface.
- Earthquakes produce two types of seismic waves, P waves and S waves, that travel out in all directions from the focus of an earthquake.
- Today, the moment magnitude scale is used to determine the magnitude of an earthquake. Other scales that geologists have used to rate earthquakes include the Mercalli scale and the Richter scale.

Key Terms

focus
epicenter
seismic waves
P waves
S waves
surface waves
seismograph
magnitude
Mercalli scale
Richter scale
moment magnitude scale

Section 3 Earthquake Hazards and Safety

Key Ideas

- Earthquakes can damage buildings and other structures through shaking or liquefaction of the ground, tsunamis, and landslides or avalanches.
- New buildings can be designed to withstand earthquakes; old buildings can be modified to make them more earthquake-resistant.
- For personal safety indoors during an earthquake, drop, cover, and hold under a desk or table, or against an interior wall.

Key Terms

liquefaction
aftershock
tsunamis
base-isolated building

Section 4 Monitoring Faults

INTEGRATING TECHNOLOGY

Key Ideas

- Geologists use instruments to measure deformation and stress along faults.
- Scientists determine earthquake risk by monitoring active faults and by studying faults where past earthquakes have occurred.

ACTIVITY
USING THE INTERNET
www.science-explorer.phschool.com

CHAPTER 2 REVIEW

Program Resources

- **Teaching Resources** Chapter 2 Project Scoring Rubric, p. 46; Chapter 2 Performance Assessment, pp. 175–177; Chapter 2 Test, pp. 178–181

Media and Technology

Interactive Student Tutorial CD-ROM F-2

Computer Test Bank Chapter 2 Test

Extend

Suggest that students contact their local government representatives to find out whether the community has any plans in place for dealing with earthquake preparedness.

You Decide

1. Students' summaries should include the major points presented in the text. Students should list structures related to public health and safety as the most important to protect against damage.
2. Encourage students to carefully think through the repercussions of more, less, and no funding for earthquake preparedness from the viewpoints of the groups they identified in their initial discussion.
3. Students may rely on the points identified in the panel discussion or may present their own ideas. In either case, make sure each student gives a well-reasoned rationale for use of the funds.

CHAPTER 2 REVIEW

Reviewing Content:

Multiple Choice

1. b **2.** c **3.** c **4.** d **5.** b

True or False

6. stress **7.** normal faults **8.** focus
9. true **10.** true

Checking Concepts

11. Stress changes the crust's volume or shape through compression, tension, and shearing.

12. Where two plates move away from each other, tension forces create many normal faults. When two normal faults form parallel to each other, a block of rock is left lying between them. As the hanging wall of each normal fault slips downward, the block in between moves upward, forming a fault-block mountain.

13. Compression forms folded mountains. Compression shortens and thickens the crust so it bends slowly without breaking. If the fold bends upward into an arch, the fold is called an anticline. If the fold bends downward to form a bowl, the fold is called a syncline.

14. A plateau is a large area of flat land that is elevated high above sea level. A plateau may form when vertical faults push up a large, flat block of rock.

15. Both the moment magnitude scale and the Richter scale measure earthquake strength. The Richter scale rates the size of seismic waves as measured by a mechanical seismograph. The moment magnitude scale estimates the total energy released by an earthquake. The Richter scale provides accurate measurements for small, nearby earthquakes but does not work well for large or distant earthquakes. The moment magnitude scale can be used to rate earthquakes of all sizes and at all distances.

16. Geologists use fault-monitoring devices to measure stress and deformation in the crust—horizontal movement along a strike-slip fault and tilting, upward movement, or downward movement along normal or reverse faults.

17. Students' letters should include a brief description of what a fault is and why earthquakes commonly occur along faults. Evaluate students' recommendations on the basis of their practicality, benefits, and attention to critical structures such as hospitals, highways, and utilities.

Thinking Visually

18. a. Tension **b.** Shearing **c.** Reverse fault **d.** Strike-slip fault *Title:* Answers may vary. Sample title, Stress Forces in Earth's Crust

Applying Skills

19. P waves arrive first, then S waves, and finally surface waves. Surface waves produce the largest ground movement.

20. approximately 1 minute and 50 seconds

21. The up-and-down spikes of the waves would be much less, perhaps even very smooth. If an aftershock occurred, the spikes would resume again.

22. The second station is farther away from the earthquake's epicenter.

CHAPTER 2 REVIEW

Reviewing Content

For more review of key concepts, see the Interactive Student Tutorial CD-ROM.

Multiple Choice

Chose the letter of the answer that best completes each statement.

1. Shearing is the force in Earth's crust that
a. squeezes the crust together.
b. pushes the crust in opposite directions.
c. forces the crust to bend and fold.
d. stretches the crust apart.

2. When the hanging wall of a fault slips downward with respect to the footwall, the result is a
a. reverse fault.
b. syncline.
c. normal fault.
d. strike-slip fault.

3. A seismograph measures
a. energy released during an earthquake.
b. friction forces along a fault.
c. ground motion during an earthquake.
d. movement along a fault.

4. Geologists use the difference in the arrival times of P waves and S waves at a seismograph to determine
a. the magnitude of the earthquake.
b. the depth of the earthquake's focus.
c. the strength of the surface waves.
d. the distance to the epicenter.

5. To monitor the upward movement along a fault, geologists would probably use a
a. laser-ranging device.
b. tiltmeter.
c. seismograph.
d. creep meter.

True or False

If the statement is true, write true. If it is false, change the underlined word or words to make the statement true.

6. Deformation is the breaking, tilting, and folding of rocks caused by <u>liquefaction</u>.

7. Rock uplifted by <u>strike-slip faults</u> creates fault-block mountains.

8. An earthquake's <u>epicenter</u> is located deep underground.

9. As <u>S waves</u> move through the ground, they cause it to compress and then expand.

10. <u>Tsunamis</u> are triggered by earthquakes originating beneath the ocean floor.

Checking Concepts

11. How does stress affect Earth's crust?

12. Explain the process that forms a fault-block mountain.

13. What type of stress in the crust results in the formation of folded mountains? Explain your answer.

14. What are plateaus and how do they form?

15. Explain how the moment magnitude and Richter scales of earthquake measurement are similar and how they are different.

16. When geologists monitor a fault, what kinds of data do they collect? Explain.

17. Writing to Learn You are a geologist studying earthquake risk in an eastern state. Your data show that a major earthquake might happen there within 5 years. Write a letter to the governor of your state explaining why there is an earthquake hazard there and recommending how your state should prepare for the earthquake.

Thinking Visually

18. Concept Map Copy the concept map about stress on a separate piece of paper. Then complete it and add a title. (For more on concept maps, see the Skills Handbook.)

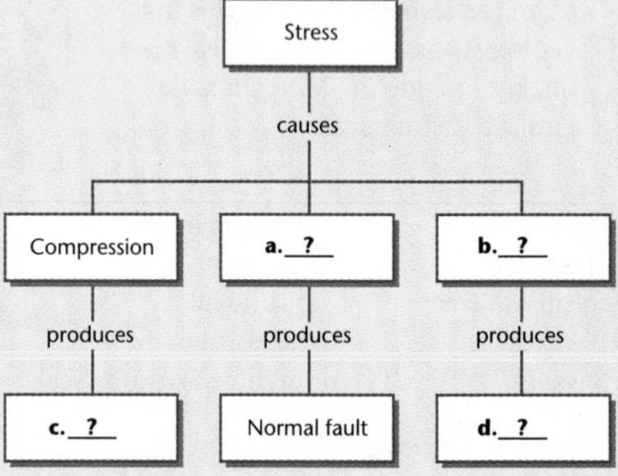

84 ◆ F

CHAPTER 2 REVIEW

Applying Skills

The graph shows the seismograph record for an earthquake. The y-axis of the graph shows the up-and-down shaking in millimeters detected at the seismograph station. The x-axis shows time in minutes.

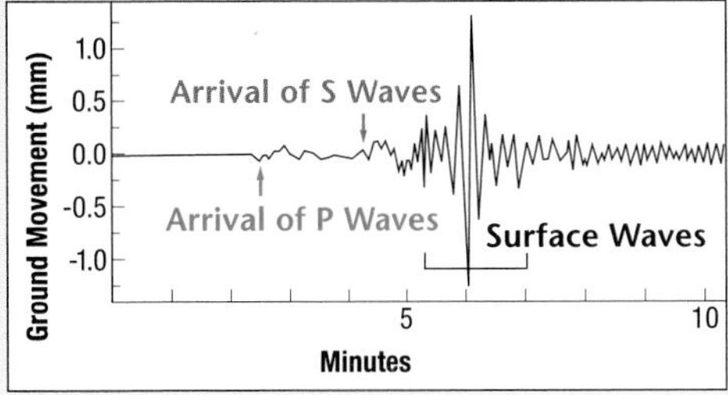

19. **Interpreting Diagrams** In what order do the seismic waves arrive at the seismograph station? Which type of seismic wave produces the largest ground movement?
20. **Interpreting Diagrams** What is the difference in arrival times for the P waves and S waves?
21. **Predicting** What would the seismograph record look like several hours after this earthquake? How would it change if an aftershock occurred?
22. **Drawing Conclusions** If the difference in arrival times for P waves and S waves is 5 minutes longer at a second seismograph station than at the first station, what can you conclude about the location of the second station?

Thinking Critically

23. **Classifying** How would you classify a fault in which the hanging wall has slid up and over the footwall?
24. **Comparing and Contrasting** Compare and contrast P waves and S waves.
25. **Predicting** A community has just built a street across a strike-slip fault that has frequent earthquakes. How will movement along the fault affect the street?
26. **Applying Concepts** If you were building a house in an earthquake-prone area, what steps would you take to limit potential damage in an earthquake?

Performance Assessment

CHAPTER PROJECT 2

Wrap Up

Presenting Your Project Before testing how your model withstands a major earthquake, explain to your classmates how and why you made changes to your model. When your model is tested, make notes of how it withstands the earthquake.

Reflect and Record How would a real earthquake compare with the method used to test your model? If it were a real building, could your structure withstand an earthquake? How could you improve your model?

Getting Involved

In Your Home If you live in an eathquake risk area, work with your family to develop an earthquake safety plan. The plan should tell family members what to do for their safety during an earthquake. It should list items your family would need if a quake cut electrical power and water lines. It should also explain where to shut off the gas if your home has a natural gas line.

Thinking Critically

23. It should be classified as a reverse fault.

24. Both P waves and S waves are seismic waves sent out from the earthquake's focus deep under ground. P waves arrive first at a seismograph. They compress and expand the ground like an accordion. P waves travel through both solids and liquids. S waves arrive second at a seismograph. They vibrate from side to side and push the ground up and down, back and forth. S waves cannot move through liquids.

Program Resources

◆ **Inquiry Skills Activity Book** Provides teaching and review of all inquiry skills

25. The street will break where it crosses the fault, and the two sides will be moved horizontally in opposite directions.

26. Build the home on solid rock and in a flat area rather than on loose soil and on a hillside. Build as far as possible from the fault itself and away from coastal areas that might be exposed to tsunamis. Use brackets to secure brick chimneys. Use connectors to strengthen joints in the house's frame. Use plywood panels to strengthen cripple walls beneath the house and on ceiling joists around the chimney to protect against falling bricks. Bolt the house to its foundation.

Performance Assessment

Wrap Up

Presenting Your Project Give each student an opportunity to explain any changes made to the model based on the results of previous tests. Then let students test their models for the last time and make final changes before their class presentations. Remind students to note any further improvements they might want to make.

Reflect and Record Use the two questions in the student text as the basis for a whole-class discussion. Then let students write in their journals.

Getting Involved

In Your Home If students made a survey of their homes in the TE activity Exploring An Earthquake-Safe House, page 75, point out that this activity is different because it focuses on personal safety and emergency planning. Strongly encourage students to do the safety planning with their families. If students do not live in an earthquake-risk area, suggest that they work with their families to devise a safety plan for another type of natural disaster that does occur in their area, such as a flood, blizzard, or tornado.

CHAPTER 3

Volcanoes

Sections	Time	Student Edition Activities	ACTIVITY Other Activities
CHAPTER PROJECT 3 **Volcanoes and People** p. 87	Ongoing (2–3 weeks)	Check Your Progress, p. 91 Check Your Progress, p. 107 Check Your Progress, p. 112 Wrap Up, p. 115	
1 **Volcanoes and Plate Tectonics** pp. 88–92 ◆ Identify where Earth's volcanic regions are found, and explain why they are found there.	2–3 periods/ 1–$1\frac{1}{2}$ blocks	**Discover** Where Are Volcanoes Found on Earth's Surface?, p. 88 **Try This** Hot Spot in a Box, p. 91 **Skills Lab** Mapping Earthquakes and Volcanoes, p. 92	**TE** Including All Students, p.90
2 **Volcanic Activity** pp. 93–102 ◆ Describe what happens when a volcano erupts. ◆ Explain how the two types of volcanic eruptions differ. ◆ Identify some hazards of volcanoes.	4–5 periods/ 2–$2\frac{1}{2}$ blocks	**Discover** What Are Volcanic Rocks Like?, p. 93 **Try This** Gases in Magma, p. 94 **Science at Home,** p. 102	**TE** Building Inquiry Skills: Inferring, p. 94 **TE** Inquiry Challenge, p. 96 **TE** Building Inquiry Skills: Comparing and Contrasting, p. 96 **TE** Demonstration, p. 99 **TE** Building Inquiry Skills: Inferring, p. 101 **IES** "The Glory of Ancient Rome," pp. 20–23 **ISLM** F-3, "Predicting Lava Flows"
3 **Volcanic Landforms** pp. 103–109 ◆ Identify landforms that lava creates on Earth's surface. ◆ Explain how magma that hardens beneath the surface creates landforms.	3–4 periods/ $1\frac{1}{2}$–2 blocks	**Discover** How Can Volcanic Activity Change Earth's Surface?, p. 103 **Real-World Lab** Gelatin Volcanoes, pp. 108–109	**TE** Inquiry Challenge, p. 105 **IES** "The Glory of Ancient Rome," pp. 24–25
4 *INTEGRATING SPACE SCIENCE* **Volcanoes in the Solar System** pp. 110–112 ◆ Explain how volcanoes on Mars and Venus compare with volcanoes on Earth. ◆ Describe the volcanic activity found on the moons of Jupiter and Neptune.	1 period/ $\frac{1}{2}$ block	**Discover** What Forces Shaped the Surface of Io?, p. 110	**TE** Using the Visuals, p. 111
Study Guide/Chapter Review pp. 113–115	1 period/ $\frac{1}{2}$ block		**ISAB** Provides teaching and review of all inquiry skills

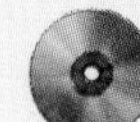

For Standard or Block Schedule The Resource Pro® CD-ROM gives you maximum flexibility for planning your instruction for any type of schedule. Resource Pro® contains Planning Express®, an advanced scheduling program, as well as the entire contents of the Teaching Resources and the Computer Test Bank.

CHAPTER PLANNING GUIDE

Program Resources	Assessment Strategies	Media and Technology
TR Chapter 3 Project Teacher Notes, pp. 68–69 **TR** Chapter 3 Project Student Materials, pp. 70–73 **TR** Chapter 3 Project Scoring Rubric, p. 74	**SE** Performance Assessment: Chapter 3 Project Wrap Up, p. 115 **TE** Check Your Progress, pp. 91, 107, 112 **TR** Chapter 3 Project Scoring Rubric, p. 74	
TR 3-1 Lesson Plan, p. 75 **TR** 3-1 Section Summary, p. 76 **TR** 3-1 Review and Reinforce, p. 77 **TR** 3-1 Enrich, p. 78 **TR** Skills Lab blackline masters, pp. 91–93	**SE** Section 1 Review, p. 91 **SE** Analyze and Conclude, p. 92 **TE** Ongoing Assessment, p. 89 **TE** Performance Assessment, p. 91 **TR** 3-1 Review and Reinforce, p. 77	Exploring Earth Science Videodisc, Unit 3 Side 1, "Everything on Your Plate" Audiotapes, English-Spanish Summary 3-1 Transparencies 12, "Earth's Active Volcanoes"; 13, "Volcanoes at Converging Boundaries" Interactive Student Tutorial CD-ROM, F-3
TR 3-2 Lesson Plan, p. 79 **TR** 3-2 Section Summary, p. 80 **TR** 3-2 Review and Reinforce, p. 81 **TR** 3-2 Enrich, p. 82 **SES** *Earth's Waters,* Chapter 2	**SE** Section 2 Review, p. 102 **TE** Ongoing Assessment, pp. 95, 97, 99, 101 **TE** Performance Assessment, p. 102 **TR** 3-2 Review and Reinforce, p. 81	Audiotapes, English-Spanish Summary 3-2 Transparency 14, "Exploring a Volcano" Interactive Student Tutorial CD-ROM, F-3
TR 3-3 Lesson Plan, p. 83 **TR** 3-3 Section Summary, p. 84 **TR** 3-3 Review and Reinforce, p. 85 **TR** 3-3 Enrich, p. 86 **TR** 3-3 Real-World Lab blackline masters, pp. 94–95	**SE** Section 3 Review, p. 107 **SE** Analyze and Conclude, p. 109 **TE** Ongoing Assessment, p. 105 **TE** Performance Assessment, p. 107 **TR** 3-3 Review and Reinforce, p. 85	Exploring Earth Science Videodisc, Unit 2 Side 2, "Flying Over America" Audiotapes, English-Spanish Summary 3-3 Transparency 15, "Exploring Volcanic Mountains" Interactive Student Tutorial CD-ROM, F-3
TR 3-4 Lesson Plan, p. 87 **TR** 3-4 Section Summary, p. 88 **TR** 3-4 Review and Reinforce, p. 89 **TR** 3-4 Enrich, p. 90	**SE** Section 4 Review, p. 112 **TE** Ongoing Assessment, pp. 111 **TE** Performance Assessment, p. 112 **TR** 3-4 Review and Reinforce, p. 89	Audiotapes, English-Spanish Summary 3-4 Interactive Student Tutorial CD-ROM, F-3
TR Chapter 3 Performance Assessment, pp. 182–184 **TR** Chapter 3 Test, pp. 185–188	**SE** Chapter 3 Review, pp. 113–115 **TR** Chapter 3 Performance Assessment, pp. 182–184 **TR** Chapter 3 Test, pp. 185–188 **CTB** Chapter 3 Test	Interactive Student Tutorial CD-ROM, F-3 Computer Test Bank, Chapter 3 Test Science Explorer Internet Site

Key: **SE** Student Edition
CTB Computer Test Bank
ISAB Inquiry Skills Activity Book
TE Teacher's Edition
SES Science Explorer Series Text
PTA Product Testing Activities by *Consumer Reports*
TR Teaching Resources
ISLM Integrated Science Laboratory Manual
IES Interdisciplinary Explorations Series

Meeting the National Science Education Standards and AAAS Benchmarks

National Science Education Standards	Benchmarks for Science Literacy	Unifying Themes
Science As Inquiry (Content Standard A) ◆ **Develop descriptions, explanations, predictions, and models using evidence** Students interpret data to find a pattern in the locations of earthquakes and volcanoes. Students model the flow of magma inside a volcano. *(Skills Lab; Real-World Lab)* ◆ **Communicate scientific procedures and explanations** Students make a documentary about life in a volcanic region. *(Chapter Project)* **Earth and Space Science** (Content Standard D) ◆ **Structure of the Earth system** Most volcanoes occur along diverging plate boundaries or in subduction zones. A volcano erupts when magma breaks through Earth's crust and lava flows over the surface. Volcanoes create a variety of landforms. *(Sections 1, 2, 3; Skills Lab)* ◆ **Earth in the solar system** Space probes show evidence of volcanic activity on other planets and moons. *(Section 4)* **Science in Personal and Social Perspectives** (Content Standard F) ◆ **Natural hazards** A volcanic eruption can cause great damage. Volcanic eruptions have affected the land and people around them. *(Section 2; Science & History)* ◆ **Risks and benefits** Students research how volcanoes have affected people in volcanic regions. *(Chapter Project)*	**1B Scientific Inquiry** Students research how volcanoes have affected people in volcanic regions. Students interpret data to find a pattern in the locations of earthquakes and volcanoes. Students investigate the flow of magma inside a volcano. *(Chapter Project; Skills Lab; Real-World Lab)* **4A The Universe** Space probes show evidence of volcanic activity on other planets and moons. *(Section 4)* **4C Processes That Shape the Earth** Most volcanoes occur along diverging plate boundaries or in subduction zones. A volcano erupts when magma breaks through Earth's crust and lava flows over the surface. Volcanic eruptions have greatly affected the land and people around them. Volcanoes create a variety of landforms. Magma inside a volcano generally moves in an upward direction. *(Sections 1, 2, 3; Skills Lab; Science & History; Real-World Lab)* **11B Models** Students use a model to investigate the flow of magma inside a volcano. *(Real-World Lab)* **12D Communication Skills** Students make a documentary about life in a volcanic region. Students locate earthquakes and volcanoes on a map using coordinates. *(Chapter Project; Skills Lab)*	◆ **Energy** A hot spot is where magma from the mantle melts through the crust. During a volcanic eruption, gases dissolved in magma rush out, carrying magma with them. *(Sections 1, 2)* ◆ **Evolution** A volcano passes through three stages: active, dormant, extinct. *(Section 2)* ◆ **Patterns of Change** Most volcanoes occur along diverging plate boundaries or in subduction zones. Earthquake zones and volcanic belts are located along plate boundaries. The buildup of lava and magma creates landforms on or beneath Earth's surface. *(Sections 1, 3; Skills Lab)* ◆ **Scale and Structure** All volcanoes have a magma chamber, pipe, and vent. *(Section 2)* ◆ **Systems and Interactions** Students research how volcanoes have affected people living in volcanic regions. A volcano erupts when magma from the mantle breaks through the crust and lava flows over the surface. Volcanic eruptions have affected the land and people around them. Students investigate how magma flows inside a volcano. *(Chapter Project; Section 2; Science & History; Real-World Lab)* ◆ **Unity and Diversity** The silica content of magma helps to determine whether a volcanic eruption is quiet or explosive. Volcanoes create a variety of landforms. There are volcanoes on other planets and moons. *(Sections 2, 3, 4)*

Media and Technology

Exploring Earth Science Videodiscs

◆ **Section 1** "Everything on Your Plate" illustrates how geologic activity occurs at divergent, convergent, and strike-slip plate boundaries.

◆ **Section 3** "Flying Over America" explores the mountains, plains, and plateaus of the United States and identifies the forces that shaped their development.

Interactive Student Tutorial CD-ROM

◆ **Chapter Review** Interactive questions help students to self-assess their mastery of key chapter concepts.

Student Edition Connection Strategies

◆ **Section 1** **Language Arts Connection,** p. 89 

◆ **Section 2** **Social Studies Connection,** p. 98 **Integrating Technology,** p. 99 

◆ **Section 3** **Integrating Environmental Science,** p. 106 

◆ **Section 4** **Integrating Space Science,** pp. 110–112

www.science-explorer.phschool.com

Visit the Science Explorer Internet site to find an up-to-date activity for Chapter 3 of *Inside Earth*.

ACTIVITY	Time (minutes)	Materials *Quantities for one work group*	Skills
Section 1			
Discover, p. 88	10	No special materials are required.	Developing Hypotheses
Try This, p. 91	15–20	**Consumable** cold water, hot water, red food coloring **Nonconsumable** plastic box, small narrow-necked bottle, flat piece of plastic foam	Making Models
Skills Lab, p. 92	40	**Consumable** outline world map showing longitude and latitude (Teaching Resources page 93) **Nonconsumable** 4 pencils of different colors	Interpreting Data, Observing, Inferring
Section 2			
Discover, p. 93	5–10	**Nonconsumable** samples of pumice and obsidian, hand lens	Developing Hypotheses
Try This, p. 94	10–15	**Consumable** 10 g baking soda, 65 mL water, 6 raisins, 65 mL vinegar **Nonconsumable** 1- or 2-liter plastic bottle	Making Models
Science at Home, p. 102	home	**Consumable** cold water, hot water, matches **Nonconsumable** 2 cups, candle	Making Models
Section 3			
Discover, p. 103	10–15	**Consumable** tape, balloon, damp sand, straw **Nonconsumable** box	Making Models
Real-World Lab, pp. 108–109	40	**Consumable** unflavored gelatin mold in bowl, pegboard, red food coloring in water, unlined paper **Nonconsumable** plastic cup, knife, tray, plastic syringe (10 cc), two books (30 cm high), rubber gloves, colored pencils	Developing Hypotheses, Making Models, Observing
Section 4			
Discover, p. 110	5	No special materials are required.	Posing Questions

A list of all materials required for the Student Edition activities can be found on pages T14–T15. You can order Materials Kits by calling 1-800-828-7777 or by accessing the Science Explorer Internet site at **www.science-explorer.phschool.com.**

CHAPTER PROJECT 3

Volcanoes and People

When students first consider volcanoes, they will undoubt-edly think of fiery eruptions and the death, injury, and destruction they cause. As significant as those effects are, other aspects of volcanoes are also important, including their influence on the art, history, and literature of the people living near them, important products obtained or produced from volcanic materials, and the effects of volcanic activity on soil fertility and agriculture. This project encourages students to consider such aspects as well.

Purpose This project will give students an opportunity to investigate a variety of ways in which people have been affected by volcanoes. Student groups will each choose a specific volcanic region and a particular topic for research. Based on their research, the group will prepare a multimedia documentary about the volcanic region for presentation to the rest of the class.

Skills Focus After completing the Chapter 3 Project, students will be able to

- classify the type of volcano chosen for the project;
- draw conclusions from a variety of source materials about the volcano's effects on people living near it;
- communicate how the volcano has affected the people living in a volcanic region in a documentary presentation, using a variety of media.

Project Time Line The project requires two to three weeks to complete. Each group should first choose a volcanic region and investigate possible topics related to its effects on people in the area. After choosing one topic, group members should research information on that topic and take relevant, well-organized notes. (Chapter 3 Project Worksheet 2 on page 73 in Teaching Resources reviews how to take research notes.) Students then should create a storyboard showing each step in the presentation, including the media materials that will be used. Posters, transparencies, videos, and other media should then be prepared—and refined, if needed—and the entire documentary rehearsed before presentation to the class. See Chapter 3 Project Teacher Notes on pages 68–69 in Teaching Resources for more hints and detailed directions.

Possible Materials

- Provide a wide variety of age-appropriate source materials for students to use in their research, including encyclopedias, nonfiction library books, magazine articles, and films on videocassette and CD-ROM. If students have access to the internet in school or at home, encourage them to use that source as well. One appropriate website is Volcano World, at **www.volcano.und.edu**.
- Also provide index cards for taking notes and self-stick removable tags for flagging appropriate information in books.
- When students are ready to prepare their multimedia materials, supply a variety of materials and devices—poster paper, art supplies, acetate sheets for making overhead transparencies, videocameras, and tape recorders for taping songs, background

CHAPTER 3 Volcanoes

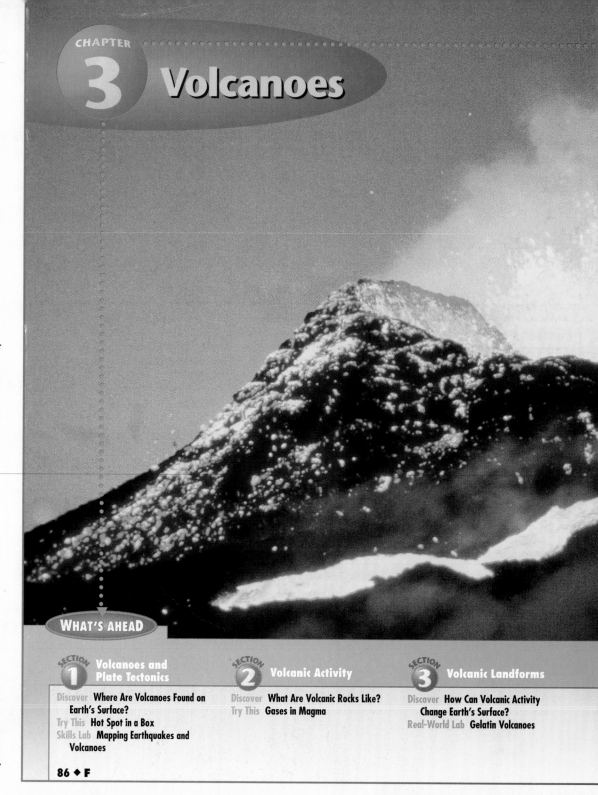

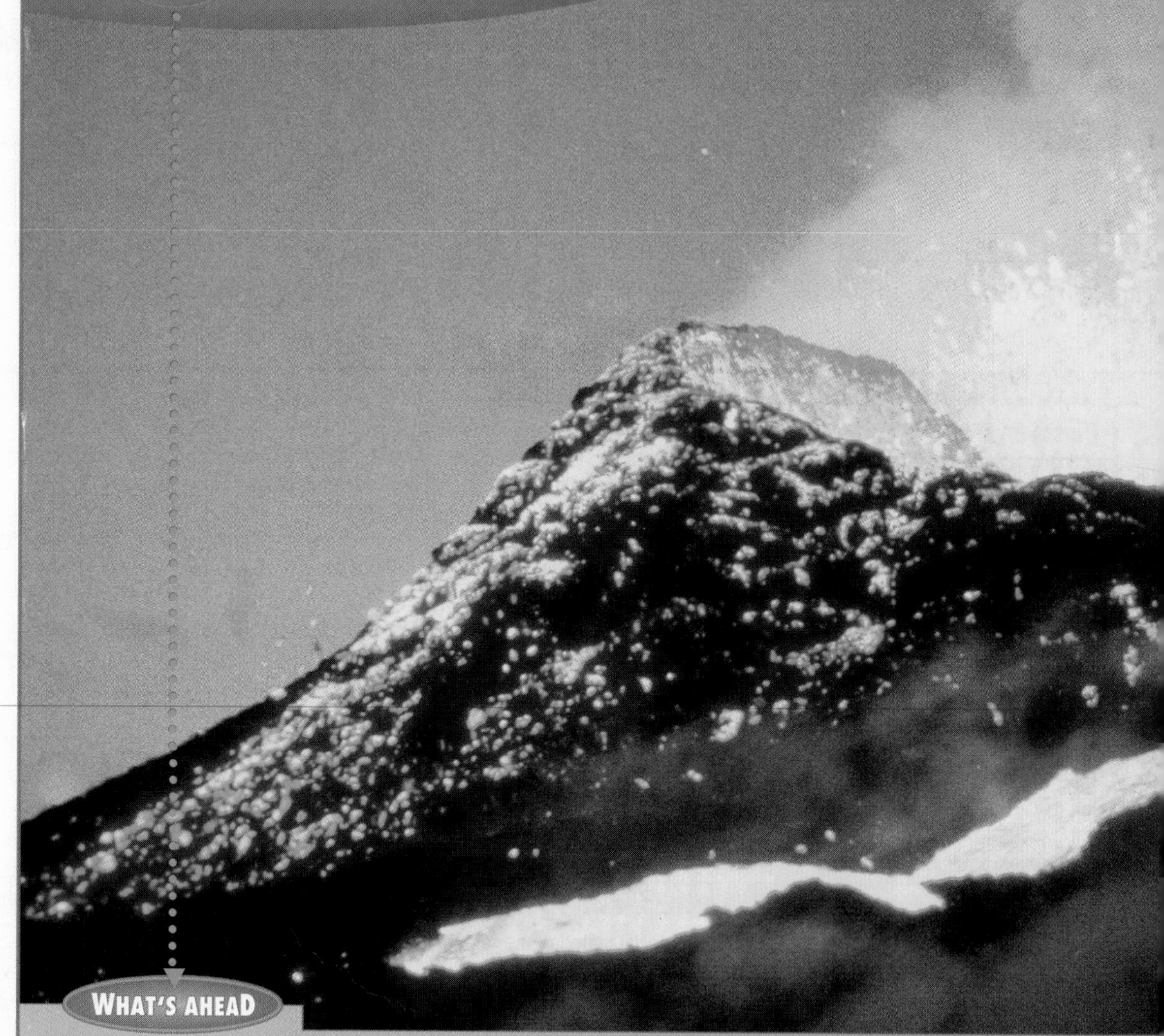

WHAT'S AHEAD

SECTION 1 Volcanoes and Plate Tectonics
Discover **Where Are Volcanoes Found on Earth's Surface?**
Try This **Hot Spot in a Box**
Skills Lab **Mapping Earthquakes and Volcanoes**

SECTION 2 Volcanic Activity
Discover **What Are Volcanic Rocks Like?**
Try This **Gases in Magma**

SECTION 3 Volcanic Landforms
Discover **How Can Volcanic Activity Change Earth's Surface?**
Real-World Lab **Gelatin Volcanoes**

86 ◆ F

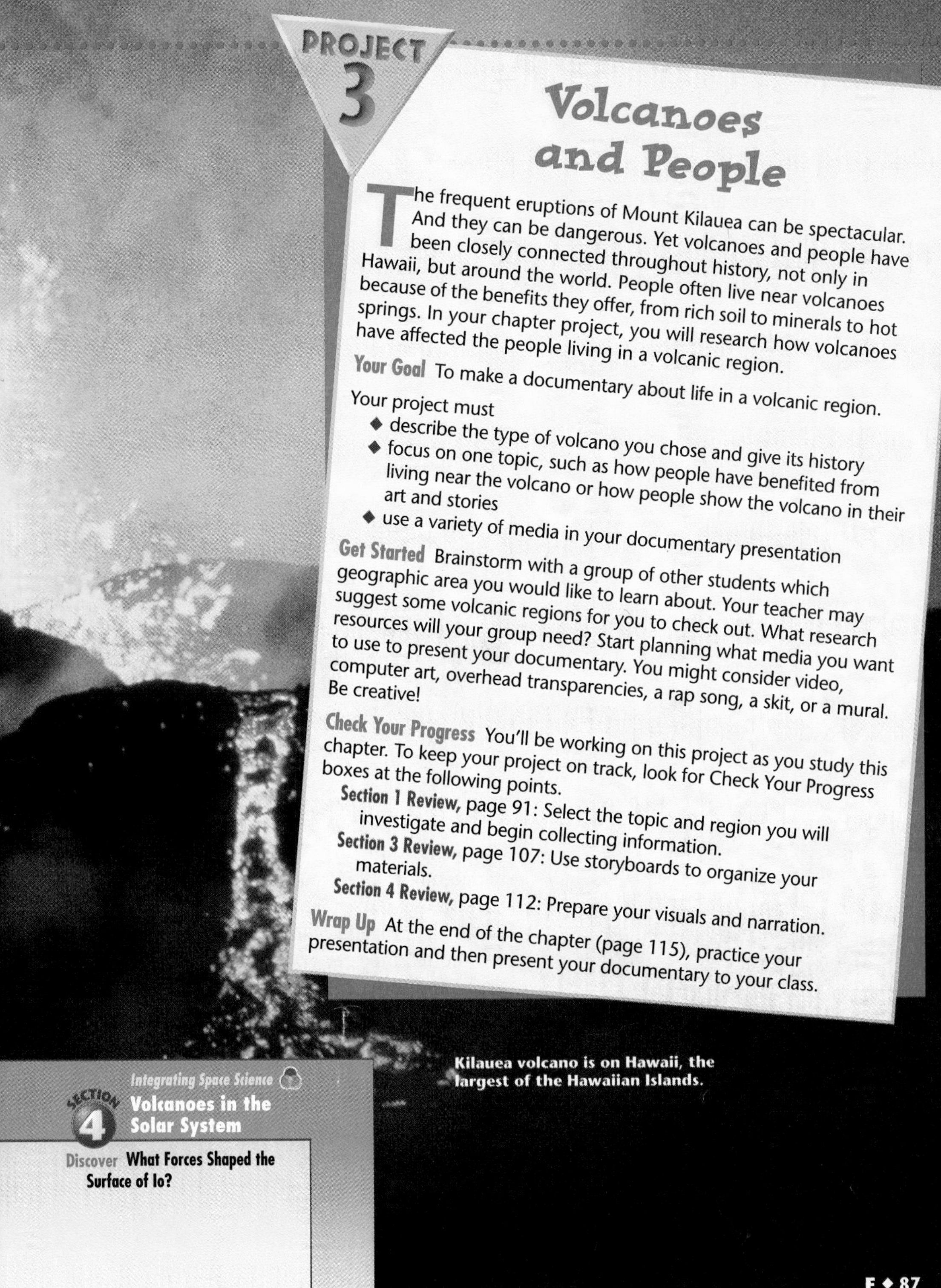

PROJECT 3

Volcanoes and People

The frequent eruptions of Mount Kilauea can be spectacular. And they can be dangerous. Yet volcanoes and people have been closely connected throughout history, not only in Hawaii, but around the world. People often live near volcanoes because of the benefits they offer, from rich soil to minerals to hot springs. In your chapter project, you will research how volcanoes have affected the people living in a volcanic region.

Your Goal To make a documentary about life in a volcanic region.

Your project must
◆ describe the type of volcano you chose and give its history
◆ focus on one topic, such as how people have benefited from living near the volcano or how people show the volcano in their art and stories
◆ use a variety of media in your documentary presentation

Get Started Brainstorm with a group of other students which geographic area you would like to learn about. Your teacher may suggest some volcanic regions for you to check out. What research resources will your group need? Start planning what media you want to use to present your documentary. You might consider video, computer art, overhead transparencies, a rap song, a skit, or a mural. Be creative!

Check Your Progress You'll be working on this project as you study this chapter. To keep your project on track, look for Check Your Progress boxes at the following points.
Section 1 Review, page 91: Select the topic and region you will investigate and begin collecting information.
Section 3 Review, page 107: Use storyboards to organize your materials.
Section 4 Review, page 112: Prepare your visuals and narration.

Wrap Up At the end of the chapter (page 115), practice your presentation and then present your documentary to your class.

Integrating Space Science
SECTION 4 Volcanoes in the Solar System
Discover What Forces Shaped the Surface of Io?

Kilauea volcano is on Hawaii, the largest of the Hawaiian Islands.

F ◆ 87

music, or sound effects. Also let students use materials and devices from home.

Launching the Project

To introduce the project, suggest that students preview Science & History on pages 100–101. Then ask: **What are some ways that each of these volcanoes may have affected the people living nearby?** *(Accept all responses at this time, and encourage creative thinking.)*

Allow time for students to read the project description on page 87 and the Chapter 3 Project Overview on pages 70–71 in Teaching Resources. Encourage discussion of the different topics students could focus on and the types of source materials they could use for their research. Also answer any initial questions that students may have.

Emphasize that although they may divide responsibilities among group members so only some prepare the visuals, *all* members of the group should take part in planning the visuals and be prepared to answer questions about them.

Distribute Chapter 3 Project Worksheet 1 on page 72 in Teaching Resources, which lists a number of volcanoes and specific topics that students might want to consider as subjects for the project. Make clear, though, that they may choose any volcanic region they wish, so long as they are able to find adequate source material for their research.

Program Resources

◆ **Teaching Resources** Chapter 3 Project Teacher Notes, pp. 68–69; Chapter 3 Project Student Materials, pp. 70–73; Chapter 3 Project Scoring Rubric, p. 74

Performance Assessment

The Chapter 3 Project Scoring Rubric on page 74 in Teaching Resources will help you evaluate how well students complete the Chapter 3 Project. You may want to share the scoring rubric with students so they are clear about what will be expected of them.
Students will be assessed on
◆ their ability to identify the type of volcano they have chosen and summarize its history;
◆ how well they have focused both their research and their presentation on a single topic related to the volcano's effect on people living in the area;
◆ their creativity in making use of a variety of media to support the narrative part of their presentation;
◆ how well they present their documentary to the rest of the class.

Section 1 Volcanoes and Plate Tectonics

Objective

After completing the lesson, students will be able to
- ◆ identify where Earth's volcanic regions are found, and explain why they are found there.

Key Terms volcano, magma, lava, Ring of Fire, island arc, hot spot

1 Engage/Explore

Activating Prior Knowledge

Ask students: **Have you ever seen a volcano in person or on TV? Was it erupting? What was happening? What effects did you see? How were people affected?** *(Answers will vary depending on students' experience. Encourage students to share their observations.)*

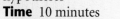

Discover Activity

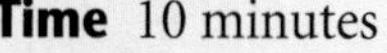

Skills Focus developing hypotheses
Time 10 minutes
Tips Direct students' attention to the map's key to answer the questions in Step 1.
Expected Outcome **1.** Triangles symbolize active volcanoes; solid lines symbolize plate boundaries. **2.** Yes, there is a pattern: volcanoes seem to be related to plate boundaries.
Think It Over *Possible hypothesis:* Volcanoes are concentrated along plate boundaries. *Exceptions:* A few volcanoes occur within plates.

Section 1 Volcanoes and Plate Tectonics

Discover Activity

Where Are Volcanoes Found on Earth's Surface?

1. Look at the map of Earth's volcanoes on page 89. What symbols are used to represent volcanoes? What other symbols are shown on the map?
2. Do the locations of the volcanoes form a pattern? Do the volcanoes seem related to any other features on Earth's surface?

Think About It
Developing Hypotheses Develop a hypothesis to explain where Earth's volcanoes are located. Are there any volcanoes on the map whose location cannot be explained by your hypothesis?

Guide for Reading
- ◆ **Where are Earth's volcanic regions found, and why are they found there?**

Reading Tip **Before you read, preview the headings in this section. Predict where volcanoes are likely to be located.**

Before 1995, the island of Montserrat sat like a beautiful green gem in the Caribbean Sea. Some residents of the small island grew cotton, limes, and vegetables. Tourists flocked to the island to enjoy the scenery and tropical climate. What could possibly spoil this island paradise? A volcano named Soufrière (soo free EHR) Hills did. In 1995, Soufrière Hills began a series of eruptions that lasted more than two years. The volcano belched volcanic ash that fell like snow on roofs and gardens. Residents were evacuated as the volcano continued to erupt, and heavy falls of ash buried entire towns on the southern half of the island.

◀ **Soufrière Hills volcano**

What Is a Volcano?

The eruption of a volcano is among the most dangerous and awe-inspiring events on Earth. A **volcano** is a weak spot in the crust where molten material, or magma, comes to the surface. **Magma** is a molten mixture of rock-forming substances, gases, and water from the mantle. When magma reaches the surface, it is called **lava**. After lava has cooled, it forms solid rock. The lava released during volcanic activity builds up Earth's surface. Volcanic activity is a constructive force that adds new rock to existing land and forms new islands.

88 ◆ F

Reading Strategies

Reading Tip Based on the headings alone, students should be able to determine that volcanoes are likely to be located in three main areas: at the boundaries between diverging plates, at the boundaries between converging plates (subduction zones), and in other areas called "hot spots."

Outlining Have students list the three main areas they identified in the Reading Tip on a sheet of paper and label these headings I, II, and III. Tell students to leave space below each heading so that as they read the section, they can add main ideas (labeled A, B, C, and so forth) below each main heading and supporting details (labeled 1, 2, 3, and so forth) below each main idea. Check students' outlines to make sure they have differentiated correctly between main ideas and supporting details and have included all important information.

Location of Volcanoes

There are about 600 active volcanoes on land. Many more lie beneath the sea. Figure 1 is a map that shows the location of Earth's volcanoes. Notice how volcanoes occur in belts that extend across continents and oceans. One major volcanic belt is the **Ring of Fire,** formed by the many volcanoes that rim the Pacific Ocean. Can you find other volcanic belts on the map?

Volcanic belts form along the boundaries of Earth's plates. At plate boundaries, huge pieces of the crust diverge (pull apart) or converge (push together). Here, the crust is weak and fractured, allowing magma to reach the surface. **Most volcanoes occur along diverging plate boundaries, such as the mid-ocean ridge, or in subduction zones around the edges of oceans.** But there are exceptions to this pattern. Some volcanoes form at "hot spots" far from the boundaries of continental or oceanic plates.

Volcanoes at Diverging Plate Boundaries

Volcanoes form along the mid-ocean ridge, which marks a diverging plate boundary. Recall from Chapter 1 that the ridge is a long, underwater rift valley that winds through the oceans. Along the ridge, lava pours out of cracks in the ocean floor. Only in a few places, as in Iceland and the Azores Islands in the Atlantic Ocean, do the volcanoes of the mid-ocean ridge rise above the ocean's surface.

Language Arts CONNECTION

The word *volcano* comes from the name of the Roman god of fire, Vulcan. According to Roman mythology, Vulcan lived beneath Mount Etna, a huge volcano on the island of Sicily in the Mediterranean Sea. Vulcan used the heat of Mount Etna to make metal armor and weapons for the ancient gods and heroes.

In Your Journal

Use the dictionary to find the definition of *plutonic* rock. Explain why the name of another Roman god was used for this term.

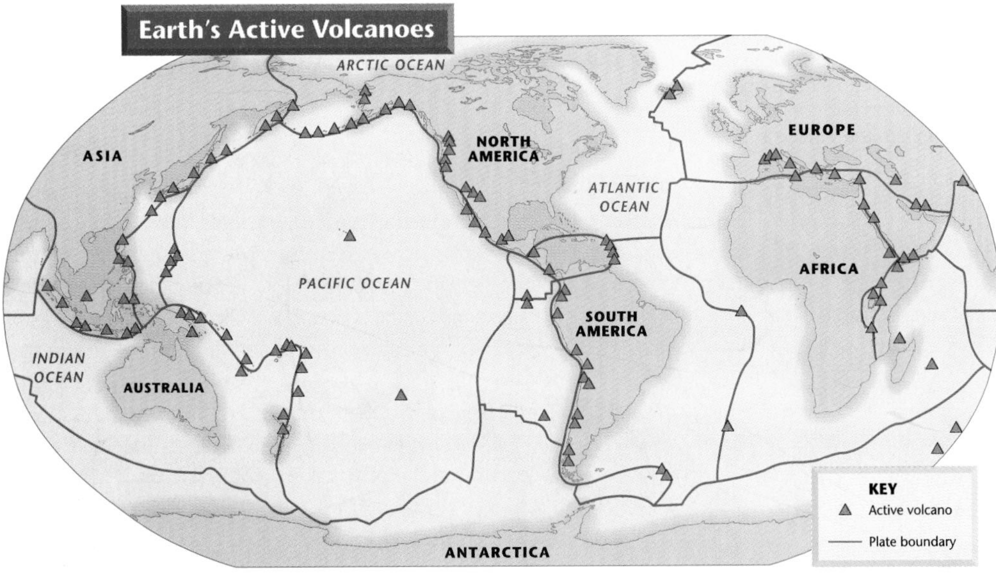

Figure 1 The Ring of Fire is a belt of volcanoes that circles the Pacific Ocean. *Observing What other patterns can you see in the locations of Earth's volcanoes?*

2 Facilitate

What Is a Volcano?

Including All Students

For students whose primary language is not English, suggest that they start a personal glossary of vocabulary terms, with each term and its definition in English on one side of an index card and in the student's primary language on the other side. Encourage students to add to their glossaries as they study other sections in this chapter. **limited English proficiency**

Location of Volcanoes

Language Arts CONNECTION

Provide a map of the Mediterranean region so students can locate Sicily and Mount Etna. Encourage students to find and read a myth about Vulcan.

In Your Journal *Plutonic* refers to rock formed when magma cools and solidifies deep below Earth's surface. Pluto was the name of the Roman god of the underworld. **learning modality: verbal**

Volcanoes at Diverging Plate Boundaries

Using the Visuals: Figure 1

Ask: **What other volcanic belts besides the Ring of Fire do you see on the map?** *(Along the boundaries between Europe and Africa and between Africa and the Saudi Arabian peninsula; within Africa; in the eastern Caribbean; along the islands between Australia and Asia)* **learning modality: visual**

Ongoing Assessment

Oral Presentation Call on students to explain what accounts for the volcanic belt known as the Ring of Fire.

Program Resources

- **Teaching Resources** 3-1 Lesson Plan, p. 75; 3-1 Section Summary, p. 76

Media and Technology

Audiotapes English- Spanish Summary 3-1

Transparencies "Earth's Active Volcanoes," Transparency 12

Answers to Self-Assessment

Caption Question

Figure 1 Volcanic belts also occur along other plate boundaries.

Volcanoes at Converging Boundaries

Including All Students

Display a large world map, and invite volunteers to locate and trace the six major island arcs mentioned in the third paragraph. Let students compare these locations with the plate boundaries shown in Figure 1 on the previous page. Repeat this procedure with the two volcanic belts mentioned in the last paragraph. Have students draw the plates and belts on a map. **learning modality: visual**

Hot Spot Volcanoes

Skills Focus making models
Materials *plastic box, cold water, hot water, red food coloring, small narrow-necked bottle, flat piece of plastic foam*
Time 15–20 minutes
Tips Tell students to make sure the water in the box is deeper than the height of the bottle.
Expected Outcome The "magma" rises out of the bottle and to the water's surface, where it hits the "tectonic plate" in a spot directly above the bottle. When the plate is moved in one direction, the magma hits it in a spot behind the original spot. If the plate continued to move in the same direction, magma would hit it in a series of spots, with the newer volcanoes closer to the "hot spot" and the older volcanoes farther away from it.
Extend Suggest that students continue the plate movement and number the volcanoes to show the sequence in which the volcanoes form. **learning modality: kinesthetic**

Volcanoes at Converging Boundaries

Many volcanoes form near the plate boundaries where oceanic crust returns to the mantle. Subduction causes slabs of oceanic crust to sink through a deep-ocean trench into the mantle. The crust melts and forms magma, which then rises back toward the surface. When the magma from the melted crust erupts as lava, volcanoes are formed. Figure 2 shows how converging plates produce volcanoes.

Many volcanoes occur on islands, near boundaries where two oceanic plates collide. The older, denser plate dives under the other plate, creating a deep-ocean trench. The lower plate sinks through the deep-ocean trench into the asthenosphere. There it begins to melt, forming magma. Because it is less dense than the surrounding rock, the magma seeps upward through cracks in the crust. Eventually, the magma breaks through the ocean floor, creating volcanoes.

The resulting volcanoes create a string of islands called an **island arc**. The curve of an island arc echoes the curve of its deep-ocean trench. Major island arcs include Japan, New Zealand, Indonesia, the Caribbean islands, the Philippines, and the Aleutians.

Subduction also occurs where the edge of a continental plate collides with an oceanic plate. Collisions between oceanic and continental plates produced both the volcanoes of the Andes mountains on the west coast of South America and the volcanoes of the Pacific Northwest in the United States.

✓ *Checkpoint* *How can oceanic crust eventually become magma?*

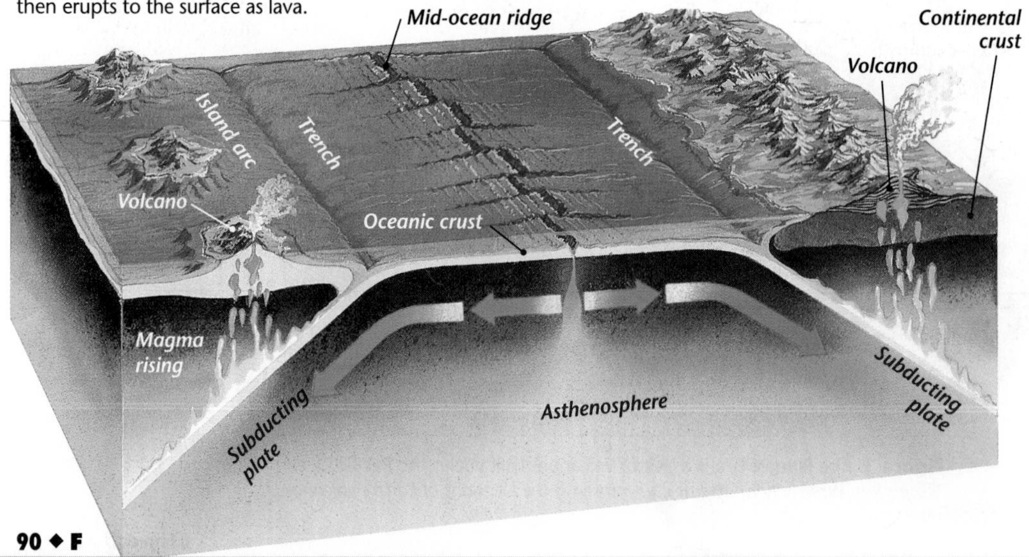

Figure 2 Converging plates often form volcanoes when two oceanic plates collide or when an oceanic plate collides with a continental plate. In both situations, oceanic crust sinks through a deep-ocean trench, melts to form magma, and then erupts to the surface as lava.

Background

Facts and Figures As plates diverge along the mid-ocean ridge, pressure on underlying rock decreases. The reduced pressure lowers the melting point of the rock, producing huge quantities of magma that rise upward. Some magma reaches the ocean floor, where it erupts in extensive lava flows. Flows can pile up to form volcanic cones, some rising above sea level. The island of Surtsey off Iceland's coast formed this way in 1963.

Media and Technology

Transparencies "Volcanoes at Converging Boundaries," Transparency 13

Exploring Earth Science Videodisc Unit 3, Side 1, "Everything on Your Plate"

Figure 3 Hawaii sits on the moving Pacific plate. Beneath it is a powerful hot spot. Eventually, the plate's movement will carry the island of Hawaii away from the hot spot. *Inferring* *Which island on the map formed first?*

Hot Spot Volcanoes

Some volcanoes result from "hot spots" in Earth's mantle. A **hot spot** is an area where magma from deep within the mantle melts through the crust like a blow torch. Hot spots often lie in the middle of continental or oceanic plates far from any plate boundaries. Unlike the volcanoes in an island arc, the volcanoes at a hot spot do not result from subduction.

A hot spot volcano in the ocean floor can gradually form a series of volcanic mountains. For example, the Hawaiian Islands formed one by one over millions of years as the Pacific plate drifted over a hot spot.

Hot spots can also form under the continents. Yellowstone National Park in Wyoming marks a major hot spot under the North American plate. The last volcanic eruption in Yellowstone occurred about 75,000 years ago.

Hot Spot in a Box

ACTIVITY

1. Fill a plastic box half full of cold water. This represents the ocean.
2. Mix red food coloring with hot water in a small, narrow-necked bottle to represent magma.
3. Hold your finger over the mouth of the bottle as you place the bottle in the center of the box. The mouth of the bottle must be under water.
4. Float a flat piece of plastic foam on the water to model a tectonic plate. Make sure the "plate" is floating above the bottle.
5. Take your finger off the bottle and observe what happens to the "magma."

Making Models Move the plastic foam slowly along. Where does the magma touch the "plate"? How does this model a hot spot volcano?

Section 1 Review

1. Where do most volcanoes occur on Earth's surface?
2. What process forms island arcs?
3. What causes hot spot volcanoes to form?
4. **Thinking Critically** **Predicting** What will eventually happen to the active volcano on the island of Hawaii, which is now over the hot spot?

Check Your Progress

CHAPTER PROJECT 3

Start by selecting the volcanic region you will study. Possible topics to investigate are myths and legends about volcanoes, the importance of volcanic soils, mineral resources from volcanoes, tourism, and geothermal power. Choose the topic that interests you the most. Begin your research and take notes on the information you collect.

3 Assess

Section 1 Review Answers

1. Most volcanoes occur along diverging plate boundaries, such as the mid-ocean ridge, or in subduction zones around the edges of the oceans.
2. When converging plates collide, the older, denser plate dives under the other plate and sinks into the asthenosphere. There it melts and forms magma, which seeps upward, creating volcanoes that can result in an island arc.
3. Magma from deep within the mantle rises and melts through the crust above it, often far from plate boundaries.
4. The volcano will no longer be active as the island of Hawaii moves with the Pacific plate and is carried away from the hot spot.

Check Your Progress

CHAPTER PROJECT 3

To avoid duplication, check each group's choice of a volcanic region. You may want to allow two groups to choose the same region so long as they focus on different specific topics. Other possible topics besides those suggested in this Check Your Progress are listed on Chapter 3 Project Worksheet 1. You may also distribute Chapter 3 Project Worksheet 2 at this time, which provides support for helping students take notes as they do their research.

Program Resources

◆ **Teaching Resources** 3-1 Review and Reinforce, p. 77; 3-1 Enrich, p. 78

Media and Technology

Interactive Student Tutorial CD-ROM F-3

Answers to Self-Assessment

Checkpoint

The oceanic crust sinks through a deep-ocean trench into the mantle, where it melts to form magma.

Caption Question

Figure 3 Kauai formed first.

Performance Assessment

Writing Have each student explain, in his or her own words, why volcanoes commonly occur along the boundaries of converging plates.

Portfolio Students can save written explanations in their portfolios.

Skills Lab

Interpreting Data

Mapping Earthquakes and Volcanoes

Preparing for Inquiry

Key Concept Earthquakes and volcanoes are concentrated together in belts.

Skills Objectives Students will be able to

- interpret data to plot the locations of earthquakes and volcanoes on a world map;
- observe areas in which earthquakes and volcanoes are concentrated;
- infer that earthquakes and volcanoes occur together in certain areas.

Time 40 minutes

Advance Planning Photocopy an outline world map for each student. (*Note:* A map is provided in Teaching Resources, page 93.)

Guiding Inquiry

Introducing the Procedure Review the terms *longitude* and *latitude* and how to use those lines on the map to determine precise locations. Make sure students know how to determine longitudes and latitudes that fall between lines.

Troubleshooting the Experiment
When students have plotted all locations, display a copy of the map that you have marked so students can check their work.

Expected Outcome
The marked map should indicate belts in which *both* volcanoes *and* earthquakes occur.

Skills Lab

Interpreting Data

Mapping Earthquakes and Volcanoes

In this lab, you will interpret data on the locations of earthquakes and volcanoes to find patterns.

Problem

Is there a pattern in the locations of earthquakes and volcanoes?

Materials

outline world map showing longitude and latitude
4 pencils of different colors

Procedure

1. Use the information in the table to mark the location of each earthquake on the world map. Use one of the colored pencils to draw a letter E inside a circle at each earthquake location.
2. Use a pencil of a second color to mark the locations of the volcanoes on the world map. Indicate each volcano with the letter V inside a circle.
3. Use a third pencil to lightly shade the areas in which earthquakes are found.
4. Use a fourth colored pencil to lightly shade the areas in which volcanoes are found.

Analyze and Conclude

1. How are earthquakes distributed on the map? Are they scattered evenly over Earth's surface? Are they concentrated in zones?
2. How are volcanoes distributed? Are they scattered evenly or concentrated in zones?
3. From your data, what can you infer about the relationship between earthquakes and volcanoes?
4. **Apply** Based on the data, which area of the North American continent would have the greatest risk of earthquake damage? Of volcano damage? Why would knowing this information be important to urban planners, engineers, and builders in this area?

More to Explore

On a map of the United States, locate active volcanoes and areas of earthquake activity. Determine the distance from your home to the nearest active volcano.

Earthquakes		Volcanoes	
Longitude	Latitude	Longitude	Latitude
120° W	40° N	150° W	60° N
110° E	5° S	70° W	35° S
77° W	4° S	120° W	45° N
88° E	23° N	61° W	15° N
121° E	14° S	105° W	20° N
34° E	7° N	75° W	0°
74° W	44° N	122° W	40° N
70° W	30° S	30° E	40° N
10° E	45° N	60° E	30° N
85° W	13° N	160° E	55° N
125° E	23° N	37° E	3° S
30° E	35° N	145° E	40° N
140° E	35° N	120° E	10° S
12° E	46° N	14° E	41° N
75° E	28° N	105° E	5° S
150° W	61° N	35° E	15° N
68° W	47° S	70° W	30° S
175° E	41° S	175° E	39° S
121° E	17° N	123° E	138 N

Analyze and Conclude

1., 2. Both earthquakes and volcanoes are concentrated in definite zones.
3. Earthquakes and volcanoes tend to occur in the same areas.
4. The west coast of North America has the greatest risk of both earthquake and volcano damage. Urban planners, engineers, and builders should use this information when placing and designing structures.

Extending the Inquiry

More to Explore Provide copies of a U.S. map that includes insets for Alaska and Hawaii and have students research and plot active volcanoes and recent earthquakes in the United States.

Program Resources

- **Teaching Resources** Skills Lab blackline masters, pp. 91–93

Section 2 Volcanic Activity

Discover Activity

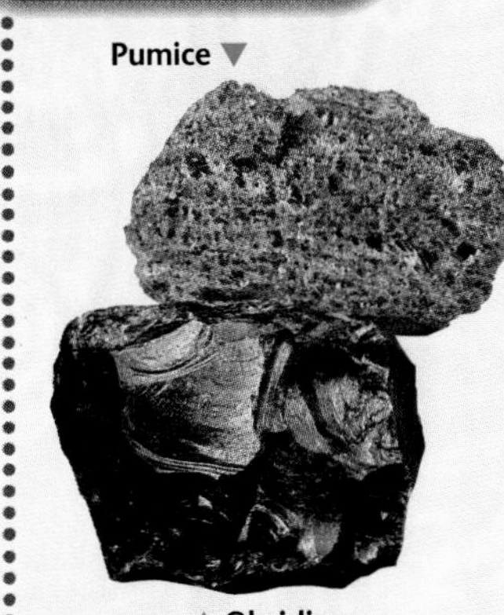
Pumice ▼

▲ Obsidian

What Are Volcanic Rocks Like?

Volcanoes produce lava, which hardens into rock. Two of these rocks are pumice and obsidian.

1. Observe samples of pumice and obsidian with a hand lens.
2. How would you describe the texture of the pumice? What could have caused this texture?
3. Observe the surface of the obsidian. How does the surface of the obsidian differ from pumice?

Think It Over

Developing Hypotheses What could have produced the difference in texture between the two rocks? Explain your answer.

In Hawaii, there are many myths about Pele (PAY lay), the fire goddess of volcanoes. In these myths, Pele is the creator and the destroyer of the Hawaiian islands. She lives in the fiery depths of erupting volcanoes. According to legend, when Pele is angry, she releases the fires of Earth through openings on the mountainside. Evidence of her presence is "Pele's hair," a fine, threadlike rock formed by lava. Pele's hair forms when lava sprays out of the ground like water from a fountain. As it cools, the lava stretches and hardens into thin strands.

GUIDE FOR READING

- What happens when a volcano erupts?
- How do the two types of volcanic eruptions differ?
- What are some hazards of volcanoes?

Reading Tip Before you read, preview *Exploring a Volcano* on page 95. Write a list of any questions you have about how a volcano erupts.

How Magma Reaches Earth's Surface

Where does this fiery lava come from? Lava begins as magma in the mantle. There, magma forms in the asthenosphere, which lies beneath the lithosphere. The materials of the asthenosphere are under great pressure.

Magma Rises Because liquid magma is less dense than the surrounding solid material, magma flows upward into any cracks in the rock above. Magma rises until it reaches the surface, or until it becomes trapped beneath layers of rock.

Figure 4 Pele's hair is a type of rock formed from lava. Each strand is as fine as spun glass.

Reading Strategies

Reading Tip Suggest that students write their questions on a sheet of paper, leaving space below each question to write the answer as they read the section. Students could use the list to review the section's content and as a basis for researching answers that are not found in the textbook.

Program Resources

◆ **Teaching Resources** 3-2 Lesson Plan, p. 79; 3-2 Section Summary, p. 80

Media and Technology

Audiotapes English- Spanish Summary 3-2

Section 2 Volcanic Activity

Objectives

After completing the lesson, students will be able to

- ◆ describe what happens when a volcano erupts;
- ◆ explain how the two types of volcanic eruptions differ;
- ◆ identify some hazards of volcanoes.

Key Terms magma chamber, pipe, vent, lava flow, crater, silica, pahoehoe, aa, pyroclastic flow, active, dormant, extinct, hot spring, geyser, geothermal energy

1 Engage/Explore

Activating Prior Knowledge

Ask students: **What does lava look like when it comes out of a volcano?** *(Based on photographs or videos they have seen, students may describe lava as red-hot and thick or gooey.)* **What else comes out of a volcano when it erupts?** *(Students may mention steam and dark clouds of volcanic dust. Accept all responses without comment at this time.)*

Discover

Skills Focus developing hypotheses
Materials *samples of pumice and obsidian, hand lens*
Time 5–10 minutes
Tips Help students with the correct pronunciations of *pumice* (PUHM is) and *obsidian* (ob SID ee un).
Expected Outcome The obsidian is smooth and glassy, whereas the pumice is rough and grainy.
Think It Over The lava that produced the pumice had more gas (air) in it than the lava that produced the obsidian. Obsidian formed when lava cooled very quickly.

2 Facilitate

How Magma Reaches Earth's Surface

Building Inquiry Skills: Inferring

Materials *2 clear, capped, plastic bottles of soda water; hand lens*
Time 5 minutes

Provide each pair of students with the materials. One student should closely watch a bottle with the hand lens while the other student slowly uncaps it. Students can then switch places and repeat with the second bottle. Ask: **What did you see in the bottle as the cap was removed?** *(Bubbles formed.)* **Why did that happen?** *(At some point, enough pressure was released to allow the carbon dioxide gas to come out of solution and form bubbles.)* **What do you think releases the pressure on gases trapped in magma?** *(When magma reaches Earth's surface, it is no longer confined to a limited space.)*
learning modality: visual

TRY THIS

Skills Focus making models
Materials *1- or 2-liter plastic bottle, 10 g baking soda, 65 mL water, 6 raisins, 65 mL vinegar*
Time 10–15 minutes
Tips You may want to supply funnels for pouring the materials into the bottle.
Expected Outcome The vinegar reacts with the baking soda solution to produce carbon dioxide gas. Bubbles of gas adhere to the raisins. As more bubbles collect, the raisins rise to the surface, where the bubbles pop. The raisins sink again, and the cycle repeats. The raisins represent magma; the bubbles represent gases trapped in the magma. In this model, the raisins and gas bubbles are not under pressure, as magma and gases are in a real volcano. Also, magma, unlike raisins, doesn't go up and down in a volcano, but rather goes up and out.
Extend Students could repeat the activity using raisins and clear carbonated soda.
learning modality: kinesthetic

Figure 5 Molten lava from Kilauea volcano in Hawaii.

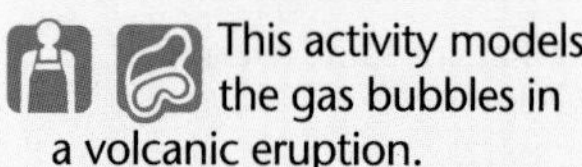

Gases in Magma

This activity models the gas bubbles in a volcanic eruption.

1. In a 1- or 2-liter plastic bottle, mix 10 g of baking soda into 65 mL of water.
2. Put about six raisins in the water.
3. While swirling the water and raisins, add 65 mL of vinegar and stir vigorously.
4. Once the liquid has stopped moving, observe the raisins.

Making a Model What happens after you add the vinegar? What do the raisins and bubbles represent? How is this model similar to the way magma behaves in a volcano?

A Volcano Erupts Just like the carbon dioxide trapped in a bottle of soda pop, the dissolved gases trapped in magma are under tremendous pressure. You cannot see the carbon dioxide gas in a bottle of soda pop because it is dissolved in the liquid. But when you open the bottle, the pressure is released. The carbon dioxide forms bubbles, which rush to the surface.

As magma rises toward the surface, the pressure decreases. The dissolved gases begin to separate out, forming bubbles. A volcano erupts when an opening develops in weak rock on the surface. **During a volcanic eruption, the gases dissolved in magma rush out, carrying the magma with them.** Once magma reaches the surface and becomes lava, the gases bubble out.

Inside a Volcano

All volcanoes have a pocket of magma beneath the surface and one or more cracks through which the magma forces its way. You can see these features in *Exploring a Volcano.* Beneath a volcano, magma collects in a pocket called a **magma chamber.** The magma moves through a **pipe,** a long tube in the ground that connects the magma chamber to Earth's surface. Molten rock and gas leave the volcano through an opening called a **vent.** Often, there is one central vent at the top of a volcano. However, many volcanoes also have other vents that open on the volcano's sides. A **lava flow** is the area covered by lava as it pours out of a vent. A **crater** is a bowl-shaped area that may form at the top of a volcano around the volcano's central vent.

☑ *Checkpoint* ***How does magma rise through the lithosphere?***

Background

Integrating Science Students may wonder how geologists are able to determine what the inside of a volcano is like when they cannot observe it directly. Some evidence is indirect. For example, geologists can determine that a large body of magma or very hot rock is present underground by measuring small delays in the arrival times of seismic waves from distant earthquakes.

Other evidence is more direct. The erosion of some ancient volcanoes has exposed their "roots," enabling geologists to examine the dikes and pipes that once connected underground magma chambers to the surface vents. Also, magma sometimes tears off pieces of the mantle as it rises. These fragments, known as ultramafic nodules, are found in erupted lava flows. The density and chemistry of these nodules have confirmed geologists' theories about Earth's interior.

EXPLORING a Volcano

A volcano forms where magma breaks through Earth's crust and lava flows over the surface.

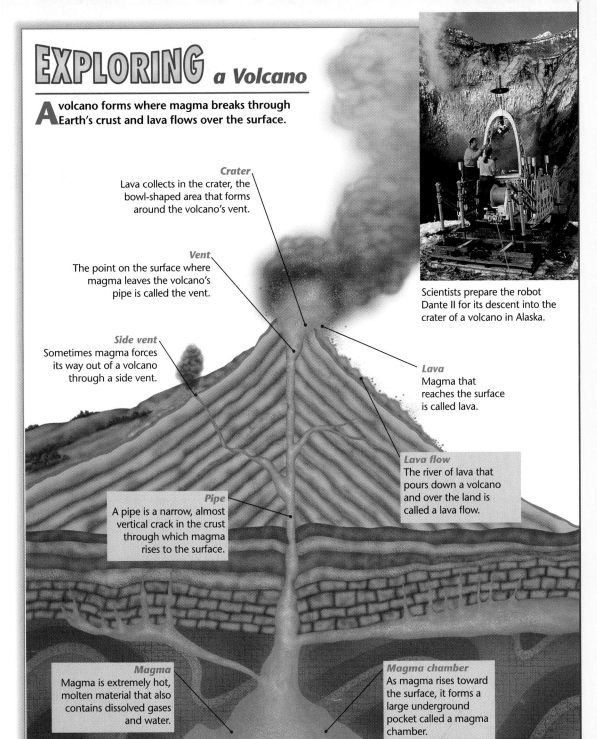

Crater
Lava collects in the crater, the bowl-shaped area that forms around the volcano's vent.
Vent
The point on the surface where magma leaves the volcano's pipe is called the vent.
Side vent
Sometimes magma forces its way out of a volcano through a side vent.
Lava
Magma that reaches the surface is called lava.
Lava flow
The river of lava that pours down a volcano and over the land is called a lava flow.
Pipe
A pipe is a narrow, almost vertical crack in the crust through which magma rises to the surface.
Magma
Magma is extremely hot, molten material that also contains dissolved gases and water.
Magma chamber
As magma rises toward the surface, it forms a large underground pocket called a magma chamber.

Scientists prepare the robot Dante II for its descent into the crater of a volcano in Alaska.

EXPLORING a Volcano

After students have examined the diagram and read the captions on their own, call on students in turn to describe the movement of magma during an eruption, starting with the magma chamber and moving upward through the pipe to the vent and then out onto the surface in a lava flow. Make sure students notice the side vent as well. Ask: **Why would magma flow to a side vent?** *(A crack in the rock layers might offer less resistance to the magma's flow than the magma-filled main pipe.)* Point out the two bodies of magma to the right and left of the pipe just above the magma chamber. Ask: **What happened to the magma there?** *It flowed sideways away from the pipe, then smaller amounts flowed upward from those bodies.)* When students read about dikes and sills in the next section, have them look back at this diagram to review how they are formed.

Draw students' attention to the photograph and caption at the upper right. Ask: **Why would scientists use a robot to explore a volcano's crater?** *(Gases, extreme heat, steep or slippery slopes, and other conditions make exploring the crater too hazardous for people to do themselves.)* **Why was the robot named "Dante"?** *("Dante" refers to Dante Alighieri, the Italian poet who wrote* The Divine Comedy, *the first book of which is* The Inferno, *a description of hell. Students probably will not know; encourage volunteers to consult an encyclopedia and report back to the class.)* **Why is "Dante" a good name for a robot that explores volcanoes?** *(With their fire, heat, and noxious fumes, volcanoes resemble people's images of hell.)* **learning modality: visual**

Media and Technology

 **Transparencies** "Exploring a Volcano," Transparency 14

Answers to Self-Assessment

☑ Checkpoint

Liquid magma in the asthenosphere is less dense than the rock in the lithosphere above it, so it flows upward through cracks in the rock. It continues upward until it reaches the surface or is trapped beneath layers of rock.

Ongoing Assessment

Drawing Have each student draw a simple cross-sectional diagram of a volcano and label the magma chamber, pipe, vent, crater and lava without referring to the diagram on this page.

Characteristics of Magma

Inquiry Challenge

Materials *fluids of different thicknesses, jars with secure tops, board covered with waxed paper, other materials of students' choice*

Time 15 minutes

Ask students: **What are some thick liquids?** *(Examples include maple syrup, hand lotion, shampoo, and liquid detergent.)* **What are some thin liquids?** *(Water, milk, juice, vinegar, and so forth)* Then challenge students with the following question: **How could you test how thick or thin a liquid is and compare it with another liquid?** *(Students' ideas will vary. They could put a small amount of each liquid in a jar, turn the jar over, and observe how quickly the liquid flows to the other end. They also could pour liquids down an inclined surface, such as a board, and time its flow rate. Accept other ideas as well.)* Allow time for students to test their ideas and report their results to the rest of the class. **learning modality: logical/ mathematical**

Building Inquiry Skills: Comparing and Contrasting

Materials *2 small paper cups, molasses, small paper cup with warmed molasses, small paper cup with chilled molasses.*

Time 15 minutes

Give each student an empty cup and an identical cup half-filled with molasses at room temperature. Let students pour the molasses from one cup to the other, observing its rate of flow. Let students repeat the pouring activity and compare the flow rate of warmed molasses and then the chilled molasses with the flow rate of the room-temperature molasses. Ask: **How did the temperature of the molasses affect its thickness?** *(The lower the molasses' temperature, the thicker it was.)* Emphasize that although magma is thousands of degrees hotter than the molasses used in this activity, its thickness also varies with temperature. **learning modality: kinesthetic**

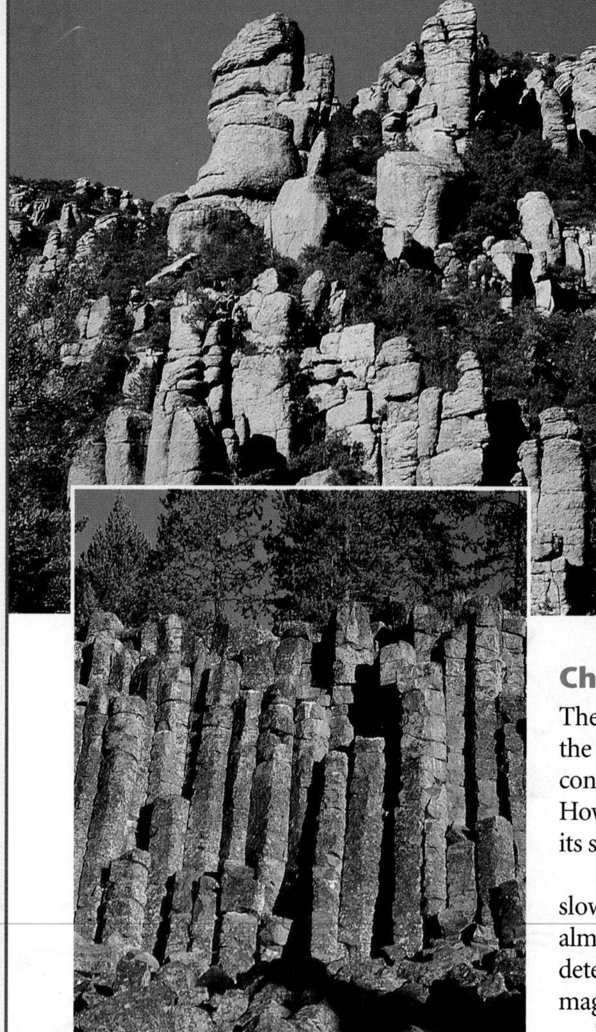

Figure 6 Rhyolite (top) forms from high-silica lava. Basalt (bottom) forms from low-silica lava. When this type of lava cools, it sometimes forms six-sided columns like the ones in the picture.

Characteristics of Magma

The force of a volcanic eruption depends partly on the amount of gas dissolved in the magma. But gas content is not the only thing that affects an eruption. How thick or thin the magma is, its temperature, and its silica content are also important factors.

Some types of magma are thick and flow very slowly. Other types of magma are fluid and flow almost as easily as water. Magma's temperature partly determines whether it is thick or fluid. The hotter the magma, the more fluid it is.

The amount of silica in magma also helps to determine how easily the magma flows. **Silica,** which is a material that is formed from the elements oxygen and silicon, is one of the most abundant materials in Earth's crust and mantle. The more silica magma contains, the thicker it is.

Magma that is high in silica produces light-colored lava that is too sticky to flow very far. When this type of lava cools, it forms the rock rhyolite, which has the same composition as granite. Pumice and obsidian, which you observed if you did the Discover activity, also form from high-silica lava. Obsidian forms when lava cools very quickly, giving it a smooth, glossy surface. Pumice forms when gas bubbles escape from cooling lava, leaving spaces in the rock.

Magma that is low in silica flows readily and produces dark-colored lava. When this kind of lava cools, rocks such as basalt are formed.

Background

History of Science Kilauea's quiet eruptions are sometimes punctuated by fiery displays, with fountains of lava spraying hundreds of meters into the air. However, such displays are generally short-lived, and the lava falls back harmlessly into lava pools.

The Hawaiian Volcanoes Observatory has been able to operate safely on the volcano's summit since 1912, despite more than 50 eruptive phases since record keeping began in 1823. Kilauea's longest and largest eruption began along a 6.5-km fissure in 1983 and still continues today.

In 1986 eruptions of pahoehoe formed a lava lake on the volcano's slope. When the lake overflowed, the fast-moving lava destroyed almost a hundred homes, covered a major roadway, and eventually flowed into the ocean. There, it cooled and solidified, adding new land area to the island.

Types of Volcanic Eruptions

A volcano's magma influences how the volcano erupts. **The silica content of magma helps to determine whether the volcanic eruption is quiet or explosive.**

Quiet Eruptions A volcano erupts quietly if its magma flows easily. In this case, the gas dissolved in the magma bubbles out gently. Thin, runny lava oozes quietly from the vent. The islands of Hawaii and Iceland were formed from quiet eruptions. On the Big Island of Hawaii, lava pours out of the crater near the top of Mount Kilauea (kee loo AY uh), but also flows out of long cracks on the volcano's sides. Quiet eruptions like the ones that regularly take place on Mount Kilauea have built up the Big Island over hundreds of thousands of years. In Iceland, lava usually emerges from gigantic fissures many kilometers long. The fluid lava from a quiet eruption can flow many kilometers from the volcano's vent.

Quiet eruptions produce two different types of lava: pahoehoe and aa. **Pahoehoe** (pah HOH ee hoh ee) is fast-moving, hot lava. The surface of a lava flow formed from pahoehoe looks like a solid mass of wrinkles, billows, and ropelike coils. Lava that is cooler and slower-moving is called **aa** (AH ah). When aa hardens, it forms a rough surface consisting of jagged lava chunks. Figure 7 shows how different these types of lava can be.

☑ *Checkpoint* ***What types of lava are produced by quiet eruptions?***

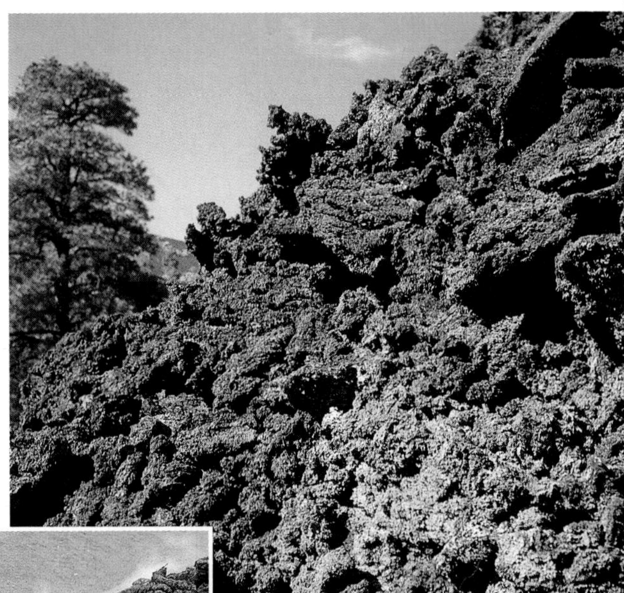

Figure 7 Both pahoehoe and aa can come from the same volcano. **A.** Pahoehoe flows easily and hardens into a rippled surface. **B.** Aa hardens into rough chunks. *Inferring What accounts for the differences between these two types of lava?*

Types of Volcanic Eruptions

Including All Students

Many excellent films are available—on both videocassette and CD-ROM—showing different types of volcanic eruptions and lava flows, including slow-moving aa flows from Kilauea advancing on and consuming homes. Try to obtain one or more such films so students can observe actual volcanoes in action. "Live" footage of lava flows, pyroclastics, fissure eruptions, and the fiery volcanic clouds known as *nuée ardente* will give students a far greater appreciation of the awesome power and drama of volcanic activity. **learning modality: visual**

Cultural Diversity

Write the terms *pahoehoe* and *aa* on the board, and tell students how to pronounce them (pah HOH ee hoh ee, AH ah). Then ask: **Where do you think these words come from?** *(They are the native Hawaiian words for these two types of lava. If students cannot make this inference on their own, remind them that Mount Kilauea is on the island of Hawaii.)* Suggest that students do research to find other native Hawaiian terms related to volcanoes. They might also enjoy reading myths about Pele, the Hawaiian goddess of volcanoes. **learning modality: verbal**

Program Resources

- **Integrated Science Laboratory Manual** F-3, "Predicting Lava Flows"

Answers to Self-Assessment

☑ *Checkpoint*

Quiet eruptions produce two types of lava: pahoehoe (a fast-moving, hot lava) and aa (a cooler, slower-moving lava).

Caption Question

Figure 7 The temperature of the lava and the speed at which it flows.

Ongoing Assessment

Writing Have each student write a brief explanation of how the temperature and silica content of magma affects its thickness.

Types of Volcanic Eruptions, continued

Using the Visuals: Figure 8

Explain that Mount St. Helens is part of the Cascade Range, which runs north-south through Washington, Oregon, and northern California. Let students find the Cascades on a map of the Northwest. Ask: **What volcanic belt are the Cascades part of?** *(The Ring of Fire; let students look back at Figure 1, page 89, if necessary.)* If possible, share with students some first-hand accounts of the eruption of Mount St. Helens from books, magazines, or videos. **learning modality: visual**

Social Studies CONNECTION

Display a large map of the Mediterranean region, and let students find Mount Vesuvius and Pompeii in Italy. You may wish to provide various source materials for students to use for their research.

In Your Journal Provide photographs showing excavated areas of Pompeii and artists' illustrations depicting daily life in the city. Encourage students to use these pictures to help them imagine what life in Pompeii was like. **learning modality: verbal**

Including All Students

Write the term *pyroclastic* on the board, and draw a line between the two word parts. Choose volunteers to find the meaning of each part in a dictionary. *(pyro: "fire"; clastic: "made of fragments")* Ask: **Why is pyroclastic a good word for a volcanic explosion?** *(The lava is fiery and is broken into pieces.)* **learning modality: verbal**

Figure 8 Mount St. Helens erupted at 8:30 A.M. on May 18, 1980. **A.** A large bulge that had formed on the north side of the mountain crashed downward.

B. As the mountainside collapsed, bottled up gas and magma inside began to escape.

Social Studies CONNECTION

In A.D. 79, Mount Vesuvius in Italy erupted. A thick layer of ash from Vesuvius buried the Roman city of Pompeii, which lay between the volcano and the Mediterranean Sea. Beginning in the 1700s, about half of the buried city was dug out, and we now know the following: Pompeii was a walled city with shops, homes, paved streets, a forum (or public square), temples, and public baths. Perhaps 20,000 people lived there.

In Your Journal

Research Pompeii to find out what scientists have learned about daily life in the city. Write a paragraph summarizing your findings.

Explosive Eruptions If its magma is thick and sticky, a volcano erupts explosively. The thick magma does not flow out of the crater and down the mountain. Instead, it slowly builds up in the volcano's pipe, plugging it like a cork in a bottle. Dissolved gases cannot escape from the thick magma. The trapped gases build up pressure until they explode. The erupting gases push the magma out of the volcano with incredible force.

The explosion breaks the lava into fragments that quickly cool and harden into pieces of different sizes. The smallest pieces are volcanic ash—fine, rocky particles as small as a grain of sand. Cinders are pebble-sized particles. Larger pieces, called bombs, may range from the size of a baseball to the size of a car. A **pyroclastic flow** (py roh KLAS tik) occurs when an explosive eruption hurls out ash, cinders, and bombs.

Look at Figure 8 to see the 1980 eruption of Mount St. Helens in the state of Washington. It was one of the most violent explosive eruptions that has ever occurred in the United States.

Checkpoint ***What causes an explosive eruption?***

Stages of a Volcano

The activity of a volcano may last from less than a decade to more than 10 million years. Most long-lived volcanoes, however, do not erupt continuously. Geologists often describe volcanoes with terms usually reserved for living things, such as sleeping, awakening, alive, and dead. An **active,** or live, volcano is one that is erupting or has shown signs that it may erupt in the near future. A **dormant,** or sleeping, volcano is like a sleeping bear. Scientists expect a dormant volcano to awaken in the future and become active. However, there may be thousands of years between eruptions. An **extinct,** or dead, volcano is unlikely to erupt again.

Background

Facts and Figures The explosive eruption of Mount St. Helens on May 18, 1980, blew out the entire north side of the mountain, leaving a gaping hole. The eruption destroyed stands of timber on the mountain's north side, leaving the trees stripped of branches and flattened like toothpicks. The eruption claimed about 60 lives, many dying from the pyroclastic flow's intense heat and suffocating cloud of ash and gases.

Mount St. Helens is one of 15 large volcanoes in the Cascade Range. Eight of the largest volcanoes have been active in the past few hundred years. Mount St. Helens' previous eruptive phase ended in 1857. Of the seven remaining active volcanoes, the most likely to erupt again are Mount Baker, Mount Shasta, Lassen Peak, Mount Hood, and Mount Rainier.

C. Shattered rock and pyroclastic flows blasted out sideways from the volcano.

D. The blast traveled outward, leveling the surrounding forest and causing mudflows that affected a wide area around the volcano.

Other Types of Volcanic Activity

Hot springs and geysers are two examples of volcanic activity that do not involve the eruption of lava. These features may occur in any volcanic area—even around an extinct volcano,

A **hot spring** forms when groundwater heated by a nearby body of magma rises to the surface and collects in a natural pool. (Groundwater is water that has seeped into the spaces among rocks deep beneath Earth's surface.) Water from hot springs may contain dissolved gases and other substances from deep within Earth.

Sometimes, rising hot water and steam become trapped underground in a narrow crack. Pressure builds until the mixture suddenly sprays above the surface as a geyser. A **geyser** (GY zur) is a fountain of water and steam that erupts from the ground.

INTEGRATING TECHNOLOGY In volcanic areas, water heated by magma can provide a clean, reliable energy source called **geothermal energy.** The people of Reykjavik, Iceland, pipe this hot water directly into their homes for warmth. Geothermal energy is also a source of electricity in Iceland as well as northern California and New Zealand. Steam from deep underground is piped into turbines. Inside a turbine, the steam spins a wheel in the same way that blowing on a pinwheel makes the pinwheel turn. The moving wheel in the turbine turns a generator that changes the energy of motion into electrical energy.

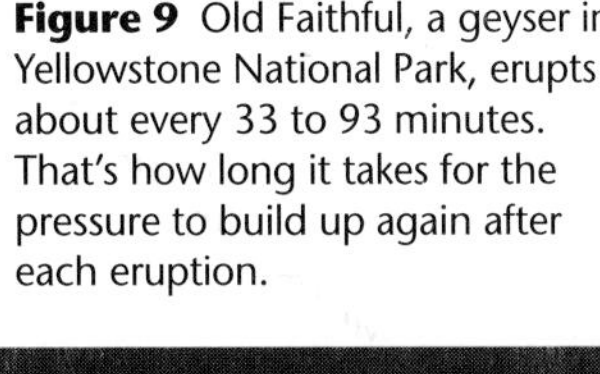

Figure 9 Old Faithful, a geyser in Yellowstone National Park, erupts about every 33 to 93 minutes. That's how long it takes for the pressure to build up again after each eruption.

Stages of a Volcano

Including All Students

Ask: **What other things have you heard described as dormant? As extinct?** *(In cold regions, animals such as bears and bats become dormant in winter. Plant and animal species that have completely died out, such as dinosaurs, are said to be extinct.)* **limited English proficiency**

Other Types of Volcanic Activity

Demonstration

Materials *water, teakettle, hot plate*
Time 5–10

Heat some water in a teakettle on a hot plate. When the water boils and steam escapes from the spout, ask: **What would happen if I plugged the spout?** *(The steam's pressure would build up to the point where it would blow the plug out of the spout.* CAUTION: *Do not try this and caution students not to do it.)* Emphasize that this is what happens when a geyser erupts. Ask: **What heated the water in the kettle?** *(the hot plate)* **What heats the water deep underground in a geyser?** *(magma)* **learning modality: logical/ mathematical**

Integrating Technology

Invite students to consider the problems and benefits involved in tapping steam and hot underground water for use in heating buildings or operating turbines by asking: **Why are the steam and water sometimes difficult to access?** *(They may be far underground, so deep wells must be drilled.)* **What dangers are involved?** *(Steam could rupture pipes and injure workers.)* **What are the advantages of geothermal energy?** *(It is clean, with no dangerous wastes or fumes; it is a renewable energy source.)* **learning modality: logical/mathematical**

Program Resources

- **Interdisciplinary Explorations Series** "The Glory of Ancient Rome," pp. 20–23
- **Science Explorer Series** *Earth's Water,* Chapter 2, can provide additional information about hot springs and geysers.

Answers to Self-Assessment

Checkpoint

Magma that is thick and sticky causes a volcano to erupt explosively.

Ongoing Assessment

Oral Presentation Ask students to describe the major differences between quiet and explosive volcanic eruptions.

Monitoring Volcanoes

Building Inquiry Skills: Applying Concepts

Prompt students to recall what they learned about tiltmeters and laser-ranging devices in the previous chapter by asking: **How are changes in the land surface along a fault detected with a tiltmeter? A laser-ranging device?** *(A tiltmeter uses two connected liquid-filled bulbs to measure the rise or fall of land surfaces along a fault. A laser-ranging device placed on one side of a fault bounces a laser beam off a reflector on the other side to measure changes in distance. If students have difficulty recalling this information, let them look back at pages 79–80.)* Then ask: **How do you think each of these instruments is used to detect signs of a possible volcanic eruption?** *(Accept all reasonable responses. Example: Both devices could be set up on the side of a volcanic mountain to detect bulges caused by magma rising to the surface.)* **learning modality: logical/mathematical**

SCIENCE & History

Focus students' attention on the introductory statement that volcanic eruptions "have greatly affected the land and the people around them." Ask: **How do you think each of these eruptions affected the people in the area?** *(Some eruptions killed people; people lost their homes and possessions; they may have had to evacuate the area; crops were destroyed when fields were covered with ash and other volcanic materials; and so forth.)*

In Your Journal Provide age-appropriate resource books so students can research these eruptions. Also remind students that if their group has chosen one of these volcanoes as the subject of its chapter project, they can add this research to their report. **learning modality: verbal**

Monitoring Volcanoes

Geologists have been somewhat more successful in predicting volcanic eruptions than in predicting earthquakes. Changes in and around a volcano usually give warning a short time before the volcano erupts. Geologists use tiltmeters, laser-ranging devices, and other instruments to detect slight surface changes in elevation and tilt caused by magma moving underground. Geologists monitor the local magnetic field, water level in a volcano's crater lake, and any gases escaping from a volcano. They take the temperature of underground water to see if it is getting hotter—a sign that magma may be nearing the surface.

Geologists also monitor the many small earthquakes that occur in the area around a volcano before an eruption.

SCIENCE & History

The Power of Volcanoes

Within the last 150 years, major volcanic eruptions have greatly affected the land and people around them.

1883 Indonesia
The violent eruption of Krakatau volcano threw 18 cubic kilometers of ash skyward. The blast was heard 5,000 kilometers away.

1915 Alaska, U.S.A.
Today, a river in Alaska cuts through the thick layer of volcanic ash from the eruption of Mount Katmai. Mount Katmai blasted out almost as much ash as Krakatau.

1850 1900

1902 Martinique
Mount Pelée, a Caribbean volcano, spewed out a burning cloud of hot gas and pyroclastic flows. Within two minutes of the eruption, the cloud had killed the 29,000 residents of St. Pierre, a city on the volcano's flank. Only two people survived.

Background

Facts and Figures Of the six volcanic eruptions presented in the time line on these pages, two—Krakatau in 1883 and Mount Pelèe in 1902—are among the five most destructive volcanic eruptions since 1700. The remaining three are Unzen, Japan, in 1792; Mt. Tambora, Indonesia, in 1815; and Nevada del Ruiz, Colombia, in 1985.

As evidence of a volcano's varying hazards, 80,000 of the 92,000 people killed as a result of the 1815 Mt. Tambora eruption died not from the volcanic activity itself but from starvation afterward. Ninety percent of Krakatua's 36,400 victims were killed by a tsunami. Pyroclastic flows claimed 23,000 lives in the Mount Pelée eruption. Mudflows killed 23,000 people in the Nevada del Ruiz eruption. Clearly, lava flows and collapsing cones are not the only volcanic hazards.

The movement of magma into the magma chamber and through the volcano's pipe triggers these quakes.

All these data help geologists predict that an eruption is about to occur. But geologists cannot be certain about the type of eruption or how powerful it will be.

Volcano Hazards

The time between volcanic eruptions may span hundreds of years. So people living near a dormant volcano may be unaware of the danger. Before 1980, the people who lived, worked, and vacationed in the region around Mount St. Helens viewed it as a peaceful mountain. Few imagined the destruction the volcano would bring when it awakened from its 123-year slumber.

People have written eyewitness accounts of famous volcanic eruptions. Research one of the eruptions in the time line. Then write a letter describing what someone observing the eruption might have seen.

1991 Philippines

Mount Pinatubo was dormant for 500 years before erupting in June 1991. Pinatubo spewed out huge quantities of ash that rose high into the atmosphere and also buried the surrounding countryside.

1950 — 2000

1980 Washington, U.S.A.

When Mount St. Helens exploded, it blasted one cubic kilometer of rock fragments and volcanic material skyward. The eruption was not unexpected. For months, geologists had monitored releases of ash, small earthquakes, and a bulge on the mountain caused by the buildup of magma inside.

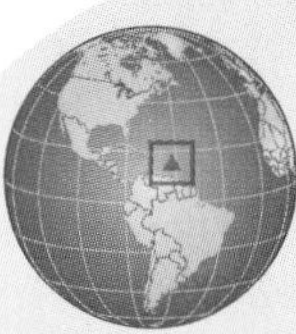

1995 Montserrat

For more than two years, eruptions of volcanic ash from the Soufrière Hills volcano poured down on this small Caribbean island. Geologists anxiously waited for the eruption to run its course, not knowing whether it would end in a huge explosion.

Including All Students

Ask: **What are some signs that a volcano may be about to become active?** *(Accept all reasonable responses. Students will probably mention steam and other gases escaping from vents, bulges in the mountainside, a changing water level in a crater lake, small earthquakes in the area.)* **learning modality: verbal**

Volcano Hazards

Building Inquiry Skills: Inferring

ACTIVITY

Materials *sealed plastic bag containing ash and cinders from a fire, hand lens*
Time 10 minutes
Advance Preparation Prepare one bagged sample for each group of four students. Seal the bag securely with tape or staples. (CAUTION: *When you distribute the bags, warn students not to open them, as the fine dust could be inhaled.)*

Let students examine the sample both with and without a hand lens and note the varying sizes of the particles, particularly the extremely small size of the finest ash. Encourage students to draw circles and dots on a sheet of plain paper to represent the particle sizes they see. Then ask: **Why would something as tiny as these smallest ash particles be hazardous?** *(People and animals can breathe them in; plants coated with ash die; ash can clog automobile engines and other machinery; and so forth.)* **learning modality: visual**

Program Resources

Interdisciplinary Exploration Series "The Glory of Ancient Rome," pp. 20–23

Ongoing Assessment

Oral Presentation Ask each student to identify at least four ways in which geologists can determine that a volcano may erupt in the near future.

3 Assess

Section 2 Review Answers

1. Magma deep underground flows upward through cracks in rock. As the magma rises, the pressure decreases, and dissolved gases in the magma begin to separate out and form bubbles. When an opening develops in weak rock on the surface, the gases and magma erupt out of the volcano.
2. Quiet eruptions occur if the magma is thin and runny. The gases dissolved in the magma bubble out gently, and the lava oozes from the vent. Explosive eruptions occur if the magma is thick and sticky. The magma slowly collects in the volcano's neck and plugs it, trapping the gases. Pressure builds up until the gases explode, pushing the magma out of the volcano with great force. The explosion breaks the lava into fragments of different sizes.
3. Students may mention any of the hazards described on this page. Accept other reasonable answers as well.
4. Pahoehoe; produced by thin lava. The speed is high, and smooth ripples are characteristic of pahoehoe.

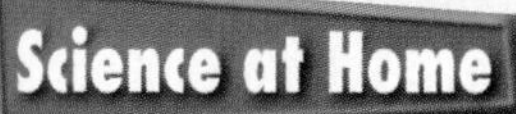

Materials *2 cups, cold water, hot water, candle, matches*
Tips You may want to let students do this activity in class before they present it at home. (CAUTION: Handle the lighted candle yourself; do not let students do so.) The wax in cold water will solidify more quickly and form a more rounded shape than the wax in hot water, with a greater temperature difference between the two cups producing more dramatic results. The model shows that quickly cooling magma forms distinct "lumps," whereas slowly cooling magma continues to spread out and forms a flatter mass.

Performance Assessment

Drawing Have each student draw and label a sketch to identify the parts of a volcano and describe what happens underground to cause an eruption.

Figure 10 A. Mudflows were one of the hazards of Mt. Pinatubo's 1991 eruption. B. People around Mt. Pinatubo wore masks to protect themselves from breathing volcanic ash.

Although quiet eruptions and explosive eruptions involve different volcano hazards, both types of eruption can cause damage far from the crater's rim. During a quiet eruption, lava flows pour from vents, setting fire to and then burying everything in their path. During an explosive eruption, a volcano can belch out hot, burning clouds of volcanic gases as well as cinders and bombs.

Volcanic ash can bury entire towns, damage crops, and clog car engines. If it becomes wet, the heavy ash can cause roofs to collapse. If a jet plane sucks ash into its engine, the engine may stall. Eruptions can also cause landslides and avalanches of mud, melted snow, and rock. Figure 10 shows some effects of mud and ash from Mount Pinatubo's eruption. When Mount St. Helens erupted, gigantic mudflows carried ash, trees, and rock fragments 29 kilometers down the nearby Toutle River.

Section 2 Review

1. What are the stages that lead up to a volcanic eruption?
2. Compare and contrast quiet and explosive eruptions.
3. Describe some of the hazards posed by volcanoes.
4. **Thinking Critically Drawing Conclusions** A geologist times a passing lava flow at 15 kilometers per hour. The geologist also sees that lava near the edge of the flow is forming smooth-looking ripples as it hardens. What type of lava is this? What type of magma produced it? Explain your conclusions.

Science at Home

Place cold water in one cup and hot tap water in another. **CAUTION:** *Handle the cup containing the hot water carefully to avoid spilling.* Ask members of your family to predict what will happen when some melted candle wax drops into each cup of water. Have an adult family member drip melted wax from a candle into each cup. Explain how this models what happens when lava cools quickly or more slowly.

Program Resources

◆ **Teaching Resources** 3-2 Review and Reinforce, p. 81; 3-2 Enrich, p. 82

Media and Technology

Interactive Student Tutorial CD-ROM F-3

3 Volcanic Landforms

Discover ACTIVITY

How Can Volcanic Activity Change Earth's Surface?

1. Use tape to secure the neck of a balloon over one end of a straw.
2. Place the balloon in the center of a box with the straw protruding.
3. Partially inflate the balloon.
4. Put damp sand on top of the balloon until it is covered.
5. Slowly inflate the balloon more. Observe what happens to the surface of the sand.

Think It Over

Making Models This activity models one of the ways in which volcanic activity can cause a mountain to form. What do you think the sand represents? What does the balloon represent?

Volcanoes have created some of Earth's most spectacular landforms. For example, the perfect volcanic cone of Mt. Fuji in Japan and the majestic profile of snow-capped Mt. Kilimanjaro rising above the grasslands of East Africa are famous around the world.

Some volcanic landforms arise when lava flows build up mountains and plateaus on Earth's surface. Other volcanic landforms are the result of the buildup of magma beneath the surface.

GUIDE FOR READING

- What landforms does lava create on Earth's surface?
- How does magma that hardens beneath the surface create landforms?

Reading Tip As you read, make a table comparing volcanic landforms. Include what formed each landform—lava, ash, or magma—as well as its characteristics.

Landforms From Lava and Ash

Rock and other materials formed from lava create a variety of landforms including shield volcanoes, composite volcanoes, cinder cone volcanoes, and lava plateaus. Look at *Exploring Volcanic Mountains* on page 105 to see the similarities and differences among these features.

◄ Mt. Fuji, Japan

3 Volcanic Landforms

Objectives

After completing the lesson, students will be able to

- identify landforms that lava creates on Earth's surface;
- explain how magma that hardens beneath the surface creates landforms.

Key Terms shield volcano, cinder cone, composite volcano, caldera, volcanic neck, dike, sill, batholith

1 Engage/Explore

Activating Prior Knowledge

Ask students: **What shape is a volcano?** Choose several volunteers to come to the board and draw what they think a volcano looks like. *(Students will most likely draw cone-shaped mountains.)* **Are all volcanoes shaped like this?** *(Accept all responses without comment at this time.)*

Discover

Skills Focus making models

Materials *tape, balloon, straw, box, damp sand*

Time 10–15 minutes

Tips Make sure the box is large enough for the balloon to fit when it is fully inflated. Tell students to inflate the balloon slowly in Step 5.

Expected Outcome As the balloon is inflated, a dome will form in the sand.

Think It Over The sand represents Earth's crust. The balloon represents a filling magma chamber.

Reading Strategies

Reading Tip Students' tables should include shield volcanoes, cinder cone volcanoes, composite volcanoes, lava plateaus, calderas, volcanic necks, dikes, sills, batholiths, and dome mountains. Suggest that students write the name of each landform on the front of an index card and a description and sketch on the back. Students can use the cards to review section content.

Program Resources

- **Teaching Resources** 3-3 Lesson Plan, p. 83; 3-3 Section Summary, p. 84
- **Interdisciplinary Explorations Series** "The Glory of Ancient Rome," pp. 24–25

Media and Technology

Audiotapes English- Spanish Summary 3-3

2 Facilitate

Landforms From Lava and Ash

Building Inquiry Skills: Classifying

Suggest that students look for photographs of the volcanoes mentioned but not pictured on these pages and of other volcanoes that exemplify the three mountain shapes. Point out to students that Kilauea—pictured on pages 86–87 and whose gentle eruptions they learned about on page 97—is a shield volcano. Encourage students to photocopy the pictures they find, label each one to identify the volcano type, and then use the pictures to create a bulletin board display, with all the pictures showing the same type of volcano grouped together. **learning modality: visual**

Addressing Naive Conceptions

Students may think that the terms *crater* and *caldera* are used interchangeably to refer to the same structure. Help them differentiate between the two by asking: **What is a crater?** *(A bowl-shaped area around a volcano's vent; if students cannot recall this information, direct their attention back to the visual essay on page 95.)* **What happens to change a crater into a caldera?** *(The vent and magma chamber empty during an eruption, and the top of the volcano collapses inward.)* **limited English proficiency**

Shield Volcanoes At some places on Earth's surface, thin layers of lava pour out of a vent and harden on top of previous layers. Such lava flows gradually build a wide, gently sloping mountain called a **shield volcano.** Shield volcanoes rising from a hot spot on the ocean floor created the Hawaiian Islands.

Cinder Cone Volcanoes A volcano can also be a **cinder cone,** a steep, cone-shaped hill or mountain. If a volcano's lava is thick and stiff, it may produce ash, cinders, and bombs. These materials pile up around the vent in a steep, cone-shaped pile. For example, Paricutín in Mexico erupted in 1943 in a farmer's cornfield. The volcano built up a cinder cone about 400 meters high.

Composite Volcanoes Sometimes, lava flows alternate with explosive eruptions of ash, cinder, and bombs. The result is a composite volcano. **Composite volcanoes** are tall, cone-shaped mountains in which layers of lava alternate with layers of ash. Examples of composite volcanoes include Mount Fuji in Japan and Mount St. Helens in Washington state.

Lava Plateaus Instead of forming mountains, some eruptions of lava form high, level areas called lava plateaus. First, lava flows out of several long cracks in an area. The thin, runny lava travels far before cooling and solidifying. Again and again, floods of lava flow on top of earlier floods. After millions of years, these layers of lava can form high plateaus. One example is the Columbia Plateau, which covers parts of Washington, Oregon, and Idaho.

Figure 11 Crater Lake in Oregon fills the caldera formed after an eruption that destroyed the top 2,000 meters of Mount Mazama nearly 7,000 years ago. *Developing Hypotheses Develop a hypothesis to explain the formation of Wizard Island, the small island in Crater Lake.*

Calderas Enormous eruptions may empty the main vent and the magma chamber beneath a volcano. The mountain becomes a hollow shell. With nothing to support it, the top of the mountain collapses inward. The huge hole left by the collapse of a volcanic mountain is called a **caldera** (kal DAIR uh). The hole is filled with the pieces of the volcano that have fallen inward, as well as some lava and ash. In Figure 11 you can see one of the world's largest calderas.

Checkpoint ***What are the three types of volcanic mountains?***

Background

Facts and Figures Shield volcanoes derive their name from the shape of a warrior's shield. Mauna Loa is one of five shield volcanoes that make up the island of Hawaii. It has taken nearly one million years and numerous eruptive cycles to build the island of Hawaii. Other islands, including Midway Island and the Galapagos Islands, were created in a similar manner.

Composite volcanoes, also called stratovolcanoes because of their layering, produce the most violent volcanic activity. Most active composite volcanoes are located in the Ring of Fire.

Cinder cones are rather small and often form on or near larger volcanoes. Because loose pyroclastic material remains stable on a slope of 30–40 degrees, cinder cones have very steep slopes. Parícutin is one of many cinder cones in central Mexico.

EXPLORING Volcanic Mountains

Volcanic activity is responsible for building up much of Earth's surface. Lava from volcanoes cools and hardens into three types of mountains.

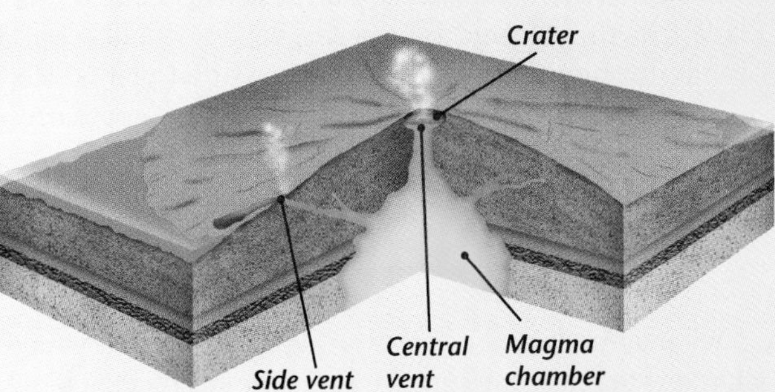

Shield Volcano
Repeated lava flows gradually build up a broad, gently sloping volcanic mountain known as a shield volcano.

▲ *Mauna Loa is a shield volcano in Hawaii.*

Cinder Cone Volcano
When cinders erupt again and again from a volcanic vent, they pile up around the vent, forming a cone-shaped hill called a cinder cone.

▲ *Sunset Crater is an extinct cinder cone in Arizona.*

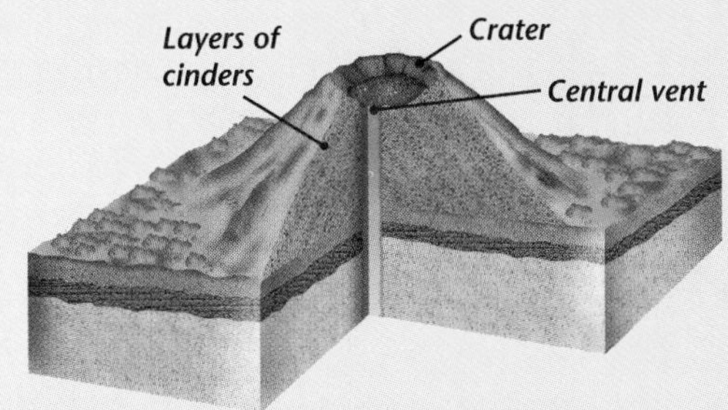

Composite Volcano
Layers of lava alternate with layers of ash, cinders, and bombs in a composite volcano, which has both quiet and explosive eruptions.

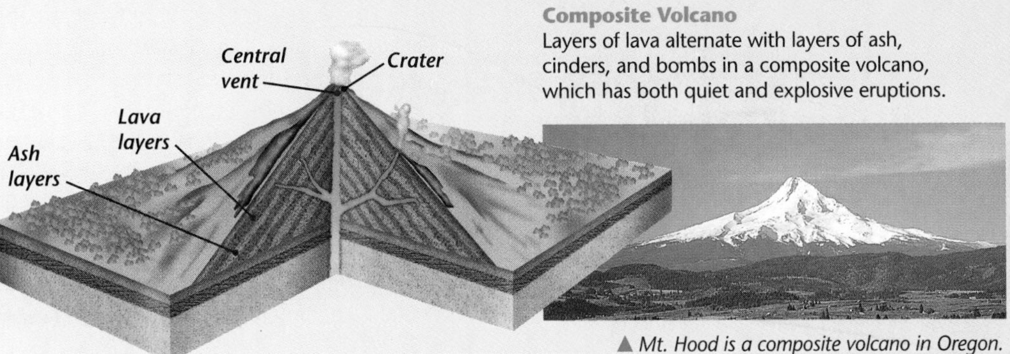

▲ *Mt. Hood is a composite volcano in Oregon.*

EXPLORING Volcanic Mountains

After students have examined the visual essay, ask: **How do the shapes of these mountains differ?** *(The cinder cone volcano is very steep-sided. The composite volcano is also steep-sided but has a wider base. The shield volcano has a very gradual slope and is not as high as the other two.)* **What causes these differences?** *(The type of material that erupts from each volcano; pyroclastic materials—ash, cinders, and bombs—seem to create a steeper slope.)* **learning modality: visual**

Inquiry Challenge

ACTIVITY

Materials *clay, fine sand, coarse sand, small pebbles, plaster of Paris or wheat paste*
Time 30 minutes

Challenge small groups to design a model that shows how a composite volcano builds up in alternating layers over time. Then allow groups to build the models with materials you provide or materials of their own choice. *(Beginning with a small hill made of clay as the "core," students could add a layer of mixed fine sand, coarse sand, and pebbles to represent ash, cinder, and bombs, then pour plaster of Paris or wheat paste over it to represent lava and let it harden, and repeat these layers alternately to build up a composite cone.)* **cooperative learning**

Media and Technology

Transparencies "Exploring Volcanic Mountains," Transparency 15

Answers to Self-Assessment

Caption Question

Figure 11 Wizard Island might be magma that hardened in the volcano's pipe.

Checkpoint

The three types of volcanic mountains are shield volcanoes, cinder cone volcanoes, and composite volcanoes.

Ongoing Assessment

Drawing Have each student draw cross- sectional views of the three volcano types, label each with its name, and add a brief explanation of how it is formed.

Students could save their sketches in their portfolios.

Soils from Lava and Ash

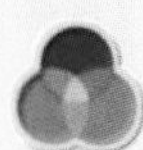

Integrating Environmental Science

Obtain (or ask students to find) photographs of the area around Mount St. Helens soon after the 1980 eruption and at intervals in the years afterward. (A good source is *Mount St. Helens, Eruption and Recovery of a Volcano* by Rob Carson, Sasquatch Books, 1990.) Let students examine the photographs to find evidence of regrowth in the area—first of small, scattered "settler" plants, then of wider areas of larger plants and saplings, and finally stands of maturing trees. Ask: **Where do you think the new plants came from?** *(Accept all reasonable answers. Examples: Seeds blew in from other, undamaged areas. Tree roots that were not destroyed grew new sprouts.)* **Were plants the only organisms that returned to the area? Why?** *(No, animals returned too because the regrowth provided food, shelter, and the like.)* **learning modality: visual**

Landforms from Magma

Building Inquiry Skills: Inferring

Ask students: **If magma is rising through the upper crust, why would it fail to reach the surface?** *(It might become trapped under a solid rock layer, or there might not be enough pressure to keep forcing the magma up. Accept other reasonable responses.)* **learning modality: logical/mathematical**

Including All Students

After students have read about domes, ask: **Where have you seen a bulging landform like this before?** *(In the Discover activity at the beginning of this section, when the inflated balloon made the sand bulge upward)* Review with students that the balloon in the model represented rising magma and the sand represented layers of rock in the upper crust. **learning modality: visual**

Soils from Lava and Ash

Integrating Environmental Science The lava, ash, and cinders that erupt from a volcano are initially barren. Over time, however, the hard surface of the lava flow breaks down to form soil. As soil develops, plants are able to grow. Some volcanic soils are among the richest soils in the world. Saying that soil is rich means that it's fertile, or able to support plant growth. Volcanic ash also breaks down and releases potassium, phosphorus, and other materials that plants need. Why would anyone live near an active volcano? People settle close to volcanoes to take advantage of the fertile volcanic soil.

☑ **Checkpoint** *How does volcanic soil form?*

Landforms from Magma

Sometimes magma forces its way through cracks in the upper crust, but fails to reach the surface. There the magma cools and hardens into rock. Or the forces that wear away Earth's surface—such as flowing water, ice, or wind—may strip away the layers of rock above the magma and finally expose it. **Features formed by magma include volcanic necks, dikes, and sills, as well as batholiths and dome mountains.**

Volcanic Necks, Dikes, and Sills A volcanic neck looks like a giant tooth stuck in the ground. A **volcanic neck** forms when magma hardens in a volcano's pipe. The softer rock around the pipe wears away, exposing the hard rock of the volcanic neck. Magma that forces itself into a vertical crack hardens into a **dike.** When magma squeezes between relatively horizontal layers of rock, it forms a **sill.**

Figure 12 Magma that hardens beneath the surface may form volcanic necks, dikes, and sills. *Compare and Contrast What is the difference between a dike and a sill?*

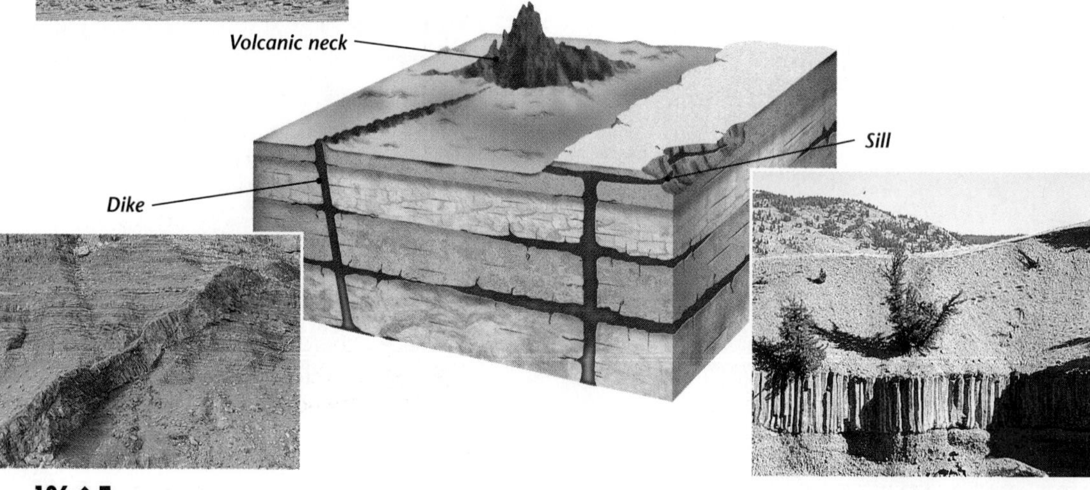

Background

Facts and Figures Like all land areas, volcanic mountains are subjected to weathering and erosion. Because they are composed of loose materials, cinder cones are most easily eroded. Thus, cinder cones are most apt to produce volcanic necks.

As erosion continues over millions of years, the looser materials surrounding the hardened magma in the pipe is worn away, leaving the more-resistant rock standing above the surrounding land long after the cone has disappeared.

One example of a volcanic neck is Ship Rock in New Mexico, shown in Figure 12. This structure stands about 450 m high, taller than many skyscrapers. Many volcanic necks dot the desert floor of the American Southwest. In time, even these necks will be worn away.

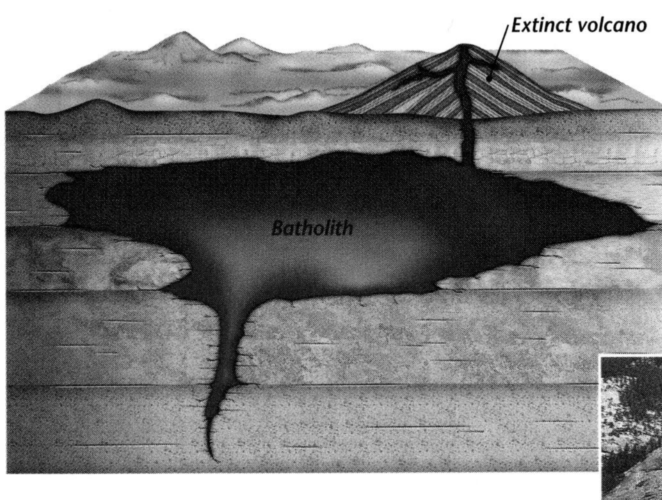

Figure 13 A batholith forms when magma cools inside the crust. One of the largest batholiths in North America forms the core of the Sierra Nevada mountains in California. These mountains in Yosemite National Park are part of that granite batholith.

Batholiths Large rock masses called batholiths form the core of many mountain ranges. A **batholith** (BATH uh lith) is a mass of rock formed when a large body of magma cools inside the crust. The diagram in Figure 13 shows how a batholith looks when it forms. The photograph shows how it looks when the layers of rock above it have worn away.

Dome Mountains Other, smaller bodies of magma can create dome mountains. A dome mountain forms when rising magma is blocked by horizontal layers of rock. The magma forces the layers of rock to bend upward into a dome shape. Eventually, the rock above the dome mountain wears away, leaving it exposed. This process formed the Black Hills in South Dakota.

Section 3 Review

1. Describe five landforms formed from lava and ash.
2. Describe the process that creates a lava plateau.
3. What features form as a result of magma hardening beneath Earth's surface?
4. Describe how a dome mountain can eventually form out of magma that hardened beneath Earth's surface.
5. **Thinking Critically** **Relating Cause and Effect** Explain the formation of a volcanic landform that can result when a volcano uses up the magma in its magma chamber.

Check Your Progress

CHAPTER PROJECT 3

By now you should have collected information about what it's like to live in a volcanic region. Do you need to do more research? Now begin to plan your presentation. One way to plan a presentation is to prepare storyboards. In a storyboard, you sketch each major step in the presentation on a separate sheet of paper. Decide who in your group is presenting each portion.

Program Resources

- **Teaching Resources** 3-3 Review and Reinforce, p. 85; 3-3 Enrich, p. 86

Media and Technology

Interactive Student Tutorial CD-ROM F-3

Exploring Earth Science Videodisc Unit 2, Side 2, "Flying Over America"

Chapter 7

3 Assess

Section 3 Review Answers

1. Students should describe shield volcanoes, cinder cone volcanoes, composite volcanoes, lava plateaus, and calderas using information from pages 104–105.
2. Thin, runny lava flows out of several long, horizontal cracks and travels far in all directions before cooling and hardening. Over time, layers of lava build up, forming a plateau.
3. Volcanic necks, dikes, sills, batholiths, dome mountains
4. Magma forces its way upward through cracks in the crust, but overlying rock layers keep the magma from reaching the surface. The magma forces the rock layers to bend upward into a dome shape. When the rock layers wear away, the dome is exposed.
5. A huge eruption can empty a volcano's magma chamber. Without magma to support it, the top of the mountain collapses inward, forming a caldera.

Check Your Progress

CHAPTER PROJECT 3

Consult with each group to determine whether the members were able to find all the information that they want to include in their documentary. If not, suggest or provide additional source materials. Discuss the storyboarding technique with the entire class to make sure each group knows what to do. Instruct students to include in their storyboards notes about the media materials they plan to use. Review each group's storyboard to make sure it includes all the required elements and to provide any help that students may need in organizing the information they have collected.

Performance Assessment

Oral Presentation Call on students to name one of the landforms discussed in this section and explain how it is formed.

Real-World Lab

How It Works

Gelatin Volcanoes

Preparing for Inquiry

Key Concept Magma inside a volcano generally flows vertically to form dikes.

Skills Objectives Students will be able to
- develop a hypothesis about how magma flows inside a volcano;
- make a model volcano to test their hypothesis;
- observe how "magma" flows inside their model.

Time 40 minutes

Advance Planning

Gelatin molds: At least five hours before students will do this lab, make a gelatin mold for each student group. You can use bowls ranging from $2\frac{1}{2}$ cups to 2 quarts in capacity. For a $2\frac{1}{2}$-cup bowl (such as a plastic margarine container), mix one 7-oz envelope of unflavored gelatin with $\frac{1}{2}$ cup of room-temperature water. Add $1\frac{1}{2}$ cups of boiling water and stir until the gelatin is completely dissolved. Add $\frac{1}{3}$ cup of cold water. Refrigerate the mold for 3–5 hours or until set. Also make a test mold in a smaller container. After 3 hours, check the hardness of the test mold by removing it from its container. If it is not completely set, refrigerate the large molds for at least another 2 hours. You may want to practice removing one mold from its bowl beforehand to make sure you can demonstrate the technique successfully to the class.

Pegboard: Use pegboard with holes 5 mm in diameter. Cut the pegboard into squares about 10 cm wider than the tops of the bowls.

Syringe: Use plastic bird-feeding syringes, which will pass through the pegboard holes and pierce the gelatin by at least 1 cm.

Layered volcano (More to Explore): Fill a bowl only half full with gelatin solution, and set aside the rest at room temperature. Add the second layer to the bowl after the first layer has been refrigerated for two hours.

Alternative Materials Instead of a pegboard square, each group could use a disposable aluminum tray with holes punched in it with a nail. Drive the nail *downward* through the tray so the upper surface stays smooth and the gelatin mold will not snag on the holes' edges.

Real-World Lab

How It Works

Gelatin Volcanoes

Does the magma inside a volcano move along fractures, or through tubes or pipes? How does the eruption of magma create features such as dikes and sills? You can use a gelatin volcano model and red-colored liquid "magma" to find answers to these questions.

Problem

How does magma move inside a volcano?

Skills Focus

developing hypotheses, making models, observing

Materials

plastic cup
knife
unflavored gelatin mold in bowl
red food coloring and water
plastic syringe, 10 cc
two books (30 cm high)
rubber gloves
unlined paper
colored pencils
pegboard
tray

Procedure 

1. Before magma erupts as lava, how does it travel up from underground magma chambers? Record your hypothesis.
2. Remove the gelatin from the refrigerator. Loosen the gelatin from its container by briefly placing the container of gelatin in a larger bowl of hot water.
3. Place the pegboard over the gelatin so the mold is near the center of the pegboard. While holding the pegboard against the top of the mold, carefully turn the mold and pegboard upside down.
4. Place the pegboard with the gelatin mold on top of the books as shown in the photograph.
5. Carefully lift the bowl off the gelatin mold to create a gelatin volcano.
6. Fill the syringe with the red water ("magma"). Remove air bubbles from the syringe by holding it upright and squirting out a small amount of water.
7. Insert the tip of the syringe through a hole in the pegboard near the center of the gelatin volcano. Inject the magma into the gelatin very slowly. It should take at least 30 seconds to empty the syringe. Observe what happens to the magma.
8. Repeat steps 6 and 7 as many times as possible. Observe the movement of the magma each time. Note any differences in the direction the magma takes when the syringe is inserted into different parts of the gelatin volcano. Record your observations.
9. Look down on your gelatin volcano from above. Make a sketch of the positions and shapes of the magma bodies. Label your drawing "Top View."
10. Carefully use a knife to cut your volcano in half. Separate the pieces and examine the cut surfaces. Observe the traces made by the magma bodies.
11. Sketch the positions and shapes of the magma bodies on one of the cut faces. Label your drawing "Cross Section."

Guiding Inquiry

Invitation Ask: **What are dikes and sills made of?** *(Hardened magma)* **What is the major difference between a dike and a sill?** *(Dikes are vertical; sills are horizontal.)*

Introducing the Procedure

Have students read the entire procedure and examine the picture of the lab set-up. Ask if they have any questions before they begin.

Troubleshooting the Experiment
- Demonstrate the mold-removal process described in steps 2–5.
- Have students wear rubber gloves in steps 6–8 to keep their hands from being stained by the food coloring.
- In Step 6, have students lightly tap the

Analyze and Conclude

1. Describe how the magma moved through your model. Did the magma move straight up through the center of your model volcano or did it branch off in places? Explain why you think the magma moved in this way.
2. What knowledge or experience did you use to develop your hypothesis? How did the actual movement compare with your hypothesis?
3. Were there differences in the direction the magma flowed when the syringe was inserted in different parts of the gelatin volcano?
4. **Apply** How does what you observed in your model compare to the way magma moves through real volcanoes?

Design an Experiment

Plan to repeat the experiment using a mold made of two layers of gelatin. Before injecting the magma, predict what effect the layering will have on magma movement. Record your observations to determine if your hypothesis was correct. What volcanic feature is produced by this version of the model? Can you think of other volcanic features that you could model using gelatin layers?

syringe before they squirt water out.

- Before students begin injecting colored water in Step 7, make sure they have put a tray under the pegboard to catch any water that drains out of the mold.
- If colored water dribbles down the syringe in steps 7 and 8, students can wrap a folded paper towel around it.
- In Step 10, make sure students cut the volcano in half *from top to bottom,* not across its diameter.

Program Resources

- **Teaching Resources** Real-World Lab blackline masters, pp. 94–95

Safety

Students should wear a lab apron during this lab to protect their clothing from food coloring. Review the safety guidelines in Appendix A.

Expected Outcome
With a slow, steady injection rate, the colored water will create thin, vertical dikes inside the gelatin.

Analyze and Conclude
1. The magma spread vertically from the point of injection into a fan-shaped dike that gradually grew until it broke through the surface of the volcano. With repeated injections, dikes may have branched off into other vertical planes. The magma moved in this way because there was upward pressure on it from the syringe.
2. Answers will vary. Students should base their answers on what they have already learned about how magma flows through a volcano and how dikes are formed in a vertical or near-vertical plane.
3. When injected into the center, the magma flowed radially outward in any direction. When injected near the edge, magma flowed to the closest surface point, following a path of least resistance.
4. The colored water flowed vertically in the direction of least resistance, much like a flow of magma in an actual volcano.

Extending the Inquiry

Design an Experiment Horizontal sills will form along the joint between the layers. Students might also be able to model dome mountains or batholiths.

Volcanoes in the Solar System

Objectives

After completing the lesson, students will be able to

- explain how volcanoes on Mars and Venus compare with volcanoes on Earth;
- describe the volcanic activity found on the moons of Jupiter and Neptune.

1 Engage/Explore

Activating Prior Knowledge

Ask: **What are the names of the planets in our solar system in order from the one closest to the sun to the one farthest away?** *(Mercury, Venus, Earth, Mars, Jupiter, Saturn, Uranus, Neptune, Pluto; if students cannot recall all the names in their correct order, teach them the following mnemonic device:* ***M****y* ***V****ery* ***E****asy* ***M****ethod:* ***J****ust* ***S****tand* ***U****nder* ***N****orth* ***P****ole.)*

DISCOVER

Skills Focus posing questions
Time 5 minutes
Tips Suggest that students compare these photographs to other photographs in this chapter showing volcanoes erupting or evidence of past volcanic activity.
Expected Outcome Accept all plausible answers when students speculate about the nature of the cloud in Photo A. Clearly, something is erupting into Io's atmosphere. In Photo B, some sort of material seems to have erupted from inside Io and flowed across its surface, much like a lava flow on Earth. Volcanoes on Io erupt molten sulfur.
Think It Over Students' questions will vary. *Examples:* What kind of material is erupting in Photo A? What material formed the riverlike flows in Photo B? Does the location in Photo A show repeated eruptions over time? Are more flows added to the location in Photo B?

INTEGRATING SPACE SCIENCE 

Section 4 Volcanoes in the Solar System

DISCOVER ACTIVITY

What Forces Shaped the Surface of Io?

Io is a moon of Jupiter. Pictures taken by the *Voyager* space probe as it passed by Io in 1979 show signs of unusual features and activity on Io.

1. Observe the blue cloud rising above the rim of Io in the top photo. What do you think it could be?
2. Look at the feature on Io's surface shown in the bottom photo. What do you think it looks like?

Think It Over

Posing Questions Is the volcanic activity on Io similar to that on Earth? State several questions that you would like to answer in order to find out.

GUIDE FOR READING

- How do volcanoes on Mars and Venus compare with volcanoes on Earth?
- What volcanic activity is found on the moons of Jupiter and Neptune?

Reading Tip Before you read, preview the headings in the section. Then predict where, besides Earth, volcanoes are found in the solar system.

Earth is not the only body in the solar system to show signs of volcanic activity. Pictures taken by space probes show evidence of past volcanic activity on Mercury, Venus, and Mars. These planets—like Earth and its moon—have rocky crusts. Scientists think these planets once had hot, molten cores. The heat caused volcanic activity. But because these planets are smaller than Earth, their cores have cooled, bringing volcanic activity to an end.

Geologists are eager for information about other planets and moons. By comparing other bodies in the solar system with Earth, geologists can learn more about the processes that have shaped Earth over billions of years.

Earth's Moon

If you looked at the full moon through a telescope you would notice that much of the moon's surface is pockmarked with light-colored craters. Other, darker areas on the moon's surface look unusually smooth. The craters mark where meteorites have smashed into the moon over billions of years. The smooth areas are where lava flowed onto the moon's surface more than three billion years ago.

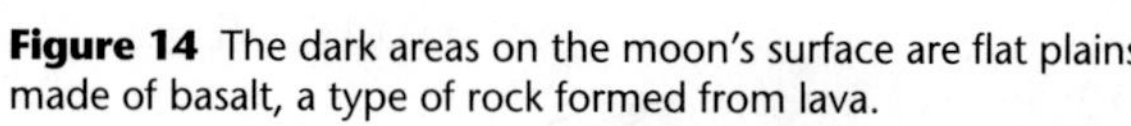

Figure 14 The dark areas on the moon's surface are flat plains made of basalt, a type of rock formed from lava.

READING STRATEGIES

Vocabulary Point out that other than Earth, the names of the planets in our solar system and many of their moons are derived from the names of gods and other characters in Greek and Roman mythology. Encourage students to find out who the mythological gods and characters mentioned in this section were. *(**Mercury:** the Roman god of trade and travel, messenger of the gods; **Venus:** the Roman goddess of love and beauty; **Mars:** the Roman god of war; **Jupiter:** the supreme Roman god; **Saturn:** the Roman god of agriculture, father of Jupiter; **Uranus:** a Greek god personifying the sky; **Neptune:** the Roman god of the sea; **Pluto:** the Roman god of the dead, ruler of the underworld; **Io:** in Greek myth, a maiden who was loved by Zeus (the Greek equivalent of Jupiter) and changed into a heifer by Zeus's jealous wife, Hera; **Triton:** a Greek god of the sea)*

Figure 15 The space probe *Magellan* observed volcanoes on Venus, but no recent or ongoing eruptions.

Volcanoes on Venus

Geologists were excited about the results of the space probe *Magellan's* mission to Venus in 1990. Venus shows signs of widespread volcanic activity that lasted for billions of years. Venus has thousands of volcanoes, more than any other planet in the solar system. There are about 150 large volcanoes measuring between 100 and 600 kilometers across and about half a kilometer high. The largest volcano on Venus, Theia Mons, is 800 kilometers across and 4 kilometers high.

Like Earth, Venus has volcanic mountains and other features that are probably made of thin, runny lava. Such lava produces gently sloping shield volcanoes with broad bases, as well as long, riverlike lava flows. One of the lava flows on Venus is more than 6,800 kilometers long!

☑ *Checkpoint* *What type of volcano is most common on Venus?*

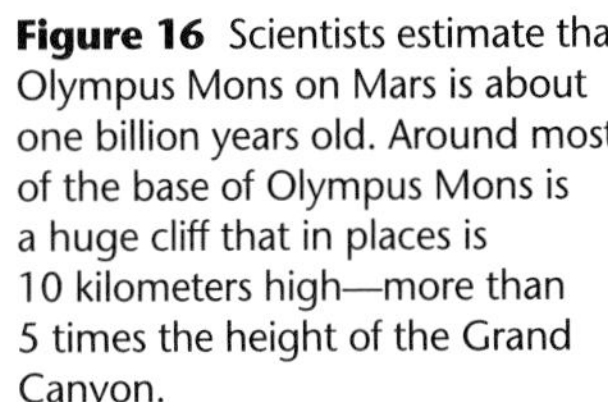

Volcanoes on Mars

Mars is a planet with a long history of volcanic activity. However, there are far fewer volcanoes on Mars than on Venus. Volcanoes are found in only a few regions of Mars' surface.

Mars has a variety of volcanic features. **On Mars there are large shield volcanoes similar to those on Venus and Earth, as well as cone-shaped volcanoes and lava flows.** Mars also has lava plains that resemble the lava flows on the moon.

The biggest volcano on Mars is the largest mountain in the solar system. This volcano, Olympus Mons, is a shield volcano similar to Mauna Loa on the island of Hawaii, but much, much bigger! Olympus Mons covers an area as large as Ohio. This huge volcano, shown in Figure 16, is over eight times taller than Theia Mons on Venus.

Figure 16 Scientists estimate that Olympus Mons on Mars is about one billion years old. Around most of the base of Olympus Mons is a huge cliff that in places is 10 kilometers high—more than 5 times the height of the Grand Canyon.

2 Facilitate

Earth's Moon

Using the Visuals: Figure 14

ACTIVITY

Point out to students that this photograph shows the side of the moon that always faces Earth. Suggest that they take their book outside on the next evening when there is a full moon and compare the photograph with the real moon. Have them sketch what they see. **learning modality: visual**

Volcanoes on Venus

Using the Visuals: Figure 15

Draw students' attention to the caption and ask: **Are the volcanoes on Venus active, dormant, or extinct? How do you know?** *(Either dormant or extinct; Magellan's photographs did not show any recent or ongoing eruptions on the planet.)* **learning modality: logical/mathematical**

Volcanoes on Mars

Building Inquiry Skills: Inferring

Ask students: **If a planet has active volcanoes erupting lava on its surface, what does that tell you about the planet's interior?** *(It must be hot, like Earth's mantle.)* **If a planet shows signs of active volcanoes in the far-distant past but no evidence of recent eruptions, what does that tell you about the planet's interior?** *(It must have cooled so there is no longer any hot magma below the surface.)* **learning modality: logical/mathematical**

Program Resources

◆ **Teaching Resources** 3-4 Lesson Plan, p. 87; 3-4 Section Summary, p. 88

Media and Technology

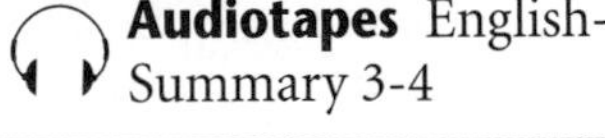

Audiotapes English- Spanish Summary 3-4

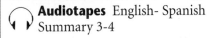

Answers to Self-Assessment

☑ *Checkpoint*

Gently sloping shield volcanoes are most common on Venus.

Ongoing Assessment

Writing Have each student briefly describe the volcanoes on Venus and Mars.

Volcanoes on Distant Moons

Including All Students

Ask: **Why would it be difficult for a space probe to observe eruptions in progress on other moons?** *(The probe would have to be flying past the right place at just the right time.)* **learning modality: logical/mathematical**

3 Assess

Section 4 Review Answers

1. Venus has many shield volcanoes and other features that are probably made of thin, runny lava. Mars has far fewer but a greater variety of volcanoes than Venus. Like Earth, both planets show signs of wide-spread volcanic activity that lasted for billions of years.
2. Io's and Triton's volcanoes erupt different materials from Earth's volcanoes—sulfur on Io and liquid nitrogen on Triton.
3. Olympus Mons, a shield volcano on Mars
4. Venus's volcanoes appear to be made of thin, runny basaltic lava, which produces long, riverlike lava flows and gently sloping shield volcanoes with broad bases. Mars has cone-shaped volcanoes as well as shield volcanoes. Venus has thousands of volcanoes; Mars has far fewer, and they are found in only a few regions.

Check Your Progress (Chapter Project 3)

Suggest that group members display the visuals to one another from across the room to check whether they are readable at a distance. Provide tape recorders, videocameras, and a separate, quiet area for making the recordings without disturbing others.

Performance Assessment

Oral Presentation Have students describe the volcanic features observed on one planet (besides Earth) or moon in our solar system.

Figure 17 The surface of Neptune's moon Triton has areas covered by frozen "lava lakes" that show where liquid material erupted from inside Triton. **Posing Questions** *Imagine that you are observing Triton from a spacecraft. What questions would you want to answer about volcanic activity there?*

Scientists estimate that volcanic activity on Mars probably goes back about 3.5 billion years, to about the same time as the volcanic activity on the moon. Lava flows on Olympus Mons may range from as little as 100 years old to more than 100 million years old.

Volcanoes on Distant Moons

Besides Earth, there are only two other bodies in the solar system where volcanic eruptions have been observed: Io, a moon of the planet Jupiter, and Triton, a moon of the planet Neptune. *Voyager 1* photographed eruptions on these moons as it sped past them in 1979. Geologists on Earth were amazed when they saw these pictures. **Io and Triton have volcanic features very different from those on Earth, Mars, and Venus.** On Io, sulfur volcanoes erupt like fountains or spread out like umbrellas above the colorful surface.

The eruptions on Triton involve nitrogen. On Earth, nitrogen is a gas. Triton is so cold, however, that most of the nitrogen there is frozen solid. Scientists hypothesize that Triton's surface, which is made up of frozen water and other materials, absorbs heat from the sun. This heat melts some of the frozen nitrogen underneath Triton's surface. The liquid nitrogen then expands and erupts through the planet's icy crust.

Other moons of Jupiter, Saturn, and Neptune show signs of volcanic activity, but space probes have not observed any eruptions in progress on these moons.

Section 4 Review

1. Describe what volcanic activity is like on Venus and Mars. Does volcanic activity on these planets resemble volcanic activity on Earth? Explain.
2. How is volcanic activity on the moons of Jupiter and Neptune different from volcanic activity on Earth?
3. What is the largest volcano in the solar system? What type of volcano is it?
4. **Thinking Critically Comparing and Contrasting** How do the volcanoes on Venus compare with the volcanoes on Mars?

Check Your Progress (Chapter Project 3)

By this time, your group should have planned your documentary and know what materials you will need. Put the finishing touches on your presentation. Make sure any posters, overhead transparencies, or computer art will be easy for your audience to read. If you are using video or audio, make your recordings now. Revise and polish any narrative, rap, or skit. *(Hint:* Check the length of your presentation.)

Program Resources

- **Teaching Resources** 3-4 Review and Reinforce, p. 89; 3-4 Enrich, p. 90

Media and Technology

 **Interactive Student Tutorial CD-ROM** F-3

Answers to Self-Assessment

Caption Question

Figure 17 Students' questions will vary. *Examples:* What kind of material formed the "lava lakes"? Do eruptions still occur, or are the volcanoes extinct? Where on Triton's surface are volcanoes located?

STUDY GUIDE

Section 1 Volcanoes and Plate Tectonics

Key Ideas

- A volcano is an opening on Earth's surface where magma escapes from the interior. Magma that reaches Earth's surface is called lava.
- The constructive force of volcanoes adds new rock to existing land and forms new islands.
- Most volcanoes occur near the boundaries of Earth's plates and along the edges of continents, in island arcs, or along mid-ocean ridges.

Key Terms

volcano
magma
lava
Ring of Fire
island arc
hot spot

Section 2 Volcanic Activity

Key Ideas

- An eruption occurs when gases trapped in magma rush through an opening at the Earth's surface, carrying magma with them.
- Volcanoes can erupt quietly or explosively, depending on the amount of dissolved gases in the magma and on how thick or fluid the magma is.
- When magma heats water underground, hot springs and geysers form.
- Volcano hazards include pyroclastic flows, avalanches of mud, damage from ash, lava flows, flooding, and deadly gases.

Key Terms

magma chamber
pipe
vent
lava flow
crater
silica
pahoehoe
aa
pyroclastic flow
active
dormant
extinct
hot spring
geyser
geothermal energy

Section 3 Volcanic Landforms

Key Ideas

- Different types of volcanic eruptions form different types of landforms.
- Lava on the surface creates landforms such as shield volcanoes, cinder cones, composite volcanoes, and plateaus.
- One benefit of volcanoes is fertile soil.
- Magma that hardens beneath the surface creates batholiths, dome mountains, dikes, and sills that are eventually exposed when the covering rock wears away.

Key Terms

shield volcano
composite volcano
cinder cone
volcanic neck
dike
sill
batholith

Section 4 Volcanoes in the Solar System

Integrating Space Science

Key Ideas

- Venus and Mars both have extinct volcanoes similar to volcanoes on Earth.
- Spacecraft have photographed volcanic activity on moons of Jupiter and Neptune.

www.science-explorer.phschool.com

CHAPTER 3 REVIEW

Program Resources

- **Teaching Resources** Chapter 3 Project Scoring Rubric, p. 74; Chapter 3 Performance Assessment, pp. 182–184; Chapter 3 Test, pp. 185–188

Media and Technology

 **Interactive Student Tutorial CD-ROM** F-3

 **Computer Test Bank** Chapter 3 Test

CHAPTER 3 REVIEW

Reviewing Content: Multiple Choice

1. c **2.** d **3.** c **4.** d **5.** c

True or False

6. true **7.** lava plateaus **8.** true **9.** true
10. Mars

Checking Concepts

11. A volcanic belt formed by volcanoes that rim the Pacific Ocean
12. The mid-ocean ridge marks a diverging plate boundary, and lava pours out of cracks in the ocean floor.
13. In the middle of continental or oceanic plates, often far from plate boundaries
14. The amount of silica in magma helps determine how easily the magma flows. Magma high in silica produces light-colored lava that is too sticky to flow very far and forms rhyolite, pumice, and obsidian. Magma low in silica flows readily and produces dark-colored lava that forms basalt.
15. Hot springs form when groundwater heated by a nearby body of magma rises to the surface and collects in a natural pool. A geyser forms when rising hot water and steam become trapped underground in a narrow crack until pressure builds and the mixture suddenly sprays to the surface.
16. Aa; forms from cooler, slower-moving lava
17. Lava repeatedly flows out of a wide fissure and hardens to form thin layers, gradually building up a wide, gently sloping mountain.
18. Geologists know that many small earthquakes occur in the area around a volcano before it erupts. These quakes are triggered by movement of magma into the magma chamber and through the pipe.
19. Students may base part of their reports on the photographs of the Mount St. Helens eruption on pages 98–99, adding details such as the sound and smell of the eruption and its effects on people, plants, and animals living in the area.

CHAPTER 3 REVIEW

Reviewing Content

For more review of key concepts, see the Interactive Student Tutorial CD-ROM.

Multiple Choice

Choose the letter of the best answer.

1. When two oceanic plates collide, the result may be
   a. volcanoes on the edge of a continent.
   b. a hot spot volcano.
   c. volcanoes in an island arc.
   d. a volcano along the mid-ocean ridge.
2. The force that causes magma to erupt at the surface is provided by
   a. heat.
   b. the shape of the pipe.
   c. geothermal energy.
   d. dissolved gases under pressure.
3. An eruption of thin, fluid lava would most likely be
   a. a cinder-cone eruption.
   b. an explosive eruption.
   c. a quiet eruption.
   d. a pyroclastic eruption.
4. Alternating layers of lava and volcanic ash are found in
   a. dome mountains.
   b. dikes and sills.
   c. shield volcanoes.
   d. composite volcanoes.
5. Which of the following has active volcanoes?
   a. Venus b. Mars
   c. Triton d. Earth's moon

True or False

If the statement is true, write true. If it is false, change the underlined word or words to make the statement true.

6. Many volcanoes are found in island arcs that form where two oceanic plates collide.
7. Thin, runny lava usually hardens into ash, cinders, and bombs.
8. An extinct volcano is not likely to erupt in your lifetime.
9. Hot spots form where a plume of magma rises through the crust from the mantle.
10. Olympus Mons, the largest mountain in the solar system, is found on Venus.

Checking Concepts

11. What is the Ring of Fire?
12. How does plate tectonics explain the volcanoes that form along the mid-ocean ridge?
13. Where are hot spot volcanoes located in relation to Earth's plates?
14. What effect does silica content have on the characteristics of magma?
15. How do hot springs and geysers form?
16. While observing a lava flow from a recently active volcano, you notice an area of lava with a rough, chunky surface. What type of lava is this and how does it form?
17. How does a shield volcano form?
18. Why can earthquakes be a warning sign that an eruption is about to happen?
19. **Writing to Learn** Pretend you are a newspaper reporter in 1980. You have been assigned to report on the eruption of Mount St. Helens. Write a news story describing your observations.

Thinking Visually

20. **Concept Map** Copy the concept map about types of volcanic mountains onto a separate sheet of paper. Then complete it and add a title. (For more on concept maps, see the Skills Handbook.)

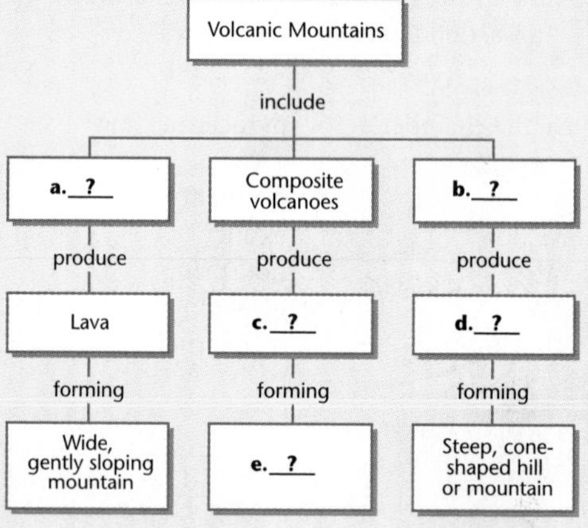

Thinking Visually

20. a. shield volcano **b.** cinder cone volcano **c.** lava flows alternating with explosive eruptions of ash, cinder, and bombs **d.** lava that hardens into ash, cinders, and bombs **e.** a tall, cone-shaped mountain

Applying Skills

21. Alternating layers of lava and ash; a composite volcano
22. A is a sill; B is a dike. A sill forms when magma squeezes between horizontal rock layers and hardens. A dike forms when magma forces into a vertical crack and hardens.
23. Explosively; the volcanic cone has layers of ash, so we know that pyroclastic materials were erupted; such eruptions are explosive, not quiet.
24. The pipe; pressure might build up to the point where the entire top of the mountain blows off in a violent explosion, or if there were cracks in the layers, a new pipe might form leading to the side of the cone. (Accept other reasonable responses.)

Applying Skills

Refer to the diagram to answer Questions 21–24.

21. **Classifying** What is this volcano made of? How do geologists classify a volcano made of these materials?
22. **Developing Hypotheses** What is the feature labeled A in the diagram? What is the feature labeled B? How do these features form?

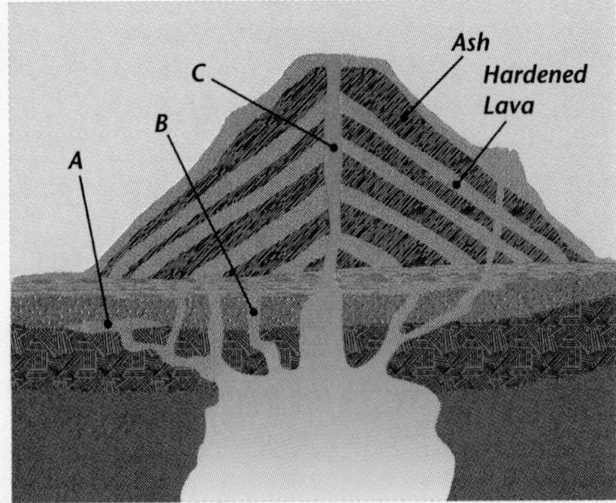

23. **Inferring** This volcano is located where oceanic crust is subducted under continental crust. Would the volcano erupt quietly or explosively? Give reasons for your answer.
24. **Predicting** What is the feature labeled C in the diagram? If this feature becomes plugged with hardened magma, what could happen to the volcano? Explain.

Thinking Critically

25. **Applying Concepts** Is a volcanic eruption likely to occur on the east coast of the United States? Explain your answer.
26. **Comparing and Contrasting** Compare the way in which an island arc forms with the way in which a hot spot volcano forms.
27. **Making Generalizations** How might a volcanic eruption affect the area around a volcano, including its plant and animal life?

CHAPTER 3 REVIEW

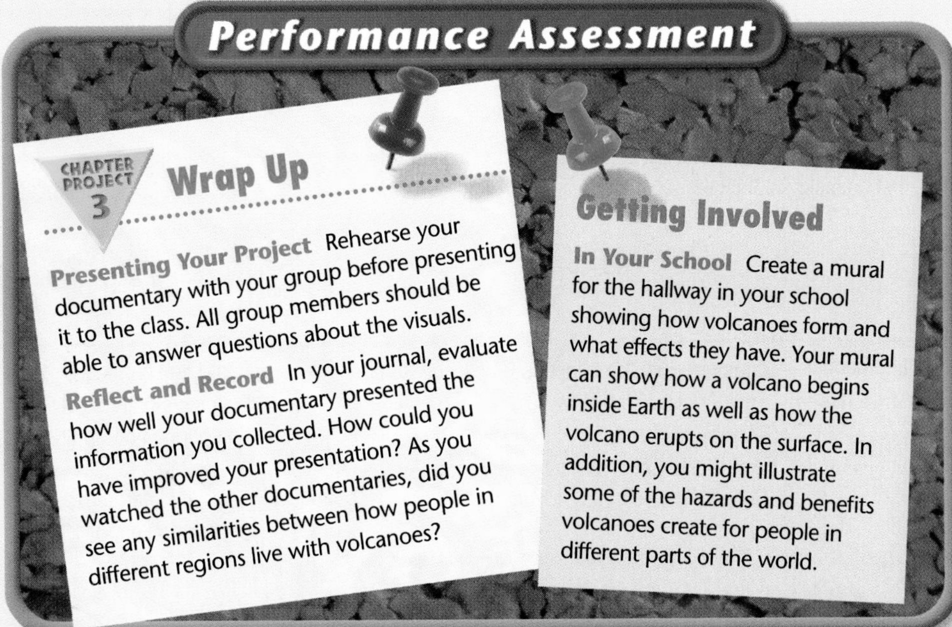

Performance Assessment
CHAPTER PROJECT 3
Wrap Up
Presenting Your Project Rehearse your documentary with your group before presenting it to the class. All group members should be able to answer questions about the visuals.
Reflect and Record In your journal, evaluate how well your documentary presented the information you collected. How could you have improved your presentation? As you watched the other documentaries, did you see any similarities between how people in different regions live with volcanoes?
Getting Involved
In Your School Create a mural for the hallway in your school showing how volcanoes form and what effects they have. Your mural can show how a volcano begins inside Earth as well as how the volcano erupts on the surface. In addition, you might illustrate some of the hazards and benefits volcanoes create for people in different parts of the world.

Thinking Critically

25. No. As shown in Figure 1, page 89, there are no active volcanoes in the eastern United States. (Students may also recall, based on the plate map on page 43, that the continental North American plate and the oceanic Caribbean plate are moving away from each other (diverging), whereas volcanoes are more common along the boundaries of converging plates where subduction occurs.)
26. An island arc forms at a converging boundary between two oceanic plates where one subducts under the other and creates a deep-ocean trench. A hot spot volcano forms in a continental or oceanic plate where magma from deep within the mantle melts through the crust. Hot spot volcanoes often lie in the middle of plates and do not result from subduction.

Program Resources

- **Inquiry Skills Activity Book** Provides teaching and review of all inquiry skills

27. Accept all reasonable responses. *Examples:* Plants and animals could be killed by lava flows, pyroclastic flows, clouds of suffocating gases, mudflows, or avalanches. The land surface would also be changed, and new landforms created. Nutrient-rich lava, ash, and cinders would in time form fertile soil.

Performance Assessment

Wrap Up (CHAPTER PROJECT 3)

Presenting Your Project
You may want to provide time for groups to practice their presentations. Inform students how much time each group will have for its presentation. Tell them that if their practice presentation runs too long, they should find ways to cut its length without jeopardizing its content or flow.
Reflect and Record Give students time to record their thoughts individually, then encourage them to discuss their ideas with the other members of their group. Let students respond to the last question in a whole-class discussion. Emphasize the similarities that students identify by listing them on the board or an overhead transparency.

Getting Involved

In Your School To encourage variety in the mural and avoid duplication, help students plan the mural in a whole-class discussion, identifying the various parts they think should be shown. List the parts on the board, then let students work in small groups, with each group responsible for one part of the mural. Advise students to make sure the various parts are integrated into a coherent whole rather than disconnected scenes. In addition to using the chapter text and illustrations as source material, encourage students to consult library books, videos, CD-ROM programs, and other references to obtain ideas and information.

Minerals

Sections	Time	Student Edition Activities	Other Activities
CHAPTER PROJECT 4 **Growing a Crystal Garden** p. 117	Ongoing (2 weeks)	Check Your Progress, p. 126 Check Your Progress, p. 132 Wrap Up, p. 143	
1 Properties of Minerals pp. 118–127 ◆ Identify the characteristics of a mineral. ◆ Identify the properties of minerals and explain how minerals are identified.	3–4 periods/ $1\frac{1}{2}$–2 blocks	**Discover** What Is the True Color of a Mineral?, p. 118 **Sharpen Your Skills** Classifying, p. 121 **Try This** Crystal Hands, p. 125 **Skills Lab: Measuring** The Density of Minerals, p. 127	TE Building Inquiry Skills: Classifying, p. 119 TE Building Inquiry Skills: Comparing and Contrasting, p. 121 TE Inquiry Challenge, p. 122 TE Building Inquiry Skills: Observing, p. 122 TE Building Inquiry Skills: Classifying, p. 123 TE Including All Students, p. 125 TE Demonstration, p. 125 TE Inquiry Challenge, p. 125 ISLM F-4, "How Tesselating!"
2 How Minerals Form pp. 128–133 ◆ Describe the processes by which minerals form.	2–3 periods/ 1–$1\frac{1}{2}$ blocks	**Discover** How Does the Rate of Cooling Affect Crystals?, p. 128	TE Building Inquiry Skills: Designing Experiments, p. 129 TE Building Inquiry Skills: Inferring, p. 130 TE Demonstration, p. 131
3 *INTEGRATING TECHNOLOGY* **Mineral Resources** pp. 134–140 ◆ Describe how minerals are used. ◆ List the three types of mines. ◆ Explain how ores are processed to obtain metals.	2–3 periods/ 1–$1\frac{1}{2}$ blocks	**Discover** How Are Minerals Processed Before They Are Used?, p. 134 **Science at Home,** p. 138 **Real-World Lab: Careers in Science** Copper Recovery, p. 140	TE Real-Life Learning, p. 135 TE Building Inquiry Skills: Comparing and Contrasting, p. 135 TE Real-Life Learning, p. 138 TE Demonstration, p. 138
Study Guide/Chapter Review pp. 141–143	1 period/ $\frac{1}{2}$ block		ISAB Provides teaching and review of all inquiry skills

For Standard or Block Schedule The Resource Pro® CD-ROM gives you maximum flexibility for planning your instruction for any type of schedule. Resource Pro® contains Planning Express®, an advanced scheduling program, as well as the entire contents of the Teaching Resources and the Computer Test Bank.

CHAPTER PLANNING GUIDE

Program Resources	Assessment Strategies	Media and Technology
TR Chapter 4 Project Teacher Notes, pp. 96–97 **TR** Chapter 4 Project Overview and Worksheets, pp. 98–101 **TR** Chapter 4 Project Scoring Rubric, p. 102	**SE** Performance Assessment: Chapter 4 Project Wrap Up, p. 143 **TE** Check Your Progress, pp. 126, 132 **TE** Performance Assessment: Chapter 4 Project Wrap Up, p. 143 **TR** Chapter 4 Project Scoring Rubric, p. 102	
TR 4-1 Lesson Plan, p. 103 **TR** 4-1 Section Summary, p. 104 **TR** 4-1 Review and Reinforce, p. 105 **TR** 4-1 Enrich, p. 106 **TR** Chapter 4 Skills Lab, pp. 115–117 **SES** Book K, *Chemical Building Blocks,* Chapter 3	**SE** Section 1 Review, p. 126 **SE** Analyze and Conclude, p. 127 **TE** Ongoing Assessment, pp. 119, 121, 123, 125 **TE** Performance Assessment, p. 126 **TR** 4-1 Review and Reinforce, p. 105	Audiotapes, English-Spanish Summary 4-1 Transparency 16, "Properties and Uses of Minerals" Interactive Student Tutorial CD-ROM, F-4
TR 4-2 Lesson Plan, p. 107 **TR** 4-2 Section Summary, p. 108 **TR** 4-2 Review and Reinforce, p. 109 **TR** 4-2 Enrich, p. 110 **SES** Book L, *Chemical Interactions,* Chapter 3	**SE** Section 2 Review, p. 132 **TE** Ongoing Assessment, pp. 129, 131 **TE** Performance Assessment, p. 132 **TR** 4-2 Review and Reinforce, p. 109	Audiotapes, English-Spanish Summary 4-2 Transparency 17, "Formation of Mineral Deposits on Ocean Floor" Interactive Student Tutorial CD-ROM, F-4
TR 4-3 Lesson Plan, p. 111 **TR** 4-3 Section Summary, p. 112 **TR** 4-3 Review and Reinforce, p. 113 **TR** 4-3 Enrich, p. 114 **TR** Chapter 4 Real-World Lab, pp. 118–119 **SES** Book H, *Earth's Waters,* Chapter 3 **SES** Book L, *Chemical Interactions,* Chapter 4	**SE** Section 3 Review, p. 138 **SE** Analyze and Conclude, p. 140 **TE** Ongoing Assessment, pp. 135, 137 **TE** Performance Assessment, p. 138 **TR** 4-3 Review and Reinforce, p. 113	Exploring Earth Science Videodisc, Unit 3 Side 1, "What a Gem!" Exploring Earth Science Videodisc, Unit 3 Side 1, "Ore What?" Audiotapes, English-Spanish Summary 4-3 Transparency 18, "Exploring Smelting Iron Ore" Interactive Student Tutorial CD-ROM, F-4
TR Chapter 4 Performance Assessment, pp. 189–191 **TR** Chapter 4 Test, pp. 192–195	**SE** Chapter 4 Review, pp. 141–143 **TR** Chapter 4 Performance Assessment, pp. 189–191 **TR** Chapter 4 Test, pp. 192–195 **CTB** Test F-4	Interactive Student Tutorial CD-ROM, F-4 Computer Test Bank, Test F-4 Science Explorer Internet Site

Key: **SE** Student Edition
CTB Computer Test Bank
ISAB Inquiry Skills Activity Book
TE Teacher's Edition
SES Science Explorer Series Text
PTA Product Testing Activities by *Consumer Reports*
TR Teaching Resources
ISLM Integrated Science Laboratory Manual
IES Interdisciplinary Explorations Series

Meeting the National Science Education Standards and AAAS Benchmarks

National Science Education Standards	Benchmarks for Science Literacy	Unifying Themes
Science As Inquiry (Content Standard A) ◆ **Use appropriate tools and techniques to gather, analyze, and interpret data** Students create a crystal garden. Students measure and compare the density of different minerals. Students recover copper from a solution. *(Chapter Project; Skills Lab; Real-World Lab)* **Physical Science** (Content Standard B) ◆ **Properties and changes of properties in matter** A mineral is a naturally occurring, inorganic solid that has a crystal structure and a definite chemical composition. Minerals can form through crystallization of melted materials and through crystallization of materials dissolved in water. *(Sections 1, 2)* **Earth and Space Science** (Content Standard D) ◆ **Structure of the Earth system** Some minerals form as magma cools inside Earth's crust or as lava hardens on the surface. *(Section 2)* **Science and Technology** (Content Standard E) ◆ **Understandings about science and technology** After miners remove ore from a mine, smelting is necessary to remove the metal from the ore. *(Section 3)* **Science in Personal and Social Perspectives** (Content Standard F) ◆ **Science and technology in society** Students examine the issue of who owns the ocean's minerals. *(Science and Society)*	**1B Scientific Inquiry** Students create a crystal garden. Students measure and compare the density of different minerals. Students recover copper from a solution. *(Chapter Project; Skills Lab; Real-World Lab)* **3A Technology and Science** After miners remove ore from a mine, smelting is necessary to remove the metal from the ore. *(Section 3)* **3C Issues in Technology** Students examine the issue of who owns the ocean's minerals. *(Science and Society)* **4C Processes That Shape the Earth** Some minerals form as magma cools inside Earth's crust or as lava hardens on the surface. *(Section 2)* **4D Structure of Matter** A mineral is a naturally occurring, inorganic solid that has a crystal structure and a definite chemical composition. Minerals can form through crystallization of melted materials and through crystallization of materials dissolved in water. *(Sections 1, 2)*	◆ **Energy** Magma heats water to a high temperature beneath Earth's surface. Smelting is necessary to remove the metal from an ore. *(Sections 2, 3)* ◆ **Scale and Structure** The repeating pattern of a mineral's particles forms a solid called a crystal. *(Sections 1, 2)* ◆ **Stability** Each mineral has its own specific properties that can be used to identify it. *(Section 1; Skills Lab)* ◆ **Systems and Interactions** Students create a crystal garden. Minerals form through crystallization of melted materials and through crystallization of materials dissolved in water. Metals are removed from ores through the process of smelting. Students remove copper from a solution. *(Chapter Project; Sections 2, 3; Real-World Lab)* ◆ **Unity and Diversity** Minerals are identified by properties such as color, luster, hardness, streak, crystal shape, cleavage, and fracture. Each mineral has a characteristic density. Minerals are formed from magma and from hot water solutions. The three types of mines are strip mines, open pit mines, and shaft mines. *(Sections 1, 2, 3; Skills Lab)*

Media and Technology

Exploring Earth Science Videodiscs

◆ **Section 3** "What a Gem!" shows how minerals are created synthetically. "Ore What?" explains the aluminum manufacturing process.

Interactive Student Tutorial CD-ROM

◆ **Chapter Review** Interactive questions help students to self-assess their mastery of key chapter concepts.

Student Edition Connection Strategies

◆ **Section 1** **Integrating Chemistry,** p. 120
Language Arts Connection, p. 123

◆ **Section 2** **Science and Society,** p. 133

◆ **Section 3** **Integrating Technology,** pp. 134–140
Science & History, pp. 136–137
Integrating Environmental Science, p. 137

www.science-explorer.phschool.com

Visit the Science Explorer Internet site to find an up-to-date activity for Chapter 4 of *Inside Earth.*

ACTIVITY	Time (minutes)	Materials *Quantities for one work group*	Skills
Section 1			
Discover, p. 118	15	**Consumable** paper towel **Nonconsumable** samples of hematite and magnetite, porcelain or ceramic tile	Observing
Sharpen Your Skills, p. 121	10	**Nonconsumable** penny, samples of talc, calcite, quartz	Classifying
Try This, p. 125	15; 10	**Consumable** table salt, Epsom salts, water, piece of black construction paper **Nonconsumable** 2 pitchers, 2 shallow pans, hand lens	Observing
Skills Lab, p. 127	40	**Consumable** water **Nonconsumable** 100-mL graduated cylinder, balance, samples of pyrite, quartz, galena	Measuring, Drawing Conclusions
Section 2			
Discover, p. 128	15	**Consumable** salol, plastic spoon, candle, matches, ice cube **Nonconsumable** 2 microscope slides, tongs, hand lens	Relating Cause and Effect
Section 3			
Discover, p. 134	10	**Nonconsumable** samples of bauxite and graphite, aluminum can, pencil	Posing Questions
Science at Home, p. 138	home	**Consumable** 3 iron nails, petroleum jelly, clear nail polish, water, vinegar **Nonconsumable** clear glass	Communicating
Real-World Lab, p. 140	30	**Consumable** 3 g copper sulfate, water, 5 iron nails **Nonconsumable** triple-beam balance, 400-mL beaker, 200-mL graduated cylinder	Measuring, Observing, Developing Hypotheses, Drawing Conclusions

A list of all materials required for the Student Edition activities can be found on pages T14–T15. You can order Materials Kits by calling 1-800-828-7777 or by accessing the Science Explorer Internet site at **www.science-explorer.phschool.com.**

Growing a Crystal Garden

When students think of minerals and their crystals, they likely think of something solid and unchanging. They may not realize that the forming of mineral crystals is one of the constructive processes that is continuous in Earth's crust.

Purpose In this project, students will design and create a crystal garden using at least two different crystal-growth solutions. During the project, they will observe and record the growth rate of the different crystals in their gardens. By doing this project, students will gain a better understanding of how mineral crystals form in Earth's crust.

Skills Focus Students will be able to
- measure and prepare a chemical solution;
- observe and sketch the various types of crystals that grow;
- compare and contrast the growth of different kinds of crystals;
- create a data table to record crystal growth rates;
- communicate results to the class.

Project Time Line The entire project will take about two weeks. Students can individually make crystal gardens or work in small groups. During the project, students may need some class time to carry out the following tasks. After the initial design and preparation, students can observe and record crystal growth at various times during the school day.
- Design and gather materials to create the garden scene.
- Prepare a solution with which to begin crystal growth in the garden scene.
- Use additional teacher-made solutions to add to their crystal gardens.
- Make a sketch of the crystal garden to keep track of which crystals are where.
- Record the growth rate of each kind of crystal in their gardens
- Make sketches of the crystals grown in their gardens.
- Present their crystal gardens to the class.

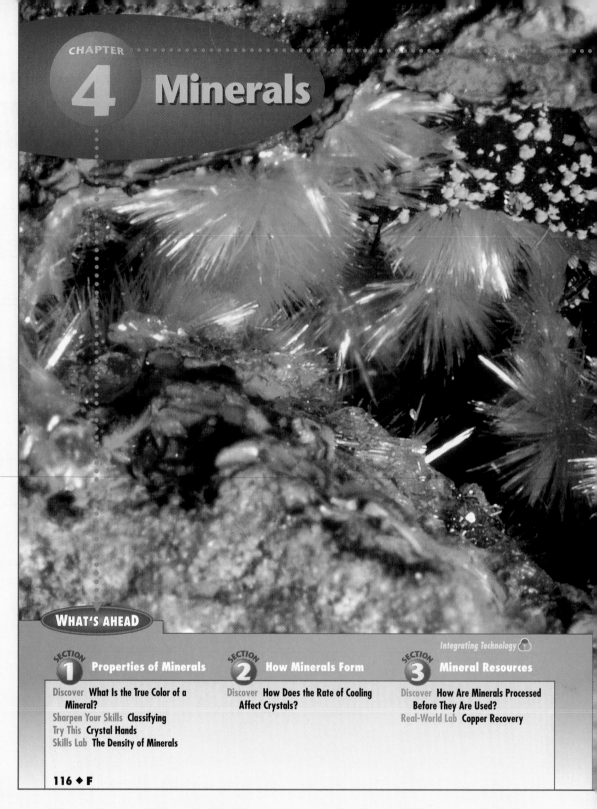

CHAPTER 4

Minerals

WHAT'S AHEAD

For more detailed information on planning and supervising the chapter project, see Chapter 4 Project Teacher Notes, pages 96–97 in Teaching Resources.

Suggested Shortcuts
- You can make this project shorter by simply having individual students grow one kind of crystal on a simple base, such as a sponge in a clear glass. Different students could grow different kinds of crystals from prepared solutions.
- For a class project, have students design and create one elaborate garden scene in an aquarium tank or similar container. Then have small groups grow different kinds of crystals at different places in the garden.

Possible Materials Possibly the best type of container in which to grow a crystal garden is a plastic shoe box, though students may find other containers that will work as well. Base materials in the garden include charcoal, brick pieces, porous rocks such as sandstone, plastic foam of various shapes, pipe cleaners, cotton

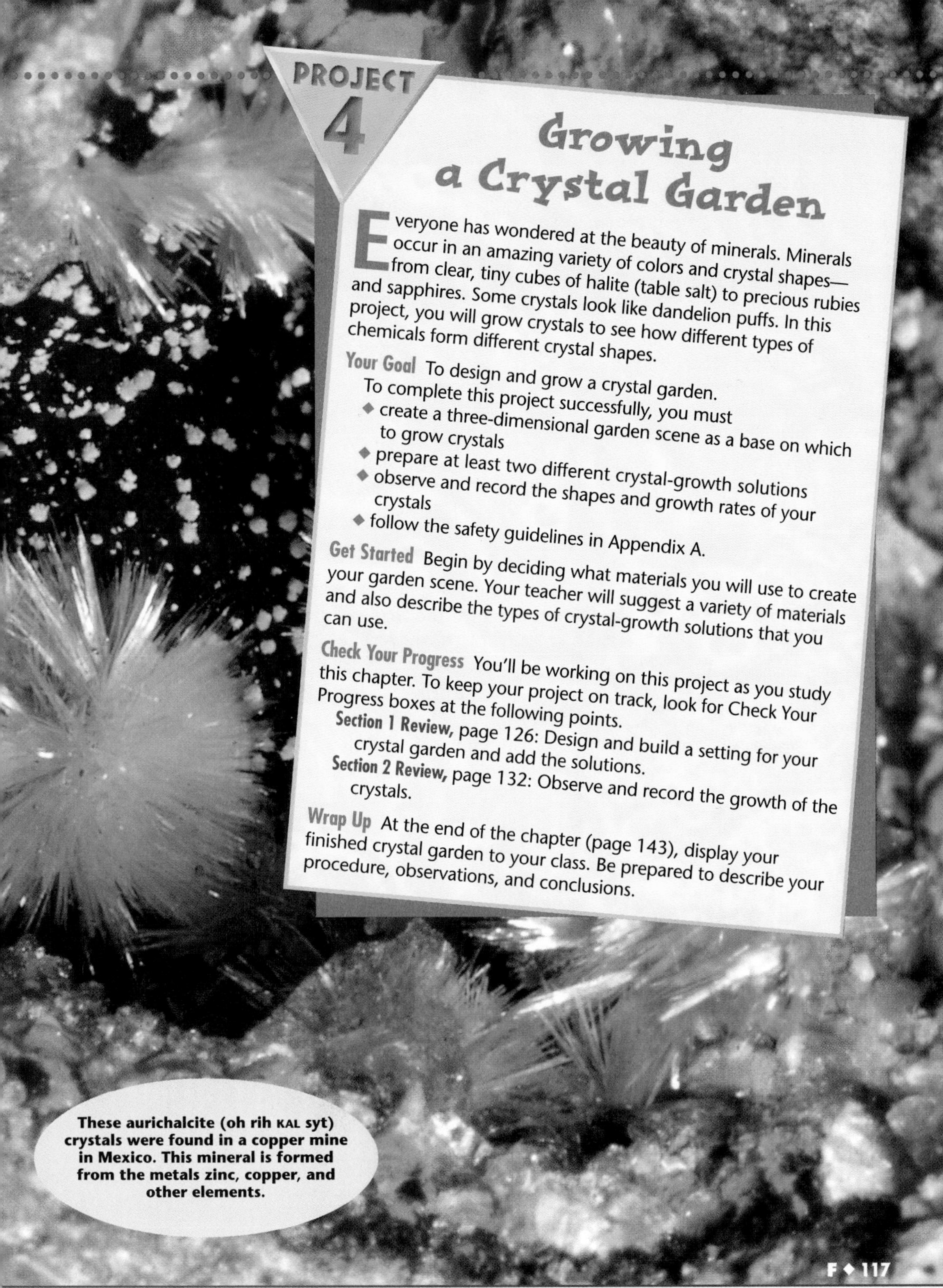

PROJECT 4

Growing a Crystal Garden

Everyone has wondered at the beauty of minerals. Minerals occur in an amazing variety of colors and crystal shapes—from clear, tiny cubes of halite (table salt) to precious rubies and sapphires. Some crystals look like dandelion puffs. In this project, you will grow crystals to see how different types of chemicals form different crystal shapes.

Your Goal To design and grow a crystal garden.

To complete this project successfully, you must

- create a three-dimensional garden scene as a base on which to grow crystals
- prepare at least two different crystal-growth solutions
- observe and record the shapes and growth rates of your crystals
- follow the safety guidelines in Appendix A.

Get Started Begin by deciding what materials you will use to create your garden scene. Your teacher will suggest a variety of materials and also describe the types of crystal-growth solutions that you can use.

Check Your Progress You'll be working on this project as you study this chapter. To keep your project on track, look for Check Your Progress boxes at the following points.

Section 1 Review, page 126: Design and build a setting for your crystal garden and add the solutions.

Section 2 Review, page 132: Observe and record the growth of the crystals.

Wrap Up At the end of the chapter (page 143), display your finished crystal garden to your class. Be prepared to describe your procedure, observations, and conclusions.

These aurichalcite (oh rih KAL syt) crystals were found in a copper mine in Mexico. This mineral is formed from the metals zinc, copper, and other elements.

F ◆ 117

swabs, and small kitchen sponges. Various chemicals can be used to create different crystalline structures, including salt (sodium chloride), sugar (sucrose), Epsom salts, alum (aluminum potassium sulfate), and magnesium sulfate. You may have to order some of these chemicals from a pharmacy a couple of weeks in advance of the start of the project. To vary the color of crystals, use dye powder, liquid bluing, or food coloring. Students will also need a hand lens to observe the crystals.

Launching the Project To introduce this project, show students pictures of mineral crystals from geology books. Then explain that they will be growing similar crystals in garden scenes that they build and design. Ask: **What are some materials you could use to build such a garden scene?** *(Practically any porous material could serve as a substrate for crystal growth.)* Explain that students will create these garden scenes, which will be the first step in creating their crystal gardens. To help students get started, pass out Chapter 4 Project Overview and Worksheets, on pages 98–101 in Teaching Resources. You may also wish to pass out the Chapter 4 Project Scoring Rubric, page 102, at this time.

Program Resources

- **Teaching Resources** Chapter 4 Project Teacher Notes, pp. 96–97; Chapter 4 Project Overview and Worksheets, pp. 98–101; Chapter 4 Project Scoring Rubric, p. 102

Performance Assessment

Use the Chapter 4 Project Scoring Rubric to assess students' work. Students will be assessed on

- how well they create a three-dimensional crystal garden;
- how well they observe and record the growth of crystals in their crystal garden;
- how effectively they present their crystal garden and growth data to the class;
- their participation in their groups.

SECTION 1 Properties of Minerals

Objectives

After completing the lesson, students will be able to

- ◆ identify the characteristics of a mineral;
- ◆ identify the properties of minerals and explain how minerals are identified.

Key Terms mineral, inorganic, crystal, element, compound, Mohs hardness scale, streak, luster, cleavage, fracture, fluorescence

1 Engage/Explore

Activating Prior Knowledge

Ask students: **What are minerals?** *(Some students may know that minerals are the chemical compounds that make up rocks, but many students will probably mention dietary minerals, such as iron and calcium.)* **Where do you think you could find minerals in nature?** *(A few students may know that some minerals, such as sulfur and copper, occur in deposits and are mined. Students might suggest minerals are found in rocks.)*

DISCOVER ACTIVITY

Skills Focus observing

Materials *samples of hematite and magnetite, porcelain or ceramic tile, paper towel*

Time 15 minutes

Tips Use black hematite rather than red. Demonstrate how to make a streak on the tile and then wipe it clean.

Expected Outcome Both hematite (Fe_2O_3) and magnetite (Fe_3O_4) are types of iron ore, and they are both dark and similar in appearance. Hematite leaves a reddish-brown streak, while magnetite leaves a black streak.

Think It Over The streak of magnetite matches its color, but the streak of hematite does not. This streak test could be used to identify them as two different minerals.

SECTION 1 Properties of Minerals

DISCOVER ACTIVITY

What Is the True Color of a Mineral?

1. Examine samples of hematite and magnetite. Both minerals contain iron. Describe the color and appearance of the two minerals. Are they similar or different?
2. Rub the hematite across the back of a porcelain or ceramic tile. Observe the color of the streak on the tile.
3. Wipe the tile clean before you test the next sample.
4. Rub the magnetite across the back of the tile. Observe the color of the streak on the tile.

Think It Over

Observing Does the color of each mineral's streak match its color? How could this streak test be helpful in identifying them as two different minerals?

GUIDE FOR READING

- ◆ What are the characteristics of a mineral?
- ◆ How are minerals identified?

Reading Tip **As you read, use the headings to make an outline showing what minerals are and how they can be identified.**

If you visit a science museum, you might wander into a room named the "hall of minerals." There you would see substances you have never heard of. For example, you might see deep-red crystals labeled "sphalerite" (SFAL uh ryt). You might be surprised to learn that sphalerite is a source of zinc and gallium. These metals are used in products from "tin" cans to computer chips! Although you may never have seen sphalerite, you are probably familiar with other common minerals. For example, you have probably seen turquoise, a blue-green mineral used in jewelry.

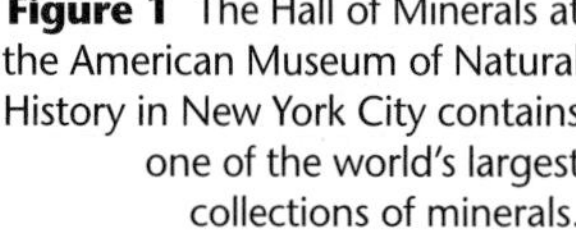

Figure 1 The Hall of Minerals at the American Museum of Natural History in New York City contains one of the world's largest collections of minerals.

READING STRATEGIES

Vocabulary Help students clarify the meaning of the term *mineral* as used in this context by addressing other common uses. *Mineral resources* includes the mineral ores discussed in this chapter but also includes oil and natural gas, which are not defined as minerals in this context because they are organic. *Mineral oil* and *mineral wax* are likewise petroleum products. *Mineral water* includes water that contains dissolved mineral salts, but also often designates water that contains dissolved carbon dioxide. *Dietary minerals* are various inorganic substances required by living things, including calcium and iron compounds. Finally, the *mineral* of "animal, vegetable, or mineral" simply designates any nonliving thing or inorganic substance and is not a scientific use of the term.

Figure 2 **A.** Red crystals of the mineral sphalerite are called ruby zinc. **B.** Borax is a mineral that forms in dry lake beds. **C.** Coal is not a mineral because it is made of the remains of ancient plants. *Comparing and Contrasting How are sphalerite and borax similar? How are they different?*

What Is a Mineral?

Sphalerite and turquoise are just two of more than 3,000 minerals that geologists have identified. Of all these minerals, only about 100 are common. Most of the others are harder to find than gold. About 20 minerals make up most of the rocks of Earth's crust. These minerals are known as rock-forming minerals. Appendix B at the back of this book lists some of the most common rock-forming minerals.

A mineral is a naturally occurring, inorganic solid that has a crystal structure and a definite chemical composition. For a substance to be a mineral, it must have all five of these characteristics. In Figure 2, you can compare sphalerite with another mineral, borax, and with coal, which is not a mineral.

Naturally Occurring To be classified as a mineral, a substance must occur naturally. Cement, brick, steel, and glass all come from substances found in Earth's crust. However, these building materials are manufactured by people. Because they are not naturally occurring, such materials are not considered to be minerals.

Inorganic A mineral must also be **inorganic.** This means that the mineral cannot arise from materials that were once part of a living thing. For example, coal forms naturally in the crust. But geologists do not classify coal as a mineral because it comes from the remains of plants and animals that lived millions of years ago.

Solid A mineral is always a solid, with a definite volume and shape. The particles that make up a solid are packed together very tightly, so they cannot move like the particles that make up a liquid. A solid keeps its shape because its particles can't flow freely.

2 Facilitate

What Is a Mineral?

Using the Visuals: Figure 2

Ask students: **Which characteristics of a mineral does coal have and which does it not have?** (*It is naturally occurring, is a solid, and has a definite chemical composition. Some students may know that it has a crystal structure. But it is not inorganic.*) Then have students find sphalerite on the table of common minerals in Appendix B. Ask: **What property of this mineral can you confirm by looking at its picture?** (*Its color, brown to light yellow*) Explain that the other properties in the table will be explained later in the section.
learning modality: visual

Building Inquiry Skills: Classifying

ACTIVITY

Materials *mineral samples such as quartz, calcite, halite, and feldspar; nonmineral objects such as brick, rubber ball, lump of coal, and bottle of water*
Time 10 minutes

To help students understand the difference between minerals and nonminerals, place mineral samples and examples of nonminerals on a table in random order. Then challenge students to classify each object as either a mineral or a nonmineral using their knowledge of the five characteristics that a substance must have to be a mineral. Allow students to handle and examine all objects and then classify each by making two lists on a piece of paper. **learning modality: logical/mathematical**

Program Resources

- **Teaching Resources** 4-1 Lesson Plan, p. 103; 4-1 Section Summary, p. 104

Media and Technology

Audiotapes English-Spanish Summary 4-1

Answers to Self-Assessment

Caption Question

Figure 2 Both are minerals. Therefore, each is a naturally occurring, inorganic solid with a crystal structure and a definite chemical composition. They are different in color and in where they form.

Ongoing Assessment

Oral Presentation Call on students at random to explain why various examples are or are not minerals, including gold, oil, cement, borax, and coal. Then call on other students to list the five characteristics of a mineral.

What Is a Mineral?, continued

Addressing Naive Conceptions

To help students differentiate between the common term crystal and the mineral characteristic, show them a piece of quartz crystal. Ask: **What is this called?** *(Many students will identify it as a "crystal.")* Explain that a common name for the crystals of the mineral quartz is simply "crystal" or "rock crystal." But quartz crystals are not the only kind of crystals. All minerals have a crystal structure, in a variety of shapes. **learning modality: verbal**

Using the Visuals: Figure 3

Ask students: **What color do you get if you mix the colors silver and yellow?** *(A typical answer might suggest light yellow.)* **What color is the mineral that is composed of silver mercury and yellow sulfur?** *(red)* Point out that the mineral cinnabar is not a mixture but a compound, in which elements have been chemically combined to form a new substance. Explain that the new substance, cinnabar, has the chemical formula HgS, which means that a molecule of cinnabar is made of 1 atom of mercury and 1 atom of sulfur. **learning modality: visual**

Integrating Chemistry

Provide students with access to the Periodic Table of the Elements. Focus students' attention on the symbol for each element. Then review how a chemical formula uses symbols and numbers to represent a chemical compound. Ask: **What does the formula for fluorite, CaF_2, tell you about that mineral?** *(A molecule of fluorite is composed of 1 atom of calcium and 2 atoms of fluorine.)* Emphasize that each mineral has its own formula and the properties of each compound the formulas represent differ from all other compounds. Then have students use the Periodic Table to write the number and name of the elements that compose these minerals: halite, NaCl; Magnetite, Fe_3O_4; Pyrite, FeS_2; Chalcopyrite, $CuFeS_2$; Galena, PbS; and Corundum, Al_2O_3. **learning modality: logical/mathematical**

Crystal Structure The particles of a mineral line up in a unique pattern that repeats over and over again. The repeating pattern of a mineral's particles forms a solid called a **crystal.** A crystal has flat sides, called faces, that meet at sharp edges and corners.

All minerals have a characteristic crystal shape. Sometimes, the crystal shape is obvious from the mineral's appearance. In other minerals, however, the crystal structure is visible only under a microscope.

Definite Chemical Composition A mineral has a definite chemical composition. This means that a mineral always contains the same elements in the same proportions. An **element** is a substance composed of a single kind of atom. All the atoms of the same element have the same chemical and physical properties.

INTEGRATING CHEMISTRY

Almost all minerals are compounds. In a **compound,** two or more elements are combined so that the elements no longer have distinct properties. The elements that make up a compound are said to be chemically joined. For example, a crystal of the mineral quartz has one atom of silicon for every two atoms of oxygen. Each compound has its own properties, which usually differ greatly from the properties of the elements that form it. Figure 3 compares the mineral cinnabar to the elements that make it up.

Figure 3 Minerals are usually a compound of two or more elements. **A.** Mercury is a metal that is a silvery liquid at room temperature. **B.** The element sulfur is bright yellow. **C.** The mineral cinnabar is a compound of the elements mercury and sulfur. Cinnabar has shiny red crystals.

Background

Facts and Figures Some 40–50 new minerals are identified each year. Two elements, oxygen and silicon, make up about 75 percent of Earth's crust. Those two elements in combination with other elements—such as iron, aluminum, calcium, and sodium—comprise the group of minerals known as the *silicates.* Silicates make up 95 percent of the volume of Earth's crust. They include such minerals as feldspar, quartz, mica, olivine, and hornblende.

Minerals that do not contain silicon are called *nonsilicates.* They include such minerals as hematite, corundum, gypsum, pyrite, cinnabar, halite, calcite, and dolomite. The elements that occur in nature in pure form are called *native elements.* These minerals, all nonsilicates, include gold, copper, diamond, sulfur, graphite, silver, and platinum.

Figure 4 An old saying warns "All that glitters is not gold." **A.** Real gold can occur as a pure metal. **B.** Pyrite, or fool's gold, contains iron and sulfur. **C.** Chalcopyrite is a compound of copper, iron, and sulfur. *Observing These minerals are very similar in color. But do you notice any differences in their appearance?*

Some elements occur in nature in a pure form, not as part of a compound with other elements. These elements, such as copper, silver, and gold, are considered to be minerals. Almost all pure elements are metals.

Checkpoint ***What does it mean to say that a mineral has a definite chemical composition?***

Identifying Minerals

During the California Gold Rush of 1848, thousands of people headed west to find gold in the California hills. Some found gold, but most found disappointment. Perhaps the most disappointed of all were the ones who found pyrite, or "fool's gold." All three minerals in Figure 4 look like gold, yet only one is the real thing.

Because there are so many different kinds of minerals, telling them apart can be a challenge. The color of a mineral alone often provides too little information to make an identification. **Each mineral has its own specific properties that can be used to identify it.** When you have learned to recognize the properties of minerals, you will be able to identify many common minerals around you.

You can see some of the properties of a mineral just by looking at a sample. To observe other properties, however, you need to conduct tests on that sample. As you read about the properties of minerals, think about how you could use them to identify a mineral.

Hardness When you identify a mineral, one of the best clues you can use is the mineral's hardness. In 1822, Friedrich Mohs, an Austrian mineral expert, invented a test to describe and compare the hardness of minerals. Called the **Mohs hardness scale,** this scale ranks ten minerals from softest to hardest. Look at the

Sharpen your Skills

Classifying

ACTIVITY

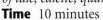

1. Use your fingernail to try to scratch talc, calcite, and quartz. Record which minerals you were able to scratch.
2. Now try to scratch the minerals with a penny. Were your results different? Explain.
3. Were there any minerals you were unable to scratch with either your fingernail or the penny?
4. How would you classify the three minerals in order of increasing hardness?

Identifying Minerals

Building Inquiry Skills: Comparing and Contrasting

Materials *mineral samples, hand lens*
Time 10 minutes

Invite students to examine several different mineral samples. Then have each student list properties that could be used to distinguish between types of minerals. **learning modality: kinesthetic**

Using the Visuals: Figure 4

Circulate samples of pyrite through the class. Ask: **Could you be fooled into thinking this is gold?** *(Many will say yes.)* Then have students turn to the table in Appendix B, find the entries for pyrite and gold, and compare these two minerals' properties. Point out the difference in their formulas. Guide students into understanding that the only property both have in common is color. **learning modality: visual**

ACTIVITY

Materials *penny, samples of talc, calcite, quartz*
Time 10 minutes
Tips Divide students into pairs, pairing students of differing abilities
Expected Outcome A fingernail scratches talc but not calcite or quartz. A penny scratches talc and calcite but not quartz. Quartz, then, cannot be scratched by either a fingernail or a penny. Therefore, the minerals in order of increasing hardness are: talc, calcite, quartz.
Extend Have students test other materials in the classroom, including chalk, wood, plastics, and various metals. At the end, have students collaborate on a hardness scale for all materials tested. **learning modality: kinesthetic**

Program Resources

Science Explorer Series *Chemical Building Blocks*, Chapter 3, has the Periodic Table of Elements and an explanation of what it contains.

Answers to Self-Assessment

Caption Question

Figure 4 The crystal structure, texture, and size of the individual particles are different.

Checkpoint

A mineral always contains the same elements in the same proportions.

Ongoing Assessment

Writing Write this question on the board: Why does each mineral have its own specific properties? Have each student write an answer, which should mention that each mineral has a different chemical composition.

Identifying Minerals, continued

Using the Visuals: Figure 5

After students are familiar with the scale, ask: **What is the hardness of your fingernail? Explain your answer.** *(Because a fingernail can scratch gypsum but not calcite, its hardness is somewhere between the two, or about 2.5).* **What is the hardness of a steel knife? Explain.** *(Because a steel knife can scratch apatite but not feldspar, its hardness is somewhere between the two, or about 5.5).* **learning modality: logical/mathematical**

Inquiry Challenge

ACTIVITY

Materials *metal nail file, penny, glass baby-food jar, scrap piece of steel, mineral samples such as quartz, pyrite, magnetite, galena, and halite*
Time 20 minutes

Divide students into small groups. Then challenge each group to give each of the mineral samples a hardness rating and place the samples in a sequence from softest to hardest, using the Mohs hardness scale for reference. After all groups have completed their work, invite a member of each to write the results on the board. Discuss any differences. **cooperative learning**

Building Inquiry Skills: Observing

ACTIVITY

Materials *hand lens, unglazed porcelain tile, numbered samples of various minerals*
Time 10 minutes

Ask students: **How does the color of a mineral compare to the color of its streak?** *(The streak color and the mineral color are often different.)* Invite students to make a data table, list the mineral samples by number, and record the color and streak characteristic of each sample. Then have students use Appendix B to identify the samples. **learning modality: visual**

Figure 5 Mohs hardness scale rates the hardness of minerals on a scale of 1 to 10. *Drawing Conclusions You find a mineral that can be scratched by a steel knife, but not by a copper penny. What is this mineral's hardness on the Mohs scale?*

Mohs Hardness Scale

Mineral	Rating	Testing Method
Talc	1	Softest known mineral. It flakes easily when scratched by a fingernail.
Gypsum	2	A fingernail can easily scratch it.
Calcite	3	A fingernail cannot scratch it, but a copper penny can.
Fluorite	4	A steel knife can easily scratch it.
Apatite	5	A steel knife can scratch it.
Feldspar	6	Cannot be scratched by a steel knife, but it can scratch window glass.
Quartz	7	Can scratch steel and hard glass easily.
Topaz	8	Can scratch quartz.
Corundum	9	Can scratch topaz.
Diamond	10	Hardest known mineral. It can cut hard glass.

table in Figure 5 to see which mineral is the softest and which is the hardest. A mineral can scratch any mineral softer than itself, but will be scratched by any mineral that is harder. How would you determine the hardness of a mineral not listed on the Mohs scale, such as sphalerite? If you scratch sphalerite with talc, gypsum, and calcite, you would find that none of them scratch sphalerite. But apatite, the next mineral on the scale, does scratch sphalerite. Therefore, you would conclude that sphalerite's hardness is about 4 on Mohs hardness scale.

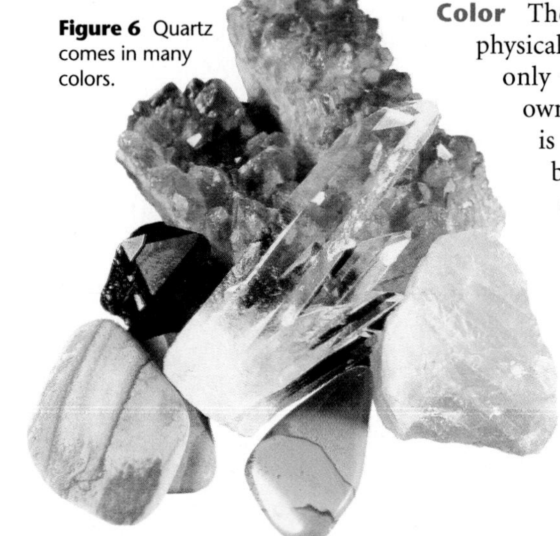

Figure 6 Quartz comes in many colors.

Color The color of a mineral is an easily observed physical property. But color can be used to identify only those few minerals that always have their own characteristic color. The mineral malachite is always green. The mineral azurite is always blue. No other minerals look quite the same as these. Many minerals, however, like the quartz in Figure 6, can occur in a variety of colors.

Streak A streak test can provide a clue to a mineral's identity. The **streak** of a mineral is the color of its powder. You can observe a streak by rubbing a mineral against a piece of unglazed tile called a streak plate. Even though the color of the mineral may vary, its streak does not. Surprisingly, the streak color

Background

History of Science When Friedrich Mohs (1773–1839) developed his hardness scale, he arbitrarily assigned the number 10 to diamond because that was the hardest mineral known. He then arbitrarily assigned numbers to other common minerals in descending order of hardness, assigning the number 1 to the softest mineral known, talc. Thus, the numbers of his scale do not represent any units of hardness. For example, topaz is much harder than fluorite but not exactly twice as hard, as their numbers might suggest.

Facts and Figures Quartz can occur in a variety of different colors because of impurities. Pure quartz, colorless and transparent, is often called rock crystal. Impurities can cause it to be yellow, black, red, banded, and other colors.

Figure 7 A. Galena, which contains lead, has a metallic luster. B. Malachite, which contains copper, has a silky luster.

and the mineral color are often different. For example, although pyrite has a gold color, it always produces a greenish black streak. Real gold, on the other hand, produces a golden yellow streak.

Luster Another simple test to identify a mineral is to check its luster. **Luster** is the term used to describe how a mineral reflects light from its surface. Minerals containing metals are often shiny. For example, galena is an ore of lead that has a bright, metallic luster. Look at Figure 7 to compare the luster of galena with the luster of malachite. Other minerals, such as quartz, have a glassy luster. Some of the other terms used to describe luster include earthy, waxy, and pearly.

Density Each mineral has a characteristic density. Recall from Chapter 1 that density is the mass in a given space, or mass per unit volume. No matter what the size of a mineral sample, the density of that mineral always remains the same.

You can compare the density of two mineral samples of about the same size. Just pick them up and heft them, or feel their weight, in your hands. You may be able to feel the difference between low-density quartz and high-density galena. If the two samples are the same size, the galena is almost three times as heavy as the quartz.

But heft provides only a rough measure of density. When geologists measure density, they use a balance to determine precisely the mass of a mineral sample. The mineral is also placed in water to determine how much water it displaces. The volume of the displaced water equals the volume of the sample. Dividing the sample's mass by its volume gives the density of the mineral.

☑ *Checkpoint* *How can you determine a mineral's density?*

Language Arts CONNECTION

Geologists use adjectives such as glassy, dull, pearly, silky, greasy, and pitchlike to describe the luster of a mineral. When writers describe the surfaces of objects other than rocks, they also use words that describe luster. Luster can suggest how a surface looks. A new car, for example, might look glassy; an old car might look dull.

In Your Journal

Think of a familiar scene to describe—a room, building, tree, or street. Make a list of objects in your scene and a list of adjectives describing the surfaces of these objects. You might use some of the adjectives that geologists use to describe luster. Now write a paragraph using sensory words that make the scene seem real.

Answers to Self-Assessment

Caption Question

Figure 5 The mineral's hardness is 4.

☑ *Checkpoint*

First, find the mass of the mineral with a balance. Second, find its volume by determining how much water it displaces. Finally, divide the mineral's mass by its volume.

Language Arts CONNECTION

Other words geologists use to describe luster include earthy, resinous, vitreous, and waxy. These terms are meant to be self-explanatory, calling to mind other common materials of the same look.

In Your Journal Before students write their paragraphs, read a description of a natural setting by a nature writer, such as in an outdoors magazine or a book of nature essays. Discuss with students the descriptive words that helped them form an image in their minds of the scene the writer described. **learning modality: verbal**

Building Inquiry Skills: Classifying

ACTIVITY

Materials *samples of metallic minerals such as pyrite, copper, silver, galena; samples of nonmetallic minerals such as olivine, hornblende, quartz, feldspar*
Time 10 minutes

Place several mineral samples in random order on a table, identifying each only by a number. Then challenge students to classify each sample as a mineral with either metallic or nonmetallic luster. After all students have classified the samples, provide the names of each mineral sample and invite students to check their classifications using the table in Appendix B. **learning modality: visual**

Ongoing Assessment

Skills Check Have each student make a table that lists each mineral property, a description of each property, and a description of the test for the property.

Identifying Minerals, continued

Using the Visuals: Figure 8

Emphasize that each mineral has its own unique combination of properties. Ask: **Why does each mineral have its own properties, different from the properties of all other minerals?** *(Each mineral has a chemical composition that is different from all other minerals.)* Point out that this chart includes one example for each of the six types of crystal shapes. **learning modality: verbal**

TRY THIS

ACTIVITY

Skills Focus observing
Materials *table salt, Epsom salts, water, 2 pitchers, 2 shallow pans, piece of black construction paper, hand lens*
Time 15 minutes the first day; 10 minutes for observation a day later
Tips Prepare ahead of time super-saturated solutions of salt and Epsom salts by adding those substances to separate pitchers of hot water, allowing the water to cool, and then adding more salt or Epsom salts. To simplify the activity, also pour the solutions into the shallow pans ahead of time, filling each to a depth of 1–2 cm. Provide a place for the hand prints to dry overnight.
Expected Outcome The water in the solutions will evaporate overnight, leaving solid crystals as hand prints. Students will observe that the halite crystals are cubic, while the Epsom salts crystals are orthorhombic, or prism-shaped. Which hand prints have more crystals can vary, depending on the conditions of the experiment.
Extend Have students make drawings of the two different types of crystals they observe. **learning modality: kinesthetic**

Crystal Shape The crystals of each mineral grow atom by atom to form that mineral's particular crystal shape. If you broke a mineral into tiny pieces, each piece would still show that same crystal shape. Geologists classify these shapes into six groups. To classify crystals, geologists consider the number and angle of the crystal faces. For example, all halite crystals are cubic. Halite crystals have six sides that meet at right angles, forming a perfect cube. If you look at Figure 8, you can see examples of minerals having each of the six types of crystal shapes, together with their other properties.

Figure 8 This chart lists some common minerals and their properties. *Interpreting Data Which mineral is lowest in density and hardness? Which mineral could you identify by using a compass?*

Properties and Uses of Minerals

Name	Magnetite	Quartz	Rutile	Sulfur	Azurite	Microcline Feldspar
Hardness	6	7	$6-6\frac{1}{2}$	2	$3\frac{1}{2}-4$	6
Color	Black	Transparent or in a range of colors	Black or reddish brown	Lemon yellow to yellowish brown	Blue	Green, red-brown, pink, or white
Streak	Black	Colorless	Light brown	White	Pale blue	Colorless
Crystal Shape	Cubic	Hexagonal	Tetragonal	Orthorhombic	Monoclinic	Triclinic
Luster	Metallic	Glassy	Metallic or gemlike	Greasy	Glassy to dull or earthy	Glassy
Special Properties	Magnetic	No	No	No	Reacts to acid	No
Density (g/cm^3)	5.2	2.6	4.2–4.3	2.0–2.1	3.8	2.6
Uses	A source of iron used to make steel	Used in making glass and electronic equipment, or as a gem	Contains titanium, a hard, light-weight metal used in air-craft and cars	Used in fungicides, industrial chemicals, and rubber	A source of copper metal; also used as a gem	Used in pottery glaze, scouring powder, or as a gem

Background

Facts and Figures The hardness of a mineral greatly depends on the strength of the bonds that hold its atoms together. For example, both diamond and graphite are pure carbon, but the strongly bonded atoms of a diamond make it much harder than graphite.

Students doing further research on minerals may find that geology books list *specific gravity* among the properties instead of density. A mineral's specific gravity is its weight compared to the weight of an equal volume of water. Since specific gravity is a ratio, it is not expressed in units, and that is why it is favored by geologists. But because 1 cm^3 of water has a mass of 1 g, the value for specific gravity and density is the same. For example, quartz has a specific gravity of 2.65 and a density of 2.65 g/cm^3. Thus, to translate a figure for specific gravity into density, just add the unit to the value.

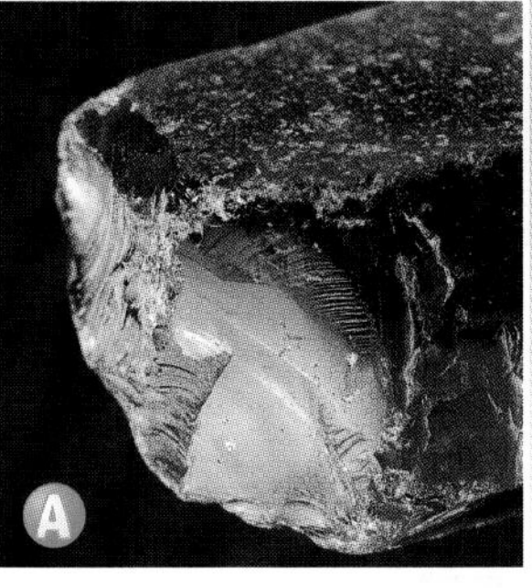

Figure 9 A. When quartz fractures, the break looks like the surface of a seashell. B. A piece of feldspar cleaves at right angles. C. Mica cleaves into thin, flat sheets that are almost transparent. *Applying Concepts How would you test a mineral to determine its cleavage and fracture?*

Cleavage and Fracture The way a mineral breaks apart can help to identify it. A mineral that splits easily along flat surfaces has the property called **cleavage.** Whether a mineral has cleavage depends on how the atoms in its crystals are arranged. Depending on the arrangement of atoms in the mineral, it will break apart more easily in one direction than another. Look at the minerals in Figure 9. Mica separates easily in only one direction, forming flat sheets. Feldspar splits at right angles, producing square corners. These minerals have cleavage.

Most minerals do not split apart evenly. Instead, they have a characteristic type of fracture. **Fracture** describes how a mineral looks when it breaks apart. Geologists use a variety of terms to describe fracture. For example, quartz has a shell-shaped fracture. When quartz breaks, it produces curved, shell-like surfaces that look like chipped glass. Pure metals, like copper and iron, have a hackly fracture—they form jagged points. Some soft minerals that crumble easily like clay have an earthy fracture. Minerals that form rough, irregular surfaces when broken have an uneven fracture.

☑ *Checkpoint How are cleavage and fracture similar? How are they different?*

Crystal Hands

ACTIVITY

You can grow two different kinds of salt crystals.

1. Put on your goggles.
2. Pour a solution of halite (table salt) into one shallow pan and a solution of Epsom salts into another shallow pan.
3. Put a large piece of black construction paper on a flat surface.
4. Dip one hand in the halite solution. Shake off the excess liquid and make a palm print on the paper. Repeat with your other hand and the Epsom salt solution, placing your new print next to the first one. **CAUTION:** *Do not do this activity if you have a cut on your hand.* Wash your hands after making your hand prints.
5. Let the prints dry overnight.

Observing Use a hand lens to compare the shape of the crystals. Which hand prints have more crystals?

Including All Students

Materials *2 paper towels* ACTIVITY
Time 10 minutes

To reinforce the concept of cleavage, provide each student with a paper towel. Ask: **In which direction does a paper towel split, or tear, evenly?** Students should find that the towel tears evenly from top to bottom but not from left to right. This is similar to a mineral with cleavage that breaks apart easily in one direction but not in another. **learning modality: kinesthetic**

Demonstration

Materials *samples of halite and hematite, modeling compound, razor blade, hammer, hand lens* ACTIVITY
Time 10 minutes

Demonstrate cleavage in halite and fracture in hematite by showing students how each breaks apart. Place a piece of halite on modeling compound to hold the halite in place. Then position the sharp edge of the razor blade on the halite and tap the blade with a hammer until the mineral breaks. It should split easily along flat surfaces. Repeat with the hematite. When it breaks, it should break irregularly. **learning modality: visual**

Inquiry Challenge

Materials *unglazed porcelain tile, mineral samples such as pyrite, galena, hornblende, feldspar, talc, hematite, quartz, olivine* ACTIVITY
Time 20 minutes

Provide each small group with 6 to 8 mineral samples. Then challenge each group to identify the properties of each mineral, including color, streak, luster, density, and cleavage/fracture. For density, they can heft each sample and place them in order from least dense to densest. For cleavage/fracture, they can closely examine the breaks and edges of each sample. Each group should make a table to record all their findings. **cooperative learning**

Program Resources

◆ **Integrated Science Laboratory Manual** F-4, "How Tesselating!"

Media and Technology

Transparencies "Properties and Uses of Minerals," Transparency 16

Answers to Self-Assessment

Caption Questions

Figure 8 Sulfur; magnetite
Figure 9 You would break a mineral apart to determine its cleavage and fracture.

☑ *Checkpoint*

Cleavage refers to when a mineral splits easily along a flat surface. Fracture describes how a mineral looks when it breaks apart.

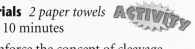

Ongoing Assessment

Drawing Have students make drawings of the six types of crystal shapes, using Figure 8 as a reference.

3 Assess

Section 1 Review Answers

1. A mineral must be a naturally occurring, inorganic solid that has a crystal structure and a definite chemical composition.
2. To determine hardness, do a scratch test and use Mohs hardness scale. To determine density, divide the mineral's mass by its volume. To determine streak, rub the mineral against a piece of unglazed tile called a streak plate.
3. An element is a substance composed of a single type of atom, while in a compound two or more elements are combined.
4. Water in its liquid form is not a mineral because it is not solid. But water as ice is classified as a mineral because it is a naturally occurring, inorganic solid with a crystal structure and a definite chemical composition.
5. Two minerals could have one or more properties that are similar or the same, such as minerals with the same color or hardness. The more tests or properties considered, the more likely it becomes to make an identification.

CHAPTER PROJECT 4

Check Your Progress

Make sure that each student has completed Chapter 4 Project Worksheet 1. Review the materials and designs, and encourage students to be creative. Help students get started with making crystals.

Performance Assessment

Oral Presentation Play a game using information in Appendix B. Choose a mystery mineral and begin by mentioning a property of that mineral, such as its streak color. Challenge students to identify the mineral. Announce more properties one by one until someone identifies the mineral.

Figure 10 Scheelite looks quite ordinary in daylight, but glows with brilliant color under ultraviolet light.

Special Properties Some minerals can be identified by special physical properties. For example, minerals that glow under ultraviolet light have a property known as **fluorescence** (floo RES uns). The mineral scheelite is fluorescent. Magnetism occurs naturally in a few minerals. Lodestone, which is a form of magnetite, acts as a natural magnet. Early magnets—such as compass needles—were made by striking a piece of iron with lodestone. Uraninite and a few other minerals are radioactive. They set off a Geiger counter. Some minerals react chemically to acid. Calcite, a compound of calcium, carbon, and oxygen, fizzes and gives off carbon dioxide when a drop of vinegar is placed on it.

A few minerals, such as quartz, have electrical properties. Pressure applied to these crystals produces a small electric current. In addition, these crystals vibrate if they come in contact with an electric current. Because of these properties, quartz crystals are used in microphones, radio transmitters, and watches.

Section 1 Review

1. What characteristics must a substance have to be considered a mineral?
2. Describe how you can test a mineral to determine its hardness, density, and streak.
3. What is the major difference between an element and a compound?
4. **Thinking Critically Classifying** According to the definition of a mineral, can water be classified as a mineral? Explain your answer.
5. **Thinking Critically Making Generalizations** Explain why you can't rely on any single test or property when you are trying to identify a mineral.

CHAPTER PROJECT 4

Check Your Progress

Select a container for your crystal garden such as a plastic shoe box or a large-mouth jar. Make a sketch showing the shapes and locations of the "plants" you plan to grow. When you have designed your garden, decide what materials to put in the box for the crystals to grow on. Decide what crystal-growth solutions you will use. Halite, Epsom salts, and alum are possibilities. Check with your teacher to make sure the chemicals you plan to use are safe.

Background

Facts and Figures Many minerals can be identified by their special properties. Gold is particularly malleable, which means it can easily be shaped. Clay minerals have an earthy odor. Talc feels soapy, and graphite feels greasy. The "greasiness" of graphite is useful in "dry" graphite-based lubricants. A transparent piece of calcite has the property of "double refraction." When it is placed over print, for example, the letters look to be doubled.

Program Resources

- **Teaching Resources** 4-1 Review and Reinforcement, p. 105; 4-1 Enrich, p. 106

Media and Technology

Interactive Student Tutorial CD-ROM F-4

Measuring

THE DENSITY OF MINERALS

Skills Lab

In this lab, you will use water to help you measure the density of minerals.

Problem

How can you compare the density of different minerals?

Materials (per student)

graduated cylinder, 100 mL
3 mineral samples: pyrite, quartz, and galena
water
balance

Procedure 

1. Check to make sure the mineral samples are small enough to fit in the graduated cylinder.
2. Copy the data table into your notebook. Place the pyrite on the balance and record its mass in the data table.
3. Fill the cylinder with water to the 50-mL mark.
4. Carefully place the pyrite into the cylinder of water. Try not to spill any of the water.
5. Read the level of the water on the scale of the graduated cylinder. Record the level of the water with the pyrite in it.
6. Calculate the volume of water displaced by the pyrite. To do this, subtract the volume of water without the pyrite from the volume of water with the pyritet. Record your answer.
7. Calculate the density of the pyrite by using this formula.

$$\text{Density} = \frac{\text{Mass of mineral}}{\text{Volume of water displaced by the mineral}}$$

(Note: Density is expressed as g/cm^3. One mL of water has a volume of 1 cm^3.)

8. Remove the water and mineral from the cylinder.
9. Repeat steps 2–8 for quartz and galena.

Analyze and Conclude

1. Which mineral had the highest density? The lowest density?
2. How does finding the volume of the water that was displaced help you find the volume of the mineral itself?
3. Why won't the procedure you used in this lab work for a substance that floats or one that dissolves in water?
4. **Apply** Pyrite is sometimes called "fool's gold" because its color and appearance are similar to real gold. How could a scientist determine if a sample was real gold?
5. **Think About It** Does the shape or size of a mineral sample affect its density? Explain.

More to Explore

Repeat the activity by finding the density of other minerals or materials. Then compare the densities of these materials with pyrite, quartz, and galena.

DATA TABLE

	Pyrite	Quartz	Galena
Mass of Mineral (g)			
Volume of Water without Mineral (mL)	50 mL	50 mL	50 mL
Volume of Water with Mineral (mL)			
Volume of Water Displaced (mL)			
Density (g/cm^3)			

Safety

Have students wear safety goggles. Review the safety guidelines in Appendix A.

Program Resources

- **Teaching Resources** Chapter 4 Skills Lab, pp. 115–117

Analyze and Conclude

1. Galena, the highest; quartz, the lowest
2. The volume of water displaced equals the volume of the mineral itself.
3. One that floats would not displace a volume of water equal to itself; one that dissolves would not displace any water.
4. First determine the density of the sample, and then compare that to the known density of gold.
5. Neither affects density because each mineral has a characteristic density.

Skills Lab

Measuring

The Density of Minerals

Preparing for Inquiry

Key Concept Each mineral has a characteristic density.
Skills Objectives Students will be able to
- measure the density of minerals;
- draw conclusions about how density helps identify minerals.

Time 40 minutes
Advance Planning Collect enough mineral samples. Make sure each sample will fit into a graduated cylinder. Students may need calculators to calculate the density of the samples.

Guiding Inquiry

Introducing the Procedure
- Ask: **What is density?** *(A measure of how much mass there is in one unit volume of a substance)* Then have students relate that definition to the formula for density in Step 7.

Troubleshooting the Experiment
- Emphasize that spilling any water when placing a sample in the graduated cylinder will distort the calculation of density.
- Demonstrate finding mass and volume of one mineral sample, and then do an example calculation on the board, using the formula given in Step 7.

Expected Outcome
In students' data tables, figures for Volume of Water with Mineral and Volume of Water Displaced will vary depending on the sample sizes. Students' calculations of density should be close to these: galena, 7.4–7.6 g/cm^3; pyrite, 5.0 g/cm^3; quartz, 2.6 g/cm^3.

Extending the Inquiry

More to Explore Challenge students to find the density of other mineral samples and then check the densities they find with the figures in Appendix B.

How Minerals Form

Objective

After completing the lesson, students will be able to

- ◆ describe the processes by which minerals form.

Key Terms solution, vein

1 Engage/Explore

Activating Prior Knowledge

Invite students to describe diamonds and other gems they have seen. Point out that all these gems are minerals mined from Earth's crust. Then ask: **What processes do you think are involved in the formation of a diamond?** *(A typical answer might mention high temperatures and pressures deep underground.)* Tell students that they will learn about the formation of minerals in this section.

DISCOVER ACTIVITY

Skills Focus relating cause and effect
Materials *salol, plastic spoon, 2 microscope slides, tongs, candle, matches, ice cube, hand lens*
Time 15 minutes
Tips Obtain salol (phenyl salicylate) from a drugstore or a chemical supply house. Students should wear goggles to make sure they do not get salol in their eyes. Caution students not to overheat the slide, especially the one placed on ice because it might break. Moving the slide from side to side over the flame will prevent overheating. Keep the slides on which the salol has hardened for remelting by other classes.
Expected Outcome The crystals that form on the two slides will be of different sizes. On the first slide, the crystals should be larger, because of the slower cooling. On the second slide, the crystals should be smaller, because of the more rapid cooling.
Think It Over The first sample should have larger crystals. The crystals formed by rapid cooling should have small crystals.

Section 2 How Minerals Form

DISCOVER ACTIVITY

How Does the Rate of Cooling Affect Crystals?

1. Put on your goggles. Use a plastic spoon to place a small amount of salol near one end of each of two microscope slides. You need just enough to form a spot 0.5 to 1.0 cm in diameter.
2. Carefully hold one slide with tongs. Warm it gently over a lit candle until the salol is almost completely melted. **CAUTION:** *Move the slide in and out of the flame to avoid cracking the glass.*
3. Set the slide aside to cool slowly.
4. While the first slide is cooling, hold the second slide with tongs and heat it as in Step 2. Cool the slide quickly by placing it on an ice cube. Carefully blow out the candle.
5. Observe the slides under a hand lens. Compare the appearance of the crystals that form on the two slides.
6. Wash your hands when you are finished.

Think It Over
Relating Cause and Effect Which sample had larger crystals? If a mineral forms by rapid cooling, would you expect the crystals to be large or small?

GUIDE FOR READING

- ◆ What are the processes by which minerals form?

Reading Tip **Before you read, rewrite the headings of the section as how, why, or what questions. As you read, look for answers to these questions.**

Imagine digging for diamonds. At Crater of Diamonds State Park in Arkansas, that's exactly what people do. The park is the former site of the only diamond mine in the United States. Visitors are permitted to prospect, or search, for diamonds. Since the area became a park in 1972, visitors have found more than 20,000 diamonds!

How did the diamonds get there? Millions of years ago, a volcanic pipe formed in the mantle at a depth of 120 kilometers or more. At that depth, great

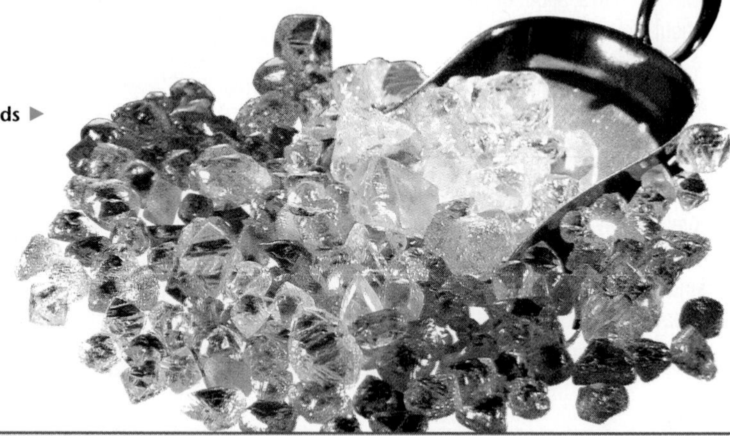

Diamonds ▶

READING STRATEGIES

Reading Tip The headings translate into these questions: What processes form minerals? How do minerals form from magma? How do minerals form from hot water solutions? How do minerals form by evaporation? Where are minerals found? Encourage students to use these questions as a study guide for the section. For each question, they should write a short paragraph that answers it succinctly but completely.

Vocabulary Remind students that a solution is a type of homogenous mixture in which substances are equally mixed throughout. The dissolved substance, called the solute, is mixed evenly throughout the dissolving substance, called the solvent. In the cases discussed in this section, the solvent is water and the solutes are elements or compounds in magma.

pressure and heat changed carbon atoms into the hardest known substance—diamond. Then the pipe erupted, carrying diamonds and other materials toward the surface. Today, geologists recognize this type of volcanic pipe as an area of unusual bluish-colored rock made up of a variety of minerals, including diamond. Volcanic pipes containing diamonds are found in only a few places on Earth. Most occur in South Africa, where many of the world's diamonds are mined today.

Processes That Form Minerals

You probably have handled products made from minerals. But you may not have thought about how the minerals formed. The minerals that people use today have been forming deep in Earth's crust or on the surface for several billion years. **In general, minerals can form in two ways: through crystallization of melted materials, and through crystallization of materials dissolved in water.** Crystallization is the process by which atoms are arranged to form a material with a crystal shape.

Minerals From Magma

Minerals form as hot magma cools inside the crust, or as lava hardens on the surface. When these liquids cool to the solid state, they form crystals. The size of the crystals depends on several factors. The rate at which the magma cools, the amount of gas the magma contains, and the chemical composition of the magma all affect crystal size.

When magma remains deep below the surface, it cools slowly over months and years. Slow cooling leads to the formation of large crystals. If the crystals remain undisturbed while cooling, they grow by adding atoms according to a regular pattern.

Magma closer to the surface cools much faster than magma that hardens deep below ground. With more rapid cooling, there is no time for magma to form large crystals. Instead, small crystals form. If magma erupts to the surface and becomes lava, the lava will also cool quickly and form minerals with small crystals.

Figure 10 This crystal of the mineral spodumene is 24 cm long. But it's not the largest crystal. Spodumene crystals the size of telephone poles have been found in South Dakota. *Inferring Under what conditions did such large crystals probably form?*

2 Facilitate

Processes That Form Minerals

Addressing Naive Conceptions

Many students may believe that mineral crystallization always results in perfectly formed crystals. In reality, fully formed crystals are relatively rare. Most crystals only partially form because they form at the same time as crystals of the same and other minerals. Pass around pieces of granite, and point out that granite is composed of such minerals as quartz, feldspar, and hornblende. Ask: **Can you see any fully formed quartz crystals in this rock?** *(No, only fragments of crystals can be seen.)* Emphasize that crystallization indicates the formation of a crystalline solid but not necessarily a complete crystal. **learning modality: visual**

Minerals From Magma

Building Inquiry Skills: Designing Experiments

Time 20 minutes

ACTIVITY

Ask: **What experiment could test the hypothesis that the rate at which a substance cools affects the size of the crystals that form?** Divide students into small groups and challenge each group to design an experiment that would test the hypothesis. *(A typical experiment would involve cooling two solutions at different rates and then comparing the crystals that form.)* Once groups have designed their experiments, examine them in a class discussion. Then help interested students carry out one of the experiments and report their findings to the class. **cooperative learning**

Ongoing Assessment

Skills Check Call on students to infer whether the formation of diamonds occurs through crystallization of melted materials or of materials dissolved in water. *(Material that erupts through a volcano is melted material, and thus diamonds form through crystallization of melted materials.)*

Program Resources

- **Teaching Resources** 4-2 Lesson Plan, p. 107; 4-2 Section Summary, p. 108

Media and Technology

Audiotapes English-Spanish Summary 4-2

Answers to Self-Assessment

Caption Question

Figure 11 The large crystals probably formed deep below the surface, where magma cooled slowly over months or years.

Minerals From Magma, continued

Building Inquiry Skills: Inferring

Materials *hand lens, rock samples of granite and rhyolite* ACTIVITY
Time 10 minutes

Invite students to examine samples of granite and rhyolite. Explain that both rocks are composed mostly of the same minerals, including feldspar and quartz. Then ask: **What can you infer about the conditions under which each formed?** *(Students should infer that the granite cooled slower than the rhyolite because it has larger mineral crystals. Few if any crystals can be seen in rhyolite.)* Explain that granite forms when magma cools slowly underground and rhyolite forms when lava cools quickly on the surface.
learning modality: visual

Minerals From Hot Water Solutions

Using the Visuals: Figure 12

Ask students: **In the solutions described in the caption, what is the solvent and what are the solutes?** *(Water is the solvent, and minerals are the solutes.)* Explain that both the water and the minerals were part of the magma. After many other minerals have crystallized, such solutions are left. The minerals in these cases are often metals, such as silver and gold. Ask: **What are other kinds of veins you know about?** *(Veins that carry blood in the body.)* Point out that a mineral vein is visually similar to a vein in the body. The difference is that a fluid flows through a vein in the body, while a mineral vein is solid and stable, at least once the mineral has crystallized.
learning modality: verbal

Figure 11 A. Silver sometimes occurs as a pure metal, forming delicate, treelike crystals.
B. Solutions containing dissolved metals form veins like the ones in this silver mine in Idaho.

Minerals From Hot Water Solutions

Sometimes, the elements that form a mineral dissolve in hot water. Magma has heated the water to a high temperature beneath Earth's surface. These dissolved minerals form solutions. A **solution** is a mixture in which one substance dissolves in another. When a hot water solution begins to cool, the elements and compounds leave the solution and crystallize as minerals. The silver shown in Figure 11A formed by this process.

Pure metals that crystallize underground from hot water solutions often form veins. A **vein** is a narrow channel or slab of a mineral that is much different from the surrounding rock. Deep underground, solutions of hot water and metals often follow cracks within the rock. Then the metals crystallize into veins that resemble the streaks of fudge in vanilla fudge ice cream. Figure 11B shows a vein of silver in a mine.

Many minerals form from solutions at places where tectonic plates spread apart along the mid-ocean ridge. First, ocean water

Figure 12 Many minerals form at chimneys along the mid-ocean ridge. Chimneys occur in areas where sea-floor spreading causes cracks in the oceanic crust. *Interpreting Diagrams What is the energy source for this process?*

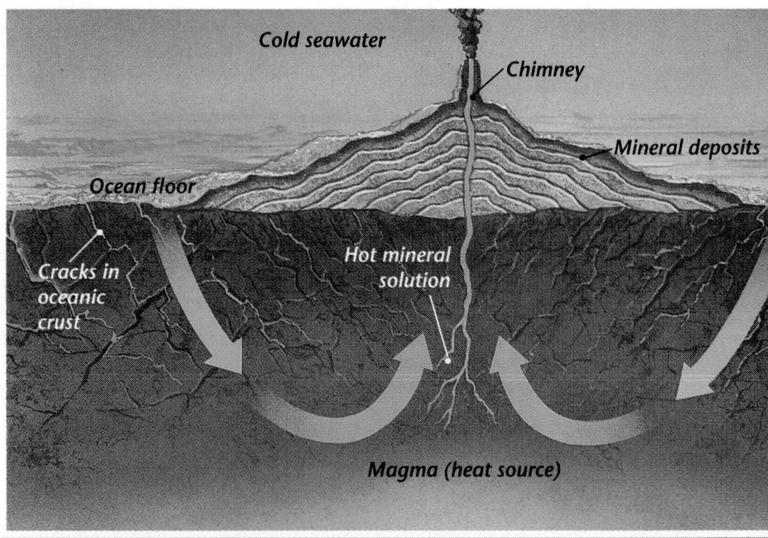

Background

Facts and Figures The explanation for the multitude of minerals is that different minerals crystallize at different temperatures as magma cools. For example, olivine crystallizes at 1200°C, while quartz crystallizes at 700°C. Thus, a complicated process occurs as magma cools. Certain minerals crystallize at certain temperatures, and as they do, they tend to deplete the magma of the elements they use, changing the makeup of the magma that remains. One reason quartz tends to crystallize late in the process is because, by that time, a lot of silicon and oxygen are left in the magma. Also left at the end are rare metals such as gold and silver, and they flow into fractures with the water that's also left over, eventually crystallizing into veins.

Figure 13 In Death Valley, California, water carries dissolved minerals from the surrounding mountains into the valley. When the water evaporates under the blazing desert sun, the minerals form a crust on the valley floor.

seeps down through cracks in the crust. There, the water comes in contact with magma that heats it to a very high temperature. The heated water dissolves minerals from the crust and rushes upward. This hot solution then billows out of vents, called "chimneys." When the hot solution hits the cold sea, minerals crystallize and settle to the ocean floor.

Minerals Formed by Evaporation

Minerals can also form when solutions evaporate. You know that if you stir salt crystals into a beaker of water, the salt dissolves, forming a solution. But if you allow the water in the solution to evaporate, it will leave salt crystals on the bottom of the beaker. In a similar way, thick deposits of the mineral halite formed over millions of years when ancient seas slowly evaporated. In the United States, such halite deposits occur in the Midwest, the Southwest, and along the Gulf Coast.

Several other useful minerals also form by the evaporation of seawater. These include gypsum, used in making building materials; calcite crystals, used in microscopes; and minerals containing potassium, used in making fertilizer.

Using the Visuals: Figure 12

After students have examined the figure and read the caption, ask: **What layer of Earth does the magma come from and why is it hot?** *(Magma comes from the mantle. It is hot because the mantle is heated by Earth's core.)* Explain that some materials dissolve better the higher the temperature of the solvent water. Ask: **What happens to the temperature of the heated water once it belches out of the chimneys?** *(The temperature drops very quickly as the water flows into the almost freezing ocean water.)* Point out that as the water temperature suddenly drops from almost boiling to almost freezing, its particles contract, leaving less room between them for the dissolved minerals. As a consequence, the minerals crystallize on the ocean floor. **learning modality: visual**

Minerals Formed by Evaporation

Demonstration

Materials *salt, water, large glass bowl, measuring cup, spoon*
Time 5 minutes for setup, observation over 2 weeks

To model how salt deposits form, set up this demonstration as students begin the chapter. Prepare a saturated salt solution by stirring 30 mL of salt into 125 mL of water. Then set the bowl in a sunny place and allow the water to evaporate. Periodically call students' attention to changes in the bowl. When the water has completely evaporated, a deposit of salt crystals will be left. Ask: **What natural process does this demonstration model?** *(The formation of halite deposits by evaporation of seawater)* **learning modality: visual**

Program Resources

Science Explorer Series *Chemical Interactions,* Chapter 3, provides information on solutions.

Media and Technology

Transparencies "Formation of Mineral Deposits on Ocean Floor," Transparency 17

Answers to Self-Assessment

Caption Question

Figure 12 The energy source is the heat from magma.

Ongoing Assessment

Skills Check Have students make three flowcharts: one that shows how veins form, one that shows how minerals form near the mid-ocean ridge, and one that shows how minerals form through evaporation.

Where Minerals Are Found

Using the Visuals: Figure 14

Have students turn back to the map of Earth's plates in Chapter 1, Section 5, and compare the location of plate boundaries with the distribution of metals shown on this map. Ask: **What pattern do you see when you compare maps?** *(The distribution of metals roughly matches the location of plate boundaries.)* **What can you infer from this?** *(Metals are formed near plate boundaries.)* **learning modality: visual**

3 Assess

Section 2 Review Answers

1. Through crystallization of melted materials and crystallization of materials dissolved in water
2. The slower the cooling rate, the larger the crystals formed.
3. Ocean water seeps through cracks in the crust. Magma heats the water to high temperatures. Heated water dissolves minerals in the crust, rushes upward, and billows out of "chimneys." In the cold sea, minerals crystallize and settle.
4. Deep underground, a solution of hot water and silver followed a fracture within rock. When the solution cooled, the silver crystallized into a vein.

Check Your Progress (Chapter Project 4)

Make sure students are recording observations, including written descriptions, drawings of crystals, and measurements of growth. Students can make line graphs comparing the growth of different crystals.

Performance Assessment

Skills Check Have each student make a concept map entitled The Formation of Minerals. The map should include the two general ways in which minerals form and then branch out into specific ways and details.

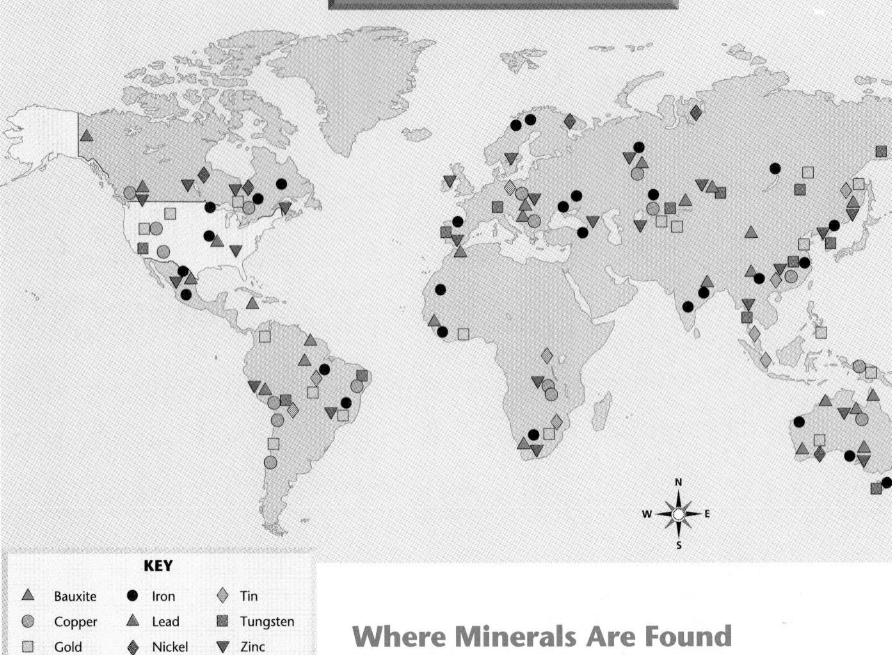

Figure 14 The map shows where important mineral resources are found throughout the world. *Interpreting Maps Which metals are found in the United States? Which ones must be imported from other countries?*

Where Minerals Are Found

Earth's crust is made up mostly of the common rock-forming minerals combined in various types of rock. Less common and rare minerals, however, are not distributed evenly throughout the crust. Instead, there are several processes that concentrate minerals, or bring them together, in deposits. Look at the map of the world's mineral resources in Figure 14. Do you see any patterns in the distribution of minerals such as gold and copper? Many valuable minerals are found in or near areas of volcanic activity and mountain building. For example, rich copper deposits are found along the Andes mountains in Chile.

Section 2 Review

1. What are the two main ways in which minerals form?
2. Describe how the cooling rate of magma affects the size of the mineral crystals formed.
3. What are the steps by which mineral deposits form along mid-ocean ridges?
4. **Thinking Critically** **Relating Cause and Effect** A miner finds a vein of silver. Describe a process that could have formed the vein.

Check Your Progress (Chapter Project 4)

Remember to record your daily observations of how your crystal garden grows. Sketch the shapes of the crystals and describe how the crystals grow. Compare the shapes and growth rates of the crystals grown from the various solutions. (*Hint:* If crystals do not begin growing, add more of the correct solution.)

Answers to Self-Assessment

Caption Question

Figure 14 Minerals found in the United States include copper, gold, iron, lead, tungsten, and zinc. Therefore, bauxite, nickel, and tin must be imported.

Program Resources

- **Teaching Resources** 4–2 Review and Reinforcement, p. 109; 4–2 Enrich, p. 110

Media and Technology

Interactive Student Tutorial CD-ROM F-4

SCIENCE AND SOCIETY

Who Owns the Ocean's Minerals?

Rich mineral deposits lie on and just beneath the ocean floor. Many nations would like to mine these deposits. Coastal nations already have the right to mine deposits near their shores. Today, they are mining minerals such as tin, titanium, diamonds, and sulfur from the continental shelf—the wide area of shallow water just off the shores of continents.

But the ocean floor beyond the continental shelves is open for all nations to explore. Mineral deposits in volcanic areas of the ocean floor include manganese, iron, cobalt, copper, nickel and platinum. Who owns these valuable underwater minerals?

▲ This sample from the floor of the Pacific Ocean near New Guinea may contain copper and gold.

The Issues

Who Can Afford to Mine? Although the ocean floor is open to all for exploration, mining the ocean floor will cost a huge amount of money. New technologies must be developed to obtain mineral deposits from the ocean floor.

Only wealthy industrial nations such as France, Germany, Japan, and the United States will be able to afford these costs. Industrial nations that have spent money and effort on mining think that they should be allowed to keep all the profits. However, developing nations that lack money and technology disagree. Landlocked nations that have no coastlines also object.

What Rights Do Other Nations Have? In 1982, 149 nations signed the Law of the Sea treaty. Among other things, this treaty stated that ocean mineral deposits are the common property of all people. It also stated that mining profits must be shared among all nations. The United States did not sign this treaty. Without American support, the treaty is not effective.

Some people think that, because of the treaty, wealthy nations should share their technology and any profits they get from mining the ocean floor.

How Can the Wealth Be Shared? What can nations do to prevent conflict over mining the ocean floor? They might arrange a compromise. Perhaps wealthy nations should contribute part of their profits to help developing or landlocked nations. Developing nations could pool their money for ocean-floor mining. Whatever nations decide, some regulations for ocean-floor mining are necessary. In the future, these resources will be important to everyone.

You Decide

1. **Identify the Problem** In your own words, state the controversy about ocean mineral rights.
2. **Analyze the Options** Compare the concerns of wealthy nations with those of developing nations. How could you reassure developing nations that they will not be left out?
3. **Find a Solution** Look at a map of the world. Who should share the mineral profits from the Pacific Ocean? From the Atlantic Ocean? Write one or two paragraphs stating your opinion. Support your ideas with facts.

You Decide

1. Statements will vary. A typical statement should mention that the minerals on the ocean floor are valuable resources and there are differing opinions about who owns those resources.
2. Answers will vary. A typical answer might suggest that the wealthy nations have a much better opportunity to exploit the ocean's resources than do developing nations. One solution is to require that wealthy nations share any profits from mining of those resources.
3. Solutions will vary. Accept any solution as long as it shows the student has thought about the problem.

SCIENCE AND SOCIETY

Science and Society

Purpose

Students will develop and express opinions about the difficult issue of ownership of the ocean's mineral resources.

Debate

Time 20 minutes for preparation, 20 minutes for debate

Have students read the feature and answer the You Decide questions individually as a homework assignment. The next day, divide the class into small groups for discussion. Have students consider these questions: Who should own the minerals on the ocean floor? Do the people of wealthy nations have any obligation to share profits from mining of these minerals with people from developing nations? Do private companies from any nation have an obligation to share profits with all the nations of the world?

- Divide the class into two groups. Arbitrarily assign one group to argue that wealthy nations and companies have no obligation to share profits from the mining of these minerals. Assign the other group to argue that the wealth should be shared equally among nations. Alternately call on students from each group to state its position or refute an idea someone from the other group has put forward.

Extend Encourage interested students to write to the U.S. State Department and to the U.S. Ambassador to the United Nations to find out about the current government's position on the ownership and use of the ocean's mineral resources. A first step might be to find these agencies' web pages on the Internet. The inquiry could then be made via e-mail, which might expedite a reply.

INTEGRATING TECHNOLOGY 

SECTION 3 Mineral Resources

Objectives

After completing the lesson, students will be able to
- ◆ describe how minerals are used;
- ◆ list the three types of mines;
- ◆ explain how ores are processed to obtain metals.

Key Terms gemstone, ore, smelting, alloy

1 Engage/Explore

Activating Prior Knowledge

Ask students: **Which things that you use every day are made of minerals?** *(Answers will vary. A typical answer might mention metallic things, such as bicycles, autos, and coins.)* **What process do you think could turn a mineral mined from the ground into a shiny piece of steel?** *(Some students may describe a steel mill, in which ore is melted in furnaces.)* Explain that this section will give some answers to these questions.

DISCOVER

Skills Focus posing questions
Materials *samples of bauxite and graphite, aluminum can, pencil*
Time 10 minutes
Tips Place samples of bauxite and graphite, as well as the aluminum can, on a table in a central location. Have students make notes of their observations.
Think It Over While bauxite is brown, crumbly, and of a dull luster, the aluminum can is silver, hard, and of a metallic luster. The graphite sample and pencil lead are much more alike, with both being soft, dark, greasy, and of almost a metallic luster. Students should pose questions about the processes involved in turning these minerals into finished products.

INTEGRATING TECHNOLOGY 

SECTION 3 Mineral Resources

DISCOVER ACTIVITY

How Are Minerals Processed Before They Are Used?

1. Examine a piece of the mineral bauxite and use your knowledge of the properties of minerals to describe it.
2. Examine an aluminum can. (The metal aluminum comes from bauxite.) Compare the properties of the aluminum can with the properties of bauxite.
3. Examine a piece of the mineral graphite and describe its properties.
4. Examine the lead in a pencil. (Pencil "lead" is made from graphite.) Compare the properties of the pencil lead with the properties of graphite.

Think It Over
Posing Questions How is each mineral similar to or different from the object made from it? What questions would you need to answer to understand how bauxite and graphite are made into useful materials?

GUIDE FOR READING
- ◆ **How are minerals used?**
- ◆ **What are the three types of mines?**
- ◆ **How are ores processed to obtain metals?**

Reading Tip **As you read, draw a concept map that explains how metal ores are located, mined, and smelted.**

More than a thousand years ago, the Hopewell people lived in the Mississippi River valley. These ancient Native Americans are famous for the mysterious earthen mounds they built near the river. There these people left beautiful objects made from minerals: tools chipped from flint (a variety of quartz), the shape of a human hand cut out of a piece of translucent mica, or a flying bird made from a thin sheet of copper.

To obtain these minerals, the Hopewell people traded with peoples across North America. The copper, for example, came from near Lake Superior. There, copper could be found as a pure metal. Because copper is a soft metal, this copper was easy to shape into ornaments or weapons.

Figure 15 The copper to make this Hopewell ornament may have come from an area in Michigan that is still a source of copper ore.

The Uses of Minerals

Like the Hopewell people, people today use minerals. You are surrounded by materials that come from minerals—for example, the metal body and window glass of a car. **Minerals are the source of metals, gemstones, and other materials used to make many products.** Are you familiar with any products that are made from minerals? You might be surprised at how important minerals are in everyday life.

READING STRATEGIES

Reading Tip Review with students how to make a concept map. They should link information on a main topic with specific related information that clarifies the main topic. Point out that they can use the headings in the section as a way to organize their concept map.

Vocabulary Before students read the section, have them speculate about what the verb *smelt* means. Some students might notice that it sounds and looks like the word *melt.* Explain that the term is used for the process to refine mineral ore and it is an old variant on the word *melt.* Melting is an integral part of the smelting process.

Gemstones Beautiful gemstones such as rubies and sapphires have captured the imagination of people throughout the ages. Usually, a **gemstone** is a hard, colorful mineral that has a brilliant or glassy luster. People value gemstones for their color, luster, and durability—and for the fact that they are rare. Once a gemstone is cut and polished, it is called a gem. Gems are used mainly for jewelry and decoration. They are also used for mechanical parts and for grinding and polishing.

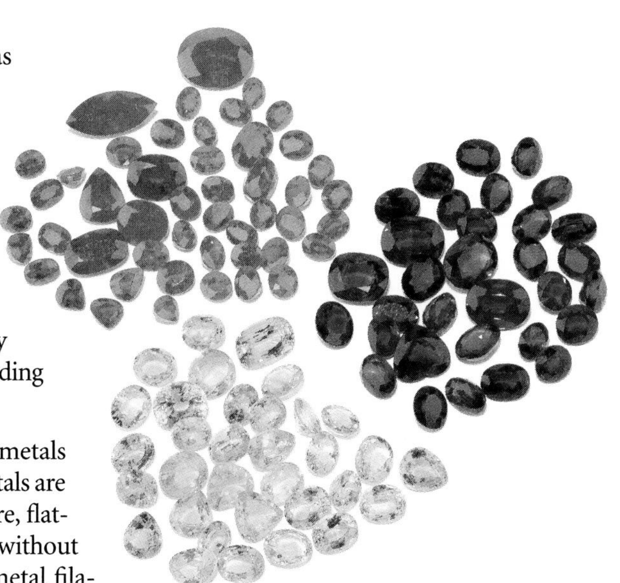

Figure 16 Gems like these red rubies and blue and yellow sapphires are among the most valuable minerals.

Metals Some minerals are the sources of metals such as aluminum, iron, copper, or silver. Metals are useful because they can be stretched into wire, flattened into sheets, and hammered or molded without breaking. Metal tools and machinery, the metal filament in a light bulb, even the steel girders used to frame office buildings—all began as minerals inside Earth's crust.

Other Useful Minerals There are many other useful minerals besides metals and gems. People use materials from these minerals in foods, medicines, fertilizers, and building materials. The very soft mineral talc is ground up to make talcum powder. Fluorite is important in making aluminum and steel. Clear crystals of the mineral calcite are used in optical instruments such as microscopes. Quartz, a mineral found in sand, is used in making glass as well as in electronic equipment and watches. Kaolin occurs as white clay, which is used for making high-quality china and pottery. Gypsum, a soft, white mineral, is used to make wallboard, cement, and stucco. Corundum, the second hardest mineral after diamond, is often used in polishing and cleaning products.

☑ *Checkpoint* *What is a gemstone? Why are gemstones valuable?*

Ores

A rock that contains a metal or economically useful mineral is called an **ore**. Unlike the copper used by the Hopewell people, most metals do not occur in a pure form. A metal usually occurs as a mineral that is a combination of that metal and other elements. Much of the world's copper, for example, comes from ores containing the mineral chalcopyrite (kal kuh PY ryt). Before metals, gemstones, and other useful minerals can be separated from their ores, however, geologists must find them.

2 Facilitate

The Uses of Minerals

Real-Life Learning

ACTIVITY

Ask other teachers, staff, and other adults who work at the school to stop by your classroom and show students gems they own and wear. (An alternative is to provide catalogues selling jewelry for students to examine.) These gems might include diamonds as well as emerald (beryl), ruby (corundum), sapphire (corundum), amethyst (quartz), jade (jadite), opal (opal), topaz (topaz), and turquoise (turquoise). Have students examine the gems, make notes about shape and color, and then find the mineral source in a dictionary or encyclopedia. **learning modality: visual**

Ores

Building Inquiry Skills: Comparing and Contrasting

Materials *cast-iron skillet, samples of magnetite and hematite*
Time 15 minutes

Display a cast-iron skillet and samples of iron ore. Explain to students that the skillet is a form of almost pure iron and that the two minerals are used as iron ore. Then have each student make a compare/contrast table that includes the name, formula, color, luster, and texture of the cast iron and the two minerals. **learning modality: visual**

Ongoing Assessment

Skills Check Encourage students to begin a table that lists all minerals in the left column and their uses in the right column. They should begin by including minerals and uses discussed on this page and continue the table by including all the minerals and uses they learn about during their study of the chapter.

Students can save their tables in their portfolios.

Program Resources

- **Teaching Resources** 4-3 Lesson Plan, p. 111; 4-3 Section Summary, p. 112

Media and Technology

Audiotapes English-Spanish Summary 4-3

Answers to Self-Assessment

☑ *Checkpoint*

Usually, a gemstone is a hard, colorful mineral that has a brilliant or glassy luster. They are valuable for their color, luster, and durability and because they are rare.

Prospecting

Addressing Naive Conceptions

From movies and television shows, students may believe that "prospectors" are grizzled old men who pan for silver and gold in the mountains of the West. Ask: **What image comes to mind when you hear about a prospector?** *(Many students will describe the stereotypical prospector.)* Explain that only a few people fit that image. Most modern prospectors are geologists who use modern techniques and technology to find ore deposits. **learning modality: verbal**

Mining

Real-Life Learning

Bring to class pictures of mines from geology books and old magazines. These should include strip mines, open-pit mines, and shaft mines. The largest copper mine in the world is the open-pit mine at Bingham Canyon, Utah, and photos of it are common in texts. Photos of strip mines and shaft mines are often of coal rather than mineral mines, but they will serve to illustrate the basic types of mines. Show the pictures to students and have them write a description of what they observe. **learning modality: visual**

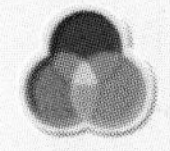

Integrating Environmental Science

Encourage student volunteers to contact their state's Environmental Protection Agency (EPA) by telephone or e-mail to ask about requirements and regulations for mine operators. Students should ask what the operators need to do to prevent pollution and to repair the land after use. The state EPA may be able to send pamphlets or brochures. If not, have students take notes and report to the class. **learning modality: verbal**

Prospecting

A prospector is anyone who searches, or prospects, for an ore deposit. Geologists prospect for ores by looking for certain features on Earth's surface. These geologists observe what kind of rocks are on the land surface. They examine plants growing in an area and test stream water for the presence of certain chemicals.

Geologists also employ some of the tools used to study Earth's interior. In one technique, they set off explosions below ground to create shock waves. The echoes of these shock waves are used to map the location, size, and shape of an ore deposit.

Mining

The geologist's map of an ore deposit helps miners decide how to mine the ore from the ground. **There are three types of mines: strip mines, open pit mines, and shaft mines.** In strip mining,

Advances in Metal Technology

For thousands of years, people have been inventing and improving methods for smelting metals and making alloys.

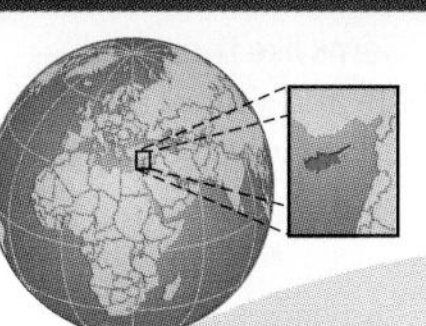

4000 B.C. Cyprus

The island of Cyprus was one of the first places where copper was mined and smelted. In fact, the name of the island provided the name of the metal. In Latin, *aes cyprium* meant "metal of Cyprus." It was later shortened to *cuprum,* meaning "copper." The sculptured figure is carrying a large piece of smelted copper.

4000 B.C. — 2500 B.C. — 1000 B.C.

3500 B.C. Mesopotamia

Metalworkers in Sumer, a city between the Tigris and Euphrates rivers, made an alloy of tin and copper to produce a harder metal—bronze. Bronze was poured into molds to form statues, weapons, or vessels for food and drink.

1500 B.C. Turkey

The Hittites learned to mine and smelt iron ore. Because iron is stronger than copper or bronze, its use spread rapidly. Tools and weapons could be made of iron. This iron dagger was made in Austria several hundred years after the Hittites' discovery.

Background

Facts and Figures A mineral is classified as an ore only if it can be mined at a profit. For example, aluminum constitutes a little over 8 percent of Earth's crust. For an aluminum deposit to be considered an ore, it must be concentrated to about four times that, or about 32 percent of the crust of an area. By contrast, copper constitutes only about 0.0135 percent of the crust. To be considered an ore, it must be concentrated to about 100 times that amount. Yet that concentration would still be only about 1 percent of the crust.

History of Science Bronze was the first metal worked, or shaped, into tools and weapons. Historians date the Bronze Age, a stage of prehistory, from about 5000–1200 B.C. in the Middle East and 2000–500 B.C. in Europe. The Bronze Age followed the Stone Age and preceded the Iron Age.

earthmoving equipment scrapes away soil to expose ore. In open pit mining, miners use giant earthmoving equipment to dig a tremendous pit. Miners dig an open pit mine to remove ore deposits that may start near the surface, but extend down for hundreds of meters. Some open pit mines are more than a kilometer wide and nearly as deep. For ore deposits that occur in veins, miners dig shaft mines. Shaft mines often have a network of tunnels that extend deep into the ground, following the veins of ore.

INTEGRATING ENVIRONMENTAL SCIENCE Mining for metals and other minerals can harm the environment. Strip mining and pit mining leave scars on the land. Waste materials from mining can pollute rivers and lakes. In the United States, laws now require that mine operators do as little damage to the environment as possible. To restore land damaged by strip mining, mine operators grade the surface and replace the soil.

In Your Journal

When people discover how to use metals in a new way, the discovery often produces big changes in the way those people live. Choose a development in the history of metals to research. Write a diary entry telling how the discovery happened and how it changed people's lives.

A.D. 1860s
England

Steel-making techniques invented by Henry Bessemer and William Siemens made it possible to produce steel cheaply on a large scale. Siemens' invention, the open-hearth furnace, is still widely used, although more modern methods account for most steel production today.

A.D. 500 — A.D. 2000

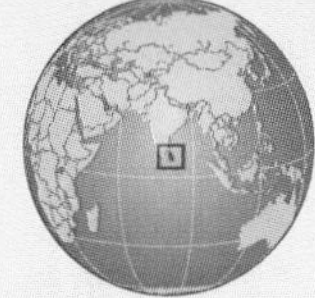

A.D. 600s
Sri Lanka

Sri Lankans made steel in outdoor furnaces. Steady winds blowing over the top of the furnace's front wall created the high temperatures needed to make steel. Because their steel was so much harder than iron, the Sri Lankans were able to trade it throughout the Indian Ocean region.

A.D. 1960s TO THE PRESENT
United States

Scientists working on the space program have developed light and strong alloys for use in products ranging from bicycles to soda cans. For example, a new alloy of nickel and titanium can "remember" its shape. It is used for eyeglasses that return to their original shape after being bent.

Smelting

SCIENCE & History **ACTIVITY**

Materials *common objects made of metal, such as copper pot, bronze candle holder, cast-iron skillet, steel tool, bendable eyeglasses frame*
Time 20 minutes

Invite volunteers to read the annotations for the entries on the time line. For each entry, display an object that is made of the metal described. Allow students to handle each object and compare characteristics. Ask: **Are there important characteristics of these useful metals that improved over time?** *(Most students will recognize that bronze is harder and more durable than copper, iron is harder and more durable than bronze, and so on.)* **What characteristic is particularly useful in modern alloys, such as those used in bicycle frames?** *(Modern alloys are lightweight as well as strong.)*

In Your Journal In doing their research, students might begin by finding out about the Bronze Age, the Iron Age, or the Industrial Revolution. Some students may want to concentrate on more modern advances, including those first developed for space travel. In their paragraphs, students should mention a specific process and a specific application that changed people's lives.

Extend Have interested students make a bulletin board showing how the development of metal technology changed the world. **learning modality: verbal**

Media and Technology

Exploring Earth Science Videodisc
Unit 3, Side 1, "What a Gem"

Chapter 7

Exploring Earth Science Videodisc
Unit 3, Side 1, "Ore What?"

Chapter 8

Program Resources

Science Explorer Series *Earth's Waters,* Chapter 3, provides information on water pollution from industrial sources.

Ongoing Assessment

Writing Have students write a short story of prospecting and mining for silver or gold in the Old West, using the information about prospecting and mining learned on these pages.

Smelting, continued

EXPLORING

Smelting Iron Ore

Have students look up the formulas for magnetite (Fe_3O_4) and hematite (Fe_2O_3) in Appendix B. Both are a compound of iron and oxygen. Then ask volunteers to read the annotations for each step in the smelting process. Ask: **What is the purpose of smelting?** *(To separate the iron from the oxygen in iron ore)* **What is added to the ore to accomplish this purpose?** *(coke and limestone)* The product of smelting can be made into either cast-iron objects or used to make steel. **learning modality: verbal**

Real-Life Learning

ACTIVITY

Bring to class something made of cast iron, such as a cast-iron skillet. Also bring something made of steel, such as a pan or a tool, and something made of stainless steel, such as utensils. Invite students to touch, visually examine, and compare the characteristics of each. Then ask students to list the major differences they observed. **learning modality: kinesthetic**

Demonstration

ACTIVITY

Materials *black copper oxide, powdered charcoal, test tube, test-tube holder, Bunsen burner, jar, water*
Time 15 minutes

To help students understand how another metal can be separated from an ore, demonstrate how to extract copper from copper oxide. First, mix copper oxide with bits of charcoal at the bottom of a test tube. Then, holding the test tube with a test-tube holder and wearing goggles, heat the mixture over a Bunsen burner. Finally, pour the heated mixture into a jar of cold water. Students should see that pieces of shiny orange copper fall to the bottom of the jar, while the charcoal floats. Explain that the heating of the mixture freed the copper from the oxygen in copper oxide. Explain that copper oxide ores are smelted in a similar way, through heating the ore in a blast furnace with materials that will free the copper from the oxygen. **learning modality: visual**

Figure 17 Plain steel rusts easily. But stainless steel—an alloy of iron, chromium, and nickel—doesn't rust. The chromium and nickel slow down the process by which the oxygen in the air combines with iron in the steel to form iron oxide, or rust.

Smelting

Ores must be processed before the metals they contain can be used. **After miners remove ore from a mine, smelting is necessary to remove the metal from the ore.** In the process of **smelting,** an ore is melted to separate the useful metal from other elements the ore contains. People around the world have used smelting to obtain metals from ores. Look at the time line in *Science and History* to see how this technology has developed from ancient times to the present.

How does smelting separate iron metal from hematite, a common form of iron ore? In general, smelting involves mixing an ore with other substances and then heating the mixture to a very high temperature. The heat melts the metal in the ore. The heat also causes the metal to separate from the oxygen with which it is combined. Metalworkers can then pour off the molten metal. Follow the steps in *Exploring Smelting Iron Ore.*

After smelting, additional processing is needed to remove impurities from the iron. The result is steel, which is harder and less brittle than iron. Steel is an **alloy,** a solid mixture of two or more metals. Steelmakers mix iron with other elements to create alloys with special properties. For stronger steel, the metal manganese and a small amount of carbon are added. For rust-resistant steel, the metals chromium and nickel are added. You can compare plain steel with rust-resistant stainless steel in Figure 17.

Section 3 Review

1. What are some of the ways that people use gems and metals?
2. Describe three different kinds of mines.
3. What process is used to separate useful metals from ores?
4. What are alloys, and why are they useful?
5. **Thinking Critically** In smelting, what causes a metal to separate from its ore?

Science at Home

You can demonstrate to your family how rust damages objects that contain iron. Obtain three iron nails. Coat one of the nails with petroleum jelly and coat the second nail with clear nail polish. Do not put anything on the third nail. Place all the nails in a glass of water with a little vinegar. (The vinegar speeds up the rusting process.) Allow the nails to stand in the glass overnight. Which nails show signs of rusting? Explain these results to your family.

Background

Facts and Figures You might want to share with students these facts and figures about smelting iron ore.

- Iron ore often contains only 30 percent iron.
- A blast furnace produces as much as 350 tons of molten iron per hour.
- The molten iron poured, or "tapped," from a blast furnace is commonly referred to as *pig iron,* a name that derives from long ago when the molten iron often was cooled in a mold shaped somewhat like a baby pig.
- Some of the pig iron is cooled to a solid and sold to foundries, which melt it and mold it into "cast iron" products. Most of the pig iron, though, remains liquid. It is carried by hot-metal "bottle" or "submarine" cars to a steel-making building.

Smelting Iron Ore

Iron usually occurs as the ores hematite or magnetite. Iron ores must be smelted to separate the iron from the oxygen and other substances in the ores. Then the iron is refined and processed into steel.

1. Iron ore is crushed and then mixed with crushed limestone and coke (baked coal), which is rich in carbon.

2. The coke and iron ore mixture is placed in a blast furnace, where extremely hot air is blown through, making the coke burn easily.

3. As the coke burns, chemical changes in the mixture produce carbon dioxide gas and molten iron.

4. The iron sinks to the bottom of the furnace. Oxygen and other substances left in the ore combine with the limestone to create slag.

5. The slag and molten iron are poured off through taps in the blast furnace.

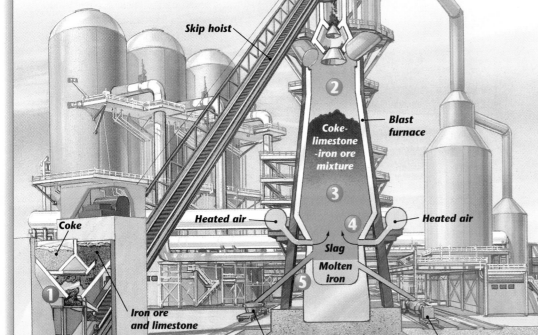

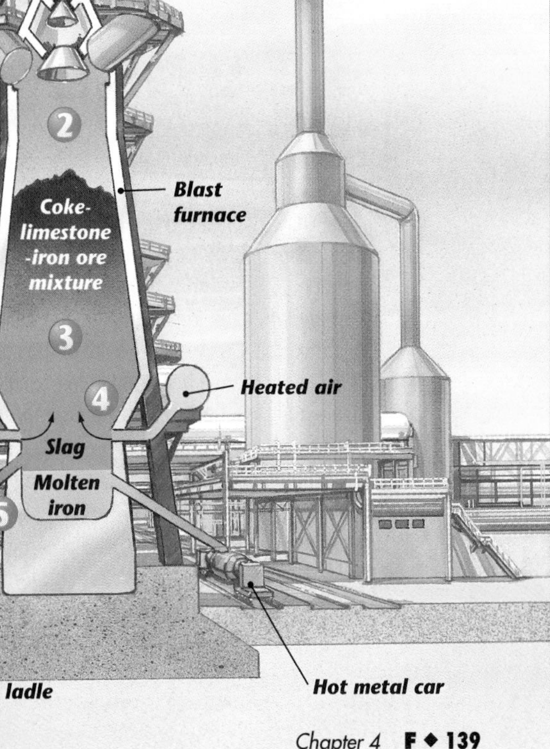

3 Assess

Section 3 Review Answers

1. Answers will vary. A typical answer might mention uses of gems in jewelry and in industry, as well as uses of metals in tools and machinery, metal filaments in light bulbs and steel girders.
2. In a strip mine, ore is exposed by scraping away the soil. An open pit mine is a tremendous pit. A shaft mine often has a network of tunnels that extends deep underground.
3. Smelting separates useful metal from other elements in ore.
4. An alloy is a solid mixture of two or more metals. Alloys have special properties that pure metals may not have.
5. The heating of the ore causes the metal to melt and separate from the oxygen it is combined with. Because the metal is heavy, it sinks to the bottom of the furnace.

Science at Home

ACTIVITY

Materials *3 iron nails, petroleum jelly, clear nail polish, clear glass, water, vinegar*
Tips Family members will notice that the uncoated nail shows signs of rusting after a night in water, while the coated nails do not. Remind students also to mention that stainless steel does not readily rust because it is a steel alloy that includes iron, chromium, and nickel.

Program Resources

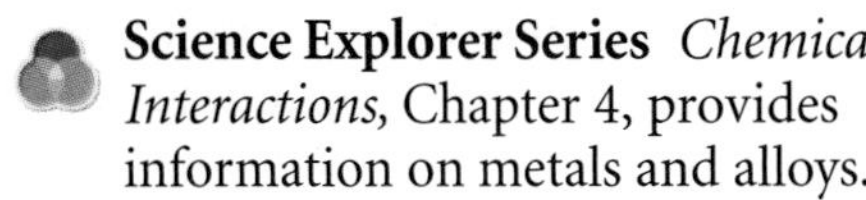

- **Science Explorer Series** *Chemical Interactions,* Chapter 4, provides information on metals and alloys.
- **Teaching Resources** 4-3 Review and Reinforcement, p. 113; 4-2 Enrich, p. 114

Media and Technology

Transparencies "Exploring Smelting Iron Ore," Transparency 18

Interactive Student Tutorial CD-ROM F-4

Performance Assessment

Skills Check Have students make a flowchart that includes information about the processes involved from the formation of an ore to its use in a manufactured process. The flowchart, then, should include a process that formed the ore as well as the processes of locating, mining, and smelting the ore.

Real-World Lab

Careers in Science

Copper Recovery

Preparing for Inquiry

Key Concept The processing of copper ore can be made more efficient by recovering copper from the waste water produced.

Skills Objectives Students will be able to

- measure amounts of copper sulfate and water to make a solution;
- observe changes in nails after adding them to the solution;
- infer that the nails draw copper from the solution;
- develop a hypothesis to describe how a mine could recover copper from mine waste water;
- draw a conclusion about why a mine operator would try to collect copper from waste water.

Time 30 minutes

Advance Planning You can simplify the procedure by making the solution yourself before class. Place it in a container from which students can pour into their beakers. If students are to remove the nails from the solutions as part of disposal, provide gloves and possibly tongs.

Alternative Materials Any small pieces of iron will do in place of the nails, as long as they fit into the beaker. Avoid steel alloys, though, since they include other elements as well as iron.

Guiding Inquiry

Invitation Help students focus on the key concept by asking: **How are most minerals mined?** *(A typical answer might suggest that mining involves digging ore from the ground.)* **Could a metal also be obtained from a solution?** *(Most students will not know if that is possible.)* Explain that copper is one mineral that can be extracted from a solution and this lab will demonstrate one such method.

Real-World Lab

Careers in Science

COPPER RECOVERY

If you were a mining engineer, one of your tasks would be to make mining and processing ores more efficient. When copper ore is processed at copper mines, waste water containing copper sulfate is produced. Mining engineers have invented a way to recover copper metal from the waste water. They make the waste water flow over scrap iron.

Problem

How is copper recovered from a solution?

Materials

copper sulfate, 3 g
triple-beam balance
beaker, 400 mL
graduated cylinder, 200 mL
5 iron nails

Procedure

1. Place 3 g of copper sulfate in a beaker. **CAUTION:** *Copper sulfate is poisonous. Handle it with care.*
2. Add 50 mL of water to the beaker to dissolve the copper sulfate. Observe the color of the solution.
3. Add the iron nails to the beaker. The nails act as scrap iron. Describe the color of the solution after the nails have been added to the solution.
4. Follow your teacher's instructions for proper disposal.

Analyze and Conclude

1. What happened to the nails after you placed them in the solution? What is the material on the nails? Explain your answer.
2. How does the material on the nails compare with the copper sulfate?
3. Form a hypothesis that describes how a mine might recover copper from mine water using the method that you have just tried.
4. What additional step would you have to perform to obtain copper useful for making copper wire or pennies?
5. **Apply** Why do you think the operator of a copper mine would want to collect copper from the waste water?

Move to Explore

Repeat the experiment. This time test the solution with litmus paper both before and after you add the nails. Litmus paper indicates if a solution is acidic, basic, or neutral. Record your results. Why do you think a mining engineer would test the water from this process before releasing it into the environment?

Program Resources

- **Teaching Resources** Chapter 4 Real-World Lab, pp. 118–119

Safety

Caution students to be careful with the copper sulfate, because it's poisonous. Since students will be working with breakable glass, they should wear goggles. Make sure they dispose of the solution per your instructions. Review the safety guidelines in Appendix A.

STUDY GUIDE

Properties of Minerals

Key Ideas

- A mineral is a naturally occurring inorganic solid that has a distinct chemical composition and crystal shape.
- Each mineral can be identified by its own physical and chemical properties.
- Some of the properties of minerals include hardness, color, streak, luster, density, cleavage and fracture, and crystal shape. Hardness is measured by the Mohs hardness scale.
- Minerals usually consist of two or more elements joined together in a compound.

Key Terms

mineral	Mohs hardness scale
inorganic	streak
crystal	luster
element	cleavage
compound	fracture

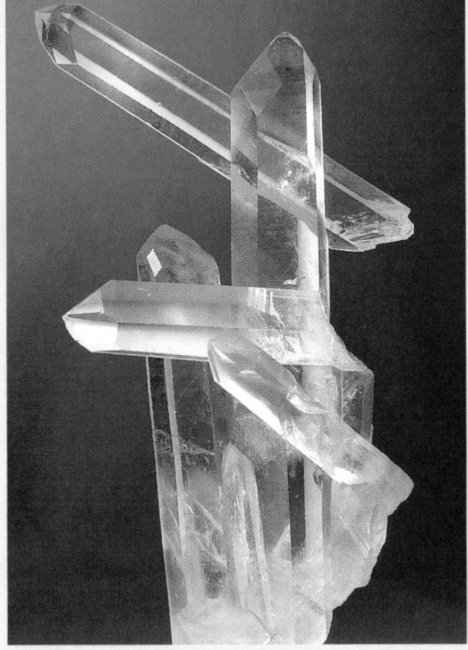

How Minerals Form

Key Ideas

- Minerals form inside Earth through crystallization as magma or lava cools.
- Minerals form on Earth's surface when materials dissolved in water crystallize through evaporation.
- Mineral deposits form on the ocean floor from solutions heated by magma along the mid-ocean ridge. The hot-water solutions containing minerals erupt through chimneys on the ocean floor, then crystallize when they come in contact with cold sea water.

Key Terms

solution
vein

Mineral Resources

INTEGRATING TECHNOLOGY

Key Ideas

- Minerals are useful as the source of all metals, gemstones, and of many other materials.
- Geologists locate ore deposits by prospecting—looking for certain features on and beneath Earth's surface.
- Ores can be removed from the ground through open pit mines, strip mines, or shaft mines.
- Smelting is the process of heating an ore to extract a metal.

Key Terms

gemstone	smelting
ore	alloy

www.science-explorer.phschool.com

CHAPTER 4 REVIEW

Program Resources

- **Teaching Resources** Chapter 4 Project Scoring Rubric, p. 102; Chapter 4 Performance Assessment, pp. 189–191; Chapter 4 Test, pp. 192–195

Media and Technology

Computer Test Bank Test F-4

Introducing the Procedure

- **What is scrap iron?** *(Fragments of discarded iron materials)*
- **What could produce a change in color in a copper sulfate solution?** *(A chemical reaction caused by the addition of another substance)*

Troubleshooting the Experiment

- Demonstrate how to add the water to the beaker so as not to splash or spill the solution.
- Allow about 10 minutes between the time students add the nails and the time when they note their observations.

Expected Outcome

Students will observe that the copper in the copper sulfate solution will coat the nails. This occurs because iron from the nails replaces the copper in a chemical reaction represented by this equation:

$$CuSO_4 + Fe = FeSO_4 + Cu$$

Analyze and Conclude

1. The nails were coated with a layer of some material. Students may correctly infer that this substance is copper, the result of a chemical reaction between the nails and the solution.
2. The material on the nails is a different color than the color of the copper sulfate before the nails were added. When the nails were added, the solution became colorless.
3. Hypotheses may vary. A typical hypothesis might suggest that iron materials, such as scrap iron, could be used to recover copper from the mine water.
4. The copper-coated iron would need to be processed further to remove the copper coating and obtain pure copper.
5. Copper is valuable, and allowing copper to leave with the water is lost money.

Extending the Inquiry

More to Explore Students will discover that before the nails are added the solution is neutral, as indicated by no change in the color of the litmus paper. After the nails are added, the solution becomes acidic, as indicated by the paper turning blue. A mining engineer would test the water because releasing acidic water into the environment could harm living things.

CHAPTER 4 REVIEW

Reviewing Content: Multiple Choice

1. b 2. b 3. c 4. c 5. d

True or False

6. true 7. streak 8. large 9. true
10. mining

Checking Concepts

11. Most minerals are compounds, composed of atoms of two or more elements. A pure element is composed of atoms of a single element.
12. Although the color of a mineral may vary, the color of a mineral's streak is always the same.
13. Cleavage is when a mineral splits easily along flat surfaces. Fracture, by contrast, describes how a mineral breaks apart when it does not split evenly.
14. In general, minerals can form through crystallization of melted materials and crystallization of materials dissolved in water. In the first way, minerals form as hot magma cools deep inside the crust or as lava hardens on the surface. In the second way, minerals crystallize as solutions cool or evaporate.
15. The process of extracting a metal from hematite ore is called smelting. It involves crushing the hematite, heating it with such materials as coke and limestone, and then separating the iron in the hematite from oxygen. The metal obtained at the end of the process is iron.
16. Answers will vary. A typical letter might mention examining the rocks of an area, testing streams for the presence of chemicals, and using explosions to map the location, size, and shape of an ore deposit. The next step would be to test for the correct properties of gold as distinct from other minerals, such as fool's gold. If gold were found, the prospector would probably feel elated.

Thinking Visually

17. a. Inorganic b. Solid.

Applying Skills

18. The color of the sample of wulfenite is yellowish orange, the luster is shiny and gemlike, and the crystal shape is rectangular, with angled edges (tetragonal).

CHAPTER 4 REVIEW

Reviewing Content

For more review of key concepts, see the Interactive Student Tutorial CD-ROM.

Multiple Choice

Choose the letter of the answer that best completes each statement.

1. In a mineral, the particles line up in a repeating pattern to form
   a. an element. b. a crystal.
   c. a mixture. d. a compound.
2. The softest mineral in the Mohs hardness scale is
   a. quartz. b. talc.
   c. apatite. d. gypsum.
3. Halite is a mineral formed by
   a. sea-floor spreading.
   b. cooling of magma.
   c. evaporation.
   d. cooling of lava.
4. Metals are useful for tools because they
   a. are compounds.
   b. have a metallic luster.
   c. are hard yet can be easily shaped.
   d. are elements.
5. Minerals from which metals can be removed in usable amounts are called
   a. gemstones. b. crystals.
   c. alloys. d. ores.

True or False

If the statement is true, write true. If it is false, change the underlined word or words to make the statement true.

6. <u>Luster</u> is the term that describes how a mineral reflects light from its surface.
7. A piece of unglazed tile is used to test a mineral's <u>hardness.</u>
8. If magma cools very slowly, minerals with <u>small</u> crystals will form.
9. Minerals form from <u>hot-water solutions</u> at chimneys on the ocean floor.
10. The process of removing an ore deposit from the ground is known as <u>prospecting.</u>

Checking Concepts

11. What is the difference in composition between most minerals and a pure element?
12. How can the streak test be helpful in identifying minerals?
13. Compare cleavage and fracture.
14. Describe two different ways that minerals can form.
15. Describe the process used to extract metal from hematite ore. What metal would be obtained?
16. **Writing to Learn** You are a prospector searching for gold. In a letter home, describe where you plan to look, how you will know if you have found gold, and how you will feel about your discovery.

Thinking Visually

17. **Venn Diagram** Copy the Venn diagram comparing the mineral hematite and the human-made material brick onto a separate piece of paper. Then complete it and add a title. (For more on Venn diagrams, see the Skills Handbook.)

19. The fairly large size of the crystals indicates that the wulfenite formed slowly.
20. A hardness of 3 is very low on the Mohs hardness scale. Since most gems are relatively hard, wulfenite would not be hard enough to be used as a gem. These crystals might be used as an ore for the metals they contain, lead and molybdenum.

Thinking Critically

21. Color and luster are similar in that they are both visually observable properties. There are fewer kinds of luster, however, than there are colors. Luster is also different in that it can describe the surface texture of a mineral.
22. Since obsidian does not have a crystal structure, one of the five characteristics of a mineral, it cannot be classified as a mineral.
23. Deep underground, a solution of hot water and metals follows a fracture within rock. When the solution cools, the metals crystallize

Applying Skills

Working as a geologist, you have found a sample of the mineral wulfenite. Testing the wulfenite reveals that it has a hardness of about 3 on the Mohs hardness scale and a density of 6.8 grams per cubic centimeter. You also determine that the mineral contains oxygen as well as the metals lead and molybdenum.

18. **Observing** Describe wulfenite's color, luster, and crystal shape.
19. **Inferring** Did the wulfenite form slowly or quickly? Explain your answer.
20. **Drawing Conclusions** Is wulfenite hard enough for use as a gem? What would you use these crystals for? Explain.

Thinking Critically

21. **Comparing and Contrasting** Color and luster are both properties of minerals. How are these properties similar? How are they different? How can each be used to help identify a mineral?
22. **Classifying** Obsidian forms when magma cools very quickly, creating a type of glass. In glass, the particles are not arranged in an orderly pattern as in a crystal. Obsidian is a solid, inorganic substance that occurs naturally in volcanic areas and has a definite chemical composition. Should it be classified as a mineral? Explain why or why not.
23. **Relating Cause and Effect** Describe how a vein of ore forms underground. What is the energy source for this process?
24. **Applying Concepts** Explain the roles of elements, solutions, and compounds in the process that forms minerals along the mid-ocean ridge.
25. **Predicting** What would happen if steel-makers forgot to add enough chromium and nickel to a batch of stainless steel?

CHAPTER 4 REVIEW

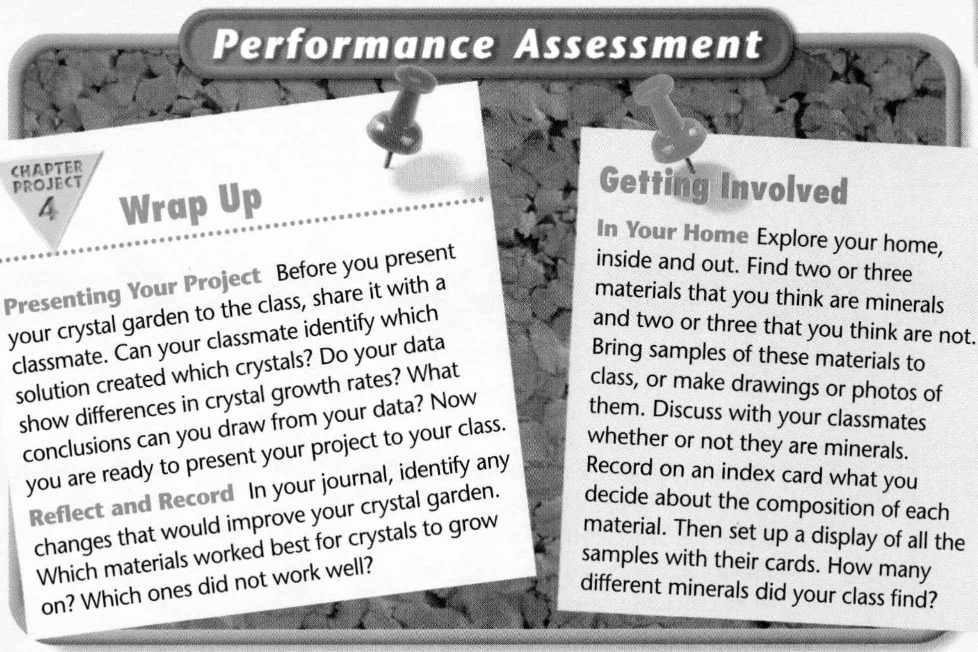

Performance Assessment

CHAPTER PROJECT 4

Wrap Up

Presenting Your Project Before you present your crystal garden to the class, share it with a classmate. Can your classmate identify which solution created which crystals? Do your data show differences in crystal growth rates? What conclusions can you draw from your data? Now you are ready to present your project to your class.

Reflect and Record In your journal, identify any changes that would improve your crystal garden. Which materials worked best for crystals to grow on? Which ones did not work well?

Getting Involved

In Your Home Explore your home, inside and out. Find two or three materials that you think are minerals and two or three that you think are not. Bring samples of these materials to class, or make drawings or photos of them. Discuss with your classmates whether or not they are minerals. Record on an index card what you decide about the composition of each material. Then set up a display of all the samples with their cards. How many different minerals did your class find?

into a vein. The energy source for the process is heat from hot magma, which is heated by Earth's core.

24. The elements and compounds that form minerals in oceanic crust dissolve in water heated by magma. The solutions that result, then, are rich in minerals. These solutions belch out of chimneys, and the minerals they contain crystallize on the ocean floor.

25. Without enough chromium and nickel in the steel, iron oxide could form on the steel; that is, the steel could rust.

Program Resources

- **Inquiry Skills Activity Book** Provides teaching and review of all inquiry skills

Performance Assessment

CHAPTER PROJECT 4

Wrap Up

Presenting Your Project Talk with each student or group before the presentation. Make suggestions and give words of encouragement. Assess the presentations on the quality of the garden scenes, the growth of the crystals in the garden, the growth data kept by the students, and the coherence of the presentation.

Reflect and Record In assessing their crystal gardens, students should reflect on the materials used, the quality and attractiveness of the scenes they made, and the growth rate of the different kinds of crystals. They should assess how their gardens compared with others in the class and suggest ways in which they could have improved their own outcome.

Getting Involved

In Your Home Encourage students to bring as many of the materials to school as possible. Then divide the class into small groups for consideration of these materials. Samples might include various metal objects, such as silverware, coins, tools, and candle holders, as well as various objects made of stone, plastic, rubber, and so on. Point out that students should look for materials that they think might stump other students in the class. Set aside a place in the classroom for students to display labeled samples.

Rocks

Sections	Time	Student Edition Activities	Other Activities
CHAPTER PROJECT 5 **Collecting Rocks** p. 145	Ongoing (3 weeks)	Check Your Progress, pp. 149, 158, 161, 169 Wrap Up, p. 173	
1 Classifying Rocks pp. 146–149 ◆ List the characteristics used to identify rocks. ◆ Identify and describe the three major groups of rocks.	1–2 periods/ $\frac{1}{2}$–1 block	**Discover** How Are Rocks Alike and Different?, p. 146	**TE** Using the Visuals: Figure 2, p. 147 **TE** Including All Students, p. 147 **TE** Building Inquiry Skills: Comparing and Contrasting, p. 148; Observing, p. 148
2 Igneous Rocks pp. 150–153 ◆ Identify the characteristics used to classify igneous rocks.	2–3 periods/ 1–1$\frac{1}{2}$ blocks	**Discover** How Do Igneous Rocks Form?, p. 150 **Sharpen Your Skills** Observing, p. 152 **Science at Home,** p. 153	**TE** Building Inquiry Skills: Comparing and Contrasting, p. 151
3 Sedimentary Rocks pp. 154–158 ◆ Describe how sedimentary rocks form. ◆ List and describe the three major types of sedimentary rocks.	2–3 periods/ 1–1$\frac{1}{2}$ blocks	**Discover** How Does Pressure Affect Particles of Rock?, p. 154 **Try This** Rock Absorber, p. 156	**TE** Building Inquiry Skills: Making Models, p. 155; Classifying, p. 156 **TE** Integrating Life Science, p. 157
4 *Integrating Life Science* **Rocks From Reefs** pp. 159–161 ◆ Describe the formation of coral reefs. ◆ Explain how coral reefs become organic limestone deposits on land.	1–2 periods/ $\frac{1}{2}$–1 block	**Discover** What Can You Conclude From the Way a Rock Reacts to Acid?, p. 159	**TE** Building Inquiry Skills: Making Models, p. 160 **ISLM** F-5, "Making Models of Sedimentary Rocks"
5 Metamorphic Rocks pp. 162–165 ◆ Describe the conditions under which metamorphic rocks form. ◆ Identify the ways in which geologists classify metamorphic rocks.	2–3 periods/ 1–1$\frac{1}{2}$ blocks	**Discover** How Do the Grain Patterns of Gneiss and Granite Compare?, p. 162 **Try This** A Sequined Rock, p. 163 **Science at Home,** p. 164 **Skills Lab: Classifying** Mystery Rocks, p. 165	
6 The Rock Cycle pp. 166–170 ◆ Describe the rock cycle. ◆ Explain the role played by plate tectonics in the rock cycle.	2–3 periods/ 1–1$\frac{1}{2}$ blocks	**Discover** Which Rock Came First?, p. 166 **Sharpen Your Skills** Classifying, p. 167 **Real-World Lab: You, the Consumer** Testing Rock Flooring, p. 170	**TE** Exploring the Rock Cycle, p. 168
Study Guide/Chapter Review pp. 171–173	1 period/ $\frac{1}{2}$ block		**ISAB** Provides teaching and review of all inquiry skills

For Standard or Block Schedule The Resource Pro® CD-ROM gives you maximum flexibility for planning your instruction for any type of schedule. Resource Pro® contains Planning Express®, an advanced scheduling program, as well as the entire contents of the Teaching Resources and the Computer Test Bank.

CHAPTER PLANNING GUIDE

Program Resources	Assessment Strategies	Media and Technology
TR Chapter 5 Project Teacher Notes, pp. 120–121 **TR** Chapter 5 Project Overview and Worksheets, pp. 122–125 **TR** Chapter 5 Project Scoring Rubric, p. 126	**SE, TE** Performance Assessment: Chapter 5 Project Wrap Up, p. 173 **TE** Check Your Progress, pp. 149, 158, 161, 169 **TR** Chapter 5 Project Scoring Rubric, p. 126	
TR 5-1 Lesson Plan, p. 127 **TR** 5-1 Section Summary, p. 128 **TR** 5-1 Review and Reinforce, p. 129 **TR** 5-1 Enrich, p. 130	**SE** Section 1 Review, p. 149 **TE** Ongoing Assessment, p. 147 **TE** Performance Assessment, p. 149 **TR** 5-1 Review and Reinforce, p. 129	Audiotapes, English-Spanish Summary 5-1 Interactive Student Tutorial CD-ROM, F-5
TR 5-2 Lesson Plan, p. 131 **TR** 5-2 Section Summary, p. 132 **TR** 5-2 Review and Reinforce, p. 133 **TR** 5-2 Enrich, p. 134	**SE** Section 2 Review, p. 153 **TE** Ongoing Assessment, p. 151 **TE** Performance Assessment, p. 153 **TR** 5-2 Review and Reinforce, p. 133	Audiotapes, English-Spanish Summary 5-2 Interactive Student Tutorial CD-ROM, F-5
TR 5-3 Lesson Plan, p. 135 **TR** 5-3 Section Summary, p. 136 **TR** 5-3 Review and Reinforce, p. 137 **TR** 5-3 Enrich, p. 138 **SES** Book G, *Earth's Changing Surface*, Chapter 3	**SE** Section 3 Review, p. 158 **TE** Ongoing Assessment, pp. 155, 157 **TE** Performance Assessment, p. 158 **TR** 5-3 Review and Reinforce, p. 137	Audiotapes, English-Spanish Summary 5-3 Transparency 19, "Formation of Sedimentary Rocks" Interactive Student Tutorial CD-ROM, F-5
TR 5-4 Lesson Plan, p. 139 **TR** 5-4 Section Summary, p. 140 **TR** 5-4 Review and Reinforce, p. 141 **TR** 5-4 Enrich, p. 142 **SES** Book H, *Earth's Waters,* Chapter 5	**SE** Section 4 Review, p. 161 **TE** Performance Assessment, p. 161 **TR** 5-4 Review and Reinforce, p. 141	Audiotapes, English-Spanish Summary 5-4 Interactive Student Tutorial CD-ROM, F-5
TR 5-5 Lesson Plan, p. 143 **TR** 5-5 Section Summary, p. 144 **TR** 5-5 Review and Reinforce, p. 145 **TR** 5-5 Enrich, p. 146 **TR** Chapter 5 Skills Lab, pp. 151–153	**SE** Section 5 Review, p. 164 **SE** Analyze and Conclude, p. 165 **TE** Ongoing Assessment, p. 163 **TE** Performance Assessment, p. 164 **TR** 5-5 Review and Reinforce, p. 145	Exploring Earth Science Videodisc, Unit 5 Side 1, "The Earth Library" Audiotapes, English-Spanish Summary 5-5 Interactive Student Tutorial CD-ROM, F-5
TR 5-6 Lesson Plan, p. 147 **TR** 5-6 Section Summary, p. 148 **TR** 5-6 Review and Reinforce, p. 149 **TR** 5-6 Enrich, p. 150 **TR** Chapter 5 Real-World Lab, pp. 154–155	**SE** Section 6 Review, p. 169 **SE** Analyze and Conclude, p. 170 **TE** Ongoing Assessment, p. 167 **TE** Performance Assessment, p. 169 **TR** 5-6 Review and Reinforce, p. 149	Exploring Earth Science Videodisc, Unit 3 Side 1, "Everything on Your Plate" Transparency 20, "Exploring the Rock Cycle" Interactive Student Tutorial CD-ROM, F-5
TR Chapter 5 Performance Assessment, pp. 196–198 **TR** Chapter 5 Test, pp. 199–202	**SE** Chapter 5 Review, pp. 171–173 **TR** Chapter 5 Performance Assessment, pp. 196–198 **TR** Chapter 5 Test, pp. 199–202 **CTB** Test F-5	Interactive Student Tutorial CD-ROM, F-5 Computer Test Bank, Test F-5 Science Explorer Internet Site

Key: **SE** Student Edition, **CTB** Computer Test Bank, **ISAB** Inquiry Skills Activity Book, **TE** Teacher's Edition, **SES** Science Explorer Series Text, **PTA** Product Testing Activities by *Consumer Reports*, **TR** Teaching Resources, **ISLM** Integrated Science Laboratory Manual, **IES** Interdisciplinary Explorations Series

Meeting the National Science Education Standards and AAAS Benchmarks

National Science Education Standards	Benchmarks for Science Literacy	Unifying Themes
Science As Inquiry (Content Standard A) ◆ **Design and conduct a scientific investigation** Students investigate what kind of stone makes the best flooring. *(Real-World Lab)* ◆ **Use appropriate tools and techniques to gather, analyze, and interpret data** Students collect, classify, and display rocks. Students use the properties of rocks to classify them. *(Chapter Project; Skills Lab)* **Life Science** (Content Standard C) ◆ **Populations and ecosystems** Coral animals build shells that grow together to form a coral reef. *(Section 4)* **Earth and Space Science** (Content Standard D) ◆ **Structure of the Earth system** There are three major groups of rocks: igneous rock, sedimentary rock, and metamorphic rock. Igneous rocks form from magma or lava. Sedimentary rocks form from particles deposited by water and wind. Coral buried by sediments can turn into limestone. Heat and pressure deep beneath Earth's surface can change any rock into metamorphic rock. Forces inside Earth and at the surface produce a rock cycle that builds, destroys, and changes the rocks in the crust. *(Sections 1, 2, 3, 4, 5, 6)* **Science and Technology** (Content Standard E) ◆ **Understandings about science and technology** Humans use rocks in different ways. *(Sections 2, 3, 5; Real-World Lab)*	**1B Scientific Inquiry** Students collect, classify, and display rocks. Students use the properties of rocks to classify them. Students investigate what kind of stone makes the best flooring. *(Chapter Project; Skills Lab; Real-World Lab)* **3A Technology and Science** Humans use rocks in different ways. *(Sections 2, 3, 5; Real-World Lab)* **4C Processes That Shape the Earth** There are three major groups of rocks: igneous rock, sedimentary rock, and metamorphic rock. Igneous rocks form from magma or lava. Sedimentary rocks form from particles deposited by water and wind. Coral buried by sediments can turn into limestone. Heat and pressure deep beneath Earth's surface can change any rock into metamorphic rock. Forces inside Earth and at the surface produce a rock cycle that builds, destroys, and changes the rocks in the crust. *(Sections 1, 2, 3, 4, 5, 6)* **5A Diversity of Life** Coral animals build shells that grow together to form a coral reef. *(Section 4)*	◆ **Energy** Igneous rocks form from hot magma or lava. Limestone that began as coral can be found in places where uplift has raised ancient sea floors. Heat and pressure deep beneath Earth's surface can change any rock into metamorphic rock. Forces inside Earth and at the surface produce a rock cycle that builds, destroys, and changes rocks in the crust. *(Sections 1, 2, 4, 5, 6)* ◆ **Evolution** The remains of living things may be preserved as fossils in sedimentary rock. In the rock cycle, rocks change over time. *(Sections 3, 6)* ◆ **Patterns of Change** Molten rock cools to form igneous rock. Compaction and cementation change sediments into sedimentary rock. The processes of the rock cycle cause rocks to change continuously from one form to another. *(Sections 2, 3, 6)* ◆ **Scale and Structure** Rocks are made of minerals. *(Section 1; Chapter Project; Skills Lab)* ◆ **Systems and Interactions** Humans use rocks in different ways. Plate movements drive the rock cycle. *(Sections 2, 3, 5, 6; Real-World Lab)* ◆ **Unity and Diversity** Rocks are classified as igneous, sedimentary, or metamorphic. Igneous rocks are classified as extrusive or intrusive. Sedimentary rocks are classified as clastic, organic, or chemical. There are three types of coral reefs: fringing reefs, barrier reefs, and atolls. Metamorphic rocks are classified as foliated or nonfoliated. The rock cycle can follow many different pathways. *(Sections 1, 2, 3, 4, 5, 6; Chapter Project; Skills Lab)*

Media and Technology

Exploring Earth Science Videodiscs

◆ **Section 5** "The Earth Library" shows how layers of rock explain the history of Earth.

◆ **Section 6** "Everything on Your Plate" illustrates how geologic activity occurs at plate boundaries.

Interactive Student Tutorial CD-ROM

◆ **Chapter Review** Interactive questions help students to self-assess their mastery of key chapter concepts.

Student Edition Connection Strategies

◆ **Section 2** Integrating Chemistry, p. 152

◆ **Section 3** Integrating Life Science, p. 157 

◆ **Section 4** Integrating Life Science, pp. 159–161 

◆ **Section 5** Visual Arts Connection, p. 164 

www.science-explorer.phschool.com

Visit the Science Explorer Internet site to find an up-to-date activity for Chapter 5 of *Inside Earth*.

Student Edition Activities Planner

ACTIVITY	Time (minutes)	Materials Quantities for one work group	Skills
Section 1			
Discover, p. 146	10	**Nonconsumable** samples of marble and conglomerate, hand lens, penny	Observing
Section 2			
Discover, p. 150	10	**Nonconsumable** samples of granite and obsidian, hand lens	Inferring
Sharpen Your Skills, p. 152	10	No special materials are required.	Observing
Science at Home, p. 153	Home	No special materials are required.	Communicating
Section 3			
Discover, p. 154	15	**Consumable** sheet of paper, 2 slices of bread **Nonconsumable** stack of books, plastic knife	Observing
Try This, p. 156	15; 10	**Consumable** water **Nonconsumable** samples of sandstone and shale, hand lens, balance, pan	Drawing Conclusions
Section 4			
Discover, p. 159	15	**Consumable** dilute (5%) hydrochloric acid, running water **Nonconsumable** samples of limestone and coquina, plastic dropper	Drawing Conclusions
Section 5			
Discover, p. 162	15	**Nonconsumable** samples of gneiss and granite, hand lens	Inferring
Try This, p. 163	15	**Consumable** modeling compound, 25 sequins, 30-cm string **Nonconsumable** metric ruler, 2 blocks of wood	Making Models
Science at Home, p. 164	Home	No special materials are required.	Observing
Skills Lab, p. 165	30	**Nonconsumable** 1 nonrock solid object such as brick or bone, 2 igneous rock samples such as granite and basalt, 2 sedimentary rock samples such as sandstone and conglomerate, 2 metamorphic rock samples such as gneiss and slate, hand lens	Observing, Creating Data Tables, Classifying
Section 6			
Discover, p. 166	10	**Consumable** 3 index cards **Nonconsumable** colored pencils	Developing Hypotheses
Sharpen Your Skills, p. 167	10	No special materials are required.	Classifying
Real-World Lab, p. 170	40	**Consumable** water, materials that form stains such as ink and paint, greasy materials such as butter and crayons **Nonconsumable** steel nail, plastic dropper, wire brush, hand lens, samples of igneous, sedimentary, and metamorphic rocks with flat surfaces	Designing Experiments, Forming Operational Definitions, Drawing Conclusions

A list of all materials required for the Student Edition activities can be found on pages T14–T15. You can order Materials Kits by calling 1-800-828-7777 or by accessing the Science Explorer Internet site at **www.science-explorer.phschool.com.**

Collecting Rocks

Rocks are such a major part of the environment that for most students they remain mostly unseen, and certainly largely undifferentiated. Collecting rocks in the field will enrich student's understanding of the natural world.

Purpose In this project, students will collect rock samples in their own community, as well as classify and identify the rocks collected. They will also create a display of their collection to be presented to the class. By doing this project, students will gain a first-hand understanding of the three major groups of rocks.

Skills Focus In completing the Chapter 5 Project, students will be able to:

- observe rocks in the field and choose interesting samples to collect;
- classify each rock sample based on its characteristics into one of the three major groups of rocks;
- draw conclusions about the identity of specific rocks by using a field guide;
- communicate what they have learned by creating a display of the rock collection and making a presentation to the class.

Project Time Line The entire project will require about three weeks. Students can do this project either individually or in small groups. Some class time may be needed for planning as well as for creating the display and preparing the presentation. The bulk of the time, though, should be spent by students in the field, collecting rocks at various locations in their community. Students can complete the project by doing the following.

- Brainstorm locations where rocks could be collected safely and legally.
- Plan excursions to parks and other places where they are likely to find many kinds of rocks.
- Collect rocks at several locations.
- Examine the collected rocks, classifying and identifying each sample through observation and tests.
- Create a display of the rock collection.
- Make a presentation to the class, explaining how each sample was classified.

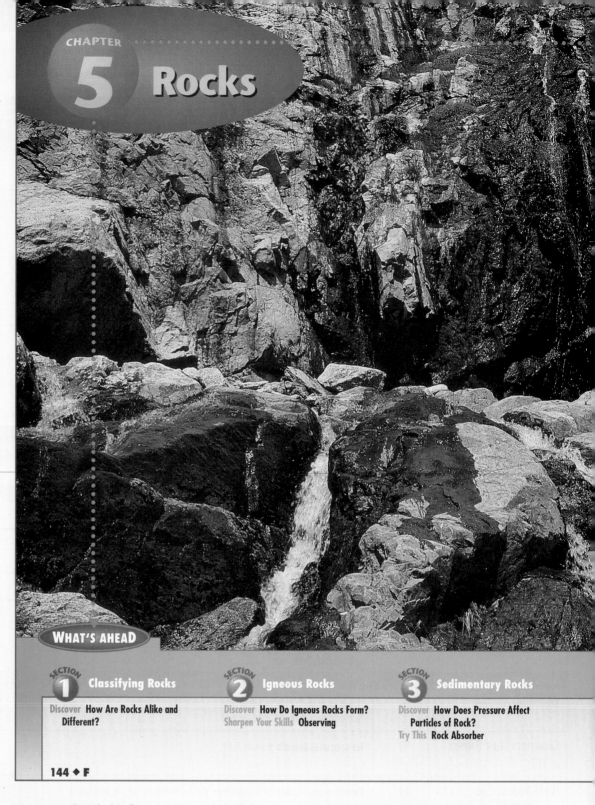

CHAPTER 5 Rocks

WHAT'S AHEAD

For more detailed information on planning and supervising the chapter project, see Chapter 5 Project Teacher Notes, pages 120–121 in Teaching Resources.

Suggested Shortcuts

- You may wish to divide the class into small groups to carry out this project.
- You can make this project shorter and less involved by having pairs of students collect only two or three rocks and bring the rocks to class. Then, either small groups or the class as a whole can classify and identify the most interesting samples. Those rocks can then be made into a display.

Possible Materials For the collection phase of the project, students will need a heavy bag in which to carry the rock samples. A canvas bag is traditional for this purpose, but an old book backpack would serve the same purpose. Resealable plastic sandwich bags are good for storing individual rock samples. For examination in the lab, students will need a hand lens and a fingernail file to do a scratch test. It may also be desirable for students to break apart

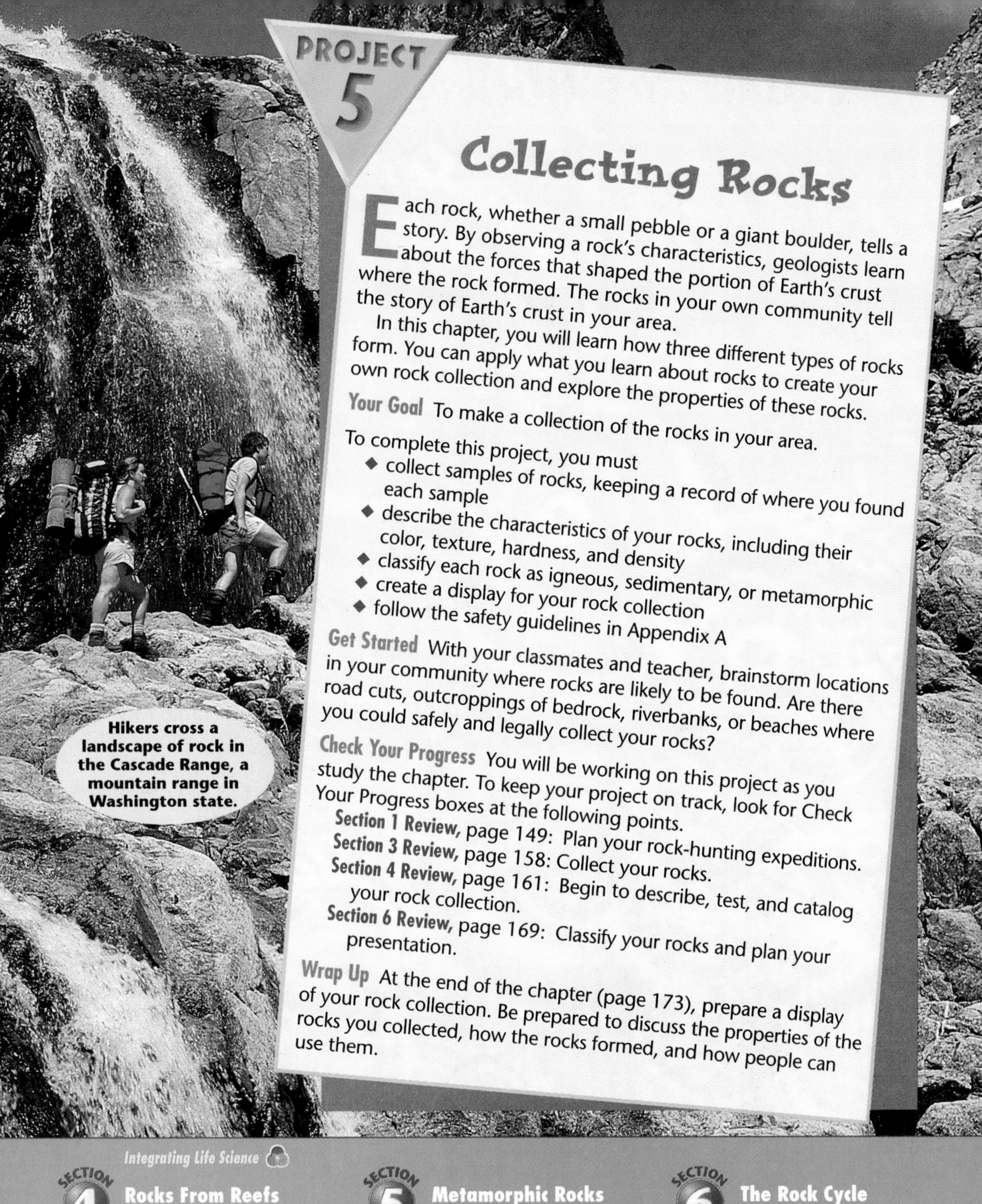

PROJECT 5

Collecting Rocks

Each rock, whether a small pebble or a giant boulder, tells a story. By observing a rock's characteristics, geologists learn about the forces that shaped the portion of Earth's crust where the rock formed. The rocks in your own community tell the story of Earth's crust in your area.

In this chapter, you will learn how three different types of rocks form. You can apply what you learn about rocks to create your own rock collection and explore the properties of these rocks.

Your Goal To make a collection of the rocks in your area.

To complete this project, you must

- collect samples of rocks, keeping a record of where you found each sample
- describe the characteristics of your rocks, including their color, texture, hardness, and density
- classify each rock as igneous, sedimentary, or metamorphic
- create a display for your rock collection
- follow the safety guidelines in Appendix A

Get Started With your classmates and teacher, brainstorm locations in your community where rocks are likely to be found. Are there road cuts, outcroppings of bedrock, riverbanks, or beaches where you could safely and legally collect your rocks?

Check Your Progress You will be working on this project as you study the chapter. To keep your project on track, look for Check Your Progress boxes at the following points.

Section 1 Review, page 149: Plan your rock-hunting expeditions.
Section 3 Review, page 158: Collect your rocks.
Section 4 Review, page 161: Begin to describe, test, and catalog your rock collection.
Section 6 Review, page 169: Classify your rocks and plan your presentation.

Wrap Up At the end of the chapter (page 173), prepare a display of your rock collection. Be prepared to discuss the properties of the rocks you collected, how the rocks formed, and how people can use them.

Hikers cross a landscape of rock in the Cascade Range, a mountain range in Washington state.

some of the samples. A hammer and goggles are necessary for this purpose. For creating a display, students will need egg cartons or some other container with compartments, with cotton padding added to each compartment. In addition, rock and mineral guidebooks are necessary if students are to identify specific rocks in their collection.

Launching the Project To introduce the project, show students a rock collection in a professional display. At this stage, students may know very little about how rocks are classified. Point out that the display shows various kinds of rocks, each with a specific name. Then ask: **Where in our community are some good places to collect different kinds of rocks?** *(A typical answer might mention parks, roadcuts, and stream beds.)* Explain that in the Chapter 5 Project they will collect rock samples from such places, classify and identify as many samples as they can, and then create a display similar to the professional one. Emphasize that students should collect rocks only where it is safe and legal. To help students get started, pass out Chapter 5 Project Overview and Worksheets, pages 122–125 in Teaching Resources. You may also wish to pass out the Chapter 5 Project Scoring Rubric, page 126, at this time.

Program Resources

- **Teaching Resources** Chapter 5 Project Teacher Notes, pp. 120–121; Chapter 5 Project Overview and Worksheets, pp. 122–125; Chapter 5 Project Scoring Rubric, p. 126

Performance Assessment

Use the Chapter 5 Project Scoring Rubric to assess students' work. Students will be assessed on

- how many rock samples they collect and describe;
- how well they classify and identify their rock samples, as well as how well they create an attractive display;
- how effectively they present their rock collections to the class;
- their participation in a group, if they worked in groups.

Section 1 Classifying Rocks

Objectives

After completing the lesson, students will be able to
- list the characteristics used to identify rocks;
- identify and describe the three major groups of rocks.

Key Terms texture, grain, igneous rock, sedimentary rock, metamorphic rock

1 Engage/Explore

Activating Prior Knowledge

Encourage students to share their knowledge of rocks and rock types. For example, ask students about two types of rocks that they could probably recognize: **How would you describe the difference between sandstone and marble?** *(A typical answer might describe a difference in texture—sandstone is grainy, while marble is smooth.)* **What could the feel of a rock's surface tell a geologist about how that rock formed?** *(Answers will vary. Some students might suggest that marble formed farther underground than sandstone.)*

Discover Activity

Skills Focus observing
Materials *samples of marble and conglomerate, hand lens, penny*
Time 10 minutes
Tips If you have only a few samples of each kind of rock, pair samples of about the same size and place pairs at strategic places around the classroom. Then invite students to examine the pair closest to them.
Think It Over Students should discover that marble is a fine-grained rock, with a crystalline texture that can easily be seen. Conglomerate has a rough texture and is clearly composed of small rocks and other materials, such as shells. Marble is harder and denser than conglomerate. Both marble and conglomerate vary in color.

Section 1 Classifying Rocks

Discover Activity

How Are Rocks Alike and Different?

1. Look at samples of marble and conglomerate with a hand lens.
2. Describe the two rocks. What is the color and texture of each?
3. Try scratching the surface of each rock with the edge of a penny. Which rock seems harder?

4. Hold each rock in your hand. Allowing for the fact that the samples aren't exactly the same size, which rock seems denser?

Think It Over
Observing Based on your observations, how would you compare the physical properties of marble and conglomerate?

Guide for Reading

- **What characteristics are used to identify rocks?**
- **What are the three major groups of rocks?**

Reading Tip **Before you read, use the headings to make an outline about rocks. Then fill in details as you read.**

Between 1969 and 1972, the Apollo missions to the moon returned to Earth with pieces of the moon's surface. Space scientists eagerly tested these samples. They wanted to learn what the moon is made of. They found that the moon's surface is made of material very similar to the material that makes up Earth's surface—rock. Some moon samples are dark rock called basalt. Other samples are light-colored rock made mostly of the mineral feldspar.

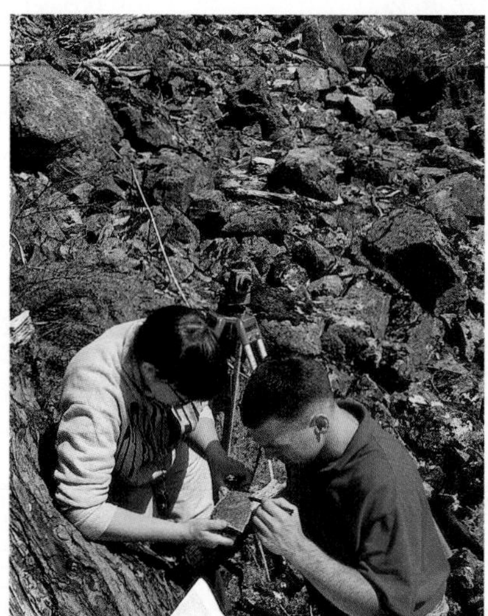

Figure 1 Geology students collect and study samples of rocks.

How Geologists Classify Rocks

For both Earth and its moon, rocks are important building blocks. On Earth, rock forms mountains, hills, valleys, beaches, even the ocean floor. Earth's crust is made of rock. Rocks are made of mixtures of minerals and other materials, although some rocks may contain only a single mineral. Granite, shown in Figure 2, is made up of the minerals quartz, feldspar, mica, and hornblende, and sometimes other minerals.

Geologists collect and study samples of rock in order to classify them. Imagine that you are a geologist exploring a mountain range for the first time. How would you study a particular type of rock found in these mountains? You might use a camera or notebook to record

Reading Strategies

Reading Tip Students should use the main headings: "How Geologists Classify Rocks," "Texture," "Mineral Composition," and "Origin." As students read the material under each heading, they should summarize the main points in a few words and add these to their outlines. Suggest that they use the sideheads under "Texture" as subheadings and write a few words under each. The finished outline can serve as a study guide for section review.

Vocabulary Have students brainstorm a list of words they commonly use to describe the feel of the surface of something, such as *rough, smooth, grainy, gritty, coarse, oily, silky, bumpy,* and *waxy.* Then point out the key term *texture* in their text. Explain that the words in their list are descriptive words of texture and they probably classify objects by texture all the time.

Figure 2 Granite is made up of quartz, mica, feldspar, and hornblende. It may also contain other minerals. *Observing* Which mineral seems most abundant in the sample of granite shown?

information about the setting where the rock was found. (In classifying a rock, it's important for a geologist to know what other types of rock occur nearby). Then, you would use a chisel or the sharp end of a rock hammer to remove samples of the rock. Finally, you would break open the samples with a hammer to examine their inside surfaces. You must look at the inside of a rock because the effects of water and weather can change the outer surface of a rock.

When studying a rock sample, geologists observe the rock's color and texture and determine its mineral composition. Using these characteristics, geologists can classify a rock according to its origin, or where and how it formed.

Texture

As with minerals, color alone does not provide enough information to identify a rock. A rock's texture, however, is very useful in identifying the rock. To a geologist, a rock's **texture** is the look and feel of the rock's surface. Some rocks are smooth and glassy. Others are rough or chalky. Most rocks are made up of particles of minerals or other rocks, which geologists call **grains.** A rock's grains give the rock its texture. To describe a rock's texture, geologists use a number of terms based on the size, shape, and pattern of the rock's grains.

Program Resources

◆ **Teaching Resources** 5-1 Lesson Plan, p. 127; 5-1 Section Summary, p. 128

Media and Technology

Audiotapes English-Spanish Summary 5–1

Answers to Self-Assessment

Caption Question

Figure 2 Answers may vary, though most students should observe that feldspar makes up the greatest proportion of granite.

2 Facilitate

How Geologists Classify Rocks

Using the Visuals: Figure 2

ACTIVITY

Materials *hand lens, sample of granite, samples of the minerals quartz, pink feldspar, hornblende, mica*
Time 15 minutes

To help students understand the relationship between minerals and rocks, provide them with a granite sample and separate samples of the primary minerals in the rock. Have students make a labeled drawing of the granite sample, with pointers to prominent crystals of each kind of mineral. **learning modality: visual**

Texture

Including All Students

Materials *samples of cloth with different kinds of weaves*
Time 15 minutes

Explain that the term texture is derived from a Latin word meaning "to weave," as is the word *textile*, another word for "cloth." Then pass around several pieces of cloth with different weaves, or textures. Have students write a description of each piece of cloth, using adjectives that describe the weaves. Call on students to share the words they used to describe the texture of each piece. Then ask: **Does color or type of thread used affect a cloth's texture?** *(The color of the cloth does not affect its texture. The kind of thread or yarn used may affect texture.)* Likewise, texture, color, and mineral composition are separate qualities in a rock. **learning modality: kinesthetic**

Ongoing Assessment

Oral Presentation Call on students at random to name and describe one of the three characteristics geologists use to identify rocks—color, texture, and mineral composition.

Texture, continued

Using the Visuals: Figure 3

Ask students: **What do "nonbanded" and "banded" refer to in the examples of quartzite and gneiss shown?** *(Those words refer to the grain pattern of each rock. The grains of gneiss are arranged in a pattern that looks like bands, or thin layers. The grains of quartzite appear to have no bands but occur randomly throughout the rock.)* **learning modality: visual**

Building Inquiry Skills: Comparing and Contrasting

ACTIVITY

Materials *cardboard box, scissors, piece of cloth, tape, samples of granite, sandstone, shale*
Time 15 minutes

To prepare for this activity, use the scissors to cut away one side of the box. Then use tape to replace that side with a piece of cloth, which serves as a curtain. Use this box to cover the three rock samples, which should be about the same size. Then invite students to reach through the curtain and, without seeing the rocks, arrange the samples from coarsest grained to finest grained, left to right. **learning modality: kinesthetic**

Mineral Composition

Building Inquiry Skills: Observing

ACTIVITY

Materials *microscope, prepared slides of thin sections of various kinds of rock, including granite, basalt, obsidian, limestone, shale, sandstone, marble, slate, schist, gneiss*
Time 15 minutes

Set up microscopes at three locations around the classroom, one each for igneous rocks, sedimentary rocks, and metamorphic rocks. Have students observe the slides and make drawings of what they see, labeling each drawing with the name of the rock. Challenge students to identify specific minerals. Give students the opportunity to observe the slides again as they learn more about differences in rocks. **learning modality: visual**

Figure 3 Texture helps geologists classify rocks. *Forming Operational Definitions* Looking at the rocks below, describe the characteristics of a rock that help you to define what a rock's "grain" is.

Fine-grained
Slate

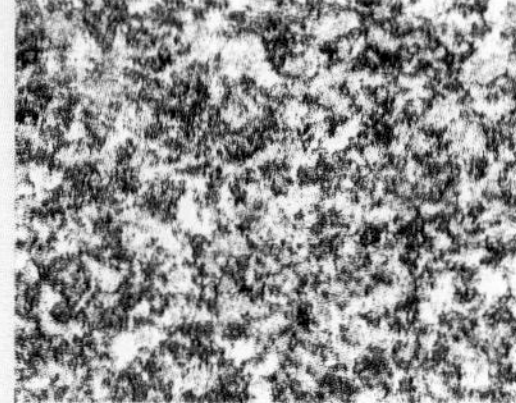

Coarse-grained
Peridotite

No visible grain
Flint

Grain Size Often, the grains in a rock are large and easy to see. Such rocks are said to be coarse-grained. In other rocks, the grains are so small that they can only be seen with a microscope. These rocks are said to be fine-grained. Notice the difference in texture between the fine-grained slate and the coarse-grained peridotite at left.

Grain Shape The grains in a rock vary widely in shape. Some grains look like tiny particles of fine sand. Others look like small seeds or exploding stars. In some rocks, such as granite, the grain results from the shapes of the crystals that form the rock. In other rocks, the grain shape results from fragments of other rock. These fragments can be smooth and rounded, like the fragments in conglomerate, or they can be jagged, like the fragments in breccia. You can compare conglomerate and breccia below.

Grain Pattern The grains in a rock often form patterns. Some grains lie in flat layers that look like a stack of pancakes. Other grains form wavy, swirling patterns. Some rocks have grains that look like rows of multicolored beads, as in the sample of gneiss shown below. Other rocks, in contrast, have grains that occur randomly throughout the rock.

No Visible Grain Some rocks have no grain, even when they are examined under a microscope. Some of these rocks have no crystal grains because when they form, they cool very quickly. This quick cooling gives these rocks the smooth, shiny texture of a thick piece of glass. Other rocks with a glassy texture are made up of extremely small particles of quartz that have been pressed together. One glassy-textured rock that forms in this manner is flint.

☑ *Checkpoint* ***What terms describe a rock's texture?***

Rounded grain
Conglomerate

Jagged grain
Breccia

Nonbanded
Quartzite

Banded
Gneiss

148 ◆ F

Background

Facts and Figures Grain size in igneous rocks depends on how slowly or rapidly the minerals in magma or solution crystallized. Grain size in metamorphic rocks is affected by the degree of metamorphism—how high the temperature or great the pressure. Low-grade metamorphism often results in a denser rock, with smaller grains. More intense metamorphism causes some minerals to recrystallize and form larger grains. Many metamorphic rocks, such as gneiss, have a texture similar to a coarse-grained igneous rock. The size of the grains in clastic sedimentary rocks is also an indication of the conditions in which the rocks formed, though it's environmental conditions that are indicated. The large particles of conglomerate, for example, might have been deposited by a fast-moving stream.

Mineral Composition

Often, geologists must look more closely at a rock to determine its mineral composition. By looking at a small sliver of a rock under a microscope, a geologist can observe the shape and size of crystals in the rock and identify the minerals it contains. To prepare a rock for viewing under the microscope, geologists cut the rock very thin, so that light can shine through its crystals.

In identifying rocks, geologists also use some of the tests that are used to identify minerals. The scratch test determines the rock's hardness on Mohs hardness scale. Testing the rock's surface with acid determines whether the rock includes minerals containing carbon compounds. Testing with a magnet detects the elements iron or nickel.

Figure 4 A scientist is preparing to cut a thin slice from a piece of moon rock. He will then examine it under a microscope to determine its composition.

Origin

There are three major groups of rocks: igneous rock, sedimentary rock, and metamorphic rock. These terms refer to how the rocks in each group formed.

Rock belonging to each of these groups forms in a different way. **Igneous rock** forms from the cooling of molten rock—either magma below the surface or lava at the surface. **Sedimentary rock** forms when particles of other rocks or the remains of plants and animals are pressed and cemented together. Sedimentary rock forms in layers below the surface. **Metamorphic rock** is formed when an existing rock is changed by heat, pressure, or chemical reactions. Most metamorphic rock forms deep underground.

Section 1 Review

1. What three characteristics do geologists use to identify a rock sample?
2. What are the three groups into which geologists classify rocks?
3. What is a rock's texture?
4. What methods do geologists use to determine the mineral composition of a rock?
5. **Thinking Critically Comparing and Contrasting** What do the three major groups of rocks have in common? How are they different?

Check Your Progress

CHAPTER PROJECT 5

Your neighborhood might be a good place to begin your rock collection. Look for gravel and crushed rock in flower beds, driveways or parking lots, and beneath downspouts. **CAUTION:** *If the area you choose is not a public place, make sure that you have permission to be there.* Begin to collect samples of rocks with different colors and textures. Plan with your teacher or an adult family member to visit other parts of your community where you could collect rocks.

Origin

Including All Students

For students who are still mastering English, explain that *origin* refers to the source or beginning of something, in this case the formation of each of the major rock groups. Ask: **Some of the rocks of which group have their origin at the surface of Earth rather than underground?** *(Some igneous rocks form at the surface.)* **limited English proficiency**

3 Assess

Section 1 Review Answers

1. Color, texture, and mineral composition
2. Igneous rock, sedimentary rock, and metamorphic rock
3. A rock's texture is the look and feel of the rock's surface.
4. Geologists look at a small sliver of a rock under a microscope to observe its crystals and identify the minerals it contains. They also use tests to identify minerals, including the scratch test for hardness, an acid test for carbon compounds, and a magnet to detect iron or nickel.
5. Rocks in each group make up Earth's crust and are composed of minerals and other materials. They are different in the way they are formed.

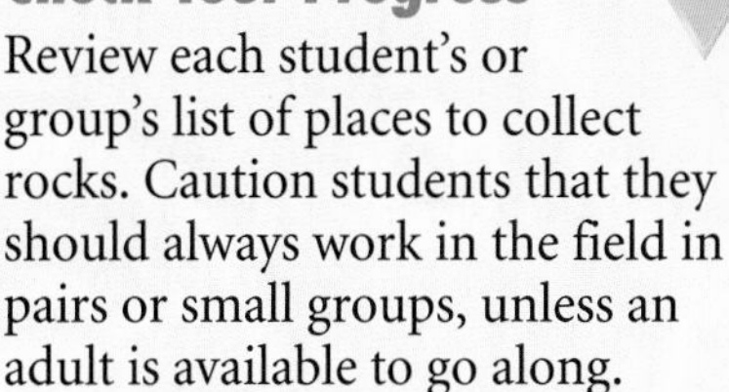

Check Your Progress

CHAPTER PROJECT 5

Review each student's or group's list of places to collect rocks. Caution students that they should always work in the field in pairs or small groups, unless an adult is available to go along.

Program Resources

◆ **Teaching Resources** 5-1 Review and Reinforce, p. 129; 5-1 Enrich, p. 130

Media and Technology

Interactive Student Tutorial CD-ROM F-5

Answers to Self-Assessment

Caption Question

Figure 3 Characteristics include grain size, grain shape, and grain pattern.

Checkpoint

Texture is described with terms based on grain size, including fine-grained and coarse-grained; grain shape, including smooth and jagged; and grain pattern, including banded and nonbanded.

Performance Assessment

Writing Have students explain in their own words what characteristics geologists use to identify rocks.

SECTION 2 Igneous Rocks

Objective

After completing the lesson, students will be able to

◆ identify the characteristics used to classify igneous rocks.

Key Terms extrusive rock, intrusive rock, porphyritic texture

1 Engage/Explore

Activating Prior Knowledge

Help students recall the knowledge they gained from earlier chapters about molten material from the mantle and where it rises into Earth's crust. Ask: **At what places does molten material rise to Earth's surface?** *(Volcanoes, hot spots, mid-ocean ridge)* **What happens to molten material from the mantle when it rises close to or onto the surface?** *(It hardens, or crystallizes.)* Help students recall how cooling rates affect the size of mineral crystals.

DISCOVER ACTIVITY

Skills Focus inferring
Materials *samples of granite and obsidian, hand lens*
Time 10 minutes
Tips If samples of granite and obsidian are unavailable, use any two igneous rocks with similar composition but obviously different textures, such as gabbro and basalt or diorite and andesite.
Expected Outcome Granite and obsidian are very similar in composition but have different textures because granite forms from magma and obsidian forms from lava. Students should observe that the granite has coarse-grained crystals, while the glassy obsidian has no crystals.
Think It Over Students should infer that the granite formed as magma slowly cooled deep beneath Earth's surface, while the obsidian formed as lava cooled quickly on the surface.

SECTION 2 Igneous Rocks

DISCOVER ACTIVITY

How Do Igneous Rocks Form?

1. Use a hand lens to examine samples of granite and obsidian.
2. Describe the texture of both rocks using the terms coarse, fine, or glassy.
3. Which rock has coarse-grained crystals? Which rock has no crystals or grains?

Think It Over

Inferring Granite and obsidian are igneous rocks. Given the physical properties of these rocks, what can you infer about how each type of rock formed?

GUIDE FOR READING

◆ **What characteristics are used to classify igneous rocks?**

Reading Tip **As you read, make a list of the characteristics of igneous rocks. Write one sentence describing each characteristic.**

You are in a spacecraft orbiting Earth 4.6 billion years ago. Do you see the blue and green globe of Earth that astronauts today see from space? No—instead, Earth looks like a glowing piece of charcoal from a barbecue, or a charred and bubbling marshmallow heated over the coals.

When Earth first formed, the planet was so hot that its surface was a glowing mass of molten material. Nearly a billion years passed before Earth cooled enough for a crust to solidify. Then lava probably flowed from Earth's interior, spread over the molten surface, and hardened. The movement of magma and lava has continued ever since.

Figure 5 A lava flow soon cools and hardens to form igneous rock.

READING STRATEGIES

Reading Tip Point out that the subheadings "Origin," "Texture," and "Mineral Composition" provide students with three main characteristics of igneous rocks. Thus, they should write one sentence for each of those characteristics. Each sentence should sum up the information under the subheading.

Vocabulary After students have read about the derivation of the term *igneous,* point out that they may use two words that are derived from the same Greek word. When you *ignite* charcoal, for example, you set it on fire. Figuratively, you can *ignite* a crowd with a "fiery" speech. Also, when you start a car, you turn the key in the *ignition* switch. Explain that turning the switch causes an electric current to *ignite* the fuel mixture that powers the engine.

Figure 6 Igneous rocks can vary greatly in texture.
A. Rhyolite is a fine-grained igneous rock with a mineral composition similar to granite.
B. Pegmatite is a very coarse-grained variety of granite.
C. Porphyry has large crystals surrounded by fine-grained crystals.
Relating Cause and Effect What conditions caused rhyolite to have a fine-grained texture?

Characteristics of Igneous Rock

The first rocks to form on Earth probably looked much like the igneous rocks that harden from lava today. Igneous rock (IG nee us) is any rock that forms from magma or lava. The name "igneous" comes from the Latin word *ignis*, meaning "fire."

Most igneous rocks are made of mineral crystals. The only exceptions to this rule are the different types of volcanic glass—igneous rock that lacks a crystal structure. **Igneous rocks are classified according to their origin, texture, and mineral composition.**

Origin Geologists classify igneous rocks according to where they formed. **Extrusive rock** is igneous rock formed from lava that erupted onto Earth's surface. Basalt is the most common extrusive rock. Basalt forms much of the crust, including the oceanic crust, shield volcanoes, and lava plateaus.

Igneous rock that formed when magma hardened beneath Earth's surface is called **intrusive rock.** Granite is the most abundant intrusive rock. Recall from Chapter 3 that granite batholiths form the core of many mountain ranges.

Texture The texture of an igneous rock depends on the size and shape of its mineral crystals. Igneous rocks may be similar in mineral composition and yet have very different textures. The texture of an igneous rock may be fine-grained, coarse-grained, glassy, or porphyritic. Rapid cooling lava forms fine-grained igneous rocks with small crystals. Slow cooling magma forms coarse-grained rock with large crystals.

Intrusive and extrusive rocks usually have different textures. Intrusive rocks have larger crystals than extrusive rocks. If you examine a coarse-grained rock such as granite, you can easily see that the crystals vary in size and color.

Some intrusive rocks have a texture that looks like a gelatin dessert with chopped-up fruit mixed in. A rock with large crystals scattered on a background of much smaller crystals has a **porphyritic texture** (pawr fuh RIT ik). How can a rock have two

2 Facilitate

Characteristics of Igneous Rocks

Using the Visuals: Figure 6

Ask students: **Which of these rocks is intrusive and which is extrusive?** *(Rhyolite is fine-grained, and thus is extrusive. Pegmatite is coarse-grained, and thus is intrusive. Porphyry has a porphyritic texture, and therefore must be an intrusive rock that cooled in two stages.)* **learning modality: visual**

Building Inquiry Skills: Comparing and Contrasting

Materials *hand lens, samples of granite and basalt*
Time 15 minutes

Explain that granite and basalt are the two most common igneous rocks. Then have students turn back to Chapter 1, Section 1, to review the text description of Earth's crust and Figure 6 of Chapter 1. Ask: **Which parts of the crust are composed mostly of one or the other of these igneous rocks?** *(Oceanic crust is composed mostly of basalt, while continental crust is composed mostly of granite.)* Then invite students to examine and handle samples of each kind of rock. Have them make sketches of mineral grains and write a description of each. In their descriptions, students should mention origin, texture, any minerals they can identify, color, and density (heft). **learning modality: kinesthetic**

Portfolio Students can keep their sketches and descriptions in their portfolio.

Program Resources

◆ **Teaching Resources** 5-2 Lesson Plan, p. 131; 5-2 Section Summary, p. 132

Media and Technology

Audiotapes English-Spanish Summary 5-2

Answers to Self-Assessment

Caption Question

Figure 6 Rapid cooling on Earth's surface caused rhyolite to have a fine-grained texture.

Ongoing Assessment

Writing Have students explain in their own words how the location where rock cools affects its texture.

Characteristics of Igneous Rocks, continued

Using the Visuals: Figure 7

Have students closely examine the figure and also re-examine the photographs in Figure 2. Then ask: **Can you identify specific mineral grains in this photograph of granite?** *(Students should be able to identify the glassy grains as quartz, the pink grains as feldspar, the dark grains as mica or hornblende.)* **Can you see the grains of this rock without the aid of a microscope?** *(Yes, because granite is an intrusive, coarse-grained rock.)* **learning modality: visual**

Sharpen your Skills

Observing

Time 10 minutes
Expected Outcome Students should be able to conclude that feldspar is the most abundant mineral in gabbro either by estimating or by counting mineral grains of approximately equal size. Similarly, they may conclude that either mica or quartz is the least abundant mineral in gabbro.
Extend Provide students with samples of gabbro to try to confirm their observations about that igneous rock's mineral composition. **learning modality: visual**

Integrating Chemistry

Some students may confuse the chemical composition of minerals, which are exact and never-changing, with the mineral composition of rocks, which can vary somewhat. To address this difference, find pictures of different varieties of granite, such as pegmatite, biotite granite, and muscovite granite, in geology texts or field guides. Explain that each of the major igneous rocks, including granite and basalt, actually encompass a range of rocks with similar but not identical mineral compositions. Geologists often talk about "granitic" rocks or the "granite family." **learning modality: visual**

Sharpen your Skills

Observing

ACTIVITY

You can learn about a rock's mineral composition by looking at a thin section.

1. The diagram shows a thin section of the igneous rock gabbro. The key identifies different minerals. Which mineral makes up most of gabbro? How did you decide?
2. Which mineral is present in the smallest amount?

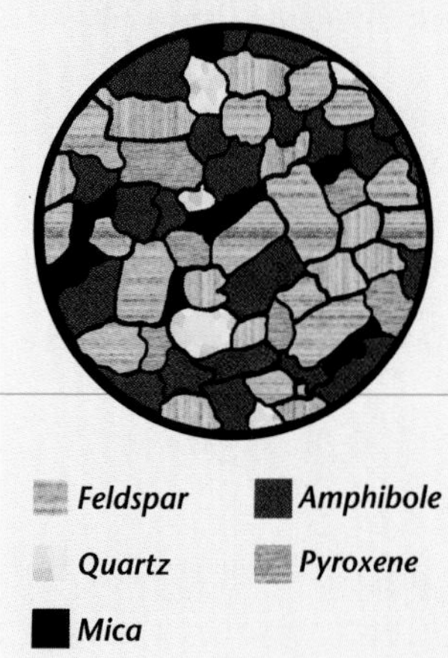

Figure 7 This thin slice of granite, viewed under a microscope, contains quartz, feldspar, mica, and other minerals.

textures? Porphyritic rocks form when intrusive rocks cool in two stages. As the magma begins to cool, large crystals form slowly. The remaining magma, however, cools more quickly, forming small crystals. The change in the rate of cooling may occur as magma moves nearer to the surface.

Extrusive rocks have a fine-grained or glassy texture. Basalt is an extrusive rock. It consists of crystals too small to be seen without a microscope.

Mineral Composition Recall from Chapter 3 that the silica content of magma and lava affects how easily the magma or lava will flow. Lava that is low in silica usually forms dark-colored rocks such as basalt. Basalt contains feldspar as well as certain dark-colored minerals, but does not contain quartz.

INTEGRATING CHEMISTRY Magma that is high in silica usually forms light-colored rocks, such as granite. However, granite comes in many shades and colors. Granite can be dark to light gray, red, and pink. Granite's color changes along with its mineral composition. Granite that is rich in reddish feldspar is a speckled pink. But granite rich in hornblende and dark mica is light gray with dark specks. Quartz crystals in granite add white specks. Geologists can make thin slices of granite and study each type of crystal in the rock to determine its mineral composition more exactly.

☑ *Checkpoint* ***How do igneous rocks differ in origin, texture, and mineral composition?***

Background

Facts and Figures About 95 percent of Earth's crust is composed of igneous rocks or metamorphic rocks formed from igneous rocks. There are six major kinds of igneous rocks: the intrusive rocks granite, diorite, and gabbro; and the extrusive rocks rhyolite, andesite, and basalt.

History of Science In the early 1800s, Scottish geologist James Hall (1761–1832) showed that magma could cool to become crystalline rock. At the time, many geologists thought that magma would always harden to a glassy texture and thus most rocks had to have crystallized from a water solution. Hall melted rocks in a glass-factory furnace and then allowed them to cool. The melted rocks that cooled quickly did have a glassy texture, but the ones that cooled slowly formed crystalline solids.

Uses of Igneous Rocks

Many igneous rocks are hard, dense, and durable. For this reason, people throughout history have used igneous rock for tools and building materials. For example, ancient Native Americans used obsidian for making very sharp tools for cutting and scraping.

Granite, one of the most abundant igneous rocks, has a long history as a building material. More than 3,500 years ago, the ancient Egyptians used granite for statues like the one shown in Figure 9. About 600 years ago, the Incas of Peru carefully fitted together great blocks of granite and other igneous rocks to build a fortress near Cuzco, their capital city. In the United States during the 1800s and early 1900s, granite was widely used to build bridges and public buildings and for paving streets with cobblestones. Thin, polished sheets of granite are still used in decorative stonework, curbstones, and floors.

Igneous rocks such as basalt, pumice, and obsidian also have important uses. Basalt is crushed to make gravel that is used in construction. The rough surface of pumice makes it a good abrasive for cleaning and polishing. Perlite, formed from the heating of obsidian, is used in place of soil for starting vegetable seeds.

Figure 8 The ancient Egyptians valued granite for its durability. This royal couple at a temple in Luxor, Egypt, was carved in granite.

Section 2 Review

1. What are the three major characteristics that geologists use to identify igneous rocks?
2. What is the difference between extrusive and intrusive rocks? Give an example of each.
3. Explain what causes an igneous rock to have a fine-grained or coarse-grained texture.
4. Why are some igneous rocks dark and others light?
5. **Thinking Critically** **Comparing and Contrasting** How are basalt and granite different in their origin, texture, and mineral composition? How are they similar?

Science at Home

When you and a family member visit a pharmacy or large food store, observe the various foot-care products. What kinds of foot products are available that are made from pumice? How do people use these products? Check other skin and body care products to see if they contain pumice or other igneous rocks. Explain to your family how pumice is formed.

Program Resources

◆ **Teaching Resources** 5-2 Review and Reinforce, p. 133; 5-2 Enrich, p. 134

Media and Technology

Interactive Student Tutorial CD-ROM F-5

Answers to Self-Assessment

Checkpoint

Igneous rocks form either from lava that erupted onto Earth's surface or from magma that hardened below the surface. They differ in texture according to the size and shape of their mineral grains. They differ in mineral composition depending on how much silica and other minerals are present in magma and lava.

Uses of Igneous Rocks

Real-Life Learning

Have student volunteers call local city or county offices to ask if there are any large granite buildings or other structures in the area. Then invite the volunteers to provide a short list of these granite structures to the class. Encourage students to visit these places with their families and closely examine the texture of the stone. **learning modality: kinesthetic**

3 Assess

Section 2 Review Answers

1. Origin, texture, and mineral composition
2. Extrusive rock, such as basalt, forms from lava that has erupted onto Earth's surface. Intrusive rock, such as granite, forms when magma hardens beneath Earth's surface.
3. Rapid cooling causes an igneous rock to have a fine-grained texture. Slow cooling causes an igneous rock to have a coarse-grained texture.
4. Dark igneous rocks form from magma or lava low in silica content, while light igneous rocks form from magma or lava high in silica content.
5. Basalt is an extrusive rock with a fine-grained texture and low silica content. Granite is an intrusive rock with a coarse-grained texture and high silica content. Both are igneous rocks that began as molten material inside Earth.

Science at Home

ACTIVITY

Remind students that pumice forms when gas bubbles escape from cooling lava. Students should find that a number of foot products include pumice, especially those used to care for calluses, rough skin, and corns. Pumice is also used in some soaps.

Performance Assessment

Skills Check Have students compare and contrast granite and basalt.

SECTION 3 Sedimentary Rocks

Objectives

After completing the lesson, students will be able to

- ◆ describe how sedimentary rocks form;
- ◆ list and describe the three major types of sedimentary rocks.

Key Terms sediment, erosion, deposition, compaction, cementation, clastic rock, organic rock, chemical rock

1 Engage/Explore

Activating Prior Knowledge

Invite students to think of a sandy beach along an ocean or lake. Then ask: **What could cause the sand to harden into sandstone?** *(A typical answer might suggest that the weight of sand piled on that sand could provide pressure enough to harden it into a rock. Some students might suggest that there would have to be something to glue the sand particles together.)*

DISCOVER ACTIVITY

Skills Focus observing
Materials *sheet of paper, 2 slices of bread, stack of books, plastic knife*
Time 15 minutes
Tips To keep the bread from sticking to the tabletop, have students fold the sheet of paper and place the slice of bread inside the fold. The amount of change in the bread will depend on how long the books are left in place. Have one student leave the bread under the books overnight, and then have all students observe the results.
Think It Over Students should observe that the weight of the books compressed the bread and that the bread's texture is rougher and harder than before. A typical prediction might suggest that pressure would affect rock particles similarly.

SECTION 3 Sedimentary Rocks

DISCOVER ACTIVITY

How Does Pressure Affect Particles of Rock?

1. Place a sheet of paper over a slice of soft bread.
2. Put a stack of several heavy books on the top of the paper. After 10 minutes, remove the books. Observe what happened to the bread.
3. Slice the bread so you can observe its cross section.
4. Carefully slice a piece of fresh bread and compare its cross section to that of the pressed bread.

Think It Over

Observing How did the bread change after you removed the books? Describe the texture of the bread. How does the bread feel? What can you predict about how pressure affects the particles that make up sedimentary rocks?

GUIDE FOR READING

- ◆ How do sedimentary rocks form?
- ◆ What are the three major types of sedimentary rocks?

Reading Tip **Before you read, preview the headings in the section and predict how you think sedimentary rocks form.**

Visitors to Arches National Park in Utah see some of the strangest scenery on Earth. The park contains hundreds of natural arches sculpted in colorful rock that is layered like a birthday cake. The layers of this cake are red, orange, pink, or tan. One arch, named Landscape Arch, is nearly 100 meters across and almost as high. Delicate Arch looks like the legs of a striding giant. The forces that wear away rock on Earth's surface have been carving these arches out of solid rock for 100 million years. The arches are made of sandstone, one of the most common sedimentary rocks.

From Sediment to Rock

Sedimentary rocks form from particles deposited by water and wind. If you have ever walked along a stream or beach you may have noticed tiny sand grains, mud, and pebbles. These are some of the sediments that form sedimentary rock. **Sediment** is small, solid pieces of material that come from rocks or living things. Water, wind, and ice can carry sediment and deposit it in layers. But what turns these sediments into solid rock?

◀ **Delicate Arch, Arches National Park, Utah**

READING STRATEGIES

Vocabulary Help students understand the names used for each type of sedimentary rock. The word *clastic* derives from a Greek word for "broken," and clastic rocks are made from broken rock fragments. *Organic* denotes an origin in living things, and organic rocks form from the remains of living things. The term *chemical* in this context denotes an origin in a chemical process, which in this case is evaporation.

Program Resources

- ◆ **Teaching Resources** 5-3 Lesson Plan, p. 135; 5-3 Section Summary, p. 136

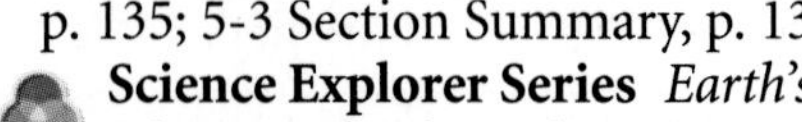

Science Explorer Series *Earth's Changing Surface,* Chapter 3, provides more information on erosion and deposition.

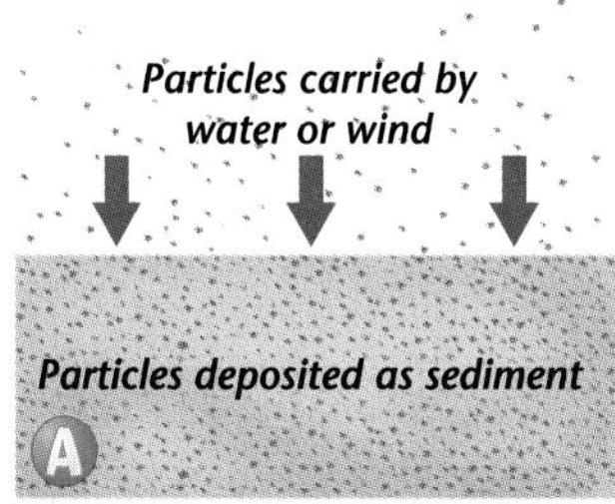

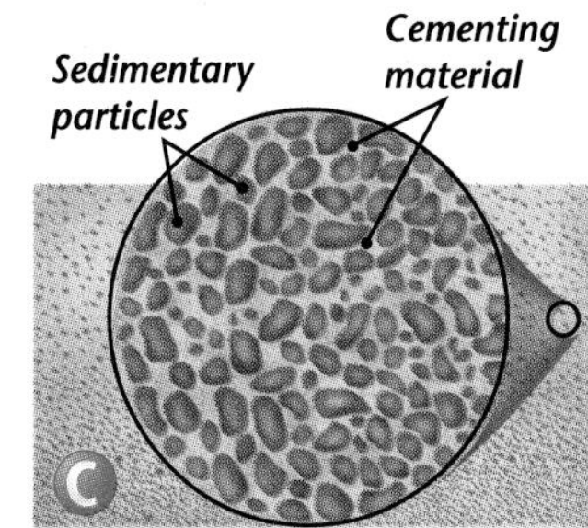

Figure 9 Sedimentary rocks form through the deposition, compaction, and cementation of sediments. **A.** Water or wind deposits sediment. **B.** The heavy sediments press down on the layers beneath. **C.** Dissolved minerals flow between the particles and cement them together. *Relating Cause and Effect What conditions are necessary for sedimentary rock to form?*

Erosion Destructive forces are constantly breaking up and wearing away all the rocks on Earth's surface. These forces include heat and cold, rain, waves, and grinding ice. **Erosion** occurs when running water or wind loosen and carry away the fragments of rock.

Deposition Eventually, the moving water or wind slows and deposits the sediment. If water is carrying the sediment, rock fragments and other materials sink to the bottom of a lake or ocean. **Deposition** is the process by which sediment settles out of the water or wind carrying it. **After sediment has been deposited, the processes of compaction and cementation change the sediment into sedimentary rock.**

In addition to particles of rock, sediment may include shells, bones, leaves, stems, and other remains of living things. Over time, any remains of living things in the sediment may slowly harden and change into fossils trapped in the rock.

Compaction At first the sediments fit together loosely. But gradually, over millions of years, thick layers of sediment build up. These layers are heavy and press down on the layers beneath them. Then compaction occurs. **Compaction** is the process that presses sediments together. Year after year more sediment falls on top, creating new layers. The weight of the layers further compacts the sediments, squeezing them tightly together. The layers often remain visible in the sedimentary rock.

Cementation While compaction is taking place, the minerals in the rock slowly dissolve in the water. The dissolved minerals seep into the spaces between particles of sediment. **Cementation** is the process in which dissolved minerals crystallize and glue particles of sediment together. It takes millions of years for compaction and cementation to transform loose sediments into solid sedimentary rock.

☑ *Checkpoint* *What are the processes that change sediment to sedimentary rock?*

2 Facilitate

From Sediment to Rock

Using the Visuals: Figure 9

Ask students: **What force is responsible for the compaction of sediment?** *(The weight of overlying sediment compacts underlying sediment. Therefore, the force of gravity is responsible.)* **For cementation to occur, what change must occur in the solution of water and dissolved minerals between particles of sediment?** *(The water must evaporate, leaving the minerals as solids between the particles.)*
learning modality: verbal

Building Inquiry Skills: Making Models

ACTIVITY

Materials *plaster of Paris, sand, pebbles of various colors, bowl, 2-L pop bottle with top cut off, scissors*
Time 20 minutes; 10 minutes 3–4 days later

Students can make a model of how sedimentary rock forms by building layers of sand and pebbles in a plastic bottle. In a bowl, students should mix sand, pebbles of one color, plaster of Paris, and a small amount of water. This mixture should be poured into the bottle. Repeating that process with different colors of pebbles, students can make several layers, one on top of the other. Once the layers have been prepared, the bottle should be placed in a warm, sunny place for several days to dry. When the layers have dried, have students cut the plastic away from the hardened "rock." Students should notice that the plaster has cemented the sediment together and that the bottom layers are more compressed than the top layers.
learning modality: kinesthetic

Media and Technology

Audiotapes English-Spanish Summary 5-3

Transparencies "Formation of Sedimentary Rocks," Transparency 19

Answers to Self-Assessment

Caption Question

Figure 9 Water or wind must be present for deposition to occur, and water must continue to be present for dissolved materials to cement particles together.

☑ *Checkpoint*

Compaction and cementation change sediment to sedimentary rock.

Ongoing Assessment

Writing Have students write a description in their own words of how sedimentary rock forms.

Students can keep their descriptions in their portfolios.

Types of Sedimentary Rock

Building Inquiry Skills: Classifying

Materials *hand lens, samples of sedimentary rocks, including sandstone, conglomerate, breccia, shale, limestone, gypsum*
Time 15 minutes

Before students have read about specific sedimentary rocks, provide small groups with representative samples of the three major groups of sedimentary rock. Challenge each group to generate a rationale for classifying the samples into three different types. **learning modality: logical/mathematical**

Clastic Rocks

Skills Focus drawing conclusions
Materials *samples of sandstone and shale, hand lens, balance, pan, water*
Time 15 minutes for setup; 10 minutes the next day
Tips Samples need to be at least 25 g to show a significant change in mass. If there are not enough samples for every student, divide the class into small groups. Make sure the pans will hold enough water to totally immerse the samples provided. Set up one or more balances in a central location so students can take each sample to a balance to find its mass. Advise students to make a data table to record the mass of each sample before and after immersing it in water.
Expected Outcome Students should observe that sandstone is rough and coarse-grained, while shale is smooth and fine-grained. The mass of each rock will vary depending on the samples used. Students should find that the mass of the shale changes little or not at all after being submerged overnight, while the mass of the sandstone increases substantially. They should conclude that sandstone has spaces between particles to absorb water, while shale does not.
Extend Have students perform the same activity with other rock samples. **learning modality: logical/mathematical**

Rock Absorber

Find out if water can soak into rock.

1. Using a hand lens, observe samples of sandstone and shale. How are they alike? How are they different?
2. Use a balance to measure the mass of each rock.
3. Place the rocks in a pan of water. Observe the samples. Which sample has bubbles escaping? Predict which sample will gain mass.
4. Leave the rocks submerged in the pan overnight.
5. The next day, remove the rocks from the pan and find the mass of each rock.

Drawing Conclusions How did the masses of the two rocks change after soaking? What can you conclude about each rock based on your observations?

Types of Sedimentary Rock

Geologists classify sedimentary rocks according to the type of sediments that make up the rock. **There are three major groups of sedimentary rocks: clastic rocks, organic rocks, and chemical rocks.** Different processes form each of these types of sedimentary rocks.

Clastic Rocks

Most sedimentary rocks are made up of the broken pieces of other rocks. A **clastic rock** is a sedimentary rock that forms when rock fragments are squeezed together. These fragments can range in size from clay particles too small to be seen without a microscope to large boulders too heavy for you to lift. Clastic rocks are grouped by the size of the rock fragments, or particles, of which they are made.

Shale One common clastic rock is shale. Shale forms from tiny particles of clay. For shale to form, water must deposit clay particles in very thin, flat layers, one on top of another. No cementation is needed to hold clay particles together. Even so, the spaces between the particles in the resulting shale are so small that water cannot pass through them. Shale feels smooth, and splits easily into flat pieces.

Sandstone Sandstone forms from the sand on beaches, on the ocean floor, in riverbeds, and in sand dunes. Sandstone is a clastic rock formed from the compaction and cementation of small particles of sand. Most sand particles consist of quartz. Because the cementation process does not fill all the spaces between sand grains, sandstone contains many small holes. Sandstone can easily absorb water through these holes.

Conglomerate and Breccia Some sedimentary rocks contain a mixture of rock fragments of different sizes. The fragments can range in size from pebbles to boulders. If the fragments have rounded edges, they form a clastic rock called conglomerate. A rock made up of large fragments with sharp edges is called breccia (BRECH ee uh).

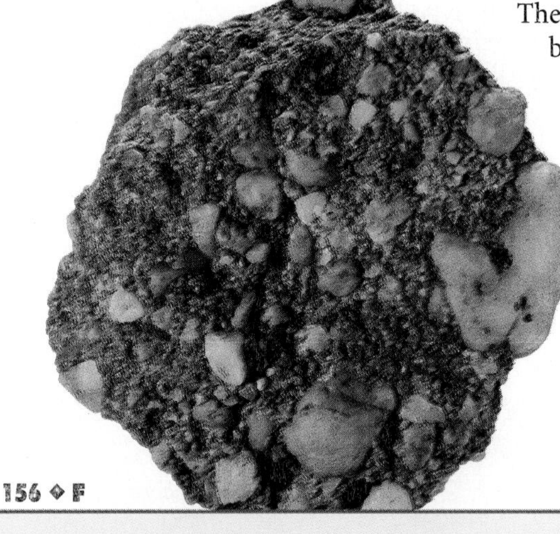

Figure 10 Puddingstone is a form of the clastic rock conglomerate. ***Observing*** *What types of particles can you observe in this sample of puddingstone?*

Background

Facts and Figures Clastic rocks contain a great variety of rock fragments and other materials, but clay minerals and quartz particles dominate in these sedimentary rocks. Clay minerals are abundant because they result from the chemical weathering of such silicates as feldspar. Quartz particles, by contrast, are abundant because they are so hard that they resist chemical weathering.

The time it takes for compaction and cementation to produce sedimentary rock varies greatly. Much depends on the availability of water and its dissolved minerals, which are necessary to cement the sediments together. Sediments in the Rocky Mountains, for example, became sedimentary rock in less than 20,000 years. But sand and gravel found today in western Montana were deposited 30–40 million years ago and still haven't become rock.

Organic Rocks

INTEGRATING LIFE SCIENCE Not all sedimentary rocks are made from particles of other rocks. **Organic rock** forms where the remains of plants and animals are deposited in thick layers. The term "organic" refers to substances that once were part of living things or were made by living things. Two important organic sedimentary rocks are coal and limestone.

Coal Coal forms from the remains of swamp plants buried in water. As layer upon layer of plant remains build up, the weight of the layers squeezes the decaying plants. Over millions of years, they slowly change into coal.

Limestone The hard shells of living things produce limestone. How does limestone form? In the ocean, many living things, including coral, clams, oysters, and snails, have shells or skeletons made of calcite. When these animals die, their shells pile up as sediment on the ocean floor. Over millions of years, these layers of sediment can grow to a depth of hundreds of meters. Slowly, the pressure of overlying layers compacts the sediment. Some of the shells dissolve, forming a solution of calcite that seeps into the spaces between the shell fragments. Later, the dissolved material comes out of solution, forming calcite. The calcite cements the shell particles together, forming limestone.

Everyone knows one type of limestone: chalk. Chalk forms from sediments made of the skeletons of microscopic living things found in the oceans.

☑ *Checkpoint* *What are two important organic sedimentary rocks?*

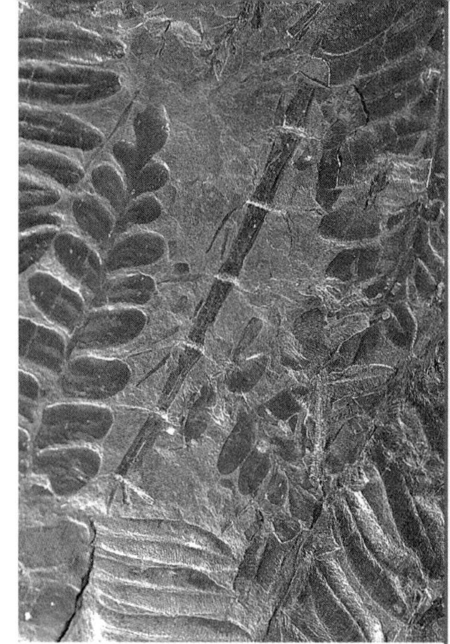

Figure 11 When broken apart, a piece of coal may reveal the impression of an ancient plant. Geologists estimate that it takes about 20 meters of decayed plants to form a layer of coal about one meter thick.

Figure 12 These limestone cliffs are along the Eleven Point River in Missouri.

Organic Rocks

Integrating Life Science

Materials *pieces of lignite or subbituminous coal, paper towels, needles, hand lens, piece of wood, modeling compound*
Time 15 minutes

Have students examine pieces of soft coal, using paper towels to handle the coal. Point out that coal is a sedimentary rock composed of layers. Have students count the layers. Then take one piece of coal and separate its layers. Flatten the modeling compound on the piece of wood and press the coal into the compound, which will hold the coal in place. Then insert needles between the layers of the coal and pry the layers apart. (If students handle the needles, caution them to be careful.) Continue prying apart layers until you find an impression of a leaf or twig. Have students examine the fossil with a hand lens. **learning modality: visual**

Chemical Rocks

Real-Life Learning

Bring to class an alabaster vase or ornament and have students note its qualities. Explain that alabaster is a fine-grained form of gypsum often carved into vases and ornaments. Ask: **What do you know about gypsum that would make this rock easy to carve?** *(Gypsum has a rating of 2 on Mohs hardness scale, and thus is a relatively soft rock.)* **How did the alabaster in this vase originally form?** *(It formed as water evaporated, leaving the minerals dissolved in the water as crystals.)* **learning modality: verbal**

Answers to Self-Assessment

Caption Question

Figure 10 Answers may vary. A typical answer will mention rock fragments of various sizes, most with rounded edges.

☑ *Checkpoint*

Coal and limestone

Ongoing Assessment

Skills Check Challenge students to draw a conclusion about whether the process shown in Figure 9 better describes the formation of clastic rocks or organic rocks. *(Students should conclude that the first step, concerning sediment carried by water or wind, only relates to clastic rocks.)*

Uses of Sedimentary Rocks

Including All Students

Invite students who need additional challenges to find out what brownstone is and what "a brownstone" refers to in some American cities, especially New York City. *(Students should learn that brownstone is a reddish brown sandstone. It was once widely used in building houses and apartment buildings, hence the name "brownstone" for many older buildings in New York City and elsewhere.)* **learning modality: verbal**

3 Assess

Section 3 Review Answers

1. The processes of compaction and cementation
2. Clastic rocks, organic rocks, and chemical rocks
3. Limestone can form when shells pile up as sediment on the ocean floor and then compaction and cementation change the sediment into organic rock. Limestone can also form when calcite dissolved in lakes, seas, or underground water comes out of solution and crystallizes to form chemical rock.
4. Shale forms from tiny particles of clay deposited in flat layers. No cementation is needed to hold the particles together. Sandstone forms from the compaction and cementation of sand particles.

Check Your Progress (Chapter Project 5)

Check that students are beginning to collect rocks and bring them to class. Provide a place where each student or group can store their rocks. Encourage students to begin classifying and identifying their rocks.

Performance Assessment

Skills Check Have students make a compare/contrast table that includes all the sedimentary rocks discussed in the section. The table should have columns for name, major group, and characteristics.

Figure 13 These rock "towers" in Mono Lake, California, are made of tufa. Tufa forms when solutions containing minerals evaporate under the hot desert sun. *Classifying What type of sedimentary rock is tufa?*

Chemical Rocks

Chemical rock forms when minerals that are dissolved in a solution crystallize. For example, limestone can form when calcite that is dissolved in lakes, seas, or underground water comes out of solution and forms crystals. This kind of limestone is considered a chemical rock.

Chemical rocks can also form from mineral deposits left when seas or lakes evaporate. Rock salt is a chemical rock made of the mineral halite, which forms by evaporation. Gypsum is another chemical rock formed by evaporation. Large deposits of rocks formed by evaporation form only in dry climates.

Uses of Sedimentary Rocks

For thousands of years, people have used sandstone and limestone as building materials. Both types of stone are soft enough to be easily cut into blocks or slabs. You may be surprised to learn that the White House in Washington, D.C., is built of sandstone. Builders today use sandstone and limestone for decorating or for covering the outside walls of buildings.

Limestone also has many industrial uses. Recall from Chapter 4 that limestone is important in smelting iron ore. Limestone is also used in making cement.

Section 3 Review

1. Once sediment has been deposited, what processes change it into sedimentary rock?
2. What are the three major kinds of sedimentary rocks?
3. Describe two ways in which limestone can form.
4. **Thinking Critically Comparing and Contrasting** Compare and contrast shale and sandstone. Include what they are made of and how they form.

Check Your Progress (Chapter Project 5)

With an adult, visit an area where you can collect samples of rocks. As you collect your samples, observe whether the rock is loose on the ground, broken off a ledge, or in a stream. Begin to classify your rocks into groups. Do any of your rocks consist of a single mineral? Do you recognize any of the minerals in these rocks? Notice the texture of each rock. Did you find any rocks made of pieces of other rocks?

Answers to Self-Assessment

Caption Question

Figure 13 Tufa is a chemical rock, because it forms when water evaporates.

Program Resources

◆ **Teaching Resources** 5-3 Review and Reinforce, p. 137; 5-3 Enrich, p. 138

Media and Technology

Interactive Student Tutorial CD-ROM F-5

SECTION 4 Rocks From Reefs

DISCOVER ACTIVITY

What Can You Conclude From the Way a Rock Reacts to Acid?

1. Using a hand lens, observe the color and texture of samples of limestone and coquina.
2. Put on your goggles and apron.
3. Obtain a small amount of dilute hydrochloric acid from your teacher. Hydrochloric acid is used to test rocks for the presence of the mineral calcite.
4. Using a plastic dropper, place a few drops of dilute hydrochloric acid on the limestone. **CAUTION**: *Hydrochloric acid can cause burns.*
5. Record your observations.
6. Repeat Steps 2 through 4 with the sample of coquina and observe the results.
7. Rinse the samples of limestone and coquina with lots of water before returning them to your teacher. Wash your hands.

Think It Over
Drawing Conclusions How did the color and texture of the two rocks compare? How did they react to the test? A piece of coral reacts to hydrochloric acid the same way as limestone and coquina. What could you conclude about the mineral composition of coral?

Off the coast of Florida lies a "city" in the sea. It is a coral reef providing both food and shelter for many sea animals. The reef shimmers with life—clams, sponges, sea urchins, starfish, marine worms and, of course, fish. Schools of brilliantly colored fish dart in and out of forests of equally colorful corals. Octopuses lurk in underwater caves, scooping up crabs that pass too close. A reef forms a sturdy wall that protects the shoreline from battering waves. This city was built by billions of tiny, soft-bodied animals that have outer shells made of calcite.

GUIDE FOR READING

- How do coral reefs form?
- How do coral reefs become organic limestone deposits on land?

Reading Tip As you read, make a list of main ideas and supporting details about coral.

Figure 14 A coral reef in the Florida Keys provides food and shelter for many different kinds of living things.

READING STRATEGIES

Reading Tip Encourage students to write one main idea for each main heading and then list two or three supporting details for each. Main ideas: "Corals are animals whose shells grow together to form a coral reef." "When coral animals die, their shells remain, and new corals build on top of them." "Limestone that began as coral can be found in places where uplift has raised ancient sea floors above sea level."

Program Resources

- **Teaching Resources** 5-4 Lesson Plan, p. 139; 5-4 Section Summary, p. 140
- **Integrated Science Laboratory Manual** F-5, "Making Models of Sedimentary Rocks"

Media and Technology

 **Audiotapes** English-Spanish Summary 5-4

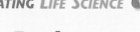

INTEGRATING LIFE SCIENCE 

SECTION 4 Rocks From Reefs

Objectives

After completing the lesson, students will be able to
- describe the formation of coral reefs;
- explain how coral reefs become organic limestone deposits on land.

Key Terms coral reef, atoll

1 Engage/Explore

Activating Prior Knowledge

Encourage students to share their knowledge of coral reefs, either from direct experience or nature shows on television. Ask: **Where are coral reefs found?** *(In warm ocean waters, such as in the Caribbean)* **How would you describe the structure of a coral reef?** *(A typical answer might describe an underwater plantlike structure.)*

DISCOVER

Skills Focus drawing conclusions
Materials *samples of limestone and coquina, dilute hydrochloric acid, plastic dropper, running water*
Time 15 minutes
Tips Coquina is a clastic rock composed of shells and shell fragments. A fossil shell can be used as an alternative. Coral itself is not recommended for this activity because of conservation concerns. Caution students that the dilute (5%) hydrochloric acid needs to be handled with extreme care. You could use white vinegar, which is a weak acid, in place of the dilute HCl, though the effect will not be as strong.
Think It Over The color and texture of the rocks will vary depending on the samples used. Students should observe that hydrochloric acid fizzes where it comes in contact with limestone and coquina, thus testing positive for the mineral calcite. Students should conclude that coral also contains calcite in its composition.

2 Facilitate

Living Coral

Including All Students

For students who need extra help, review some of the basic concepts related to biology that need to be understood to grasp how coral reefs originate. Explain that photosynthesis is a process carried out by plants, algae, and some other organisms that uses the energy of sunlight to produce a sugar. Then have students use dictionaries, encyclopedias, and biology books to write descriptions of corals and algae. **learning modality: verbal**

How a Coral Reef Forms

Using the Visuals: Figure 16

Ask students: **What is a fringe on a dress or shirt?** *(A border of different material that serves as an ornament)* Point out that a fringing reef is a fringe around an island. **What part of this picture will remain once the volcano is worn away?** *(The circular fringe around the volcano.)* Explain that an atoll is sometimes large enough to be inhabited, as some are in the equatorial Pacific Ocean. The middle of an atoll, where a volcano once was, becomes a lagoon at the center of the island. **learning modality: visual**

Building Inquiry Skills: Making Models

Materials *wooden board, modeling compound*
Time 15 minutes

Challenge pairs of students to make a model of a reef, randomly assigning one of the three types to each pair. Students can form their clay models on a wooden board. When all groups have finished, have students compare the different models, analyzing which models best represent the three types of coral reefs. **learning modality: kinesthetic**

Figure 15 Coral animals feed on even smaller living things carried their way by the movement of ocean water. (This view has been magnified to show detail.)

Living Coral

Coral animals are tiny relatives of jellyfish that live together in vast numbers. Most coral animals are the size of your fingernail, or even smaller. Each one looks like a small sack with a mouth surrounded by tentacles. These animals use their tentacles to capture and eat microscopic creatures that float by. They build shells that grow together to form a structure called a **coral reef.**

Coral reefs form only in the warm, shallow water of tropical oceans. Coral animals cannot grow in cold water or water low in salt. Reefs are most abundant around islands and along the eastern coasts of continents. In the United States, only the coasts of southern Florida and Hawaii have coral reefs.

Tiny algae grow within the body of each coral animal. The algae provide substances that the coral animals need to live. In turn, the coral animals provide a framework for the algae to grow on. Like plants, algae need sunlight. Below 40 meters, not enough light penetrates the water for the algae to grow. For this reason, almost all growth in a coral reef occurs within 40 meters of the water's surface.

How a Coral Reef Forms

Coral animals absorb the element calcium from the ocean water. The calcium is then changed into calcite and forms their protective outer shells. **When coral animals die, their shells remain, and new corals build on top of them.** Over thousands of years, reefs may grow to be hundreds of kilometers long and hundreds of meters thick. Reefs usually grow outward toward the open ocean. If the sea level rises or if the sea floor sinks, the reef will grow upward, too.

Figure 16 The island of Bora Bora in the South Pacific Ocean is ringed by a fringing reef. Someday, erosion will wear away the island, leaving an atoll. *Inferring As the sea floor beneath an atoll sinks, what happens to the living part of the coral reef?*

Background

Integrating Science The relationship between corals and the green alga Zooxanthella is a type of symbiosis called *mutualism,* in which two species live together in such a way that both benefit. The corals provide the algae with a place to live as well as the carbon dioxide needed to carry out photosynthesis. The algae provide the coral animals with the food produced through photosynthesis. Nearly all of the body of a coral animal is transparent, allowing sunlight to penetrate to the algae. One square centimeter of coral may contain as many as 1 million individual algae cells. Corals do eat other organisms, mostly microscopic protists, by capturing them with their tentacles. But that provides only about 2 percent of a coral's nutritional needs. The other 98 percent is provided by the algae.

There are three types of coral reefs: fringing reefs, barrier reefs and atolls. Fringing reefs lie close to shore, separated from land by shallow water. Barrier reefs lie farther out, at least 10 kilometers from the land. The Great Barrier Reef that stretches 2,000 kilometers along the coast of Australia is a barrier reef. An **atoll** is a ring-shaped coral island found far from land. An atoll develops when coral grows on top of a volcanic island that has sunk beneath the ocean's surface. How can a volcanic island sink? As the oceanic crust moves away from the mid-ocean ridge, it cools and becomes more dense. This causes the sea floor to sink.

☑ *Checkpoint* *What are the three types of coral reefs?*

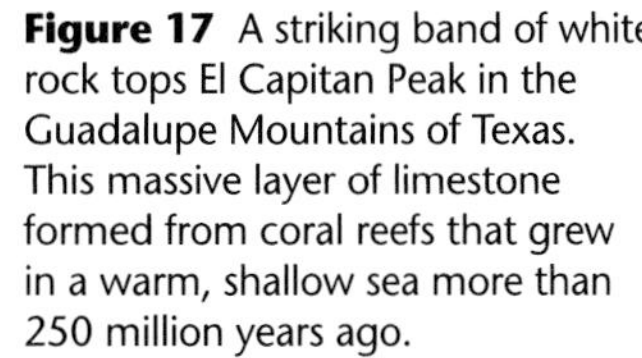

Figure 17 A striking band of white rock tops El Capitan Peak in the Guadalupe Mountains of Texas. This massive layer of limestone formed from coral reefs that grew in a warm, shallow sea more than 250 million years ago.

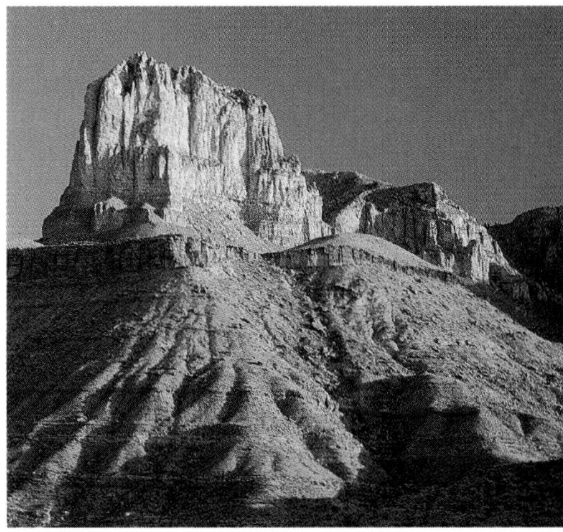

Limestone Deposits From Coral Reefs

Over time, coral buried by sediments can turn into limestone. Like modern-day coral animals, ancient coral animals thrived in warm, tropical oceans. Their limestone fossils are among the most common fossils on Earth. **Limestone that began as coral can be found on continents in places where uplift has raised ancient sea floors above sea level.**

In parts of the United States, reefs that formed under water millions of years ago now make up part of the land. The movement of Earth's plates slowly uplifted the ocean floor where these reefs grew until the ocean floor became dry land. There are exposed reefs in Wisconsin, Illinois, and Indiana, as well as in Texas, New Mexico, and many other places.

Section 4 Review

1. Explain how coral reefs form.
2. How does coral become limestone?
3. Why are living coral animals only found in water that is less than 40 meters deep?
4. **Thinking Critically Predicting** The Amazon is a great river that flows through the tropical forests of Brazil. The river dumps huge amounts of fresh water, made cloudy by particles of sediment, into the South Atlantic Ocean. Would you expect to find coral reefs growing in the ocean near the mouth of the Amazon? Explain your answer.

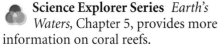

Check Your Progress (CHAPTER PROJECT 5)

Begin to make an information card for each of your rocks, and decide how to store the rocks. Each rock's card should include the following information: where and when the rock was found; the type of geologic feature where you found the rock; a description of the rock's texture; a description of the minerals that make up the rock; and the results of any tests you performed on the rock. Are any of your rocks organic rocks? How could you tell?

Limestone Deposits From Coral Reefs

Using the Visuals: Figure 17

After students have examined the figure, have them turn back to Figure 29, on pages 46–47, in Chapter 1. Ask: **How has the land we call Texas changed in the last 250 million years?** *(Texas was once part of the supercontinent Pangaea. Since then, plate movements have changed its position dramatically.)* **learning modality: visual**

3 Assess

Section 4 Review Answers

1. Coral reefs form as the shells of coral animals grow together. When coral animals die, their shells remain, and new corals build on top of them.
2. Coral becomes limestone where uplift has raised ancient sea floors above sea level.
3. Living corals depend upon tiny algae within their bodies. Like plants, these algae need sunlight. Below 40 meters, not enough sunlight penetrates the water for the algae to live. Therefore, coral animals cannot live below 40 meters deep.
4. You would not expect coral animals to grow near the mouth of the Amazon because the particles of sediment would block the sunlight needed by the algae in the body of corals. The fresh water from the river would lower the salt content of the water, and the coral animals could not survive.

Check Your Progress (CHAPTER PROJECT 5)

Make sure students understand how to make an information card on each of their rocks. You may want to make a sample card and display it on a bulletin board.

Program Resources

Science Explorer Series *Earth's Waters,* Chapter 5, provides more information on coral reefs.

◆ **Teaching Resources** 5-4 Review and Reinforce, p. 141; 5-4 Enrich, p. 142

Media and Technology

Interactive Student Tutorial CD-ROM F-5

Answers to Self-Assessment

Caption Question

Figure 16 The living part of the coral dies as the island sinks more than 40 meters below the water's surface.

☑ *Checkpoint*

Fringing reefs, barrier reefs, and atolls

Performance Assessment

Writing Have students write a description of how each of the three types of coral reefs form.

Metamorphic Rocks

Objectives

After completing the lesson, students will be able to

- describe the conditions under which metamorphic rocks form;
- identify the ways in which geologists classify metamorphic rocks.

Key Term foliated

1 Engage/Explore

Activating Prior Knowledge

Help students recall forces that could change rocks beneath Earth's surface. For example, ask: **What occurs at convergent plate boundaries?** *(Plates collide, resulting in subduction, mountain building, and volcanic activity.)* **What effect do you think plate collisions would have on the rocks involved or on rocks in the area?** *(Students might mention increases in pressure and temperature that could deform or change rocks.)*

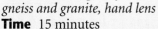

DISCOVER ACTIVITY

Skills Focus inferring
Materials *samples of gneiss and granite, hand lens*
Time 15 minutes
Tips Since the color of both gneiss and granite varies, try to obtain samples of each that are of similar color in order to focus students' attention on the more relevant characteristic of texture.
Expected Outcome Students should observe that both granite and gneiss are coarse-grained. In granite, the grains are more angular or rounded than those in gneiss. The grains in gneiss appear flattened and more compact. Students' sketches should reflect these differences.
Think It Over Answers may vary. A typical answer might suggest that tremendous pressure and heat could cause such a change to occur.

Section 5 Metamorphic Rocks

DISCOVER ACTIVITY

How Do the Grain Patterns of Gneiss and Granite Compare?

1. Using a hand lens, observe samples of gneiss and granite. Look carefully at the grains or crystals in both rocks.
2. Observe how the grains or crystals are arranged in both rocks. Draw a sketch of both rocks and describe their textures.

Think It Over

Inferring Within the crust, some granite becomes gneiss. What do you think must happen to cause this change?

GUIDE FOR READING

- **Under what conditions do metamorphic rocks form?**
- **How do geologists classify metamorphic rocks?**

Reading Tip **Before you read, rewrite the headings in the section as questions. As you read, look for answers to those questions.**

Every metamorphic rock is a rock that has changed its form. In fact, the word *metamorphic* comes from the Greek words *meta*, meaning "change," and *morphosis*, meaning "form." But what causes a rock to change into metamorphic rock? The answer lies inside Earth.

How Metamorphic Rocks Form

Heat and pressure deep beneath Earth's surface can change any rock into metamorphic rock. When rock changes into metamorphic rock, its appearance, texture, crystal structure, and mineral content change. Metamorphic rock can form out of igneous, sedimentary, or other metamorphic rock.

Collisions between Earth's plates can push the rock down toward the heat of the mantle. Pockets of magma rising through the crust also provide heat that can produce metamorphic rocks.

The deeper rock is buried in the crust, the greater the pressure on that rock. Under pressure hundreds or thousands of times greater than at Earth's surface, the minerals in a rock can change into other minerals. The rock has become a metamorphic rock.

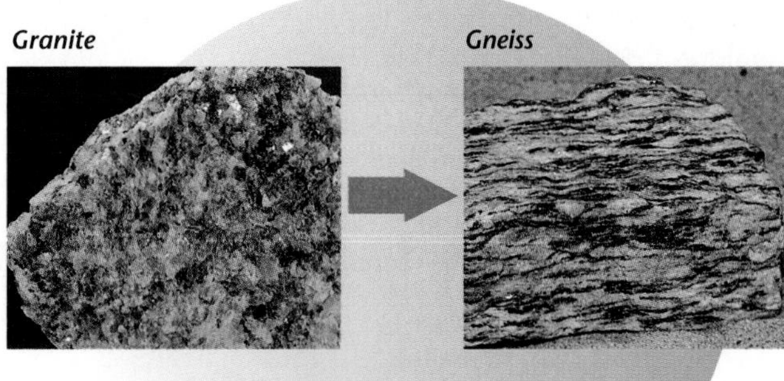

Figure 18 Great heat and pressure can change one type of rock into another. Granite becomes gneiss, shale becomes slate, and sandstone changes to quartzite. *Observing How does quartzite differ from sandstone?*

READING STRATEGIES

Reading Tip Sample questions derived from the section headings are: "How do metamorphic rocks form?" "How are metamorphic rocks classified?" "What are some uses of metamorphic rock?" Encourage students to answer each question in two to three sentences just as if these were questions on a quiz. Students can later use their questions and answers for review.

Program Resources

- **Teaching Resources** 5-5 Lesson Plan, p. 143; 5-5 Section Summary, p. 144

Media and Technology

Audiotapes English-Spanish Summary 5-5

Classifying Metamorphic Rocks

While metamorphic rocks are forming, high temperatures change the size and shape of the grains, or mineral crystals, in the rock. In addition, tremendous pressure squeezes rock so tightly that the mineral grains may line up in flat, parallel layers. **Geologists classify metamorphic rocks by the arrangement of the grains that make up the rocks.**

Metamorphic rocks that have their grains arranged in parallel layers or bands are said to be **foliated.** The term *foliated* comes from the Latin word for "leaf." It describes the thin, flat layering found in most metamorphic rocks. Foliated rocks—including slate, schist, and gneiss—may split apart along these bands. In Figure 18, notice how the crystals in granite have been flattened to create the foliated texture of gneiss.

One common foliated rock is slate. Heat and pressure change the sedimentary rock shale into slate. Slate is basically a denser, more compact version of shale. During the change, new minerals such as mica and hornblende form in the slate.

Sometimes metamorphic rocks are nonfoliated. The mineral grains in these rocks are arranged randomly. Metamorphic rocks that are nonfoliated do not split into layers. Marble and quartzite both have a nonfoliated texture. Quartzite forms out of sandstone. The weakly cemented quartz particles in the sandstone recrystallize to form quartzite, which is extremely hard. Notice in Figure 18 how much smoother quartzite looks than sandstone.

☑ *Checkpoint* *What is a foliated rock?*

A Sequined Rock

ACTIVITY

1. Make three balls of clay about 3 cm in diameter. Gently mix about 25 sequins into one ball.
2. Use a 30-cm piece of string to cut the ball in half. How are the sequins arranged?
3. Roll the clay with the sequins back into a ball. Stack the three balls with the sequin ball in the middle. Set these on a block of wood. With another block of wood, press slowly down until the stack is about 3 cm high.
4. Use the string to cut the stack in half. Observe the arrangement of the sequins.

Making a Model What do the sequins in your model rock represent? Is this rock foliated or nonfoliated?

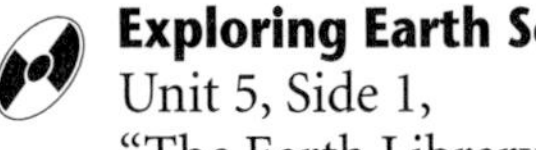

Exploring Earth Science Videodisc
Unit 5, Side 1,
"The Earth Library"

Chapter 3

Answers to Self-Assessment

Caption Question

Figure 18 Quartzite looks much smoother than sandstone because heat and pressure have caused the weakly cemented particles in sandstone to recrystallize.

☑ *Checkpoint*

A foliated rock is a metamorphic rock whose grains are arranged in parallel layers or bands.

2 Facilitate

How Metamorphic Rocks Form

Using the Visuals: Figure 18

Ask students: **How could you tell the difference between granite and gneiss?** *(The grains in granite occur randomly, while the grains in gneiss occur in bands or layers; that is, gneiss is foliated, while granite is not.)* **Are all rocks classified as metamorphic foliated?** *(No. Quartzite is an example of a nonfoliated metamorphic rock.)* **learning modality: visual**

Classifying Metamorphic Rocks

TRY THIS

Skills Focus making models
Materials *modeling compound, metric ruler, 25 sequins, 30-cm string, 2 blocks of wood*
Time 15 minutes
Tips Cut string ahead of time. Experiment to find how much modeling compound each student will need, and then prepare the appropriate number of mounds of compound.
Expected Outcome When students cut the ball in half, they should observe that the sequins are spread randomly. When they cut the stack in half, they should observe that the sequins are arranged in a layer or band. Students should infer that the sequins model rock grains and that the model rock made after flattening represents a foliated rock.
Extend Ask: **What did you model when you pressed down on the clay?** *(Pressing down modeled the pressure that changes rock into metamorphic rock.)* **learning modality: kinesthetic**

Ongoing Assessment

Drawing Challenge students to make two drawings—one of a foliated metamorphic rock and one of an nonfoliated metamorphic rock.

Uses of Metamorphic Rock

Visual Arts CONNECTION

Architects often use symmetry and repetition. A likely example is the front of the school building; there is often a central door with the same number of windows and other structures on either side.

In Your Journal Suggest that students write a letter of at least one paragraph. They should mention the use of symmetry and repetition as well as the effect that a surface of polished marble has on the observer. **learning modality: verbal**

3 Assess

Section 5 Review Answers

1. Heat and pressure caused by plate collisions, rising magma, or the weight of the crust can cause metamorphic rocks to form.
2. The arrangement of the grains that make up the rocks
3. As a rock becomes metamorphic, its appearance, texture, crystal structure, and mineral content may change.
4. Pressure can change the minerals in a rock into other minerals and cause the grains to line up in layers.
5. The temperature and pressure that cause metamorphic rock to form would likely destroy any fossils that were in the parent sedimentary rock.

Science at Home

ACTIVITY

Review the characteristics of marble, granite, limestone, and sandstone so students can recognize these rocks. Invite volunteers to present their findings to the class.

Performance Assessment

Skills Check Challenge students to create a flowchart that describes how sandstone forms and becomes quartzite.

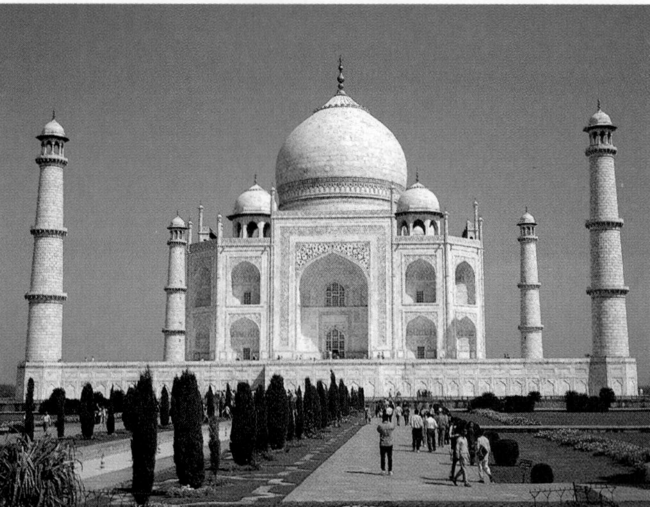

Figure 19 The pure white marble for the Taj Mahal came from a quarry 300 kilometers away. It took 20,000 workers more than 10 years to build the Taj Mahal.

Visual Arts CONNECTION

The unknown architect of the Taj Mahal used symmetry and repetition to design a beautiful building. Notice how the left side mirrors the right side, creating balance. Also notice how different parts of the building, such as domes, arches, and minarets (towers), are repeated. Repetition of these shapes creates rhythms as you look at the building.

In Your Journal

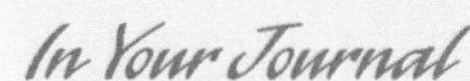

Write a letter to a friend describing what you feel walking toward the Taj Mahal. Explain how the building's symmetry and other features help to create this effect.

Uses of Metamorphic Rock

Marble and slate are two of the most useful metamorphic rocks. Because marble has a fine, even grain, it is relatively easy to cut into thin slabs. And marble can be polished so that its surface is smooth and mirrorlike. These qualities have led architects and sculptors to use marble for many buildings and statues. For example, one of the most beautiful buildings in the world is the Taj Mahal in Agra, India. An emperor of India had the Taj Mahal built during the 1600s as a memorial to his wife, who had died in childbirth. The Taj Mahal, shown in Figure 19, is made of gleaming white marble.

Slate, because it is foliated, splits easily into flat pieces that can be used for flooring, roofing, outdoor walkways, or chalkboards. Like marble, slate comes in a variety of colors, including gray, black, red, and purple, so it has been used as trim for stone buildings.

Section 5 Review

1. Describe the process by which metamorphic rocks form.
2. What characteristics are used to classify metamorphic rocks?
3. Which properties of a rock may change as the rock becomes metamorphic?
4. How does pressure change rock?
5. **Thinking Critically Relating Cause and Effect** Why are you less likely to find fossils in metamorphic rocks than in sedimentary rocks?

Science at Home

How are rocks used in your neighborhood? Take a walk with your family to see how many uses you can observe. Identify statues, walls, and buildings made from rocks. Can you identify which type of rock is used? Look for limestone, sandstone, granite, and marble. Share a list of the rocks you found with your class. For each rock, include a description of its color and texture, where you observed the rock, and how it was used.

Background

Facts and Figures Pure limestone is composed of a single mineral, calcite. When this sedimentary rock is metamorphosed, its small calcite crystals combine, or recrystallize, to form large, interlocking crystals. The result is marble. Marble is white when the limestone is pure calcite. Impurities in the original sedimentary rock can make the marble pink, green, gray, or black.

Program Resources

- **Teaching Resources** 5-5 Review and Reinforce, p. 145; 5-5 Enrich, p. 146

Media and Technology

Interactive Student Tutorial CD-ROM F-5

Classifying

MYSTERY ROCKS

Skills Lab

Problem
What properties can be used to classify rocks?

Materials
1 "mystery rock"
hand lens
2 unknown igneous rocks
2 unknown sedimentary rocks
2 unknown metamorphic rocks

Procedure
1. For this activity, you will be given six rocks and one sample that is not a rock. They are labeled A through G.
2. Copy the data table into your notebook.
3. Using the hand lens, examine each rock for clues that show the rock formed from molten material. Record the rock's color and texture. Observe if there are any crystals or grains in the rock.
4. Use the hand lens to look for clues that show the rock formed from particles of other rocks. Observe the texture of the rock to see if it has any tiny, well-rounded grains.
5. Use the hand lens to look for clues that show the rock formed under heat and pressure. Observe if the rock has a flat layer of crystals or shows colored bands.
6. Record your observations in the data table.

Sample	Color (dark, medium, light, or mixed colors)	Texture (fine, medium, or coarse-grained)	Foliated or Banded	Rock Group (igneous, metamorphic, sedimentary)
A				
B				

Analyze and Conclude
1. Infer from your observations which group each rock belongs in.
2. Decide which sample is not a rock. How did you determine that the sample you chose is not a rock? What do you think the "mystery rock" is? Explain.
3. Which of the samples could be classified as igneous rocks? What physical properties do these rock share with the other samples? How are they different?
4. Which of the samples could be classified as sedimentary rocks? How do you think these rocks formed? What are the physical properties of these rocks?
5. Which of the samples could be classified as metamorphic rocks? What are their physical properties?
6. **Think About It** What physical property was most useful in classifying rocks? Why?

More to Explore
Can you name each rock? Use a field guide to rocks and minerals to find the specific name of each rock sample.

Analyze and Conclude
1. Students should classify two rocks each as igneous, sedimentary, and metamorphic.
2. Students' reasons for identifying the nonrock will depend on what it is.
3. Answers may vary. Students might say all the rocks have grains. These rocks have no evidence of sediment or metamorphic change.
4. Answers may vary. Students might mention evidence of sediments or cementation. Students should describe in general terms how sedimentary rocks form.
5. Answers may vary. Students might mention foliation or evidence of pressure and heat.
6. Answers may vary. Students might suggest that texture was most useful because it reflects how rocks form.

Program Resources
- **Teaching Resources** Chapter 5 Skills Lab, pp. 151–153

Skills Lab

Classifying

Mystery Rocks

Preparing for Inquiry
Key Concept Properties of rocks can be used to classify rock samples as igneous, sedimentary, or metamorphic.

Skills Objectives Students will be able to
- observe properties of each rock sample;
- create a data table to organize their observations;
- classify each rock sample as one of the three major groups of rocks.

Time 30 minutes

Advance Planning Select and label the samples ahead of time. Suggested rock samples and labels: A. sandstone, B. gneiss, D. granite, E. conglomerate, F. slate, G. basalt. Also label as C the "mystery rock," an object that is not a rock. This could be a piece of brick, bone, wood, or pottery. Number the samples by painting a small spot of correcting fluid on each and then using a marker to write the number on the spot. Provide each group or student with a complete set of seven samples.

Guiding Inquiry
Introducing the Procedure
- **Why is a hand lens helpful in observing the texture of rocks?** *(The individual grains of fine-grained rocks are too small to be seen with the naked eye.)*

Troubleshooting the Experiment
- Demonstrate how to examine a rock sample and record observations in a data table using a sample not included in the students' samples, such as a sample of marble.

Extending the Inquiry
More to Explore Provide rock and mineral field guides for students to use to identify their samples. Have students share results and resolve differences.

SECTION 6 The Rock Cycle

Objectives

After completing the lesson, students will be able to

- ◆ describe the rock cycle;
- ◆ explain the role played by plate tectonics in the rock cycle.

Key Term rock cycle

1 Engage/Explore

Activating Prior Knowledge

Encourage students to brainstorm a list of Earth processes that affect rock in Earth's crust. *(Weathering, erosion, volcanic activity, and plate tectonics)* **Do you think rocks are ever completely destroyed?** *(Yes, when oceanic plates are subducted and become part of the mantle and when rocks are completely weathered and form soil.)* Point out that these forces affect all rocks in the crust, and thus no rock is permanent.

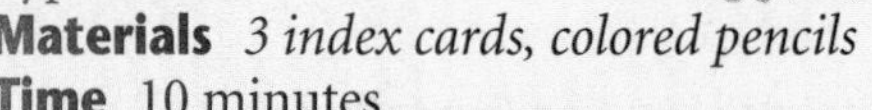

Skills Focus developing hypotheses
Materials *3 index cards, colored pencils*
Time 10 minutes
Tips If possible, provide samples of quartzite, granite, and sandstone to give students real objects to examine and draw.
Expected Outcome Students' sketches should reflect the colors and textures of the rocks pictured in their text. They should identify quartzite as metamorphic, granite as igneous, and sandstone as sedimentary.
Think It Over Answers may vary. A typical answer might suggest that granite formed first from cooling magma. Weathering, erosion, deposition, compaction, and cementation then formed sandstone from granite particles. Pressure and high temperatures then changed the sandstone into quartzite. Some students may also suggest that both quartzite and sandstone could melt in the mantle and form again as granite or that quartzite could weather and its particles could form into sandstone.

SECTION 6 The Rock Cycle

DISCOVER ACTIVITY

Which Rock Came First?

1. Referring to the photos below, make sketches of quartzite, granite, and sandstone on three index cards.
2. In your sketches, try to portray the color and texture of each rock. Look for similarities and differences.
3. To which major group does each rock belong?

Think It Over

Developing Hypotheses How are quartzite, granite, and sandstone related? Arrange your cards in the order in which these three rocks formed. Given enough time in Earth's crust, what might happen to the third rock in your series?

Quartzite

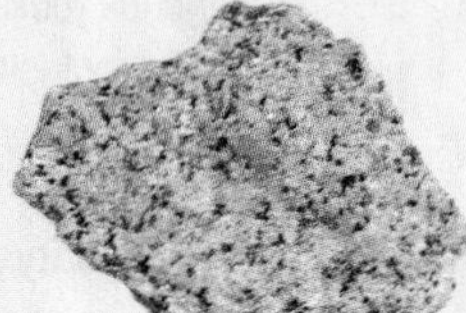

Granite

Sandstone

GUIDE FOR READING

- ◆ **What is the rock cycle?**
- ◆ **What is the role of plate tectonics in the rock cycle?**

Reading Tip **Before you read, preview *Exploring the Rock Cycle* on page 168. Write a list of questions you have about the rock cycle. Then look for answers to the questions as you read.**

The enormous granite dome that forms Stone Mountain in Georgia looks as if it will be there forever. The granite formed hundreds of millions of years ago as a batholith—a mass of igneous rock beneath Earth's surface. But this rock has stood exposed to the weather for millions of years. Bit by bit, the granite is flaking off. Washed away in streams, the bits of granite will eventually be ground down into sand. But that's not the end of the story. What will become of those sand particles from Stone Mountain? They are part of a series of changes that happen to all the rocks of Earth's crust.

A Cycle of Many Pathways

Earth's rocks are not as unchanging as they seem. **Forces inside Earth and at the surface produce a rock cycle that builds, destroys, and changes the rocks in the crust.** The **rock cycle** is a series of processes on Earth's surface and inside the planet that slowly change rocks from one kind to another. What drives the rock cycle? Earth's constructive and destructive forces—including plate tectonics—move rocks through the rock cycle.

The rock cycle can follow many different pathways. You can follow the rock of Stone Mountain along one of the pathways of the rock cycle.

READING STRATEGIES

Reading Tip Students' questions will vary. Typical questions might include these: "Do rocks always continue through the complete cycle?" "What causes rocks to melt?" and "What causes rocks to follow alternate pathways?" Students may write questions that are not answered in their text. In such cases, invite others in the class to answer the questions with what they have learned in this and previous chapters. If the question is still not answered, encourage students to do research in other books to find the answer.

Vocabulary Point out that this section focuses on a *cycle* in nature. Explain that a cycle is a series of events or processes that regularly recur and usually lead back to a starting point. A good synonym for *cycle* is *wheel.*

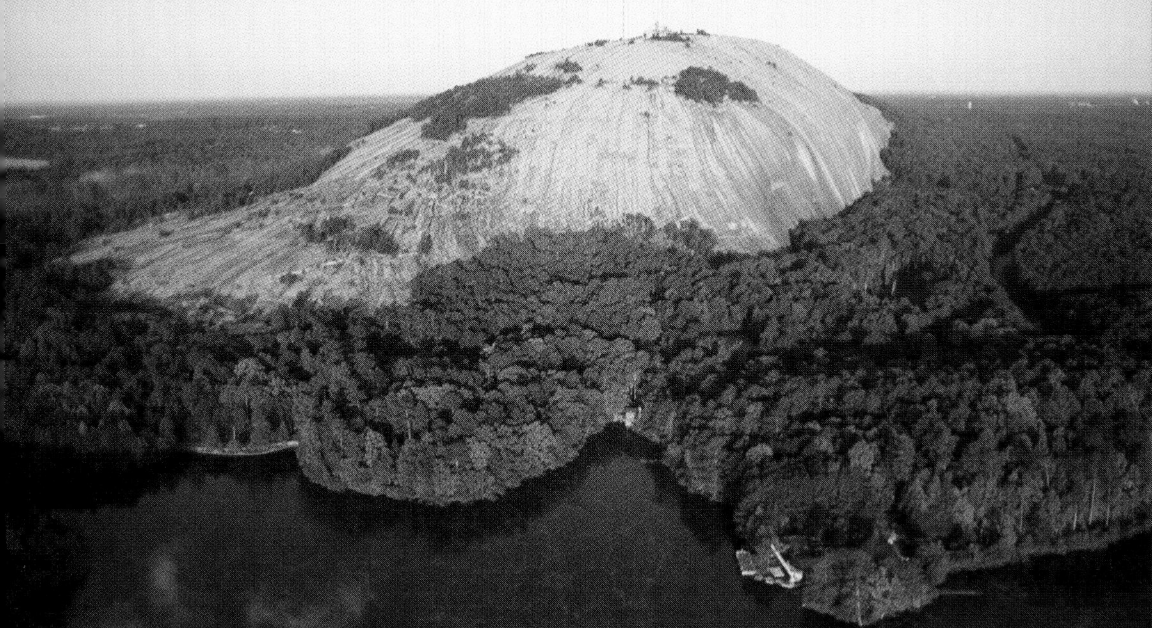

Figure 20 Stone Mountain, near Atlanta, Georgia, rises 210 meters above the surrounding land.

One Pathway Through the Rock Cycle

In the case of Stone Mountain, the rock cycle began millions of years ago. First, a granite batholith formed beneath Earth's surface. Then the forces of mountain building slowly pushed the granite upward. Over millions of years, water and weather began to wear away the granite of Stone Mountain. Today, particles of granite still break off the mountain and become sand. Streams carry the sand to the ocean.

Over millions of years, layers of sediment will pile up on the ocean floor. Slowly, the sediments will be compacted by their own weight. Dissolved calcite in the ocean water will cement the particles together. Eventually, the quartz that once formed the granite of Stone Mountain will become sandstone, a sedimentary rock.

More and more sediment will pile up on the sandstone. As sandstone becomes deeply buried, pressure on the rocks will increase. The rock will become hot. Pressure will compact the particles in the sandstone until no spaces are left between them. Silica, the main ingredient in quartz, will replace the calcite as the cement holding the rock together. The rock's texture will change from gritty to smooth. After millions of years, the sandstone will have changed into the metamorphic rock quartzite.

What will happen next? You could wait tens of millions of years to find out how the quartzite completes the rock cycle. Or you can trace alternative pathways in *Exploring the Rock Cycle.*

Classifying

ACTIVITY

Some metamorphic rocks form out of igneous rocks, and other metamorphic rocks form out of sedimentary rocks.

1. If you find a fine-grained metamorphic rock with thin, flaky layers, from which group of rocks did it probably form? Explain.
2. If you find a metamorphic rock with distinct grains of different colors and sizes arranged in parallel bands, from which group of rocks did it probably form? Explain.

Program Resources

- **Teaching Resources** 5-6 Lesson Plan, p. 147; 5-6 Section Summary, p. 148

Media and Technology

Audiotapes English-Spanish Summary 5-6

Transparencies Transparencies "Exploring the Rock Cycle," Transparency 20

2 Facilitate

A Cycle of Many Pathways

Including All Students

Challenge students to describe other natural cycles. These might include the cycle of seasons, the cycle of night and day, the water cycle, and the carbon-oxygen cycle. Point out that these cycles are continuous, with no beginning or end, just as the rock cycle is. **learning modality: verbal**

One Pathway Through the Rock Cycle

Sharpen your Skills

Classifying

Time 10 minutes
Expected Outcome
1. Such a metamorphic rock probably formed from sedimentary rock, because sedimentary rocks form in layers. Some students might suggest that this description fits the metamorphic rock slate, which forms from the sedimentary rock shale. **2.** Answers may vary. Such a metamorphic rock probably formed from igneous rock, because igneous rocks have distinct grains of different colors and sizes. Some students, though, may correctly suggest that such a rock could form from conglomerate, a sedimentary rock.
Extend Ask: **Could igneous rock form from sedimentary rock?** *(Yes. Through the process of subduction at convergent plates, sedimentary rock melts and becomes part of the mantle. That mantle material could then rise as magma and harden into igneous rock.)* **learning modality: logical/mathematical**

Ongoing Assessment

Writing Have students explain in their own words how grains in the granite of Stone Mountain eventually became part of quartzite.

One Pathway Through the Rock Cycle, continued

EXPLORING
The Rock Cycle

Materials *3 crayons of different colors, pocket pencil sharpener, aluminum foil, large piece of wood, hot plate, pan*
Time 20 minutes; 5 minutes the next day

ACTIVITY

After students have examined the feature, demonstrate a model of the rock cycle using crayons. Explain to students that the three crayons represent different kinds of rock. Then use the pencil sharpener to shave the crayons, one after another, onto a piece of aluminum foil so that the shavings create three layers. Ask: **What does this process represent?** *(Weathering, erosion, deposition, and the formation of sedimentary rock)* Then fold the aluminum foil over the shavings, place the piece of wood on top, and press moderately. Show students the compressed results. Ask: **What does this represent?** *(The formation of metamorphic rock)* Then place the "rock" and aluminum foil into a pan and heat the pan on the hot plate. Ask: **What does this process represent?** *(The melting of rock at a convergent plate boundary)* Allow the crayon material to harden overnight, and show students the results. Ask: **What does this hardening represent?** *(The formation of igneous rock)* To conclude, call on students to explain how the demonstration represented the rock cycle. **learning modality: visual**

The Rock Cycle and Plate Tectonics

Using the Visuals: Figure 21

Ask students: **Through what processes did the fossil trilobite—once a sea creature—become part of a Vermont mountain?** *(Movement of material in the asthenosphere caused crustal plates to move. Plate collisions resulted in an uplift of the land on a continental plate, raising the ocean floor above sea level to become part of a mountain.)* **learning modality: verbal**

EXPLORING the Rock Cycle

Earth's constructive and destructive forces build up and wear down the crust. Igneous, sedimentary, and metamorphic rocks change continuously through the rock cycle. Rocks can follow many different pathways. The outer circle shows a complete cycle. The arrows within the circle show alternate pathways.

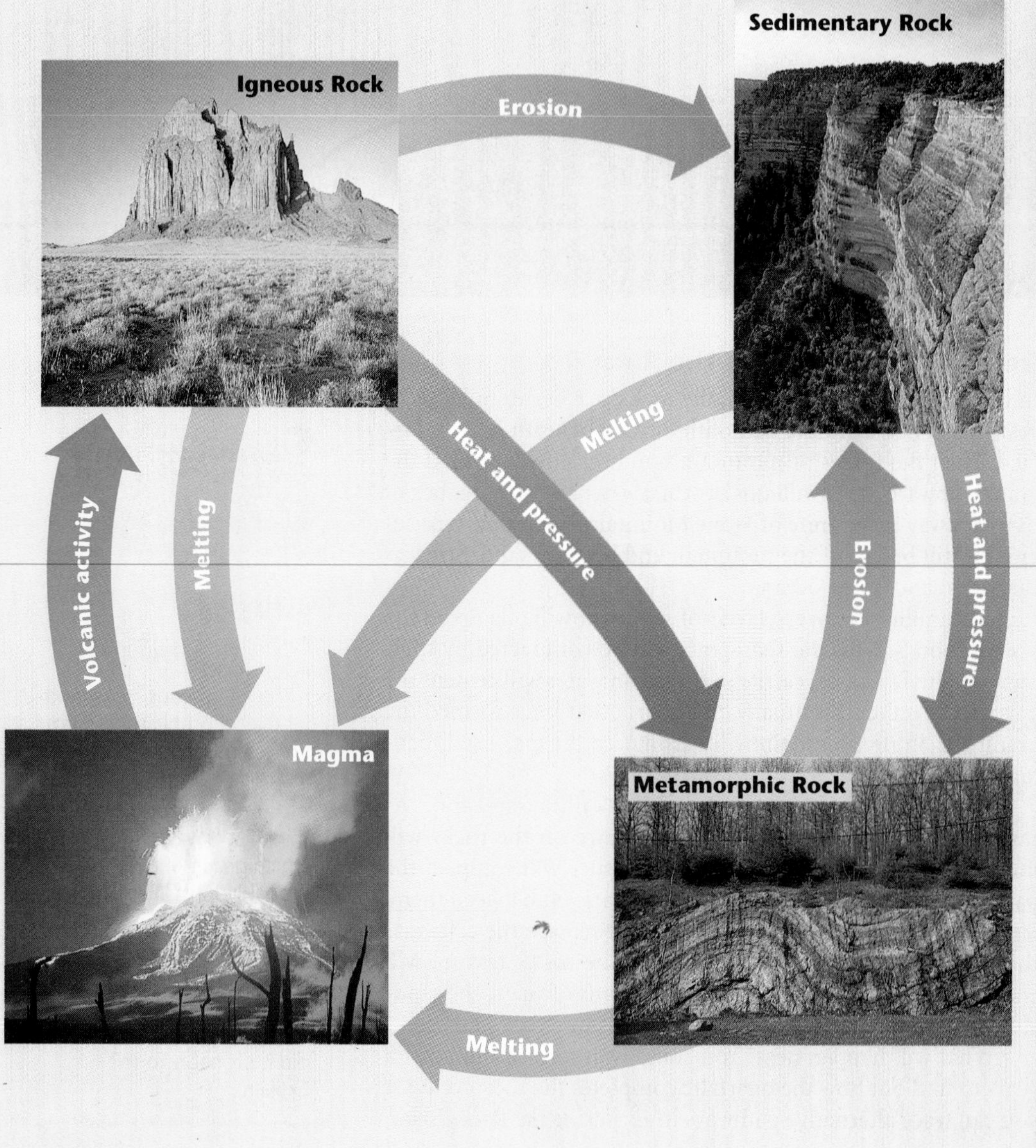

Background

Facts and Figures The rock cycle is simply a way to express the concept that all rocks are impermanent over geologic time. A diagram of the cycle could actually be more complex than that shown on this page. For instance, some sedimentary rock is neither melted nor metamorphosed. Rather, it is weathered, eroded, and reformed as sedimentary rock. A further complexity might be to show the cycle as two interlocking subcycles, one for continental crust and one for oceanic crust. The subcycle for continental crust would look much like the one here. The subcycle for oceanic crust, though, would be simpler, as magma rises from the mantle, becomes igneous rock, and then is subducted to the mantle at trenches.

The Rock Cycle and Plate Tectonics

The changes of the rock cycle are closely related to plate tectonics. Recall that plate tectonics causes the movement of sections of Earth's crust called plates. **Plate movements drive the rock cycle by pushing rocks back into the mantle, where they melt and become magma again. Plate movements also cause the folding, faulting, and uplift of the crust that move rocks through the rock cycle.** Two types of plate movement advance the rock cycle. One type is a collison that involves subducting oceanic plates. The other type is a collision between continental plates.

Subducting Oceanic Plates Consider what could happen to the sand grains that once were part of Stone Mountain. The sand may become sandstone attached to oceanic crust. On this pathway through the rock cycle, the oceanic crust carrying the sandstone drifts toward a deep-ocean trench. At the trench, subduction returns some of the sandstone to the mantle. There, it melts and forms magma, which eventually becomes igneous rock.

Figure 21 This fossil trilobite lived on an ocean floor about 500 million years ago. As plate tectonics moved pieces of Earth's crust, the rock containing this fossil became part of a mountain in Vermont.

Colliding Continental Plates Collisions between continental plates can also change a rock's path through the rock cycle. Such a collision can squeeze some sandstone from the ocean floor. As a result, the sandstone will change to quartzite. Eventually, the collision could form a mountain range or plateau. Then, as the mountains or plateaus containing quartzite are worn away, the rock cycle continues.

Section 6 Review

1. What process gradually changes rocks from one form to another?
2. How can plate movements move rocks through the rock cycle?
3. What rock comes before marble in the rock cycle? What rock or rocks could come just after marble in the rock cycle? Explain your answer.
4. **Thinking Critically** **Applying Concepts** Begin with a grain of sand on a beach. Describe what happens as you follow the grain through the rock cycle until it returns to a beach as a grain of sand again.
5. **Thinking Critically** **Making Judgments** In your opinion, at what point does the rock cycle really begin? Give reasons for your answer.

Check Your Progress CHAPTER PROJECT 5

Now that you have collected, described, tested, and recorded your rocks, classify them as igneous, sedimentary, or metamorphic. Are any of your rocks foliated? Try to identify specific types of rock. Compare your rock samples with pictures of rocks in a field guide or other library reference sources.

Program Resources

◆ **Teaching Resources** 5-6 Review and Reinforce, p. 149; 5-6 Enrich, p. 150

Media and Technology

Interactive Student Tutorial CD-ROM F-5

Exploring Earth Science Videodisc Unit 3, Side 1, "Everything on Your Plate"

3 Assess

Section 6 Review Answers

1. The rock cycle
2. Subducting oceanic plates can return rock to the mantle. There, it melts and forms magma, which eventually becomes igneous rock. Collisions between continental plates can also change rocks. A collision can cause sandstone to become quartzite. It can also form mountains or plateaus. Then, as the mountains or plateaus are worn away, the rock cycle continues.
3. Sandstone comes before quartzite, since quartzite is formed from sandstone. Quartzite could change into either a sedimentary rock or an igneous rock, depending on which pathway it took in the rock cycle.
4. Answers may vary. A typical answer will describe the formation of the sedimentary sandstone, a change into the metamorphic quartzite, a change into an igneous rock through plate movement, weathering of the igneous rock to form sand, and erosion of the sand to a beach.
5. Answers may vary. Some students may argue that the cycle must begin with the formation of igneous rocks as minerals in magma crystallize. Others can logically argue that the rock cycle has no beginning or end.

Check Your Progress CHAPTER PROJECT 5

Help students or groups organize their rocks into a display. Make sure that each has the necessary materials, and provide suggestions for those who seem to be having trouble. Some students may still be having difficulty in using the field guides. Help them understand how such guides are organized.

Performance Assessment

Oral Presentation Call on students at random and name one of the three major groups of rocks. Then challenge the student to describe a path in the rock cycle that rock might follow to eventually become the same type of rock again.

Real-World Lab

You, the Consumer

Testing Rock Flooring

Preparing for Inquiry

Key Concept Different kinds of rocks have different properties that determine how useful each is in specific situations.

Skills Objectives Students will be able to:

- design an experiment to determine which building stones are easiest to maintain and keep clean;
- form operational definitions using observations gained from testing various building stones;
- draw conclusions about which building stones would make the best flooring.

Time 40 minutes

Advance Planning Gather enough rock samples to provide each group with at least one igneous, sedimentary, and metamorphic rock. Granite, sandstone, and marble are good choices, though testing any rock sample is useful for students to learn about characteristics of rocks. If your samples are limited, you could assign different rock samples to each group. In addition, provide a variety of stains and greasy materials.

Alternative Materials If rock samples are in short supply, provide commercial products such as brick, ceramic, or vinyl flooring. Make sure, though, that all groups test at least two rock samples.

Guiding Inquiry

Invitation Show students a commercial square tile. Then ask: **If this material were on your kitchen floor, how well do you think it would hold up under normal use?** *(Answers may vary depending on the material. In answering, students should begin to think about what sort of abuse a floor tile takes.)*

Helping Design a Plan

- Divide students into pairs or small groups, and encourage them to brainstorm qualities of good flooring.
- Encourage students to write down a procedure that details how they will perform each type of test on their rock samples.

Real-World Lab

You, the Consumer

TESTING ROCK FLOORING

You are building your own house. For the kitchen floor, you want to use some building stones such as granite, marble, or limestone. You need to know which material is easiest to maintain and keep clean.

Problem

What kind of building stone makes the best flooring?

Skills Focus

designing experiments, forming operational definitions drawing conclusions

Suggested Materials

steel nail, wire brush, water, plastic dropper, hand lens, samples of igneous, sedimentary, and metamorphic rocks with flat surfaces, materials that form stains, such as ink and paints, greasy materials such as butter and crayons

Procedure 

1. Brainstorm with your partner the qualities of good flooring. For example, good flooring should resist stains, scratches, and grease marks, and be safe to walk on when wet.
2. Predict what you think is the best building stone for a kitchen floor. Why?
3. Write the steps you plan to follow to answer the problem question. As you design your plan, consider the following factors:
   - What igneous, sedimentary, and metamorphic rocks will you test? (Pick at least one rock from each group.)
   - What materials or equipment will you need to acquire, and in what amounts?
   - What tests will you perform on the samples?
   - How will you control the variables in each test?
   - How will you measure each sample's resistance to staining, grease, and scratches?
   - How will you measure slipperiness?
4. Review your plan. Will it lead to an answer to the problem question?
5. Check your procedure and safety plan with your teacher.
6. Create a data table that includes a column in which you predict how each material will perform in each test.

Analyze and Conclude

1. Which material performed the best on each test? Which performed the worst on each test?
2. Which material is best for the kitchen flooring? Which material would you least want to use?
3. Do your answers support your initial prediction? Why or why not?
4. The person installing the floor might want stone that is easy to cut to the correct size or shape. What other qualities would matter to the flooring installer?
5. **Apply** Based on your results for flooring, what materials would you use for kitchen counters? How might the qualities needed for countertops differ from those for flooring?

More to Explore

Find out the cost per square meter of some materials used to build kitchen floors in your community. How does cost influence your decision on which material to use? What other factors can influence the choice of materials?

Evaluating Student Plans

- Make sure each group has developed a procedure for performing tests for staining, grease, scratch, and slipperiness.

Troubleshooting the Experiment

- Observe each pair or group as they test one of their rock samples.
- Make sure that the results of each test are recorded in the data table.

Safety

Caution students to be careful when performing the scratch test and to wear their lab aprons when testing with grease or stains. Review the safety guidelines in Appendix A.

STUDY GUIDE

CHAPTER 5 REVIEW

Section 1 Classifying Rocks

Key Ideas
- A rock is a hard piece of Earth's crust.
- Geologists classify rocks according to their color, texture, mineral composition, and origin.
- The three kinds of rocks are igneous, sedimentary, and metamorphic.

Key Terms
texture igneous rock metamorphic rock
grain sedimentary rock

Section 2 Igneous Rocks

Key Ideas
- Igneous rocks form when hot, liquid magma or lava cools and hardens.
- Igneous rocks are classified according to their origin, texture, and composition.

Key Terms
extrusive rock porphyritic texture
intrusive rock

Section 3 Sedimentary Rocks

Key Ideas
- Most sedimentary rocks are formed from sediments that are compacted and cemented together.
- Sedimentary rocks are classified according to the origin of the materials from which the rocks are made.
- The three types of sedimentary rocks are clastic rocks, organic rocks, and chemical rocks.

Key Terms
sediment compaction organic rock
erosion cementation chemical rock
deposition clastic rock

Section 4 Rocks From Reefs

INTEGRATING LIFE SCIENCE

Key Ideas
- When coral animals die, their shells remain and new coral grows on top of them, eventually forming a coral reef.
- Over millions of years, the movement of Earth's crust can bring to the surface deposits of limestone formed by ancient coral reefs.

Key Terms
coral reef atoll

Section 5 Metamorphic Rocks

Key Ideas
- In a process that takes place deep beneath the surface, heat and pressure can change any type of rock into metamorphic rock.
- Geologists classify metamorphic rock according to whether the rock is foliated or nonfoliated.

Key Term
foliated

Section 6 The Rock Cycle

Key Ideas
- The series of processes on and beneath Earth's surface that change rocks from one type of rock to another is called the rock cycle.
- Plate movements drive the rock cycle by pushing rocks back into the mantle, where they melt and become magma again. Plate movements also advance the rock cycle by causing folding, faulting, and uplifting of the crust.

Key Term
rock cycle

ACTIVITY
USING THE INTERNET
www.science-explorer.phschool.com

Program Resources

- **Teaching Resources** Chapter 5 Real-World Lab, pp. 154–155
- **Teaching Resources** Chapter 5 Project Scoring Rubric, p. 126; Chapter 5 Performance Assessment, pp. 196–198; Chapter 5 Test, pp. 199–202

Media and Technology

Interactive Student Tutorial CD-ROM F-5

Computer Test Bank Test F-5

Expected Outcome
The harder, smoother rocks will prove more resistant to scratches, stains, and grease but will be slipperier when wet.

Analyze and Conclude
1. Answers will vary depending on the samples tested. In a stain test, granite, slate, and marble are hard to stain, while limestone and sandstone are easy to stain. In a scratch test, all rock samples will scratch, though granite and marble may be the hardest to scratch. Limestone and sandstone, by contrast, should scratch easily. In a slipperiness test, the smoothest rocks, such as marble, are more slippery than more porous rocks, such as sandstone. In a grease test, the porous rocks, such as sandstone, are much harder to clean than the smoother rocks, such as marble.
2. Answers may vary. Most students will mention marble, granite, or slate as best for kitchen flooring and sandstone or limestone as least desirable. But because of the slipperiness factor, some students may decide that sandstone, for example, may be a good choice.
3. Answers will vary depending on students' predictions. Students should cite results from their tests to explain why or why not their answers supported their predictions.
4. Answers may vary. Students might suggest that brittleness and weight would be qualities that would matter to a floor installer. Cost and availability would also be important considerations.
5. Answers may vary. Of the qualities tested, resistance to staining and grease would be more important than slipperiness or resistance to scratches. On that basis, students might choose a different material for counters than they did for flooring.

Extending the Inquiry

More to Explore Suggest that students call retail stores that sell building materials, ask what rock flooring is available, and record the cost. Students will likely have to convert cost per square foot to cost per square meter. Most students will answer that cost would influence their decision about which material to use. They may also suggest that such considerations as color and luster might also influence their decision.

CHAPTER 5 REVIEW

Reviewing Content: Multiple Choice

1. c 2. d 3. a 4. b 5. c

True or False

6. mineral composition 7. coarse-grained 8. chemical rocks 9. atoll 10. true

Checking Concepts

11. An igneous rock with a glassy or fine-grained texture cooled rapidly near the surface. An igneous rock with coarse-grained texture cooled slowly deep underground. An igneous rock with a porphyritic texture cooled in two stages, first far below the surface and then nearer to the surface.
12. Water can pass through sandstone because the cementation process does not fill all the spaces between sand grains, leaving small holes. In shale, the spaces between the clay particles are too small for water to pass through.
13. Shells get trapped with other sediment as it is deposited on the bottom of a lake or ocean. Slowly these sediments harden to become sedimentary rock.
14. When rock changes into metamorphic rock, its appearance, texture, crystal structure, and mineral content change.
15. Collisions between Earth's plates push rock down toward the heat of the mantle. Pockets of magma rising through the crust also provide heat that can produce metamorphic rock.
16. The remains of a dead fish could have been covered by sediment before the fish decayed. The sediments could then have hardened into sedimentary rock. The movement of Earth's plates then could have resulted in mountain building.

Thinking Visually

17. **a.** Igneous rock forms **b.** Igneous rock wears away **c.** Sediments build up **d.** Sedimentary rock forms **e.** Lava erupts; **Title:** The Rock Cycle

Applying Skills

18. Students should describe rock A as being a foliated rock with a fine-grained texture, rock B as having a coarse-grained texture, and rock C as having coarse-grained crystals mixed with fine-grained crystals.
19. Rock A is a metamorphic rock because it is the only one of the three that is foliated.
20. From the texture of rock B, students can infer that it is a sedimentary rock formed from rounded pieces of other rocks that were cemented together.

Thinking Critically

21. The tremendous pressure and heat that creates metamorphic rock packs the grains closer together than in sedimentary rock. Therefore, the metamorphic marble and quartzite resist being worn away better than the sedimentary limestone and sandstone.
22. The environment was probably swampy, since coal forms from swamp plants buried in water. The shale is further evidence of a wet environment, since it forms from clay particles deposited by water.
23. Clastic rocks and organic rocks are similar in that they are both sedimentary rocks composed of sediments deposited in layers.

CHAPTER 5 REVIEW

Reviewing Content

For more review of key concepts, see the Interactive Student Tutorial CD-ROM.

Multiple Choice

Choose the letter of the best answer.

1. Which of the following sedimentary rocks is a chemical rock?
   a. shale
   b. sandstone
   c. halite
   d. breccia
2. Metamorphic rocks can be formed from
   a. igneous rocks.
   b. sedimentary rocks.
   c. metamorphic rocks.
   d. all rock groups.
3. The rock formed when limestone changes to a metamorphic rock is
   a. marble. b. basalt.
   c. granite. d. pumice.
4. Which of the following helps create both metamorphic and sedimentary rocks?
   a. cementation b. pressure
   c. evaporation d. heat
5. Millions of years ago, a deposit of organic limestone was probably
   a. a swampy forest. b. a lava flow.
   c. a coral reef. d. an intrusive rock.

True or False

If the statement is true, write true. If it is false, change the underlined word or words to make the statement true.

6. Igneous rocks are classified by how they formed and by their color, texture, and <u>shape</u>.
7. Granite is a <u>fine-grained</u> igneous rock.
8. Sedimentary rocks that form when minerals come out of solution are classified as <u>porphyritic</u>.
9. A <u>barrier reef</u> is a ring-shaped coral island found in the open ocean.
10. The forces that wear away, transport, and deposit <u>sediment</u> are that part of the rock cycle which takes place on Earth's surface.

Checking Concepts

11. What is the relationship between an igneous rock's texture and where it was formed?
12. Why can water pass easily through sandstone but not through shale?
13. How do shells end up being trapped in solid rock?
14. How do the properties of a rock change when the rock changes to metamorphic?
15. What are the sources of the heat that helps metamorphic rocks to form?
16. **Writing to Learn** You are a camp counselor taking your campers on a mountain hike. One of your campers cracks open a rock and finds a fossil fish inside. The camper wants to know how a fish came to be trapped inside a solid rock on the side of a mountain. What explanation would you give the camper?

Thinking Visually

17. **Cycle Diagram** Copy the cycle diagram of the rock cycle onto a sheet of paper. To complete the diagram, match each of the following with the correct letter: sediments build up, igneous rock wears away, sedimentary rock forms, igneous rock forms, lava erupts. Add a title. (For more on cycle diagrams, see the Skills Handbook).

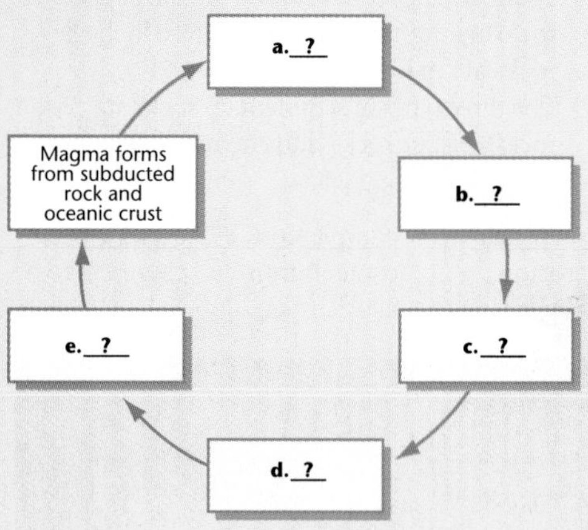

Applying Skills

Answer Questions 18–20 using the photos of three rocks.

18. Observing How would you describe the texture of each rock?

19. Classifying Which of the three rocks would you classify as a metamorphic rock? Explain your answer.

20. Inferring A rock's texture gives clues about how the rock formed. What can you infer about the process by which rock B formed?

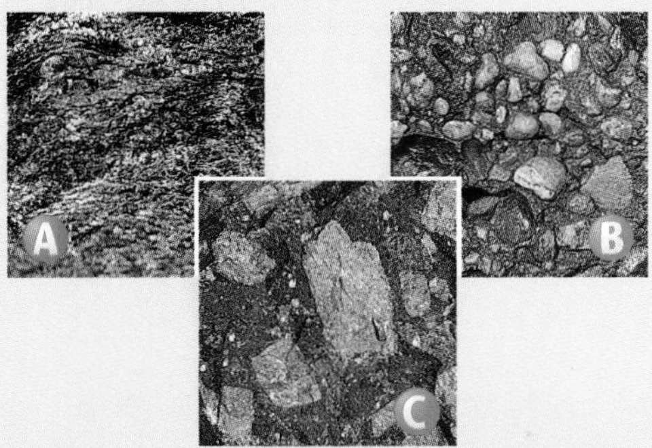

Thinking Critically

21. Applying Concepts The sedimentary rocks limestone and sandstone are used as building materials. However, they do not withstand weathering as well as marble and quartzite, the metamorphic rocks that are formed from them. Why do you think this is so?

22. Inferring As a geologist exploring for rock and mineral deposits, you come across an area where the rocks are layers of coal and shale. What kind of environment probably existed in this area millions of years ago when these rocks formed?

23. Comparing and Contrasting How are clastic rocks and organic rocks similar? How are they different?

24. Relating Cause and Effect Look at the sample of rhyolite in Figure 6 on page 151. Rhyolite is very similar to granite in mineral composition. But the two types of rock look very different. Explain why this is so.

CHAPTER 5 REVIEW

CHAPTER PROJECT 5 Wrap Up

Presenting Your Project Construct a simple display for your rocks. Your display should clearly give your classification for each of your rock samples. In your presentation, describe where you went hunting for rocks and what kinds of rocks you found. Describe which of your discoveries surprised you the most.

Reflect and Record In your journal, write about how you developed your rock collection. Were there any rocks that were hard to classify? Did you find rocks from each of the three major groups? Can you think of any reason why certain types of rocks would not be found in your area?

Getting Involved

In Your School Rock is often used in the construction of a school. With your classmates and teacher, find places in and around your school where rock has been used as a building material. Draw or photograph these materials. Then write captions for each picture identifying the rocks and explaining their origin. Display the pictures on a poster for other students in your school.

Performance Assessment

CHAPTER PROJECT 5 Wrap Up

Presenting Your Project
As each student or group presents the rock collection, assess how well the rocks are displayed and how effectively the rocks were classified and identified. For example, students should give reasons for classifying a rock as igneous or identifying a rock as sandstone. These reasons might be related to observation or to tests performed on the rock.

Reflect and Record In writing about how the rock collection was developed, the student should describe where and how the rocks were collected, what observations and tests led to classification and identification of the rocks, and how the display was constructed. Some students may not have collected metamorphic rocks. If so, they might conclude that the reason is that they live far away from plate boundaries or that such rocks are probably buried deep underground.

They are different in that clastic rocks are formed when rock fragments are squeezed together, while organic rocks are formed when the remains of plants and animals are deposited in thick layers.

24. The two rocks look different because of a difference in grain size. Rhyolite's fine-grained texture indicates that it formed from lava that cooled near or at Earth's surface, while granite's coarse-grained texture indicates that it cooled deep below the surface.

Program Resources

- **Inquiry Skills Activity Book** Provides teaching and review of all inquiry skills

Getting Involved

In Your School One way to organize this effort is to encourage an artistically talented student to make a drawing of the school to use in the center of the poster. Then photographs of various structures could be arrayed around the drawing, with lines to various parts of the school. Students might find that rock has been used on the school's facade, as well as well as elsewhere around the school.

The Noble Metal

This interdisciplinary feature presents the central theme of gold as a mineral by connecting four different disciplines: science, social studies, language arts, and mathematics. The four explorations are designed to capture students' interest and help them see how the content they are studying in science relates to other school subjects and to real-world events. The unit is particularly suitable for team teaching.

1 Engage/Explore

Activating Prior Knowledge

Help students recall what they learned in Chapter 4, Minerals, by asking questions such as: **What is a mineral?** *(A mineral is a naturally occurring, inorganic solid with a crystal structure and a definite chemical composition.)* **What is a mineral vein and how does it form?** *(A mineral vein is a narrow channel or slab of a mineral that is much different from the surrounding rock. A vein forms when a solution of hot water and metals follow cracks in underground rock. When the metals crystallize, they form veins in the rock.)*

Introducing the Unit

Have students turn to Appendix B, Identifying Common Minerals, and examine the entry for gold. Ask: **What properties does gold have that might make it valuable or desirable?** *(It is a metallic mineral, and metals have many uses. Its color is a rich yellow. It can be pounded into various shapes and drawn into wires. It does not tarnish.)* **What are some of the ways you know gold was used in the past and is used today?** *(Students might mention use of gold in coins, jewelry, and many ornaments. Some students might also suggest that gold bars are valuable and used like money.)*

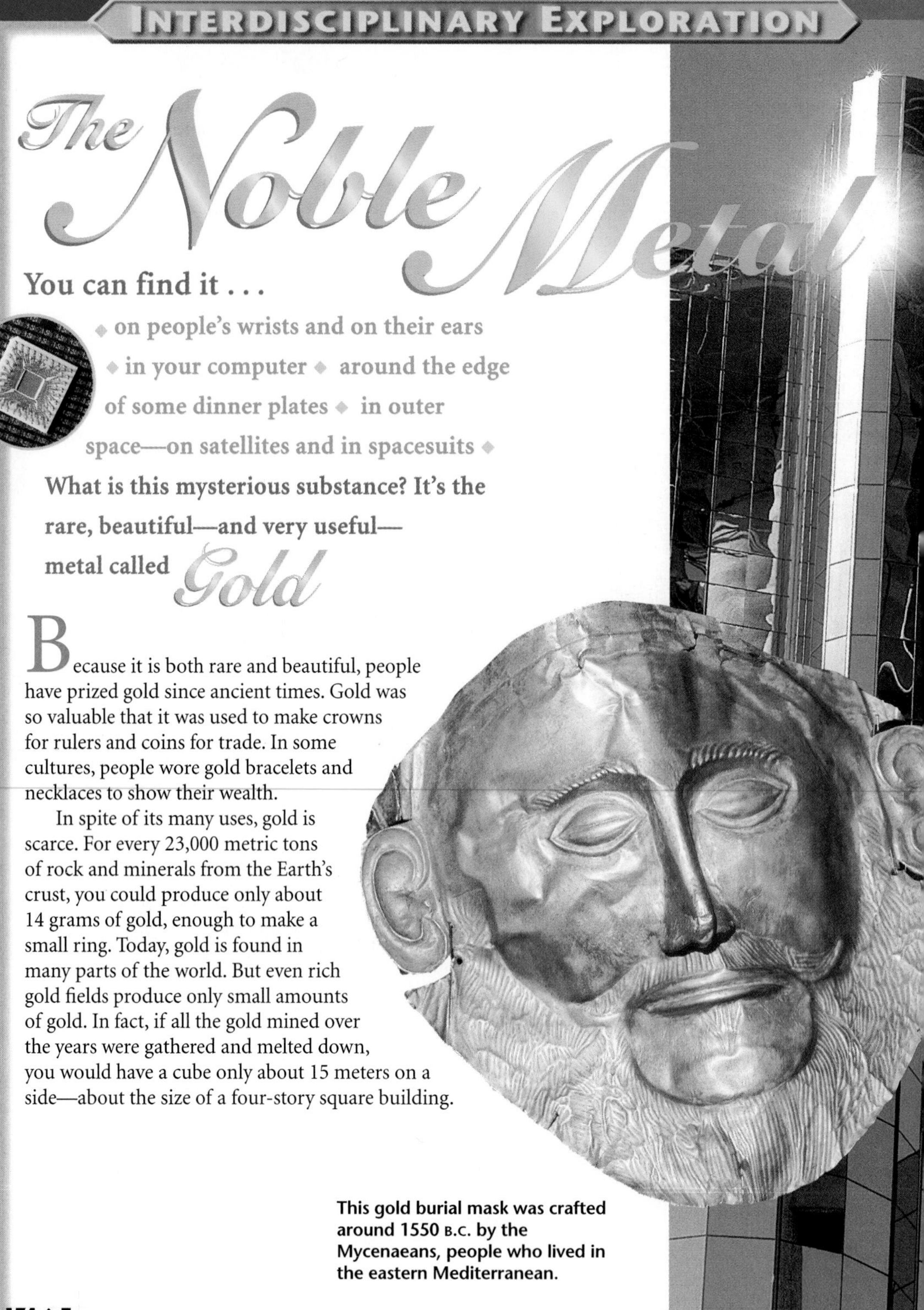

INTERDISCIPLINARY EXPLORATION

The Noble Metal

You can find it . . .

◆ on people's wrists and on their ears ◆ in your computer ◆ around the edge of some dinner plates ◆ in outer space—on satellites and in spacesuits ◆

What is this mysterious substance? It's the rare, beautiful—and very useful—metal called *Gold*

Because it is both rare and beautiful, people have prized gold since ancient times. Gold was so valuable that it was used to make crowns for rulers and coins for trade. In some cultures, people wore gold bracelets and necklaces to show their wealth.

In spite of its many uses, gold is scarce. For every 23,000 metric tons of rock and minerals from the Earth's crust, you could produce only about 14 grams of gold, enough to make a small ring. Today, gold is found in many parts of the world. But even rich gold fields produce only small amounts of gold. In fact, if all the gold mined over the years were gathered and melted down, you would have a cube only about 15 meters on a side—about the size of a four-story square building.

This gold burial mask was crafted around 1550 B.C. by the Mycenaeans, people who lived in the eastern Mediterranean.

Program Resources

◆ **Teaching Resources** Interdisciplinary Explorations, Science, pp. 156–160; Social Studies, pp. 161–162; Language Arts, pp. 163–165; Mathematics, pp. 166–167

Properties of Gold

Why is gold used for everything from bracelets to space helmets to medicine? You'll find the answers in this precious metal's unusual chemical and physical properties. Gold is deep yellow in color and so shiny, or lustrous, that its Latin name, *aurum,* means "glowing dawn." Gold's chemical symbol—*Au*—comes from that Latin word.

Gold is very stable. Unlike iron, gold doesn't rust. It also doesn't tarnish in air as silver does, so its luster can last forever. Ancient chemists thought that gold was superior to other metals. They classified it as one of the "noble" metals.

Gold is very soft and malleable. That is, it's easy to bend or hammer into shapes without breaking. It can be pounded into very thin sheets called gold leaf. In fact, you can pound 30 grams of gold into a sheet that's large enough to cover the floor of a small room. Gold is also the most ductile metal. You can draw out 30 grams of gold into a fine thread as long as 8 kilometers without breaking it.

Ancient people of Egypt, Greece, and China found ways to dig gold from mines. But most of the gold that people have used in the last 6,000 years has come from Earth's surface, often from streams and riverbanks. Gold is very heavy—one of the densest metals. Over centuries, mountain streams have washed away dirt and pebbles from veins of gold-bearing rocks and minerals and left the heavy gold in the streambeds.

Gold reflects heat and, when combined with other materials, filters sunlight. For this reason, gold is used in spacesuits and face visors. This astronaut wears a face visor coated with gold. The window glass in some skyscrapers is tinted with gold to keep out heat and protect people's eyes.

Science Activity

Many of the gold hunters who flocked to California during the Gold Rush of 1849 were searching for gold in streams and rivers. Although they had very simple equipment, their technique worked because gold is so dense. Using pans, miners washed gold-bearing gravel in running water. Try your own gold panning.

Procedure:
Set up your own model of gold panning, using a large pan, a gravel mixture, and a very dense material as a substitute for gold. Use a sink trap. Under running water, shake and swirl the pan until the lighter materials wash away. What's left is your "gold."

- Why is "gold" left in the pan while other materials are washed away?

Background

Integrating Science and Technology
Because of gold's properties, the uses of gold have expanded greatly from its traditional uses in jewelry and coins. Gold is used in electronics because of its good conducting properties. Thus, televisions, radios, and computers often have parts made of a gold alloy. Gold alloys are used in dental work, including fillings and crowns. Gold's reflective properties make gold film useful not only in space suits but also on the outside of spacecraft, as backing for mirrors in scientific equipment, and on the outside windows of office buildings. In addition, gold is used to make compounds to treat some medical conditions, such as rheumatoid arthritis.

Science

2 Facilitate

- Have students read about the properties of gold. Then ask: **What properties give gold its great value?** *(Its luster, stability, malleability, and ductility)* Review each of these properties to make sure students understand what they mean.

Science Activity

Make a mixture of sand and gravel in a bucket. Then mix in some heavy material, such as iron filings from a machine shop. Show students before they begin the activity what the "gold" is that they are looking for. An alternative to using a sink would be to set up several large washtubs or other containers filled with water. Try the activity ahead of time so that you can advise students on how to move the pan in the most advantageous ways. (See the worksheet, Panning for Gold, on page 158 for more detailed instructions.)

Teaching Resources The following worksheets correlate with this page: Eureka!, page 156; Gold in a Stream, page 157; Panning for Gold, page 158; and Gold From Start to Finish, pages 159–160.

3 Assess

Activity Assessment

Have students write a description of their experience in panning for "gold." Evaluate these descriptions on the basis of how earnestly they attempted to learn and use the technique of panning. Also assess their understanding of how the process works through their answer to the question of why the "gold" was left in the pan. *("Gold" is the heaviest material in the pan, so it sinks to the bottom and remains in the pan when the other materials wash out.)*

Social Studies

2 Facilitate

- Have students refer to the map on this page, and ask: **Where was the Kingdom of Ghana?** *(In West Africa, below the Sahara Desert)* **Where were there salt deposits, and where was salt needed?** *(Salt deposits were in the north, while salt was needed in Ghana.)* **Where were gold deposits, and where was gold desired?** *(Gold deposits were south of Ghana, and gold was desired north of the Sahara.)*
- Review supply and demand. Ask: **In commerce, what is supply?** *(The quantity of a substance that is available to be traded)* **What is demand?** *(The quantity of a substance desired by buyers of that substance)*

Social Studies Activity

Divide the class into teams of four or five students each. Then give each team several sandwich bags, some teams bags filled with salt and other teams bags filled with objects such as paper clips that represent gold. Have groups move to different parts of the room and discuss strategies for getting the best deals for their gold or salt. Next, invite traders to meet. At each meeting, announce a change in situation, such as a discovery of a gold deposit in Europe or an increased demand for salt in Africa.

Teaching Resources The following worksheets correlate with this page: An African King, page 161, and The Forty-Niners, page 162.

3 Assess

Activity Assessment

Invite teams to report to the class about how well their silent trading worked and what happened each time the value of gold or salt was changed. Have each student write an answer to the final question. *(If supply exceeds demand, the price will go down. However, if demand exceeds supply, the price will go up.)*

Social Studies

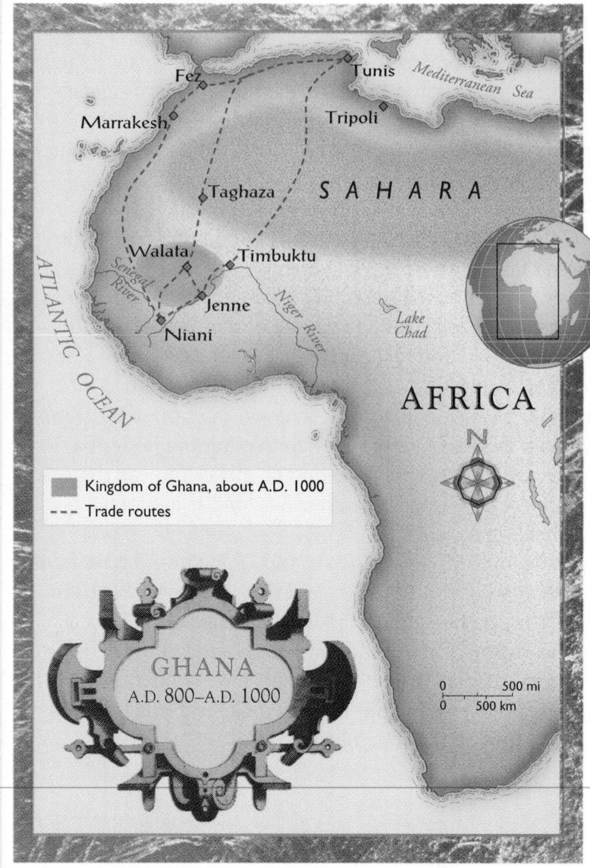

Golden Trade Routes

In West Africa nearly 1,000 years ago, salt was said to be worth its weight in gold. If you get your salt from the supermarket shelf, it may be hard to imagine how valuable this mineral was to people. But if you lived in a very hot, dry climate, you would need salt. It would be as valuable to you as gold. In West Africa, salt and gold were the most important goods traded in a busy north-south trade.

Camel caravans crossed the desert going south, carrying slabs of salt from mines in the desert. Trade centers, such as Jenne and Timbuktu, flourished. In the area around Taghaza, people built houses with walls of salt slabs. But several hundred kilometers south in the Kingdom of Ghana, salt was scarce and gold was plentiful. Salt traders from the north traveled deep into the forests of Ghana to trade salt for gold.

African gold became the basis for several rich cultures and trading empires that grew up in West Africa between 800 and 1400. At that time, most of the gold that Europeans used for crowns, coins, and jewelry was carried north from Africa.

Around 1100, Arab travelers in Africa wrote about the fabulous wealth of the Kingdom of Ghana. The most popular tale was that the salt traders and gold miners never met, as a way of keeping secret the location of gold mines. Traders from the north left slabs of salt in an agreed-upon trading place, pounded their drums to indicate a trade, and then withdrew. Miners from the south arrived, left an amount of gold that seemed fair, and withdrew. The salt traders returned. If they thought the trade was fair, they took the gold and left. If they were not satisfied, the silent trade continued.

Social Studies Activity

How would you succeed as a gold or salt trader? Find out by carrying out your own silent trade. Work in teams of Salt Traders and Gold Miners. Before trading, each team should decide how much a bag of gold or a block of salt is worth. Then, for each silent trade, make up a situation that would change the value of gold or salt, such as, "Demand for gold in Europe increases."

- Suppose you are selling a product today. How would the supply of the product affect the value or sale price of the product?

Background

History The ancient Kingdom of Ghana flourished from about the fifth century to the thirteenth century A.D., in what is now southern Mauritania and Mali. This ancient kingdom has no direct connection with the modern country of Ghana, which took its name to honor the past. Trade was a major factor in the kingdom's early importance and subsequent growth. In about the fifth century, the camel was introduced to cross-desert traffic, giving a boost to trans-Saharan trade. The gold fields were in the woodlands to the south of Ghana, on the Senegal River. After Ghana's decline in the mid-1200s, the Mali Empire dominated that region of West Africa until about 1500, when the Songhay Empire rose. The gold trade continued throughout those centuries. Both Timbuktu and Jenne (or Djenne) were associated with the later empires.

*RUNE OF RICHES

I have a golden ball,
A big, bright, shining one,
Pure gold; and it is all
Mine—It is the sun.

I have a silver ball
A white and glistening stone
That other people call
The moon;—my very own!

The jewel things that prick
My cushion's soft blue cover
Are mine,—my stars, thick, thick,
Scattered the sky all over.

And everything that's mine
Is yours, and yours, and yours,—
The shimmer and the shine!—
Let's lock our wealth out-doors!

—*Florence Converse*

Go for the gold

What do these sayings have in common?

- It's worth its weight in gold.
- Speech is silver, silence is golden.
- All that glitters is not gold.
- Go for the gold!

All of these sayings use gold as a symbol of perfection and value. Because gold has always been beautiful and scarce, it has for centuries been a symbol of excellence and richness—things that people want and search for. When writers use *gold* or *golden,* they are referring to something desirable, of value or worth. These words may also represent the beauty of gold.

In literature, writers and poets often use *gold* to make a comparison in a simile or metaphor. Similes and metaphors are figures of speech.

- A simile makes a comparison between two things, using *like* or *as* in the comparison. Here's an example: "An honest person's promise is as good as gold."
- A metaphor is a comparison without the use of like or as, such as, "When you're in trouble, true friends are golden."

Look for similes and metaphors in the poem by Florence Converse.

- What similes or metaphors has Converse made?
- What would this poem be like without the comparisons?

**A rune is a song or poem.*

Language Arts Activity

What does gold symbolize for you? Think of some comparisons of your own in which you use gold in a simile or metaphor. After jotting down all of your ideas, choose one (or more) and decide what comparison you will make. Write a short saying, a proverb, or a short poem that includes your own simile or metaphor.

◆ How does your comparison make your saying or poem more interesting?

Background

History The word *metaphor* comes from a Greek word meaning "to transfer." In a metaphor, the meaning of one word or image is transferred to another, providing insight through a comparison between the two. With a metaphor, a writer can often convey using a familiar example a thought that would be difficult to convey in only a few words. But a good metaphor does not just suggest a similarity between unlike things. Rather, it causes the reader to call up images and emotions that enlarge on the meaning. Thus, for example, the phrase, "days of golden dreams," evokes in a reader complex feelings of happiness, well-being, and warmth by using the word *golden.*

2 Facilitate

- Call on volunteers to read aloud the examples given in the exploration. Then ask: **What does the word *gold* mean in the saying "All that glitters is not gold"?** *(Something of the highest value)* Point out that in this use, the word can literally refer to gold, but it can also stand for anything of high value. **In your own words, what does this saying mean?** *(Students might suggest that it means that not all attractive things are of great value.)*
- Reinforce the difference between a simile and a metaphor by asking, **Which of the opening examples are similes?** *(None)* **What words in a phrase indicate that it is a simile?** *(Like or as)*
- To extend the exploration, encourage interested students to look for quotations that include the word *gold* or *golden* in books of famous quotations.

Language Arts Activity

Begin by having the whole class brainstorm a list of words that *gold* brings to mind, such words as *wealth, beauty,* and *value.* Write the list on the board. Then encourage students individually to think of comparisons that include the word *gold.*

Teaching Resources The following worksheets correlate with this page: Similes and Metaphors, page 163; An Ancient Folk Tale, page 164; and Same Sound, Different Meaning, page 165.

3 Assess

Activity Assessment

Check to see that each student has jotted down some ideas about gold. Evaluate students' sayings or poems on whether they used *gold* in a symbolic way as well as on how creatively that idea is expressed.

Mathematics

2 Facilitate

- Have students review what alloys are and why they are made. Ask: **What is an alloy?** *(An alloy is a solid mixture of two or more metals.)* **Why are alloys made?** *(To improve the usefulness of a metal, such as by making it stronger or rust resistant)*
- To extend the exploration, interested students could make an appointment with the owner or manager of a jewelry store. To prepare for the interview, students should make a list of questions they will ask related to gold and gold alloys used in rings and other jewelry. Invite these students to report to the class what they find out about the uses and prices of gold.

Mathematics Activity

Have students complete the activity on their own. Remind them that when rounding decimals to the nearest hundredth, they should round the second number to the right of the decimal point. If the third number to the right of the decimal point is 5 or above, round up; if it is below 5, keep the second number as it is.

Teaching Resources The following worksheets correlate with these pages: The Price of Gold, page 166, and Gold Mining Around the World, page 167.

3 Assess

Activity Assessment

- The 14 K gold ring is 58 percent gold ($14 \div 24 = 0.583$). Copper is 42 percent of the ring ($100\% - 58\% = 42\%$).
- The 12 K ring is 50 percent gold ($12 \div 24 = 0.5$) The 20 K ring is 83 percent gold ($20 \div 24 = 0.833$).
- The 20 K gold ring contains more gold, and therefore it would be more desirable to own.
- The 24 K gold ring is pure gold, and therefore it would be most expensive.

Mathematics

Measuring Gold

People often say that something is "worth its weight in gold." But how do you measure the weight of gold? Most gold that's mined today is used to make jewelry. But modern-day jewelry is seldom made of pure gold. Because gold is so soft, it is usually mixed with another metal to form an alloy—a mixture of two or more metals.

Most commonly the other metal in a gold alloy is copper, although alloys of gold can also contain silver, zinc, or other metals. A gold alloy keeps most of the properties of gold but is harder and resists denting and scratching. The other metals affect the color. More copper produces "red gold," while "white gold" may contain gold and copper along with nickel, palladium, or silver.

Suppose you are shopping for a gold ring. You see two rings that look the same and are exactly the same size. How do you decide which one to buy? If you look carefully at the gold jewelry, you'll probably see small letters that read "18 K," "20 K," "14 K," or "12 K." The "K" here stands for karat. That's the measure of how pure an alloy of gold is. Pure gold—used very rarely—is 24 karat. Gold that is 50 percent pure is $\frac{12}{24}$ gold, or 12 karat. The greater the amount of gold in a piece of jewelry, the higher the value.

Background

Facts and Figures The main purpose of adding other minerals to gold is to make the gold harder. The strongest alloy of gold and silver contains about 50 percent gold. But that alloy is a dull white color, and it easily tarnishes. "Green gold," an alloy often used in jewelry, is 75 percent gold and 25 percent silver. "White gold" contains roughly 80 percent gold, 16 percent nickel, 3 percent zinc, and 1 percent copper. "Red gold," which contains varying amounts of gold and copper, has been widely used in making coins. Goldware, such as cups and bowls, is often made of "yellow gold," which designates alloys containing gold, silver, and copper. Such alloys are gold colored and hard but still very workable. "Solid gold" jewelry in the United States is mostly made with 10–21 karat gold.

Look at the display of rings above. The 18-karat ring has copper in it. What percent of the 18 K gold ring is gold? What percent is copper?

Analyze. You know that pure gold is $\frac{24}{24}$ gold. In order to find out what percent of an 18 K ring is gold, you need to write a proportion.

Write the proportion.

$$\frac{\text{number of gold parts}}{\text{number of parts in the whole}} \rightarrow \frac{18}{24}$$

Simplify and solve.

$$\frac{18}{24} = \frac{3}{4} = 75\%$$

Think about it. If 75% of the ring is gold, then 25% of the ring must be copper.

Math Activity

Look at the other gold rings to determine what percent of each is gold.

- What percent of the 14 K gold ring is gold? What percent is another metal? Round decimals to the nearest hundredth.
- What percent of the 12 K ring is gold? What percent of the 20 K ring is gold?
- Which ring would you like to own—the 12 K or the 20 K? Why?
- Which ring in the display would probably be the most expensive?

Tie It Together

Gold Producers

1. South Africa
2. United States
3. Australia
4. Canada
5. Russia
6. China

A Treasure Hunt

Work in small groups to make a World Treasure Map of one of the countries where gold is mined today. Use the information above to get you started. Then use the library to learn about these gold-producing countries.

On a large map of the world, use push pins to mark the location of the gold sites. In the United States and Canada, mark the states and provinces that are the largest producers. Make up fact sheets with information that will answer questions such as the following:

- Where are gold sites located in each country?
- When was gold first discovered there?
- Did a gold rush influence the history of that area?

If possible, collect photographs to illustrate gold products in each country. Post your pictures and fact sheets at the side of the World Treasure Map.

Tie It Together

Time 1 week (3 days for research and collection of photographs, 2 days for making up the fact sheets and preparing the map)

Tips Have students work in groups of three or four. Encourage students to meet with their groups to agree on research strategies and then work individually or in pairs to gather the information. Help each group with questions about research avenues, as well as with the materials they might need to make their maps and pictures.

- In the research stage, suggest that students first examine articles and entries in encyclopedias and almanacs to make a list of countries, states, and provinces in which gold is produced. From that list, they can dig deeper in more specialized books and magazine articles.
- Encourage students familiar with the Internet to search for facts and figures using such key words as *gold* and *mining*.
- Have groups make their maps on poster board or a length of butcher paper. Advise them that their maps need not be exactly accurate. They can draw the continents, provinces, and states free form, using different pencil colors for boundaries.
- If students are unsuccessful in collecting photos, they can make drawings from photographs they see in books and magazines.

Extend Groups can choose a country or continent on which to focus their attention and then prepare a more detailed report on the areas where gold is produced and the processes involved in production and trade. Invite each group to make a presentation to the class.

- The same groups could also investigate a topic suggested by the explorations included in this feature, such as uses of gold, the California gold rush, and early African gold trade. Other similar topics include the Klondike gold rush of the 1890s and the modern trade in gold as a commodity.

Developing scientific thinking in students is important for a solid science education. To learn how to think scientifically, students need frequent opportunities to practice science process skills, critical thinking skills, as well as other skills that support scientific inquiry. The *Science Explorer* Skills Handbook introduces the following key science skills:

- Science Process Skills
- SI Measuring Skills
- Skills for Conducting a Scientific Investigation
- Critical Thinking Skills
- Information Organizing Skills
- Data Table and Graphing Skills

The Skills Handbook is designed as a reference for students to use whenever they need to review a science skill. You can use the activities provided in the Skills Handbook to teach or reinforce the skills.

Think Like a Scientist

Observing

ACTIVITY

Before students look at the photograph, remind them that an observation is only what they can see, hear, smell, taste, or feel. Ask: **Which senses will you use to make observations from this photograph?** *(Sight is the only sense that can be used to make observations from the photograph.)* **What are some observations you can make from the photograph?** *(Answers may vary. Sample answers: The boy is wearing sneakers, sport socks, shorts, and a tee shirt; the boy is sitting in the grass holding something blue against his knee; the boy is looking at his knee; there is a soccer ball laying beside the boy.)* List the observations on the chalkboard. If students make any inferences or predictions about the boy at this point, ask: **Can you be sure your statement is factual and accurate from just observing the photograph?** Help students understand how observations differ from inferences and predictions.

Inferring

ACTIVITY

Review students' observations from the photograph. Then ask: **What inferences can you make from your observations?** *(Students may say that the boy hurt his knee playing soccer and is holding a coldpack against his injured knee.)* **What experience or knowledge helped you make this inference?** *(Students may have experienced knee injuries from playing soccer, and they may be familiar with coldpacks like the one the boy is using.)* **Can anyone suggest another possible explanation for these observations?** *(Answers may vary. Sample answer: The boy hurt his knee jogging, and he just happened to sit beside a soccer ball his sister left in the yard.)* **How can you find out whether an inference is correct?** *(by further investigation)*

Predicting

ACTIVITY

After coming to some consensus about the inference that the boy hurt his knee, encourage students to make predictions about what will happen next. *(Students' predictions may vary. Sample answers: The boy will go to the doctor. A friend will help the boy home. The boy will get up and continue playing soccer.)*

Think Like a Scientist

Although you may not know it, you think like a scientist every day. Whenever you ask a question and explore possible answers, you use many of the same skills that scientists do. Some of these skills are described on this page.

Observing

When you use one or more of your five senses to gather information about the world, you are **observing.** Hearing a dog bark, counting twelve green seeds, and smelling smoke are all observations. To increase the power of their senses, scientists sometimes use microscopes, telescopes, or other instruments that help them make more detailed observations.

An observation must be factual and accurate—an exact report of what your senses detect. It is important to keep careful records of your observations in science class by writing or drawing in a notebook. The information collected through observations is called evidence, or data.

Inferring

When you explain or interpret an observation, you are **inferring,** or making an inference. For example, if you hear your dog barking, you may infer that someone is at your front door. To make this inference, you combine the evidence—the barking dog—and your experience or knowledge—you know that your dog barks when strangers approach—to reach a logical conclusion.

Notice that an inference is not a fact; it is only one of many possible explanations for an observation. For example, your dog may be barking because it wants to go for a walk. An inference may turn out to be incorrect even if it is based on accurate observations and logical reasoning. The only way to find out if an inference is correct is to investigate further.

Predicting

When you listen to the weather forecast, you hear many predictions about the next day's weather—what the temperature will be, whether it will rain, and how windy it will be. Weather forecasters use observations and knowledge of weather patterns to predict the weather. The skill of **predicting** involves making an inference about a future event based on current evidence or past experience.

Because a prediction is an inference, it may prove to be false. In science class, you can test some of your predictions by doing experiments. For example, suppose you predict that larger paper airplanes can fly farther than smaller airplanes. How could you test your prediction?

Use the photograph to answer the questions below.

Observing Look closely at the photograph. List at least three observations.

Inferring Use your observations to make an inference about what has happened. What experience or knowledge did you use to make the inference?

Predicting Predict what will happen next. On what evidence or experience do you base your prediction?

Classifying

Could you imagine searching for a book in the library if the books were shelved in no particular order? Your trip to the library would be an all-day event! Luckily, librarians group together books on similar topics or by the same author. Grouping together items that are alike in some way is called **classifying.** You can classify items in many ways: by size, by shape, by use, and by other important characteristics.

Like librarians, scientists use the skill of classifying to organize information and objects. When things are sorted into groups, the relationships among them become easier to understand.

ACTIVITY Classify the objects in the photograph into two groups based on any characteristic you choose. Then use another characteristic to classify the objects into three groups.

Making Models

Have you ever drawn a picture to help someone understand what you were saying? Such a drawing is one type of model. A model is a picture, diagram, computer image, or other representation of a complex object or process. **Making models** helps people understand things that they cannot observe directly.

Scientists often use models to represent things that are either very large or very small, such as the planets in the solar system, or the parts of a cell. Such models are physical models—drawings or three-dimensional structures that look like the real thing. Other models are mental models—mathematical equations or words that describe how something works.

ACTIVITY This student is using a model to demonstrate what causes day and night on Earth. What do the flashlight and the tennis ball in the model represent?

Communicating

Whenever you talk on the phone, write a letter, or listen to your teacher at school, you are communicating. **Communicating** is the process of sharing ideas and information with other people. Communicating effectively requires many skills, including writing, reading, speaking, listening, and making models.

Scientists communicate to share results, information, and opinions. Scientists often communicate about their work in journals, over the telephone, in letters, and on the Internet. They also attend scientific meetings where they share their ideas with one another in person.

ACTIVITY On a sheet of paper, write out clear, detailed directions for tying your shoe. Then exchange directions with a partner. Follow your partner's directions exactly. How successful were you at tying your shoe? How could your partner have communicated more clearly?

SKILLS HANDBOOK

On what did you base your prediction? *(Scientific predictions are based on knowledge and experience.)* Point out that in science, predictions can often be tested with experiments.

Classifying — ACTIVITY

Encourage students to think of other common things that are classified. Then ask: **What things at home are classified?** *(Clothing might be classified by placing it in different dresser drawers; glasses, plates, and silverware are grouped in different parts of the kitchen; screws, nuts, bolts, washers, and nails might be separated into small containers.)* **What are some things that scientists classify?** *(Scientists classify many things they study, including organisms, geological features and processes, and kinds of machines.)* After students have classified the different fruits in the photograph, have them share their criteria for classifying them. *(Some characteristics students might use include shape, color, size, and where they are grown.)*

Making Models — ACTIVITY

Ask students: **What are some models you have used to study science?** *(Students may have used human anatomical models, solar system models, maps, stream tables.)* **How did these models help you?** *(Models can help you learn about things that are difficult to study, either because they are too big, too small, or complex.)* Be sure students understand that a model does not have to be three-dimensional. For example, a map in a textbook is a model. Ask: **What do the flashlight and tennis ball represent?** *(The flashlight represents the sun, and the ball represents Earth.)* **What quality of each item makes this a good model?** *(The flashlight gives off light, and the ball is round and can be rotated by the student.)*

Communicating — ACTIVITY

Challenge students to identify the methods of communication they've used today. Then ask: **How is the way you communicate with a friend similar to and different from the way scientists communicate about their work to other scientists?** *(Both may communicate using various methods, but scientists must be very detailed and precise, whereas communication between friends may be less detailed and precise.)* Encourage students to communicate like a scientist as they carry out the activity. *(Students' directions should be detailed and precise enough for another person to successfully follow.)*

Making Measurements

Measuring in SI

Review SI units in class with students. Begin by providing metric rulers, graduated cylinders, balances, and Celsius thermometers. Use these tools to reinforce that the meter is the unit of length, the liter is the unit of volume, the gram is the unit of mass, and the degree Celsius is the unit for temperature. Ask: **If you want to measure the area of the floor in this classroom, which SI unit would you use?** *(meter)* **Which unit would you use to measure the amount of matter in your textbook?** *(gram)* **Which would you use to measure how much water a drinking glass holds?** *(liter)* **When would you use the Celsius scale?** *(To measure the temperature of something)* Then use the measuring equipment to review SI prefixes. For example, ask: **What are the smallest units on the metric ruler?** *(millimeters)* **How many millimeters are there in 1 cm?** *(10 mm)* **How many in 10 cm?** *(100 mm)* **How many centimeters are there in 1 m?** *(100 cm)* **What does 1,000 m equal?** *(1 km)*

Length ACTIVITY *(Students should state that the shell is 4.6 centimeters, or 46 millimeters, long.)* If students need more practice measuring length, have them use meter sticks and metric rulers to measure various objects in the classroom.

Liquid Volume ACTIVITY *(Students should state that the volume of water in the graduated cylinder is 62 milliliters.)* If students need more practice measuring liquid volume, have them use a graduated cylinder to measure different volumes of water.

Making Measurements

When scientists make observations, it is not sufficient to say that something is "big" or "heavy." Instead, scientists use instruments to measure just how big or heavy an object is. By measuring, scientists can express their observations more precisely and communicate more information about what they observe.

Measuring in SI

The standard system of measurement used by scientists around the world is known as the International System of Units, which is abbreviated as SI (in French, *Système International d'Unités*). SI units are easy to use because they are based on multiples of 10. Each unit is ten times larger than the next smallest unit and one tenth the size of the next largest unit. The table lists the prefixes used to name the most common SI units.

Common SI Prefixes

Prefix	Symbol	Meaning
kilo-	k	1,000
hecto-	h	100
deka-	da	10
deci-	d	0.1 (one tenth)
centi-	c	0.01 (one hundredth)
milli-	m	0.001 (one thousandth)

Length To measure length, or the distance between two points, the unit of measure is the **meter (m).** One meter is the approximate distance from the floor to a doorknob. Long distances, such as the distance between two cities, are measured in kilometers (km). Small lengths are measured in centimeters (cm) or millimeters (mm). Scientists use metric rulers and meter sticks to measure length.

Common Conversions

1 km = 1,000 m
1 m = 100 cm
1 m = 1,000 mm
1 cm = 10 mm

ACTIVITY The larger lines on the metric ruler in the picture show centimeter divisions, while the smaller, unnumbered lines show millimeter divisions. How many centimeters long is the shell? How many millimeters long is it?

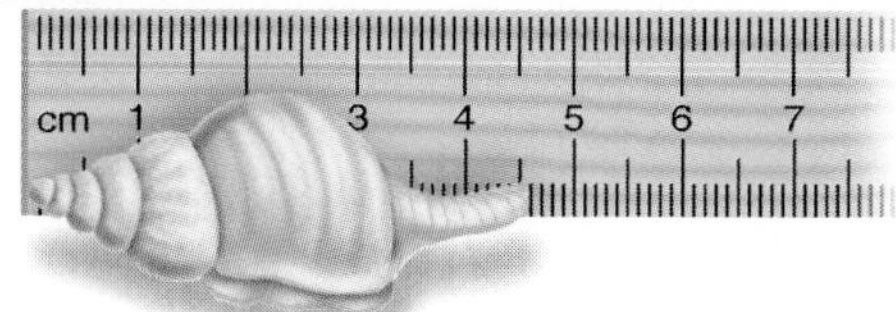

Liquid Volume To measure the volume of a liquid, or the amount of space it takes up, you will use a unit of measure known as the **liter (L).** One liter is the approximate volume of a medium-sized carton of milk. Smaller volumes are measured in milliliters (mL). Scientists use graduated cylinders to measure liquid volume.

Common Conversion

1 L = 1,000 mL

ACTIVITY The graduated cylinder in the picture is marked in milliliter divisions. Notice that the water in the cylinder has a curved surface. This curved surface is called the *meniscus*. To measure the volume, you must read the level at the lowest point of the meniscus. What is the volume of water in this graduated cylinder?

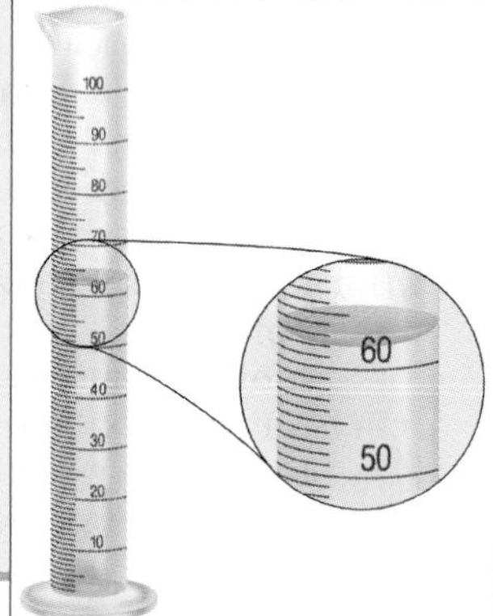

Mass To measure mass, or the amount of matter in an object, you will use a unit of measure known as the **gram (g)**. One gram is approximately the mass of a paper clip. Larger masses are measured in kilograms (kg). Scientists use a balance to find the mass of an object.

Common Conversion

1 kg = 1,000 g

ACTIVITY The electronic balance is measuring the mass of an apple in kilograms. What is the mass of the apple? Suppose a recipe for applesauce called for one kilogram of apples. About how many apples would you need?

Temperature

To measure the temperature of a substance, you will use the **Celsius scale.** Temperature is measured in degrees Celsius (°C) using a Celsius thermometer. Water freezes at 0°C and boils at 100°C.

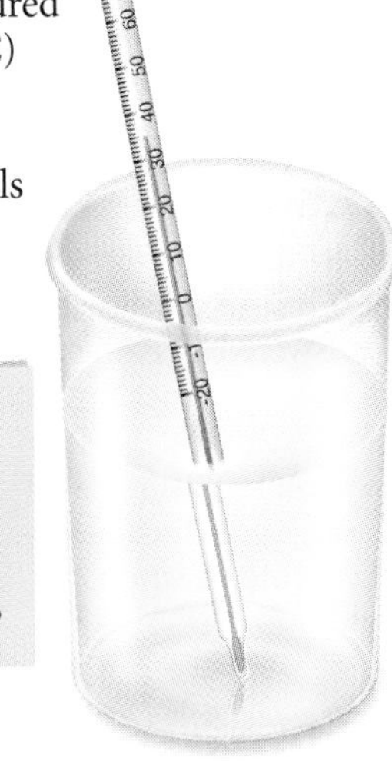

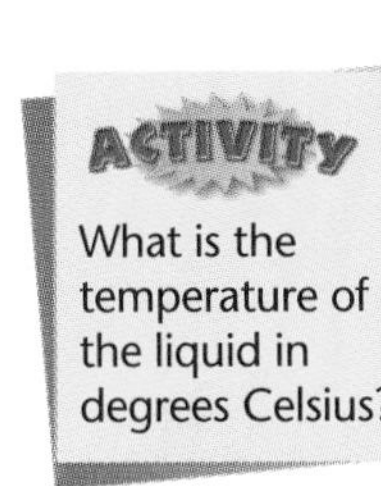

ACTIVITY What is the temperature of the liquid in degrees Celsius?

Converting SI Units

To use the SI system, you must know how to convert between units. Converting from one unit to another involves the skill of **calculating**, or using mathematical operations. Converting between SI units is similar to converting between dollars and dimes because both systems are based on multiples of ten.

Suppose you want to convert a length of 80 centimeters to meters. Follow these steps to convert between units.

1. Begin by writing down the measurement you want to convert—in this example, 80 centimeters.
2. Write a conversion factor that represents the relationship between the two units you are converting. In this example, the relationship is *1 meter = 100 centimeters.* Write this conversion factor as a fraction, making sure to place the units you are converting from (centimeters, in this example) in the denominator.
3. Multiply the measurement you want to convert by the fraction. When you do this, the units in the first measurement will cancel out with the units in the denominator. Your answer will be in the units you are converting to (meters, in this example).

Example

80 centimeters = __?__ meters

$$80 \text{ centimeters} \times \frac{1 \text{ meter}}{100 \text{ centimeters}} = \frac{80 \text{ meters}}{100}$$

$$= 0.8 \text{ meters}$$

Convert between the following units.

1. 600 millimeters = __?__ meters
2. 0.35 liters = __?__ milliliters
3. 1,050 grams = __?__ kilograms

SKILLS HANDBOOK

Mass *(Students should state that the mass of the apple is 0.1 kilograms. They would need 10 apples to make 1 kilogram.)* If students need practice measuring mass, have them use a balance to measure the mass of various common objects, such as coins, paper clips, and books.

Temperature *(Students should state that the temperature of the liquid is 35°C.)* If students need practice measuring temperature, have them use a Celsius thermometer to measure the temperature of various water samples.

Converting SI Units

Review the steps for converting SI units and work through the example with students. Then ask: **How many millimeters are in 80 centimeters?** *(Students should follow the steps to calculate that 80 centimeters is equal to 800 millimeters.)*

Have students do the conversion problems in the activity. *(**1.** 600 millimeters = 0.6 meters; **2.** 0.35 liters = 350 milliliters; **3.** 1,050 grams = 1.05 kilograms)* If students need more practice converting SI units, have students make up conversion problems and trade with a partner.

Conducting a Scientific Investigation

Posing Questions

Before students do the activity on the next page, walk them through the steps of a typical scientific investigation. Begin by asking: **Why is a scientific question important to a scientific investigation?** *(It is the reason for conducting a scientific investigation and how every investigation begins.)* **What is the scientific question in the activity at the bottom of the next page?** *(Is a ball's bounce affected by the height from which it is dropped?)*

Developing a Hypothesis

Emphasize that a hypothesis is a prediction about the outcome of a scientific investigation, but it is *not* a guess. Ask: **On what information do scientists base their hypotheses?** *(Their observations and previous knowledge or experience)* Point out that a hypothesis does not always turn out to be correct. Ask: **In that case, do you think the scientist wasted his or her time? Explain your answer.** *(No, because the scientist probably learned from the investigation and maybe could develop another hypothesis that could be supported.)*

Designing an Experiment

Have a volunteer read the Experimental Procedure in the box. Then call on students to identify the manipulated variable *(amount of salt added to water)*, the variables that are kept constant *(amount and starting temperature of water, placing containers in freezer)*, the responding variable *(time it takes water to freeze)*, and the control *(Container 3)*.

Ask: **How might the experiment be affected if Container 1 had only 100 mL of water?** *(It wouldn't be a fair comparison with the containers that have more water.)* **What if Container 3 was not included in the experiment?** *(You wouldn't have anything to compare the other two containers to know if their freezing times were faster or slower than normal.)* Help students understand the importance of keeping all variables constant except the manipulated variable. Also be sure they understand the role of the control. Then ask: **What operational definition is used in this experiment?** *("Frozen" means the time at which a wooden stick can no longer move in a container.)*

Conducting a Scientific Investigation

In some ways, scientists are like detectives, piecing together clues to learn about a process or event. One way that scientists gather clues is by carrying out experiments. An experiment tests an idea in a careful, orderly manner. Although all experiments do not follow the same steps in the same order, many follow a pattern similar to the one described here.

Posing Questions

Experiments begin by asking a scientific question. A scientific question is one that can be answered by gathering evidence. For example, the question "Which freezes faster—fresh water or salt water?" is a scientific question because you can carry out an investigation and gather information to answer the question.

Developing a Hypothesis

The next step is to form a hypothesis. A **hypothesis** is a prediction about the outcome of the experiment. Like all predictions, hypotheses are based on your observations and previous knowledge or experience. But, unlike many predictions, a hypothesis must be something that can be tested. A properly worded hypothesis should take the form of an *If... then...* statement. For example, a hypothesis might be *"If I add salt to fresh water, then the water will take longer to freeze."* A hypothesis worded this way serves as a rough outline of the experiment you should perform.

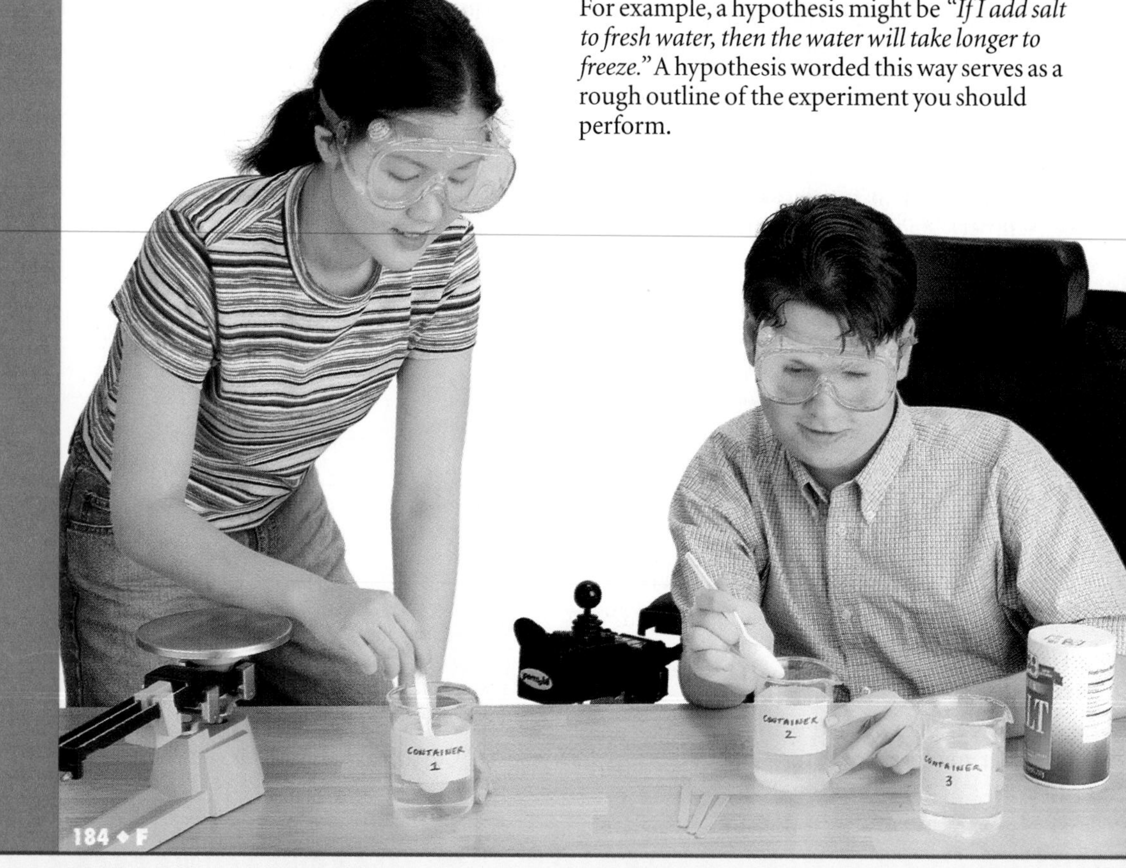

Designing an Experiment

Next you need to plan a way to test your hypothesis. Your plan should be written out as a step-by-step procedure and should describe the observations or measurements you will make.

Two important steps involved in designing an experiment are controlling variables and forming operational definitions.

Controlling Variables In a well-designed experiment, you need to keep all variables the same except for one. A **variable** is any factor that can change in an experiment. The factor that you change is called the **manipulated variable.** In this experiment, the manipulated variable is the amount of salt added to the water. Other factors, such as the amount of water or the starting temperature, are kept constant.

The factor that changes as a result of the manipulated variable is called the responding variable. The **responding variable** is what you measure or observe to obtain your results. In this experiment, the responding variable is how long the water takes to freeze.

An experiment in which all factors except one are kept constant is a **controlled experiment.** Most controlled experiments include a test called the control. In this experiment, Container 3 is the control. Because no salt is added to Container 3, you can compare the results from the other containers to it. Any difference in results must be due to the addition of salt alone.

Forming Operational Definitions
Another important aspect of a well-designed experiment is having clear operational definitions. An **operational definition** is a statement that describes how a particular variable is to be measured or how a term is to be defined. For example, in this experiment, how will you determine if the water has frozen? You might decide to insert a stick in each container at the start of the experiment. Your operational definition of "frozen" would be the time at which the stick can no longer move.

EXPERIMENTAL PROCEDURE

1. *Fill 3 containers with 300 milliliters of cold tap water.*
2. *Add 10 grams of salt to Container 1; stir. Add 20 grams of salt to Container 2; stir. Add no salt to Container 3.*
3. *Place the 3 containers in a freezer.*
4. *Check the containers every 15 minutes. Record your observations.*

Interpreting Data

The observations and measurements you make in an experiment are called data. At the end of an experiment, you need to analyze the data to look for any patterns or trends. Patterns often become clear if you organize your data in a data table or graph. Then think through what the data reveal. Do they support your hypothesis? Do they point out a flaw in your experiment? Do you need to collect more data?

Drawing Conclusions

A conclusion is a statement that sums up what you have learned from an experiment. When you draw a conclusion, you need to decide whether the data you collected support your hypothesis or not. You may need to repeat an experiment several times before you can draw any conclusions from it. Conclusions often lead you to pose new questions and plan new experiments to answer them.

ACTIVITY

Is a ball's bounce affected by the height from which it is dropped? Using the steps just described, plan a controlled experiment to investigate this problem.

SKILLS HANDBOOK

Interpreting Data

Emphasize the importance of collecting accurate and detailed data in a scientific investigation. Ask: **What if the students forgot to record the times that they made their observations in the experiment?** *(They wouldn't be able to completely analyze their data to draw valid conclusions.)* Then ask: **Why are data tables and graphs a good way to organize data?** *(It often makes it easier to compare and analyze data.)* You may wish to have students review the Skills Handbook pages on Creating Data Tables and Graphs at this point.

Drawing Conclusions

Help students understand that a conclusion is not necessarily the end of a scientific investigation. A conclusion about one experiment may lead right into another experiment. Point out that in scientific investigations, a conclusion is a summary and explanation of the results of an experiment.

Tell students to suppose that for the Experimental Procedure described on this page, they obtained the following results: Container 1 froze in 45 minutes, Container 2 in 80 minutes, and Container 3 in 25 minutes. Ask: **What conclusions can you draw about this experiment?** *(Students might conclude that the more salt that is added to fresh water, the longer it takes the water to freeze. The hypothesis is supported, and the question of which freezes faster is answered—fresh water.)*

ACTIVITY

You might wish to have students work in pairs to plan the controlled experiment. *(Students should develop a hypothesis, such as "If I increase the height from which a ball is dropped, then the height of its bounce will increase." They can test the hypothesis by dropping balls from varying heights (the manipulated variable). All trials should be done with the same kind of ball and on the same surface (constant variables). For each trial, they should measure the height of the bounce (responding variable).)* After students have designed the experiment, provide rubber balls and invite them to carry out the experiment so they can collect and interpret data and draw conclusions.

Thinking Critically

Comparing and Contrasting

Emphasize that the skill of comparing and contrasting often relies on good observation skills, as in this activity. *(Students' answers may vary. Sample answer: Similarities—both are dogs and have four legs, two eyes, two ears, brown and white fur, black noses, pink tongues; Differences—smooth coat vs. rough coat, more white fur vs. more brown fur, shorter vs. taller, long ears vs. short ears.)*

Applying Concepts

Point out to students that they apply concepts that they learn in school in their daily lives. For example, they learn to add, subtract, multiply, and divide in school. If they get a paper route or some other part-time job, they can apply those concepts. Challenge students to practice applying concepts by doing the activity. *(People add antifreeze to the water in their car's radiator to lower the temperature at which the solution will freeze, and thus keep the water in the radiator from freezing.)*

Interpreting Illustrations

Again, point out the need for good observation skills. Ask: **What is the difference between "interpreting illustrations" and "looking at the pictures"?** *("Interpreting illustrations" requires thorough examination of the illustration, caption, and labels, while "looking at the pictures" implies less thorough examination.)* Encourage students to thoroughly examine the diagram as they do the activity. *(Students' paragraphs may vary, but should describe the internal anatomy of an earthworm, including some of the organs in the earthworm.)*

Thinking Critically

Has a friend ever asked for your advice about a problem? If so, you may have helped your friend think through the problem in a logical way. Without knowing it, you used critical-thinking skills to help your friend. Critical thinking involves the use of reasoning and logic to solve problems or make decisions. Some critical-thinking skills are described below.

Comparing and Contrasting

When you examine two objects for similarities and differences, you are using the skill of **comparing and contrasting.** Comparing involves identifying similarities, or common characteristics. Contrasting involves identifying differences. Analyzing objects in this way can help you discover details that you might otherwise overlook.

Compare and contrast the two animals in the photo. First list all the similarities that you see. Then list all the differences.

Applying Concepts

When you use your knowledge about one situation to make sense of a similar situation, you are using the skill of **applying concepts.** Being able to transfer your knowledge from one situation to another shows that you truly understand a concept. You may use this skill in answering test questions that present different problems from the ones you've reviewed in class.

You have just learned that water takes longer to freeze when other substances are mixed into it. Use this knowledge to explain why people add a substance called antifreeze to their car's radiator in the winter.

Interpreting Illustrations

Diagrams, photographs, and maps are included in textbooks to help clarify what you read. These illustrations show processes, places, and ideas in a visual manner. The skill called **interpreting illustrations** can help you learn from these visual elements. To understand an illustration, take the time to study the illustration along with all the written information that accompanies it. Captions identify the key concepts shown in the illustration. Labels point out the important parts of a diagram or map, while keys identify the symbols used in a map.

Blood vessels
Reproductive organs
Hearts
Brain
Mouth
Bristles
Digestive tract
Nerve cord
Waste-removal organs
Intestine

▲ **Internal anatomy of an earthworm**

Study the diagram above. Then write a short paragraph explaining what you have learned.

Relating Cause and Effect

If one event causes another event to occur, the two events are said to have a cause-and-effect relationship. When you determine that such a relationship exists between two events, you use a skill called **relating cause and effect.** For example, if you notice an itchy, red bump on your skin, you might infer that a mosquito bit you. The mosquito bite is the cause, and the bump is the effect.

It is important to note that two events do not necessarily have a cause-and-effect relationship just because they occur together. Scientists carry out experiments or use past experience to determine whether a cause-and-effect relationship exists.

> ACTIVITY
>
> You are on a camping trip and your flashlight has stopped working. List some possible causes for the flashlight malfunction. How could you determine which cause-and-effect relationship has left you in the dark?

Making Generalizations

When you draw a conclusion about an entire group based on information about only some of the group's members, you are using a skill called **making generalizations.** For a generalization to be valid, the sample you choose must be large enough and representative of the entire group. You might, for example, put this skill to work at a farm stand if you see a sign that says, "Sample some grapes before you buy." If you sample a few sweet grapes, you may conclude that all the grapes are sweet—and purchase a large bunch.

> ACTIVITY
>
> A team of scientists needs to determine whether the water in a large reservoir is safe to drink. How could they use the skill of making generalizations to help them? What should they do?

Making Judgments

When you evaluate something to decide whether it is good or bad, or right or wrong, you are using a skill called **making judgments.** For example, you make judgments when you decide to eat healthful foods or to pick up litter in a park. Before you make a judgment, you need to think through the pros and cons of a situation, and identify the values or standards that you hold.

> ACTIVITY
>
> Should children and teens be required to wear helmets when bicycling? Explain why you feel the way you do.

Problem Solving

When you use critical-thinking skills to resolve an issue or decide on a course of action, you are using a skill called **problem solving.** Some problems, such as how to convert a fraction into a decimal, are straightforward. Other problems, such as figuring out why your computer has stopped working, are complex. Some complex problems can be solved using the trial and error method—try out one solution first, and if that doesn't work, try another. Other useful problem-solving strategies include making models and brainstorming possible solutions with a partner.

Relating Cause and Effect

Emphasize that not all events that occur together have a cause-and-effect relationship. For example, tell students that you went to the grocery and your car stalled. Ask: **Is there a cause-and-effect relationship in this situation? Explain your answer.** *(No, because going to the grocery could not cause a car to stall. There must be another cause to make the car stall.)* Have students do the activity to practice relating cause and effect. *(Students should identify that the flashlight not working is the effect. Some possible causes include dead batteries, a burned-out light bulb, or a loose part.)*

Making Generalizations

Point out the importance of having a large, representative sample before making a generalization. Ask: **If you went fishing at a lake and caught three catfish, could you make the generalization that all fish in the lake are catfish? Why or why not?** *(No, because there might be other kinds of fish you didn't catch because they didn't like the bait or they may be in other parts of the lake.)* **How could you make a generalization about the kinds of fish in the lake?** *(By having a larger sample)* Have students do the activity to practice making generalizations. *(The scientists should collect and test water samples from a number of different parts of the reservoir.)*

Making Judgments

Remind students that they make a judgment almost every time they make a decision. Ask: **What steps should you follow to make a judgment?** *(Gather information, list pros and cons, analyze values, make judgment)* Invite students to do the activity, and then to share and discuss the judgments they made. *(Students' judgments will vary, but should be supported by valid reasoning. Sample answer: Children and teens should be required to wear helmets when bicycling because helmets have been proven to save lives and reduce head injuries.)*

Problem Solving

ACTIVITY

Challenge student pairs to solve a problem about a soapbox derby. Explain that their younger brother is building a car to enter in the race. The brother wants to know how to make his soapbox car go faster. After student pairs have considered the problem, have them share their ideas about solutions with the class. *(Most will probably suggest using trial and error by making small changes to the car and testing the car after each change. Some students may suggest making and manipulating a model.)*

Skills Handbook

Organizing Information

Concept Maps

Challenge students to make a concept map with at least three levels of concepts to organize information about types of transportation. All students should start with the phrase *types of transportation* at the top of the concept map. After that point, their concept maps may vary. *(For example, some students might place* private transportation *and* public transportation *at the next level, while other students might have* human-powered *and* gas-powered. *Make sure students connect the concepts with linking words. Challenge students to include cross-linkages as well.)*

Compare/ Contrast Tables

ACTIVITY

Have students make their own compare/contrast tables using two or more different sports or other activities, such as playing musical instruments. Emphasize that students should select characteristics that highlight the similarities and differences between the activities. *(Students' compare/contrast tables should include several appropriate characteristics and list information about each activity for every characteristic.)*

Organizing Information

As you read this textbook, how can you make sense of all the information it contains? Some useful tools to help you organize information are shown on this page. These tools are called *graphic organizers* because they give you a visual picture of a topic, showing at a glance how key concepts are related.

Concept Maps

Concept maps are useful tools for organizing information on broad topics. A concept map begins with a general concept and shows how it can be broken down into more specific concepts. In that way, relationships between concepts become easier to understand.

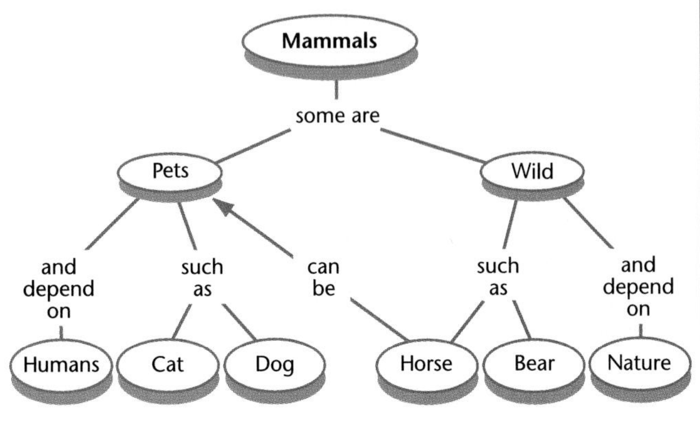

A concept map is constructed by placing concept words (usually nouns) in ovals and connecting them with linking words. Often, the most general concept word is placed at the top, and the words become more specific as you move downward. Often the linking words, which are written on a line extending between two ovals, describe the relationship between the two concepts they connect. If you follow any string of concepts and linking words down the map, it should read like a sentence.

Some concept maps include linking words that connect a concept on one branch of the map to a concept on another branch. These linking words, called cross-linkages, show more complex interrelationships among concepts.

Compare/Contrast Tables

Compare/contrast tables are useful tools for sorting out the similarities and differences between two or more items. A table provides an organized framework in which to compare items based on specific characteristics that you identify.

To create a compare/contrast table, list the items to be compared across the top of a table. Then list the characteristics that will form the basis of your comparison in the left-hand column. Complete the table by filling in information about each characteristic, first for one item and then for the other.

Characteristic	Baseball	Basketball
Number of Players	9	5
Playing Field	Baseball diamond	Basketball court
Equipment	Bat, baseball, mitts	Basket, basketball

Venn Diagrams

Another way to show similarities and differences between items is with a Venn diagram. A Venn diagram consists of two or more circles that partially overlap. Each circle represents a particular concept or idea. Common characteristics, or similarities, are written within the area of overlap between the two circles. Unique characteristics, or differences, are written in the parts of the circles outside the area of overlap.

To create a Venn diagram, draw two overlapping circles. Label the circles with the names of the items being compared. Write the unique characteristics in each circle outside the area of overlap. Then write the shared characteristics within the area of overlap.

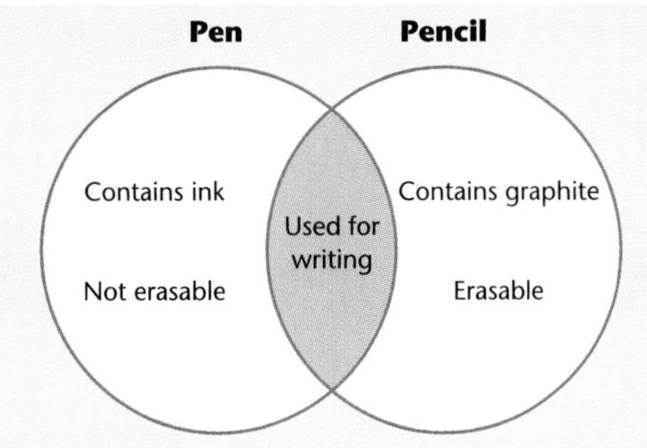

Flowcharts

A flowchart can help you understand the order in which certain events have occurred or should occur. Flowcharts are useful for outlining the stages in a process or the steps in a procedure.

To make a flowchart, write a brief description of each event in a box. Place the first event at the top of the page, followed by the second event, the third event, and so on. Then draw an arrow to connect each event to the one that occurs next.

Preparing Pasta

Boil water → Cook pasta → Drain water → Add sauce

Cycle Diagrams

A cycle diagram can be used to show a sequence of events that is continuous, or cyclical. A continuous sequence does not have an end because, when the final event is over, the first event begins again. Like a flowchart, a cycle diagram can help you understand the order of events.

To create a cycle diagram, write a brief description of each event in a box. Place one event at the top of the page in the center. Then, moving in a clockwise direction around an imaginary circle, write each event in its proper sequence. Draw arrows that connect each event to the one that occurs next, forming a continuous circle.

Steps in a Science Experiment

Pose a question → Develop a hypothesis → Design an experiment → Interpret data → Draw conclusions → Pose a question

SKILLS HANDBOOK

Venn Diagrams — ACTIVITY

Students can use the same information from their compare/contrast tables to create a Venn diagram. Make sure students understand that the overlapping area of the circles is used to list similarities and the parts of the circles outside the overlap area are used to show differences. If students want to list similarities and differences among three activities, show them how to add a third circle that overlaps each of the other two circles and has an area of overlap for all three circles. *(Students' Venn diagrams will vary. Make sure they have accurately listed similarities in the overlap area and differences in the parts of the circles that do not overlap.)*

Flowcharts — ACTIVITY

Encourage students to create a flowchart to show the things they did this morning as they got ready for school. Remind students that a flowchart should show the correct order in which events occurred or should occur. *(Students' flowcharts will vary somewhat. A typical flowchart might include: got up → ate breakfast → took a shower → brushed teeth → got dressed → gathered books and homework → put on jacket.)*

Cycle Diagrams — ACTIVITY

Review that a cycle diagram shows a sequence of events that is continuous. Then challenge students to create a cycle diagram that shows how the weather changes with the seasons where they live. *(Students' cycle diagrams may vary, though most will include four steps, one for each season.)*

Creating Data Tables and Graphs

Data Tables

Have students create a data table to show how much time they spend on different activities during one week. Suggest that students first list the main activities they do every week. Then they should determine the amount of time they spend on each activity each day. Remind students to give this data table a title. *(Students' data tables will vary. A sample data table is shown below.)*

Bar Graphs

Students can use the data from their data table above to make a bar graph showing how much time they spend on different activities during a week. Help students understand that on this particular graph, the time spent on each activity is the responding variable, because it is the result being measured. Therefore, the vertical axis should be divided into units of time, such as hours. Remind students to label both axes and give their graph a title. *(Students' bar graphs will vary. A sample bar graph is shown below.)*

Creating Data Tables and Graphs

How can you make sense of the data in a science experiment? The first step is to organize the data to help you understand them. Data tables and graphs are helpful tools for organizing data.

Data Tables

You have gathered your materials and set up your experiment. But before you start, you need to plan a way to record what happens during the experiment. By creating a data table, you can record your observations and measurements in an orderly way.

Suppose, for example, that a scientist conducted an experiment to find out how many Calories people of different body weights burn while doing various activities. The data table shows the results.

CALORIES BURNED IN 30 MINUTES OF ACTIVITY

Body Weight	Experiment 1 Bicycling	Experiment 2 Playing Basketball	Experiment 3 Watching Television
30 kg	60 Calories	120 Calories	21 Calories
40 kg	77 Calories	164 Calories	27 Calories
50 kg	95 Calories	206 Calories	33 Calories
60 kg	114 Calories	248 Calories	38 Calories

Notice in this data table that the manipulated variable (body weight) is the heading of one column. The responding variable (for Experiment 1, the number of Calories burned while bicycling) is the heading of the next column. Additional columns were added for related experiments.

Bar Graphs

To compare how many Calories a person burns doing various activities, you could create a bar graph. A bar graph is used to display data in a number of separate, or distinct, categories. In this example, bicycling, playing basketball, and watching television are three separate categories.

To create a bar graph, follow these steps.

1. On graph paper, draw a horizontal, or x-, axis and a vertical, or y-, axis.
2. Write the names of the categories to be graphed along the horizontal axis. Include an overall label for the axis as well.
3. Label the vertical axis with the name of the responding variable. Include units of measurement. Then create a scale along the axis by marking off equally spaced numbers that cover the range of the data collected.
4. For each category, draw a solid bar using the scale on the vertical axis to determine the appropriate height. For example, for bicycling, draw the bar as high as the 60 mark on the vertical axis. Make all the bars the same width and leave equal spaces between them.
5. Add a title that describes the graph.

Calories Burned by a 30-kilogram Person in Various Activities

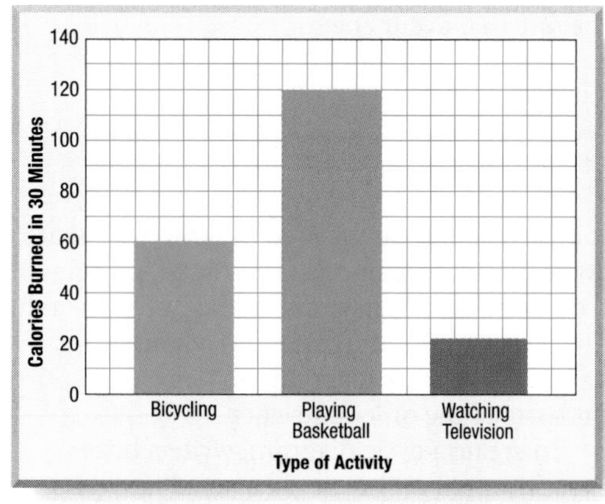

Time Spent on Different Activities in a Week

	Going to Classes	Eating Meals	Playing Soccer	Watching Television
Monday	6	2	2	0.5
Tuesday	6	1.5	1.5	1.5
Wednesday	6	2	1	2
Thursday	6	2	2	1.5
Friday	6	2	2	0.5
Saturday	0	2.5	2.5	1
Sunday	0	3	1	2

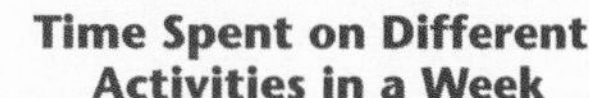

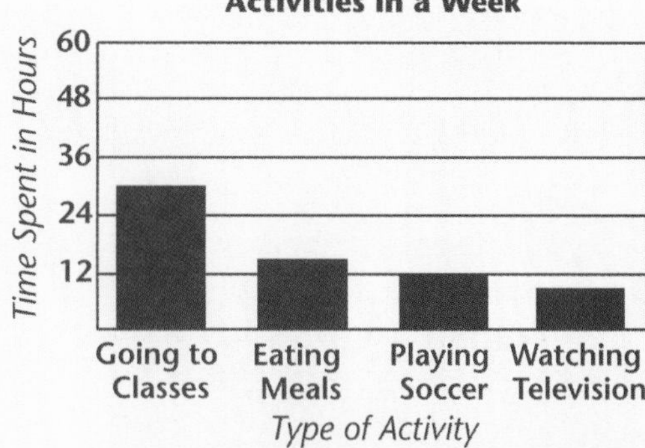

Line Graphs

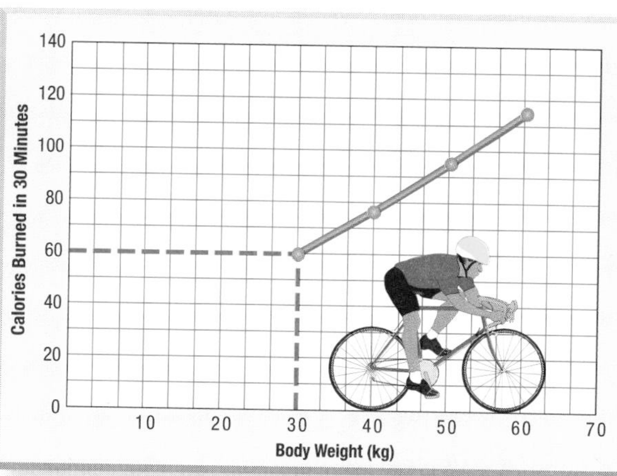

To see whether a relationship exists between body weight and the number of Calories burned while bicycling, you could create a line graph. A line graph is used to display data that show how one variable (the responding variable) changes in response to another variable (the manipulated variable). You can use a line graph when your manipulated variable is *continuous*, that is, when there are other points between the ones that you tested. In this example, body weight is a continuous variable because there are other body weights between 30 and 40 kilograms (for example, 31 kilograms). Time is another example of a continuous variable.

Line graphs are powerful tools because they allow you to estimate values for conditions that you did not test in the experiment. For example, you can use the line graph to estimate that a 35-kilogram person would burn 68 Calories while bicycling.

To create a line graph, follow these steps.

1. On graph paper, draw a horizontal, or *x*-, axis and a vertical, or *y*-, axis.
2. Label the horizontal axis with the name of the manipulated variable. Label the vertical axis with the name of the responding variable. Include units of measurement.
3. Create a scale on each axis by marking off equally spaced numbers that cover the range of the data collected.
4. Plot a point on the graph for each piece of data. In the line graph above, the dotted lines show how to plot the first data point (30 kilograms and 60 Calories). Draw an imaginary vertical line extending up from the horizontal axis at the 30-kilogram mark. Then draw an imaginary horizontal line extending across from the vertical axis at the 60-Calorie mark. Plot the point where the two lines intersect.
5. Connect the plotted points with a solid line. (In some cases, it may be more appropriate to draw a line that shows the general trend of the plotted points. In those cases, some of the points may fall above or below the line.)
6. Add a title that identifies the variables or relationship in the graph.

ACTIVITY

Create line graphs to display the data from Experiment 2 and Experiment 3 in the data table.

ACTIVITY

You read in the newspaper that a total of 4 centimeters of rain fell in your area in June, 2.5 centimeters fell in July, and 1.5 centimeters fell in August. What type of graph would you use to display these data? Use graph paper to create the graph.

SKILLS HANDBOOK

Line Graphs

Walk students through the steps involved in creating a line graph using the example illustrated on the page. For example, ask: **What is the label on the horizontal axis? On the vertical axis?** *(Body Weight (kg); Calories Burned in 30 Minutes)* **What scales are used on each axis?** *(10 kg on the x-axis and 20 calories on the y-axis)* **What does the second data point represent?** *(77 Calories burned for a body weight of 40 kg)* **What trend or pattern does the graph show?** *(The number of Calories burned in 30 minutes of cycling increases with body weight.)*

ACTIVITY Have students follow the steps to carry out the first activity. *(Students should make a different graph for each experiment with different y-axis scales to practice making scales appropriate for data. See sample graphs below.)*

ACTIVITY Have students carry out the second activity. *(Students should conclude that a bar graph would be best to display the data. A sample bar graph for these data is shown below.)*

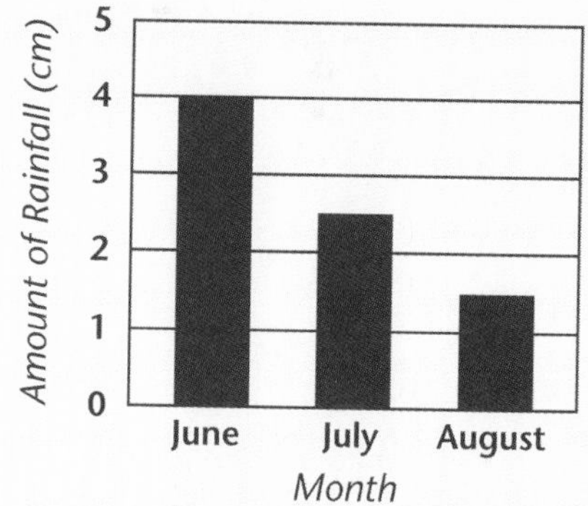

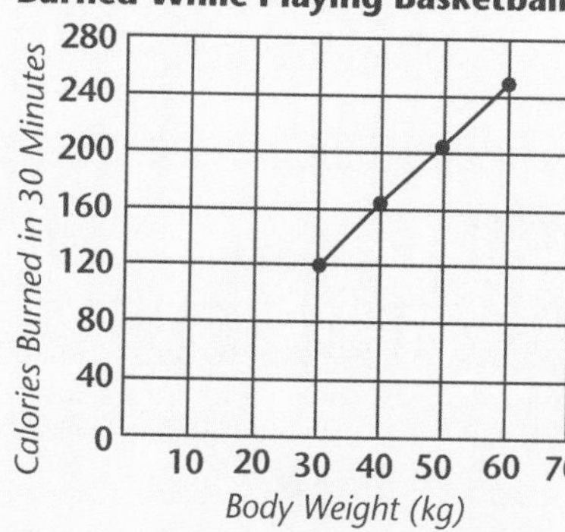

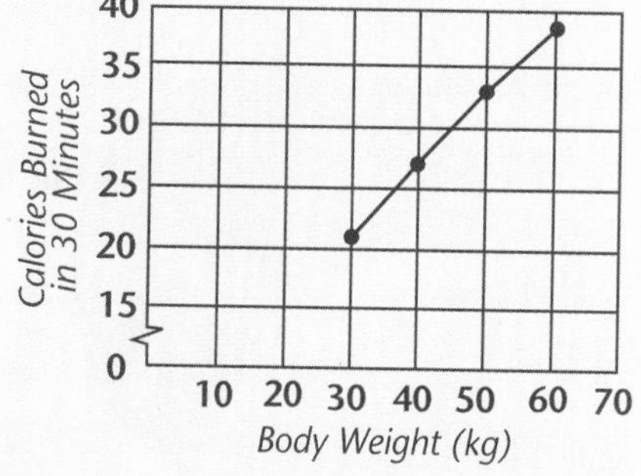

Circle Graphs

Emphasize that a circle graph has to include 100 percent of the categories for the topic being graphed. For example, ask: **Could the data in the bar graph titled "Calories Burned by a 30-kilogram Person in Various Activities" (on the previous page) be shown in a circle graph? Why or why not?** *(No, because it does not include all the possible ways a 30-kilogram person can burn Calories.)* Then walk students through the steps for making a circle graph. Help students to use a compass and a protractor. Use the protractor to illustrate that a circle has 360 degrees. Make sure students understand the mathematical calculations involved in making a circle graph.

You might wish to have students work in pairs to complete the activity. **ACTIVITY** *(Students' circle graphs should look like the graph below.)*

Circle Graphs

Like bar graphs, circle graphs can be used to display data in a number of separate categories. Unlike bar graphs, however, circle graphs can only be used when you have data for *all* the categories that make up a given topic. A circle graph is sometimes called a pie chart because it resembles a pie cut into slices. The pie represents the entire topic, while the slices represent the individual categories. The size of a slice indicates what percentage of the whole a particular category makes up.

The data table below shows the results of a survey in which 24 teenagers were asked to identify their favorite sport. The data were then used to create the circle graph at the right.

FAVORITE SPORTS

Sport	Number of Students
Soccer	8
Basketball	6
Bicycling	6
Swimming	4

To create a circle graph, follow these steps.

1. Use a compass to draw a circle. Mark the center of the circle with a point. Then draw a line from the center point to the top of the circle.
2. Determine the size of each "slice" by setting up a proportion where x equals the number of degrees in a slice. (NOTE: A circle contains 360 degrees.) For example, to find the number of degrees in the "soccer" slice, set up the following proportion:

$$\frac{\text{students who prefer soccer}}{\text{total number of students}} = \frac{x}{\text{total number of degrees in a circle}}$$

$$\frac{8}{24} = \frac{x}{360}$$

Cross-multiply and solve for x.

$$24x = 8 \times 360$$

$$x = 120$$

The "soccer" slice should contain 120 degrees.

Sports That Teens Prefer

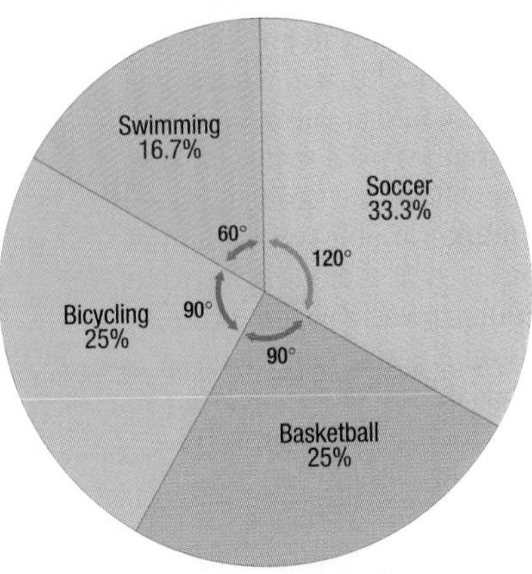

3. Use a protractor to measure the angle of the first slice, using the line you drew to the top of the circle as the 0° line. Draw a line from the center of the circle to the edge for the angle you measured.
4. Continue around the circle by measuring the size of each slice with the protractor. Start measuring from the edge of the previous slice so the wedges do not overlap. When you are done, the entire circle should be filled in.
5. Determine the percentage of the whole circle that each slice represents. To do this, divide the number of degrees in a slice by the total number of degrees in a circle (360), and multiply by 100%. For the "soccer" slice, you can find the percentage as follows:

$$\frac{120}{360} \times 100\% = 33.3\%$$

6. Use a different color to shade in each slice. Label each slice with the name of the category and with the percentage of the whole it represents.
7. Add a title to the circle graph.

ACTIVITY In a class of 28 students, 12 students take the bus to school, 10 students walk, and 6 students ride their bicycles. Create a circle graph to display these data.

Ways Students Get to School

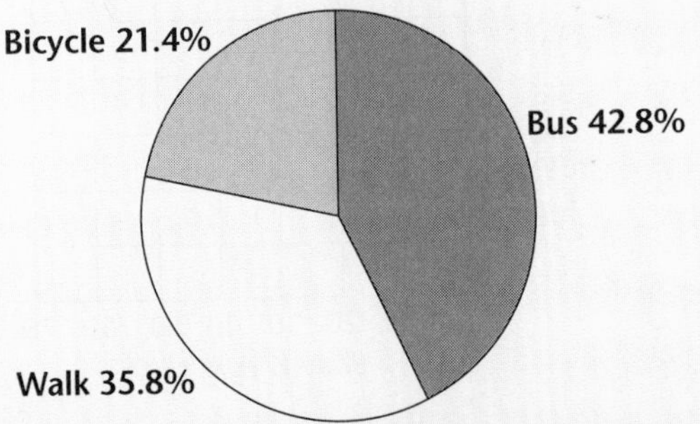

Laboratory Safety

Safety Symbols

These symbols alert you to possible dangers in the laboratory and remind you to work carefully.

Safety Goggles Always wear safety goggles to protect your eyes in any activity involving chemicals, flames or heating, or the possibility of broken glassware.

Lab Apron Wear a laboratory apron to protect your skin and clothing from damage.

Breakage You are working with materials that may be breakable, such as glass containers, glass tubing, thermometers, or funnels. Handle breakable materials with care. Do not touch broken glassware.

Heat-resistant Gloves Use an oven mitt or other hand protection when handling hot materials. Hot plates, hot glassware, or hot water can cause burns. Do not touch hot objects with your bare hands.

Heating Use a clamp or tongs to pick up hot glassware. Do not touch hot objects with your bare hands.

Sharp Object Pointed-tip scissors, scalpels, knives, needles, pins, or tacks are sharp. They can cut or puncture your skin. Always direct a sharp edge or point away from yourself and others. Use sharp instruments only as instructed.

Electric Shock Avoid the possibility of electric shock. Never use electrical equipment around water, or when the equipment is wet or your hands are wet. Be sure cords are untangled and cannot trip anyone. Disconnect the equipment when it is not in use.

Corrosive Chemical You are working with an acid or another corrosive chemical. Avoid getting it on your skin or clothing, or in your eyes. Do not inhale the vapors. Wash your hands when you are finished with the activity.

Poison Do not let any poisonous chemical come in contact with your skin, and do not inhale its vapors. Wash your hands when you are finished with the activity.

Physical Safety When an experiment involves physical activity, take precautions to avoid injuring yourself or others. Follow instructions from your teacher. Alert your teacher if there is any reason you should not participate in the activity.

Animal Safety Treat live animals with care to avoid harming the animals or yourself. Working with animal parts or preserved animals also may require caution. Wash your hands when you are finished with the activity.

Plant Safety Handle plants in the laboratory or during field work only as directed by your teacher. If you are allergic to certain plants, tell your teacher before doing an activity in which those plants are used. Avoid touching harmful plants such as poison ivy, poison oak, or poison sumac, or plants with thorns. Wash your hands when you are finished with the activity.

Flames You may be working with flames from a lab burner, candle, or matches. Tie back loose hair and clothing. Follow instructions from your teacher about lighting and extinguishing flames.

No Flames Flammable materials may be present. Make sure there are no flames, sparks, or other exposed heat sources present.

Fumes When poisonous or unpleasant vapors may be involved, work in a ventilated area. Avoid inhaling vapors directly. Only test an odor when directed to do so by your teacher, and use a wafting motion to direct the vapor toward your nose.

Disposal Chemicals and other laboratory materials used in the activity must be disposed of safely. Follow the instructions from your teacher.

Hand Washing Wash your hands thoroughly when finished with the activity. Use antibacterial soap and warm water. Lather both sides of your hands and between your fingers. Rinse well.

General Safety Awareness You may see this symbol when none of the symbols described earlier appears. In this case, follow the specific instructions provided. You may also see this symbol when you are asked to develop your own procedure in a lab. Have your teacher approve your plan before you go further.

Laboratory Safety

Laboratory safety is an essential element of a successful science class. It is important for you to emphasize laboratory safety to students. Students need to understand exactly what is safe and unsafe behavior, and what the rationale is behind each safety rule.

Review with students the Safety Symbols and Science Safety Rules listed on this and the next two pages. Then follow the safety guidelines below to ensure that your classroom will be a safe place for students to learn science.

- Post safety rules in the classroom and review them regularly with students.
- Familiarize yourself with the safety procedures for each activity before introducing it to your students.
- Review specific safety precautions with students before beginning every science activity.
- Always act as an exemplary role model by displaying safe behavior.
- Know how to use safety equipment, such as fire extinguishers and fire blankets, and always have it accessible.
- Have students practice leaving the classroom quickly and orderly to prepare them for emergencies.
- Explain to students how to use the intercom or other available means of communication to get help during an emergency.
- Never leave students unattended while they are engaged in science activities.
- Provide enough space for students to safely carry out science activities.
- Keep your classroom and all science materials in proper condition. Replace worn or broken items.
- Instruct students to report all accidents and injuries to you immediately.

Laboratory Safety

Additional tips are listed below for the Science Safety Rules discussed on these two pages. Please keep these tips in mind when you carry out science activities in your classroom.

General Precautions

- For open-ended activities like Chapter Projects, go over general safety guidelines with students. Have students submit their procedures or design plans in writing and check them for safety considerations.
- In an activity where students are directed to taste something, be sure to store the material in clean, *nonscience* containers. Distribute the material to students in *new* plastic or paper dispensables, which should be discarded after the tasting. Tasting or eating should never be done in a lab classroom.
- During physical activity, make sure students do not overexert themselves.
- Remind students to handle microscopes and telescopes with care to avoid breakage.

Heating and Fire Safety

- No flammable substances should be in use around hot plates, light bulbs, or open flames.
- Test tubes should be heated only in water baths.
- Students should be permitted to strike matches to light candles or burners *only* with strict supervision. When possible, you should light the flames, especially when working with sixth graders.
- Be sure to have proper ventilation when fumes are produced during a procedure.
- All electrical equipment used in the lab should have GFI switches.

Science Safety Rules

To prepare yourself to work safely in the laboratory, read over the following safety rules. Then read them a second time. Make sure you understand and follow each rule. Ask your teacher to explain any rules you do not understand.

Dress Code

1. To protect yourself from injuring your eyes, wear safety goggles whenever you work with chemicals, burners, glassware, or any substance that might get into your eyes. If you wear contact lenses, notify your teacher.
2. Wear a lab apron or coat whenever you work with corrosive chemicals or substances that can stain.
3. Tie back long hair to keep it away from any chemicals, flames, or equipment.
4. Remove or tie back any article of clothing or jewelry that can hang down and touch chemicals, flames, or equipment. Roll up or secure long sleeves.
5. Never wear open shoes or sandals.

General Precautions

6. Read all directions for an experiment several times before beginning the activity. Carefully follow all written and oral instructions. If you are in doubt about any part of the experiment, ask your teacher for assistance.
7. Never perform activities that are not assigned or authorized by your teacher. Obtain permission before "experimenting" on your own. Never handle any equipment unless you have specific permission.
8. Never perform lab activities without direct supervision.
9. Never eat or drink in the laboratory.
10. Keep work areas clean and tidy at all times. Bring only notebooks and lab manuals or written lab procedures to the work area. All other items, such as purses and backpacks, should be left in a designated area.
11. Do not engage in horseplay.

First Aid

12. Always report all accidents or injuries to your teacher, no matter how minor. Notify your teacher immediately about any fires.
13. Learn what to do in case of specific accidents, such as getting acid in your eyes or on your skin. (Rinse acids from your body with lots of water.)
14. Be aware of the location of the first-aid kit, but do not use it unless instructed by your teacher. In case of injury, your teacher should administer first aid. Your teacher may also send you to the school nurse or call a physician.
15. Know the location of emergency equipment, such as the fire extinguisher and fire blanket, and know how to use it.
16. Know the location of the nearest telephone and whom to contact in an emergency.

Heating and Fire Safety

17. Never use a heat source, such as a candle, burner, or hot plate, without wearing safety goggles.
18. Never heat anything unless instructed to do so. A chemical that is harmless when cool may be dangerous when heated.
19. Keep all combustible materials away from flames. Never use a flame or spark near a combustible chemical.
20. Never reach across a flame.
21. Before using a laboratory burner, make sure you know proper procedures for lighting and adjusting the burner, as demonstrated by your teacher. Do not touch the burner. It may be hot. And never leave a lighted burner unattended!
22. Chemicals can splash or boil out of a heated test tube. When heating a substance in a test tube, make sure that the mouth of the tube is not pointed at you or anyone else.
23. Never heat a liquid in a closed container. The expanding gases produced may blow the container apart.
24. Before picking up a container that has been heated, hold the back of your hand near it. If you can feel heat on the back of your hand, the container is too hot to handle. Use an oven mitt to pick up a container that has been heated.

Using Chemicals Safely

- When students use both chemicals and microscopes in one activity, microscopes should be in a separate part of the room from the chemicals so that when students remove their goggles to use the microscopes, their eyes are not at risk.

Using Glassware Safely

- Use plastic containers, graduated cylinders, and beakers whenever possible. If using glass, students should wear safety goggles.
- Use only nonmercury thermometers with anti-roll protectors.
- Check all glassware periodically for chips and scratches, which can cause cuts and breakage.

Using Chemicals Safely

25. Never mix chemicals "for the fun of it." You might produce a dangerous, possibly explosive substance.
26. Never put your face near the mouth of a container that holds chemicals. Never touch, taste, or smell a chemical unless you are instructed by your teacher to do so. Many chemicals are poisonous.
27. Use only those chemicals needed in the activity. Read and double-check labels on supply bottles before removing any chemicals. Take only as much as you need. Keep all containers closed when chemicals are not being used.
28. Dispose of all chemicals as instructed by your teacher. To avoid contamination, never return chemicals to their original containers. Never simply pour chemicals or other substances into the sink or trash containers.
29. Be extra careful when working with acids or bases. Pour all chemicals over the sink or a container, not over your work surface.
30. If you are instructed to test for odors, use a wafting motion to direct the odors to your nose. Do not inhale the fumes directly from the container.
31. When mixing an acid and water, always pour the water into the container first and then add the acid to the water. Never pour water into an acid.
32. Take extreme care not to spill any material in the laboratory. Wash chemical spills and splashes immediately with plenty of water. Immediately begin rinsing with water any acids that get on your skin or clothing, and notify your teacher of any acid spill at the same time.

Using Glassware Safely

33. Never force glass tubing or thermometers into a rubber stopper or rubber tubing. Have your teacher insert the glass tubing or thermometer if required for an activity.
34. If you are using a laboratory burner, use a wire screen to protect glassware from any flame. Never heat glassware that is not thoroughly dry on the outside.
35. Keep in mind that hot glassware looks cool. Never pick up glassware without first checking to see if it is hot. Use an oven mitt. See rule 24.
36. Never use broken or chipped glassware. If glassware breaks, notify your teacher and dispose of the glassware in the proper broken-glassware container. Never handle broken glass with your bare hands.
37. Never eat or drink from lab glassware.
38. Thoroughly clean glassware before putting it away.

Using Sharp Instruments

39. Handle scalpels or other sharp instruments with extreme care. Never cut material toward you; cut away from you.
40. Immediately notify your teacher if you cut your skin when working in the laboratory.

Animal and Plant Safety

41. Never perform experiments that cause pain, discomfort, or harm to mammals, birds, reptiles, fishes, or amphibians. This rule applies at home as well as in the classroom.
42. Animals should be handled only if absolutely necessary. Your teacher will instruct you as to how to handle each animal species brought into the classroom.
43. If you know that you are allergic to certain plants, molds, or animals, tell your teacher before doing an activity in which these are used.
44. During field work, protect your skin by wearing long pants, long sleeves, socks, and closed shoes. Know how to recognize the poisonous plants and fungi in your area, as well as plants with thorns, and avoid contact with them.
45. Never eat any part of an unidentified plant or fungus.
46. Wash your hands thoroughly after handling animals or the cage containing animals. Wash your hands when you are finished with any activity involving animal parts, plants, or soil.

End-of-Experiment Rules

47. After an experiment has been completed, clean up your work area and return all equipment to its proper place.
48. Dispose of waste materials as instructed by your teacher.
49. Wash your hands after every experiment.
50. Always turn off all burners or hot plates when they are not in use. Unplug hot plates and other electrical equipment. If you used a burner, check that the gas-line valve to the burner is off as well.

Using Sharp Instruments

- Always use blunt-tip safety scissors, except when pointed-tip scissors are required.

Animal and Plant Safety

- When working with live animals or plants, check ahead of time for students who may have allergies to the specimens.
- When growing bacteria cultures, use only disposable petri dishes. After streaking, the dishes should be sealed and not opened again by students. After the lab, students should return the unopened dishes to you. Students should wash their hands with antibacterial soap.
- Two methods are recommended for the safe disposal of bacteria cultures. *First method:* Autoclave the petri dishes and discard without opening. *Second method*: If no autoclave is available, carefully open the dishes (never have a student do this) and pour full-strength bleach into the dishes and let stand for a day. Then pour the bleach from the petri dishes down a drain and flush the drain with lots of water. Tape the petri dishes back together and place in a sealed plastic bag. Wrap the plastic bag with a brown paper bag or newspaper and tape securely. Throw the sealed package in the trash. Thoroughly disinfect the work area with bleach.
- To grow mold, use a new, sealable plastic bag that is two to three times larger than the material to be placed inside. Seal the bag and tape it shut. After the bag is sealed, students should not open it. To dispose of the bag and mold culture, make a small cut near an edge of the bag and cook in a microwave oven on high setting for at least 1 minute. Discard the bag according to local ordinance, usually in the trash.
- Students should wear disposable nitrile, latex, or food-handling gloves when handling live animals or nonliving specimens.

End-of Experiment Rules

- Always have students use antibacterial soap for washing their hands.

Identifying Common Minerals

GROUP 1
Metallic Luster, Mostly Dark-Colored

Mineral/ Formula	Hardness	Density	Luster	Streak	Color	Other Properties/Remarks
Pyrite FeS_2	6–6.5	5.0	Metallic	Greenish, brownish black	Light yellow	Harder than chalcopyrite and pyrrhotite; called "fool's gold," but harder than gold and very brittle
Magnetite Fe_3O_4	6	5.2	Metallic	Black	Iron black	Very magnetic; important iron ore; known as "lodestone"
Hematite Fe_2O_3	5.5–6.5	4.9–5.3	Metallic or earthy	Red or red brown	Reddish brown to black; also steel gray crystals	Most important ore of iron; known as "red ocher"
Pyrrhotite FeS	4	4.6	Metallic	Gray black	Brownish bronze	Less hard than pyrite: slightly magnetic
Sphalerite ZnS	3.5–4	3.9–4.1	Resinous	Brown to light yellow	Brown to yellow	Most important zinc ore
Chalcopyrite $CuFeS_2$	3.5–4	4.1–4.3	Metallic	Greenish black	Golden yellow, often tarnished	Most important copper ore; softer than pyrite and more yellow; more brittle than gold
Bornite Cu_5FeS_4	3	4.9–5.4	Metallic	Gray black	Copper, brown; turns to purple and black	Important copper ore; known as "peacock ore" because of iridescent purple color when exposed to air for a time
Copper Cu	2.5–3	8.9	Metallic	Copper red	Copper red to black	Can be pounded into various shapes and drawn into wires; used in making electrical wires, coins, pipes
Gold Au	2.5–3	19.3	Metallic	Yellow	Rich yellow	Can be pounded into various shapes and drawn into wires; does not tarnish; used in jewelry, coins, dental fillings
Silver Ag	2.5–3	10.0–11.0	Metallic	Silver to light gray	Silver white, tarnishes to black	Can be pounded into various shapes and drawn into wires; used in jewelry, coins, electrical wire
Galena PbS	2.5	7.4–7.6	Metallic	Lead gray	Lead gray	Main ore of lead; used in shields against radiation, plumbing
Graphite C	1–2	2.3	Metallic to dull	Black	Black	Feels greasy; very soft; used as pencil "lead" and as a lubricant

196 ◆ F

GROUP 2
Nonmetallic Luster, Mostly Dark-Colored

Mineral/ Formula	Hardness	Density	Luster	Streak	Color	Other Properties/Remarks
Corundum Al_2O_3	9	3.9–4.1	Brilliant to glassy	White	Usually brown	Very hard; used as an abrasive; transparent crystals used as gems called "ruby" (red) and "sapphire" (blue and other colors)
Garnet $(Ca,Mg,Fe)_3(Al,Fe,Cr)_2(SiO_4)_3$	7–7.5	3.5–4.3	Glassy to resinous	White, light brown	Red, brown, black, green	Used in jewelry and as an abrasive
Olivine $(Mg,Fe)_2SiO_4$	6.5–7	3.3–3.4	Glassy	White or gray	Olive green	Found in volcanic rocks; sometimes used as a gem
Augite $Ca(Mg,Fe,Al)(AlSi)_2O_6$	5–6	3.2–3.4	Glassy	Greenish gray	Dark green to black	Found in volcanic rocks
Hornblende $NaCa_2(Mg,Fe,Al)_5(Si,Al)_8O_{22}(OH)_2$	5–6	3.0–3.4	Glassy, silky	White to gray	Dark green to brown, black	Found in igneous and metamorphic rocks
Apatite $Ca_5(PO_4)_3F$	5	3.1–3.2	Glassy	White	Green, brown, red, blue, violet, yellow	Sometimes used as a gem; source of the phosphorus needed by plants
Azurite $Cu_3(CO_3)_2(OH)_2$	3.5–4	3.8	Glassy to dull	Pale blue	Intense blue	Ore of copper; used as a gem
Biotite $K(Mg,Fe)_3AlSiO_{10}(OH)_2$	2.5–3	2.8–3.4	Glassy or pearly	White to gray	Dark green, brown, or black	A type of mica, sometimes used as a lubricant
Serpentine $Mg_6Si_4O_{10}(OH)_8$	2–5	2.2–2.6	Greasy, waxy, silky	White	Usually green	Once used in insulation but found to cause cancer; used in fireproofing; is a form of asbestos
Limonite Mixture of hydrous iron oxides	1–5.5	2.8–4.3	Glassy to dull	Yellow brown	Brown black to brownish yellow	Ore of iron, also known as "yellow ocher," a pigment; a mixture that is not strictly a mineral
Bauxite Mixture of hydrous aluminum oxides	1–3	2.0–2.5	Dull to earthy	Colorless to gray	Brown, yellow, gray, white	Ore of aluminum, smells like clay when wet; a mixture that is not strictly a mineral

F ◆ 197

GROUP 3
Nonmetallic Luster, Mostly Light-Colored

Mineral/ Formula	Hardness	Density	Luster	Streak	Color	Other Properties/Remarks
Diamond C	10	3.5	Brilliant	White	Colorless and varied	Hardest known substance; used in jewelry, as an abrasive, in cutting instruments
Topaz $Al_2SiO_4(F,OH)_2$	8	3.5–3.6	Glassy	White	Straw yellow, pink, bluish, greenish	Valuable gem
Quartz SiO_2	7	2.6	Glassy, greasy	White	Colorless, white; any color when not pure	The second most abundant mineral; many varieties are gems (amethyst, cat's-eye, bloodstone, agate, jasper, onyx); used in making glass
Feldspar (K,Na,Ca) $(AlSi_3O_8)$	6	2.6	Glassy	Colorless, white	Colorless, white, various colors	As a family, the most abundant of all minerals; the different types of feldspar make up over 60 percent of Earth's crust
Fluorite CaF_2	4	3.0–3.3	Glassy	Colorless	Light green, yellow, bluish green, other colors	Some types are fluorescent (glow when exposed to ultraviolet light); used in making steel
Dolomite $CaMg(CO_3)_2$	3.5–4	2.8	Glassy or pearly	White	Colorless, white, pinkish, or light tints	Used in making concrete and cement; fizzes slowly in dilute hydrochloric acid
Calcite $CaCO_3$	3	2.7	Glassy	White to grayish	Colorless, white, pale tints	Easily scratched; bubbles in dilute hydrochloric acid; frequently fluorescent
Halite NaCl	2.5	2.1–2.6	Glassy	White	Colorless or white	Occurs as perfect cubic crystals; has salty taste
Gypsum $CaSO_4 \cdot 2H_2O$	2	2.3	Glassy, pearly, silky	White	Colorless, white, light tints	Very soft; used in manufacture of plaster of Paris; form known as alabaster used for statues
Sulfur S	2	2.0–2.1	Resinous to greasy	White	Yellow to yellowish brown	Used in making many medicines, in production of sulfuric acid, and in vulcanizing rubber
Talc $Mg_3Si_4O_{10}(OH)_2$	1	2.7–2.8	Pearly to greasy	White	Gray, white, greenish	Very soft; used in talcum powder; found mostly in metamorphic rocks; also called "soapstone"

Glossary

A

aa A cooler, slow-moving type of lava that hardens to form rough chunks; cooler than pahoehoe. (p. 97)
active Said of a volcano that is erupting or has shown signs of erupting in the near future. (p. 98)
aftershock An earthquake that occurs after a larger earthquake in the same area. (p. 73)
alloy A solid mixture of two or more metals. (p. 138)
anticline An upward fold in rock formed by compression of Earth's crust. (p. 60)
asthenosphere The soft layer of the mantle on which the lithosphere floats. (p. 21)
atoll A ring-shaped coral island found far from land. (p. 161)
atom The smallest unit of an element that retains the properties of that element. (p. 120)

B

basalt A dark, dense rock with a fine texture, found in oceanic crust. (p. 20)
base-isolated building A building mounted on bearings designed to absorb the energy of an earthquake. (p. 76)
batholith A mass of rock formed when a large body of magma cooled inside the crust. (p. 107)

C

caldera The large hole at the top of a volcano formed when the volcano's magma chamber collapses. (p. 104)
cementation The process by which dissolved minerals crystallize and glue particles of sediment together into one mass. (p. 155)
chemical rock Sedimentary rock that forms when minerals crystallize from a solution. (p. 158)
cinder cone A steep, cone-shaped hill or mountain made of volcanic ash, cinders, and bombs piled up around a volcano's opening. (p. 104)
clastic rock Sedimentary rock that forms when rock fragments are squeezed together under high pressure. (p. 156)
cleavage A mineral's ability to split easily along flat surfaces. (p. 125)
compaction The process by which sediments are pressed together under their own weight. (p. 155)
composite volcano A tall, cone-shaped mountain in which layers of lava alternate with layers of ash and other volcanic materials. (p. 104)
compound A substance in which two or more elements are chemically joined. (p. 120)
compression Stress that squeezes rock until it folds or breaks. (p. 55)
conduction The transfer of heat through solid materials. (p. 26)
constructive force A force that builds up mountains and landmasses on Earth's surface. (p. 17)
continent A great landmass surrounded by oceans. (p. 17)
continental drift The hypothesis that the continents slowly move across Earth's surface. (p. 29)
controlled experiment An experiment in which all factors except one are kept constant. (p. 185)
convection The transfer of heat by movements within a heated fluid. (p. 26)
convection current The movement of a fluid, caused by differences in temperature, that transfers heat from one part of the fluid to another. (p. 26)
convergent boundary A plate boundary where two plates move toward each other. (p. 46)
coral reef A structure of calcite shells built up by coral animals living in warm, shallow ocean water. (p. 160)
crater A bowl-shaped area that forms around a volcano's central opening. (p. 94)
crust The layer of rock that forms Earth's outer surface. (p. 20)
crystal A solid in which the atoms are arranged in a pattern that repeats again and again. (p. 120)

D

deep-ocean trench A deep valley along the ocean floor through which oceanic crust slowly sinks towards the mantle. (p. 38)
deformation A change in the volume or shape of Earth's crust. (p. 55)
density The amount of mass in a given space; mass per unit volume. (p. 26)
deposition The process by which sediment settles out of the water or wind that is carrying it. (p. 155)
destructive force A force that slowly wears away mountains and other features on the surface of Earth. (p. 17)
dike A slab of volcanic rock formed when magma hardens in a vertical crack. (p. 106)
divergent boundary A plate boundary where two plates move away from each other. (p. 45)
dormant Said of a volcano that does not show signs of erupting in the near future. (p. 98)

E

earthquake The shaking that results from the movement of rock beneath Earth's surface. (p. 54)
element A substance composed of a single kind of atom. (p. 120)
epicenter The point on Earth's surface directly above an earthquake's focus. (p. 64)

erosion The destructive process in which water or wind loosen and carry away fragments of rock. (p. 155)
extinct Said of a volcano that is unlikely to erupt again. (p. 98)
extrusive rock Igneous rock that forms from lava on Earth's surface. (p. 151)

fault A break in Earth's crust where slabs of rock slip past each other. (pp. 44, 56)
fault-block mountain A mountain that forms where a normal fault uplifts a block of rock. (p. 58)
fluorescence The property of a mineral in which the mineral glows under ultraviolet light. (p. 126)
focus The point beneath Earth's surface where rock breaks under stress and causes an earthquake. (p. 64)
fold A bend in rock that forms where part of Earth's crust is compressed. (p. 59)
foliated Term used to describe metamorphic rocks whose grains are arranged in parallel layers or bands. (p. 163)
footwall The block of rock that forms the lower half of a fault. (p. 56)
fossil A trace of an organism that has been preserved in rock. (p. 30)
fracture The way a mineral looks when it breaks apart. (p. 125)

gemstone A hard, colorful mineral that has a brilliant or glassy luster. (p. 135)
geologist A scientist who studies the forces that make and shape planet Earth. (p. 17)
geology The study of planet Earth. (p. 17)
geothermal energy Energy from water or steam that has been heated by magma. (p. 99)
geyser A fountain of water and steam that builds up pressure underground and erupts at regular intervals. (p. 99)
grain A particle of mineral or other rock that gives a rock its texture. (p. 147)
granite A usually light-colored rock that makes up most of the continental crust. (p. 20)

hanging wall The block of rock that forms the upper half of a fault. (p. 56)
heat transfer The movement of heat from a warmer object to a cooler object. (p. 25)
hot spot An area where magma from deep within the mantle melts through the crust above it. (p. 91)
hot spring A pool formed by groundwater that has risen to the surface after being heated by a nearby body of magma. (p. 99)
hypothesis A prediction about the outcome of an experiment. (p. 184)

igneous rock A type of rock that forms from the cooling of molten rock at or below the surface. (p. 149)
inner core A dense sphere of solid iron and nickel in the center of Earth. (p. 21)
inorganic Not formed from living things or the remains of living things. (p. 119)
intrusive rock Igneous rock that forms when magma hardens beneath Earth's surface. (p. 151)
island arc A string of islands formed by the volcanoes along a deep ocean trench. (p. 90)

lava Liquid magma that reaches the surface. (p. 88)
lava flow The area covered by lava as it pours out of a volcano's vent. (p. 94)
liquefaction The process by which an earthquake's violent movement suddenly turns loose soil into liquid mud. (p. 73)
lithosphere A rigid layer made up of the uppermost part of the mantle and the crust. (p. 20)
luster The way ia mineral reflects light from its surface. (p. 123)

magma The molten mixture of rock-forming substances, gases, and water from the mantle. (p. 88)
magma chamber The pocket beneath a volcano where magma collects. (p. 94)
magnitude The measurement of an earthquake's strength based on seismic waves and movement along faults. (p. 67)
manipulated variable The one factor that a scientist changes during an experiment. (p. 185)
mantle The layer of hot, solid material between Earth's crust and core. (p. 20)
Mercalli scale A scale that rates earthquakes according to their intensity and how much damage they cause. (p. 67)
metamorphic rock A type of rock that forms from an existing rock that is changed by heat, pressure, or chemical reactions. (p. 149)
mid-ocean ridge The undersea mountain chain where new ocean floor is produced; a divergent plate boundary. (p. 34)

200 ◆ F

mineral A naturally-occurring, inorganic solid that has a crystal structure and a definite chemical composition. (p. 119)

Mohs hardness scale A scale ranking ten minerals from softest to hardest; used in testing the hardness of minerals. (p. 121)

moment magnitude scale A scale that rates earthquakes by estimating the total energy released by an earthquake. (p. 68)

normal fault A type of fault where the hanging wall slides downward. (p. 56)

operational definition A statement that describes how a particular variable is to be measured or a term is to be defined. (p. 185)

ore Rock that contains a metal or economically useful mineral. (p. 135)

organic rock Sedimentary rock that forms where remains of organisms are deposited in thick layers. (p. 157)

outer core A layer of molten iron and nickel that surrounds the inner core of Earth. (p. 21)

P wave A type of seismic wave that compresses and expands the ground. (p. 65)

pahoehoe A hot, fast-moving type of lava that hardens to form smooth, ropelike coils. (p. 97)

Pangaea The name of the single landmass that broke apart 200 million years ago and gave rise to today's continents. (p. 29)

pipe A long tube through which magma moves from the magma chamber to Earth's surface. (p. 94)

plate A section of the lithosphere that slowly moves, carrying pieces of continental and oceanic crust. (p. 42)

plate tectonics The theory that pieces of Earth's crust are in constant motion, driven by convection currents in the mantle. (p. 43)

plateau A large area of flat land elevated high above sea level. (p. 61)

porphyritic texture A rock texture in which large crystals are scattered on a background of much smaller crystals. (p. 151)

pressure The amount of force pushing on a surface or area. (p. 19)

pyroclastic flow The expulsion of ash, cinders, and bombs from a violent volcanic explosion. (p. 98)

radiation The transfer of heat through empty space. (p. 25)

responding variable The factor that changes as a result of changes to the manipulated variable in an experiment. (p. 185)

reverse fault A type of fault where the hanging wall slides upward. (p. 57)

Richter scale A scale that rates seismic waves as measured by a particular type of mechanical seismograph. (p. 67)

rift valley A deep valley that forms where two plates move apart. (p. 45)

Ring of Fire A major belt of volcanoes that rims the Pacific Ocean. (p. 89)

rock The material that forms Earth's hard surface. (p. 17)

rock cycle A series of processes on the surface and inside Earth that slowly change rocks from one kind to another. (p. 166)

S wave A type of seismic wave that moves the ground up and down or side to side. (p. 65)

scientific theory A well-tested concept that explains a wide range of observations. (p. 43)

sea-floor spreading The process by which molten material adds new oceanic crust to the ocean floor. (p. 35)

sediment Small, solid pieces of material that comes from rocks or organisms. (p. 154)

sedimentary rock A type of rock that forms when particles from other rocks or the remains of plants and animals are pressed and cemented together. (p. 149)

seismic wave A vibration that travels through Earth carrying the energy released during an earthquake. (pp. 18, 64)

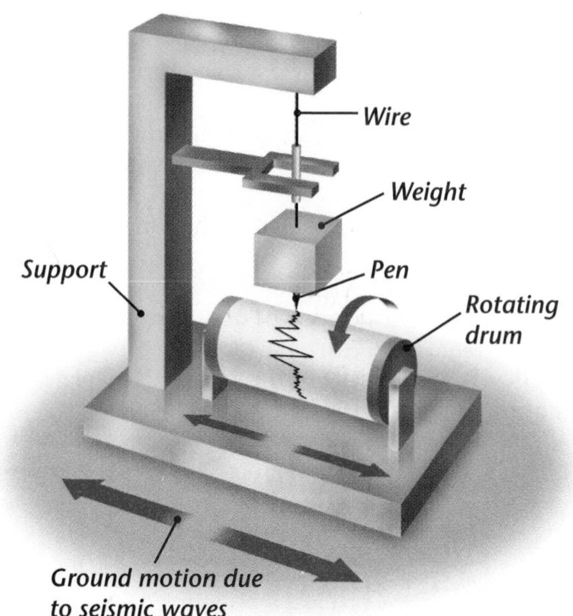

seismograph A device that records ground movements caused by seismic waves as they move through Earth. (p. 66)

shearing Stress that pushes a mass of rock in opposite, horizontal directions. (p. 55)

shield volcano A wide, gently-sloping mountain made of layers of lava and formed by quiet eruptions. (p. 103)

silica A material that is formed from the elements oxygen and silicon; silica is found in magma. (p. 96)

sill A slab of volcanic rock formed when magma hardens in a horizontal crack. (p. 106)

smelting The process by which ore is melted to separate the useful metal from other elements. (p. 138)

solution A mixture in which one substance is dissolved in another. (p. 130)

sonar A device that determines the distance of an object under water by recording echoes of sound waves. (p. 34)

streak The color of a mineral's powder. (p. 123)

stress A force that acts on rock to change its shape or volume. (p. 54)

strike-slip fault A type of fault where rocks on either side move past each other sideways with little up-or-down motion. (p. 56)

subduction The process by which oceanic crust sinks through a deep-ocean trench and back into the mantle; a convergent plate boundary. (p. 38)

surface wave A type of seismic wave that forms when P waves and S waves reach Earth's surface. (p. 66)

syncline A downward fold in rock formed by tension in Earth's crust. (p. 60)

tension Stress that stretches rock so that it becomes thinner in the middle. (p. 55)

texture The look and feel of a rock's surface. (p. 147)

transform boundary A plate boundary where two plates move past each other in opposite directions. (p. 44)

tsunami A large wave produced by an earthquake on the ocean floor. (p. 74)

variable Any factor that can change in an experiment. (p. 185)

vein A narrow slab of a mineral that is sharply different from the surrounding rock. (p. 130)

vent The opening through which molten rock and gas leave a volcano. (p. 94)

volcanic neck A deposit of hardened magma in a volcano's pipe. (p. 106)

volcano A weak spot in the crust where magma comes to the surface. (p. 88)

202 ◆ F

Index

F ◆ 203

204 ◆ F

F ◆ 205

206 ◆ F

Acknowledgments

Illustration

Carol Barber: 26
Kathleen Dempsey: 40, 48, 62, 70, 92, 108, 127, 140, 165, 170
John Edwards: 74
Chris Forsey: 13r, 27, 34t, 35, 38, 44, 45, 91
Geo Systems: 11m, 29, 30, 34b, 43, 51, 58t, 69, 70b, 81, 82, 89, 132
Jared D. Lee: 178–179t,
Martucci Design: 71b, 85, 115,
Morgan Cain & Associates: 22, 23, 24, 36, 37, 55, 60, 65tl, 66, 76, 77, 79, 80, 95, 105, 106, 152, 155
Matt Mayerchak: 50, 84, 114, 124, 142, 172
Ortelius Design Inc.: 11m, 46, 47, 100, 101, 136, 137, 176
Matthew Pippin: 65br, 75, 90, 130, 138
J/B Woolsey Associates: 44, 56, 57, 58b, 59

Photography

Photo Research Paula Wehde
Cover image Paul Chesley/TSI

Nature of Science
Page 10, 12, Paul Mann; **11,** Carol Prentice/US Geological Survey.

Chapter 1
Pages 14–15, Earth Satellite Corporation/Science Photo Library/Photo Researchers; **16,** Gardar Palsson/Mats Wibe Lund; **17t,b,** M. W. Franke/Peter Arnold; **18,** Michael Nichols/Magnum; **19,** Tracy Frankel/The Image Bank; **20–21t,** Linde Waidhofer/Liaison International; **20m,** E. R. Degginger; **20b,** Breck P. Kent; **24,** Runk/Schoenberger/Grant Heilman; **25,** Richard Haynes; **28t,** Russ Lappa; **28b,** The Granger Collection, NY; **30,** Breck P. Kent; **31,** Francois Gohier/Photo Researchers; **32,** Bildarchiv Preussischer Kulturbesitz; **33,** Emory Kristof/National Geographic Image Collection; **36tl,** Woods Hole Oceanographic Institute/Sygma; **36tr,** USGS/HVO 3cp/U. S. Geological Survey; **37,** SCRIPPS Oceanographic Institute; **39,** Norbert Wu; **40 all,** Richard Haynes; **41t,** Richard Haynes; **42t,** Russ Lappa; **49t,** The Granger Collection, NY.

Chapter 2
Pages 52–53, Science Museum/Michael Holford; **54,** Ben S. Kwiatkowski/Fundamental Photographs; **56t,** David Parker/Science Photo Library/Photo Researchers; **56b,** David Muench Photography; **57,** Sharon Gerig/Tom Stack & Associates; **58,** Stan Osolinski/TSI; **59,** Phillips Petroleum; **60–61,**Tom Bean; **63b, inset,** Richard Haynes; **64, 66t,** Richard Haynes; **66b,** Russell D. Curtis/Photo Researchers; **67,** Leonetto Medici/AP Photo; **68,** EERC/Berkeley; **72t,** Richard Haynes; **72b,** Natsuko Utsumi/Gamma Liaison; **73,** EERC/Berkeley; **76,** Esbin-Anderson/The Image Works; **78,** Terraphotographics/BPS; **83,** Science Museum/Michael Holford.

Chapter 3
Pages 86–87, Soames Summerhays/Photo Researchers; **88,** Savino/Sipa Press; **93 all,** Breck P. Kent; **94,** E. R. Degginger; **95,** B. Ingalls/NASA/Liaison International; **96t,** Ed Reschke/Peter Arnold; **96b,** E. R. Degginger; **97l,** Dave B. Fleetham/Tom Stack & Associates; **97r,** William Felger/Grant Heilman Photography; **98l, r,** Alberto Garcia/Saba Press; **99l, r,** Alberto Garcia/Saba Press; **99b,** Norbert Rosing/Animals Animals/Earth Scenes; **100tl,** North Wind; **100tr,** Kim Heacox/Peter Arnold; **100b,** Robert Fried Photography; **101,** Alberto Garcia/Saba Press; **102l,** Pat Roqua/AP/Wide World; **102r,** Antonio Emerito/Sipa Press; **103t,** Richard Haynes; **103b,** Hela Lade/Peter Arnold; **104,** Greg Vaughn/Tom Stack & Associates; **105t,** Picture Perfect; **105b,** Manfred Gottschalk/Tom Stack & Associates; **106tl,** Brownie Harris/The Stock Market; **106bl,** Tom Bean/DRK Photo; **106br,** David Hosking/Photo Researchers; **107,** Bob Newman/Visual Unlimited; **109,** Richard Haynes; **110t, m,** NASA; **110b,** Chris Bjornberg/Photo Researchers; **111t, b, 112,** NASA; **113,** Norbert Rosing/Animals Animals/Earth Scenes.

Chapter 4
Pages 116–117, Thomas R. Taylor/Photo Researchers; **118t,** Richard Haynes; **118b,** Richard B. Levine; **119t,** Mark A. Schneider/Visuals Unlimited; **119m,** Ben Johnson/Science Photo Library/Photo Researchers; **119b,** E.R. Degginger; **120l,** Richard Treptow/Visuals Unlimited; **120r,** Gregory G. Dimijian/Photo Researchers; **120m,** McCutcheon/Visuals Unlimited; **121l,** Ken Lucas/Visuals Unlimited; **121r,** Breck P. Kent; **122,** Paul Silverman/Fundamental Photographs; **123l, r,** Breck P. Kent; **124 sulfur,** E. R. Degginger; **124 all others,** Breck P. Kent; **125l,** A. J. Copley/Visuals Unlimited; **125tr,** Paul Silverman/Fundamental Photographs; **126l, r,** E. R. Degginger; **128t,** Richard Haynes; **128b,** Gerhard Gscheidle/Peter Arnold; **129,** Jeffrey Scovil; **130l,** Ken Lucas/Visuals Unlimited; **130r,** Ted Clutter/Photo Researchers; **131,** Jay Syverson/Stock Boston; **133,** Nautilus Minerals Corp.; **134,** C. M. Dixon; **135t,** Runk/Schoenberger from Grant Heilman; **135b,** Mike Husar/DRK photo; **136t,** C. M. Dixon; **136bl,** Scala/Art Resource, NY; **136br,** C. M. Dixon; **137,** The Granger Collection, NY; **138t,** Charles D. Winters/Photo Researchers; **138b,** Russ Lappa; **139,** Visuals Unlimited; **140,** Richard Haynes; **141t, b, 143,** Breck P. Kent.

Chapter 5
Pages 144–145, Jim Nelson/Adventure Photo; **146t, m,** Breck P. Kent; **146b,** Jeff Zaroda/The Stock Market; **147tl, bl,** E. R. Degginger; **147tr, m,** Breck P. Kent; **147br,** Barry L. Runk/Grant Heilman; **148 slate, gneiss,** E. R. Degginger; **148 quartzite,** Jeff Scovil; **148 all others,** Breck P. Kent; **149,** Martin Rogers/Stock Boston; **150tl,** Breck P. Kent; **150tr,** Doug Martin/Photo Researchers; **150b,** Greg Vaughn/Tom Stack & Associates; **151tl, tm,** Breck P. Kent; **151tr,** E. R. Degginger; **152,** Alfred Pasieka/Science Photo Library/Photo Researchers; **153,** Michele & Tom Grimm/TSI; **154,** Clyde H. Smith/Peter Arnold; **156,** Specimen from North Museum/Franklin and Marshall College/Grant Heilman Photography; **157t,** E. R. Degginger; **157b,** Kevin Sink/Midwestock; **158,** Grant Heilman/Grant Heilman Photography; **159t,** Ted Clutter/Photo Researchers; **159b,** Stephen Frink/Waterhouse; **160,** Norbert Wu/The Stock Market; **160b,** Jean-Marc Truchet/TSI; **161,** Grant Heilman/Grant Heilman Photography; **162tl,** E. R. Degginger; **162bl,** Barry L. Runk/Grant Heilman Photography; **162br, 163bl,** Andrew J. Martinez/Photo Researchers; **164,** David Hosking/Photo Researchers; **166tl, tr,** Jeff Scovil; **166tm,** Breck P. Kent; **167,** Corbis; **168tl,** Tom Algire/Tom Stack & Associates; **168bl,** Breck P. Kent; **168br,** N.R.Rowan/Stock Boston; **169,** Breck P. Kent; **170t, m, b,** Russ Lappa; **171,** Greg Vaughn/Tom Stack & Associates; **173l, r,** E. R. Degginger; **173m,** Breck P. Kent.

Interdisciplinary Exploration
Page 174tl, Rosenfeld Imaged Ltd/Rainbow; **174br,** Michael Holford; **174–175m,** B. Daemmrich/The Image Works; **175 inset,** NASA/The Image Works; **176 border,** Marilyn "Angel" Wynn; **178b,** John Coletti/Stock Boston.

Skills Handbook
Page 180, Mike Moreland/Photo Network; **181t,** Foodpix; **181m,** Richard Haynes; **181b,** Russ Lappa; **184,** Richard Haynes; **186,** Ron Kimball; **187,** Renee Lynn/Photo Researchers.

F ◆ 207